Religion As Belonging
A General Theory of Religion

John S. Cumpsty
Department of Religious Studies
University of Cape Town

UNIVERSITY
PRESS OF
AMERICA

Lanham • New York • London

Copyright © 1991 by
University Press of America®, Inc.
4720 Boston Way
Lanham, Maryland 20706

3 Henrietta Street
London WC2E 8LU England

Library of Congress Cataloging-in-Publication Data

Cumpsty, John S.
Religion as belonging : a general theory of religion
/ John S. Cumpsty.
p.   cm.
1. Religion.   I. Title.
BL48.C79 1991
200—dc20   91-23554 CIP

ISBN 0–8191–8358–X (hard : alk. paper)
ISBN 0–8191–8359–8 (pbk., alk. paper)

This book is dedicated to four extraordinary persons. They entered my life within a decade and each left a major impression. They are, in the order in which they appeared:

David Leighton, pastor extraordinary, then of St.Andrew's Pittsburgh, later of the diocese of Maryland, who followed conviction where it led.

James March, teacher extraordinary, then of Carnegie Tech, later of Stanford, who set a new standard of open-mindedness.

Alex Whitehouse, theologian extraordinary, then of the University of Durham, later of Kent, who thought it out anew before your eyes.

Bill Wright, industrial chaplain extraordinary, then of Teesside, still of Teesside, who insisted that faith be grounded where real people live.

I doubt if any would own its content.

The chief contributors to this book have been my graduate students. Their needs conjured it into existence and their pressing of the boundaries refined it. Two of these, who later became colleagues, have been involved throughout and at depth. They are Janet Hodgson and Jannie Hofmeyr.

Others worked with parts of the model appropriate to their projects and in making new demands upon it, pushed it further. They include Don Aeschliman, Gina Buijs, John Clarke, Herbert Diaz, Asher Flegg, James Leatt, Aviva Schein, Jacques de Wet, Anda Wayland, Jacquelin Winter. There have been many other students whose contributions have been less sustained but without whom something would have been missing.

There were two colleagues who came late on the scene, but who nevertheless exerted considerable influence upon the final package. They are David Chidester, whose concern for *epoché* led him in the nicest possible way to anathematize the whole project, thereby forcing me to secure many loose ends, and Gabriel Setiloane, who offered enormous encouragement by confirming in many ways that the model did offer a bridge between the world views of Africa and the West. It was perhaps providential that they arrived together.

Three institutions have rendered my project possible without being in any way responsible for the final content. They are my own University of Cape Town, The Human Sciences Research Council of South Africa, and The Institute for the Advanced Study of Religion in the Divinity School of the University of Chicago.

Should any part of this text surrender its meaning gracefully to anyone who does not already know more of the subject than the author, it will be because Joseph Levitt, a doctor of medicine and my father-in-law, not only labored mightily to reveal the obstacles, but also walked the difficult path between responsibility and civility with aplomb.

To all of the above, and to all who have encouraged, typed, read, criticized, or simply borne with me, my heartfelt thanks.

CONTENTS

This is a developmental text and there is advantage in the reader knowing, from the start and throughout, how the text will unfold. Changes in direction of thought are signaled, where appropriate, at the beginning of each new part or chapter and this extended table of contents provides a birds-eye-view of the whole theoretical development. A few moments spent considering this table will provide the first-time reader with the desired overview. Subsequently, the table will serve as a chart for the location and interrelation of whatever parts of the theory the reader may wish to draw upon.

PART I

FOUNDATIONS FOR A SCIENTIFIC STUDY OF RELIGION

THE NATURE OF RELIGION AND RELIGIOUS DISCOURSE

PART II

A GENERAL THEORY OF RELIGION   169

GLOSSARY

Every discipline develops a set of technical terms. They are a short-hand for ideas used frequently. This glossary is intended to familiarize the reader with such technical terms as are used in this book. It is in two sections. One is for the general reader and contains words common in the discipline but less familiar outside of it. The other is for all readers and contains terms that I have had to coin deliberately or common words that I have employed in a special sense.

Sometimes I use a word, for example "myth", in a more general sense than it has come to serve in other disciplines. Sometimes I have needed to restrict the meaning of a word, for example "monotheism", in order to express a concept more precisely. Meanings will be filled out in context, but some preliminary familiarity with the way in which a word has been used will be helpful.

Terms are capitalized within the text where a cross- reference to that term will assist understanding of the term under consideration.

SECTION I - TERMS IN GENERAL USE

ABRAHAMIC — Abrahamic is the best corporate appellation for those religions, faiths or traditions, who trace their origins to the call of Abraham. That is Judaism, Christianity and Islam. In the English speaking world it is common to find MOSAIC or even WESTERN, used to describe these same traditions. Islam, however, while acknowledging Moses as a prophet, does not trace its roots to him in the same way as it does to Abraham, nor does it contrast itself with the East in the way suggested by the title "Western".

ADHERENT

Any person who adheres to a recognizable religious tradition. Early in the book I use THEIST for any person who believes in a god or gods, but later I need to speak of religions which have no god or have more concern with BEHAVIOR than with BELIEF. I then use the more general term "adherent".

AFFECTIVE

Having to do with feeling, used particularly of judgments or decisions made on the basis of feeling. I use feeling and therefore affective in a very broad sense. It includes everything that the word can convey beyond raw tactile sensation, emotion as well as evaluation, mood as well as motivation. That is, it includes all human response to raw experience save the COGNIT-IVE process in which it is conceptualized, and rationally located.
See COGNITIVE and VOLITIONAL.

ANIMISM

Belief in spirits, more particularly the belief that personal spirits or the spirits of the departed make their dwelling place in trees, springs, hills, etc., and can influence these and other aspects of nature and human existence for the good or detriment of human beings.

ANIMATISM

A particular form of animism. The belief that many things in nature, which the modern West would regard as inanimate, have their own spirits in much the same way as human beings are thought to have theirs, that is, they are animate objects and can be appealed to as such.

DYNAMISM

A form of animism in which natural objects are believed to have a power in them which can harm or benefit humankind and can usually be manipulated by persons with the necessary skills. It differs from animatism in that the power is not thought of as personal.

COGNITIVE

Having to do with thought or reason. It is contrasted with AFFECTIVE or VOLITIONAL.

DUALISM
DUALIST
DUALISTIC

Dualism or Dualist is used: (i) of a belief or person who believes in two gods or powers, of relative equality, probably in opposition, and (ii) as the opposite of Monism or Monist. This is the way in which it will be used in this book. It refers not to gods or powers, but to reality. People who are Monotheists, in the sense of believing in one transcendent god, are Dualist in their belief about reality. They believe that reality is two and not a single closed system. On the one hand there is the god, and on the other there is everything else that they experience. For them nature is not an extension of nor an emanation from the divine, but a quite separate reality. The universe is not divine, nor is the god a part of the universe.

IMMANENT

Used of a god or gods and to mean present within and pervading the universe. That is, fully available here and now. It is the opposite of TRANSCENDENT. It might include being readily accessible but a transcendent god might also be readily accessible while not being available in his or her fulness.

MONISM
MONIST
MONISTIC

The belief that all reality is one closed system. If there is a god or gods in the system, then they are higher than humankind just as humankind is higher than the lower animals, but still part of the same system. A monist who believes that all reality is a unity and that it is all divine is therefore, in the literal sense of that word, a monotheist. In this book monist is used of a person or tradition that holds reality to be one, whether personally or impersonally conceived, and MONOTHEIST is restricted to mean a person who believes in one TRANSCENDENT God. See DUALISM.

MONOTHEISM
See THEISM.

MYSTICISM   Used of that sort of religion which is overwhelm-
MYSTICAL   ingly concerned to know and relate directly to a
                     god or to the ultimate reality, however it is
                     conceived. It is the opposite, therefore, of
                     natural, historical or ethical religions which are
                     at least equally concerned with how the powers-
                     that-be relate to nature and history and how
                     human beings should relate to them and to each
                     other.

MYTH   Sometimes used of a particular type of story as
                     one might speak of folk-tale, saga, legend.
                     Sometimes used of a story that is not true. In this
                     book "myth" refers to a verbal form of symbolic
                     expression. It is a story, whether historically true
                     or not, which is told not to communicate the
                     facts which the story contains, but to communi-
                     cate or simply to express, the feelings which
                     adherents have about the nature of reality and
                     their relation to it.

PARADIGM   A controlling idea that sets the pattern for
PARADIGMATIC   whatever develops from it. It is used in this book
                     of a particular understanding of religion itself
                     and then, generated by that, of the three ways of
                     understanding reality which, in turn, generate
                     three logically coherent types of religious
                     tradition.

RELIGION   Religion is not easy to define and much of this
                     book is concerned to do just that. Do not limit
                     your understanding of religion to that which you
                     happen to believe or which you see people
                     practising around you. For the moment think of
                     it as: "the ways in which human beings, of all
                     times and all places, have tried to conceptualize
                     and communicate their feelings about whatever
                     ultimate reality lay within or behind their
                     transitory experience of life". Think of it as: "the
                     means by which human beings seek to be secure
                     in their relation to the ultimate reality".

SOLIDARY

Used to describe traditions that are neither corporate in a sense that includes everything from the immediate to the universal, nor individualistic, but rather, having objectives beyond those of the individual adherent, cause their adherents to form into groups for the forwarding of common objectives. Such groups may differ in their interpretation of the objectives and therefore come into conflict with each other, or simply seek to impose their objectives on the adherents of other traditions or on the environment in general.

THEISM
THEIST
THEISTIC

Belief in a god or gods.

POLYTHEISM

Belief in many gods

MONOTHEISM

Literally, belief in only one god. It will be used here of belief in one TRANSCENDENT god. See MONISM

HENOTHEISM

Belief that there is one god to which the believer and his tradition community can relate, without denying the reality of the gods of other people or their right to relate to them.

ATHEIST

One who positively believes that there is no god. Compare AGNOSTIC, one who does not know, or one who believes that it cannot be known, whether there is a god.

PANTHEON

All the gods of a polytheistic religion, usually arranged in some hierarchical order.

PANTHEISM

This *does not* mean belief in a PANTHEON, that would be POLYTHEISM. Pantheism is used of the belief that all is god. It is necessarily IMMANENTIST but not all immanentist religion is pantheistic. A MONISTIC and personal view of reality is necessarily pantheistic and vice versa.

TRANSCENDENT
TRANSCENDENCE

Loosely used, frequently in the form of "transcendental", of any religion having a high god and not simply spirits or ancestors, or of religions which concern themselves with "spiritual" or mystical matters rather than the worldly needs of humankind. In this book it will be used with the meaning more familiar in the ABRAHAMIC family of religions, that is, that there is a radical gulf between what the god is and what everything else is. It expresses the "wholly otherness" of the divine in relation to humanity and nature in spatial, temporal and qualitative terms. see (ii) under DUALISM).

VOLITIONAL

Having to do with will, and the freedom of choosing. See AFFECTIVE and COGNITIVE.

SECTION II

SPECIAL TERMS, OR TERMS USED IN A SPECIAL WAY

BELIEF-PATTERN

The interwoven collection of beliefs about spirits, gods, ultimate reality, the world around, humankind and the relationship between these, held in a particular religious tradition or by a group of people. It would include doctrine, that is, the official teachings of a religion.

BEHAVIOR-
          PATTERN

The ways in which the members of a group habitually relate to the powers-that-be, to each other, to other groups and to the world around them. It will include ritual, that is, a form of behavior which is not necessary for everyday living, or is carried out in a manner, or with an attitude of mind, not necessary for everyday living, which is done not for its own sake, or not only for its own sake, but to symbolize or achieve some other purpose usually communal or overtly religious.

LOGIC OF BELONGING	The set of conditions which, it is believed, make it possible for an adherent's belonging to the ULTIMATELY REAL to be established or maintained.
MODE OF BELONGING	The understanding within a religious tradition of the manner of the individual adherent's relating to the ULTIMATELY REAL. It will include elements of the LOGIC OF BELONGING.
MODE OF ENGAGEMENT	The understanding held within a tradition of the manner of the individual's and community's relating to their IMMEDIATE-WORLD-OUT-THERE. This must be clearly distinguished from the MODE OF BELONGING in those situations where the immediate world-out-there is not the ultimately real or is not experienced as the ultimately real.
REALITY THE REAL THE ULTIMATELY REAL	"Reality" or "the real", is not used in this work as though it had some objective referent external to the observer, but with the understanding that what is real for any individual is that with which he or she desires to be in long run relation.

In traditions of the type found in the ABRAHAMIC family a distinction is made between a "real" and an "ultimately-real". In that case what has just said applies to the ULTIMATELY-REAL, and only with qualification to the REAL.

Because "real" is sometimes a synonym for "ultimately-real" and sometimes defined over against it, no usage can be ideal, but the referent should be clear in context.

I have used "real" or "reality" when speaking of what individuals may feel about their world-out-there before any religious interpretation enters.

When speaking of that to which adherents of religious traditions are thereby seeking to relate, I decided in general to use "ultimately-real". Only where I am speaking of a MONISTIC tradition and wish to emphasize its monism, do I use "real" for that to which the individual seeks to relate in religion.

TOTAL
EXPERIENCE

This term is used early in the book before development of the ideas enables it to be replaced by more specific terms. It has two interrelated meanings.

The first meaning refers to what an individual would consciously call to mind if they had the time and the inclination to stand back from the bustle of life and ask "what is it all about?".

What would be called to mind would be things personally experienced and things credibly reported by others. Whatever its source, it is now the individual's own total experience. It is unique. He or she cannot know any other.

The second meaning is all the experience, first or second hand, that determines how the individual will feel about, or respond to situations that are neither trivial, nor habitual, but consciously involve the whole person.

Should the distinction between these two meanings be significant it will be clear in context. See WORLD-OUT-THERE.

TRADITION
COMMUNITY

The permanent element in a religion is the Tradition Community. The tradition may change over time and certainly the individual members who comprise the community will change. The form of the institution or institutions which serve the needs of the Tradition Community can also change dramatically. Continuity is provided by the processes that knit together the tradition and the contemporary members of the community. If these processes cease the Tradition Community will disappear.

WORLD-OUT-
THERE

ALL-THAT-OUT-
THERE

IMMEDIATE-
WORLD-OUT-
THERE

These are terms used to make distinctions concerning the experience of individuals of the world in which they find themselves.

WORLD-OUT-THERE is used of all that the individual experiences and *as the individual experiences it*, not as it is in itself. It is the individual's own perception of reality. When there is need to emphasize that the reference is to what is actually out there then CONTEXT OF EXPERIENCE will be used.

Because some traditions have separated experience of spiritual realities from other experience, it is sometimes necessary to make it clear that what is being spoken of is *all* that the individual experiences, spiritual or otherwise. In that case ALL-THAT-OUT-THERE will be used. Equally it is sometimes necessary to speak of experience before any deeper realities are discerned in or through it, or come to be-understood to be masked by its appearance. Then I will speak of experience of the IMMEDIATE WORLD-OUT-THERE.

PREFACE

I have long believed that it is less than adequate to observe without pressing on to seek explanation. Perhaps this is because my roots lie in the applied sciences and law rather than the humanities. When I came to consider the body of theory which should have provided for the conceptual integration of religious data, I thought it inadequate. It had been drawn from many disciplines and was unnecessarily fragmented. When I moved to Southern Africa I became equally unhappy with the fact that most existing theory treated religion typical of Africa as though it were a bit of the primitive past. So, finding myself largely cut off from the debate among my colleagues, I followed the example of Lionel Bart's remodelled Fagin and *thought I'd better think it out again.*

To attempt this is to tread where many have gone before. Therefore I must offer the results of my *"reviewing the situation"* with apologies for the use of any ideas that may have filtered through, but which remain unacknowledged.

This text is not in direct debate with any other work. It is a contribution to theory and, as such, it stands or falls by its power to integrate data in a simpler and more fruitful manner than any other theory. My aim has been the creation of a sense of the whole to which the reader could say yes or no, not the elaboration of the contents by frequent referencing.

I have in fact, tried to stand back from extant opinions and to consider instead individual human beings in the world in which they find themselves. Then to ask what they need, beyond the basics of food and sleep, sex and sunshine, if they are to survive as human beings. The result of that consideration, painted in bold brush strokes, is as follows:

To survive, human beings must locate themselves in context. For this they need two things:

i) some way of conceptualizing how the various bits and pieces of experience relate to one another and to themselves

ii) some way of expressing how they feel about all-of-it-taken-together.

On this last depends how they will value each and every aspect that is beyond the immediacies of survival and sensual satisfaction, and in the same process come to identify themselves.

It is this dual need to speak of the parts as well as of the whole, which sets up, not two sorts of experience, but two modes of discourse. It is the fact that there are two ways of conceiving and communicating the one world of experience, which seems to divide it so radically into fact and value, science and religion. The raw material of experience is not divided. It is the direction of approach that differs.

Science begins with the bits and pieces and moves toward an understanding of the whole, religion begins with an understanding of the whole and assigns meaning to the parts. Both are essential to any creative process, both are verified by their success in doing what needs to be done.

"Anomie" and "Alienation" may be western words, but they are potentially universal problems. Meaning may not have to be very complex, but each person needs to relate to his or her world-out-there in a manner that will provide the bare bones of an identity or find some way of compensating for its absence. If that identity is to be satisfactory it must develop in relation to that which feels most real in all-that-out-there and, if it is to feel secure, the relation itself must be secured.

In short, one needs to have a feeling for what is the really real and some way of assuring one's relation to it. That, in human terms, is the religious drive.

The book, therefore, takes a positive view of religion. Human beings need to deal with reality as a whole and religion is, traditionally, the way in which they have done so.

Ways of conceptualizing the real, when one is wanting to secure a relationship with it, are severely limited and it is this, rather than anything in human nature or human experience, which sets limits to the ways in which human beings are religious. An examination of the ways in which people can be religious is the central theme of this book.

The book is in two parts. Part I lays the foundation for the theory that is presented in Part II.

The elements of a theory, precisely because they are close knit, arc also a set of individual tools. Tools can be taken out from here and there, as and when necessary. This text provides a set of tools for the student of religion. An eminent colleague described the ground plan as "a student's *vade mecum* in the study of religion". It is certainly that. It is intended to accompany the student of religion from the time that he or she begins an academic study to the point where they begin to research it for themselves. Because these tools may be drawn upon for particular purposes, the table of contents is something of a chart and is more detailed than would otherwise be the case.

The text is not a substitute for the study of actual religious traditions. It will offer its greatest contribution alongside such a study. It does provide, however, both a way of entering into other traditions and a frame in which those traditions can be compared.

A real attempt has been made to introduce ideas in a sequence which enables them to build upon one another and this has more or less coincided with an increasing level of difficulty. However, it has also been necessary to keep similar things together, so a few quite demanding ideas are introduced as early as chapter 1. It is better that the reader new to the field does not linger over these. They will clarify as the book proceeds.

AN INTRODUCTION

FOR READERS FAMILIAR WITH THE FIELD

While what follows is not prescribed, I believe that readers familiar with the field will gain more at first reading if I make clear just what it is that I have attempted and why certain choices were made as to method. Such readers will have to forgive a slight repetition later in the book as I introduce some of the same ideas to those new to the field.

In chapter 1 I locate the book in three ways. It is located within the type of approach associated with Durkheim rather than Weber; then as an approach for which religion itself is the primary concern rather than some other aspect of human functioning; and finally, as an approach which seeks to explain religion rather than to describe or serve it. There are five rather more complex points of location which I believe will be helpful to readers familiar with the field. It is not my purpose to drag such readers through the ancient battlefields, only to make clear to those who have already traversed them, where I stand.

The points that follow are not essential to an understanding of the text and those who would prefer to see what the text has to offer, rather than to locate it in relation to others, might pass over this introduction, returning to it at the end. To persist with this section, if you are not familiar with the debates that surround it, would be like watching a fight with only one contestant.

FIVE POINTS OF LOCATION CONCERNING THE DISCIPLINE OF RELIGIOUS STUDIES AND THE QUESTION OF EXPLANATION

I begin with two matters concerning the discipline of Religious Studies and its subject matter, and then turn to three issues concerned with how explanation takes place in the study of religion.

1. THE DISCIPLINE OF RELIGIOUS STUDIES AND
A THEORY OF RELIGION

The stage, at which the phenomenological approach came together with the textural and historical approach, was absolutely necessary to the development of the discipline of Religious Studies. The discipline, however (not being one defined by a method) will not become normative, that is be genuinely a discipline in its own right, setting its own limits and objectives, until its overt primary concern becomes the understanding of religion as a universal human phenomenon and not simply the understanding of one or more traditions in however wide a context.

Whenever Religious Studies has sought to move beyond description to explanation, it has been heavily dependent upon sociology, anthropology and psychology, for both definition and theory.

As a student of religion, one is grateful for all that one is heir to, but that this situation may not be satisfactory for anyone in the long term, becomes clear from a consideration of that criterion of good theory which has been called fruitfulness.[1] The question is raised, fruitful for what? Fruitful for the understanding of society or of the human psyche, or fruitful for the understanding of religion? It is this question which suggests that a body of theory, developing in the hands of those whose primary concern is a better understanding of religion, would be more holistic and better integrated, than the body of theory which arises out of the necessarily fragmented insights of those whose primary concerns lie elsewhere.

Psychological, sociological, economic, and aesthetic evaluation of religion will properly remain. Elements of religion, identified as such within an integrated understanding, would again take their place in explanations within other disciplines, whether they were previously labelled as such or not. Now, however, they could well carry with them depths of meaning born of relationships previously unrecognized. I am persuaded that such a body of theory developing in the hands of the student of religion *per se*, would serve the purpose of all disciplines better than anything we have now, or could hope to have in the prevailing situation. Thus, while bridges between disciplines are always important, at this time I believe that Religious Studies must:

a) become truly a discipline in its own right, by

b) defining its own object of study (however tentatively) in terms of the object itself, that is, as non-reductively as possible,

---

[1] Ian G Barbour, *Issues in Science and Religion*, (London: S.C.M., 1968), p.144f.

or it will not be in a position to fulfill the other criterion of the normative discipline, which is to:

c) develop and evaluate its own theory in terms of what enriches understanding of its own object of study.

When this is being done we may speak accurately of a science of religion as distinct from, for example, a science of society in which religion, as understood by scholars in that field, figures. We then have, without any detriment to study at lower levels of generality, the dynamic interaction between theory and experiment (the latter being broadly understood to include fieldwork and historical studies) that typifies science.

In Part II of this book I have made a beginning upon a theory of religion that would enable Religious Studies to become, in the manner just described, a discipline in its own right.

The preceding problem is a potential one. How different a body of theory would be that was generated in the hands of those whose primary concern was religion, one cannot say. There is, however, another consequence of the present situation in religious studies that is all too actual. The problem has to do with the setting of limits to the phenomenon of religion, or to the class "religious phenomena", whichever is preferred. It is concerned with the generation of a normative understanding of religion.

2. THE NORMATIVE UNDERSTANDING OF RELIGION

The title does not, of course, refer to a normative understanding of whatever is generated within a single religious tradition and which its adherents hold and proclaim, but to the understanding, such as practitioners of religious studies might be expected to have, of what is to be included in religion as a human phenomenon. This normative understanding of religion is something that every serious student in the field must work with, even if sub-consciously, and there should be a commitment to seek its constant refinement.

To the student whose primary concern is society, or the psyche, or indeed anything other than religion, it simply cannot matter whether some phenomenon is labeled religious, provided that it is real, that is, provided it is effective within the processes that are being investigated. It is also the case that scholars in other disciplines frequently have a particular interest in extreme forms of what they regard as religion. It is not simply that pathological and near pathological forms stick out like the proverbial sore thumb but that they are indicators of the pressures in individual and social life in which these scholars are likely to be interested. This emphasis cannot have good consequences for the accurate conceptualization of religion, and it is all too easy to pass from non-normal religion, to religion as abnormal.

What is to be regarded as normative cannot be determined solely by those manifestations of religion which appear the most obvious candidates. We cannot assume that their very obviousness is not the result of some pathology. Nor can what is normative be determined by that which is currently the most widespread, for that is to foreclose with the present. One must allow for the possibility that religion is the seeking of something beyond that which has been achieved or that its adherents, in the pressures of their context, have made religion something other than it has in itself to be. One might look to discover what the founders and reformers of great traditions thought they were offering, but then that is not necessarily the same as understanding why its adherents, down through history, have taken hold of what was offered.

Because we are confronted with that familiar circularity in which we cannot know what to look at until we have defined it and cannot define it until we have looked and discovered what it is, we must begin as best we may, but long remain tentative. In general we must seek to distil the nature of religion in the widest context, that is, by taking account of the greatest number of different considerations, including all those mentioned above and also the internal logic or logics operating within religion itself.

The most responsible normative understanding, and thence the most responsible choice of a definition, would be the one which, in the end, is likely to embrace in one integrated understanding, the widest range of phenomena understood to be religious.

Although it cannot matter to other social scientists what some quasi-religious phenomenon is called, what is included or excluded from the category of religion is of vital importance to the student of religion *per se*. The decision concerning what should constitute religion, therefore, must be faced by the student of religion and not left to other disciplines. I have tried in what follows to be responsible in the above sense. In particular, my years in Africa have persuaded me that *South* is at least as important as *East* and *West* in any general assessment of what is normative religion.

I now turn to three points concerned with explanation in the study of religion. They have to do with its power, its level and its form.

3. POWER OF EXPLANATION

I am here concerned with the *power* of different kinds of explanation.

There is the weaker, or *ex post facto* type which reveals the steps by which an existing state of affairs developed. Tracing backwards from a completed state of affairs, it can follow a single path from, as it were, leaf tip, along a branch, through junctions and down the stem to the tap root. The path is clear, there are no choices to be made. This type of explanation identifies all the parts in an existing system and shows how they are inter-related. Then there is the stronger, or *a priori* type which moves the other way. That is, from root to tip, and in which explanation means nothing less than the power to predict which path would be chosen at each divide in the way.

There are those who maintain that only the former type of explanation is available to the social sciences, because they deal with individuals exercising freewill and with groups of such individuals. Equally, there are those who see freewill as a mere epiphenomenon of potentially predictable biological or economic processes.

I would not identify solely with either position but would argue that the quest for predictive power ought not to be given up lightly, even if one feels that ultimately it cannot be achieved. It includes all that the weaker type has to offer and, being the more exacting, the choice is methodologically better. In addition, one of the things that I will be seeking to show is that the choices in question are not unlimited and to know these limits is already to be able to predict something.

What I have sought, therefore, is a model of religion which will make possible the prediction of religious change in a known contextual disturbance.

4. LEVELS OF EXPLANATION

Contained within, but not identical to, the levels at which religion may be studied are levels at which it might be explained.

The first thing that must be said is that the present venture, should it succeed, will never be a substitute for explanations taking place in other and usually more immediate frameworks. That levels of explanation can be hierarchically "nested" is more obvious in the hard sciences than in the social sciences, but something of the same principle applies, and some consideration of the former may throw light upon the latter.

In the physical sciences, a phenomenon observed by a botanist will be given an explanation in terms of entities appropriate at the life sciences level. It will also have explanations in terms of entities appropriate at the levels of chemistry and physics and indeed of sub-levels within these. To have explained at the most basic and universal level, in this case that of sub-atomic physics, is not to have exhausted explanation. New levels of complexity create new entities which observe regularities of their own. Those regularities also stand in need of explanation. The migration of animals is not best understood at the level of physics although it might contribute much to the total picture.

Socio-biology is the attempt to relate explanation at the levels of society and of biology. If it adds explanation at the level of life science entities to explanations at the level of social entities, we are enriched. If it thinks to replace the latter by the former, it threatens to impoverish us. Significant people are not only genes. They are as much defined by their environment as by what they are in themselves. That is not to say that genes do not set limits to the way that humanity can value courses of action and still survive.

All of this is true *mutatis mutandis* of religion. There are multiple levels at which explanation can be offered, for religion is overtly present at many levels. Religion may be explained as an ultimate context for meaning or as an essential factor in social existence. It may be understood as an instrument for social control or as the way in which individuals organize to cope with inadequacies. It may be understood as a factor in the development of individual identity. It has not generally been supposed that religion is present at levels lower than that of the human individual, but I doubt if we have heard the last of the gene as the linchpin in such a quest.

In this book I have not supposed that explanation of religion at one level renders explanation at other levels superfluous. Indeed this paradigmatic approach needs to demonstrate the power of the paradigm chosen to integrate explanations at other levels. This is not an overt theme of the book but I believe that it will be sufficiently obvious.

5. FORMS OF EXPLANATION

It is said that any explanation must include relationship with at least one entity outside of that which is to be explained, otherwise what is said is merely description. This is a persuasive statement and if one defines explanation in these terms then it is true, but it is not very practical. A consequence of this position, namely that there could be no ultimate explanations because there would then be nothing outside the system to relate to, is a well recognized problem but it does little to diminish the authority of explanations at lower levels.

My present concern is with the form of explanation appropriate to a large, relatively closed system, in which it could be much more important to know the relationship of the parts to each other than to know how the whole is related to something beyond itself. It is useful, and certainly the custom, to speak of the description of such relationships as an "explanation" and not just a "description". "Description" suggests something that might be superficial and incomplete. "Explanation" suggests a certain rigor. Perhaps we need another word, but for present purposes I will use the word "explanation" for descriptions that include a term outside what is to be explained, as well as for the description of interrelations within a system where there is a rigorous framework such as the one that will be created here by the unpacking of a paradigm.

The question of what form properly comprises an explanation has implications for both the definition of religion and its scientific study, I will deal with it under those headings.

THE DEFINITION OF RELIGION

Beyond the normative understanding of religion, of which I spoke earlier, comes the quest for a definition. Any quest for a theory requires at least a tentative definition. The study of religion inevitably includes comparison, and comparison presupposes that there is something called religion in different cultures and in different individuals which can be compared. Unless one has a workable definition of religion, one cannot begin serious study. The more discriminating, that is the more restrictive the conditions for membership of the class "religion", the more precise the possible comparisons.[2]

I will leave aside the definition of religion as institution because, as will become clear, the corporate form cannot be primary in religion. The defining condition of religion then may be either a factor external to the individual and to which religion is understood to be the response, or a factor within the individual. If it is the latter, then inevitably it will also be a factor within that which one ends up defining as religion.

Definitions of religion in terms of a response to some factor external to the individual may themselves be divided into two kinds, namely, those in which the response is positive (that is, the relationship is sought or affirmed) and those in which the response is negative (that is, flight or compensation).

In the external and positive kind of definition the external factor may be empirical or it may be non-empirical. The empirical kind could be satisfactory as a starting point for a scientific study, but, because these relate to something valued, they tend to be culture specific.

In external positive definitions of the non-empirical kind, for example, "religion is a response to a super-human being", the reality of the non-empirical external factor may be simply affirmed or, more frequently, be assumed not to be an issue in the usefulness of the definition. I would maintain that such a definition is useless, unless it can be made plain to what experience in the adherent the name given to the external factor refers. Five persons saying "I believe in a super-human being" could mean five different things and refer to five different experiences. I would have no means of

---

[2] For this reason the substitution of Wittgenstein's "family traits" for an essential definition as suggested by Rem Edwards is to be resisted. See Rem B Edwards, *Reason and Religion*, (New York: Harcourt Brace Jovanovich, 1972), p.14f.

determining in which, if any, religion was present. If to say "I believe in a super-human being" is itself understood to be religious, then religion has been trivialized. Nevertheless, within a particular religious tradition, it may be possible to say to what experience the name given to the external factor refers. That is, it may be possible to point to an empirical factor.

This "positive relationship with an external factor" type of definition, is the way in which most of my readers, having grown up in the western world, would begin to define religion, that is, as some relation to God. This book will also begin in that way. To universalize such a definition to include all religious traditions, however, defeats simplicity in language and it is not the type of definition with which I finally work.

Definitions which include a negative response to an external factor are common in the social sciences. Religion is defined as a response to the threat of death, of chaos, or of powerlessness. Religions need have nothing in common except that they are all forms of a refusal to see or accept reality. This type of definition can be useful to those whose primary concern is with society or the individual psyche. It relates easily to those extreme experiences of religion in which social scientists are frequently interested and, as I said, it cannot matter to them what the phenomenon is called.

For the student of religion *per se*, because to them it is crucial what is included in the conceptual corral "religion", a definition based on a negative response to some external factor is too imprecise. Even if one were to select a particular focus of fear, the styles of avoidance could be virtually limitless.

When the defining characteristic with which one works is something going on within the individual, the definition is a description rather than a explanation in the hard sense. Some aspect of individual functioning is described and then named "religion". It might be a quest, it might be a way of engaging with experience. This is the type of definition with which I finally work. The defining characteristic is drawn from within religion itself and relates to its objective. As will become clear, I regard it as leading to more than mere description.

In developing a theory one is seeking to contribute to a precise and universal language. By drawing my defining characteristic from within the individual and, therefore, from within religion itself, I have sought to model religion in its own terms. I make no claim that religious people will recognize my language as their own, but I do believe that I have isolated elements that religious people will admit describe, albeit at a different level of generality, something of their own experience.

THE SCIENTIFIC STUDY OF RELIGION

The question of whether the social sciences are truly scientific and how their style of study relates to that of the physical sciences has provoked much debate. I do not wish to enter that debate head on. I wish to deal only with religion and to say how that can be studied scientifically. I begin with how it may *not* be studied scientifically.

The usual and, I think, *wrong* understanding of what constitutes a scientific approach to religion might be presented as follows:

> If the final aim of scientific enquiry, (following upon description and the identification of regularities) is explanation, then that explanation must include entities other than that which is to be explained, otherwise the explanation is no more than description.

> That which is to be explained therefore, in this case religion or perhaps religious phenomena, must be understood to be one thing among others, in human experience.

> The first task is to establish some criterion by which religion or religious phenomena can be identified.

> The next, if one conceives of religion as a single entity, is to show how it is related to other realms of human experience of a reasonably cognate kind.

> If one prefers not to think of religion as a single entity, but as the name of a class in which a plurality of religious phenomena might be conceptually corralled, then the task is to show how these phenomena are related to each other and then to non-religious phenomena.

The problem with this inevitably reductionist approach lies in the criterion for identifying religion or religious phenomena. Presumably the statement "Religion is X" (or the statement "P and Q are religious phenomena") would need to be falsifiable if it were to provide the first step in a scientific approach to religion. This goes back to my earlier statement that an external positive defining condition for membership of the class religion must be meaningful to both adherent and (scientific) observer. This is the case even where the observer is dependent upon the adherent's testimony as to the presence (or otherwise) of such a defining factor.

It has to be admitted that religion can give rise to strange behavior, but the serious researcher cannot write off all religiousness as a form of sickness. The observer must be able to feel assured that the one offering testimony is, in this particular regard, a rational human being. How can this be judged if the defining condition for the presence of religion is not meaningful to the observer, which in this case means that he or she knows to what experience in the adherent the defining factor refers.[3] In what I have described as the wrong approach, terms such as "god" and "transcendence", would have to be commutable into terms meaningful to the observer if he or she was to be able to say whether relation to them was present or not. I believe that the word "god" can be commuted within particular and appropriate traditions and the word "transcendence" has meaning in a dualistic world view. However, religion in general (which includes the non-theistic and the monistic) cannot be defined in terms of such words.

I have already said that criteria based on avoidance, such as the flight from meaninglessness or the quest for security, would be too imprecise, unless it were intended that all flight from all forms of meaninglessness were to be what comprises religion, and that could hardly be the case.

An alternative way of stating my problem, with this understanding of what constitutes a scientific approach, is to say that it is contrary to the self-understanding of the religious adherent. Religion is about an ultimate of one kind or another. Either it relates the adherent to that which establishes everything else, or sets him apart from everything else as that appears, or maintains him in harmonious relation within everything else. To seek to use criteria lifted out of that "everything else" to decide what shall and what shall not count as religion, seems to me to have changed the very nature of that which one is considering and to be a self-defeating programme.

I conclude that a scientific approach to the study of religion which begins in the way described is simply not possible. Equally I do not believe that that is the only way in which one may begin an enquiry into religion which may be properly described as scientific. I do not think it necessary to begin a study of religion by considering it to be one thing among others of its kind. If one understands science to be defined by its method rather than by the nature of what it looks at, then religion may be investigated as a self-contained realm of experience and the approach remain scientific.

THE PARADIGMATIC APPROACH

The scientific method by which humankind has sought to get to grips with its physical environment and, in modified form with the social environment, functions with paradigms. That is, it functions within overall ways of seeing which are shaped by, or focused in, key theories. Within these overall ways of seeing, explanation takes place. It is accepted that there are

---

[3] "Experience" as it is used here cannot refer directly to what the individual feels but only indirectly, and a step at a time, via describable contexts of experience which, it might be supposed, generate similar feelings in similar people. See chapter 2 for a variety of such "experiences".

no ultimate explanations and the paradigms can change quite dramatically.[4] Paradigms are not true or false, simply better or worse; verifiable, *qua* paradigm, only in that they do for us whatever we feel needs to be done. Paradigms, by their very nature, do not arise directly out of the study of the phenomena under investigation. Rather they emerge as dawning insight enters a new contender in the lists for the sole accolade, "paradigm". The duel is decided by the contender's power to usefully illuminate in depth and breadth the whole phenomena under investigation in the simplest possible terms.

Religion is not best understood as one thing among others to be explained within whatever paradigm is operable in some other field. Rather, religion is such that an understanding of it operates at the paradigmatic level. An understanding of religion is a paradigm within which explanation takes place by establishing coherence in the structure and function of its component elements.

If explanation requires seeing religion as one thing among others, it cannot be explained, but an understanding of religion may serve to explain the structural and functional interrelation of its own elements and thence the relation of these elements to other factors in human experience.

THE APPROACH EMPLOYED IN THIS BOOK

I begin Part II of the book with the understanding that religion is:

the quest for, maintenance or realization of belonging to an ultimately-real. The ultimately-real being that to which the individual most feels the need to belong in order to secure, give meaning to, or otherwise enrich his or her existence.

I then proceed in a largely deductive manner from that starting point, showing:

a) what the potential elements of religion are when it is understood in this way and how they interrelate

and, given that religion will change in socio-cultural disturbance so as to maintain or restore a sense of belonging,

---

[4] See Thomas Kuhn, *The Structure of Scientific Revolutions*, 2nd edition,(Chicago: University of Chicago Press, 1970). See also the literature generated in the debate that still goes on. For an application to religion studies see C Strug, "Kuhn's Paradigm Thesis: A Two Edged Sword for Philosophy of Religion," in *Religious Studies*, Vol.20, p.269f.

b) what are the conditions which would be likely to predispose particular movements within this frame of interrelated elements.

I say "largely deductive manner" because one is seeking to illuminate the development and interrelation of elements of religion normatively understood; and both the starting point and the directions in which one subsequently chooses to go are inevitably guided by that consideration. In my view, this approach not only remains scientific but, given the nature of that which we are investigating, is the only approach that can be considered scientific.

What is advocated is, as to sources of knowledge, empiricist, history being understood to provide the experimental data. As to the verification of knowledge, or better, as to the verification of the more ultimate ways of seeing that make verification in general possible, it is pragmatist. I will say later why I think Bertrand Russell's criticism of William James, on this score, misunderstood what James intended.

SOME PROBLEMS OF THE PARADIGMATIC APPROACH

This approach requires a specific definition of religion. The more specific the definition of religion with which one works, the more likely it is that one will have to say of certain phenomena and indeed of certain persons regarded as, or regarding themselves as religious, that they are not so, and (no less provocatively) *vice versa*. I see no help for this. If one is to be scientific, in the sense of seeking to explain religious phenomena in the most rigorous theoretical frame available, then one must begin with a definition that is both functional and appropriate to the most normative understanding of religion.

Another problem is that I am proposing a procedure in which the scientific study of religion would not provide a body of knowledge that could be integrated with the body of knowledge provided by the scientific study of the physical realm. More seriously, the body of knowledge provided by the social sciences would only be integratable to the degree that its paradigms were acknowledged, and then found their place within those proposed for religion rather than vice versa. I say this because, just as physics, operating at the most basic level, is in some sense the ultimate science, giving a sense of unity to all the hard sciences, so religious studies is in some sense the ultimate social science because it deals with humanity's attempts to understand experience at the most ultimate level.

This is perhaps what it sounds, a claim to hegemony, a return to *credo ut intelligam*. Unfortunately, I do not see how this can be avoided. Every conscious engagement, on anything more than an immediate day to day level, with the world-out-there presupposes an ontology. That is, it presupposes some understanding of the nature of that with which one is engaging, if not consciously, then by implication. The study of religion, as presented here, is *inter alia* the study of the ultimate models of reality and of attempts to hold these together and to locate all else within them.

Finally, it could be asserted that this approach runs foul of "Occam's razor" by masking the fact that only religious traditions actually exist, while religion is only an idea in the mind of the scholar. This is not the place to enter into a debate concerning the nature and limits of what might properly be regarded as "existents" of which knowledge can be had, but the divide represented in what has just been said must be clarified.

It is clear that there are, if one can agree to some broad definition, religious traditions available to public scrutiny. Is there not also something more universal within the human situation, which, in accounting for the existence and form of the traditions, deserves the title "religion"? If one rejects such a thing as a possibility, then knowledge of the external world would be limited to what could be observed at a surface. The model of what lies behind a surface, verified by its being the model that best enables one to engage with whatever is there, would not constitute knowledge of an existent, but would be simply a construct or, at best, an abstraction.

It is my view that the academic task is not primarily about accurately describing surfaces, but about discovering the most enriching mode of engagement with whatever is out there. I also hold that it is the better practice to make the model of that with which one is engaging, overt, rather than to function as if there were no reality there. A model it certainly remains, but that of which it is a model is not less real because it is not immediately available to the senses. There is no such thing as religion in much the same way as there was no such thing as an atom. Nevertheless, whatever was out there made a very large disturbance when scientists acted as if to split the atom they had posited.

Given that we could not in a multitude of lifetimes know all the riches of actual religious traditions, may we not (if we prefer it to living with little bits of immediately available experience) seek to grasp as much as we can of the whole? This we may do by learning something of the human drives and the limits set upon the fulfillment of these drives that together generate the religious traditions. I would not then claim to have experienced the whole of religion, although I might claim to have, in one way, understood it.

THE ADVANTAGE OF THE PARADIGMATIC APPROACH

On the positive side, this method shares a structure with that which is being studied and this has at least an affective advantage. Religion, at the conscious and cognitive level, begins with an understanding of an ultimate reality and draws out the consequences of that understanding for life. Likewise, this method of approach begins with a paradigm for religion and then seeks to draw out the consequences of that understanding for the directions and forms that it will take in human life. It does not have the appearance of judging an ultimate by its component parts (or even its own creation), which is what so alienates the adherent of a religious tradition from the scientific study of religion as that has usually been understood.

I have given considerable space to arguing for an approach to the study of religion in which, after careful consideration of the phenomenon, one simply states a definition. One does not argue its truth, but rather concentrates on demonstrating its power to relate structurally and functionally the elements that are generally considered to constitute religion. This one must do until a paradigm is suggested that proves to be more all embracing, more fruitful, or to have the virtue of greater simplicity. Having argued for that as a method, it is not the way I begin. One reason for this is that while the proof of the paradigmatic pudding is very definitely in the eating, and therefore authentication must necessarily emerge late in the process, there is something that can be said in preliminary justification of the choice of paradigm. It seems to me that what can be said ought to be said, in order to assure the reader that her or his investment of time is likely to be profitable.

Part I, apart from laying the foundations for a scientific study of religion by teasing out the threads of what constitutes religion, is a "persuasive" concerning the reasonableness of the point from which Part II begins, that is, with the paradigmatic understanding of religion as belonging. If one simply begins with the general theory in Part II, one must suspend judgment upon the validity of the starting point until the usefulness, or otherwise, of the framework to which it gives rise, can be evaluated.

PART I

FOUNDATIONS FOR A SCIENTIFIC STUDY OF RELIGION

THE NATURE OF RELIGION AND RELIGIOUS DISCOURSE

The purpose of Part I is to lay a foundation for a scientific study of religion. The meaning of the word "scientific" in this context will be dealt with in the first chapter.

Many different things can be built upon a foundation, but foundations are not normally laid without a particular building in mind. The construction that I will have in mind throughout Part I is developed in Part II. Because a foundation is never self-justifying, but is justified by what is (or what could be) built upon it, I will sometimes need to point forward in order to justify the choices made. Nevertheless, these are not foundations that could only support one theory of religion. They are conceptual foundations for a scientific study of religion and will serve the reader in that purpose whether or not he or she approves the theoretical proposals of Part II.

A WORD TO READERS NEW TO THE FIELD

Studying religion is not the same as studying other subjects. The probing into aspects of religion that are familiar can be disturbing for believers and non-believers alike. Yet there are benefits in refining the knowledge of what is believed or not believed, particularly in relation to the beliefs of others. To refine this sort of knowledge, however, one must be prepared to dig under the surface of things long taken for granted.

A word is only a sound, or marks on a surface, until it is related to the experience that gives it meaning. Religious words are not different in this respect. In this chapter we will be asking, to what experiences in the believer does the word "religion" relate and, more narrowly, to what experience could the word "god" relate. Believers often find this question uncomfortable. It seems to diminish god, particularly when the experience is spoken of in everyday terms. Yet an inquiry into how best to speak of an experience, in order to compare it with others, cannot diminish that which is being experienced.

To say that reality can only be understood by human beings creating mental models of it, is not to say, of whatever is out there, that it is not worth engaging with as though it were at least the entity that it is modelled to be.

Try to remain as detached as the study will allow until you have a total picture of the matter under discussion. If at that stage you find the approach helpful it can become your own. If not, at least you will have considered another point of view.

CHAPTER 1

APPROACHES IN THE STUDY OF RELIGION

Religion is studied by people in a variety of disciplines and for many different reasons. Unfortunately, those who study it are not blessed with a common understanding of what should comprise the thing that they study. There is no clarity on what should be regarded as central to religion and what peripheral, nor even on what should be included and what excluded. It is not surprising, therefore, that the field is strewn with unresolved debates about method of approach or that so many different styles of scholarship have emerged.[1]

The situation requires that anyone writing about religion begin by helping the reader to locate what is about to be offered within all the possible approaches.

There are many points that could be made in order to locate the book. Fortunately readers need only be aware of two of them before they start, these require little background and are relatively simple to explain.

The points concern:

a) long standing traditions in basic approach to the study of religion

b) the multiple levels upon which religion can and must be studied.

---

[1] This diversity is ably surveyed in the introductions to the two volumes edited by Frank Whaling, *Contemporary Approaches to the Study of Religion*, (New York: Mouton 1984 and 1985.)

TWO TRADITIONS IN THE APPROACH TO RELIGION

There are two long standing traditions in the scientific study of religion. What distinguishes them at root is the way in which their representatives understand the word "religion". They understand the word to refer to two related but very different things. My present purpose is not to evaluate these usages, but to make clear which of the two will be employed in this book.

One may understand the word "religion" to refer to something external and publicly observable. That is, it may refer to an institution or institutions, among other institutions, in the history of humankind, identifiable in relation to such things as communities sharing a tradition (that is beliefs, attitudes and practices), also in relation to functionaries (such as priests or rabbis), to scriptures, to special times, places and buildings. One may evaluate such institutions, or parts thereof, positively or negatively, but either way one must conceive of the possibility that they will cease to exist and that human history will continue without them. This was the position of such leaders in the field as Max Weber, Karl Marx and Sigmund Freud.

This view has the advantage that religion, being one rather stable socio-historical fact among others, can be described in terms of its relationship with other facets of social existence and therefore in clear and literal language. One has the sense of dealing with something tangible.

The disadvantages of the view are, first, that it tends to fix the conceptualization of religion in a world where everything else is changing and therefore renders it highly vulnerable. Second, few adherents of any religious tradition would feel that the descriptions offered approximate the heartland of experiential religion and this makes dialogue between adherent and scholar difficult, if not impossible.

On the other hand the word "religion" may be understood to refer to some essential aspect in the process of being human, or at least of being part of a social humanity. If so, then as long as human beings or human societies remain there will be religion. This was the position espoused by scholars such as Emile Durkheim and Carl Jung.

This position has the advantage of a certain affinity with what adherents of religious traditions might say of their own experience. On the other hand, it becomes far less tangible, because it must be conceived that religion may take many different forms. Religion in the future may bear little or no resemblance to that which we now know, yet remain religion because it performs the same function.

From time to time I will have to use the word "religion" to refer to the institutionalized forms, but basically religion will be understood as an essential function in normal human existence which may mutate, but not disappear, as long as humanity survives.

I do not suppose religion to exist in splendid isolation in the realm of ideas, uninfluenced by the material conditions of life. On the other hand I do not suppose its existence, or its form, to be best explained in material terms, whether these are presented as modes of production, genes, or in any other way.

I believe that there is a universal drive for the development and maintenance of individual identity which has sometimes proved more important than the drive for physical survival. Religion is related to both, but more closely to the former.

MULTIPLE LEVELS IN THE STUDY OF RELIGION

The second point of location that I need to make concerns the multiple levels upon which religion can and must be studied. In particular, I must make clear to what level of study this book is intended to be a contribution. This point will take longer than the previous one but the ideas are no more complex.

There are different styles in the study of religion. The ones that will concern me here are those that depend on the choice, not always conscious, to study religion at a particular level of generality. This may range from the study of one individual's experience within a particular tradition, right up to the study of religion as a universal human phenomenon. Between these two extremes lie many other levels including, for example, the study of one tradition, and the comparative study of two or more traditions.

I will speak of "higher levels" when I refer to those styles of study that approach the phenomenon of religion on the more universal levels. It is not in any way suggested that a higher level of study is better than a lower one. In fact the higher levels of study are absolutely dependent upon the results achieved at lower levels.

I will begin with some simple but significant distinctions that are intended to enable readers new to the field to locate and integrate what will be offered to them here, with material offered to them on other levels and within different disciplines.

SOME PRELIMINARY DISTINCTIONS

I begin with the observation that all studies of religion fall into two broad categories. These are:

i) studies conducted by scholars whose primary concern is an improved understanding of religion itself

ii) studies undertaken by those whose primary concern lies elsewhere, for example, with the understanding of society or the human psyche.

The former are usually to be found in departments of theology or of religious studies or (hopefully where the differences are clearly defined and observed) in departments that combine both. The latter studies are better conducted where their primary interest is supported, in departments of sociology or psychology; philosophy, history or anthropology.

i) Studies in which Religion is the Primary Concern

Studies, by those whose primary concern is religion, may be further broken down into those in which the concern is to DO religion; those in which the concern is to OBSERVE religion; and those in which the concern is to EXPLAIN, that is to model, religion.

Because observation is not possible without the doing, nor explaining without both the observation and the doing, these activities comprise a hierarchy of levels at which religion can be studied.

I will speak of the "doers", those scholars whose purpose is to serve a particular religious tradition, as theologians, although, of course, they would not be literally that in non-theistic traditions. The scholarly observation of religions has traditionally been spoken of as History of Religions, but since the dominant approach to history of religions became phenomenological it has become the fashion to speak of the Phenomenology of Religion. Scholars working at this level seek to observe and record manifestations of a particular religious tradition or some behavior or experience regarded as religious, *as it is in itself*. That is, they seek to observe it without imposing any external categories, without imposing any interpretation or evaluation upon it. Explaining on the other hand proceeds by creating models. It is to do Science of Religion.

The word "science" may be used in its literal sense of "knowledge" (usually the systematic quest for knowledge) and thus even detached observation, that is, history of religions or phenomenology, is widely spoken of as science of religion, but I will restrict my use of "science" to the quest for a theoretical understanding. Those doing science of religion in this restricted sense necessarily impose ways of seeing upon the data gathered by those operating at the level of observation.

I have avoided the familiar term "comparative religion" because it is debatable on which level some of its sub-activities such as defining, classifying and comparing, lie.

Thus there are three interacting levels in the study of religion, Doing (at the intellectual level), Observing and Explaining.

STUDIES BY THOSE WHOSE PRIMARY CONCERN IS RELIGION

Science of Religion (explanation)

o

Phenomenology of Religion (observation)

o

"Theology" (serving a tradition)

---

ii) Studies in which Religion is not the Primary Concern

Studies of religion by those whose primary concern is other than religion may also be usefully sub-divided. This will serve to clarify their relation to the heartland of religious studies and, in particular, to indicate their strong points.

The limitation (in relation to religious studies) of all such approaches is that they necessarily operate with a partial model of religion. This is not the fault of the scholars concerned, but is a limitation set by the nature of their discipline. For example, one discipline may be adapted to the study of the behavior of groups, while another may be adapted to the study of the behavior of individuals. Religion involves both. Logic has no place for feeling nor feeling for logic, but a study of religion must embrace both.

Because religion must be considered in terms of its outward and institutional manifestations as well as in terms of something inward (done or experienced by the individual) it is appropriate to divide these disciplines into:

i) those whose general approach is to something already existent "out there", which one requires to understand, be it a society or a logic,

ii) those whose concern is with what goes on within an individual faced with a world of such existent entities.

The first group, the disciplines with an "outer focus", may be further divided into those whose method is largely empirical, that is experimental and observational, and those whose method is almost entirely cognitive. The empirical group includes the disciplines of history, sociology and anthropology and those specialized by culture, such as Indology, and African, Oriental, Middle-Eastern and, perhaps, Modernization studies. The cognitive group includes the various sub-disciplines that comprise philosophy.

The second group, the one with the largely "inner focus", includes psychology and also those humanities that are strong in affective expression.

These divisions, together with some suggested strong points of each, are summarized in the following table:

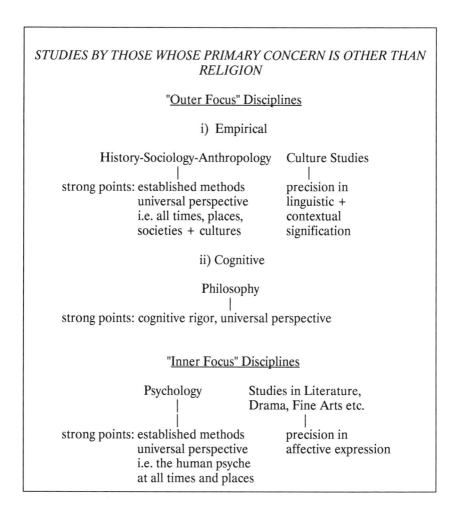

STUDIES BY THOSE WHOSE PRIMARY CONCERN IS OTHER THAN RELIGION

"Outer Focus" Disciplines

i) Empirical

History-Sociology-Anthropology   Culture Studies
| |
strong points: established methods   precision in
      universal perspective   linguistic +
      i.e. all times, places,   contextual
      societies + cultures   signification

ii) Cognitive

Philosophy
|
strong points: cognitive rigor, universal perspective

"Inner Focus" Disciplines

Psychology   Studies in Literature,
| Drama, Fine Arts etc.
| |
strong points: established methods   precision in
      universal perspective   affective expression
      i.e. the human psyche
      at all times and places

Religious Studies must aim to offer what these other disciplines cannot, even when they are taken together, that is, a holistic understanding of religion.

The introductory framework that I have been presenting is a very simplified one. Studies of religion have been divided in terms of what was being attempted by the scholars concerned. Thus they were divided into studies which sought to support, to observe or to explain religion; or to contribute (by a study of religion in particular) to the general understanding of human corporate or individual functioning. None of these distinctions is based on any feature of religion itself.

It will now serve my purpose better to return to the level of generality at which religion is being studied and draw my distinctions that way.

Because scholars who are "doing", "observing" or "explaining" religion necessarily work at different levels, the levels now to be described will include what has already been said about them. Looked at in this way, however, it can be seen where the levels shade into one another and why this can become a source of potential confusion.

An additional and highly significant reason for setting out these levels of generality, is that it enables me to show the variation from level to level of the way in which a statement (made about religion) is judged to be true or false. The criteria for what shall constitute a valid statement are not the same at each level and if the levels are not clear nor can the criteria be.

Students in departments of religious studies used to be told "Do not make faith statements in an academic essay.", but, more and more, one finds theology, biblical studies and comparative religion being taught in the same context. It is even possible that students enroled in the same course may be there for quite different reasons. The criteria for validity, appropriate to phenomenology of religion, would be totally inappropriate in both the scientific study of religion and in theology. It is important to be clear at all times which level of approach is in operation and what are the appropriate criteria for the validity of a statement. This section asks a little more of the reader but it is important.

A MORE DETAILED BREAKDOWN OF STUDIES OF RELIGION BY THEIR LEVEL OF GENERALITY

I begin at the lower levels of generality and therefore where I was when I considered the "doers", those people who are academically involved with aspects of their own tradition.

LEVEL (I) - STUDIES IN OR OF A SINGLE RELIGION

Study from Within a Tradition

For present purposes I begin with the general study of a single religious tradition from within, usually, of course, by a scholar who is also an adherent.

It will be seen that even within this one level there are styles which operate with different understandings of the generality of the theological enterprise. The higher includes the lower, but not *vice versa*, so that they constitute a sub-hierarchy of levels within the one level.

First, there is the style that functions, consciously anyway, only at the cognitive level. It applies the established principles of interpretation, the criteria for what constitutes a valid statement within the community concerned   (I will speak of these as the grammar)   to the study of the received tradition without conscious reference to anything outside of it. It deals with tradition as a timeless truth. In any setting that lays claim to being academic, the sociologies of knowledge and of language represent a challenge to the validity of this style.

Second, there is the style that recognizes that the tradition exists in a context to which it must relate, perhaps by engagement, perhaps by flight. It is recognized that the context, in posing questions to which adherents of the tradition must respond, provides not only questions but also factual evidence in the process of interpretation.

Finally, there is the style that recognizes that the tradition is not only shaped by responding consciously and overtly to the questions posed by ongoing experience, but that its very meaning at any point in time arises in a dynamic relationship with its context. It recognizes that feelings are shaped by a context seen in varying degrees through the spectacles of the tradition itself. These feelings then play a significant part in influencing the questions that are chosen, the evidence that seems appropriate, the acceptability of alternative solutions and in the end, therefore, the acceptable grammar of the tradition itself. What feels real, as well as the meaning of the language in which it is expressed, is recognized to be heavily dependent on the context.

Excursions to the more general levels in this sub-hierarchy of approaches may enrich the questions being asked at lower levels, but they may also weaken symbols and disrupt the grammar.

In certain circumstances, for example when cultures compete, there may be those who study two or more traditions from the inside. Those with a commitment to Christianity and to African culture and perhaps also to a Materialist interpretation of history, would be in this position. In such situations the criteria for what constitutes a valid statement will inevitably be confused. It is because the need is to integrate, or at least to bridge these traditions (so as to operate from within a united tradition), that I mention it at this level.

Study of a Single Tradition from Without

The next style within this level of generality is one that has moved from study within a tradition while recognizing its context, to studying a context with special reference to a tradition. This is what I take the Indologist or Africanist, with a special interest in religion, to be doing. A form of comparative study emerges here when different and independent methods, historical, sociological, textual, are used to investigate the one tradition.

At this stage we must recognize that something has had to give. Generality at one level means contraction at another and given equivalent ability, time and dedication, the scholar who opts for a higher level of generality cannot gain the same detailed knowledge, at first hand, as the one who opts for a lower level. It is this that makes dependence of the higher levels on the lower absolute, while dependence of the lower on the higher is conditional upon immediate needs and purposes.

Study of a single tradition from without is generally undertaken by someone other than an adherent, but not always so. This can lead to confusion about the criteria of validity that are in operation. The grammar of the tradition can no longer be appealed to when one has moved out of it and when the criteria are those of the linguistic, textural and historical disciplines, and perhaps also those of sociology, psychology and anthropology. Old Testament studies have been highly susceptible to confusion concerning which set of criteria is, or ought to be, in operation.

LEVEL (II) - THE STUDY OF TWO OR MORE RELIGIONS BY THE METHODS OF A PARTICULAR DISCIPLINE DEFINED OTHERWISE THAN BY A CONCERN WITH RELIGION

This level is the one found typically in the social science disciplines. In terms of religion it is more general than the previous one and has a universal interest in society, the psyche etc.. However, in other ways it is as restricted as studies defined by a culture. An Indologist may be concerned with all things Indian and have a special interest in religion, likewise a sociologist or psychologist has a concern with the functioning of society or the individual psyche and may have a special interest in religion. Philosophy of religion usually functions at this level. Likewise, the missiologist (a theologian concerned with mission) may have a commitment within a particular religious tradition and have a special interest in viewing other religions from within it.

As I said earlier, all of the above may and perhaps optimally should take place elsewhere than within departments dedicated to the discipline of religious studies. For example, one would expect anyone making a psychological study of religion to be working within the supportive environment of the discipline of psychology, not within religious studies.

LEVEL (III) - THE STUDY OF TWO OR MORE RELIGIONS UNRESTRICTED AS TO METHOD

The level of generality which is familiar within departments of Religious Studies and the first level which could only appear there, is the same as the above save that *religious traditions* themselves have become the primary concern. Two or more religions are studied without restriction as to method. Something of individual cultures is sacrificed in order to make a comparative study of their religions. Comparative now, because more than one tradition is being studied, but also in the earlier sense that many or all methods are employed - textural, historical, philosophical, sociological, psychological. Inevitably, the first hand knowledge of methods and tools, that one would expect in the practitioners of any of these normative disciplines, would be absent.

Styles of Study: Many styles of scholarship are possible at this level. For example, the study of two traditions in considerable first hand depth with finely honed linguistic, textural and cultural-historical skills; or perhaps an interest in any and every tradition and every available method, in absolute dependence on those who work in more restricted styles.

This last style would inevitably raise some academic eyebrows, and rightly so. While synthesizing skills are useful, this would not be a style that would make any sense until the bulk of work in more restricted styles began to cause indigestion. On the other hand, if what I am saying about levels of study has any validity, then there is an important task of translation from grammar to grammar to be performed. Freud and Marx both made significant contributions to our understanding of those very limited aspects of religion with which they were concerned. The need is always with us to integrate and reintegrate their contributions within an ever-developing view of religion as a whole.

The Phenomenology of Religion: At this level of study and in appropriate styles earlier, there has long been a struggle to establish the principle of not imposing the observer's values and ways of seeing (both personal and cultural) upon what is being observed. The aim is to let what is observed speak for itself, not least about its own evaluations of its experience. In so far as this "attentive openness" is achieved one has established the *epoché* of phenomenology. The values and constructs that must not be imposed are not only the conscious and unconscious ones of the missionary or western cultural chauvinist, but also those enshrined in the theory of western disciplines. Anthropology in particular has had to be sensitive to this problem. It can even seriously be questioned whether the scientific attitude itself is not laden with western values. It is doubtful if total freedom from presuppositions is a possibility, for constructs lay buried deep in the language in which observers think and in which they must record their findings.

Needless to say, advocates of the phenomenological method fear the loss of their hard-fought-for ground. One thing that threatens it is theorizing about the nature of religion *per se*, the more so when this is focused in the quest for a definition.

Yet the comparative study of religions is inevitably a move toward definition. At the very least it is a move toward a consensus among scholars, assumed rather than spelled out, of what phenomena are to be included in the conceptual corral "religion". It is not clear to me how the scholar working genuinely in one culture, without imported presuppositions, would determine what constituted religion there. In fact it seems to me, that if phenomenologists would maintain their phenomenological stance, they must dispense with any desire to know when they are studying religion. They must be content just to observe human behavior. Perhaps those early students of African groups, who decided that there was no religion present, were nearer to a truly phenomenological stance than the modern writers who mock them.

There is a genuine and serious tension here between, on the one hand, not imposing values, and, on the other hand, the need to label what one is looking at so that comparative statements become meaningful.

Phenomenology and the Community of Scholars: The ideal criterion of validity in the phenomenological method must be that those who are observed agree with the observer's description. Clearly this has difficulties. Just the need to express what is observed in images and language familiar to a broad group of scholars makes it unlikely that such an account would be sufficiently understood by those observed.

In practice the criterion becomes a general agreement, in a community of scholars in dialogue with one another, concerning what is being seen. This is clearly more reliable than the observations of an individual observer, although a whole community may share presuppositions, as the major shifts which have taken place in theoretical positions in the social sciences testify.

Limitations of the Phenomenological Approach: A particular problem has arisen because those, who think of themselves as observing the phenomenological norms in the study of religion and speak of what they do as Phenomenology of Religion, have passed beyond observing and recording data to the "observation" of regularities and to typing and classifying. Unfortunately one does not simply "observe" regularities and it is just here that value laden theory can operate in the most insidious manner. Leaving aside the question of whether one perceives or conceives wholes and meanings, it is clear that one does not observe regularities across traditions without some priority or framework being involved, if only at the subconscious level.

Some among those who have tried to teach the results of such "observations" have become increasingly disturbed by the pretence of a value-free stance and have asked if it is not time to make it clear that one is inevitably exercising judgments upon religion.[2]

It is my understanding that the observation of regularities and the construction of types belong to the next level, that is, to the science of religion. Science of religion and phenomenology are, as methods, incompatible. One cannot do both at the same time. Science demands precision in definition, classification and theory. It necessarily imposes judgments, the validity of which is determined by the power of the theory that develops. The moment one begins to observe regularities one has moved out of the phenomenological stance. Thus there is no way one can extend the phenomenological method into a quest for a general theory of religion. When the time comes for the latter, one must back off and make a new approach and be aware that one is doing it.

When all the criticisms of phenomenologists are tabled, it still remains that they have achieved much in a long and necessary battle. As a goal, phenomenology is impossible to achieve, but as a direction of striving it remains the only approach to observation that has academic validity.

LEVEL (IV) - THE STUDY OF RELIGION AS A UNIVERSAL PHENOMENON

One could not, in a life-time, exhaust the study possibilities of just one of the major traditions. It is necessary, therefore, to say to any who would limit the study of religion to the phenomenological-historical level, that it is possible to gain some understanding of the entire human phenomenon of religion, by understanding the building bricks and processes out of which humankind weave the rich tapestries of religious traditions. This, however, entails analysis and analysis entails constructs.

Thus scholars working at this last level, wishing to go beyond observation, via the recognition of regularities, to modelling, that is, to explanation, have no choice but to impose constructs upon the data.

Explanation, in the case of religion, is limited to the attempt to hold together, in a single conceptual framework, as many as possible of the phenomena generally regarded as religious. If in the process, some

---

[2] See for example the debate initiated by Martin Prozesky in "Is There a Place in Religious Studies for the Criticism and Reformulation of Religion?", *Religion in Southern Africa* v.6 No 1.

phenomena regarded as religious are excluded and some regarded as not religious are included, that cannot be helped.

The criterion for the validity of the framework constructed is simply that it works and works better than any alternative. To "work" is to meet a number of criteria but the *sine qua non* is that the construct fits the data. That is, that it explains, by interrelating in the one conceptual frame, the widest range of the phenomena generally regarded as religious.

THE PURPOSE OF THIS BOOK

This book is intended to lay the foundations for, and introduce the reader to, the study of religion at the last of the levels described above. It is an introduction to the scientific study of religion. It is not an introduction to a social scientific study of religion, but an introduction to the scientific study of religion for its own sake. Such a scientific study may be narrowly defined as:

    i) a quest for explanation - which establishes

    ii) a process in which a particular understanding of religion as a whole (not just some aspect of it) is being refined, used and tested.

Part I of the book remains at the level of foundations. That is at the level of a search for the best "understanding of religion as a whole" with which to begin a scientific study. The best understanding being the one that is likely to prove the most powerful in the explanation of particular religious phenomena. Only in Part II is a beginning made upon a scientific study proper.

This "beginning upon a scientific study" is initiated by a deliberate reversal of earlier procedures. All the earlier chapters are an enquiry into the nature of religion as it actually exists in human experience. In chapter 8, however, I will take the understanding of religion arrived at and will draw out its consequences, creating in the process a framework within which phenomena regarded as religious, can be located and interrelated.

The power of the framework developed to locate and interrelate religious phenomena constitutes a testing of the understanding of religion from which it was generated. The understanding of religion with which one begins will survive until some other understanding of religion generates a framework that integrates more phenomena, or does it more simply, or more fruitfully.

Part I of this book, therefore, invites the reader to participate in a quest for that understanding of religion which would seem to have the greatest potential for survival, as the generator of the explanatory framework in a scientific study of religion. Part II begins that scientific study, by unpacking the consequences of the understanding of religion arrived at, into a conceptual framework.

Religion is something that is experienced. It takes place within the individual. If it is not significant at that level, it has no power to become significant at any other level. In the individual, religion is something that is felt, but it is also something that is concretized in concepts and behaviors. When religion becomes institutionalized within a community it can only be communally possessed in its concretized form, that is, as tradition. Communities do not feel, only individual members can do that.

This enquiry into the nature of religion begins with the individual and with the nature of religious experience. The following chapter takes that understanding of religious experience and shows how it might be related to the development of a religious tradition within a community. Then, because one cannot discuss the nature of religion for long without confronting the special nature of religious language, the book turns to a discussion of the nature of religious discourse.

What I will be offering is no substitute for the study of actual religious traditions living and past, nor, of course, for the living of a tradition. The living of a tradition is where the quest for reality begins and ends. After that, it is only harvesting and winnowing and inevitably some comparison and evaluation of the yields, together with a quest for understanding of the systems which produce them.

CHAPTER 2

THE NATURE OF RELIGIOUS EXPERIENCE

This chapter explores aspects of religion which are within the experience of most readers in the western world. The purpose is to get behind the familiar ways of thinking and speaking about these aspects and to express them in terms that are more universal. These more universal ways of thinking are intended to form a bridge that will help the reader enter meaningfully into what can be learned of the experiences of others, relating their unfamiliar aspects to that which lies within the reader's own experience. Some such universal concepts are absolutely necessary in any comparative study of religions.

Religion, I have said, is essentially something that is done or experienced within the individual. Therefore, this enquiry into the nature of religion begins with the individual and with the nature of religious experience. The following chapter takes the understanding of religious experience arrived at and shows how it might be related to the development of a communal tradition. Then, because one cannot discuss the nature of religion for long without confronting the special nature of religious language, the book turns to a discussion of the nature of religious discourse.

THREE PRELIMINARY ISSUES:

i) How the Subject will be Approached.

There is a problem which confronts all those who presume to teach others about religion. It is that everyone already knows what it is. Non-believers as well as believers have an investment in their understanding of religion. Even in the modern West, religion is potentially too important just to ignore. Most people, by the time that they have left school, have taken a stance in relation to it, a stance that contributes significantly to their self-understanding.

Being defensive of whatever firm ground has emerged in our self-understanding, the study of religion touches us in a way that mathematics never could, and is more consciously threatening than the more subtle invasions of studies in literature. The difficulty that faces many new students of religion is not that they cannot understand what is said, but that they cannot allow themselves to accept what is said, lest the firm ground of self-understanding should shift under their feet.

The study of religion could begin with some tradition that is not our own. This we could dissect intrepidly and with true academic detachment. The trouble would then be that what we studied would not feel like religion. Perhaps it would be interesting as a collection of myths and practices of some unfamiliar peoples, but it would have no personal significance. To study religion like that is not to study it at all. We could never come close to understanding what it signified to those whose tradition it was.

I am going to begin, therefore, be it threatening or not, with religion as it is understood by most readers of a text written in English, that is, with religion that has a god. Only then will I turn to religions with many gods or no god at all. Inevitably the majority of illustrations will have a Christian flavor but most of them have become common currency in western culture.

Religion, I said, has at least two aspects. It can be an inner personal experience and it can be an institution. Central to the institution will be a tradition, an interwoven system of beliefs and practices. Gathered around and legitimated by the tradition will be other institutional factors; functionaries, buildings, educational and financial organizations, all designed to service, promote and continue the tradition.

I will begin by asking about the nature of individual religious experience as the adherent of the Abrahamic faiths, Judaism, Christianity and Islam, might know it. Later I will seek to show how this experience gives rise to and is in turn shaped by a tradition. I will only be concerned with institutional factors other than the tradition insofar as they directly effect the shaping and maintenance of the tradition itself.

ii) Normal Religious Experience.

Religious experience, in the thinking of the western world, has become divorced from the rest of experience. "Religious" and "Secular" have become polar opposites. One result of this is that people who generally believe that information is received only through the five senses, either set a question mark against the reality of religious experience, or they think of it as something quite other than everyday experience.

While I would in no way deny the reality of conversion, or of charismatic, mystical or other numinous experiences, I will conclude that normal religious experience is something other than these. In fact I will go further and show that these and other experiences which Westerners typically associate with certain types of churches and the religious *officianado*, being discrete experiences, are only validated when it is shown how they contribute positively to experience as a whole.

This present chapter is concerned with *normal* religious experience. It begins with an approach which may seem to reduce religion to a quite ordinary, and therefore insignificant, experience. To be ordinary is not, however, to be insignificant. The process forces one to ask of religious experience, in what way it differs from other experience and whether any or all experiences can become religious.

iii) The Need for a Definition.

To set out to study religion in general, as distinct from studying a particular religious tradition, presupposes that there is something in different cultures that can be identified as religion. These manifestations of religion do not have to be the same in every culture but they have to belong to the same class or classes, and that class, in order to be really useful, needs to be as restricted as possible.

It is only possible to compare apples and wishes in the most general and vague way as members of the class "factors in human experience". Apples and pears could be compared merely as "physical objects", or better as members of "the vegetable kingdom", or more precisely as members of the class "edible fruits" and much more precisely as members of the biological natural order *Rosaceae*.

The same principle applies to religion. If we are to compare religion in different cultures in a satisfactory manner we need to work with the most restricted class that is currently available to us. As comparative study proceeds we should be able to define the class "religion" ever more precisely and thus compare it more accurately.

What is true of religion in different cultures is true of religion in different sub-cultures and, in the end, of the religion of different individuals in the same culture.

Unless we can say precisely what we mean by "religion", that is, unless we can discover the defining conditions for membership of the class "religion" or perhaps, in the case of individuals, the defining conditions for the class "religious experience", we cannot begin a serious study. The more precise the definition and therefore the more restricted the class, the more precise will be the possible comparisons.

I begin therefore, in spite of my opening remarks about everyone knowing what religion is, with the quest for an adequate definition of religion.

THE DEFINITION OF RELIGION

There is no shortage of definitions of religion. Adequate definitions, however, are not so easy to find. Indeed there are scholars who propose that the search for a universal definition of religion should be abandoned, at least for the time being.

It has been suggested that, instead of seeking a universal definition, one might work with a group of family traits which are recognizable as being common to religion in general without any particular religion having all of them. One supposes that it might be possible that two religions have none of these traits in common.[1]

Alternatively, it has been suggested that one should make a start with a working definition that appeals to common sense in the culture within which one is working.[2]

From the perspective of a science of religion, such moves are methodologically unsound. No holistic understanding of religion would be being refined and tested by being used.

The whole of Part I of this book is a quest for an understanding of religion. Within that quest I will not arrive at my own definition until the last paragraphs of chapter 7. I must make clear, therefore, the particular role of this chapter which has an overt concern with the definition of religion.

I am not about to present the reader with a long list of existing definitions and I have no interest in the reader remembering any existing

---

[1] Rem B Edwards, *Reason and Religion*, (New York: Harcourt Brace Jovanovich, 1972), p.14f.

[2] Melford E Spiro, "Religion: Problems of Definition and Explanation" in Michael Banton (Ed.), *Anthropological Approaches to the Study of Religion*, (London, Tavistock, 1968) p.85f.

definitions that I may quote. I am interested in discovering what religion is and then stating it clearly and concisely in universally acceptable terms.

That, however, is a tall order. I need to know what is the most promising point from which to start. I need to know how best to proceed from there, and I need to know what are the pitfalls along the way. One way to achieve insight into these questions is to examine how others have attempted the task. It is this examination that will occupy the rest of this chapter.

In the latter part of the chapter I will examine two specific definitions in detail. The first concerns the theist's referent for the word "god", the second is a definition of A.N.Whithead's. That examination will allow me to explore the nature of individual religious experience and to show why that is the primary aspect. It will also allow me to associate some universally meaningful terms with experiences that will be familiar to most readers.

In the mid-part of the chapter, under the heading "Some Types of Definition", I will consider how religion has been or could be defined. I will impose order upon the mass of possibilities by distinguishing between those definitions which conceptualize religion in corporate terms and those which focus upon the individual. I will then further sub-divide the latter group.

This process will expose the difficulties involved in defining religion. It will suggest what must be included in any definition if it is to be considered adequate. It will contribute to an understanding of what is likely to be the best starting point for a scientific study of religion, not least by revealing the weakness in other possibilities.

In the first part of the chapter I will say something about definition in general. In distinguishing and interrelating the processes of describing, explaining and defining, I will say that not all definitions are explanations, but that any definition of religion must belong to the explanatory type. In the case of religion, explanation is limited to a description of the interrelation of its parts.

DESCRIPTION, EXPLANATION AND DEFINITION

It is not my purpose to enter into a philosophical discussion concerning the differences between describing, explaining and defining, but I must try to make clear, first, what is special about a definition, and second, what is special about defining religion. I begin with some very general statements.

To explain something is always to offer some description of it. To define something is always to describe it, at least in the limited sense of linking an object or concept, to a word or symbol and usually (but not always) to define is to explain. These statements are not true the other way around. Not every description is an explanation, not every explanation is a definition. We will see that religion does not quite fit these statements. I must now ask, therefore, "What makes certain descriptions into explanations?" and "What makes certain descriptions or explanations, into definitions?".

In general, as one moves from description through explanation to definition, one is becoming more precise and also becoming more central to the matter in hand, but a very precise description could be neither an explanation nor a definition. The key thing about an explanation is that it usually relates what is being explained to something beyond itself. If it does not do that, then what is offered is no more than a description.

For example, if one were asked for a description of an Education Resources Centre, one might say "It is a building or suite of rooms, set out very much like a library, with shelves full of books, maps and other things, and a reception desk. It will be open late afternoons, evenings and probably Saturdays." That would be one possible description, but it is not an explanation. To explain it one would need to say how it relates to other things.

To relate the Resource Centre to other things one could say either; how it came into existence and gained its current form, that is, what caused it or shaped it; or (more likely in this case) what it was for. Thus the explanation could be *causal* (what caused it) or *functional* (how it functions in relation to other things).

An example of the latter might be, "It exists to improve the standard of education in schools. It is a place where teachers can go to improve their teaching skills, to get information not in the text books and to borrow visual and other teaching aids in order to give impact to their lessons." The Resource Centre has now been related to teaching skills and to the quality of lessons, and thence to all the other things to which they in turn are related.

Insofar as definitions are explanations, they too can be causal or functional. I will return to this below.

There is an exception to what I have said about explanation. If what one wishes to explain is big enough, or otherwise a relatively closed system, it may not be possible, or useful, to relate it to something beyond itself. In that case to explain it can only be to describe the interrelation of its parts.

Consider, for example, how one would define a national education system. One might begin by speaking of its relationship to the needs of the economic, domestic and cultural sectors of the wider community, but it would not suffice without a careful description of its parts and their interrelation. Whereas if one only had the latter, one would still have a useful definition. Religion, is even more self-contained than is an education system and can only be satisfactorily explained by describing the interrelation of its parts.

While to define something is always to describe it, to define is not always to explain. In the Social Sciences, to define something is usually to explain it, but there are two important exceptions to this rule.

There are what are called ostensive definitions. These are little more than a circumscribing and naming process. One indicates clearly the limits of something that can be pointed to, or otherwise shown, and says "That is what is meant by ... ." The name now has a clear referent. In the case of religion there is no obvious "something" to which one could point. The word "religion" does not have a clear referent.

Then there are definitions that are purely mental constructs and are what is called "tautological", that is, they are other ways of saying the same thing. No information, that was not included within the first form of the statement, is imparted by the second. To say that a bachelor is an unmarried man would be an example. The word "bachelor" already contains the ideas male and unmarried and nothing else. One meets more complex definitions of this type in mathematics and theoretical physics. However, when we are dealing with religion we are not dealing with mental constructs only. There is always something out there to be explained. These two exceptions are really the points where precise language begins.

Between the extremes of a purely mental construct that is not necessarily related to anything in the world of things, and things out there that can be clearly indicated and are only in need of a name, lie all those things which exist, but are not easy to delimit. They are usually part of a bigger whole and do not make sense until they have been related to as least something beyond themselves. Relation to something else is of their essence. To define such entities is to explain them. Religion belongs to this general class because, on the one hand, it is not simply a mental construct and on the other hand it is not easily delimited. Nevertheless it is an exception to the statement that such entities belong to a bigger whole, that relation to something outside themselves is of their essence.

I have said that not every definition is an explanation, I must now say that not every explanation is a definition. To show why this is the case I must go back to the basic statement about explanation.

I said that it is usually the case that to explain something is to relate it to something beyond itself. The key word here is "*it*". To relate something to that which is beyond itself is to say what caused *it* to come into existence, or to take *its* present shape, or to say what *it* does for other things, or what they do to *it*. One could do a lot of explaining in that way and never get near to saying whether there is an *it* at the centre of the web of relationships being established, and if so, what that *it* comprises.

Many definitions of religion, the prime concern of which is to relate religion to some aspects of human social existence or to the inner life of the individual, simply assume that everyone knows what *it* is. They are definitions justified by what they are needed to do. Frequently they do not come close to expressing the essence of religion as an adherent might experience it.

To define something is to get to the heart of the matter, that is to the essence, to be seeking to say what *it* is in itself. Anyone who has ever owned a dog will know that to relate it to something beyond itself and to say "A dog is an animal on the wrong side of a door" is all too annoyingly true as a partial explanation of the word "dog". It does not, however, get to the essence of "doggieness", any more than the perfectly true *description* of an Education Resource Centre got to its essence.

The sort of definition that we are looking for, therefore, might be said to be an explanation of the essence of something, or simply, an essential explanation. In the case of religion where, because of the scale of what we are talking about, explanation can only be a description of the interrelation of its parts, a definition can be said to be an essential description. For present purposes and keeping in mind that the quest is for the essence of religion, I will use the two terms, define and explain, interchangeable. I will return to the question of what constitutes an explanation when I come, in chapter 4, to the discussion of myth and whether it is intended to explain.

NOTE: TO DEFINE CAN BE TO DIMINISH

There is a problem with explanation and with explanatory definitions, particularly in the Social Sciences and particularly in the consequences for religion. It has to do with the adequacy of the frame of reference. To make this clear I must go back once again to the beginning of the previous discussion.

I said that an explanation usually includes a relationship with an element beyond that which is to be explained. In the example of the Education Resource Centre the explanation related that which was to be explained, to teaching skills and to lesson quality and, through these, to a whole network of other factors such as the enthusiasm and therefore the happiness and health of children, and the provision of a future generation of skilled workers and potential leaders. This growing network around that which is to be explained, is the frame in which explanation is taking place. The more adequate the frame and the more clearly that it is related to the matter in hand, the greater the potential for explanation. On the other hand, to insist upon an explanation within an inadequate or inappropriate frame of reference will almost certainly have the effect of diminishing that which is being explained. This would be true of many things. In particular it is a problem for religion. What frame of reference would be adequate and appropriate for the explanation of something so ultimately concerned as religion?

To seek an explanation of religion, even within the whole frame of human social existence, represents a reversal of what religion understands itself to be. Religion, which might be thought to touch all aspects of life and to be the frame which holds much of it together, must be diminished if it is explained as the effect upon an individual or community of one or more, even most, of life's bits and pieces.

This is another reason why it is better to explain religion by showing the interrelation of its parts, and if possible their organizing principle, than by seeking to relate it to something beyond itself.

SOME TYPES OF DEFINITION

An adequate definition of religion needs to get to its essence. The essence lies at the level of inner personal experience. It may be appropriate to define specific aspects of religion for specific purposes, but if one is interested in religion as a universal human phenomenon, and if an attempt is being made to integrate in one conceptual framework all phenomena regarded as religious, then one must begin with the inner experience of the individual. The whole of this revue of the possible types of definition is directed to showing why this must be the case, but I will make two preliminary points. The essence of religion lies in inner personal experience because:

If religion did not somehow "work" for each adherent individually it would have no authority and so, save where they could be maintained by external pressure, the institutional forms would crumble.

A corporate body can only possess religion conceptually. Only an individual can experience. Religious experience must exist before it can be conceptualized in symbols. Therefore the essence of religion lies in individual religious experience not in any aspect of corporate religion.

I need say no more about the first point.

That religious experience must exist before it can be conceptualized in symbols, flies in the face of the common presumption that religion begins with commitment to certain beliefs. That this is not the case (important though symbols are) will become clear in the discussion of A.N.Whithead's definition of religion in the last section of this chapter.

That communities can only possess religion conceptually is a consequence of the fact that communities cannot feel. Only the individuals who comprise the communities can feel. Communities, therefore, can only share beliefs and consciously performed practices. Even religious symbols can only be known to be shared at the conceptual level. What a symbol means to individuals at the vital level of feeling, might be shared, but it cannot be known to be shared. Individuals can hardly know in themselves what a symbol means in its fullness. Still less can an outsider, looking in, know how a symbol is being experienced.

It follows that if one begins a study of religion at the corporate level one is precluded from dealing with the essence of religion.

Understandably, definitions used by those whose primary concern lies with human social existence begin with the public and therefore institutional aspects of religion. One is standing on the outside of corporate religion looking in. One can describe it, of course, but if one would explain it, one is limited to causal and functional explanations, limited to saying what caused it or how it functions. One cannot say what it is in itself.

Any discussion of the ways in which religion has been or could be defined, therefore, must maintain the distinction between religion as inner personal experience and religion as corporately possessed tradition.

Between definitions that conceptualize religion corporately and those which conceptualize it individually lie, on the one hand, those where the primary concern is with the corporate but where the need to root the corporate aspect in the individual is recognized and, on the other hand, those which focus on the individual but emphasize the formative effects of external factors. I will deal with each of these four types, sub-dividing the two which focus on the individual when I come to them.

Before I do this, however, there are a few more general things to be said about causal and functional definitions, for definitions of both individual and institutional religion can be of this sort.

NOTE: CAUSAL AND FUNCTIONAL DEFINITIONS OF RELIGION

Definitions of religion in terms of what brings it into existence or determines its form became popular after Darwin, that is, in the period when evolutionary thinking spilled over from biology into the social sciences. They were around, however, centuries earlier. In ancient Rome, Petronius declared that "Fear first made gods in the earth".

The literature is replete with causal definitions of religion. Some are expressed in negative terms, such as religion is the flight from finitude, chaos or death: some in positive terms such as religion is the quest for meaning, health or security: some just as matters of fact, such as religion is a "projection" of the psyche, or a "sigh" in the face of oppression. Such a variety of causal definitions suggests the question, "Is there not, what might be called, a religious cause for religion?", "Can religion not be understood as self-generating?". I will return to this question in chapter 7.

The originating and moulding causes of religion, while important to a full understanding, need have no necessary connection with why religion is significant in the lives of those who presently embrace it. That connection is more likely to be found in functional definitions.

Definitions dependent upon how religion functions in relation to other aspects of human life, have the same reductionist possibilities as causal ones. Some aspect of human, individual or social functioning, is described and then it is said to be religion. An example of this might be the establishment and maintenance of the set of shared values which constitute a society out of a number of separate individuals.[3] Equally, it might be a mechanism in the development of individual identity.[4]

Religion touches most aspects of human life, so any definition in terms of one or more of them, while possibly adequate for a specific purpose, will necessarily be inadequate as a definition of religion in general. To be adequate to the manner in which the adherent apprehends religion, a functional definition would have to be on the grand scale, that is, it would need to be in relation to life as a whole, or at least to what could be regarded as life's most significant aspects.

I now return to the main theme and to the consideration of corporate and individual definitions of religion. Causal and functional definitions will recur in both types.

i) Definitions of Corporate Religion

At the corporate level, one not infrequently finds statements which purport to sum up religion. They are not essential definitions however. They are causal or functional. They are reductionist and usually deprecatory, for example, "religion is an instrument for social control". These not only relate religion to something outside itself, but identify it with something quite other than its adherents and most observers would hold it to be. This is not to deny that religion has been employed in a variety of ways, not all of them laudable. A specific example of an institutional definition is that of Melford Spiro.

> Religion (is) an institution consisting of culturally patterned interaction with culturally postulated superhuman beings.[5]

---

[3] This I take to be the meaning of Emile Durkheim's affirmation that "Society is the soul of religion".

[4] Such would be the role of religion in the process of personal "Individuation" described by Carl Jung.

[5] *Ibid*, p.96.

This definition is apparently functional but, in my view, does not succeed. It does not say what "super-human beings" are, culturally postulated or otherwise, so that no one could know what it would mean for an individual to interact with them or when such interaction was taking place. I will return to this problem below.

Spiro does not pretend that this is an essential definition. He suggests that it is the best practical definition with which to begin a study of religion given that an essential definition is not available.

There are definitions of corporate religion that recognize the importance of personal experience. Clifford Geertz made a significant attempt to root the institutional aspect of religion in the personal with his definition:

> *a religion* is a (cultural) system of symbols which acts to establish powerful, pervasive, and long-lasting moods and motivations in men by formulating conceptions of a general order of existence and clothing these conceptions with such an aura of factuality that the moods and motivations seem uniquely realistic. [6]

The effort that Geertz made to relate his understanding of corporate religion to what the individual feels, and to portray a dynamic relationship between symbols and experience, has been very significant. His emphasis, however, remains with the corporate, and what I said about the inaccessibility of the essence of religion, if one begins from the corporate perspective, applies to all definitions of this type.

As a general definition of religion I believe this one would be too cognitive and too western. Geertz makes it clear, however, that he is defining the institutional aspect. He speaks of "a religion" not of "religion".

When we come to definitions in which religion is conceptualized as individual experience, the emphasis may still be upon external factors to which the individual relates rather than upon the experience and orientation of the individual. These types are the important ones for my purpose and I will treat them in greater detail than I did the ones with a corporate emphasis.

I will begin with definitions of personal religion which relate the individual to some external factor.

---

[6] Clifford Geertz, Religion as a Cultural System, in Michael Banton (Ed.), *Anthropological Approaches to the Study of Religion*, (London, Tavistock, 1968) p.1.

ii) Definitions of Individual Religion in Relation to External Factors

Definitions of individual religion in terms of a relationship with something, as it were, out there, may be usefully sub-divided into those in which the relationship is positive and those in which it is negative. That is, into relationships that are sought and affirmed, and relationships that are to be avoided or compensated for. I will refer to these as the external positive and the external negative sub-types.

External Positive Definitions

The external positive type of definition may be further sub-divided. There are those in which the external factor is empirical, at least in part, and there are those where the external factor is non-empirical, that is, there is nothing that can be observed or pointed to.

An example of an external factor that is partly empirical, appears in the second of the two scenarios contained within the discussion of the next sub-type. The example comprises a number of different events coinciding in a constellation that has particular value for an individual such that he or she regards it as providential. The events are a matter of public record, the value that they have for the individual will be less public, but nevertheless remain something that is assessable by an outsider. When I come to discuss the first of the definitions to be dealt with in detail, I will speak of "an adequation between individual needs and that which life provides". This is a lower intensity but more permanent example of the same kind.

Because I will be dealing with an example of the sub-type in detail I will not say more about it here. The sub-type provides a useful way of defining religion within a particular culture. However, it will become apparent later that, because what is valued is culture specific, it is difficult to extend definitions of this type into ones with universal validity.

"Religion is a response to a super-human being" is an example of the sub-type in which the external factor is non-empirical, not such that it can be observed. Sometimes the reality of this external factor is simply affirmed, in other cases it is assumed not to be an issue in the usefulness of the definition. In the latter case, religion is judged to be present whenever an individual or community believe that they are relating to a super-human or super-natural being, to spirits or to the Transcendent, whether or not such things are real.

The danger in a definition of this type is that, while it can seem very attractive and appear to be on a grand enough scale, it can so easily be *pseudo*. That is, it can define one unknown in terms of another unknown and therefore achieve nothing. Words such as "spirit", are almost impossible to define. "Transcendence", as we will see, has a clear meaning in a particular type of religion but not in others. Thus a general definition of religion in terms of such entities will almost certainly fail. The words "super-natural", "super-human" and to a lesser extent "super-normal" are so frequent in the literature and so seemingly self-evident that I must dwell on them for a moment.

If "super-human" were to refer to an ability to pass through walls we could be speaking of X-rays; if it referred to a high degree of self-sacrificial behavior, we could be speaking of a certain type of ant. Neither would be super-natural nor even super-normal for modern man. If "super-human" were to refer to levels in the quality of human characteristics supposedly better than those possessed by ordinary human-beings, then we would be in two kinds of trouble. What would "better" mean, and what would delimit "human"?

If that which was described as super-human was beyond suffering and perfect in every human talent, where would be the richness of the human experiences of struggle and of co-operation in the face of seeming inadequacy? In other words, if "super-human" were to mean "human without the defects", how would one decide, on the one hand, what are in fact defects and, on the other hand, what seemingly defective components could not be removed without destroying the very concept of humanity? Even if one could decide these issues, one could still be left in doubt about what would render relating to such a being, religious.

The term "super-natural" (or "super-normal") is no better. If it is to mean more than "something outside of normal experience", it might refer to experiences which are available but not through the five senses. If that is the case, then for the term to mean anything, one must be able to say clearly to what experiences the word does relate and how they are experienced. To this end, Rudolf Otto went to the extreme of positing the existence of a sixth sense, which he called the "faculty of divination", whereby one could detect the presence of the "numinous" which had the quality of a *mysterium tremendum et fascinans*, a mysterious experience which overawes but also attracts.[7] I must postpone saying why this solution is unacceptable, but Otto's phrase enables me to make another point.

"Super-natural" or "super-normal" might be used to refer to experiences observed by the five senses, but which are not explicable within what is known to be the law of nature. I do not wish to enter the whole field of miracle, precisely because it is my present concern to deal with the normal, but it can be said that Abrahamic religion has more to do with providence than it does with miracle. That is, it has more to do with the discernment of

---

[7] Rudolf Otto, *The Idea of the Holy*, J W Harvey (trans.), (Harmondsworth, Penguin, 1959).

value in a constellation of events than it does with an unexplained event or breach in natural law. For while the latter may be "overawing" it is not necessarily "attractive". Consider the following scenarios:

a) I fill the kettle with water and switch it on. A short time later I am aware that the kettle is not boiling. I lift the lid and discover that the water is turning into ice.

b) I have a major problem. I decide, in my desperation, that I should seek the help of a friend in a distant city. I reserve a seat on the early morning fight. My children have a pillow-fight, they break the alarm clock and I miss my flight. I get into conversation with the man sitting next to me on the fight following. It turns out that he has the solution to my problem.

It is unlikely in scenario (a), for all that I could not explain what was happening, that I would drop the lid of the kettle and flee into the street shouting Miracle!, Miracle!. In scenario (b) it is exceedingly likely that "miracle" would cross my lips, or at least "providential", yet all is explained. I am sitting in this seat, on this flight, next to this man, because my children broke the alarm clock.

Because of the degree of value involved, even scenario (b) has startling qualities and I do not wish to diminish the significance of the startling in religion. Nevertheless, I am currently exploring normal religious experience and when I return shortly to a consideration of the importance of value in the generation of religious belief, it will be at the level of an everyday adequacy, not miracle. To focus the problem, let me leave words like "super-human" and "super-natural" and return simply to the word in common use, "god".

In the western world, the definition of religion offered by the person in the street would undoubtedly be one which spoke of some relation with a god. I will begin there also. The word "god", however, is only a sound or a cypher. It is different in various traditions and languages. Such a definition must remain pseudo until agreement has been reached upon to what experience the word "god" refers. To what that experience might be I will turn shortly.

External Negative Definitions

Definitions which include a negative response to an external factor, are perhaps the most common in the literature of the social sciences. They could be functional, but are more likely to be causal. Religion is defined, therefore, as a response to the threat of such things as death, finitude, chaos or powerlessness. Thus religions need have nothing in common save that they are all forms of a refusal to look reality in the eye or to accept what one sees there. If religious experience has any of the positive meaning that adherents find in it, it is assumed not to be of its essence, or not sufficiently available or universalizable to be the object of scientific enquiry. Religion is some form of crutch, perhaps it is useful, perhaps it is the best that can be achieved in the circumstances, but it nevertheless implies defective reality testing.

This type of definition may be useful to those social scientists whose primary concern is not with religion, but with the functioning of society or the individual psyche. It is the type which most easily contains the extreme experiences of religion, even the bizarre or pathological, that social scientists are frequently interested in as a barometer of the human condition. It cannot matter to them, of course, what the phenomenon is called. That is, it cannot matter whether it is really religion, or some aberration, or some compensation for the absence of religion. It only matters that it really effects what they are studying.

Because it is of crucial concern to the student of religion *per se*, what is included and what is excluded from the field of study, a definition based on a negative response to some external factor is, of all definitions, the least adequate. It has no precision, for there are many foci of fear and the possible styles of avoidance are virtually limitless. There is nothing to be gained by labelling as "religion" all examples of social and psychological avoidance.

Sometimes this type of definition is expressed in positive form. For example "religion is the quest for security". To this might be added "meaning", "power", "health", "peace of mind". The very fact that this list could be extended almost indefinitely reveals a problem. Is religion the quest for anything which is valued and is any quest for a valued thing religion?

iii) Definitions of Personal Religion in Terms of the Inner Experience of the Individual

At this end of the spectrum it becomes possible to attempt an essential definition. Definition is in terms of something that is going on within the individual, or in terms of what the individual is doing when being religious. It may be something that is being sought, it may be a particular orientation, perhaps just a way of seeing.

The danger in this kind of definition is again its tendency to be reductionist. It identifies religion with some aspect of human experience, one perhaps that has the advantage of being clearly defined, but, in the process, it is likely to render religion other than that which the adherent feels it to be and almost certainly less significant. While anthropologists, sociologists and others more concerned to describe how people function in their context than with the nature of religion itself, tend to use the functional type of definition, those who want to say what religion actually is, frequently those with a more philosophical interest, favour this internal type.

Thus religion has been defined as:

a hypothesis supposed to render the universe comprehensible
(Herbert Spencer)

This would fit the type of internal definition associated with the seeking of some goal, in this case meaning.

the recognition of all our duties as divine commands
(Immanuel Kant)

This points to a particular perspective upon experience as the defining characteristic of religion.

morality touched with emotion
(Matthew Arnold)

This also is orientational.

the consciousness of the highest social values
(Ames)

This again stresses the individual's orientation, this time to the good of society. Meaning, morality, emotion, social values, and much else besides, have all been indicated as the essence of religious experience. [8]

While each definition of this type may fail to do justice to a phenomenon which touches the whole of life, as with functional definitions, a study of a number of them at least serves to paint some of the total picture. A definition of this type would be saved from being reductionist if the experience to which it pointed could really be supposed to be the essence of religion. The definition that I will propose in chapter 7 is of this type.

---

[8] These examples are borrowed from a much longer list in Eric S Waterhouse, *The Philosophical Approach to Religion,* (London, Epworth, 1960) p.20.

TYPES OF DEFINITION - A SUMMARY

Definitions of religion can be offered on many levels because religion itself is overtly present on many levels.

Religion may be explained as an ultimate context for meaning and value. It may be explained as a social entity, for example, the authoritative symbol set, adherence to which creates a society out of a group of individuals. At a slightly lower level, it may be understood as an instrument for social control. It may be understood as the way in which individuals organize to cope with social change and other threats in their environment. It may be understood as a factor in the development of individual identity, or as the individual reaching for timeless and undifferentiated experience.

There can be no universal objection to reductionism, that is, to the explanation of religion in non-religious terms. Left to itself, however, the explaining of religion in such terms is as potentially divisive as the areas of life touched by religion are numerous. Such an approach to definition could hardly be expected to open up the heartland of religion.

I have chosen to emphasize definition at the level of inner personal experience, because it is here that the essence of religion must lie. I have said that the defining characteristic of religion at this inner personal level can be either an objective (that is, a quest for or maintenance of some state of affairs) or it can be a mode of engagement with experience, an orientation; perhaps just a certain way of perceiving the data of experience.

Where the defining characteristic is an objective it must be such that whenever it is present religion is present and when it is absent religion is absent. It cannot be just one of a number of objectives such as those which I suggested were a positive expression of a negative response to an external factor. For example, it may be the case that religion is always in some sense a quest for health, but it would not be generally useful to claim that every quest for health is religion.

The purpose in this book is to understand religion in its own terms, to isolate and describe variables which belong to the heartland of religion, and then to go some way to showing how these variables generate the extraordinary variety that comprises the religious experience of humankind. It is vital, therefore, that the definition with which I begin is on a grand enough scale and that the variables employed are recognizably religious. Only then could the definition be expected to embrace, in a single understanding, the greatest variety of phenomena regarded as religious.

Shortly, I will consider a definition by Alfred North Whitehead that comes as close to this requirement of "embracing the greatest variety" as any in the literature. It is of the internal type in which a goal is sought. First, however, I wish to return to the definition of religion that might be offered by the western world's person in the street, namely that: religion is belief in, or relation to, a god. This, clearly, is of the external positive kind. I will, however, consider it in a way that will enable me to hold together definition of religion in terms of something "out there", and definition in terms of the believer's experience.

I will do this by asking, not, "What is religion?", but the prior question, "To what experience do theists refer when they use the word 'god'?". A theist, of course, is a believer in a god or gods.

This section will inevitably seem removed from living religion, but it is the exercise which begins the process of transforming some familiar aspects of religion into the universally relevant concepts that will be needed later.

THE THEIST'S REFERENT FOR THE WORD "GOD"

In order to move quickly to the central ideas, I will not build up gradually to an answer to the question "To what experience do theists refer when they speak of God?". Rather, I will proceed in reverse fashion. I will first offer an answer to the question. Then I will explain it and, in explaining it, seek to justify it. My answer to the question would be:

God is that quasi-personal factor which meets the theist in or through his or her total experience.

"Quasi" is a useful word in this context, precisely because its meaning is not too exactly defined. Dictionaries suggest "sort of", "almost", "as it were" or "apparently" as its equivalents. My preference would be for "at least", so that the phrase would read at-least-personal, but I do not wish to over emphasize the idea of person. The usage will become clearer in context. A theist, of course, could be any believer in a god or gods but for the present purpose I have in mind a monotheist, that is, a believer in one god.

I have said "in" as well as "through" in order to make it clear that while I am for the moment concerned with those who have a dualist view of reality, that is, those to whom God is quite other than the rest of experience, the definition might well include those with a monistic world view whose gods are a part of the one reality.

In order to explain and justify this definition, I will first show why the reference has to be to "total experience" and then say what is meant by the "quasi-personal factor" which meets the believer in or through total experience and which promotes his or her reference to God.

TOTAL EXPERIENCE

If God were not experienced primarily in total experience then He would have to be experienced in one or more particular experiences, if He were to be experienced at all. This would create a problem.

The problem in trying to define "God" (if God were indeed one thing among others in experience, one piece of the furniture of the universe) is that one would not be able to say what He was until one had located Him and, on the other hand, to locate Him (that is to identify Him) one would need some previous understanding, some sort of a measure. I will speak of this as a "yardstick of divinity".

We would need a yardstick of divinity before we could locate the presence of the divine and so know what it was like. We would need to know what divinity was like in order to arrive at a yardstick of divinity. The problem is a circular one. Till you know what He is you cannot find Him, until you find Him you cannot know what He is.

It might be supposed that one could begin by finding the divine in a person, a book or an event. Yet, how could one find God in one event, say the exodus of Israel from Egypt, but not in another, say the holocaust; or (from a Christian perspective) in the life of Jesus Christ but not in the life of Mahatma Ghandi; in the book of Isaiah, but not, say, in the book of Mormon? It is not a question of whether the Divine is revealed in the book, the person or the event. It is a question of the identification of an unknown. How do I identify it if I do not know already what it is?

One might try the experiment of asking a Christian how he or she knows what God is like. Probable answers include the following chain of reasoning: "He is like Jesus Christ. Jesus Christ came to earth, lived out his life, taught, died and rose again. Those who knew him, the Disciples, communicated to the Evangelists the accounts which they then wrote down. These have been enshrined in the New Testament and therefore we know what God is like.".

If one caught the same Christian at some other time and said to him or her, "Why do you call Jesus divine?" the reply might be, "Because he is like God". The statements have then become circular. They call Jesus divine because he is like God and they know what God is like because he is like Jesus Christ.

If one were to point out this problem of circularity to the Christian he or she might then claim to know what God is like from the Old Testament, from the message of the prophets in particular. The problem would not have been solved. It would have been pushed back a stage. The question would then become how the prophet decided that it was God who was speaking, or that some idea that came to mind was from God. In this, the prophet's problem was not different from ours. When the prophets have delivered their word we have to make up our minds whether it is revelation or not. In much the same way the prophet had to distinguish revelation from hallucination. How did he or she decide that God was speaking in a dream rather than that he or she had eaten too much goats' milk cheese for supper? After all, hallucination might be supposed to be more common in human experience than revelation.

However far one presses back in the tradition, to Abraham or beyond, one would face the same problem: If one does not possess some previous knowledge of what God is, how does one find Him, and if one cannot find Him how does one come to know what He is?

Revelation may have come with some traumatic event, fire, thunder, earthquake, or simply some inner glow. That sort of impact may be very convincing at the time, but it would probably not last long for the person who received it and certainly it could mean very little to humankind thousands of years later. There has to be something more than that. It is the content of the revelation that matters, not the super-added events, or the inner traumatic experience of the prophet. So we are left with the same problem: If we begin by supposing that God is one bit of experience amongst others, we cannot find Him because we do not know what He is and we cannot know what He is until we find Him.

For those who are prepared to accept that God is not just a piece of furniture of the universe, a possible move in the argument would be to say that God is transcendent, that He is not part of our general experience of the world, He is beyond it.

If He were only transcendent then we could not know Him at all. It would be claimed, however, that, from time to time, this transcendent God breaks into the world and makes Himself known in certain events or to particular people. This would not help. We are right back to the old problem of how to recognize where He is breaking in, how to identify a special person, book, or event, among all the other persons, books or events with which we are surrounded. It is because of this absence of a yardstick of divinity that special events, like conversion experience, charismatic or inner spiritual experience, cannot be regarded as normative religious experience, but must themselves be validated within such normative experience.

All that one is left with, if God is not met as a part of the universe, nor as totally beyond it and breaking in, is the possibility that our experience of God is via some quality in our total experience. That is, that *we give the name* "God" to something we discern in or through our total experience.

This move worries some people. It seems to them that there is a difference between meeting God and having an experience that we name "God". There are, however, two things. There is an experience and there is a name. It cannot matter which we know first. The difference between this and what (according to the prophet) the pagans of old did, when they set up their idols of wood or stone and called them gods, is not in the naming process, but in the nature of the god conceived. That which is here named God, that quasi-personal factor in or behind total experience, is big enough to bear that name in all the religions of the Abrahamic family.

So we come to the position that, if we are to know God, and particularly if we are to conceptualize Him so that we can talk about Him meaningfully, He must be known through some quality of our total experience. In the totality, God is big enough to be God, he is not just a pillar of wood or stone which mankind has declared to be a god. On the other hand He is but vaguely discerned. He needs to become crystallized in a particular book, person, or event. We could not identify Him in the particular unless we were able to discern the same hand at work in the event, person or book, which we discerned, however vaguely, in total experience. *The concrete adds clarity to the total, the total gives authority to the concrete.*

That we should first find God in total experience and then in the particular is the logical way around, but for most people it is the very opposite of what happens. Normally, one accepts the god portrayed in the book, the person, or the event. That is to say, one accepts an understanding of God handed on with the authority of parent, imam, rabbi or minister, long before one comes to any direct religious experience of one's own. The time should come however, when one asks for oneself, concerning this inherited tradition, Is it right? At that point, if what has been received is to feel authentic, it must fit our own developing experience of life.

The total experience to which I refer is not simply one's own direct experience but also includes the experience of others that we have made our own, for example, the history we have read, cultures we have studied and, of course, the inherited religious tradition itself. There are two meanings to the phrase "total experience" as I have been using it, both of which are relevant to our purpose.

The first lies at the conscious and largely conceptual level. If in a relaxed moment one were trying to decide what life and the world one lives in is all about, then that which would be brought to mind would be what I have called "total experience". It would include all that has happened to one, all that one has seen and known, all that one has learnt from others that is credible.[9]

The other meaning of "total experience", which is equally important and in operation more frequent, is all that which has made a person what he or she is. Whether it is that which has happened to one directly, or whether it is experience which conditioned one's parents and one's wider society and was then inherited, does not matter. One inherits conscious traditions, one can

---

[9] "Total experience" in this sense includes more than the individual's world-out-there, for it embraces experience of the self. The more of the self, including one's most personal traits, that is looked upon as a passing possession, the more the ego approximates to that purely conscious centre that has sometimes been called the witness.

also inherit the inward conditioning of an ongoing experience. So this meaning of "total experience" is all that has made us what we are and which governs how we intuitively respond to some particular situation. It is that which triggers in us an evaluating response. I am, of course, speaking of a response which involves the total self and is not merely some relatively detached, episodic adjustment. I will return to this in chapter 6 when I deal with the "felt sense of reality".

THE QUASI-PERSONAL FACTOR

I must now deal with the meaning of the phrase "quasi-personal" in this definition. It concerns the *quality* of the total experience through which the theist discerns God, or comes to have a conviction concerning God. Quasi-personal would include all such things as order, meaningfulness, harmony, but if that were all, then while the definition might conceivably embrace other families of religions, it would not embrace the Abrahamic. The latter requires that mind or will should also be included. That is, it must include the sense that what is out there knows the believer, knows his or her needs, and responds to them. The word that best sums up all of these factors is, I think, "adequacy". There is a felt quality of adequacy or better perhaps, an adequation, between the believer's needs in the deepest and broadest sense and what is provided in total experience.

It being important to my purpose that I clarify what is meant by this sense of an adequation, I ask the reader to consider for a moment a rather simplistic illustration.

> Suppose that a man walks to work each day. As he does so he passes a hut. The hut has a chute emanating from a hole in its wall which ends up over a basket. He cannot get into this hut and there are no windows. On a day when he has put on his last pair of socks without holes in them, he walks past the hut and a packet slides down the chute and drops into the basket. He picks it up, opens it, and lo and behold a pair of socks. On another occasion he is conscious that he has left his pen at home and wonders with what he is going to write. The packet from the hut contains a ballpoint. On a further occasion, after some interminable meeting, his stomach is in knots and he thinks how much he would like a smoke. As he passes the hut a packet drops into the basket. It contains chewing gum. On a hot day when he has been rushing, and is dying of thirst the little packet that drops out contains a block of sticky, semi-molten chocolate. On a day when he

had promised to take someone out to lunch and was aware that he had insufficient money, the packet contains the necessary amount.

Consider the consequences for belief of this unlikely situation.

If the procedure went on day by day and there emerged a fairly high degree of adequation between that which came out of the hut and the needs of the recipient, he could quite reasonably come to the conviction that in the hut or behind its operation, was a mind that knew him and perhaps even cared for him.

This would not be knowledge, either empirical or logical. He could not get into the hut and, if he were purely objective about it, he would have to admit that whereas he had had a run of adequacy, he might now experience a run of inadequacy. Nevertheless, if the degree of adequacy was reasonably high and he were not an entirely skeptical person, he would come to the conviction (conviction not knowledge) that there was a mind in or behind the operation of the hut that knew his needs. This would be a perfectly reasonable thing to do. It would even be quite reasonable to shout his thanks or to put a bunch of flowers outside the hut. As in all inductive processes there is no way of proving logically what is believed, yet holding the conviction may nevertheless be the act of a reasonable person.

If one came to the conviction that there was somebody in or behind the hut's operation (there is no choice, you either have a conviction or you do not) then one would have to do something about the chewing gum and the chocolate, because, on the face of it, they do not fit the conviction. One would probably say of the chewing gum received when one wanted a smoke, "He knew better than I did what was good for me". The milk chocolate, the sticky molten mess, received when one wanted a sparkling cool drink, one cannot accommodate. It stands, as random suffering does for the theist, as a piece of evidence against the conviction that he or she still holds.

On the other hand, if the degree of adequacy between that which came out of the hut and the man's needs was low, he would probably come to the conclusion that what came out of the hut was the result of pure chance. The things which did happen to fit he could account for by attributing them to coincidence. We may note in passing, that at the other extreme, should everything which came out of the hut be precisely what was not needed, one could conclude that there must be "mind" there, but one which was antagonistic.

For the most part, however, the theist is a person who is confronted in the totality of his or her experience with such a level of adequacy that he or she is led to the conviction that there is mind behind it. That is, total experience confronts the theist as quasi-personal and not as inanimate.

Just as it was necessary to distinguish knowledge from reasonable conviction, so I must make it quite clear that I am not speaking of affluence when I speak of adequacy. The person who lives in a big house with a swimming pool and cocktail bar and has a big balance in the bank is not necessarily aware of adequacy. Adequacy appears most clearly at the extremities of life. When we are coming to the end of our own tether, we may discover resources in ourselves which we did not know were there, and when we are really "down on our uppers", other people, whom we never thought would care, may respond to our need and become supportive. It is then that we begin to think of adequacy. At the extreme, however, there are people who have such an inadequate experience of life that it is for them dehumanizing. Such are the people the Salvation Army are said to have referred to as "gospel-proof". This then is what I mean by adequacy. It is this which conditions experience, so that it confronts the theist as quasi-personal. It is this sense of adequacy, and what is conceptualized as lying behind it, that is referred to when the word "God" is used. The word "God", therefore, refers to that quasi-personal factor which meets the theist in, or behind, his or her total experience.

Returning to where we began with the western person-in-the-street, religion is defined as the knowledge of God and the fact of relating to Him, or, at least, the quest for such knowledge and relationship. That definition is no longer pseudo. The second unknown, that is, "God", has been related to an identifiable human experience. If "quasi-personal" in this definition is understood as a conviction that there exists something akin to mind which knows and cares for one, a conviction born out of a deep sense of continuing adequacy between one's needs and what life provides, then, whether they lie in the personal experience of the observer or not, both "God" and "religion" are meaningful concepts. A further advantage of insisting that God is to be found, in the first instance, in the total experience of the believer rather than in particular aspects of experience, is that one is not reduced to the seemingly impossible task of finding criteria for distinguishing religious from other sorts of experience.

Before seeking to draw any general conclusions from this understanding of western religious experience, I must recognize that, even for many in the Abrahamic family, religion is not felt to begin with the experience of something out there, nor necessarily, with such a personal concept of the ultimately-real. Rather it consists in an inner experience, very personal to the believer, and perhaps of a mystical kind. I will therefore explore that kind of understanding. We will not end up in a very different position to that arrived at above, but it will afford the opportunity to explore the same situation in a psychological, rather than philosophical manner. I therefore turn to a second definition.

I have come to regard a definition offered by Alfred North Whitehead as the most inclusive of religion in the western style. It is not however the least opaque. The definition seems to report a highly individual, even autobiographical, experience of religion, yet Whitehead never deals with it as such. Rather he turns, in the evolutionary fashion of his time, to a description of the ascent of religion in the human race and then to metaphysics.

What religion meant for Whitehead as an individual experience never becomes clear. He treats it as though that were an obvious contemporary datum of experience. One that called for explanation in terms of how the human race had arrived at this point, but not in terms of how they presently experienced it. I must confess to having pondered his definition many times before I could relate it to anything in individual religious development. When I did, it was because I had in the meantime become aware of the model of religious development suggested by H.C. Rümke. I may, therefore, in what I am about to say, import meanings into Whitehead that he never intended.

Nevertheless, it would not be strange that Whitehead, a philosopher and mathematician, and Rümke, a psychotherapist, should illuminate each others thoughts for they were both concerned to model religious development in its own terms, and neither of them was content to understand the process of change in the individual as an accumulation of accidental episodes.[10]

It is not, of course, crucial to my purpose that Whitehead understood his words as I do, or as Rümke might have done. His definition now has an existence of its own and it certainly serves to focus the understanding of religion implicit in Rümke's developmental theory.

WHITEHEAD'S DEFINITION OF RELIGION IN THE LIGHT OF RÜMKE'S MODEL OF RELIGIOUS DEVELOPMENT

Whitehead writes:

> Religion is what the individual does with his own solitariness, it runs through three stages if it evolves to its final satisfaction, it is a transition from God the void to God the enemy, and from God the

---

[10] What Rümke reported as the distillation of his years of therapeutic experience, was the beginnings of a theory of religious personal development and its possible inhibitors. Had it been taken more seriously it might have done much to overcome the divide that exists between pastoral psychology and pastoral theology, coming as they do from opposite ends and never quite meeting. It provided the opportunity to locate human development within a theory of religious development, broadly understood, instead of trying to explain religion, narrowly understood, within theories of human development that had begun without any reference to religion.

enemy to God the companion. Thus religion is solitariness. If you were never solitary, you were never religious. [11]

The first thought and the last are often quoted. They are beloved of all people who feel that religion is a highly individualistic and mystical affair. The seemingly unrelated middle section tends to be omitted. Indeed, it is not easy to see how solitariness is related to transition and the struggle which the middle section portrays. I said that it was a model of normative religious development, presented by H.C. Rümke, which cast light upon Whitehead's definition. While we cannot know whether the interpretation of Whitehead's definition which emerges from a consideration of Rümke's model is exactly what Whitehead had in mind, it is certainly more in keeping with the philosophical position he espoused, than the usual meaning set upon his words. For far from being a definition of a mystical individualism it will turn out to be something of a very different kind.

RÜMKE'S MODEL OF NORMAL RELIGIOUS DEVELOPMENT.

Rümke, a psychologist of the Freudian school, suggests that there are two levels in the religious development of the person. The one has to do with words and therefore with conceptualization, and the other has to do with experience. The structure of what follows I owe to Rümke, the illustrations I have added. Schematically Rümke's model may be represented as follows:

Shapes Behind Words

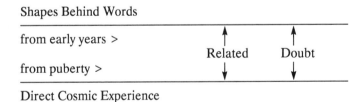

Direct Cosmic Experience

"*SHAPES BEHIND WORDS*" - Beginning in childhood, the individual undergoes a development which, in the first place, has to do with sounds. The child learns a sound and learns to associate shapes with it. The parent picks up the child's paw and utters the sound "hand", or gives it a long silver object with a round end and says "spoon", places in front of it a steaming mess in a bowl

---

[11] Alfred North Whitehead, *Religion in the Making*, (Cleveland and New York, The World Publishing Company, 1960), p.16

and says "porridge". One learns to associate images with sounds. Thus the sounds gain meaning and become words.

Once we have a basic set of images associated with certain sounds we can progress without direct experience. It might be said that if the porridge were white and if it were more finely grained, then it would be cornmeal. A new word has been added without direct experience of its referent. The child can then begin to put words into relationship, associating more complex images with more complex sets of words.

In the specific field of religion, one learns the sound "God" and begins to associate images with it. "God" refers to somebody who cares for us somewhere in the sky; or God is rather like a father - only more so; or (if they have seen a king in a story book) He is like a king - only more so. All this is at the level of what Rümke calls "Shapes Behind Words".

There are, of course, feelings associated with most of these sounds as well as images. The sounds "ice-cream" and "spinach" suggest very different feelings to most children. In the development of religious language, feeling is of central importance. For example, the child hears the word "God" in a place where its parents have taken it from playing in the sunshine, having scrubbed its knees, and where it sits for a long time on a hard bench. There they insist on giving the child a coin to put into a receptacle when it is passed round and, should he drop the coin, everybody glares. The man with a very stern face stands up in a sort of box talking about God and all are listening to him with great seriousness. Then too there is the expression on Auntie Mary's face when Uncle Bill drops a brick on his toe and says "Oh God!" All these contribute not just to the images associated with the sound "God", but primarily to the feelings associated with it.

The child then learns other sounds like "sin", "guilt", "forgiveness", "redemption", "grace", "heaven", "hell", "damnation". Sin, in early years, is simply what Mummy does not like. Guilt is what the child comes to feel when aware that it has committed such a sin. Forgiveness could be what the child feels when released from confinement in its room following Mother's wrath upon sin, and grace the chocolate biscuit received because Mummy feels more guilty about her wrath than the child does about its sin. When the child has learnt to associate images and feelings with these sounds they become words which can be built into networks of relationships.

If the child grows up in the Christian world and goes to Sunday School, people will teach him or her that once there was a creation and humans were perfect. That they sinned and God had to set about redeeming them. Then would follow the history of Israel, culminating in the story of forgiveness on the basis of Christ's death on the Cross, and the hope of heaven. So the words are linked together. Not only can these shapes be put together into an elaborate theology, but the feelings associated with each sound can be strung together into a symphony of feeling. Thus children can be led through a feeling of guilt about their sinfulness, then through the experience of feeling forgiven and restored to the fold, and a sense of looking forward to heaven and all that that implies. Both the cognitive picture of interrelated images and the symphony of feelings may become very sophisticated.

The erstwhile children may go on from school to university and perhaps read religious studies, so that they can now discourse with some ability not only on their own tradition but on other religious traditions as well. What is more they can do all this (and this is the point that Rümke would have us register) *without ever having had a religious experience of their own in their entire life*. All this experience of which I have spoken is second-hand.

That is not to say that second-hand experience may not be very like the real thing and so prepare the child to recognize his or her own religious experience when it comes. Particularly would this be the case if the persons leading the child had first hand experience of their own. Nevertheless, at this stage the experience is all second-hand.

"DIRECT COSMIC EXPERIENCE" - Rümke's second line of development is that of experience. It begins with the young child not distinguishing itself clearly from its surroundings. It may cry because of discomfort without knowing where the discomfort lies. The child, by being clothed, named, and gaining some possessions is somewhat separated from its environment and is gradually able to identify itself more clearly as a separate entity. Yet it never quite loses its sense of existing as part of the family.

It is not until one approaches those critical years around puberty that one begins the process of climbing out of the family relationship and into a new individualism. It is then that one starts to develop a sense of being an ego and, therefore, a sense of over-againstness with all that is non-ego, all that is out there in the world, be it people, things, or ideas. It is at this stage of individual development that Rümke understands religious experience to begin.

At psychological puberty one begins the climb out of a set of relationships which can be positively porridge-like. One does not look at a bowl of porridge and say "Oh! what a wonderful unity". On the other hand one might look into the back of a watch and register a wonderful unity, precisely because the parts are all individual and all working together in harmony. So the young person in the years of puberty begins to develop a strong sense of individuality and to climb out of those very real but amorphous relationships into which he or she was born and in which he or she has grown up. These are the difficult years. The time when even the advances of love from the parent have to be rejected in order that the individual may stand on his or her own feet, and pass from the relationship of child into the relationship of voluntariness, which is that of a friend of the parent. Usually a strong sense of individuality begins its development in middle to late teenage years, but as a clearer sense of individuality goes on developing so does the sense of being over against all-that-out-there.

I remember clearly in my own undergraduate days standing in my room at the top of an old Victorian house looking out over the lights of the city and experiencing, not so much a cognitive enquiry, but the sort of feeling which might be expressed as "There is the arena in which I have to find myself. What does it have to offer me? What will my future in it be? or There's the oyster, where is my pearl?". The lights of the city had become symbolic of a whole world and a whole future.

This sort of feeling, that of being an individual looking out on all-that-out-there, all that is non-ego, sensing that that is the arena in which one has to find oneself and that one is therefore dependent upon it, a feeling of something important and yet undefined, is I think, the beginning of what Whitehead meant by the experience of "God the void".

The next stage in the development of the person, according to Rümke's understanding, and which is important for our purpose, is the sense of demand laid upon one by the world-out-there. Once one has gained a sense of self, there is a sub-conscious awareness that one must come to self-knowledge. Now that I know *that I am*, the quest is on to know *who I am*. This cannot be achieved in a vacuum, but only in terms of that world-out-there. One is, as it were, the centre of a cobweb and comes to self-knowledge in establishing a set of relationships with people, with things, with sets of values. Whether one is the sort of person who thinks it is fun to get off the bus without putting the fare into the box, if the conductor has failed to collect it, or whether one is the sort of person who insists that it be handed over, is but one of a thousand little things which come to create a knowledge of self.

This knowledge of self cannot arise without one going back into relationship with the world-out-there and all its demands. One may not like that world, one may want to change it, but relate to it one must. Because of the need for a self-image one is drawn into obedience to the demands of the world. They may be regulations of a degree course, laws of the state, or simply the expectations of one's employer or peers. In order to know oneself, one must relate to that world. In order to relate to it, one must submit to certain demands. Even if one defines oneself over against the *status quo*, the world still calls the name of the game. All this is felt as a threat, for one has only just climbed out of the porridge and now one feels sucked back into it.

This is the stage which many reach in university years where, because of the threat of losing that very newly won sense of freedom, one is against all the structures. One generation seeks to change things this way and the next generation seeks to change them back again, for somehow the demands have to be resisted. Religiously speaking this is the stage of law, of the demand upon one to be obedient, and this I think is the experience which Whitehead refers to as "God the enemy".

Then, according to Rümke's model, comes a stage in which we surrender to the demand. We allow ourselves to be drawn back into relationship with the world-out-there with all its imposed structures and find, surprisingly, that we are not going back into porridge, but rather into that unity of individual differences which is more like the inside of the watch. One begins to come to self-knowledge because one establishes relationships (free relationships) with other people, with institutions, with things, with ideas. This is the time when the young get their hair cut, have a shave, put away their jeans for gardening at the week-ends, put on a suit and take themselves to work. Gradually one begins to discover where one's talents lie and where they do not, where one succeeds and how one succeeds in relation to peers. One creates a self-image in a hundred and one different ways. This ability to build the self-image, to discover a way in which one can evaluate and understand oneself is experienced as grace. This I believe is the experience which Whitehead refers to as "God the companion".

Therefore, says Whitehead, religion is transition and if it progresses to its final end, one has moved through all these levels of experience.

It must be recognized, however, that one could pass through all these experiences without being able to put them into words, let alone religious words, for they remain at the level of experience. While all that one receives at the level of words is second-hand, however sophisticated the set of images and the feelings related to them may be, that which we receive at the level of experience is our own, and hence Rümke calls it Direct. Also, because it is an experience of all that is out there, because it is all that is non-ego that one is relating to, or being confronted by, he calls it Cosmic, thus Direct Cosmic Experience.

Some Corollaries:

There are some corollaries of this understanding of Direct Cosmic Experience. It cannot, for example, be had by anybody before psychological puberty and is unavailable to anybody who has not in fact become an ego. If, therefore, in some childhood trauma one developed an inability to let go of mother's apronstrings and could not become an ego, one could not have direct cosmic experience. One could not, in Rümke's terms, have religious experience for oneself.

Likewise, the ability to have direct cosmic experience requires that one is able to become aware of the world-out-there symbolically in order to have the necessary relation to it. If after those years from 9 to 11, during which boys in particular become so analytical, tending to the mechanical and despising the poetic, they should move on toward technology and the like, then they may well develop an overly analytical cast of mind and become what Rümke calls "symbol blind". That is to say, they will not be able to see holistically, not be able to feel the importance of the totality of that-which-is-out-there, not gain a sense of all that is non-ego, and so not be able to feel its demand, nor their resistance to it. The development which Rümke describes may not, therefore, take place at all.

Even if the development does take place, it may do so purely at the experiential level. If there is no suitable or acceptable set of words available, the experience will fail to be conceptualized and never become consciously religious. The experiential level, however, is what religion is about. Consider two people:

> The first is on the top line of Rümke's developmental model, having a very sophisticated set of words but no personal religious experience.

> The second person is on the lower line, having had what Rümke called direct cosmic experience but is unable to identify himself or herself as religious because he or she has never found the right set of words to conceptualize the experience.

There is no doubt which of these two people one would say was the more religious.

It comes as something of a shock, especially if one was brought up in the sort of Protestant Christian tradition which emphasizes right belief, to recognize that experience is so obviously primary to the set of words in which one seeks to describe it. Yet direct cosmic experience does not have to be symbolized in words at all. Earlier humankind danced, carved and painted their religion insofar as it was separated from the affairs of everyday living. Such experience can be expressed in many ways. It may never be conceptualized in words. It may never therefore, become explicitly religious. Nevertheless, human beings are cognitive beings and for religion to embrace the whole of life, it too must have an adequate conceptual aspect. It might be said that religion becomes more fully religious if and when the time comes that a set of words, perhaps the tradition which one has inherited, is found to fit with one's own experience.

Many conversions, or returns to a serious concern with religion, take place in the late teenage years. Although one may have felt that one was a believer all the time, this is the stage where the set of words which one has learnt, suddenly for some, more gradually for others, is felt to relate to something in one's own experience. The words that one used for years, now describe something that is experienced within oneself. A link has been formed between the development that has gone on from childhood, at the level of "shapes behind words", and the other development, which has gone on since puberty only, at the level of direct cosmic experience. In William James' words, one now has "religion in possession".

Rümke also lays emphasis on the need for doubt, a healthy doubt, which in his model is a continual interplay between words and experience. One needs to keep asking, of the words whether they are adequate to conceptualize one's experience, and of the experience whether it is being viewed as well as it might be through the tradition that one has inherited or accepted. This maintains the dynamic relationship between them. The problem in some sectarian forms of Christianity, for example, is that great emphasis is laid on loyalty to a set of words. This means that a person who is converted and has found a set of words to fit his experience may then be taught to feel guilty about doubting them. One cannot hold back experience, however, which goes on developing willy-nilly until, perhaps in middle age, some crisis arises. The adherent may then turn to his or her religion, only to find there a teenage set of words. Then the believer is likely to reject the whole system as being inadequate and go into what Rümke calls "radical unbelief". The preventative for radical unbelief is a healthy doubt actively keeping belief and experience in line with each other.

WHITEHEAD'S DEFINITION IN THE LIGHT OF RÜMKE
- ITS STRENGTHS AND THREE WEAKNESSES

If this is indeed the meaning that Whitehead intended in his definition, then it is not simply an individual and rather mystical definition of religion, but in fact involves every possible aspect. It involves the individual, who has really become an individual, in confrontation with all that is out there, whether it be nature, society, or abstract ideals. It combines all those other definitions to which we referred, not only the strictly individual definitions but also the functional ones, precisely because it is about the individual's developing relationship with all that is non-ego. Dependence, morality, meaning, harmony, are all included here. It is, within my knowledge, the most inclusive definition in the literature. Whitehead's definition has three weaknesses.

The Problem of Terminology

The first weakness of the definition is simply its language. As I said when introducing it, I had read the definition a number of times without being able to understand it in the individual terms in which it is cast; wondering why somebody, who was very much a hard-headed philosopher-mathematician on the one hand, should have proposed a mystical and individualistic definition of religion on the other.

Once one has found the key, of course, it is nothing of the kind. He says "religion is what the individual does with his own solitariness". The key lies in the meaning of "solitariness". Solitariness is not to be understood as "being on one's own", but as "having become an individual". If, in Rümke's terms, one translates "solitariness" as "having become an ego" then the last line of Whitehead's definition would read "if you have never become an ego you have never been religious" and the rest falls into place. Nevertheless, the language is opaque.

The Western Stance

The second problem is that, in this interpretation, and also I believe in Whitehead's intention, it is strictly western.[12] It depends on the pressure to gain self-knowledge once the sense of self has been attained, and upon self-knowledge arising only out of the ego's relationship with all that is non-ego. This means not only affirming the reality of the self and all that confronts the self, but also embracing just those humanly contrived relationships and categories which the developed forms of some eastern religions seek to escape.

In the terms of this definition, it may be said that while western religion presses on to "God the Companion" the East sees the pinnacle of religious experience in a careful refinement of the "God the Void" stage. Why this is necessarily the case, given their different world views, will become clear later. For the moment it should be recognized that God the Companion is not necessarily a stage reached once and for all, even in western experience. Aspects of identity and of a sense of cosmic belonging can be lost and have to be sought again.

The Reduction of Religious Experience

The third and final problem with Whitehead's definition, as I have interpreted it, is more apparent than real, but threatening nevertheless. I must deal with it at some length.

Many readers have felt that there is a problem with this definition, or anyway with my interpretation of it, that they cannot identify. What usually emerges in discussion is a sense of reduction. "If this is what the definition means, then it seems to reduce religion to bits of everyday psycho-social experience. Feelings about the world-out-there suddenly become experience of God by selecting the right set of words with which to symbolize them." The same problem, of course, existed with the definition I presented earlier. There are a number of parallels between the two. In the first I spoke of that

---

[12] Whitehead considers what he calls "the three traditions", Christianity, Buddhism, and Science, and advocates openness between them, but there is no doubt where he thinks the truth lies. *ibid*, p.134 f.

which meets the believer through total experience. In the second Whitehead attributed religious significance to the processes of change (transition) in total experience. Rümke spoke of the ego confronted by all that is non-ego. I attributed the same meaning to Whitehead's solitariness. As statements about the source of religious experience and therefore of religious understanding they stand or fall together.

The problem for the contemporary western believer that ordinary experiences of life, viewed through the spectacles of a learnt set of words, should suddenly become religious experiences, is nevertheless a very real one. It would not be a problem in other world religions nor, perhaps, in the West until recent times. It is, I think, the consequence of a growing sense that everyday experience is secular. The spiritual dimension having, as it were, retreated to heaven, only to manifest in different degrees on recognizably religious occasions such as a conversion, a charismatic experience, or simply a run-of-the-mill religious service.

There are two consequences for Westerners of being brought up to think of religious experience in this way. On the one hand, it leads to an unrealistic expectation and therefore frequent disappointment, in those who get involved in recognizably religious activities. On the other hand, it creates a block in many of us against viewing the experience that we do have as religious. I would maintain, however, that the view presented earlier of a god known in everyday life experience, let me call it history, is in fact orthodoxy in the two Biblical faiths and at least orthopraxis in Islam.

The divine name, given in answer to Moses' question "Who shall I say sent me?", unlike the images associated with the gods of Egypt and Mesopotamia, had no immediate content. It might possibly have contained a promise of self revelation in future events. That anyway is where the prophets came to look for the divine hand and therefore for the divine character. He was above all "the one who brought us out of the land Egypt". I will return this in the next chapter.

The desert, either literal or figurative, plays a major role in the insight of the mystic and spiritual genius. It is not however a retreat from experience. The desert is redolent of totality, forcing those who enter it to place the bits and pieces of life in context, *sub specie aeternitatis*. It is a place where people are driven to find symbols (insights) in which to express their felt sense of the nature of that totality. If their experience were something other than this, then the words they subsequently offer to those of lesser insight, time, or inclination, would not in fact be experienced as insight.

The problem arises because believers in the Abrahamic faiths typically think of themselves as having knowledge (probably revealed knowledge) both of and about God. They have never before separated out knowledge, as Rümke invites us to do, into experience (knowledge of) and words (knowledge about). There are many issues here, including how one uses the word "knowledge". I try to use the terms "experience of" and "knowledge about", but not "knowledge of", save where concept and experience merge. The two issues important for my purpose are:

    i) the process in which experience becomes acceptable as knowledge,

    ii) the limitation that experience places on both words and knowledge.

I will deal with the last first.

i) Experience, the Limitation upon Words and Knowledge

In discussing Rümke, I outlined the process by which sounds become related to experiences and, therefore, to mental images and probably also to feelings. Thus they become words. Words can then be used to communicate experiences including those which have not been had at first-hand. Clearly, there can be no verbal communication of an experience from the one having it, to one not having it, if there are simply no words to express it.

There is no problem in describing to a person, who has only experienced oatmeal porridge, what cornmeal porridge looks like, if he or she has also learnt to communicate about colour and grain size. However, there can be no words to express that which is beyond the experience of the hearer at every level. Consider another storybook illustration. It is one that is obviously related to religion with a transcendent deity.

> A fruit worm burrows its way into the middle of an orange where it meets a pip to whom it wishes to describe the outside world. This would include the tree on which the orange hangs, with its green leaves, the multicolored song birds in its branches and the sun in the blue sky.
> The pip's vocabulary is of necessity limited to its experience. Its experience is limited to what we would call juice, membranes, pith and other pips. That is, to a limited range of shapes and sizes and to colours from white through creamy yellow to orange, with perhaps a memory of green. The pip might be persuaded to believe that there is something beyond its immediate environment in order to account for the cycles of temperature and the pulses of some growth generating force, if it could be aware of growth when everything expands together. If this were really a storybook, the pip, in dying, could become a tree and come to know for itself what the world beyond the orange was like, but that is of no help to our present concern.

The meaning I think is clear. However inspired the fruit worm may be it is absolutely limited, in that which it can communicate, to the experience and therefore the vocabulary of the pip. Revelation must have at least as much to do with the long process of preparing a vocabulary through experience, as it does with the specific insight which finally emerges in the words made available. To paraphrase Heinrich Ott, revelation presupposes two parties, the revealer, and the one to whom revelation takes place, and the latter in his concrete situation. [13]

ii) Experience, Reality and Knowledge

Experience is not necessarily knowledge except, in the most primitive sense of knowledge, as awareness of the sensations which comprise the experience. Experience needs to be tested in some way before it is acceptable as knowledge, for it might be judged to be hallucination. In my view it is tested within a sense of reality which is itself distilled from the individual's every significant experience. It is in relation to what I have been calling "total experience" that an individual experience may become knowledge.

In order to illustrate this, let me go back to the fruit worm for a moment. It could be asked, why an inspired fruit worm could not project into the mind of the pip, images of tree, birds and sun? The answer is that it might, but it could only be an impression. Save, insofar as it fell within the rest of the experience and therefore the vocabulary of the pip, it would be without the possibility of signifying anything. It would not become knowledge of anything, save of the sensation itself, unless it were somehow testable within what the pip already felt to be real.

The problem (for western religion anyway) may be stated like this. If experience comes to us through our five ordinary senses how can it give rise to religious knowledge, and if it is somehow projected into our mind, how can it be validated as knowledge rather than hallucination? Otto's move, to which I referred earlier, was to posit a sixth sense through which experience of what he called the *numinous* was received. I am unable to see the value in such a move.

Over against those who would see religious experience as arising in some special faculty or sixth sense, I would maintain that it arises in, or must certainly be authenticated in, a sense of reality distilled from the individual's total experience received through all five (or even six) senses. The notion of a sixth sense with direct awareness of that which cannot be felt, seen, smelled, tasted or heard, is not in itself absurd, but the notion that it can be a quite separate source of knowledge is absurd. Consider another illustration.

---

[13] Heinrich Ott, "The Problem of Non-objectifying Thinking and Speaking in Theology" in *Journal for Theology and the Church* vol 3, (New York, Harper & Row, 1967) p.129 f.

When one smells burning one may not always check on the sense of smell, but, if one does and then one cannot see fire or feel heat, one begins to worry. When one hears voices one naturally believes that there are people, or at least a radio around, but if one becomes aware that one's other senses do not support that view, then one may be driven to the conclusion that one is hallucinating. While we may frequently trust a single sense, we in fact weave our sense of reality out of the warp and woof of all the data our senses receive. To have one sense go "maverick" is a truly frightening experience.

So while one may conceive of receiving experience, that is untested data, through a sixth sense, there is no way of testing it, save in the arena of a sense of reality distilled from the data provided by all the senses. If it has to be tested in the arena of total experience before it can become knowledge, then it is better thought of as arising there, even if provoked and perhaps later symbolized by discreet experiences. The religious experience of most folk is not well described by Otto's *mysterium tremendum et fascinans*. It is more likely to be of a god who "saw that I was never without bread in the bread bin".

This limit, set by the manner in which human beings test new experience against an established sense of reality, does not exclude what Otto also seems to have had in mind, that some people, or all people at some time, may have a heightened sensitivity to a religious dimension within experience.

I do not intend to carry this form of argument further, but when I come, in the next section, to the relation between total experience and the concrete particular, I will be addressing the relation of knowledge to experience in another way.

Earlier, I made a distinction between religion as personal experience and religion as tradition and institution. Up to this point I have dealt only with the former now I must turn to the latter. Institutionalized religion has many facets, but that which holds it all together is the tradition community - that group of people who share a body of beliefs and practices which is handed on from generation to generation. For each adherent, and even for others in the same culture, the tradition is a part of their world-out-there and of their images behind words. It shapes thinking and valuing from early years onward. This being the case I must now spend a little time considering how a religious tradition develops out of the individual experiences of the people sharing the tradition, that is, the tradition community. I will illustrate what I have to say from the Biblical tradition.

CHAPTER 3

THE SHAPING OF A TRADITION

Chapter 2 began with the question "To what experiences in human beings does the word "religion" relate?" and within that, "To what experience might the word "god" relate?".

The answer thus far proposed is that religion has to do with the other side of the life-long question "Who am I?", namely "What is all that out there and how do I relate to it?". religion, therefore, is not about any or all of the bits and pieces of experience but about the whole of experience, or about a reality which may be distilled from that totality.

This reality is often symbolized by certain of its own parts. In order of time, its characteristics may first be reported to one by reference to them. It may even be felt to be particularly present in certain of them, but it is not known in any bit or piece without being known primarily in the totality. The value assigned to any one of the bits and pieces of experience remains arbitrary until it is placed in relation to the totality or to the reality distilled therefrom.

This chapter is concerned to relate this highly individual experience to the other aspect of religion. that is, the corporately possessed religious tradition, with its beliefs and practices; its history, institutions and functionaries.

I have described, in western vein, what I understand to be the source and nature of normal religious experience in the individual. In so doing I have not been able to avoid some reference to religious tradition. This present chapter will show how a religious tradition might develop out of the interplay between some concrete particular, for example, some event, person, or book, and ongoing total experience.

Logically speaking, it is total experience that is prior. In practice, it is usually the concrete particular within the developing tradition, accepted on authority, which first engages the adherent's attention. Yet it does not matter which way around it comes, the result will be the same. Consider a short illustration and then an example.

INTERPLAY BETWEEN A CHARACTERISTIC CONCRETE PARTICULAR AND ONGOING TOTAL EXPERIENCE

Let it be supposed that total experience is represented by a wall covered with unsigned paintings. One might, after looking at them for some time, recognize that a particular picture over there, was clearly the work of the same artist as this one over here; then, that the artist who painted these, also painted the one down in the corner. Perhaps one could not directly relate this one over here, to the one in the corner, but one can trace the link through the one over there.

Then one might spot a highly characteristic painting, which enabled one to see that the painter of that was also responsible for most, or all, of the others. Perhaps one spots two such characteristic pictures, indicating that two artists are represented on the wall. If no such characteristic picture could be found, the pictures, while still perhaps recognizably the work of the same or a limited number of artists, would remain in largely accidental relation. If a characteristic picture could be found, then each picture would gain in meaning from its relation to that one and from its place in a more strongly related whole.

In the faith of Israel the event of the Exodus was such a characteristic picture. God, in that tradition, becomes above all else "The one who brought us out of the land of Egypt". The understanding of the god active in that event was constantly in interplay with, and challenged by, ongoing experience. Each generation had to reinterpret the character of that god, and the meaning of that event, in terms of every significant new experience. As each generation added its own understanding - the tradition grew.

Christians were later to swop the Exodus, as their most characteristic picture, for that of the life, teaching, death and resurrection of Jesus of Nazareth. They did not, however, reject the Exodus as a characteristic picture. In that new concrete, historical event, Christians saw most clearly the hand which they discerned to be at work in the totality of their experience.

Many Christian doctrines gain central elements of their meaning in just this way. One of the meanings of the resurrection, in Christian faith, is that the personality discerned in Jesus the Carpenter of Nazareth is the same personality which is discerned in the Spirit, that all pervasive presence of the divine in the period succeeding his death. To speak of Christ as pre-existent, is to make the same sort of connection between previous total experience expressed in the symbol of God as the Creator and Father of the Old Testament period and the Carpenter of Nazareth. Already that puzzling doctrine of the Trinity begins to emerge.

Having illustrated the process in an abstracted way it might be helpful to trace, by way of example, the development of a particular strand of biblical tradition. I will trace what is perhaps the most persistent question in the Old Testament, the inexplicable suffering of the covenant people.

AN EXAMPLE FROM THE TRADITION OF ISRAEL

Leaving aside the burning bush and other miraculous elements in the Exodus story (not because they could not have happened, but because they are not normal experience) we might ask what a people who had been in bondage in Egypt, would be likely to believe about a god whom they supposed to have been involved in their escape.

Presumably they would believe him to be powerful, to have set his care upon them and to have some destiny for them, or else why would he have rescued them. All this they could come to believe, simply as a consequence of believing that this god was involved in that particular piece of history.

Yet any naive belief that they might have had, that they would inevitably prosper because this god had entered into a special relationship with them, was soon to be challenged. It was challenged in turn, by the lack of meat and bread, the lack of water and the failure to enter the land in the way expected. On the other hand, the belief would be felt to be confirmed and revitalized when they did enter the land.

There again things went wrong for them. In consequence some turned to the Ba'als (the fertility deities of the land) and Yahweh, the god of the desert, was left behind; others did not take this step. Their experiences, therefore, of suffering at the hands of the Midianites and the resurgent Canaanites, the difficulties of civil strife and finally, in this period, the crushing pressure of the Philistines, had to be understood in terms of that same god who brought them out of Egypt. Their simple faith had been challenged. It must grow or be rejected.

The direction taken by this growth is to be found in the second chapter of the book of Judges, where the history of the period is summarized. We are told that the people sinned and that God raised up an oppressor who oppressed them. The people cried unto the Lord in their distress and He raised up a Judge who delivered them from the oppressor. They served the Lord all the days of the Judge. Then the Judge died, they turned back to their wicked ways, and the cycle began again.

In short, they had come to see their suffering as punishment but within the context of a covenant with a powerful and faithful God. In fact they had come to that extension of the tradition which is referred to as the "deuteronomic theory of retribution". In this it was maintained that the good prosper and the evil suffer. In eternal perspective this may prove to be true, but it would not suffice to account for all the present sufferings of life. So, in its turn, this newer orthodoxy was challenged.

There are two separate but related issues here. First, there is the corporate issue, of understanding the nature of the covenant relationship between Israel and her God in the light of a history of almost continual suffering. Second, there is the problem of the righteous but suffering individual.

This last problem was an ancient theme in the land of Israel's origins, but it became a particularly sharp one for a people who had come to understand the character of the divine as righteous and faithful to his promises. It was more difficult because they had not yet come to believe in a possible compensation in a life beyond death.

The suffering of the righteous stands as a challenge to either the power or the perceived character of the divine. A whole nation could never be thought of as totally righteous so the issue is most sharply focused in the case of the righteous individual. I will deal with this first, although the book of Job in which the problem is examined, probably originates late in the biblical period.

We find Job, the suffering one, with his friends. They are steeped in the orthodoxy of the time, so they say to him in many different ways "Job, you are suffering, therefore you must be a sinner. You had better repent". Job, however, protests against this and looks to God for vindication.

The prologue to the book interprets his suffering in terms of refinement. God allows Satan to progressively tempt Job because he trusts his servant to be faithful and to show the mettle of his faith. But the heart of the book is a great deal more existential than this.

The picture we get of God from the friends, is rather like that of a puppet which one plays by pulling strings. If we are good he must prosper us, if we are evil he must punish us. God is caught in the meshes of an over simplified orthodoxy. Job, however, is invited by the voice from the whirlwind to consider the mighty works of nature (in much the same way as the classical prophets had examined the events of Israel's history) in order to understand better the god who stood behind them. Nature is immediately available to the suffering individual. The history of Israel is not within the immediate experience of the individual, but becomes the appropriate reference when the suffering of the nation is the problem.

Job considers the greatness of God in Behemoth (the hippopotamus) and Leviathan (the alligator), in the wonders that the miners find under the earth, in Pleiades and Orion in the sky and perhaps also in a whirlwind. Job takes a great leap from a god understood in terms of his own immediate problem and of current dogma to faith in the god of a more total experience. He says with his whole attitude what was a fortuitously bad translation earlier in the book, "I will trust him though he slay me". Perhaps this is the final answer for an individual but it cannot be satisfying when we consider the suffering of a nation. The nation is not expected to die. If it were, the meaning of belonging to it will also seem to die.

On the national level of suffering, Isaiah of Jerusalem, the prophet who had watched the northern tribes of Israel disappear into captivity in the Assyrian empire, had already taken the step of going beyond the deuteronomic orthodoxy by saying, not, "If you are righteous you will be blessed", but rather, "Whatever happens is for the best because God is sovereign".

Later, Jeremiah, believing that his people needed to have the law written into their hearts rather than on tablets of stone, was to welcome the Babylonians as they came to carry away all that was left of Israel into another bondage. This he did because he understood the event as the act of a loving God who would bring them, through another exodus, to a new covenant.

It is to Isaiah of Babylon, however, that we have to look for the greatest modification in the understanding of suffering at the national level.

Deutero-Isaiah quite clearly sees that Israel suffers because Israel has sinned, but it is also clear to him that Israel suffers more than the other nations and that there is something more in her suffering than punishment. Perhaps he saw a process of growth in the cycle - sin, repentance and return to God - which left those who had been through it in a better position than those who had never sinned. It is almost as though sin were a necessity if one was to learn of the grace of God. But whatever the exact process Isaiah had in mind, it is clear that he comes to see Israel's suffering as something borne vicariously for the redemption of others. Indeed, he sees that to suffer in this way is to be counted a privilege.

Yet Isaiah, passing beyond a corporate image of the servant to the individual image of the servant, looks for something greater than this. Israel had sinned and her suffering could be counted as punishment for sin. When Israel had been punished for her sins she had called down God's wrath on those who had oppressed her. Isaiah looks toward the ideal, which stands at the end of this learning process, of one who, even though sinless, suffers. One who goes voluntarily to the suffering and does not call down wrath upon those who persecute him.

Consider how far from the point at which we started is this understanding of Israel's covenant relationship with her god. From the covenant promising freedom from suffering, suffering becomes very nearly its *raison d'être*.

Israel's understanding of its own suffering, however, is not my primary concern. My purpose is to illustrate the manner in which the understanding of God's relationship to humankind grows as a tradition - a tradition which is challenged by each new experience and must either develop to take account of it, or cease to feel real and be rejected. It will be understood that this form of historical revelation can only take place within a religion of the Abrahamic type, that is, one in which one God is in control of the nation's destiny. If Deutero-Isaiah were not forced to declare "I am Yahweh there is none other, I create darkness and light, goodness and chaos" he would not be compelled to understand his nation's suffering within the will of that one God. He could have blamed it, in a style possible to the Zoroastrian, on the ascendancy in that period of the spirit of evil.

The development of a tradition such as I have described, does not take place in a vacuum. It requires a tradition community. Nor does it develop on its own. It requires that different roles be played out by individuals within the community. I now turn to a consideration of these roles within the tradition community.

NECESSARY ROLES IN THE DEVELOPMENT OF A TRADITION
- *PROPHET, PRIEST AND PRAGMATIST*

I begin with the nature of prophecy as it was found in Israel, and then consider its relation to other roles extant in that society. Finally, I will draw some conclusions which would be applicable to any dynamic tradition.

If the word "prophet" were defined broadly enough, it could be said that prophets have existed down through the ages and in all the world's religions. Even if we use a narrow definition of a prophet, as one who believed himself called by his god to deliver a message, usually ethical, often condemnatory, frequently directed to the most powerful of persons, then examples of prophets can still be found in other religious traditions, both before and after the classical period of Israel's prophecy. Yet there does seem to be something different about the classical Hebrew prophet and the attempt to distill his unique essence has persisted.

It is not helpful to assume, as it was assumed in the period of scholarship heavily influenced by evolutionary notions, that prophecy was the one feature of Israel's religious tradition which really made a contribution to posterity; the priest and the cult being understood as a hangover of an earlier and not so valuable tradition. Nor is it helpful to rush into the opposite and more recent stance, and see the prophet as a functionary of the cult. For, although the evidence shows frequent conflict between priest and prophet, we cannot prefer one to the other, or worse, understand one without the other.

The quest for the essence of Israel's prophecy has sometimes taken the path of recognizing the existence within Israel of a prophetic activity which parallels that in other religions, but then seeking to demonstrate that this is not the true, or at least not the important, prophecy in Israel.

Mantic prophecy (seeking to find out from God what humankind wanted to know by the casting of lots or other impersonal means) is present in the biblical tradition, with no suggestion that it did not produce the truth.

Ecstatic prophecy is also present in the biblical tradition, but any attempt to use the distinction between the ecstatic and calm ethical type to distinguish the false from the true is doomed to failure, if only because Elijah was both on the same day. Having been the very epitome of the calm ethical type, as against the frenzied performance of the prophets of Melqart, Ba'al of Tyre, he then "with the hand of the Lord upon him", ran all the way back to Jezreel before Ahab's chariot. Nor will it do to see the calm ethical type as a later and higher development of the ecstatic type which Israel had once shared with her pagan neighbors. Ecstatic behavior is to be found as late as Ezekiel.

Anyone who is brought up in the Hebrew-Christian tradition has an almost instinctive preference for the solitary, anti-cultic, reluctant, amateur, proletarian preacher of woe, as the type of the true prophet. This also is contradicted by the biblical evidence. There are those who, on every other ground, one would wish to regard as true prophets, who are either to be found in the bands of prophets, or associated with the cult, or are willing and even professional prophets, aristocratic and, on occasion anyway, preachers of weal.

It is possible to move into the subjective realm and say that the true prophet is one who has the spirit of God, but then there is at least one occasion in which it is recorded that God, for His own purposes, sent a lying spirit.

Then one can do what the Bible seems to do in two places. That is, to lay emphasis on forecasting, rather than upon admonition, encouragement or instruction; saying that the true prophet is the one whose prophecies come true. There are, of course, all sorts of problems with this as a criterion for recognizing the true prophet. One finds, in retrospect, prophecies from the mouth of the same prophet, some of which were fulfilled and some of which were not. This criterion of true prophecy either makes no room for repentance on the part of those addressed or tends to render the prophecy self-fulfilling. It is certainly of little help to the hearer who must decide, then and there, not years, maybe generations into the future, on the significance of what the prophet has to say.

The book of Deuteronomy adds the criterion of loyalty to that of proving to be right. The true prophet is one who is "sound". To hearers (who could not enter the prophet's inner self) that could only mean that he or she stood firmly in the tradition as that was understood. This takes our attention off the person of the prophet and fixes it on the tradition. That is as it should be. The primary concern is to distinguish true from false prophecy, not true from false prophet. If we would look for the uniqueness in Israel's prophets, it is to be found in the tradition out of which, and into which, they spoke. It does not lie primarily in any other quality or circumstance appertaining to the prophet.

I will attempt to show that the role of the prophet is an essential element in any growing tradition, although it may be fulfilled in widely differing ways, even within the same tradition. The role of the prophet in Israel was different to that in most other religious traditions, because the tradition itself was consciously open ended, historically revealed, not a "once given to the ancestors" tradition.

The difference had its roots in the Mosaic tradition itself not in the prophets. What it was that made this difference will be considered in chapters 5 and 8.

THE CRITERIA FOR AUTHORITATIVE PROPHECY

In order to make clear how the prophetic address could be <u>immediately</u> authoritative to at least some of its hearers; to explain the relation between priest and prophet and make clear the primacy of tradition in prophecy; I ask that the reader consider another imaginary situation.

Suppose that your door burst open and a man rushed in proclaiming that god was angry with you, because on the previous evening you drank milk while you were eating meat.

If your reaction were anything like mine you would soon be wanting to send for someone with a strait-jacket.

Suppose, however, that the man who rushed in proclaimed that god was angry with you because last evening, when driving home in the dusk, you passed a figure lying beside the road and you did not stop. Again, if you were like me and the circumstances of which the man spoke were true, then what he had to say would bite home and you would acknowledge to yourself that you ought to have stopped.

The question is, where does the difference between the two cases lie? If in the first instance the person addressed were an orthodox Jew or a member of certain Hindu sects, then the man's words would also have bitten, provided that his account of the event was correct. For some people, it is deeply significant that they do not mix milk with meat.

If the person addressed in the second case stood in some highly deterministic tradition, then the second statement would have been, not so much false, as irrelevant. In that situation the Christian parable of the Good Samaritan has no authority. If there is nothing that one can do about a situation then one cannot be held responsible for it. If the man beside the road is to die he will die. If, on the other hand, the one addressed stood in a tradition which charged him with his brother's welfare, then he would indeed feel guilt as the statement bit home. We can distill from this imaginary example the criteria which have to be fulfilled if the prophet's words are to have immediate authority for the hearer.

> a) The Prophet and the hearer must share the same basic principles of belief; in the examples these might be expressed as "There is a certain natural order in things which shall not be transgressed", or "A man is his brother's keeper".

> b) The hearer must accept the description of the situation as true. In the examples that would be that he did mix milk with meat or did pass the figure beside the road.

> c) The hearer must follow and agree the logic in which the former is applied to the latter in order to achieve the conclusion.

If the hearer shares with the prophet some basic principle of belief, if he accepts the description of the event and if he agree the logic by which one is applied to the other, then he can do nothing but accept the truth of the conclusion.

Neither the word "logic" nor the phrase "principle of belief" as they are used here must be understood too cognitively. In chapter 6 I will be discussing the development and role of the "felt sense of reality". This will indicate what more is included in belief and in the testing activity that I have referred to here as "agreeing the logic".

Consideration of the criteria for authoritative prophecy lead to certain conclusions.

SOME CONSEQUENCES OF THE CRITERIA FOR AUTHORITATIVE PROPHECY

i) Prophecy does not have to come from a Recognized Prophet.
  Prophecy is Prior to the Prophet.

Prophecy is not essentially mysterious. It does not have to come from a recognized prophet, still less does it have to come from a crystal ball. It is as likely to emerge out of agony as out of ecstasy. It comes out of a situation, a set of believed-in principles, and the logic by which the latter is applied to the former. When the situation and the tradition are out of step, prophecy is already in the air and awaiting someone to speak it.

Being "out of step" can go either way. When, in biblical Israel, the people were over-confident and forgot their god (usually in times of affluence) the prophets sought to bring them down to earth by preaching the conditional covenant of Sinai - "only if you keep my law will you be my people". If, on the other hand, the people were in despair and losing faith, then the prophets sought to lift them up by preaching the unconditional covenant first made with Abraham, - "God has promised and is faithful - underneath are the everlasting arms". It is worth noting that if the situation and the tradition are not particularly out of step there will be little or no prophecy. So it might be quite wrong to assume, as some have, that the gaps in the period of Israel's classical prophecy represent times of a lowered spirituality. It is true that prophecy can be quietened down when it would normally be taking place, perhaps because the spiritual and secular leadership have merged (as they did early and late in Israel) or because the two have merged their interests. Perhaps, also, because the tradition is deliberately protected from the challenge of ongoing experience. Nevertheless, it is better to recognize that Israel's prophets appeared in clutches when the tradition and the situation were out of step and prophecy was in the air, than to argue from silence concerning the periods in between.

Prophecy, I said, is prior to the prophet. The prophet is simply a voice - a person who speaks, writes or sometimes symbolizes the prophecy. It is true that the insight, and sometimes the agony, may be the prophet's, but the essential source of the prophecy lies elsewhere. It can even be spontaneous. If the man in my example were driving home on some later occasion, he might see a newspaper banner concerning apathetic citizenship, or simply a log of wood, which in the dusk suggested a body, and say to himself "I should have stopped". This would be much like the sight of fire, locusts and plumb-line, which triggered prophecy in the mind of the prophet Amos, who was already so aware of the disparity between the professed tradition as he understood it and the actual situation in Samaria. It was a prophecy which he resisted for a long time, because it spelled doom for a people that he understood to be God's.

ii) Prophecy can only take place in a Community Sharing a Tradition

The prophet speaks out of, and back into, a living tradition. If the prophet and his hearers do not share the same principles of belief there can be no prophecy.

We live in an age when the prophet is a highly respected figure while the priest or pastor cuts a somewhat pathetic one. Yet there could not have been a Samuel without the old priest Eli, not only because Samuel would not have known the traditions of Yahweh, but because neither would his hearers.

In any age, if there were not the faithful pastors to feed the tradition to the people from cradle to grave, breaking it small, putting it into liturgies, creeds and symbols, preserving it from generation to generation, then prophecy could not take place. For prophecy to occur there must be both the conserver of the truth, the priest or pastor, and the one who breaks it out anew in the contemporary situation, the prophet.

The prophet over against the conserver is just that, the breaker-out, the idealist who sees the spirit in the letter.

The pastoral spirit tends to fossilize the tradition, for when it is broken small and enshrined in creeds, liturgies and symbols he does not want his boat to be rocked.

Circumstances change however. What was an expression of the truth in one situation or generation, can be quite false in another. To be loyal to a tradition one needs to dig for the principle and re-apply it. The older form of words can have come to mean something quite different in a changed situation. The prophet therefore, as one steeped in the basic principles of the tradition and applying them to the contemporary situation, seeks to discover the right word for that situation. The pastoral spirit may then be threatened.

This is a tension evident in the biblical record but, it is a tension necessary for the growth of the tradition.

Without the prophet there would be no growth of the tradition, without the priest there would be no tradition to grow.

iii) The Existence of a Community Requires the Pragmatist

The condition that prophecy can only take place in a tradition community requires not only that there be a tradition but also that there be a community, and adds to the necessary roles of priest and prophet, that of the pragmatist, the conserver of the community.

There is a sense in which the prophet himself is a conserver, the conserver of an ideal over against the pragmatist, who, in seeking to achieve something however inadequate, or even simply to prevent things from running down hill, is prepared to compromise the ideal.

The pragmatist, the secular leadership essential to the maintenance of the community, was, in Israel of the prophetic period, preeminently the monarchy. It is no accident that Israel's classical period of prophecy was virtually coterminous with its monarchy. During that period the religious and secular leadership were separate and the latter was publicly addressed by the former.

There is always a potential conflict between idealism and pragmatism in any dynamic society. The pragmatist is the one who, in material terms, shapes and maintains the community. In doing this he is author of that which the prophets address and whose history they interpret; and of the vehicle which bears the tradition and houses the priests.

When the pragmatist has made his compromises and has established a functioning structure for his community, he is then in favour of the *status quo*. This is why the priest and the pragmatist tend to make common cause in their dread of the boat-rocking idealist, and to be the joint object of the prophet's strictures. On the other hand, priest and prophet have in common the besetting sin of thinking themselves to be the only truly religious members of the community. The pragmatist's besetting sin is either, having compromised, to say "I am a profitable servant" or to think of himself as not religious at all ("I am not worthy, I am a man set in authority"), while in fact all three are necessary to the growth and maintenance of a religious tradition.

I have spoken of the necessary roles of prophet, priest and pragmatist. I have not implied that the roles cannot exist in the same person. In the biblical period from Moses to Samuel the roles were hardly distinguishable. The conflict of interest had to be worked out within the same individual.

iv) A Tradition Develops Organically

A tradition grows, not like a wall, one previously unrelated brick at a time, but like a seed growing into a tree. On the one hand it is unable to escape its own nature, on the other it is totally dependent upon its environment for what is available to enter into it, and in other ways determine its growth. It puts out branches which continue to grow if they prove fruitful, but will be pruned back if their fruit proves unpalatable. New elements may be grafted on but only if they are compatible with the root stock. One requires a very special set of environmental conditions to get a new seed to grow.

The prophet, if he is to receive a hearing, can only speak out of the existing tradition. When he addresses his understanding of the character of the divine (distilled from that tradition) to a new situation, he adds to the tradition. He is (he believes) seeing as God sees. This may be because he has distilled the divine character consciously and cognitively from his total experience, including the tradition to which he is heir. Alternatively, it may be because (in the other meaning to total experience) he is responding intuitively, as a result of what his experience has made him. Either way, he will say with confidence "Thus saith the Lord".

I exemplified the development of Israel's tradition with a consideration of their growing understanding of suffering in the context of a belief in a just and powerful god who had engaged them in covenant. The role of the prophet in that process was that of a man standing at the growing edge of a tradition. He is the one who recognized that the tradition and the situation, frequently a political, economic, or social one, were out of step. That either the situation must be conformed to the tradition, or the tradition must accept the challenge of something new and grow to take account of it. Either way, priest and pragmatist would resist it. If, however, the new truth were accepted in the community, then before long it was taken by the priest and built into the tradition he conserved.

It was the priestly group who, for the most part, wrote down the tradition. The prophet's concern to address his contemporaries rendered prophecy a primarily oral phenomenon.

v) The Criteria Apply for the Prophet Himself

It is important to understand that the criteria for authority, which I presented in terms of the prophet's hearers and what would bite into them, also holds for the prophet himself.

No matter how a prophetic thought arises, be it in calm and deliberate application of the tradition to the situation, or triggered by something that for the moment becomes symbolic, or via an inner voice or dream of the night, or by some chance word overheard in a crowd, that thought must satisfy the criteria if it is to be immediately authoritative, and the possibility of hallucination be set aside.

No matter where a statement of valuation or obligation comes from, or to whom it comes, it can only be tested in the long run within a tradition. Only in the short term can a recipient be convinced by some external authority or unusual accompanying phenomenon.

vi) False Prophecy is the True Prophecy of a Tradition that has Gone Astray.

If the immediate validity of a prophecy depends, not on the inspiration of the individual who utters it, but upon it meeting the criteria set out above, then it not only follows that one cannot deny the truth of a prophecy one does not like, but also that one may be forced to accept the truth of a prophecy that later turns out to be false.

I do not have to dwell on the fact that the prophecy one does not like, if it fulfills the criteria, cannot be just rejected. It was for this reason that Ahab could neither ignore nor laugh off Miciah ben Imlah or Elijah. Rather, he said "I hate him", because the prophets' words did take hold even though he did not wish to know them.

The situation is as though one had picked up a book of social poetry and read it, then wished that one had not. You cannot deny the truth of what it is saying, for it applies what you already believe to what you know to be the situation, with a logic you cannot refute.

Nevertheless, the application of such criteria within an organic growth process leaves room for error. The prophet can interpret something in the wrong way. He may read the situation wrongly, he may bring wrong parts of the tradition to bear on the situation, or he may draw the wrong conclusions. Even if he derives the right conclusion for his own time, his successors may hang on to that conclusion as an eternal, God-given word until, the situation having changed, it becomes false. Any or all of these may be the beginning of a development which comes to be judged as false in the light of the tradition itself, at some future time.

As I said tradition grows organically. It can go in the wrong direction until it turns sour and people reject it, or until history proves it false and prunes it back.

If what I have been saying is correct, then false prophets are not prophets who simply speak what people want to hear. False prophecy cannot be just wishful thinking, for then it would not bite and in the longer run it would be rejected. One does not get a lot of satisfaction out of hearing what one knows not to be true, however much one might want to believe it.

The status of false prophecy is well summed up in the statement "The false prophets are the true prophets of a decadent tradition".[1] It makes it clear that the prophet is secondary in the matter, that it is the tradition that is primary. Even if one is operating within a tradition that history will subsequently show to be false, if that tradition is out of line with the situation prophecy is in the air. Because the prophet and his hearer share the same tradition, what is said will bite.

Had any one of us been brought up in Jerusalem prior to the time of Jeremiah, we would have been heirs to the statement of the first Isaiah that the Assyrian would not take Jerusalem, as well as the knowledge that Jerusalem had not fallen. We would also have been heirs to the conclusions drawn therefrom, that is, to the so-called Zion-David Covenant, the notion that as long as there was a Davidic king on the throne and God was in the holy of holies, Jerusalem was inviolable. With them we would have lost sight of the Sinai Covenant's conditional element, "*If* you keep my law then I will be your God".

If we had been brought up within that tradition then, even with the Babylonians on the horizon, Jeremiah's coming from Anathoth saying "You forget the Law. You exploit the poor. Jerusalem will fall and the temple be

---

[1] This is a statement that I noted many years ago. It came from a book by a Roman Catholic Old Testament scholar but I can no longer trace it.

destroyed just as God destroyed Shiloh when it housed the ark.", would have seemed foolishness to us. That his contemporaries did not believe him, was not simply because they did not want to, nor simply because they preferred to believe the false prophets who kept saying "Peace, peace, where there was no peace". It was because they genuinely stood in a tradition which held that as long as there was a Davidic king on the throne and God's presence was in the temple, Jerusalem could not fall. They stood in what history determined to be a decadent tradition.

When Jerusalem did fall and the people were in captivity in Babylon, then they went back behind the David-Zion covenant to Sinai and to the acceptance of what Jeremiah had said. History had proved the branch of the tradition that he represented to be the better one.

It is in this way that there is an historical verification of tradition and a pruning back of what proves to be a wrong direction.

This process is not something limited to the biblical period, it goes on all the time. Wherever there is growth in a tradition, there is also the danger of false paths being taken. Any tradition which is still alive is necessarily open ended and exploring, never absolute, but the best that those who share it can know at that point in time and therefore demanding their commitment.

vii) Prophecy is a Feature of all Dynamic Societies

If a people, any people, are to survive as a recognizable developing entity, they will need to have a continuing tradition, a set of shared values giving rise to reasonably common goals. Prophecy, therefore, is not just a phenomenon of the past but must exist in any culture with a dynamic tradition, as must the three contributing roles of prophet, priest and pragmatist.

In the modern world politicians and business men would be the pragmatists. The faithful pastors, and other conserving elements, fulfill the role of the priest. Political, as well as religious, figures attempting to apply anew and to extend the tradition in which they stand, are the prophets. Now, as then, when the pragmatist has succeeded he becomes protective of his achievement and tends to make common cause with the conserver.

Overtly religious traditions continue to grow. Every time a Beth Din or Moslem Judicial Council hands down a decision relating to some new situation, the tradition has potentially grown. Whenever Christians are faced with a new situation, theologian and preacher will confront it with the tradition in which they stand. Whether it be organ transplants, euthanasia or abortion, community or private ownership of the means of production, each demands an extension of the tradition. Each new technical possibility demands a moral choice, whether to realize it or to reject it. For the religious, that represents a growth in their tradition which may turn out to be supported by subsequent experience, or it may someday turn sour and be pruned back.

Finally in this section I must reaffirm the centrality of the tradition. Allowing something for the personality of the prophet and for the situation in which he or she prophesied, it is the different character of the tradition in which the prophet stands that determines most strongly the character of the prophecy. It was above all the unique character of Israel's basic tradition which gave rise to whatever was unique in her tradition.

I have dealt with the development of a tradition in the situation where there is only one on offer. That is not always the case, nor was it always the case in Israel of the biblical period. I deal with the problem of mixed or competing traditions elsewhere.[2]

---

[2] I deal with more complex tradition communities in terms of the processes, rather than the roles, to be found in them, in chapters 9 and 13.

The nature of religious discourse has concerned many of the best minds of our time. If the position arrived at in the next chapter is correct, then at least since the enlightenment, many critically minded people in the western world have been haunted by an approach that is simply mistaken. Having begun with the words of religion, rather than with the nature of the experience that the words were required to serve, they have been led to look for historical and factual verification of religious belief. It has led them to apply the logic of literal discourse to the language of religion and find it wanting. It is an approach that is as inappropriate as taking a thermometer to look for warm personalities and when it does not help, concluding that warm personalities are not real.

That we cannot speak literally of the primary object of religious concern does not mean that there is nothing to speak about or that religious discourse is nonsense.

CHAPTER 4

THE NATURE OF RELIGIOUS DISCOURSE

This chapter deals with the mode of communication that is operative in religious discourse.

It will be seen that because religion is concerned with the totality, or with a reality distilled therefrom, literal discourse, which functions by relating one thing to another within an agreed frame of reference, is rendered inoperable. The totality is necessarily unique. There can be no other to which it could be related. the whole, as also anything that one chooses to treat as unique, can only be communicated about in terms of what it feels like to be confronted by it. If the form of communication is verbal, myth is what is offered. that is, the whole can be likened or contrasted affectively to its own parts but not related to them literally.

The truth of a literal statement is tested within the agreed framework that gives it meaning, but whether the framework itself enjoys a degree of reality status can only depend upon whether or not it is felt to do what is asked of it better than any other contender for the job. that, in the end, is an affective judgment.

Reality is tested in feeling, not in cognitive process, however much cognitive process may have contributed to feeling along the way.

I began with a discussion of religious experience because one could not discuss the nature of religious discourse in any seriousness until one had decided upon the nature of the experience that people are seeking to communicate. Unfortunately this does not dispense with the problem, for we are caught in circularity. How shall we know how the mode of discourse functions, until we know what people are seeking to communicate? How shall we know what people are seeking to communicate, until we know how the discourse functions? For this reason also, I began with those forms of religious experience which I could presume to be the most familiar to my readers. I point out these problems in order to make it clear that this present consideration of the nature of religious discourse cannot be complete. What is said about the nature of the discourse will surely help to illuminate the nature of the experience, but then I will have to return over and again to each, as understanding of the other progresses.

I have tried to show that religious conviction arises out of a quality of total experience, and that religious experience, that is, the experience itself, is not necessarily different from any other experience as to its immediate source or manner of apprehension. Why then, it must be asked, is there such a seeming gulf between ordinary experience and what is thought of as religious experience? It is not because the data of experience is different nor that we experience it through a different sense or senses. The difference lies in the way in which we must speak about it. There are not two realms of experience but there are two modes of discourse. In other words, while there is only one realm of experience, not all experience can be spoken of in the same language. While much experience can be spoken of in literal language, I am here concerned with the sort of language in which one would attempt to answer the questions "who am I?" and "what is all-that-out-there?". As we will see, it is symbolic language. It can take many forms, including dance and music, art and architecture. Perhaps the most important form is simply the behavior patterns of everyday life. In its verbal form it is myth, and it is to this in particular that I now wish to direct attention.

SECTION A   MYTH - THE LANGUAGE OF PRIMARY RELIGIOUS EXPERIENCE

i) MYTH AND HISTORY

Myth is a word which is used in all sorts of ways. It is used, along with words like saga, legend and folk-tale, to describe a literary form. I am not, for present purposes, interested in such distinctions and would include in myth all of these others if they serve the same end. Myth in this context is simply verbal symbol. Myth in popular usage is the equivalent of false. I shall never use the word in that sense. Indeed the questions to ask about a myth do not concern the truth or falsehood of its story.

I am going to relate myth to history. I must, therefore, make it clear that the word "history" has two different meanings. Sometimes we use it to refer to past events and sometimes to the written accounts of such events. History as past event (because it shapes a people's sense of reality) is always present in myth, but the purpose of myth is not to recount history, so the story used in a myth may be historically true or historically false, or simply non-historical.

Frequently, one of our problems with a story embedded in a religious tradition is to know, not only whether it is historically true or false, but whether it is being told as a piece of history or as myth. It is perfectly possible that a story which is historically true is told, not because of the historical truth it contains, but because of its mythological significance. The stories of creation in the early chapters of the Bible are not being told in order to communicate historical truth. They could not be being told for that reason, simply because creation is inconceivable as history. It may help understanding of the relation between myth and history if I stay with this issue for a moment.

Creation is portrayed as a process of making, and a process is something which is only conceivable in time and space. If one wants to describe the creation of something as the making of it, then one has to do it by saying something like, "you take this piece, shaped like this, and you move it to this place, and then you take this piece shaped like that, and you fit it in here". The whole description is in a time sequence and with spatial reference, and without these one cannot conceptualize or describe a process.

God, as understood in Abrahamic tradition, be it Jewish, Christian or Islamic, is simply not in time and space. If He were so conceived, then time and space would share His eternal status, set limits upon Him, and therefore somehow be over against Him. In any case, without the objects of creation one could not conceptualize time and space. We conceive space as distance between objects, and time we have to relate to the movement of objects relative one to another. One cannot think of God being involved in creation as a process therefore, unless one also thinks of God as a human being writ large, that is, as occupying time and space and giving new shape to some pre-existent objects. I am not, of course, concerned here with what God can do, or with what He did or did not do, but only with what human beings can conceive. We cannot conceive as a process, creation from nothing.

Fortunately, whenever the Old Testament again refers to God as creator it is not with reference to the creation stories of the book of Genesis, but simply to affirm His sovereignty over all things, that is, to affirm that things in the world are as they are because He wills it. It does not ask anyone to believe in a god who did certain things one after the other in a time span of six days, and then took a rest.

The creation myth occurred in other parts of the then known world. What is really important to note, therefore, are the changes which the Hebrew authors made in the myth that they received. These key changes in fact relate to sovereignty and to transcendence. The significance of this will become clear in the next chapter. Here then is a type of myth which on the surface could be supposed to be a statement of historical truth. Many people, it seems, would go to the stake for that opinion to this day, but it is not conceivable historically.

For the same reasons, eschatological myth, that is, myth about the end of the world, cannot be history because it cannot be expressed in literal language. Anything up to the end of time might be history, that is, it might be a literal description of an expected state of affairs. Beyond the end of the time we know, it cannot be literal, it must be myth. Literal discourse presupposes continuity in the space-time framework. Frequently, the nature of the discourse is made clear by the fanciful images employed but that is not always the case.

On the other hand, the evidence for the historical truth of the exodus from Egypt, is very firm. One cannot reasonably deny that some of those who were the ancestors of Israel were in Egypt as slaves, and that they escaped and had a significant experience in the desert at a place they called Sinai. After all there is evidence such as that of the stele of Marniptah, who succeeded Ramases II as pharaoh, recording his battle with Israel in the desert, quite apart from the firmness of the tradition in the Bible itself. Few therefore, would doubt that there is a core of historical truth in the story of the exodus. Yet, historically speaking, it is trivial. There have been many peoples in bondage in the course of history, and no doubt, many escaped. The Bible itself records other such occasions. There can be little doubt that from time to time, in Egypt as elsewhere, little bands of slaves broke away, escaped into the desert and were never heard of again. Nobody bothered much about it, and we would not be bothering now, if there were not something very much more significant about that particular piece of history than the history itself.

Its value lies in the fact that a certain group of people understood that there was a god involved in this particular event. That this god had not only set his care on them, but that he was powerful, and that presumably he had a destiny for them, otherwise he would not have bothered with their rescue. Herein lies the root of the Hebrew and in the end, therefore, Christian and Islamic faith. Here is to be seen the basic character of the god who will from then on be understood primarily as "the God who brought us out of the land of Egypt". A character that has had to be wrestled with, and the understanding of it refined, through many centuries of diverse experience.

The story is historically true, but as history it is almost irrelevant. As myth it is basic to the whole Abrahamic and western development.

One of the problems in a study of the biblical tradition is being able to distinguish when it is offering history and when it is offering myth, for history is also important in the Bible. History, as history, was not important in the background religions of Mesopotamia or Egypt nor in any other religion of that type, nor is it important in the religions typical of the East. Once one has moved into a religion with a transcendent god it is vital for one comes to an understanding of the character of the god, precisely through an interpretation of divine involvement in history. As indicated earlier, monotheism has to be radical. It is only if one has a radical monotheism, such as that of Isaiah, that one has to attribute everything that happens to the will of this one god. In great empire under David, or suffering in Babylon, the empire destroyed and the temple gone, all must be attributed to the will of God. All must be understood in terms of His character. The agony of doing this is the agony of the prophet who stands on the frontier of the developing tradition.

History is important in the Bible, and in all the Abrahamic traditions, for an understanding of the character of God depends on it, but that character can only be expressed in myth. It is important, therefore, to ask of a particular story, "Is it being told because it is important historically or because it is important as myth?" and, if it is being told as myth, "Have liberties been taken with the history in order to improve the story for the purpose of communicating the meaning of the myth?".

Probably the most difficult question of all concerning myth is whether it would matter if we were to discover that the Israelites had never been in Egypt, or, for Christians, whether it would matter if the tomb were not empty and that Jesus' body was still buried outside Jerusalem. These are crunch questions, but in fact no such discovery in relation to the history would destroy the myth. The myth might change somewhat in its significance, but its value would not be destroyed. Myth may begin in a particular piece of history, but it comes to transcend it and symbolize something much more broadly founded. It speaks of what the adherent feels to be the nature of reality; a sense of reality distilled from the totality of his or her experience. It is unlikely that a changed understanding of the small piece of history which gave birth to the story will greatly modify the sense of reality which that story has come to express as myth. The Christian belief in the empty tomb, for example, had consequences that shaped the Christian mode of engagement with the world-out-there. Insofar as that mode of engagement is fruitful, it supports belief in the myth, regardless of how one feels about the likelihood of the historical event.

I will return to discussion of myth and history in chapter 8 when I consider attitudes to time in a world-view like that traditional in Africa and what happens to history in a non-literate society.

ii) THE FUNCTION OF MYTH

S.H. Hooke says of myth that it:

> is a product of human imagination arising out of a definite situation and intended to do something.

He goes on to say that:

> the right question to ask about myth is not, "Is it true?", but "What is it intended to do?".[1]

He then proceeds to classify myths of the ancient world into five types on the basis of function. This is not wholly accurate, for what he distinguishes are five functions of myth rather than five types of myth, and a myth may fulfil more than one of these functions at the same time. Nevertheless his emphasis upon function is absolutely correct.

My purpose however, is not to classify myths of the ancient world but to understand the function of myth, both past and present, and to face squarely the question "Are not myths either primitive science or primitive history, such that they are now superseded by science or scientific history, and therefore of no further use?" Henri Frankfort seems to suggest that the answer to this question is "yes", while Mircea Eliade and Ernst Cassirer seem to take the opposite view, but then they are not considering myth in quite the same way.[2] The answer depends upon what one considers to be the function of myth, and this I must now explore in some depth.

I will begin by tentatively dividing myths into two types, those which function as explanation, and those whose function is other than that of explanation. I will leave the description of what this last category contains until I deal with it. Since it has been suggested that a principal function of myth is explanation, albeit of a primitive kind, we need to ask, "what is explanation?". The answer I would suggest, is that:

> an explanation is a series of relationships within a framework comprised by an accepted set of categories such that the mind rests.

There are no ultimate explanations. When we were considering the definition of religion, I said that there were both causal and functional definitions because there were causal and functional explanations. If we are dealing with an explanation in terms of how a thing came into existence, then the inquiry can always be pushed a little further back. There are no ultimate explanations there. Likewise, with an explanation in terms of how a thing

---

[1] S H Hooke, *Middle Eastern Mythology* (Harmondsworth, Penguin, 1963), p.11f.

[2] Henri Frankfort *et al*, either *Before Philosophy*, (Harmondsworth, Penguin, 1951) or *The Intellectual Adventures of Ancient Man*, (Chicago, University of Chicago Press, 1946). Ernst Cassirer, *Language and Myth*, (New York, Dover, 1953). Mircea Eliade, for example see, *Myths, Dreams and Mysteries*, (London, Collins, 1968) or *The Sacred and The Profane*, (New York, Harcourt, Brace, World, Inc., 1959).

functions in relation to other entities, one can only include certain chosen factors, never the totality of possibilities, so there are no ultimate explanations there either. All one can do is talk about causal or functional relationships until the mind rests. Consider an example:

My small child may say to me, "Why is it that the light comes on when you press that switch ?". I am left wondering how to explain such a thing to a child. I need to find categories of thought that are already familiar to her.

Thinking that she has often seen the bath water running, I say, "Well a switch is like a tap, when I press the switch, it is like turning on a tap, and something called electricity flows through a wire, just like the water flows through the pipe, until it gets to the bulb and makes it light up". This is fine, she is happy with it, her mind rests.

When she gets a little older and a bit more critical, she wants a better explanation. She says, "Dad why is it that when the electricity running through the wire gets to the bulb it lights up?". Now I need some other familiar category of experience. I say, remembering getting burns sliding down a haystack, "Well it's like friction. If you press your hand hard onto the table and rub it backwards and forwards for long enough it becomes hot. That is because of what is called friction or resistance. Resistance is the force you have to push against to get your hand to move along the table, and the hard work you are putting into it turns into heat. Well, there is a great big engine (called a generator) in the power station, and it pushes the electricity through the wire until it comes to that very thin piece of wire in the bulb. The resistance that the electricity meets when it is pushed through that very thin wire is so great that its energy is turned into heat. When the wire gets as hot as the fire, it glows". Hopefully her mind rests.

When she moves on to science at school, she may see bits of paper picked up by a comb that has been rubbed with a piece of silk, she will hear of positive and negative charges and of conductors, perhaps see sparks jumping across gaps. Later still, the explanation will come in terms of electrons. By this time people are consciously using models to grasp that which cannot be seen or known directly. There is still no explanation in any ultimate sense.

Explanation is never ultimate. It only takes place in the categories which we decide are useful. The only difference between the myths of ancient man which were explanations, if such there were, and science or scientific history, is that in some way or another the methods of science and scientific history are more successful than the old myths. Under the description "successful" are included their ability to predict and control. After all, why is it better to know that somewhere out in the middle of the ocean the barometer registers a depression and therefore that the drought may be broken in the next 48 hours, than to believe that Imdugud, the giant bird with black wings, will come and swallow up the bull of heaven who is busy consuming the crops with its fiery breath?

Science is preferred because it enables one to predict more accurately, it sometimes enables one to control more successfully. It does more than this, of course, like ancient mythologies, it enables one to integrate explanation into ever more over-arching hypotheses. To the extent that it is more integrative, it tends to be more satisfying. It is important, however, to recognize that the models and paradigms of science are no more ultimate than myth. They are just more successful in doing for us some things which we have decided that we want done. Had our world view been different we might have wished to do quite other things. If we had not decided that we wanted to control the world out there, and if we did not want to predict what it was going to do, then science might be no more successful than the more ancient forms of explanation.

Finally, it is doubtful if the myths of primitive man were ever purely concerned with explanation. If the story of Imdugud and the Bull of Heaven was a meteorological explanation, it was also much more than that. It expressed how human beings felt about the sky under which they lived, and also the conflicted quality of that life. Even today, it is interesting to explore the reasons for the different feelings one has, when someone says "Jupiter spoke" rather than "It thundered". Nevertheless, insofar as myth was explanation, it is undoubtedly superseded by science and the scientific study of history.

I must now turn to the other group of myths, those which cannot be understood as myths of explanation. This type, we shall see, could not be superseded. I will begin by considering a myth which Mircea Eliade includes in his collection From Primitives to Zen.[3] It has the advantage of not forming part of the religious tradition of most readers and we can consider it with detachment. It is a belief of certain Indians of the Labrador Peninsula and is as follows:-

> In the interior between Ungava Bay and Hudson's Bay is a distant country where no Indians will go under any consideration for the following reason. There is a range of big mountains pure white in colour formed neither of snow, ice, nor white rock, but of caribou hair. They are shaped like a house and so they are known as Caribou House. One man of the Petisigabau band says there are two houses.

---

[3] Mircea Eliade, *From Primitives to Zen*, (London, Collins, 1967). Quoted from F G Speck, *Naskapi*, (Norman, University of Oklahoma Press, 1935)

In this enormous cavity live thousands upon thousands of caribou under the over-lordship of a human being who is white and dressed in black. Some say there are several of them and they have beards. He is master of the caribou and will not permit anyone to come within some one hundred and fifty miles of his abode, the punishment being death. Within his realm the various animals are two or three times their ordinary size. The few Indians who have approached the region say that the caribou enter and leave their kingdom each year, passing through a valley between two high mountains about fifteen miles apart. And it is also asserted that the deer hair on the ground here is several feet in depth, that for miles around the cast-off antlers on the ground form a layer waist deep, that the caribou paths leading back and forth there are so deep as to reach a man's waist, and that a young caribou going along in one would be visible only by its head.

For the purpose of understanding how this type of myth could function, we must place it in a context. In the most general terms only, I believe that the context that I have assumed approximates to that of the people whose myth it was. The detail I have simply had to invent. My present purpose, however, is not to explore the mythology of the Indians, but to investigate, in a variety of situations, the kind of needs that any myth might be called upon to meet, and how this might be done. Perhaps to avoid all possibility of confusion, I should have invented the myth also, but this one serves my purpose well. All I ask is that the reader should not confuse my speculations with the real situation, present or past, in the Labrador peninsula.

The Indians, we will assume, live in an area where they have to migrate in spring and autumn, in order to get to the summer and winter pastures. They do not herd caribou, rather the caribou migrate and the Indians migrate with them. They depend upon them not only for milk and meat, for tents and clothing, but for bones for needles and sinews for thread. In fact the whole of their existence is to an extent wrapped up with the caribou and therefore the meaning of life also.

In such a situation there would be times when life appeared to be very insecure. If the caribou did not migrate in time to get across to the spring pastures before the ice melted, then both they and the Indians would perish. Every year the question would be, "Will they migrate in time, will we get across?".

Notice certain things about the myth.

Clearly one is not to ask "Is it true?", for there are contradictions in it. On the one hand nobody may go nearer than 150 miles under punishment of death and on the other hand we get eye-witness reports. We must, however, ask "What is it intended to do?", "What would the telling of the myth do in a situation such as that suggested?"

If one believed the myth to be true, that is, if one believed that in the interior there is a place where thousands upon thousands of caribou live, that these caribou are two or three times bigger than ordinary caribou, and that they have been there for so long a time that they have worn tracks in the ground, so deep, that one can only see a young caribou in them by its antlers, and further, that the cast off antlers are waist deep all over the place, and that the hair is piled up in high mountains, then one must gain a sense of both the quantity (size and number) and permanence of caribou. What is more, these caribou do not migrate, they move in and out of the place between the mountains, but they are under the control of the Master of the Caribou, who is a man like the Indians. That he is white and dressed in black is a symbol that is lost on me, but if the Indians were to lose their caribou, if they did not migrate in time and were drowned, then somehow there would be more available.

Understood in this way, the myth of the Master of the Caribou would inculcate a sense of security. It is a security myth.

We must then ask, "Did the Indians believe the myth to be literally (physically and geographically) true?" One would suppose that the young believed it literally and also those who never quite grew up, but for the most part the adult Indians would not believe it literally, probably because they had ventured that way.

Given that they did not believe it literally, we must ask "Did the myth still work for them?" "Did it still impart a sense of security?" The answer has to be "Yes". After all, the myth survived.

A myth, told to impart or maintain a sense of security, cannot be trivial. It cannot simply be wishful thinking rehearsed to make people feel better. Such a myth would not survive. If the myth fulfills its purpose and survives it can only be because it is "true", but to conceive of truth in spatial and literal terms, is to miss the point. Truth, in this context, means that the story corresponds to reality at the deepest level, that is, that the story feels real.

I will re-state what I have said in a slightly different way.

Myth does not describe an immediate situation in literal terms. Rather, it expresses the conviction that life as a whole has the character that it would have if the myth were literally true. This particular myth testifies to a security lying deeper than the seeming insecurity on the surface of life. It is saying that underneath the seeming insecurity of the migration, and all that its failure would mean, there exists that degree of real security that there would be if indeed there was a man out there controlling caribou, big caribou, thousands of caribou, caribou which had been there since time immemorial.

The myth is not true literally but nor is it simply a placebo. It testifies to a belief about the character of reality. For such a myth to feel real, for it to go on having authority, it must be supported by the evidence of experience. This myth is certainly supported by such evidence.

If the Indians and their caribou had not crossed the ice year in and year out, neither they nor the caribou would be there now. Perhaps they have heard of some that failed to do so, but over all, the evidence is on the side of success.

The myth, therefore, is an invitation to step back from the immediate problem of the moment and trust in a quality to be discovered in the totality of life. One does not have to believe a myth literally. It does not even matter if it has literal contradictions within it. The point lies in "what it is meant to do". This one is meant to establish and maintain a sense of security, by testifying to a conviction that has arisen out of an experience which is longer and deeper than that of any one spring thaw. It bears the distilled experience of the community.

Far from being wishful thinking, myth complies with the instinctive move of the reasonable person when confronted with an extreme situation, that is, to stand back and get it into perspective. If, having enrolled in the novices' program of the local Mountain Club, one was presented with a very thin rope on which to lower oneself over the edge of a very high cliff, one would do some very swift standing back, metaphorically as well as literally. Have the other people been given the same type of rope? Have others been over the cliff on it before? What are the credentials of the people giving the instruction, and what is the reputation of the mountain club? What can I call to mind about new man-made fibres, and where, if anywhere, have I seen them in use? How thick, compared with this one, was the tow rope that I bought for the car, and what sort of load is that likely to have to bear? In this wider perspective, the immediate prospect may look a little less terrifying.

Such was the situation of the Biblical Job to whom I referred earlier. Having lost everything, goods, family and health, he was not asked, by the voice from the whirlwind, to go on believing against the evidence, but rather to consider. To consider the mighty works of nature, and therefore place himself and his god in the perspective of a more total experience. Similarly, in a time of travail, the Deuteronomic writers presented their countrymen with a total history of what they understood to be God's mighty works on their behalf.

The moment of crisis tends to grasp not only those who are primarily involved, but also the sympathy of others. Immediacy is a threat to any who would take a longer term view. Every present situation is indeed real, and a part of that experience from which is being distilled continually a sense of total reality, yet it is never the distilled reality itself.

Myth, because it provides a distilled picture of the longer term reality with which the community is engaging, should also serve to lend stability to a life experience that is potentially a roller-coaster.

I will press the myth of the Master of the Caribou a little further:

> Suppose the Great American Oil Company arrived in Labrador and sank an exploratory well. They set up camp for this purpose and inveigled some of the Indians away from following the caribou to work for the company. Around the camp fire the Indians tell the story of the Master of the Caribou.

It will still succeed in encouraging them in their feeling of underlying security even though they now have nothing to do with caribou. Most urban dwellers have never seen shepherds, but they can still talk about God in shepherd language. If one wished to remythologize the myth, that is, cash it in terms of other and more immediate symbols for felt security, one would no longer speak of caribou but in terms that expressed the permanence of the oil company; perhaps in terms of its financial reserves in the United States. In fact one does not need to do that, it works anyway. The myth goes on working because it was never primarily about caribou. Rather, it was about the nature of reality in a situation where caribou dominated everyday experience.

> Suppose, however, that the Great American Oil Company disappears from the scene and after a little while the Great American Railroad comes and the railroad encourages other industry, and so begins the development of various institutions which come, go, and are replaced. Before long the experience of the Indian becomes that of the typical Westerner, the experience of constant change.

Now if he wants to remythologize his myth he cannot do it in terms of any one institutional factor, because they arrive today, last for a while, and when they go are replaced by something else. In such a situation the story of the Master of the Caribou would cease to express or support a feeling of underlying security, save perhaps among the older generation by its remembered associations with a security they had once experienced. For the rest, the myth would cease to have any value. It would cease to have value because it functions by rooting security in permanence, and permanence has ceased to be a feature of life. Its testimony to security is set in the old static frame.

The frame in which a myth operates must be the same as that distilled from one's everyday experience or the myth will not be felt to have authority. If our total experience is characterized by underlying permanence, then the myth to be effective also has to operate in a static frame. If our experience of everyday existence is one of flux, then a myth set in a static frame will seem unreal. In such a situation, for a security myth to succeed, it would have to be rooted in some permanent feature in the processes of change.

It is not many decades since anyone advertising a product in the western world needed to appeal to the fact that Great-Grandma used it. Now, it needs to be tomorrow's model today, or it will not gain the authority of participating in the dynamic nature of the real.

The historical materialism of Karl Marx has been the successful dynamic myth of our time. It points to a constant struggle throughout history, that is, to the class struggle. It points to struggle in the past, struggle now, and then to a classless future utopia. It is negatively defined, it does not say what will be, only that the things which now cause suffering will be absent, but it is dynamic. It is about flux, and therefore it shares the ethos of modern man's everyday experience.

Attempts, within the Christian church, to re-express the faith in dynamic terms are to be seen in various forms of process theology. One such is associated with the name of Teilhard de Chardin. Those who have read Teilhard de Chardin's Phenomenon of Man will be aware that he set out to present the Christian religion as part of a dynamic process.[4] He traces evolution from energy to hydrogen atoms, to the rise and fall of different accidental molecules, until autocatalysts (which predispose the production of molecules of their own kind) emerge, from there to megamolecules and on to self-reproducing cells, that is, to life. Then cells growing into complexities of different kinds until we get to man and to intelligence. From there he looks forward to a time when these intelligences will converge in a new hyper-personal complexity which he calls the "Christosphere".

Because he is tracing a dynamic process out of the past and into the future, although it is said to be not very good science and not very orthodox theology, it has been read all over the world, and all over the world people formed Teilhard de Chardin societies. He had his frame right. It was dynamic. It fitted the daily experience of contemporary western man.

One of the problems with experiencing the world out there as flux is that the old quiet images of heaven, such as that expressed in the line of hymnody concerned with the beatific vision, "... gaze and gaze on Thee", are altogether too static. Young people say, "If heaven is like that I don't want to go there". Then again, if God is cast in too static a frame He becomes unreal. Some modern theology, therefore, has gone so far as to let go of the unchangeable

---

[4] Teilhard de Chardin, *Phenomenon of Man*, (London, Collins, 1965).

nature of the divine, and to see God himself in process. These theologies understand God to be becoming more fully Himself in the experience of creation. When God too is on the move, He feels real again. This, however, has its own problems.

The affective affinity between Marxism and the Christian liberation theologies which have manifested in recent years in various parts of the world is grounded in their dynamic quality, whatever else may contribute to it.

Basic to the myth with which I began, is not only security in existence, but also continuity of meaning. If the only dominant feature of one's experience is caribou, then the whole meaning of one's life is wrapped up in relationship with them. It was absolutely vital to the Indians that they believed that they would never be without caribou, for they had no experience of an alternative frame of meaning. After their move into the oil camp, while the story is still told in terms of caribou, it becomes obvious that the immediate source of security lies elsewhere, and could conceivably shift again.

We live in a world in which there is no permanence. There is no structure in society that we can suppose to be permanent. The farmyard becomes a battery of chickens, work becomes automated, family life and national life change their shape. We cannot pin anything down, nor can we find a secure identity in relation to these things, unless we discern something within the process which is permanent. Not permanence in the things themselves, but a direction, or intention of change, to which we can ally ourselves, and find in it the meaning of life.

The convinced Marxist, it seems, would not have to ally himself or herself to a particular state establishment, nor to a certain style of living, nor a particular educational system. If one believed that the revolutionary process generated progress, that would give meaning to life. When I come to deal with what will be called post-paradigmatic religion, however, I will want to say that I see problems with such an open-ended world-view.

The myth which began the Hebrew-Christian tradition was itself strongly future-oriented. It looked for a time of dignity, prosperity, peace and social justice, and is well described as a religion of promise and fulfillment. The difference in our situation is that we have entered the technological age. We can take the whole physical environment, as well as society, and change it. If Teilhard's evolution myth appeals, one can be a technological man and believe that one is moving to an inevitable destiny, which paradoxically, sets one free to be at risk in the present.

If, in one's sense of reality, permanence gives way to change, then security can only lie in something permanent about the change itself. The permanence may lie in the direction of change, or perhaps in the intention which brings it about. Permanence in the direction of change may be expressed in terms of the inevitability of some key aspect or quality of the end point. My examples have been "classlessness" and "christosphere". More subtly, when the end remains open and unknown, then a sense of security lies in belief that a particular mode of engagement with the world-out-there will move it in the most enriching direction. Evangelistic crusades, Christian socialism, science, Maoism and even what is called Critical Theory, can all be understood as falling into this class of myth. Security in change is made possible by a belief that the change is inevitably going somewhere worthwhile. The "somewhere" does not have to be clearly defined or even strongly emphasized, but in the longer run there will have to be evidence for the "worthwhileness" of involvement in the process of change.

It will be seen later that, in spite of the images that are used to express it, myth is never about something that has been achieved. It is not history, nor is it some unattested hope. It represents, and enables one to relate to, reality as it is experienced now, good or bad. What is felt to be reality may include a movement to a future, and that may be described in terms of a lost past, but what is described is reality as it is experienced currently.

Myth can, and frequently does, employ significant experiences to describe reality, but it is not concerned, in the first place, to explain those significant experiences, but to describe the total reality to which humankind would relate. It may later, in the process of establishing or maintaining the integrity of reality, need to account for aberrant behavior in some aspects of experience.

Myths, of course, gain their own momentum, that is, they gain a power to shape how things are experienced, and thus they damp down potential swings in the sense of reality, or even provide a short term escape from reality. If it is an escape, however, it will be temporary, for the myth will lose its authority if it does not reflect the structure of reality as that is actually experienced. Myth that ceases to meet the test of reality, may survive in the community as mere narrative, with the possibility that in some future decade, it may again become myth.

This relationship of the myth to reality is so important, that certain myths deliberately return the hearer to the exigencies of every day life. For example, many African hero myths end with the death or banishment of the hero, often at the hands of those whom he or she has served. This necessity, if the myth is to feel real, of maintaining the disjunction between the real but abstracted world of the myth, and the realities of the immediate situation, may also explain why tradition emanating from the land of Israel maintained that Moses was not allowed to enter it. The land was immediate, Moses and the era to which he belonged had to become symbolic, rather than remain in historical continuity with the present.

(iii) MYTH - THE LANGUAGE OF THE UNIQUE

I now come to what is the heart and core of myth and therefore of communication in religion.

I have already said that I see no value in positing a sixth sense in the area of religion, nor in that sort of understanding of religious experience which renders it something quite other than everyday experience. We develop a sense of what is real from our total experience, and therefore, with the involvement of all our senses. We exclude things from reality, as being hallucination or illusion, when they do not fit that wider reality. If a particular religious experience begins as something seemingly separate from ordinary experience, it still has to take the step over the gulf from extra-ordinary to ordinary and be tested there, if it is to be accorded reality status. Therefore I maintained that religious experience, the experience itself, does not have to be different from any other experience. The difference lies in the way that we have to speak about it. We do not have two realms of experience but two realms of discourse. I am now in a position to deal directly with these matters.

Earlier I indicated why the Genesis creation stories could not be meant to be understood as history. Let me again bring into focus what I am about to say by reference to those stories:-

> The story of creation is good myth but bad science, while the theory of evolution may be good science but it is bad myth. There is no problem in these two accounts of "origins" coexisting because there can be no possible conflict between them.

If I succeed in making plain what I have to say in this section it will be clear to the reader why this must be so.

As long ago as 1916, Martin Buber had planned the book which was to arrive in the English-speaking world in 1937 as I and Thou.[5] He distinguished and labelled the two possible relationships in which one could stand to some other person or object as I-it and I-thou. The I-it relationship is the ordinary detached or objective stance we take up to things and (hopefully, only when appropriate) people. It is the relationship deliberately fostered in scientific method. The I-thou relationship is the one we typically take up in relation to

---

[5] Martin Buber, *I and Thou*, Ronald Gregor Smith (trans). Quotations are from *I and Thou*, Walter A Kaufmann (trans.), (Edinburgh, T & T Clark, 1970).

a person as person, but it can also be taken up in relation to any other object. Buber's example was a tree. When this happens the thou:

> is no thing among things nor does he consist of things. He is no longer He or She, limited by other He's or She's, a dot in the world grid of space and time, nor a condition that can be experienced and described, a loose bundle of named qualities. Neighborless and seamless he is You and fills the firmament. Not as if there were nothing but he; but everything else lives in his light. 6

These two possibilities of relationship, the I-it and the I-thou, exist in all situations save one. In that situation, only the I-thou possibility exists. I will return to this. These two relationships, the I-it and the I-thou, give rise to two different modes of discourse. These two modes of discourse are quite separate yet interdependent in human existence.

The first mode of discourse is that of a detached relationship, in which factual information is communicated. It is the language of most everyday conversation. It functions by relating one thing to another within agreed frames of reference. At simple levels it can function solely in the spatial or temporal frame.

If one says "The power station is three miles north of the town.", one has communicated something about the power station by situating it in relation to the town. This has been done by employing the previously established parameters of compass bearing and an arbitrary measure of distance, the mile. If one wanted to do it in more universal terms one would give latitude and longitude, so relating it to an arbitrary point at Greenwich and to the equator. In matters of time, one might relate to the position of the sun or to another arbitrary point, the birth of Christ. Everything is fixed or explained in relation to some other point.

This mode of discourse becomes very much more elaborate. It can locate in hierarchies of experience. For example, if one says that something is warm, then one means that it is somewhere in the middle of a spectrum of experience that runs from ice to steam. If one says something is smooth it is at the baby's bottom end of the hierarchy running from there to sandpaper. In each case one is communicating by relating, that is by placing one experience into relationship with others that are public and repeatable. On a more complex level we place things into categories according to properties, and then relate the categories. For example, there are certain substances which chemists have called "acids", others "bases", others "salts". Add an acid to a base and the reaction gives a salt and water.

---

6 *ibid.*, p.59.

Science is the process whereby mankind systematically seeks to understand and describe the relationship between things. In the process, therefore, it must render this relating, or literal mode of discourse, ever more precise. If one seeks precision, one organizes to measure. If one cannot be limited to saying that something is freezing, cold, chilly, tepid, warm, hot or scalding, then one must produce a thermometer, which, being graduated in a completely arbitrary way between what ice does to the mercury and what steam does to it, enables one to say that the temperature is 23.5 degrees.

The second mode of discourse is the one appropriate to the I-thou relationship. An example will make its functioning clear:

> If one is confronted by a person, one may choose to relate to that person in the I-it mode. One might then speak of the experience by saying that here is an animal, a human animal, a female human animal, she has brown hair cut short, grey eyes and is of medium height.
>
> If one happens to have those preferences, then this description may be evocative, but it is nevertheless relating or classifying language. It places the person in a series of pigeon holes. That is, female, in the possible groups male and female; grey eyed in the possible groups, blue, brown, green, grey, black. It is all factual material of a public kind, which could be fed into a computer and printed on an identification document.
>
> Suppose that one now wishes to relate to the person as person, rather than as object. This decision is the decision to treat the person as unique, as a unique totality. As Buber put it, he or she is "neighborless and seamless". If I am to treat the person who confronts me as unique then I cannot either relate them to another of their kind nor break them down into interrelating parts. Relating language is excluded. A unique totality cannot be related without denying its uniqueness or its wholeness.
>
> All that remains, if one would speak of the experience of a unique relationship, is the language of feeling. One can speak of what it feels like to be confronted by the other. For this purpose one might use words like warm, vibrant, still or deep and not mean by those words that he or she is moving or stationary, three-dimensional or at some particular temperature. These words are drawn from the literal realm of discourse and used by some analogy of feeling.

One can, of course, do exactly the same thing with a work of art or any other object. If one is confronted by a painting, one can decide for the I-it relation and speak of its period and its school, of the artist and the stage of his development. One can speak of the degree of reality, the use of perspective, of the colour and the texture, but (enriching as all this may be) one has not done what the artist intended. One has not allowed oneself to be confronted by the work and to know what it feels like to be so confronted. When one does this, one again enters the realm of discourse associated with the I-thou relationship. Although the painting is quite still, at room temperature and all on one plane, one speaks of vibrance, warmth, depth. The words as before are taken, by analogy of feeling, from the literal realm of discourse.

The language which Buber used is a little misleading for, as I have indicated, it is perfectly possible to have an I-it relation with a person and an I-thou relationship with an object. Buber's own example of a tree, is perhaps more compelling than that of a painting, for one is used to having feelings about the latter. One is more inclined to say of a tree, "tall, deciduous, oak", than to feel its presence, including its beauty and the limitations it sets on one's freedom of action. However, if one is so confronted then one must repair to feeling language.

Both realms of discourse are necessary and have their appropriate function. Later I will discuss their inter-dependence but, at this point, I must emphasize their independence. They are independent in the sense that there is no logic by which we can pass from one to the other. One cannot demythologize a myth. That is, one cannot express its meaning in literal language. One can only remythologize it, that is express its meaning in other symbols. When a myth seems to be demythologized it is because universal and somewhat remote symbols are replaced by a number of much more immediate and familiar ones, symbols that one does not think of as symbols at all.

This lack of a bridge between the realms of discourse is experienced as there being no way of saying precisely, from the relationships in which some object stands to others, how one will feel when confronted by it. Even if one takes a thoroughly physiological view of the mechanisms of feeling, the variables are altogether too complex for such a prediction to be made with any certainty. One might believe oneself to have a preference for hair with a touch of auburn and deep-brown eyes, and one might be able to say what sort of feelings they are likely to produce, but one cannot guarantee it. Buber goes so far as to describe the separateness of the I-it and I-thou realms as "the real boundary".[7]

When we come to discuss myth and value, it will be clear that, in spite of this lack of predictability about feeling, there is nevertheless a pressure for the same precision in the I-thou mode of discourse as exists in the I-it mode. It does not seem possible of achievement, but perhaps those concerned with linguistics may lead us in that direction.

---

[7] *ibid.*, p.63.

One can decide, when confronted by a person or work of art, which is the relationship appropriate at the time and enter the appropriate mode of discourse when one wishes to speak of it. It should perhaps be noted that that of which we speak does not become less real because we treat it as unique and speak of it in feeling language. There is one, and I think only one, situation in which experience is necessarily unique, and simply cannot be related to in the I-it mode or spoken of in literal language. This is where one is attempting to arrive at some understanding of the nature and significance of the totality of one's experience, for that is necessarily unique.

It is for this reason that the language of science grows quiet when it moves toward the totality. It is said that picturability is lost. The reason for this is that there ceases to be a frame of reference in which to conceive things. More and more it is the total frame of reference itself which is under consideration. At the macro extreme, popular science speaks of the universe as finite but unbounded. It then goes on to speak of the radius of the universe. Perhaps there is a term in an equation which, when operating within the system, is what we normally picture as radius, namely the distance from the focus to the boundary. If that equation were adapted to the universe itself, the term would remain, but it would have lost its picturability and could only be called radius if the quality of analogy in the use was recognized. One would then speaking of the whole in terms of an experience gained within it, which exactly reverses the normal functioning of literal explanation.

If this last statement needs explanation, think how one might describe an orange. One would place it in a wider context, either by describing how and where it grew, its place on the colour spectrum, its acidity, its vitamin C content. Now think of the limits of language to which the pip, which had never been outside the orange, would be subject in describing its environment as that moved toward totality. In the same way humankind has no better way of modelling the ultimately-real than that which it draws from its own experience.

There are, of course, ways to extend picturability, the principal one being mathematics. Theoretical physicists live on this frontier. Long gone is talk of three and four dimensions, or even the fifth of science fiction. In the quest for integration of forces and the elegance of simplicity, physicists working in the area of theory appropriately labelled "supersymmetry", have postulated very many more. At these reaches of human exploration it is sometimes said that truth and beauty have come together. Perhaps this is because it appears that, when empirical verification has been outrun, the only criterion for truth is the simplicity of a theory. It seems a short step from simplicity, via elegance, to beauty, but it is not wise to mix what begins to sound like the language of value with the language of fact. For however close to the frontier of totality the physicist may come, he or she is struggling to relate parts in a whole. If one then begins to think and speak about that whole, one has leapt from the one mode of discourse into the other. That there is no bridge from one to the other must remain clear.

However much we may come to understand the physiological base and the mechanisms which are in operation when human beings have feelings, and however far the theoretical integration of factual knowledge may go, there remains the distinction between the language mode which functions by relating one thing to another in a publicly available frame of reference, and that which confronts the unique, and tries to say what it feels like to be so confronted. If it is said that the language of feeling is also a relational language then, of course, I have to agree that it is. The relationships, however, are not expressed in publicly available frames of reference but by a process of trial and error in which one can never be quite sure what has been communicated. I will return to this opacity of the feeling language shortly. For the present it must suffice to say, that even if one could understand the feeling language in relational terms, there would still remain all the difference in the world between understanding it and actually being involved in the feeling relationship. Values arise in a feeling relation to the totality, not in the realm of fact, however much knowledge of the latter may influence the former.

The problem is not a new one. Long ago Plato, after lengthy and very precise dialectic, would shift suddenly into mythological style. Scholars are apparently divided upon the issue of whether Plato believed that dialectic could arrive at an understanding of the good, or whether he thought that at the end of a dialectic enquiry, one came to it, as it were, intuitively, or as a yogic practice might bring one to "realization".[8] Whatever the truth of what Plato thought on the issue, it is clear what he was doing. He was approaching as closely to the whole as he was able to do in literal discourse, but switching to feeling language, when he came to evaluate the whole that he had been approaching. That last moment might be strange to experience, what Buber spoke of as being "seized" by "the power of exclusiveness", but it is not mysterious.[9] It is the transition from Buber's I-it relationship to his I-thou, and to the appropriate mode of discourse.

Returning specifically to religion - if it can be accepted that religion is primarily concerned with relationship with an ultimately-real, and that the conviction concerning the ultimately-real arises out of the totality of one's experience, then there is no way of relating it to anything else in its class. One knows no other totality of experience. All-that-out-there is solitary,

---

[8] The debate arises from Book VI of The Republic.

[9] Buber, *ibid.*, p.58.

there is no other, and what one may come to know of another's experience of it, has already become a part of one's own.

Primary religious experience is unique because, on the one hand, it is entirely personal, and on the other, it is about all-that-out-there. Whether one wishes to speak, as in a dualistic view of reality, of a monotheos, a transcendent "wholly other" or, as in a monistic world-view, of the "all-that-is-one"; the object of the discourse is necessarily solitary and cannot be described by relating it to other entities of similar characteristics within an agreed and publicly demonstrable frame of reference.

The unique may be that which for a moment we choose to treat as unique, be it a person, a painting, or Buber's tree; or that which mankind has not yet learned to relate within an agreed frame, for example, an eclipse for pre-scientific man; or that which is always and necessarily unique, God, Brahman, or one's total experience. These things can only be spoken of in terms of what it feels like to be confronted by them. They can only be spoken of in a symbolic language, in which the totality is likened to one or more of its parts.

There is no way in which this divide in language can be thought to be overcome by a theory of revelation. The limit is set by what humankind can conceptualize and therefore speak about, not by the knowledge or power of the Divine. Because it is sometimes easier to grasp the idea than to accept what it means for one's own tradition, let me just press the point in relation to the Abrahamic religions.

If to exist is to occupy a particular place at a particular time, God does not exist. He is not in Abrahamic religion a piece of the furniture of the universe, and it is better to picture Him as the ground of all that does exist. He who is no man, is spoken of as personal, as a Father, King and Judge.

Although it may be shocking to some, it has to be said, that when Christians speak of Jesus as the Son of God they cannot be using literal language. For whatever may be said literally about the historical Jesus of Nazareth, nothing can be said literally of God. There is really no problem in this except a break with a habit of thought.

When we use the word "son", it implies a male child produced by sexual intercourse between a man and a woman, that there was a time when the parents existed but the child did not, that he is therefore younger than the father and that he was provided for, taught and probably chastised by the father. Christians do not mean any one of these things when they use the word "son", of Jesus. The word is being used by analogy, to speak of a relationship which they feel but cannot describe literally. Jesus was somehow felt to be related to God more closely than any concept of election or inspiration could embrace, not least when it was felt that God suffered as Jesus hung upon the cross. "Son" is the only word that comes near to expressing such a relationship.

I have spoken, up to this point, of words taken from one realm of discourse and used by analogy in the other, but single words do not take us very far. If one was confronted by the young lady of my earlier example, perhaps in the moonlight, and all one could find to say was "warm", "vibrant", "deep", she would soon go home. We need a more elaborate and precise way of expressing feeling and if we do it in words, we begin to tell stories to convey subtleties of feeling. It matters not whether the story is true or false in literal terms. What matters is that the stories express with subtlety what it feels like to be confronted by the other. When one speaks of one's totality of experience in this way, one is creating or using myth.

As I said earlier, I am not for present purposes interested in the division of stories into such categories as saga, legend, myth, or folk-tales, and the reason should now be clear. If a fairy story survives, it is in all probability because it has within it some deep expression of what it feels like to be confronted by life. In which case, it is myth.

Similarly a traditional system of ethics or set of commandments is myth. It is an understanding of what, given a context, would lead to the fullest human flourishing. Its truth cannot be demonstrated. It is a hypothetical story told about a human situation, and it is myth.

The story in myth may be an imaginative creation, prose or verse or in the form of a play, it may be historically true or have the appearance of philosophical argument, it may even be presented as a set of laws, but it remains myth. Myth is verbal symbol, it is just one way of symbolizing one's feeling for the ultimately-real. Primitive man danced, carved and painted his religious feeling and even more important created a life-wide behavior pattern to express it. Some high points in western expression are its religious architecture and music. Myth is the verbal fulfillment of the same need. It expresses the deepest and most significant of feelings about reality as a whole.

Individual myths, like individual words, are inadequate. Humankind, therefore, creates traditions, that is, concatenations of myths, rituals and other symbols, including, for this purpose, patterns of life.

If one returns to the question, "Can myth be superseded?". Manifestly, it cannot. With all the factual knowledge one may have of the possibilities of one's time (whether these be economic, sociological, technological or educational) one cannot create a thing, save under the pressure of necessity, unless one has a value system that enables one to decide which possibilities to realize and which to reject, for many are mutually exclusive. In the end values are based in one's feeling about the nature of the whole and only symbol can express this. Myth may not be the most moving form of symbol but it is the most precise.

Frankfort, writing about what he calls the "mythopoeic age", the time when man was a myth-maker, suggests that primitive people made myths because they related to things as Thou rather than It. They did not ask the question, "How does something happen?" but rather "Who caused it to happen?". They thought that things happened because they were willed.[10] This may be true, but the real basis of the difference to which Frankfort points is that for primitive people more of life's experiences were unique. Because they had not asked the relational questions in a scientific and impersonal sense so many things seemed to happen to them for the first time. The reason for the great quantity of myth in this type of world-view lies elsewhere and will be dealt with later.

The problem in the modern world is that there is so little in experience that is unique. We are so conditioned to think of things as in relationship with other things, that even when something appears unique, we believe that we shall soon be able to relate it. There is very little pressure on us to function in the I-thou mode and therefore we live in a world which is highly impersonal. Perhaps this is why our language for describing facts is so very much better developed than our language for discussing values.

SECTION B - THE AUTHORITY OF MYTH

I must now move to an examination of what it is that determines the authority which a myth may or may not have for the potential adherent. We have already touched upon the issue and this section will serve to draw together some of the things said about the source and development of a religious tradition, with what has been said about the nature of religious discourse.

i) AUTHORITY OF A PART AND OF THE WHOLE

I have already indicated that belief in an individual myth, or indeed a whole tradition, can arise from the acceptance of a secondary authority, which may be a person, a book, or some extraordinary experience. A new convert, for example, will accept the beliefs of the group within which he or she is converted without knowing very much about them. I have also expressed the view that in a healthy maturity such acceptance on secondary

---

[10] Frankfort, *ibid*.

authority would not survive beyond the point at which belief, on the basis of one's own direct cosmic experience, became possible. It is with the sources of authority appropriate in this mature stage that I will now deal.

The question of authority must be dealt with on two levels. The first has to do with the verification within the whole tradition of any individual belief that is proposed as part of it. The second has to do with the authority of the whole tradition.

Verification Within a Tradition

When we are concerned with the authority of an individual myth or other symbolic element within a tradition, we may turn in the direction of either cognitive or affective verification.

If we turn to cognitive processes a logic is the criterion of authority. We ask, does this particular myth or symbolic statement arise logically from the tradition, as the statement "a man is his brother's keeper" seems to arise logically from a tradition maintaining the fatherhood of God and the freedom and responsibility of humankind.

If we turn to affective verification, the criterion becomes the felt coherence of the myth with other elements of the tradition and with the tradition as a whole. An unmixed affective verification is the basic one in religion, personal experience being prior to its symbolization. Only when experience has been conceptualized in symbol can any sort of a logic function.

A myth, as with other forms of symbol, while not being true in the literal sense can be right or wrong in the sense that it expresses the feeling which correctly represents the tradition in which it is offered. What is beautiful is not necessarily right.[11]

Evaluation of the Whole Tradition

At the second level, that is the recognition of authority in the tradition as a whole, only affective verification is a possibility. There is no logical procedure appropriate to the verification of a tradition as a whole save its own internal coherence. Internal coherence may guarantee that the tradition is a castle, but not that it is other than a castle in the air. If it is to be grounded in the rest of experience, the proof of the tradition pudding can

---

[11] For example, the excessive despair of the *Libera me*, and the total discontinuity between that and *In Paradisum* in Fauré's Requiem are not Christian orthodoxy however beautiful the work may be.

only be in what one feels like having eaten it. There are, however, some things to be noted about this proving process:

a) the evaluation is not of knowledge but of conviction

I said that man's response to total experience is not knowledge of the factual or scientific type, but a conviction. I illustrated this by the story of the hut from which objects emerged but into which the recipient could not gain entry, and the reasonableness, not the logical necessity, of coming to a conviction that there was mind in or behind the functioning of the hut.

The falsification test for the meaningfulness of an assertion, that is, being able to say ahead of time what sort of evidence one would accept as falsifying one's assertion, simply does not apply to convictions. One is never able to say ahead of time what will change a conviction.

Having held the conviction for years, for example, that A loves B, one can wake up one morning without it. One can say what sort of events are likely to put an end to the conviction, for example if A leaves B. However, it is always open at the time of the event, for the conviction to continue, for one to interpret A's leaving B as a self-sacrificial move for the latter's benefit.

In order to make clearer the gulf between feelings and facts, I will press this independence of conviction a little further. If X says to Y, "My wife loved me", and Y rejects the claim, then X might respond with, "But she gave me beautiful presents for Christmas", to which Y could reply, "That was because she hoped to receive a new hat for Easter". X, having in mind the text "Greater love hath no man..", could then say, "But she laid down her life for me", to which it is open to Y to respond with, "She always did have an exaggerated martyr complex". No such statement of personal feeling or evaluation is provable, nor can one ever say with certainty what would change one's mind. Myth expresses conviction. Therefore it is not true or false but dead or alive. It bites or it does not.

b) convictions are knowledge related

The lack of a one-to-one relationship between conviction and fact does not, of course, mean that conviction is unrelated to the facts, or that to hold a conviction is not the act of a reasonable person. Hindsight usually allows one to see the last straw and some of the build-up that broke the back of a conviction.

It seems that convictions concerning the more ultimate levels of which I have been speaking, continually adapt to experience, but that a radical change in conviction, such as would involve a virtual un-selfing, is only likely to take place in extremely traumatic circumstances. Even in the individual, a tradition is an organic thing that puts out branches that sometimes develop and sometimes are pruned back.

Allowing for some cultural inertia, a tradition will survive only while it in some way enriches human existence. In the short term, and in part, the tradition itself will teach people what enriches them, creating its own plausibility, but in the longer run this is not the case. No tradition can shut the world out completely and for ever. The greater the variety of experience to which the basic elements of a tradition have been related, the greater the degree of verification. The verification of a religious tradition, therefore, is not dissimilar to the verification of a scientific paradigm.

c) reality is tested in feeling

Reality, in the sense of "that which is worth hanging onto", is in the final assessment tested in feeling, not only in religion, but in all areas of experience.

Science has many empirical demonstrations, logic has many necessary conclusions from premises, but in the long run humankind would do neither science nor logic if it were not enriched by them. Enrichment, although it might be fed and clarified by reason, is in the end an affective judgment.

The Two Levels of Verification

Logic can operate within a tradition. An ethical system, for example, may be developed by a cognitive exercise taking place within a tradition, but the tradition itself is only testable in experience. If it fails to enrich it will lose its authority. [12]

I believe that it was the failure to distinguish between these two levels of verification and the radicallity of the divide between the two modes of discourse, that led Bertrand Russell into a less than worthy criticism of William James in particular, and pragmatism in general. Russell sought to rebut the pragmatist doctrine that:

> the true is that which works best, leads to the greatest advantage, or creates the greatest good

---

[12] When it is said that the power to enrich is the only criterion for the reality status of a paradigm, then it is long term enrichment that is in mind. This is not simply because the tradition may itself determine what is enriching in the short term, but because enrichment cannot be narrowly anthropocentric. It must be assumed that humankind is diminished in the long run if any part of its eco-system is diminished in any way that is not itself required by the long run benefit of humankind.

He did this by offering an example which confused verification (evaluation) of a frame of reference with verification within a frame.

It is true, to use Russell's example, that once one has accepted a calendrical system, there are processes for establishing the date of an event that have nothing to do with ones feelings about it, but equally, there is no way of judging which is the best calendrical system which, after all the evidence has been considered, does not reduce to a matter of feeling.

In the sense that there could be no verification within a frame, unless the frame itself had been approved and that presumably as "the one which works best", all knowledge can be said to be tested pragmatically.[13]

(ii) THE AUTHORITY OF MYTH AND RAPID CHANGE

I have already pointed to the need to shift the frame in which a myth operates from static to dynamic if the myth is to remain authoritative in a world of rapid change. There are numerous other ways in which rapid change can have consequences for the authority of myth.

It takes time for the authority of a myth, or indeed of any symbol, to become ubiquitous within a community. In a situation of change, a symbol might already have lost much of its relevance before it can become ubiquitous. Therefore, in societies subject to rapid change, the myth system and the values that are expressed by it, will almost certainly become fragmented. This fragmentation of the myth system is undoubtedly a contributing factor to the pluralistic nature of modern western culture. While this pluralism may free individuals within their own immediate spheres, it can hamstring societies, for the common base of decision making is eroded. This sets up a further chain of consequences.

Rapid change puts an end to the sense of a knowable destiny and, if it stops short of chaos, produces a sense of openness to the future. With this goes a decline in the significance of secondary authorities, whether secular or religious, and value then becomes a matter of individual feeling. If society is to function, these feelings have somehow to be distilled into corporate preferences in decision making and this requires, in any society that pretends to democracy, some method for polling individual opinions and of dealing with the differences. In summary, rapid change can lead, for good or bad, to the politicization of ethics and, in the process, to the replacement of myth by political slogans.

---

[13] Bertrand Russell, *A History of Western Philosophy*, (London, George Allen and Unwin, 1946), p.844f.

Examples of this are to be found not only in the world at large, but also in religious institutions. When this happens, not only justice, but also truth, is assumed to flow from the ballot box.

A further consequence of rapid change is that myth may cease to have authority, not only because the sense of reality has changed from being static to dynamic, but also because the facts which comprise the story of the myth are no longer familiar. I say this despite what I said earlier about the lack of this effect on the Indians who moved from following the caribou to working for the oil company. There would be no problem if people distinguished the message from the vehicle. However, if the facts of the story are too far removed from the picture people have of their world, there is a tendency for myth to appear as fairytale, and for it not to be considered to have serious import. Pastoral images seem to retain their grip in an urban context, perhaps because they are known to exist somewhere, but myth which depends on a three-tiered picture of the universe, for example, tends not to. The Christian resurrection and ascension myth suffers in this way. [14]

SECTION C - MYTH AND LITERAL DISCOURSE

I have emphasized throughout that myth is the language in which primary religious experience must be expressed. There is simply no other verbal means for its expression, nevertheless, religious traditions contain much which is not myth. I have already mentioned the importance of history in the Abrahamic traditions, and there is much legal and ethical material which appears to be expressed in literal language. This mixing of the two modes of discourse is often necessary, and it is best understood by considering the independence and the interdependence of fact and value. With this purpose in mind, I must first say something about my understanding of the relation between values and religion.

RELIGION AND VALUES

It is clear that there are facts without science, but science, in the modern sense of the word, is the deliberate, methodologically self-conscious quest for fact. I believe that religion stands to values much as science stands to fact.

---

[14] I consider what controls the choice of the experiences that become the building bricks of myth in chapter 10.

Values, of course, are espoused quite apart from religious traditions. They have been debated down through history by the remote giants of the philosophical tradition, who may or may not have tried to live them. Religious traditions, however, whatever else they might be, are corporate ways of valuing the different aspects of experience within as ultimate a context as possible, that is, they are value sets which have been embraced, not just by individuals, but by whole cultures. They have been tested and refined over long periods of time and in a great variety of conditions.

I have simply assumed in the preceding pages that religion is to be identified as the source of values. This obviously requires some justification, for so-called non-religious people also operate with values. I say "so-called" because I will be concluding later, that given those who are swamped with the bits and pieces of life and those who are asleep, the only non-religious persons are those for whom the world-out-there is chaos and without meaning. Whatever the truth of this, adherents of all religions seek to relate to an ultimately-real communicated in or through total experience. It is within that ultimate context that all other aspects of life gain their appropriate value. To seek to speak about the whole is not mystification because it cannot be spoken of in literal language, for this is the source of values and one cannot do without them. An example might make this clearer:

Parent ... Please do your homework.
Child   ... Why should I?
Parent ... Because I want you to do well at school.
Child   ... Why should I do well at school?
Parent ... Because then you will get into university
          and a university education will enable
          you to get the most out of and put the
          most into the sort of society in which
          we live.
Child   ... Why do I want to live in this sort of a
          society?

Before long, it becomes apparent that one needs to express a view of humankind's proper flourishing in this world and that that in turn will depend upon one's view of the most general context of experience and of humankind's role within it. That is, one must express a religious view, whatever those who are disenchanted with a particular set of dogmas may choose to call it. To stop at any point in the progression towards the most ultimate available context for values would be arbitrary. One might just as well resort to violence or bribery at the child's first objection.

A more generalized example may help. Consider the following progression:

> How a parent decides to treat one child in relation to the others will depend on his or her view of the ideal family.
>
> How much one should seek for one's own family in competition with other families will depend on one's view of the ideal community.
>
> How much one may seek for one's community will depend on a view of the ideal nation.
>
> How much one may seek for one's own nation will depend on a view of the ideal community of nations.
>
> How much one should seek for humanity in relation to all the non-human creation would depend on a view of the ideal world. That in turn would depend on the model one embraced for the ultimately-real.

I have not filled in all the possible levels, but there should be sufficient to show that:

> a) the way in which one makes judgments at any level is controlled by one's view of the level above, and
>
> b) the natural sanction for proper performance at any level is one's desire to belong to the level above.

These levels exist in a hierarchy from the immediate to the universal. If that hierarchy is broken at any point the values below the break cease to be controlled by those above, in that sense they become arbitrary. Most of us function, most of the time, with medial axioms, that is, with general statements of what comprises good action appropriate to a particular level of involvement. These may be barely conscious, being more of an habitual pattern for behavior than a set of beliefs. Nevertheless, medial axioms will not long maintain their sense of authority in a community, if they cease to fit the changing sense of reality.

I will return to the question of whether a set of values can be seriously embraced without embracing religion, but for the moment I will assume that religion and values belong together. This will enable me to discuss the interrelation of the two modes of discourse in regard, not simply to fact and value, but in terms of the most organized forms of the quest for these, namely science and religion. I begin with the independence of science and religion.

The Independence of Science and Religion

Religion is the opposite of science, not in the sense that we receive experience from a different source, or through different faculties, or verify what we have received in a different way, but rather that they begin at different ends of the spectrum of experience and proceed in different directions.

Science begins with the concrete particulars around us, seeking to show how they are related to each other, and it delves deep into their constituent elements in order to do so. In moving ever more to the micro level, it also moves toward a more integrated understanding of all things, toward a single over-arching theory, but as it draws toward a statement about the totality, its mode of discourse fails. Insofar as the scientific enterprise is true to its methodological presupposition, its developed body of knowledge will all be in literal, non-valuing discourse, even though, as a human and community activity, it cannot be free from values.

Religion begins at the other end, asking about the nature of the totality (which can only be expressed in symbolic language) whence it moves down, developing at every level the consequences for particular situations (described in literal language) of the answer it gave about the totality. Thus it builds an ethical system. In practice, of course, the process is not unidirectional. One is engaged within a living tradition, and there is feed-back from the consequences of embracing the ethic to the felt sense of the total reality. A religious tradition, therefore, will contain both modes of discourse. This is illustrated in the adjacent table.

The primary and most formative material in a tradition are the myths which communicate the nature of the totality. In the example these declare that the totality meets us as meaningful rather than chaotic, perhaps as quasi-personal rather than impersonal, like a king perhaps, but more like a father. None of these are in literal discourse. Some quite primary myth, however, may be interpretation of historical experience (for example, the Exodus of Israel from Egypt) in which case the history will be in literal discourse, the interpretation in symbolic, and sometimes it is difficult to know which ends where.

In order to bring these primary myths to bear upon the concrete situation, and so produce prescriptions for immediate action, medial axioms of differing degrees of generality are developed. Only a little way down from a primary myth of the fatherly nature of the ultimately-real, would come the medial axiom of great generality "All men are brothers" which is still a "feeling" statement. It is not suggested that all men are literally brothers, nor that they should treat each other as real brothers do, but rather as ideal brothers should. The story of how ideal brothers should relate to one another is myth and it is empirically authenticated. It is constituted, at the

LEVEL OF LANGUAGE	*EXAMPLE*

THE LEVEL OF PRIMARY MYTH
  expressed in I-Thou or
  feeling language
	Total experience is felt to be meaningful
	Total experience is felt to be quasi-personal
	The character of the quasi-personal is felt as
	Sovereignty (King), Righteousness (Judge)
	and Love (Father)

| |	

THE LEVEL OF MEDIAL AXIOMS
  of decreasing generality and
  increasing I-It language
  content
    OR
DESCRIPTIONS OF HUMAN
FLOURISHING IN A CONTEXT
	All men are brothers
	Love one another
	It is better to give than receive
	Love thine enemy
	Thou shalt not kill, steal or covet

|	

THE LEVEL OF PRESCRIPT OR
DIRECTIVE FOR ACTION
	I ought and will take this man to hospital
	  "I ought .... " is I-thou language
	  "I will .... " is I-it language

|	

THE LEVEL OF FACTUAL
INFORMATION
  expressed in I-It or
  literal language
	This man is sick
	There is a hospital
	I have a car

The top three levels, over time and with a variety of historical contexts to relate to develop into a religious tradition containing everything from the most general myths concerning God and creation down to the most specific and context-bound prescriptions for action.

conscious level, by those relationships which seem to be the most enriching in the long run and in the broadest perspective of human experience. Alternatively, if one is not being cognitive, it is constituted by a statement about the ideal brotherly relationship that resonates with a felt sense of reality that has been shaped by all that one has experienced in life, directly or vicariously.

A little further from the primary myth, down toward the prescription for action in the concrete situation, come the more specific medial axioms. These are of the type that might not hold in certain circumstances, such as "Thou shalt not kill", or "Go a second mile". When these are brought to bear on a concrete situation conceptualized in literal language as, for example, "This man is sick. There is a hospital. I have a car.", we arrive at the prescript, "I must take this man to hospital". This might be said to be a shortened form of, "I ought and will take this man to hospital" in which "I will take this man to hospital" is a statement entirely in literal discourse, whereas "I ought ...", is not literal, but is derived from the application of the primary myth to the concrete situation.

Clearly, there is sort of logic in the process by which one comes to the conclusion, "I must take this man to hospital". All men are brothers, brothers must care for one another, this man is sick, therefore I must care for him. The conclusion, "I must take him to hospital", assumes, on the one hand, a great deal about the nature of hospitals, about the goals of human life and therefore of what constitutes caring action. On the other hand, it assumes something about the limits set to human freedom of action and therefore to responsibility. If one believed in a strongly operative fate, there would be neither point in nor responsibility for taking him to hospital. Nevertheless, given the context and the tradition, there is a logic by which the conclusion is drawn.

Thus ethics of the discursive kind (philosophical or theological), or in more general terms, detailed directives for the mode of engagement with the immediate-world-out-there, emerge at the point where the two modes of discourse meet. That is, they emerge where, in the example, the feeling language progression,- from "Experience is meaningful" through "It is quasi-personal" and "Like king and judge but more like father", down to "All men are brothers" - meets the relational language conveying the facts, - "This man is sick", "There is a hospital", "I have a car".

While there is clearly a logic in operation when a particular tradition and a specific context are brought together, I do not believe that there can be a meta-logic whereby one can justify what is brought together. There is nothing in the context that can necessitate the application of a particular tradition, or of one part of a tradition rather than another. If such were the case there would be a logical bridge between the two modes of discourse and it would follow that they were really one. That cannot be so, for they do not function in the same way.

A religious tradition, therefore, will contain, in addition to the undiluted myth expressing its primary elements, material which will be, for the greater part, in the language of the literal mode. That is, prescripts for concrete situations as well as less general axioms and bits of historical material. The important thing is to be conscious of which language is in use, otherwise errors may be made in either direction. People can make a major issue of the literal truth of a statement which simply cannot be in literal discourse; and minds which have been brought up to critically test literal statements, may unwittingly reject symbolic statements on quite the wrong criteria. Even though words in the two realms of discourse are shared, to bring the logic of literal discourse to bear upon statements made in the symbolic mode, is absurd. It is as though, having decided that a thermometer is the only proper criterion for the determination of temperature levels, one took a thermometer to seek out warm personalities. To reject the reality of what religious language speaks about on the grounds that it does not meet the logical requirements of literal discourse, is as absurd as rejecting the existence of warm personalities, when a thermometer is shown not help in the task of identifying one.

I believe that the confusion of these two modes of discourse and the bodies of knowledge which they communicate is a primary cause of the rejection of religious belief in this critically-minded scientific age. It is for this, among other reasons, that I would like to reserve the word "truth" for statements in literal discourse, and to make it clear that symbolic discourse is not true or false, but dead or alive. Either it expresses our feeling for reality or it does not. That which one is seeking to speak about, is no less real because it cannot be spoken about in literal discourse.

The Interdependence of Religion and Science
I have endeavored to show the logical independence of religious and scientific discourse, by showing their opposite directions of movement, as they seek to come to grips with, and communicate about, the same world of experience. The table which illustrated the last point, also reveals their interdependence. There can be no concrete directive for action which does not include both fact and value. No amount of technical know-how will create anything, unless one also has a value system by which to choose between alternative possibilities. In the same way a value system with no technical possibilities, is sterile.

A doctor faced with a problem patient may have many possibilities for treatment. Drug A will achieve X, while drug B will achieve Y. If she operates now, there is a great risk to life, but a good chance of a 100% physical recovery. If she waits a while, the danger to life will be reduced, but the chance of a complete physical recovery is also diminished. There will be some non-medical factors to take into account. The patient may be a sport-loving bachelor, or he may be a man with a physically undemanding job but with a young family to support. When all the available facts are in, there remains a value decision. The value criterion is a model of optimum individual flourishing given the possibilities. It may not be conscious in the doctor. She may simply ask, what she herself would want if she were in that situation.

In much the same way, a group of town councillors may discuss the question of whether to spend allotted funds on a new school, a new clinic or a new community centre. If they seem to come to a common mind on the basis of what already exists and such factors as the likely level of use, they must still have operated, at least sub-consciously, with a model of corporate flourishing in the given possibilities.

This model of flourishing is a myth. It is a description of or feeling for, an ideal individual or corporate life. It is unverifiable in any scientific or logical way. For many, this model of human flourishing is indeed subconscious, a distillation of total experience which leads them to respond intuitively. It cannot remain sub-conscious, however, when a society is confronted with a variety of competing possibilities and there is a pressing need to come to a reasonably common mind on how to deal with them. Every technical possibility establishes a moral choice.

One of the features of our time is a lack of precision in the myth which sets the values for dealing with many and varied possibilities. Yet the very complexity of the technical possibilities requires that the language of feeling be precise to a commensurate level. We are left wondering which way to turn, and with mounting frustration, in the face of a sea of exciting possibilities. Such precision will always be hard to achieve. It is true that we develop a general framework of feeling, such that it is not absolutely absurd to ask "What was the name of the deep, vibrant person we met last night?", rather than "What was the name of the blonde, blue-eyed person?", but precision is limited. I will return to interdependence shortly.

The Opacity of Myth
In addition to the lack of precision in the language of feeling resulting from the impossibility of establishing clear public frames of reference, there is the problem of entering into experiences that lie outside one's own immediate culture.

Factual language is easily translated. Anyone who has a word for needle, thread, hole, perpendicular, and push, can tell or be told how to thread a needle. On the other hand, when an Eskimo says "A child is like a needle", the barriers to understanding are enormous - particularly for anyone from a culture where needles are 10 cents per dozen. "He cannot simply mean that they have eyes. Perhaps he means that they are sharp"

Anyone who (in order to enable their family to survive the cold) must invest laborious hours in carving, with very inadequate tools, a fragile needle from the bone of an animal, before they can sew the skin of the animal with its own sinews into tent or clothing, has feelings associated with the word "needle", which those outside the culture can hardly begin to share. However long one lived in the culture, one would never know what it was like to be unaware that one could walk away from it. One could learn of the high investment in the needle and how fragile and how easily lost it is, but its felt value one could never be sure that one knew. One could never know that one had entered fully into "A child is like a needle." It is always thus, when one seeks to understand a word which has taken on symbolic significance.

Although one may feel that one has understood, and in fact, one may have come very close to understanding, one can never know that one has entered fully into the meaning that a symbol has for the adherents. Any serious attempt to know how they feel presumes both an informed imagination, and a great deal of empathy in the investigator. It also presumes that attempts have been made to feed back the perceived meaning to the adherents for their agreement. This, however, is never conclusive, for although a new set of words has replaced the myth, they too may mean different things to the two parties.

This attempt to enter the world of another is fraught with difficulties, particularly in relation to the specifics of the context, but as will become clear, the possibilities for basic conceptualizations of reality are not limitless. Also, recognizable patterns of relationship emerge between these basic beliefs and particular contexts of experience. One need not enter a new tradition totally unprepared for what one will find there.

Myth in Everyday Discourse

It is sometimes suggested that religion in the western world only continues to exist at the level of the nation and therefore as what is called a "civil religion", and in the private worlds of the individual and the family, but that it has disappeared from the great public area in between.[15] The claim is

---

[15] See for example Richard J Neuhaus, *The Naked Public Square*, (Grand Rapids, Eerdmans, 1984). Not everyone is of this opinion, Peter Berger, for example, is careful to speak of the removal of sectors of society and culture from the domination of religious institutions and symbols, rather than from religion, *The Social Reality of Religion*, (London,

that no one draws upon religion anymore when arguing a case in workshop, boardroom or parliament, not, at least, without causing embarrassment, particularly to fellow believers, but this simply cannot be the case. If religion remains in the private sphere there is no way that it can disappear from the public sphere. This points to another problem in the use of symbolic discourse.

Consider a group of people, let us say the heads of the various welfare departments of a city, gathered to divide up the annual funds voted for welfare purposes by the city authority. Let us suppose that they all want to do their best for the city and not simply acquire the maximum funding for their own activity. Then each will present his or her own department's case, and weigh the claims of all of them out of his or her own sense of priorities. The more "religiously" they go about this task, the more they will draw upon their sense of the "really real" in human values. No word recognizably of Catholic, Protestant, Jewish, or other religious origin may be uttered, but, if in their private worlds these heads of departments are religious, then what operates in that decision-making process are senses of ultimate values shaped within particular religious traditions. Judaism, Catholicism and Protestantism could clearly operate around that table.

Paradoxically, the more they seek to do their task "religiously" in another sense of that word, that is in harmony and respect for each other, the greater the pressure against the divisive introduction of the religious symbols of particular traditions. It is this tension between the pressure to include one's own values while excluding their language, which forces the development of a new value-language common to the group.

If one pictures a situation in which one of the heads retires after some years in office, one would expect the replacement to feel out of the discussion and his colleagues to fail to understand the reason. Over the years a new language would have formed within the group by which they communicated with one another concerning priorities in values. Old symbols could have acquired new or more ubiquitous meanings, and an informal case law of precedents might have arisen, for example, "This is very like the situation in the Probation Department in '87 except that .. ". Whatever the source, the pressure for a shorthand, for a new set of symbols with meanings precise and common within the group would have had its effect.

This example makes it clear that religious language, the value language of a culture or sub-culture, may be divisive in relation to others. For that or other reasons, it may be suppressed and replaced by another. That new

---

Faber and Faber, 1969) p.107, and Thomas Luckmann is clear that religion has not so much disappeared, as become invisible. *The Invisible Religion,* (London, Collier - Macmillan, 1970) and "Secularization - A Contemporary Myth" in *Life-World and Social Realities*, (London, Heinemann, 1983) p.124.

language would not be obviously religious even to those who invent and use it. It is also clear that such a language is absolutely necessary at every level.

Any gathering of individuals which becomes a society, if it is not a dictatorship or a bureaucracy, is constituted by its common values. These values are ultimate for that society, in the sense that they are the sine que non of the group. They need a common language for their expression. Civil religion, operating at the national level, is but one case of this. Durkheim, when considering a relatively isolated culture in Australasia from his perspective within the relatively monochrome culture of intellectual Europe, could conceive that this was what religion was, the "ideal" which shapes and is shaped by a society. Civil religion in the U.S.A. only became consciously such, when the U.S.A. ceased to be a protestant country with minorities, and became consciously a plural society in which particular traditions were an embarrassment in public life. Having "discovered" a civil religion cast in symbols drawn from the Abrahamic tradition and from their national history together with a case law for the discussion of values suitable for internal purposes, the western nations must now discover a "multicivil religion". For in a shrinking world even Abrahamic symbols, such as God, are an embarrassment, and commonly interpreted historical symbols are hard to find. To understand this necessary quest is to see purpose in the continual verbal dance that takes place at the United Nations.[16]

It is not only in the macro direction that new groupings have emerged which de-emphasize the importance of the nation in individual consciousness and call for a new value language ubiquitous in the group. Ethnic group, religious group, generation group, economic group, and others can all become an entity to which individuals have a sense of belonging. Every minority group that becomes significant in identity formation will be perceived to have a shared set of values, and need a language for their conceptualization, communication and implementation.

The need for a value language that is both universal and precise, as a first step toward holding all these together, is as obvious as it would be difficult to achieve.

Myth and Religion in the Modern World
Religion has consequences for all the bits and pieces of life, but if discourse begins and ends with the bits and pieces of life it fails to be religious discourse. Primary religious discourse is concerned with the totality

---

[16] Consider, for example, how the phrase "South Africa" functions as a symbol in discourse at the United Nations and thence in world media. It would serve no purpose to try to more accurately relate the phrase to the reality. There comes a stage when the actual referent must not be allowed to interfere with the symbolic meaning whether one is speaking of the Exodus, Gettysburg or South Africa.

of experience and its primary question is, "What is all-that-out-there and how do I relate to it?". That being the case, literal discourse is excluded at this primary level even though, as we have seen, it must reenter when the findings at this primary level are applied to the bits and pieces of life.

That we cannot speak literally of the totality, however, should not lead us to act as if it was not there. It should not lead us to relate only to its bits and pieces, trying perhaps to relate these bits into a greater and greater whole but never jumping the gulf between the modes of discourse, in order to speak of the totality itself. It is entirely reasonable to suppose that there is something out there. It is entirely reasonable to ask what it is, not only as a multitude of bits and pieces, but as a whole. That we cannot speak literally of that whole does not make nonsense of religious discourse.

It is clear that religious people do communicate something to each other in religious discourse and to suppose that they do not is to fly in the face of evidence from all places and all times. Yet all is not well. It is not only some of those who are deeply involved in the scientific quest to understand the bits and pieces of experience and the relationship between them, who fail to understand religious language. Many who feel drawn to, and partly fulfilled by religion, can have the disturbing experience of suddenly feeling outsiders to a religious conversation. They are left asking "What are these people talking about?".

One does not want to threaten the faith of adherents by pressing them to explain what they think they are talking about, particularly if one believes that religion, as properly understood, is an essential part of being human. The danger of insisting that god-language is not literally true, is that one is understood to be saying that the experience people refer to by the word "god" is not real. At the very least, it makes it harder for people to go on grasping as true with their minds what their seemingly less reliable feelings make them want to believe. It hardly matters how people understand god-language in Church or Mosque, whether they know anything about a distinction between literal and symbolic discourse, provided that it communicates to them what it is intended to communicate, and serves its ritual purpose. All sorts of unfortunate things can happen, however, when that same language is applied to life by means of a logic that is simply not appropriate by people functioning as though god-language were literally true.

Scientists, because they now know that knowledge exists only within particular ways of seeing, that is, within paradigms, and therefore that they can never possess absolute truth, have not ceased to do science. Nor have they ceased to believe that that with which they are engaged is real. Rather, they continue to act and indeed feel, that the best they now know is the truth (which for all practical purposes it is) even while being alert to discover a better truth.

Likewise, there should be no intellectual problem about remaining committed to the symbols with which one grew up, or later came to recognize as those which resonated best with one's felt sense of reality, for there is no better way to operate.

The applied science model, perhaps best seen in medicine, is all that can be done in religion. That is, to act as if our model of the moment were an actual description of reality, but always to watch the outcome with care, so that we may do better next time. All this, provided that commitment is not idolatry, that we do not lose perspective on the status of our model as model, and therefore cease to respect other people's models. The proof of the pudding is in the eating, but in this case the eating is not complete, nor in the nature of the case - a feeling language speaking of the unique - can it ever be.

I will conclude this discussion of religious discourse by summarizing what I take to be a reasonable minimum position for a critically-minded Westerner approaching religion.

A CONCLUDING STATEMENT

Unless one takes the solipsist view that all exists in my mind one must agree that

THERE IS SOMETHING OUT THERE

- THE ONLY QUESTION IS WHAT

Unless one decides that what is out there is chaos, or at most some accidentally related bits and pieces which in the course of time have adapted to each other, had their corners rubbed down, and taken on an appearance of fit, then:

WHAT IS OUT THERE COHERES

If it coheres, and if we are to be able to place its parts in a value-generating relation to the whole, then we must attempt to say what it is. Examination of its parts and of their relation to each other will contribute toward our feelings about the whole, but all possible examination of the parts will not replace the necessity, finally, to stand back from it all, and to enter into I-thou relation with it and to say what it feels like to be confronted by it.

That is:

> *THERE IS SOMETHING TO BE SAID,*
> *IN ADDITION TO WHATEVER MIGHT BE SAID ABOUT THE*
> *BITS AND PIECES AND THEIR RELATION TO EACH OTHER,*
> *ABOUT THE NATURE OF THE WHOLE*

Unless we are to remain content with an identity that is constructed and maintained in relation to arbitrarily chosen bits and pieces of experience, and with an ethic constructed in an arbitrary frame, humankind must attempt to

> *DISCERN AND CONCEPTUALIZE THE NATURE OF A WHOLE*
> *THAT CAN ONLY BE SPOKEN OF*
> *IN MYTH, THE SYMBOLIC LANGUAGE OF FEELING*

and recognize that there is no logical bridge between that and the literal mode of discourse.

In the next chapter I will begin to explore how this exercise relates to the recognizably religious traditions. It will be seen that there are further limits set to how human beings can speak about a reality to which they would belong.

CHAPTER 5

TYPES OF RELIGIOUS TRADITION

In this chapter I return to religion as a corporately possessed tradition, I remain concerned with its conceptualization. Having begun with the individual and corporate forms of religion with which readers would be familiar I now broaden the area of enquiry to include all the major types of religious tradition.

It is suggested that if one begins with the most obvious external feature of corporate religion, namely how the community engages with their immediate world-out-there, then religious traditions of the world fall into three families. These modes of engagement with the immediate world-out-there are, logically speaking, mutually exclusive although they may have an uneasy co-existence in practice.

The three different modes of engagement seem to be consequent upon three different understandings of reality. The three understandings of reality can be associated with three internally coherent, ideal types of religious tradition. Few religious traditions fit without remainder into any one of these types but the types provide a useful framework for locating, and therefore for observing movements within, actual traditions.

THE VARIETY OF RELIGIOUS TRADITIONS

A survey of what has counted as religion in East, West and South, in both ancient and modern times, suggests that types of religious expression constitute a spectrum. The spectrum begins with a form of religion that meets a need to know about and to plug into the powers-that-be, so that they may be manipulated for the good of human life in the here and now. There is little concern to know the powers for their own sake. It begins where the use of herbs, medicines and a primitive science passes over into (what Westerners would consider) magical religion.

The spectrum then includes many varieties of religion that seek knowledge of the powers, or power, for its own sake, mixed with use of, service of and co-operation with, the power in this world. This might be called ethical religion.

Finally the spectrum includes the sort of religion that seeks to withdraw as completely as possible from this world in order to know intimately, even fuse with, reality. This we may call mystical religion.

This spectrum may be presented in a simplified form as follows:

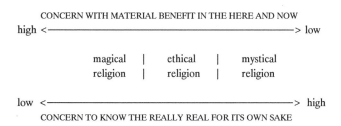

CONCERN WITH MATERIAL BENEFIT IN THE HERE AND NOW

high <————————————————————————————————————> low

      magical | ethical | mystical
      religion | religion | religion

low <————————————————————————————————————> high

CONCERN TO KNOW THE REALLY REAL FOR ITS OWN SAKE

While the spectrum of ways in which religion manifests is interesting, it takes us no further forward in understanding. It records distinctions, but it does nothing to explain them.

If we return to the religions of the world, with a different eye, we may observe that the most obvious visible difference between them lies is the manner in which their adherents relate to their immediate world out there. I will speak of this as their mode of engagement. Although they are frequently mixed in practice, there seem to be three basic modes of engagement, each one of which seems to dominate in a particular family of religion.

In the family of religions that we have been considering, the Abrahamic family, the mode of engagement with the immediate world of experience is an individual and corporate taking-hold-and-shaping. This may simply be the adherents seeking to move their society toward what they consider to be the proper standards of righteousness. On the other hand it may include all manner of technological, administrative and educational effort to overcome poverty, disease and ignorance.

In another family of religions the dominant mode of engagement seems to be a mode of disengagement. On the physical level this withdrawal seems to vary from a reasonable discipline to the extremely severe, on the affective level the withdrawal seems to be as total as can be achieved. In the third family the mode of engagement is one of conforming oneself to the patterns and rhythms of the existing order of things, of respecting and maintaining "the given".

Although these three modes of engagement appear in actual religious traditions in uneasy mixtures, they are, logically speaking, mutually exclusive. At the same time one cannot do more than one of, take hold and shape, withdraw from, or fit into the patterns and rhythms of the immediate world-out-there.

If we take a slightly deeper look, asking what it is that tradition communities are seeking to do which gives rise to these mutually exclusive modes of engagement, we discern some further differences.

In the order used above, we find that the adherents of these three families of religion are people who:

i) seek relationship with a not yet fully present reality.

ii) assume their oneness with reality but need to realize it

iii) assume their oneness with a present reality and seek to maintain it

With these two factors in mind (the mode of engagement and the relation to reality) it becomes possible to describe three ideal types of religious tradition. These are coherent within themselves and logically mutually exclusive, although they are rarely unmixed in practice. At this stage I must be content with description. In chapter 8 I will seek to show why there are only three types and why they develop as they do.

The rest of this book will be concerned with these ideal types and therefore they need names. I have chosen to name them descriptively, having regard to significant aspects of their modes of engagement.

Thus the most obvious thing to an outsider about the last of the types identified above, is that it treats the natural order (nature) as the real, handling it with respect and seeking to maintain its harmonies. I have therefore called it Nature Religion. The second type is most clearly identified by withdrawal, both physical and affective, from the immediate world of experience and hence I have called it Withdrawal Religion. The first type is marked by its adherents strong affirmation of the reality of the immediate world of experience while at the same time denying its ultimateness. I have therefore called it Secular World Affirming Religion.

Nothing in this book has been criticized as much as these names. It has been suggested that the first is derogatory and the second is both derogatory and deceptive. They are, however, clearly defined in terms of outward appearance and they are only derogatory if one loads them with western meaning, for example, if one thinks of nature as being worshiped in place of God. From those, whose traditions these were and who still know and respect them, I have received no complaint.

I did at one stage seek to meet the felt difficulty by calling the first one Natural Religion for, as will appear later, there is justification for that title. I was then asked if that meant that the others were unnatural, which in a sense they are, but it certainly suggested a derogatory implication. Finally I tried types I, II and III and was asked if the order implied some judgment concerning their respective merits. I then gave up the quest and went back to the obvious.

THE THREE IDEAL TYPES OF RELIGION

(i) NATURE RELIGION

In the first ideal type immediate experience is monistic and real. Therefore the environment or significant parts of it are dealt with as divine and eternal or (if those personal and philosophical concepts are not present) as a given without a beginning and without a destiny and, beyond certain limits, not to be interfered with by humankind.

Occurrence:
Examples of existing and historic religions most nearly approximating to this type would be the great majority of the religions of pre-literate peoples, the religions of ancient Egypt and Mesopotamia, of the Indus Valley civilization and the continuing Hinduism of the common people, the religions of China, where they have not come under major influence from Buddhism, and the traditional religions of Africa.

General Description:
In this type there is no radical gap between the gods or powers-that-be and the other entities which comprise the world of experience. All belong to the one monistic reality. Religion is not separate from life in general.

In this type, more than in the others, it is apparent that the nature of the ultimately-real and the relation of men and women to it, will depend very directly upon the immediate experience of the community concerned. Thus, if there are gods which are personifications of significant aspects of life's experience, they are, to the outsider, strangely ambivalent. They have aspects of creativity and preservation on the one hand and destructiveness on the other, and a fair degree of capriciousness to go with it. It must be remembered, however, that these are deities drawn largely from nature and nature is itself both creative and sustaining, destructive and depriving, and with it all, largely unpredictable. Without death there would be no new life and all has its part in the given cycles. Clearly, deities drawn from social experience will manifest a similar ambivalence.

Further, humankind, particularly insecure and often nomadic peoples, have needed both aspects in their gods. The benevolent aspect for themselves, the malevolent aspect to direct towards their enemies. The trick, indeed much of what their ritual is about, is in persuading, or perhaps causing, an often capricious power to do just that. In the biblical tradition the Yahweh of the exodus and conquest days seems to have retained some of this ambivalence.

When a people become settled and agricultural, both their experience and their needs change, and the nature of their gods with them. What they then need is creativity and order, a certain predictability, while retaining the destructive qualities for emergencies. Hence the destructive and creative aspects tend to get separated into different deities - not at this stage gods and demons, for both receive worship. It seems odd to a Westerner to find in India and Africa the recognition of destructive deities, yet it is natural.

Nevertheless, emphasis now goes onto the creative and sustaining deities and upon order. Fertility is now a central concern and there is a discernible tendency to move from the militant masculine deities to female fertility deities. There are, of course, male fertility deities and female deities who, though perhaps originally fertility deities, became the most ferocious of destroyers when the need arose.

This dependence of the character of the gods upon life experience is clearly illustrated by a comparison of the elaborate nature religions of ancient Egypt and Mesopotamia.

Egypt spread out along the highly fertile Nile, protected by the desert to east and west and the mountains to the south, came to have a pantheon of deities virtually all of whom were creative and sustaining. The god of the order that is rooted in reality itself, Ma'at, was central to their thinking. The one significant exception, the one destructive element, was the god Seth. He, significantly, was originally the god of a district on the north-east of the delta, the one point at which Egypt was exposed to military attack and other forms of external influence.

So secure, fertile and ordered was life in Egypt, that the realms of men and gods seemed to interflow one another. On the other hand the search for meaning seems not to have been satisfied in this life. It was projected onto an after-life and an elaborate cult of the dead developed.

The experience of the Mesopotamians was quite different. They were widely exposed to attack and therefore to constant change in the political structure. The Tigris and Euphrates were not nearly as fertile as the Nile and their confluence was in a low lying delta exposed to incursions of fertility-destroying salt water.

A constant experience of conflict and the struggle to survive became central to their understanding of reality. The gods were not infrequently represented as in conflict with one another and even creation was depicted as the result of primeval conflict. The struggle for existence ensured that religion remained focused on this world and it was said that the gods gave life to humankind but retained eternal life for themselves.

While in Egypt the very distinction between gods and humanity, this life and the next, disintegrated (beginning with the divine pharaoh), in Mesopotamia a gulf between gods and humanity existed, even a sort of conflict. Although the king was the servant of the gods, he could not be thought divine.

Time, Change and the Ideal Person:
Returning to the main theme and to the general description of Nature Religion, there are some other aspects to be noted which follow from this view of reality.

The world out there being a given, without beginning or end, time does not run in linear fashion but is cyclical. "Whatever will be has been already ... there is nothing new under the sun".[1] Change is experienced, of course, but this is accounted for as rhythms in the real; spring, summer, autumn, winter; birth, growth, fruition, death; flooding of the river, settling of the silt, the growing of the crops, the ripening of the harvest, the arid period and again the floods.

The ideal person, in relation to nature, is relatively passive fitting himself or herself into the given rhythms. They may build storehouses to bridge the years of dearth and plenty but they do not radically take hold of the world around and seek to shape it, for it is divine, or at least permeated by the divine spirit or spirits, or by some all-pervasive vital force.

In this type of religion (more in the harmonious than in the conflicted form of it) the ideal person is the one who contributes to the maintenance and, where necessary, the restoration of harmony with others (both living and departed) and with nature itself. Social coercion, perhaps in the extreme an accusation of witchcraft, is brought to bear on those who threaten the harmony.

Because the system is a closed one, neither chance nor new beginnings are possible. There is an explanation for all that happens and every action must have its effect.

The Mode of Engagement with the World Out There:
The world-out-there is itself the ultimately-real, it is also monistic, that is to say, it coheres in itself. Therefore, a person can secure his or her life by maintaining relationship with the people and things that are immediate,

---

[1] Koheleth 1:9

probably including the recently dead, because all of these are in turn related to those beyond them. Hence the importance of rites of passage or reintegration at each stage in life; also of such rites as that of "breathing out" (getting rid of) anger before communal decision-making.

In a more general sense, belonging is maintained by entering into the rhythms of nature by taking nature "at the flood". Quite literally in the case of Egypt, where it seems they inaugurated the rule of a new pharaoh when the Nile went into flood. It is a world view still represented in popular astrology. "Venus and Mars are in conjunction this month, time to reconsider your personal relationships" or some such connecting of the natural cycle with a directive for action.

In nature religion, the relationship with all else is assumed, it needs only to be maintained or at worst restored.

(ii) WITHDRAWAL RELIGION

In the second ideal type, the immediate environment is regarded as real but deceptive. The adherent, therefore, seeks to withdraw from it (withdraw in terms of both physical involvement and affective attachment) seeking instead the reality that lies behind the appearance. Reality remains monistic, so that it can be sought in the depth of one's own being, or by seeking to peel away the structures imposed upon the way humans see or feel about experience as a whole.

Occurrence:
Existing religions which best fit this type are the developed forms of those cradled in India, Vedanta Hinduism and Buddhism, but are to be found elsewhere in certain forms of mysticism.

General Description:
The development of withdrawal religion out of its roots in nature religion, was almost certainly the result of a search for meaning in the face of a deep pessimism about the natural order and a pre-existing belief in reincarnation.

When, for the Egyptians, this life became relatively secure and affluent, they were able to retain a sense meaning by understanding life as a prelude to an after-life. With a pre-existing belief in reincarnation such a move would have been impossible. With reincarnation one cannot even commit suicide without coming back again. In a life affirming situation reincarnation seems an attractive idea - within a pessimistic world view it is the ultimate threat.

It is significant that the founders of two of the withdrawal religions of India (Janism and Buddhism) and the hero of the most influential text of Hinduism, were all of the military Kshatriya caste. To be members of the officer class of a people who have ceased to conquer and have settled as the dominant group on a well watered plain, protected to a large extent by sea and mountains, is to have a question mark set against life's meaning.

Withdrawal religion is inevitably individualistic and creates the minimum social structure for existence. Vedanta Hinduism, of course, inherited the caste system. Buddhism logically rejected it in favour of its religious communities, but it would be wrong to suppose that these were forms of communalism in which the group is the link with reality. They were not, as some see the church, a foretaste of a coming kingdom. They were groups of individuals mutually supporting each other in their individual quest for enlightenment.

There is little immediately corporate in this type of religion. All is ultimately one, of course, but even love, in the sense of attachment, is excluded, making way, strangely, for a greater empathy, a greater availability at the particular moment.

Time, Change, and the Ideal Person:

In withdrawal religion the monistic conception of reality remains and is more consciously emphasized than in nature religion where it is usually assumed. In consequence reality can be, and frequently is, conceived in impersonal terms. Time, if important at all, remains cyclical, although the cycles, being far abstracted from the direct experience of nature, tend to be expressed in aeons rather than seasons. The cycles are so long that time practically disappears into a universal now. What matters is that each individual, whenever and wherever he or she might exist, achieve release or enlightenment.

Change is not a rhythm in the life of the real, nor is it even desirable. It is a mark of the transient nature of the apparent reality from which the adherent is seeking release.

The ideal person, therefore, is one who (perhaps after having fulfilled the essential duties which life has laid upon him or her) seeks, by whatever path is believed to be the most suitable, the achievement of personal release or enlightenment. This implies respect for the similar quests of all other manifestations of the reality in which he or she participates.

The Mode of Engagement with the World Out There:

Being in a monistic system and unable to overcome a pessimism concerning this world by projecting the ground of its meaning onto an afterlife (because one would only come back) withdrawal religion takes a more drastic step. It denies reality to the immediate world as experienced, seeing it as deceptive and a snare - a merely transient manifestation of reality - appearing to humans as worthy of their attachment. The transient manifestations can teach humankind of the infinite possibilities latent in the reality from which all comes and to which all returns, but they also constitute a temptation to humankind to value them for themselves.

In withdrawal religion, relation to the really real is assumed, it needs only to be realized.

(iii) SECULAR WORLD AFFIRMING RELIGION

The third ideal type affirms the environment as real but secular. The divine is transcendent, that is, something wholly other than the immediate world of sense experience. Evidence of the divine may be discerned in and through the environment but the environment is not divine.

Occurrence:
The traditions of this type, or in which this type dominates, are probably coterminous with the religions of the Abrahamic family, Judaism, Christianity and Islam. It is possible that Zoroastrianism in its more monotheistic phase is best located here, as might the high-god religion of some pre-literate peoples, but the monistic influence remains strong in this last group.

Time, Change, and the Ideal Person:
Time is of the essence of secular world affirming religion, but not the seasons and life cycles of nature religion. The focus that controls the conceptualization of time is that future moment when this and that which transcends it will come together and, in addition, those moments in which events expected to contribute to the final goal will be fulfilled along the way.

Transcendence leads inevitably to the concept of the world having a beginning, otherwise it would share the divine status of eternity, always being over against the divine, setting upon it some sort of limit. Furthermore this beginning must be creation out of nothing, rather than an emanation or manifestation of the divine substance, otherwise transcendence is lost. The creation, being an act of the divine will, must also be supposed to have a purpose or destiny. Time, therefore, ceases to be cyclical and becomes linear, running from creation to destiny.

The world being God's creation is viewed as essentially good, although its present condition may be far from this. It is real because He creates it but not as real as He.

With linear time the very basis for the evaluation of life changes. No longer is it judged on the present quality of corporate existence, nor on the individual's state of consciousness, but upon its contribution or otherwise towards the creation's destiny.

Change is no longer just a rhythm in the real, nor a mark of impermanence, but a positive step for or against a divine purpose.

In consequence the ideal person is no longer one who passively fits into the rhythms of nature, nor one who withdraws from it. Rather, it is the person who actively takes hold of this real, secular and essentially good environment, seeking to shape it in conformity to the divine will.

This is necessarily a corporate goal, a kingdom being its symbol. Previously this meant the production of the righteous society, but given the technical possibilities, it must now include conforming the physical environment.

The Mode of Belonging and Mode of Engagement with the World Out There:

In secular world affirming religion, with its dualistic view of reality, it is important to distinguish between the mode of belonging to the ultimately-real and the mode of engagement with the world-out-there. Relation to the divine is not assumed but must be sought.

Whereas in the other two types the ultimately-real may be personally or impersonally conceived, in this type it is always understood in personal terms.

If God is transcendent humankind cannot relate to what they understand to be the ultimately-real either by fitting into the rhythms of nature or by finding the spark of the real in themselves, but only by entering into some form of volitional covenant with the divine. The human part in that covenant lies in seeking to co-operate with the divine in bringing about His will for the world. This responsibility involves a freedom to change the world. The level of human freedom is a matter of theological debate and is closely related to the perceived character of the divine. Nevertheless, freedom is a distinctive characteristic of this type of religion.

In contrast, the monistic systems are closed systems of cause and effect. Withdrawal religion with its individual emphasis, has a strong sense of karma. The result of every negative act remains in the residue of the individual's deeds until it is worked out by a positive act. Nature religion has a much less karmic sense, but only because, being more communal than individual, the wider community absorbs consequences and enables the individual, or individual grouping, to escape the full weight of them. There is, however, no such thing as chance, every eventuality must have its explanation.

Finally, it should be noted of the secular world affirming type, that if the real is diminished markedly in favour of the ultimately-real, then transcendence is lost rather than increased. This is because it moves the religion toward a virtual monism, to a single reality not fully known, that is toward the withdrawal religion type. If the ultimately-real is diminished, the move can be either toward nature religion or to some form of secularity.[2]

---

[2] I deal with the possibility of a secular cosmos in chapter 12.

A FURTHER NOTE ON NATURE RELIGION

Experience shows that it is frequently more difficult for students to gain a feeling for this type of religion than for either of the other two and it is not only those new to the field who manifest a mistaken understanding of it.

For those who are unfamiliar with the nature of myth, to be confronted by a description of Egyptian religion, for example, is to enter fairyland. Is the sky believed to be a sea over which the barque of the sun-god sails, or a desert over which the scarabaeus beetle rolls its ball of dung, or the belly of the cow-goddess Hathor, or Shu the sky-goddess bending over Geb the earth-god in creative interaction. "If it is one, surely it cannot be the others, and how could they have believed it was any of them?"

Having looked at the nature of myth and reminding ourselves that it is feeling language, the seeming contradictions disappear. One can have many different feelings, coherent or conflicting, about the same object of experience. The sun-filled sky may easily be understood to create feelings of awe-full sovereignty and dependence, of persistence, of fruitfulness and aridity, of protectiveness and fearfulness. All of which one may wish to express.

We have also seen that myth may be believed on different levels and there is little difficulty with the idea that a myth expresses a believed-in quality of total reality, such as immediate experience would have if the myth were literally true.

Even with these understandings it remains difficult to enter the world-view of nature religion. The difficulty that I deal with here is the problem which arises when the distinction between personal and impersonal is imposed upon a monistic understanding of reality.

Commentators on nature religion have often described it as animist or animatist. That is to say that the adherents are said to perceive all, or many, of the natural objects which Westerners would regard as inanimate, to be the dwelling place of spirits or to themselves have spirits. Africans, for example, have responded by asking "What do you mean by spirit?" or "What is the problem with that? You Westerners, at least since the advent of nuclear physics, admit to power in everything.".

In secular world affirming religion, the ultimately-real is necessarily conceived as having volition and therefore as being quasi-personal. I will explain why this must be the case in chapter 8. For the moment, it is sufficient to recognize that this identification of the ultimately-real with the personal has conditioned all western thinking. In religions with a monistic view of reality, the power, or powers, do not have to be perceived as personal and in many cases are not. That does not mean that they are impersonal, only that the personal-impersonal distinction is not felt to be significant.

That there is a tendency in all religions to speak of the powers in personal terms is the result, in part, of something already discussed. Because humankind's most typical experience of the unique is another person, when treated as person, there is a tendency to carry the feeling over to other unique experiences and to transfer a sense of the personal to the unique *per se*.

In the world-view of the West, the divide between the personal and the impersonal is deeply ingrained. Transcendence holds them apart. The ultimately-real is preeminently personal, the real is preeminently an impersonal realm with persons in it. Secular world affirming religion is self-reinforcing in this. The self-reinforcement processes might be summarized as follows:

Secular world affirming religion sees God as transcendent, He therefore becomes personal and the world becomes secular. In secularizing the world, unique experience is almost entirely reduced to experiences of the other person and of the totality. There is, therefore, a tendency to carry over feeling of person into the experience of the totality.

Western thinking is strongly goal orientated. Goals are inseparable from the idea of volition and of values. Volition and values are personal categories.

Values arise out of a matter's location in relation to the ultimately-real. The ultimately-real is therefore felt to be preeminently the source of the personal. The real is the source of impersonal fact.

None of the above is true of the monistic religions.

To return to the African's question "What do Westerners mean by spirit?" the answer must be something like "a power with volition of its own and therefore personal".

It is this deeply felt divide between the personal and the impersonal, between power with or without volition, which must not be imported into the nature religion world-view if we are to understand it.

An over emphasis on God as person, even in western thinking, can become difficult. Because volition is not a necessary feature, the more cognitive forms of religions such as Vedanta Hinduism and Buddhism, are able to dispense with personal language altogether when speaking of the ultimate.

A monistic world view is just that, monistic. It holds all things together, including fact and value, personal and impersonal.

It is one thing to understand another world-view, it is something else to enter it empathetically. For the sake of empathy, I include a short illustration.

When a religiously-inclined Westerner drives over a hill and is confronted with a particularly beautiful or fertile panorama he or she may say silently, to one they perceive to be somehow out there or up above, "My! that's really something.", expressing both appreciation and gratitude. How would the nature religionist respond?

Only that world-out-there could be addressed, there is no transcendent. The world-out-there is not just the land, nor just the ancestors, nor just a personally conceived high god, if there is one, but the vitality which is all of them.

Frequently, an African's ancestors are not simply in the land, they are the land in an inter-penetration which leads to respect for all things animate and inanimate and an emphasis on the maintenance of harmony.

Nature religion is not likely to again become humankind's sense of reality in such a mixed and changing world, but it is very much the ideal end-point of the other religious types. Its view of the unspoiled texture of life is one in which there are no oppositions to be overcome and the really real is immediately and permanently present. It is both Nirvana and the heavenly eschaton of the Abrahamic religions.

Nature religion has been called primitive and primal. It would be better to call it primary.

I have described each of the three types of religious tradition as though it were an undivided whole. Any consideration of world religion will show that this is not so and that each type has sub-divisions within it. It will not be possible to consider many of these sub-divisions, but it is important to understand what sort of divisions they might be. One example, drawn from the secular world affirming type, will serve this purpose. It concerns the manner in which the individual understands his or her relation to the ultimately-real.

MODES OF BELONGING TO THE ULTIMATELY-REAL
IN SECULAR WORLD AFFIRMING RELIGION

In secular world affirming religion, with its belief in a transcendent god, humankind cannot relate to him by fitting into the rhythms of nature, nor by withdrawing into the self, but only in some form of volitional covenant.

Within that very general understanding of how humanity and history are potentially linked to the divine, there is the need for every individual to feel linked. This calls for cognitive support.

There are two ways in which the individual's relation to the divine can be modelled and perhaps a third, a compensatory move, which may be employed if the former paths are for any reason excluded.

The two normative relations, I have called Direct Cosmic Belonging and Indirect Cosmic Belonging. I have called the compensatory move Reduced Reality Belonging.

I have employed the word cosmic, in the same sense as Rümke uses it, to indicate that the relationship includes all that is non-ego, all that is out there, the real and the ultimately-real. The reason for this will become clear when we consider the compensatory move.

While these modes of belonging are frequently mixed in practice, there is some evidence that a mixed logic of belonging presents some difficulties for a secure faith.

The modes of belonging which I will be considering are only appropriate to secular world affirming religion with its dualistic view of reality. Nevertheless, there is at least an affective affinity between direct cosmic belonging and withdrawal religion, and between indirect cosmic belonging and nature religion.

i) DIRECT COSMIC BELONGING

In direct cosmic belonging, which is the traditional emphasis of Islam and of protestant and pietistic Christianity, the believer relates directly and individually to the ultimately-real and in that relationship to the rest of experience. God initiates the relationship and the individual responds.

Because the principle of belonging lies within the individual, this mode of belonging tends to be associated with societies which place a premium on social or geographical mobility. Overall it is a brittle form of belonging for, while it tends to keep one in, if one moves out, one is right out, there is nothing left. It can also become that sort of ultra-demanding, face-to-face relationship which finds expression in that line of hymnody, "Oh what a worm am I".

The principle of belonging is usually what is called faith. It necessarily includes belief, but also the elements of trust and obedience.

When it is left like that, those of tender conscience never know whether they were being trusting or obedient enough. The need for a sense of assurance presses a tradition community toward formalizing the requirement of obedience in a prescribed behavior pattern, and the requirement of trust, as either a prescribed belief or a prescribed inner experience. Faith understood in these terms, particularly in the case of prescribed belief, can become dogmatic and as divisive between groups as it is cohesive within them.

ii) INDIRECT COSMIC BELONGING

In indirect cosmic belonging, which is the traditional emphasis of Judaism and of the catholic forms of Christianity, the believer relates to the ultimately-real by relating to that which is already so related, and in that relationship to the rest of experience. That is, God is seen to have established upon earth an institution which belongs to Him and in belonging to that the individual belongs to God. For the Jew, this institution is the elect people into which one is born but from which one can opt out. In the more catholic end of Christianity, it is the Church which is the divine institution, the extension in the world of the presence of Christ. To be initiated and retained in the Church, therefore, is to belong to God.

This is a much less brittle form of belonging than the direct cosmic mode. Perhaps the way in which the two traditions used as examples are sometimes caricatured may help to catch their feeling and their strengths.

Within the Jewish tradition one can be breaking every rule in the book, including eating the odd piece of bacon, but if one is not eating ham then one is still in some way Jewish.

Likewise if one is baptized, one can spend one's life in the Mafia and hope to make a good confession on one's death-bed and in some way remain a Catholic.

Such caricatures are, needless to say, grossly unfair. They nevertheless serve to convey an important quality of this mode of belonging, namely, that those born or initiated into the divinely related institution have a sense that the divine has a hold upon them at times when they feel unable to hold onto the divine.

This mode of belonging is also more comfortable in the sense that it is less face-to-face and limits are set to the sense of demand, the individual conscience being partially integrated within the institution. The institution is likely to be more realistic in its expectations than many an individual conscience and one can more easily feel assured that the minimal requirements for acceptance have been met.

A danger of this mode of belonging lies in the potentially corrupting power that is vested in an institution set between the individual and God. It can also, less dramatically but just as seriously, undermine personal responsibility.

It is not, of course, necessary that the bridge institution be as large as a church or a nation, in fact one other person will do if he or she is believed to be specially related to God. This is the significance of the charismatic figure who emerges particularly in times of turmoil and of the tendency for new departures in religion to manifest this direct relation in charismatic features.

This mode of belonging, being corporate, tends to maintain the societal status quo. All must change or nothing changes.

iii) SUBSTITUTE OR REDUCED REALITY BELONGING

In the absence of a cosmic sense of belonging, intensive belonging to a small, tightly knit, clearly delimited and manageable group, can provide a substitute sense of belonging. The group will have reduced its reality to virtually the group itself, all the rest of experience being understood to be bad, transient, or at least markedly inferior.

It is reduced reality belonging which generates sectarian groups. Those whom it attracts, those for whom a more cosmic sense of belonging is unobtainable, could be the bulk of a population in times of major socio-cultural disturbance. It will attract certain psychological types at all times. In practice it probably constitutes a part of most adherents' sense of belonging.

Representing as it does a deliberate withdrawal from the rest of experience, it will not satisfy the integrative nature of most people when socio-cultural conditions stabilize.

What matters in this type is, not so much what is believed or practiced, but the intensity with which it is believed or practiced. Religious beliefs are not cashed in terms of their meaning in everyday life, but become symbols which operate as flags. These "flag beliefs" serve to unite the group all the better because they are unrelated to the chaotic world outside.

Marks for inclusion and exclusion become important, dress, hairstyle, food laws, rejection of dancing, cinema, television, alcohol, etc., the social or ethical significance of which is assumed rather than justified.

The important elements are the fervor with which the symbols are affirmed, and the rigidity with which the marks, of who belongs and who does not, are complied with. These are the source of the sense of belonging.

It is a characteristic of reduced reality belonging, that there is no way of knowing the ultimately-real except in the sense of togetherness in the group. The symbols for the ultimately-real are flags that unite. Their meaning cannot be cashed in terms of the divine attitudes to all the details of a world-out-there, save only that he is against it. Thus the character of the divine and its related ethic do not emerge in terms of the adherent's real and immediate world. The divine becomes a rescuing power with minimal personal characteristics.

This defensive solution, which closes down on experience, is not to be confused with the situation in which experience itself is limited. That is, when either the adherent's world-out-there is experientially small but open to expansion, or when depth in one area of experience has been preferred to breadth, for both of these situations can remain cosmic in spirit.

Reduced reality belonging is not, I think, orthodox within any of the Abrahamic family of faiths, for it overly diminishes the creator aspect of divinity in favour of the saviour aspect. Clearly the sense of belonging is gained at the cost of breadth and, one supposes, of the possible richness and meaningfulness of experience. One would not propose it as the long term solution within this type of religion, but it may be for many in times of crisis, always for some, the only available mode of belonging.

A GENERAL COMMENT ON THE MODES OF BELONGING

The modes of belonging which we have been considering concern the relation of the individual to the divine. In the secular world affirming type of religion, humankind relates to the divine in a volitional covenant. The individual's part in that covenant is to seek to co-operate with the deity and, where appropriate, with the community, in bringing about the divine will in and for the creation. The goal is therefore symbolized corporately as a kingdom. The adherent needs the sense that his or her individual belonging is related to this corporate goal.

In indirect cosmic belonging, the relation of individual belonging to the corporate goal will be automatic if the divinely constituted institution (in belonging to which one belongs to the divine) is of sufficient size and significance to be seen as having a formative influence on human history.

Reduced reality belonging usually rejects the possibility of humanity improving the creation, so the kingdom is seen as the result of divine intervention, even as a new creation, that is, as discontinuous with human history.

In direct cosmic belonging, or in indirect cosmic belonging where the institution is not of great secular significance, the existence of a corporate level of purpose is presupposed. This may be in the form of what has become known as a civil religion.

That is to say, if the individual's daily involvement with his or her world out there is to have ultimate significance, then it must be seen contribute to a community, which is understood to contribute to some wider purpose, such as Pax Britannica, the American Way of Life, or a Liberation Movement, which in turn is understood, however subliminally, to be part of the divine purpose.

THE ADVANTAGES AND DANGERS OF A
TYPOLOGICAL APPROACH TO RELIGION

Throughout this chapter I have been establishing what are called ideal types. I first established the ideal types of religious tradition and then the ideal models of belonging within one of those types. As types they are conceptually coherent. In practice, however, one would find few, if any, traditions or individual adherents who would fit without remainder into any one of them.

The potential advantage of a typological approach, is that it reduces the chaos of almost unlimited variety to some manageable order. It liberates one from bondage to historical manifestations of religion, so that one might discern more clearly the relatively limited, basic elements comprising them.

Precisely because types are fixed they offer a framework within which movements may be observed. Insofar as a living tradition can be located within a particular type, it assists access to areas that happen to be obscure. It enables one to know what to expect and to ask questions when it is not found. It enables one to know which symbols are consequential to a particular religious type, and which are serving the secondary role of seeking to hold together elements from two or more types.

The dangers of a typological approach are that the ideal types can all too easily become realities in one's thinking and be substituted for the more complex and sometimes awkward actualities. Also, in the desire to fit actual religions into the types, one may fail to notice the factors which do not fit, and perhaps lose much of their richness. One may also, without knowing it, be forcing western, or even personal values upon the reality. One needs to be aware of these dangers if the benefits are to outweigh the detriments.

CHAPTER 6

RELIGIOUS EXPERIENCE AND RELIGIOUS DISCOURSE

A UNIFYING PERSPECTIVE

It has served my purpose to distinguish clearly between how one thinks and speaks about experience and the experience itself and to that end I employed H.C.Rümke's model of the two levels of development. However, new experience is not just raw data but is received into consciousness already interpreted and evaluated, partly under the influence of previous experiences possessed conceptually. This interaction between what is believed and what is experienced, is now made overt and explored. The model that is developed will be seen to be that of Rümke with added feedback loops and some further conceptual handles. The consequences of this dynamic inter-relation between experience and the discourse in which it is conceptualized, are then drawn out and used to further elaborate a number of the items dealt with earlier under the separate heads of Experience and Discourse.

In chapter 2 I attributed two related but distinguishable meanings to the phrase "total experience". The first meaning was conscious and partly cognitive. It was all the significant experience, whether one's own or acquired, that would be called to mind in the process of asking, "What is life all about? What is all-that-out-there? What reality, if any, lies within or behind it?".

The second meaning was largely unconscious and affective. It arose in the recognition that individuals, responding intuitively to those significant situations which call for a personal engagement, do so as a result of all the experience that has contributed to making them what they are. This meaning of "total experience" and the first are clearly related, but not necessarily identical.

Up to this point, I have been concerned largely with the first meaning and have continued to ask the reader to stand in the shoes of adherents as they think about or consciously feel towards their world-out-there. I now wish to change perspective in order to consider the development, within the individual, of the largely unconscious and responsive aspect of total experience. By doing this I will be able to draw into a single model much that I have said about the ego and the world-out-there, about religious language, and about the types of religious tradition. Where it is necessary to distinguish the model that I am about to present from what has gone before, I will speak of it as the "internal model".

SECTION A - THE FORMATION AND EXPRESSION OF
THE FELT SENSE OF REALITY

i) THE FELT SENSE OF REALITY

Central to the understanding of an individual's religion is what I will call the "felt sense of reality". In each person there develops a sense of what is real, or better, a sense of the nature of reality. It is not for the most part conscious. It outcrops into consciousness when one either accepts or rejects a story of how life is. If one hears a sermon or political address one may either respond with "Yes! that is right", or "No! that is false", or simply get irritated because it seems irrelevant. This is partly a cognitive process. There is a rational evaluation going on as one hears what is being said, but the judgment is not primarily cognitive. It is a matter of feeling. We say, "It rings a bell." or "It touches a cord." or "It finds an echo." and mean deep inside us.

I speak of *felt* sense of reality because one can only speak of reality in terms of what it feels like to be confronted by it. I will use *sense* of reality when speaking of the primary experience as it exists before it is conceptualized in symbol, and *nature* of reality or *symbolized* reality for the conceptualization given to that felt sense. In considering how the felt sense of reality is formed it will be useful to break the process down and present it diagrammatically. See Fig.6.1.

ii) THE FORMATION OF THE SENSE OF REALITY

I begin in reference to Fig.6.1 with what is labelled as the context of experience. This is simply the world out there as it could be experienced, the sum total of the possibilities of raw experience.

That which we experience, however, is by no means everything that is available. There are always things in our field of vision and auditory range, that we do not notice, or do not notice consciously.

We may rush to catch a bus and, only when sitting on it, realize that a person passed on the way was an old acquaintance not seen in a long time. Somehow one has seen them but not consciously registered the fact. It is only when one relaxes that it comes to consciousness. We seem to know what to register and when it is appropriate for what is registered to become conscious. We have learnt of what, in our total field of sensory awareness, to become conscious, either because it constitutes a threat or because it offers some advantage. This is a highly culture dependent conditioning.

We might walk on veld or mountain and never see spoor, but if we were dependent upon hunting for our food, we would be conditioned to register every broken blade of grass. Thus there is a sort of filter on raw experience, a selection process at work, which determines what we actually become conscious of and, one suspects, what we register at all, even sub-consciously. The rural dweller visiting the city jumps at every sound precisely because the proper filter is not in place. In Fig.6.1 this filter is presented as the fact selection process.

Fig.6.1

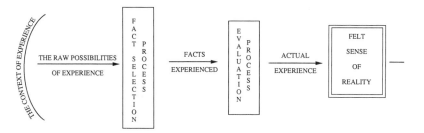

Even the selected facts do not constitute our actual experience. The same facts of experience are felt by different people and even by the same people at different times, in different ways. At the fringes of society there are people who experience prison as security and keep wanting to return there, while at the other extreme there are people who, even in the most liberal society, experience it as some sort of straitjacket. According to their expectations and experience, two people may value a similar set of observed facts in quite different ways.

There is a process in which we value the selected raw experience. It is that valued fact, which constitutes the experience we have. Unless, of course, we quite consciously set aside the valuing activity and ask what it is that we are actually observing. If I enter my home and smell supper cooking, I do not register the fact and later feel good about it. The experiences comes as one. What we experience most of the time is a valuation of the facts that are consciously observed, not the raw data of the actual context. This step I have presented in Fig.6.1 as the evaluation process. It is this selected and evaluated experience which shapes our sense of reality.

There may be aspects of the felt sense of reality which are inherited or simply a given of being human. It is the point at which faith might locate the secret work of divine grace. Here, however, I am only concerned with that which is part of the process of human development and open to investigation.

iii) THE SYMBOLIZATION OF THE SENSE OF REALITY

When people have gained a sense of reality they need to be able to picture it, to express it and to move from a sense of reality to a course of action. This last requires what is usually called an ethic. In short the felt sense of reality needs to be symbolized in a concatenation of symbols of reality. The symbols can, as I have indicated, be dance, carving, painting, architecture, as well as music. They may be ritual behavior or simply prescribed relationships with the people and the world around. Frequently they are words, in which case we are dealing with myth.

Whatever the form of symbols chosen the end point is a symbolized sense of reality (Fig.6.2) and a language in which one can express the felt nature of reality. To the extent that this becomes shared, we can speak of a tradition.

Fig.6.2

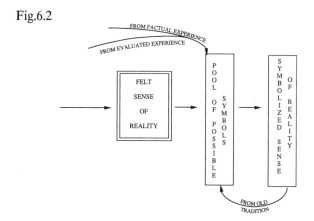

iv) THE SOURCE OF THE SYMBOLS FOR THE SENSED REALITY

When individuals seek to symbolize their sense of reality, it is clear that they draw upon, what I will call, a pool of possible symbols (Fig.6.2). One source of the symbols in this pool will be the individual's own earlier symbolized reality and any tradition he or she may have received. It is important to emphasize the fact, that when one looks for a way of expressing a present sense of reality and draws symbols from an existing tradition for that purpose, one is probably using the symbols in a modified way. When one observes that different communities and different generations have used the same symbol, one must not assume that the symbol expressed the same feeling. It is necessary to have understood a symbol in the context of the particular experience, before one can hope to understand what it really expressed.

The pool of possible symbols is fed also from contemporary experience, so that, whereas once the pool of possible symbols included sheep, wolves and shepherds, fishes and nets, it now includes also models of atoms, radio waves, computers and a host of other possible models. This is just as well, for while, as was noted earlier, symbols of permanence sufficed for a rather static sense of reality, now that the sense of reality is highly dynamic, we are in need of new symbols

From experience in one's community come bits of already interpreted history. The exodus is one example, the cross another. These enter into the pool of possible symbols.

The actual exodus, the actual cross, because fact selection and evaluation processes operated differently, would have been experienced differently by those who were present. Then the first generation of Jewish and Greek Christians would have experienced the message of the cross differently. However it was filtered, the cross influenced their sense of reality, which in turn influenced their symbols and the developing tradition. These developments eventually fed into our experience and therefore into our sense of reality and into our pool of possible symbols.

The bare uninterpreted fact of the events, to the extent that we know them, are fed into our raw experience simply as recounted history and thence into our sense of reality and into our pool of possible symbols. These are of lesser significance. The cross for modern Christians does not belong to direct experience. It has fed into their sense of reality as historical fact; it has fed into their sense of reality through other people's understanding of it (conveyed in the inherited tradition) and through the impact that this has had on their society and culture.

If the cross is significant for people today it is because its meaning to them in some way meshes with their sense of reality, a sense of reality which was not only created by the cross and by other people's understanding of the cross, but by everything else that they have registered and evaluated, in fact by their total experience.

v) THE CLOSING OF THE SYSTEM

Having emphasized the importance of the individual's sense of reality and its long run dependence upon experience, it is perhaps necessary to emphasize that tradition is not unimportant. Words are carriers of change and religious symbols have the power to shape both culture and society. This is made clear by the manner in which the symbols of Hebrew-Christianity, having first needed to be rendered palatable in order to gain access to the Graeco-Roman world, in the longer run imported into that world much of what was most distinctive in the Hebrew experience. Consider the feed-back loops in the following figure.

Fig.6.3

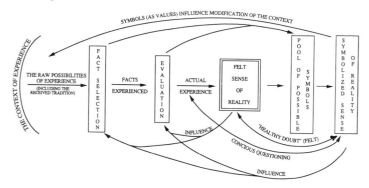

If we return to the selection and valuation processes operating on raw experience, it is clear that both are influenced by the symbolized reality, the beliefs and practice in which we express our understanding of the nature of reality, as well as by the felt sense of reality itself. That is to say, how we have symbolized our sense of reality will control in some measure how we experience the world and thence will control how our sense of reality is modified.

Our symbolized reality also influences the shape of the world we build around us, that is, what we choose to do individually and especially corporately to shape the context of experience. Those changes feed back into the system as raw experience.

While the individual may continue to operate at the level of feeling, the community can only act corporately if it has conceptualized the feelings of its members. Thus, in the process of deciding how to modify the context of experience, the community comes to possess a corporate symbolized reality. That also becomes a part of the context and feeds back to the individual as raw experience.

The necessary healthy doubt of which Rümke writes, must operate affectively in this model between the symbolized reality and the felt sense of reality, and cognitively, between the symbols and a conscious review of the actual experience feeding into the felt sense of reality.

SOME GENERAL COMMENTS ON THE MODEL

(a)   In terms of Rümke's model, religion, understood as direct cosmic experience, is not available before puberty. In terms of the present model it should be recognized that in the years after the dominance of fantasy and before puberty, insofar as a child can be said to have a sense of reality, it is largely a received one. Socialization provides a symbol set for reality.

With reference to the diagram, it is as though the felt sense of reality, the pool of possible symbols and the symbolized reality were all lumped together in what might be called the received tradition. Then with the move to individuality at puberty, the individual stands back from that tradition and begins to explore both it and the context, thus developing his or her own feeling about reality. The old received tradition may then provide the basis of the pool of possible symbols from which the individual draws in symbolizing his or her developing sense of reality.

While it is clear that the major revolt against the received tradition will take place around puberty, this model is not quite as excluding of the young as was the earlier one, for there is little doubt that the process of questioning aspects of the received symbol set, can and does begin before puberty.

There is a difference here, therefore, between the felt sense of reality and Rümke's direct cosmic experience. While it is clear that a child cannot have the direct experience that Rümke calls cosmic, until they have developed the necessary sense of individuality, it is equally clear that they have a strong sense of belonging unless some trauma has determined otherwise.

This is not the sense of belonging that earlier I likened to the workings of a watch, in which clearly defined units relate to each other and therefore to the whole, but the more unconscious sense, of not thinking of oneself as apart from a family, extended family, or local community and of these as not separated from whatever lies beyond.

A child's world view tends to remain monistic. Perhaps because they tend to a literal interpretation of received myth, but also because transcendence asks that they recognize two entities that are non-ego, when they cannot yet have a sense of one. If there is a sense of a divide in their experience, it is more likely to approximate the withdrawal religion paradigm, in which, behind the dull face of immediate experience, an imagined world has the greater reality.

People whose developing sense of reality does not differ markedly from the relatively unconscious one of childhood, would have affinity with the nature religion paradigm.

Belonging is possible at all ages. However, it changes from being little more than the lack of a sense of being out, to the conscious sense of being in, and therefore toward the "watch mechanism" sense of participation. The change may come gradually or suddenly, but it will almost certainly require that Rümke's two levels have come together, that is, that cosmic experience has found expression in an acceptable set of words. This will lead in turn, as I noted earlier, to the sense of what William James called "having religion in possession".

(b)   The ideal types of religion that I set out in chapter 5 are themselves paradigms, that is, they are the determinants of the frameworks within which the symbolized sense of reality of the present model can be built.

Religion is more than a felt sense of reality, more also than the symbolized reality. It requires in addition a mode of belonging to that experienced and symbolized reality. Within the symbolized reality, therefore, will lie a logic for belonging. Within the felt sense of reality will lie whatever sense of belonging has been achieved.

It should be noted that the symbolic elaboration of a felt sense of reality can be severely limited by the content of the pool of possible symbols. In most situations where the nature religion paradigm has prevailed undisturbed, nature itself, including the human body and a relatively simple social structure, are all that can be drawn upon. History, science and technology only become serious sources, when there is a background of literacy.

(c)   In speaking of the felt sense of reality I have avoided speaking of the ultimately-real, for the distinction between real and ultimately-real belongs only to a symbolized reality within the secular world affirming type.

SECTION B - SOME IMPLICATIONS OF THE MODEL

i) FEELINGS ARE PRIOR TO SYMBOLS

The model that I have presented in this chapter is, of course, that of H.C. Rümke, now turned on its side and elaborated with feed-back loops. This elaboration makes it clear that the two levels of development are not as independent of each other as I suggested in presenting Rümke's model. However, the distinction between experience, and the words in which people seek to express that experience, remains significant.

One can restate Rümke's point in the terms of the present model and say that whereas, when people speak of religion they are usually referring to what is here called the symbolized sense of reality, it is in fact the felt sense of reality which is basic. What is made clearer in this model is the dynamic relationship between the felt sense of reality and the symbolized sense of reality. Symbols can be seen to play a part in the shaping of the felt sense of reality although very much more feeds into it. It is there that the synthesis of experience takes place and there that symbols are authenticated.

If this point had been recognized by those who studied religion as well as by those who taught it, a lot of misdirected effort might have been spared. The debate concerning conflicting truth claims between religions might have been, if not avoided, at least conducted at a level where the beginnings of a real debate between the traditions was possible. Likewise, the classroom torture of making affectively supple young people sit under an authoritarian presentation of "religious facts" could have been reformed far earlier than it was.

It would also have been clear that religion can operate strongly in situations where its symbols have become an embarrassment.

A comment on Christian mission in Africa from an essay by Desmond Tutu illustrates the importance of recognizing the centrality of the felt sense of reality.

> ... Christianity has failed to be rooted sufficiently deeply in the African soil, since (most missionaries) have tended to make us feel somewhat uneasy and guilty about what we could not alter even if we tried until doomsday - our Africanness.
> "No positive religion that has moved men has been able to start with a *tabula rasa* to express itself as if religion was beginning for the first time; *in form if not in substance*, the new system must be in contact all along the line with the older ideas and practices which it finds in possession. A new scheme of faith can find a hearing only by appealing to *religious instincts and susceptibilities* that already exist in its audience, and it cannot reach them without taking account of the *traditional forms* in which religious *feeling* is embodied, and without speaking a language which men accustomed to these forms can understand."[1]

Africanness, like Jewishness or Christianness, is not just a set of beliefs or practices, but a deeper form grasped, not so much in intellect, as in the "instincts and susceptibilities", that is, in feeling. Perhaps this is truer in African tradition that some others, but it is true for all. The new (whatever its words and practices) must answer in some manner to the same instincts and susceptibilities, that is, it must relate to the old in deep structure, not just superficial content, if it is to find acceptance.

---

[1] Desmond M Tutu. "Some African Insights and the Old Testament" in *Relevant Theology for Africa*, (Mapumulo, Missiological Institute, 1973), p.45. His quotation is from Robertson Smith, *Religion of the Semites*.

If under the pressure of circumstances a radical conversion seems to take place at the level of beliefs and practices only, unrelated to the old structure, then it must be considered as an escape; a conversion out of the old rather than a conversion into the new. The people concerned will be in an affective vacuum and conversion will last only as long as the circumstances promoting the change exist.

Stability, "sufficient rooting" in Tutu's words, requires that what is new gain sufficient plausibility by its grounding in the felt sense of reality, and that for the most part, will have the structure of the old.

Just how transient content can be while structure remains, and just how deceptive this can be for our understanding of the human ability to change, is well illustrated by an example which appears in George Orwell's literary critical essay, "Inside the Whale".[2] In this essay Orwell considers what is apparently a major swing in allegiance between two groups of English-speaking intellectuals. These are the poets of the mid 1920s, among whom it was the done thing to be received into the Catholic Church, and the poets of the mid 1930s, who were equally busy joining the Communist Party. That is, from attitudes which seemed near to fascism (by the standards of the 1930s) to communism, all in a decade. By implication these two groups are compared with the English speaking poets before the watershed of the 1914-18 war.

According to Orwell, the moves of both the '20s and the '30s were escape routes for those who could no longer face the possibilities of life in the ordinary middle-class way, as soldier, clergyman, stockbroker, or Indian civil servant. Each transcended loyalty to King, Anglican Church and Empire. Each had "..a world-wide organization, ... a rigid discipline, ... power and prestige behind it". Each had "a Church, an army, an orthodoxy, a discipline .... a Fatherland and .....a Fuehrer.. ".[3]

Both were, to use Orwell's words for the latter, "the patriotism of the deracinated"; a new universalism for one that had ceased to be such. Three very different sets of beliefs and practices with little change in the underlying structure of the felt sense of reality, the ground which rendered the beliefs plausible.

Orwell indicates how much people are prisoners of their structuring of reality. Not of the bits and pieces with which they en-flesh the skeleton (his example shows how fast those can change) but of the structure itself. People are indeed "inside the whale" being borne along.

---

[2] George Orwell, *Inside the Whale*, Harmondsworth, Penguin, 1962).

[3] *ibid.*, p.35.

His example also shows that liberty may not mean throwing away mythology as soon as people become aware that it is mythology, for then, in craving belonging, they may grab at anything on offer, provided that is not the old one.

Given that people can accept as real only that which fits with what they already feel to be real, change at the roots can be either a very slow process or an exceedingly traumatic unselfing.

People need to belong but to be aware that they are working with a structure for that to which they belong. This structure is not ultimate, is not the only one, is open to modification or exchange. Such modification or exchange is not without cost.

ii) FURTHER THOUGHTS ON RELIGION AND SCIENCE, FACT AND VALUE

The internal model adds to our understanding of the similarities and differences between religious and scientific knowledge. Not only is the former expressed in symbolic language and the latter in literal language. The former, whether the symbols come from, history, imagination, other people's tradition, or wherever, is authenticated in the felt sense of reality, while the latter is (at one level) verified against unevaluated experience. The two worlds even at this level are not totally separate, for that same experience serves to modify the felt sense of reality.

The distinction between science as a human enterprise and science as a method, has become clearer in recent years. The aim of science, to verify theories against unevaluated experience, is no doubt carried through, but what data is considered in the first place and therefore what theories emerge, is an area haunted with competing special interests. Science is not working impartially with raw experience. At the very least, the tradition of the scientific community itself, exercises some control over what I have called the fact selection process.

Another distinction to be made is that between the observation of data, together with any regularities in it (laws), and the interpretation of those regularities within a theoretical frame work.[4] The former is potentially value free, the latter it seems, is not. Theories tend to develop as a body around a particular area of concern. In that body there may develop an overall

---

[4] The critical theorists, Horkheimer, makes the distinction between "Forschung" (scientific research or analysis) and "Darstellung" (the functioning within a frame of reference which gives rise to the analysis and recomposes the material analyzed), the former is value free within its own limits, the latter essentially valued, whether consciously or not. See Paul Connerton, *The Tragedy of Enlightenment*, (Cambridge, Cambridge University Press, 1980), p.30.

theoretical position, perhaps stemming from one key (paradigmatic) theory within it.

While the validity of a paradigmatic theory may, as theory, be tested against unevaluated experience, as paradigm, there is good evidence that it is tested to a significant degree within the felt sense of reality.

Freedom from bias and presuppositions in the conduct of whatever experiments have *already* been decided upon and in the interpretation of the resulting data within the *current* theoretical frame, is all the freedom from values that could properly be claimed. The closed nature of the model that we have been considering indicates that any knowledge which arises from humanity's engagement with its context, cannot be value free in any broader sense than this. The selection, not only of the experiment, but also of the theoretical frame, cannot be value free.

The debate about the relation of fact and value, is a long standing one. For the social sciences, where it is always a live issue, some have suggested setting aside the distinction by using a stimulus-response model of human beings. In this, the individual is considered to receive input through the five senses then to respond to what is received with a sign. The observer records that certain sets of sense inputs occur together with certain outputs and relates these regularities into more general laws and thence into generalized theories with predictive power.

This stopping at the observable surface of the individual, however, neglects the difference between the two modes of discourse and sets up potential confusion in the interpretation of a response. Is it literal or is it symbolic, and if the latter, how shall it be interpreted without access to the inner frame of reference that generates its meaning?

The model which we have been considering, at least retains the experiential difference between head and heart. The model is constructed on the understanding that all signs are in fact a response to the same type of sense inputs, but it also takes account of the fact that they function in two ways.

In the first function, they gain their meaning by location in an agreed cognitive frame of reference, derived ultimately from the external world. The examples I used in chapter 4. it may be recalled, apart from the spatio-temporal framework, were spectra running from hot to cold and rough to smooth.

In the second function they gain their meaning, not in a cognitive frame of reference, but from some analogy of feeling, the examples I used were those of warmth, depth and vibrance, when no reference to temperature, dimension or movement was intended.

This statement now needs qualification because we seem to communicate feelings with some precision. It is arguable, therefore, that, as for literal discourse, there must be external publicly observable points of reference. For example, feelings of anxiety may be referred to facial expressions, or to involuntary movements.

While it is clear that we do develop a community meaning for feeling symbols and that external factors like facial expression play a part in this, it is by no means certain that all symbols gain their power to communicate in that way.

People who play the aura game for the first time are usually surprised by how often people assign the same colour to a common acquaintance's personality. Colours and shapes seem to generate common feelings, at least in people in the same culture. These colours and shapes can then be used to express feelings. There can be little doubt that natural symbols are a fact of experience, alongside those symbols whose meaning is culturally assigned.

In whatever way a symbol for feeling gains its communal meaning, it is clear that the mode of its being "cashed" and verified by the receiver is different to that for signs in the other mode of discourse. We select the form in which we will cash a received sign. We either, as it might be said, send it up to the head or down to the guts. We ask about its meaning and then its appropriateness, either by reference to a conceptual frame only, or by reference to feeling and perhaps an associated conceptual frame.

The matter is further complicated because we reduce our feelings to symbols and then in a conceptual frame of reference deduce courses of action from them, as in an ethical or perhaps legal decision. Whether such a deduced course of action could have a sense of authority for us, if it were not supported directly by the felt sense of reality, is doubtful. The source of authority for a "rational" ethic is hard to pinpoint.

iii) THE IDEAL TYPES OF RELIGION

The internal model provides a way of describing the ideal types of religious tradition in terms which lays greater emphasis on what goes on inside the adherent. It allows me to present a clearer picture of the relative significance of the received tradition. The previous model, being more external, might have over-stressed the role of the adherent's world-out-there.

Nature Religion
If a community exists in a very static context or if, perhaps because it is either a privileged or a threatened group, it deliberately fosters the status quo, then our model becomes completely closed. There is no new input of raw experience and total experience has a monistic feel to it. Because of the felt unity of experience and because belief can become dogmatic and therefore divisive, religion will tend toward being the sort which pervades all of life and to be symbolized in behavior of a natural rather than of a

separated out, specifically religious kind. The concern with texture rather than goals is automatic in this situation.

Withdrawal Religion

Withdrawal religion, although it is not a belief pattern, has a strongly cognitive base which can be seen to arise out of some elaborated form of this present model. Once the paradigm is established, this type of tradition becomes largely a behavior pattern.

The behavior pattern in this type relates to the natural order so as to limit involvement with it and is, for the most part, un-natural in the literal meaning of that word. It is highly ascetic and internally focused.

It begins by recognizing that the felt sense of reality has priority for religion and also that it is to a degree culture bound. It therefore seeks a path by which the individual (and it has to be the individual) may escape from bondage to the received tradition and the culturally limited pool of possible symbols. In its quest to feel reality as it is in itself, to experience things as pure phenomena unforced into humanly constructed categories, it also seeks escape from the functioning of the fact selection and evaluation filters.

Secular World Affirming Religion

When the context of a group's experience is in flux, or becomes otherwise unacceptable, the felt sense of reality tends to transcend present experience. This may be expressed in terms of returning to a lost paradise or as a not-yet-ness. However it is expressed it lies in the future, it becomes, in temporal imagery, eschatological or, in spatial imagery, transcendent.

This present model helps to show what happens when this experience has been long enough, or profound enough, for the tendency towards transcendence to become built into the symbolized sense of reality.

Because the pool of possible symbols is fed largely from the older tradition, the transcendence symbol tends to remain even in times when the context is calmer and more acceptable. The fact selection and evaluation processes will also be programmed to give preference to "progress", that is, they will maintain a goal orientation.

The changes wrought in the context, on the basis of the values contained in the symbolized sense of reality, will themselves render a goal oriented sense of reality plausible. In short, once the symbol of transcendence enters a system it prevents the absolutization of anything within the system and therefore tends to be self authenticating.

The symbol of transcendence is only likely to be lost if goal orientation itself is called into question. This happened in the modern western world for a variety of reasons, including the feeling that it led to excesses in conflict or other loss of texture, or simply because the goals were achieved, proved unobtainable, or turned sour. Some conflict is always the price of a goal orientation.[5]

iv) THE AUTHENTICATION OF THE PART AND THE WHOLE

The model illustrates and refines what was said concerning the authentication of tradition, that is of the authentication of the whole and of the part within the whole.

A potential part of a tradition is authenticated in two ways. First, it is authenticated quite consciously and logically by its coherence with and enrichment of the other symbols in the individual's symbolized reality which, insofar as it shares in a tradition, is corporately determined. Second, it is authenticated if it is felt to fit the felt sense of reality. The felt sense of reality, however, is not conscious. If the authentication process at this stage becomes a conscious quest, the question asked is not usually "does the symbol feel right?" but "does the symbol fit my experience?", that is, does it fit total experience in the first meaning of that term. There is, however, *no logic for relating a symbol to a literal description of experience*, whether it be a symbol of a part or of the whole.

What actually happens is, as I have stated, the experience creates a felt sense of reality (the second meaning of total experience) and the symbol either feels right within it or it does not.

The tradition as a whole can only be tested by its long term power to enrich. In relation to the model, it can be said, that the tradition as a whole is tested, not simply in the felt sense of reality, for that generates the symbolized reality in the mature person, but in the fact that the felt sense of reality is an integrated and a satisfying one. If it is not then all the contributing elements in the model, including the tradition, will be called into question.

v) CONVERSION, EDUCATION AND BELONGING

I now wish to show, in relation to the model, what contributes to the sense of religious belonging, and to do it in such a way as to assist

---

[5] It is interesting to note how Koheleth, having lost his faith in an historical salvation and returning to a cyclical view of nature, cannot accept it as a nature religionist would. The seed of goal orientation having been sown, he confronts a grand but cyclical nature with deep pessimism, unlike Job, who in his individual suffering allows nature to point to something greater beyond itself and so maintain his trust in the future.

understanding of both the phenomenon of conversion and the pastoral and educational tasks.

Within the protestant tradition of Christianity there is a strong emphasis on right belief, and prayer is thought of in very verbal terms, whether it be praise or petition.

Within the Catholic tradition one finds a greater emphasis upon meditation, and upon mood, whether it be one of adoration, penitence, or simply contemplation.

This same divide between the more cognitive and more mystical wings, is to be found in Judaism and in Islam.

The model, in making clear the relationship between the felt sense of reality and the symbolized sense of reality, shows these two emphases to be different aspects of the same religious quest.

Meditation of the less cognitive kind serves to develop and integrate the felt sense of reality and therefore to facilitate a personal and well grounded sense of belonging.

Meditation of the cognitive kind serves, as does theology, to integrate the symbolized reality, but it is also a mild form of Rümke's "doubt" and serves to keep the felt sense of reality and the symbolized reality, in relationship to one another.

Symbols play a vital role in the formation of the felt sense of reality, so the quest for an integrated felt sense of reality will clearly be aided by the integration of the symbolized sense of reality.

A sense of belonging can come suddenly or gradually and this raises the issue of what may be called conversion, healing, release or enlightenment, according to the tradition involved. A consideration of the present model shows that the move toward a sense of belonging (I will speak of it as conversion) can take place at a number of different levels.

Conversion may be a change at the level of the symbolized reality only, at the level of the felt sense of reality only, or involve both levels.

If the focus is the symbolized reality, conversion may involve gaining a new centre to the symbolized reality, one which better fits the existing felt sense of reality. It may include the surrender of part or all of the previous symbolized reality. On the other hand it may be simply an integration of a previously divided symbolized reality.

If the focus is the felt sense of reality, conversion may be a major shift of the whole, or it may be an integration of a previously fragmented felt sense, either of which might be triggered by a shift at the level of the symbolized reality.

What Leon Salzman calls "expedient conversion" would be, in terms of this model, to swop one symbolized reality for another, neither of which relates exclusively or with any profundity to the felt sense of reality. [6]

Conversion which only involves change at the level of symbol can still be a deeply felt emotional experience. Particularly will this be the case if it swops, for one that is better related, a symbolized reality with little fit, or even one that is in conflict with the felt sense of reality. This change may take place because of peer group pressure, or to legitimate some deeply felt emotion, each of which could dramatically improve the personal sense of integrity and of belonging.

It must be emphasized that a conversion at the level of the symbolized sense of reality, far from being a change in identity, may be an identity legitimating or otherwise preserving move. [7]

Clearly, religious institutions seeking converts should be aiming at modification of the felt sense of reality and the modification of symbols as a step in that direction.[8]

It is exceedingly doubtful if a complete conversion at the level of the felt sense, as distinct from an integration or recentering, could ever be sudden. The felt sense of reality is the other side of personal identity; and while identity and its conscious representation, self-image, may be lost in some sudden traumatic experience, it is notoriously difficult to rebuild.

One can understand sudden conversion in religion of the secular world affirming type, in terms of a shift in symbols for what remains largely the same felt sense of reality. One cannot understand a sudden sense of release or of enlightenment in religion of the withdrawal type, in the same way. These would be better understood as either an integration of the felt sense of reality or as a realization of what the felt sense of reality has become, when the necessary surrender of previously cherished symbols for the self and its immediate world-out-there is made.

The model also makes clear why conversion should be looked upon as a particular manifestation of a continuing adjustment process, as Rümke's "healthy doubt" and Whitehead's "transition" suggest, and not as a single discrete event.

---

[6] Leon Salzman, "Types of Religious Conversion", in *Pastoral Psychology vol.17:1966*, p.8.

[7] *ibid.*, p.18b. See Salzman's understanding of "regressive" conversion as the legitimation of hate and the ensuing conflict with the "real" self.

[8] In withdrawal religion, this primary concern is explicit, in nature religion it would be understood as the health or wholeness of the individual, in the Catholic tradition of Christianity as the nurture of the soul, and in the Protestant tradition perhaps as sanctification, or perhaps as the hidden work of the Spirit in the assurance of salvation.

Even Whitehead's "God the Companion" is not a final stage in the sense of being static. If the context of experience shifts and with it the felt sense of reality, the symbolized reality could once again reflect "God the Enemy", or even "God the Void".

Attempts at adjustment must go on all the time that experience changes, walking the tightrope between a symbolized reality that is too flexible and never defined (anomie) and a symbolized reality that is too rigid and for ever out of step with the felt sense of reality (alienation).

It is not, of course, only the symbolized reality that can be rigid and out of step with experience. The felt sense of reality may also be resistant to change and become fragmented or completely alienated. This leaves the individual concerned with a limited number of choices if he or she is to achieve reasonable integration of the felt sense of reality, of the symbolized reality, and of these with each other.

Consider, for example, young people who are of this more rigid type and whose identity has been formed in a liberal religious background with an idealistic view of the world. On leaving the nest and entering the real world and finding it to be quite other than they have been led to believe, they are either completely alienated from it, or to the degree that their felt sense of reality does change, become alienated from their inherited symbols. The remedies are limited.

They may *change*. With the help of psychotherapy (or some personality changing cult) they may manage to loosen up and bring into some conformity with the real world, both their symbols for reality and whatever part of their felt sense that has hitherto resisted change. If they cannot loosen up then their limited choices include *flight* from the problem (hyper-activity, alcohol, drugs, or worse), or *attack*, that is seeking to change the real world (political or social activism of the driven kind). Alternatively they can seek *legitimation* by moving into an institution with the same faith as their upbringing but one with a much more authoritarian stance. What they need now, is to know assuredly that the world out there is not the real. The real is as it was portrayed in their received sense of reality and its symbol set. They are right! The world is wrong! The world out there needs to be written off and their alienation from it legitimated. A return to the liberal institution of their youth would not serve that purpose.

It is not only the overtly religious who can be rigid enough to have their felt sense of reality and their symbolized reality out of step. There is what might be called, from a religious perspective, "the good materialist", the individual who has a sort of cosmic trust, who is recognizably religious, but denies it. This might arise from a situation of inner alienation in which the felt sense of reality is out of line with the symbolized reality, but this in not necessarily the case.

The experience of individuals in community can give rise to a widely shared symbolized reality, which in turn gives rise to a corporately held set of values and then to directions of socio-cultural development. When this happens it is possible for the individuals within the community to gain a sense of identity significant belonging by embracing the values of the community (or even its directions of development) as the symbols for their self-knowledge, commitment and a limited modelling of reality. This is because both sets of symbols are related to the same felt sense of reality. This is not to say that ultimate symbols are unimportant, as what was said about the symbol of transcendence indicates, but to function without them is not always the tension producing situation that it might appear.

vi) SOME PROBLEMS POSED BY THE MODEL

Considering the model from the position of those within a specific religious tradition, a number of dichotomies appear which leave the educator or pastor walking a tightrope.

It is clear that one does not wish to produce a symbolized reality which shackles the felt sense of reality. Therefore one must not present a tradition in so authoritarian a manner that it inhibits the development of the felt sense of reality by damping down active ferment concerning its relation to the symbolized sense. This indicates the need to encourage a healthy doubt.

On the other hand, one would not wish to leave the young without an adequate pool of possible and sufficiently authoritative symbols by which to express and conceptualize their own developing sense of reality. Nor would one wish to leave them unaided in that development.

The model also indicates that the advocates of a tradition should be trying to develop in their potential adherents the most genuine possible sense of reality. This would mean exposing them to the widest variety of raw experience and ensuring that this experience was a genuine sample, not a deliberately selected one. Part of religious education, therefore, would seem to be provision of a broad and stimulating raw experience in order to nurture the developing felt sense of reality. At the same time it would serve to generate the words and other symbols that adherents would need, in order to express that felt sense of reality.

Against this, many traditions regard major aspects of the world as tainting and feel that they must encourage not only their rejection but also the pretence that they are not there or not significant.

Then again, the model calls for the recognition of the historical and cultural conditioning of the fact selection and evaluation procedures. This would seem to suggest, on the one hand, that it is an educator's job to help individuals climb out of this historical and cultural bondage, so that they might ask ever more objective questions about the facts they choose to observe and how they evaluate them. On the other side it must be recognized that any society needs a fairly uniform sense of reality in its members (hopefully drawn out from the community rather than imposed) and also that any pastor would wish to offer the cumulated wisdom of his or her tradition.

We are here confronted with the need for the socialization of the young, as well as the inclusion of the more mature, into the ongoing quest of a community.

Both educator and pastor therefore, need to balance their attempts to liberate the fact and evaluation filters, with the attempt to set them in the direction that the tradition community believes to be important. It is certain that the hunting community would be taking its children out to get them spoor conscious. What is the parallel in a religious tradition?

Whatever decision individual teachers or pastors may come to on the foregoing issues, it is clear that they ought to know how the fact selection and evaluation procedures of those for whom they are responsible are programmed. To know that they need to observe their responses to actual or simulated situations.

vii) INHIBITORS OF THE DEVELOPMENT OF RELIGIOUS BELIEF

Before leaving this elaboration of Rümke's model it is appropriate to consider potential inhibitors of the development of religious belief. I will begin with those suggested by Rümke himself and then turn to those that emerge from the elaborated model.

Inhibitors of Belief in
  H.C. Rümke's model of Religious Development

a) Failure to become an ego

According to Rümke, direct cosmic experience is only available to the post-puberty individual. The individual must have climbed out of the psychological structure of the family background in which he or she grew up, in order to become the potential nucleus of a new family. Only when a strong ego sense has developed will the person have that strong sense of over-against-ness with all that is non-ego, which makes cosmic experience possible. Only then is it likely that they will stand back from all-that-out-there and ask what it is all about and how they relate to it.

To the degree that some trauma or other personal factor deprives the individual of the power to let go of old structures, to that degree will direct cosmic experience be inhibited.

b) Symbol Blindness

Even an individual who has developed a sense of being an ego, can still fail to have direct cosmic experience. This may be because he or she fails to see holistically and therefore symbolically.

In the process of the breakdown of their older psychological structures, the pre-puberty young frequently develop a highly analytical sense, a sense which is reinforced in modern technological society by an emphasis on analytical education. Looking out of their window they see houses, roads, railways and factories rather than a community. Still less do they see a symbol of the whole world-out-there to which they must relate if they are to add self-knowledge to their sense of individuality.

Because their socialization has indicated that it provides the only reliable access to reality, they remain in the I-it stance when the I-thou might be appropriate.

To the degree that individuals develop in this one-sided, over analytical way, they will be what Rümke calls symbol blind and fail to enjoy direct cosmic experience.

c) Failure of Shapes Behind Words to Mesh with Direct Cosmic Experience

I have emphasized the priority of experience to words or other symbols. Nevertheless, a full religious experience is one which has become conscious, can conceptualize and communicate experience, and pass from experience to action.

A learnt set of words which has no felt relationship with cosmic experience would inhibit this fuller religious development, as would the possession of a set of words which, while fitting the felt sense of reality, was received from such a source or in such a manner that it cannot be embraced.

d) Failure of Doubt

Should an individual, at the time when a set of words is accepted as relating to his or her personal experience, be under the influence of a religious environment which regards doubt as sin, then that set of words will almost certainly become fixed.

Experience, however, cannot be fixed. If in adult years, the adherents meets some crisis which makes major demands upon their religious belief, they may turn to their religion and find there a teenage set of words. They may then go into what Rümke calls, radical unbelief. "Doubt" may be too strong a word for some, but it means no more than a serious and honest contemplation, which constantly asks if the symbols truly fit experience and if the symbols are being truly used in the interpretation of experience. In that way the two may remain in relation.

e) Failure to Surrender

If all previous stages are successfully negotiated and individuals come to the stage of religion which A.N. Whitehead calls "God the Enemy", they may still fail to achieve the experience of God the Companion if, for one of many reasons, they cannot or will not surrender back into relationship with the reality that they discern in or behind total experience. Both to become an ego and to surrender back into the supportive relationship, requires that the individual has learnt to trust, a possibility which according to Erik Erikson may be lost very early in life.[9]

Unwillingness to surrender back will be directly related to the cost of the struggle experienced when breaking out.

Inhibitors of Belief in the Elaborated Model

As I have indicated, the present model is an elaboration of Rümke's basic structure and all the inhibitors to which he draws attention apply within this one.

The difference between Rümke's direct cosmic experience and what I have called the felt sense of reality is that one can understand the felt sense of reality to develop from childhood. It will, of course, contain much fantasy in early years and become fragmented as puberty approaches. It will be in considerable bondage to received ways of seeing, whether from parents, teachers or peers. In fact, a considerable part of education consists of plugging culturally programmed sub-units into the felt sense of reality. The problem of balancing the development of a critical intelligence with the necessary socialization was discussed above.

Inhibitors of belief which do not appear in Rümke's model are as follows:

f) Failure to Integrate or Legitimate Divisions in the Felt Sense of Reality

This has been discussed under conversion and is referred to here only for the sake of completeness.

---

[9] Erik Erikson, "Identity and the Life Cycle: Selected Papers", *Psychological Issues,* (New York, International University Press, 1959), I:1.

g) Bondage to Symbolized Reality, to Fact Selection and Evaluation Processes. - Paucity of Possible Symbols

If what I called total experience is to be wide enough to provide, not only an adequate ground for the evaluation of received tradition, but also to provide for its growth, then the individual will need to be constantly breaking out of existing limitations upon fact selection and evaluation processes and be questioning his or her symbolized reality. The last of these is what Rümke calls "healthy doubt", but the former, the critical reappraisal of fact selection and evaluation processes, is achieved by a questioning of one's values, by an enquiring and open approach to experience, and by maintaining that level of search for enrichment of experience which the post-puberty young have when they are engaged in a search for self-identity.

Limitation of the pool of possible symbols would include the situation implied by Rümke's model - that words may not fit experience - but in addition, that the words may simply not be sufficient in number and variety for the adequate conceptualization of experience.

h) Undeveloped Sense of Reality

Finally we must recognize that the felt sense of reality can be undeveloped and there is need for what in certain traditions would be referred to as "spiritual exercises" or "the practice of the presence of God".

Some people's experience is so limited that it has very little creative effect on their sense of reality, which likewise remains limited. It is interesting to get together a group of people having approximately the same context of experience, or alternatively a group to respond to a deliberately presented story or role play, and then to ask them to speak about what they see and how they feel about it.

Not only does this sharpen their experience and presumably, therefore, its effect on their sense of reality, but it can also indicate to them that they are both seeing and evaluating in a different way to others and reveal how their fact selection and evaluation procedures are programmed. Experience may be wide but still not create a lively sense of reality, unless people are stirred to feel holistically.

Some people, of course, are simply shy of expressing their deepest feelings, even to themselves, and this should not be confused with either the underdevelopment of the sense of reality or the paucity of symbols with which to express it.

CHAPTER 7

THE NATURE OF RELIGION - A SUMMARY

In this chapter I return to the religious experience of the individual and seek to draw together what can now be said of that.

It will be my conclusion that religion is related to two human drives, the one for physical and material survival, the other for the development and securing of identity, but more to the latter than the former. It will be said that religion is concerned with the human quest to "belong" to that which is perceived to be the ultimately-real.

Having arrived at the last chapter of Part I I must now seek to distil the "essential understanding of religion as a universal human phenomenon" necessary for the development of the conceptual framework in Part II. I begin by sketching in stark outline the path that has been followed.

I began this enquiry in western vein, understanding religion to be grounded in *belief about* and *relation to* a god, a god understood to be out there, above and beyond the immediate world of experience even though available within it.

I distinguished between religion as individual experience and religion as institution including tradition.

Beginning with religion as individual experience, I offered a definition, not directly of religion, but of the personal experience that the theist refers to when he or she uses the word "god". I spoke of a quasi-personal factor which met the theist in or through his or her total experience. I unpacked the words quasi-personal in terms of an experience of deep adequation between needs and provision, such that a conviction arose concerning a mind that knew and perhaps cared for one.

Recognizing that, even in the Abrahamic traditions, God is not always conceived in such personal terms, I used Whitehead and Rümke to further explore the relationship between the individual and all that is non-ego, all-that-out-there, in terms of a sense of dependence, of demand, and, once again, of adequacy or support.

In discussing the source of human knowledge of that to which one would relate ultimately, I laid emphasis upon its being known in, or distilled from, total experience. It was not to be found in any particular experience, however much that experience might be prior in time or serve to trigger awareness. I did that because:

i) I rejected the possibility of reality being tested by a single sense,

ii) because it seemed to me that all the world's major traditions have sought an integration of experience into a cosmic understanding, and

iii) because I accepted, along with Rümke, that personal religious experience begins with the experience of being an ego over against all that is non-ego. This last, is also what I understood Whitehead to have meant by "solitary" when saying that "religion is what the individual does with his own solitariness".

I then examined the processes whereby many individual experiences can build into a religious tradition and how this in turn informs and shapes the personal religious experience of those who adhere to it.

Having recognized that religious experience is rooted in total experience, it followed that the language necessary for speaking about primary religious experience must be a language for speaking of the unique. That is, it must be a symbolic language, a language expressive of inner feeling rather than overt relationship.

I then broadened the scope of the enquiry to identify and describe the distinctive types of religious tradition as these manifest in world religion.

The threads of this enquiry were then drawn together in a discussion of the "felt sense of reality" as the seat of religion in the individual.

Returning to the intention with which I began these "Foundations for a Scientific Study of Religion", I must now ask:

"What can be learned from these beginnings concerning the universal religious experience of humankind?" and therefore

"What understanding of religion promises to survive the longest as the jumping off point in a scientific study of religion proper?".

THE RELIGIOUS EXPERIENCE OF HUMANKIND

In the attempt to uncover a universal core in the religious experience of humankind I could have begun by modifying my first definition. This would have required that the meaning of the phrase "quasi-personal" be modified so that a definition in terms of it would fit those forms of Hinduism and Buddhism, among others, in which the ultimately-real is not understood to be personal. The experience of what I called "adequacy" would then have had to be accounted for in more internal terms and within a monistic system, rather than within the strongly external sense of a transcendent god and secular creation world-view. I made some suggestions about how this might be done when I considered that definition.

It will have been recognized, however, even when speaking only of the Abrahamic religious traditions, how much language is strained. How much more difficult it would be to modify a definition, such as the one used, to include non-theistic religions. I begin, therefore, in a different way.

If we no longer ask, of those manifestations of religion which we have considered, "What is the nature of the ultimately-real believed in?" and "To what experience in the believer does that belief refer?" (for these things are very tradition specific) but if we ask instead, "What activity is the individual engaged in when being religious, and why?" we may arrive at defining characteristics of religion that have a more general application.

In the process, it should be noted, we will have moved from a definition of religion in terms of a positive relationship with something external, to one in terms of some quality of the religious experience itself. I begin with the first part of the question.

i) IN WHAT ACTIVITY IS A PERSON ENGAGED WHEN BEING RELIGIOUS ?

As a minimum statement, drawn from all that we have considered, it might be agreed that:

Religion is concerned with belonging, affectively and cognitively, individually and probably corporately, to that which emerges within the whole transitory parade of experience as the ultimately-real.

This "ultimately-real" would be understood as that to which the individual most feels the need to belong in order that life might, in the long run, have meaning, security, warmth, or be otherwise enriched.

This belonging will have two aspects; a feeling for, and a minimal understanding of, the nature of the ultimately-real and an appropriate mode of belonging to the ultimately-real so perceived.

Such a minimum definition of religion, drawn largely from a consideration of religion in the Abrahamic tradition, does, I believe, represent the essence of all religion.[1]

When I considered what has seemed to count as religion east, west and south, both ancient and modern, I suggested that there was a whole spectrum of religious expression that began with the concern to plug into and manipulate the causal nexus in things for the good of human life in the here and now. This was followed by many varieties of religion that seek knowledge of the power for its own sake, mixed with use of, service of and co-operation with that power in this world. Finally it included religion that seeks as complete a withdrawal as possible from this life in order to know intimately, indeed to fuse with, the ultimately-real. In this spectrum, however much the perceived nature of the ultimately-real may change and with it the mode of belonging, the need for belonging remains the common factor.

I noted in chapter 5, that while in monistic traditions belonging is assumed and only needs to be maintained or realized, in those traditions in which reality is twofold, belonging must be established.

All other proposed satisfactions of religion such as meaning, control, security, are either a part of belonging or they necessarily presuppose it. Meaning, for example, is in part the cognitive aspect of the sense of belonging and control presupposes a relationship with the source of power.

It has sometimes been said that all religions are about salvation. This is unhelpful. The variety of possibilities, not only in the positive aspect, of those ends *for* which one could be saved, but also in the negative aspect, of those situations *from* which one could be saved, makes a mockery of the use of the single word "salvation". Belonging, on the other hand, for all its range of

---

[1] The two statements, "religion is about belonging affectively and cognitively to the ultimately-real" and "the ultimately-real is understood as that to which the individual most feels the need to belong in order that life might have meaning, security, warmth, or be otherwise enriched", may appear to be circuitous. Why not just cancel out the difficult middle term, ultimately-real? Then we could say religion is the quest to belong to that which provides meaning, security, warmth etc. This, however, fails to express the sense of unity in all-that-out-there, which Rümke labeled cosmic. There could then be many fragments meeting many needs, but nothing to belong to. Belonging presupposes the self and at least one other, or not more than a handleable number of integratable others, expressed perhaps as a Pantheon or Trinity, otherwise I am pulled apart and belonging is destroyed.

meaning, is restricted to the positive sense and has an element of common significance which transcends variety in world-views.

In summary then, the activity in which I understand the individual to be engaged when being religious, is *the quest for, realization or maintenance of, a sense of belonging to the ultimately-real.* That sense of belonging requires both a feeling for, and understanding of, *the nature of the ultimately-real* and *a mode of belonging thereto.* The mode of belonging will vary in both its cognitive and affective elements as the perceived nature of the ultimately-real varies.

Completeness requires that both the ultimately-real and the mode of belonging thereto are symbolized, so that adherents have knowledge of them in the cognitive and public sense. This, however, is not primary in religious experience, whereas a *felt* sense of the ultimately-real, and a quest for and realization of a *felt* belonging, certainly are.

I must now ask the second question with which I started this section and press behind the *what* to the *why* of religious activity.

ii) WHY DO HUMAN BEINGS ENGAGE IN RELIGIOUS ACTIVITY ?

The human drive to belong to an ultimately-real may be *sui generis*, it may not be open to further explanation. That I believe to be the case. Nevertheless, it is useful to speak of it in terms which are more familiar and this I will now do.

Human beings appear to have two basic drives. The one is for physical survival, not just the fight against death, but including also the quest for the space and material resources necessary for the realization of physical potential. The other is for the development and maintenance of identity. These two basic drives, in various combinations, give rise to other drives such as those for the survival of nation or culture group.

It may be that in the future, these two drives will come to be regarded as aspects of one life-drive. It has already been suggested that ethical behavior, such as individual self-sacrifice or otherwise, is controlled by the need to ensure the survival of genes. We are not, however, at the point where there is utility in treating identity survival and physical survival as the same quest. On the contrary, precisely because "it is sometimes more important to know that life has meaning than to go on living"[2] and because the two drives can all too

---

[2] Peter Bertocci credits this statement to a student of his. *Introduction to a Philosophy of Religion*, (Englewood Cliffs, Prentice-Hall, 1951), p.25.

easily exist in competition with each other, it is better to treat them as separate. [3]

Religion is related to both drives. There is no doubt that human beings turn to the powers-that-be when their material and physical survival is threatened. There have been those who understood religion in its entirety in this light, and in particular there have been those who understood religion to be humanity's attempt to deal with the threat of death.

Certainly, at the lower end of the spectrum of religious expressions described earlier, religion is almost indistinguishable from magic, a sort of primitive science, seeking to know the environment's cause and effect nexus so that the right button might be pressed. But ritual, however much focused on the attainment of some this-worldly physical benefit, can never be purely that. It always requires knowledge of and a link with the powers-that-be and this inevitably has implications for self-understanding.

There is considerable evidence that the drive for identity is the more important factor in religion.

Anyone who has been involved in a religious healing movement for any length of time becomes aware that, while there is much talk about successful healings, there is little or no attempt to examine the evidence. Certainly the benefit that adherent's feel, both the sick and those who are not sick (usually the majority), is out of all proportion to any physical healing that may take place.

Likewise there is evidence that supporters of prophetic movements do not fall away when the material predictions of the prophet fail but, on the contrary, in the increased chaos of the situation, support is likely to grow both in numbers and in intensity. [4]

There is also much evidence that religion is not simply reaction to the physical fact of death. The religion of biblical Israel survived for many centuries without any emphasis on a life after death. When the issue became pressing, it arose out of a concern with justice, that is, that neither the very good nor the very bad seemed to get their just desserts in this life. It was not simply a concern with physical survival for everyone nor for its own sake.

Then again, a list of what religion might be supposed to provide in relation to the drive for physical fulfillment is potentially so long, that, if it is not simply about the threat of death, one must suspect that the essence of religion does not lie here - that we have not arrived at the heart of the

---

[3] For example, see the final section on Israel in Theme (II) of Chapter 9.

[4] See for example Janet Hodgson, "A Study of the Xhosa Prophet Nxele" in *Religion in Southern Africa* vols 6:2 and 7:1.

matter. After all, life at university provides fellowship, culture, sport, perhaps even a health service and job placement. It clearly functions as a marriage agency. All of these, however, are spin offs from the one central purpose of higher education.

Such spin offs are not unimportant. They contribute substantially to one's frame of mind, to confidence in one's university and to drawing students to this university rather than that. So it is with religion, but we must not confuse spin offs with essence.

There are always certain "blessings", as a certain group of Christians tend to speak of them, that serve to authenticate a particular religious system to its adherents. Without the blessings to authenticate the system it could not succeed in creating a sense of belonging, but belonging is what it is all about, not the blessings.

On the other hand, against the position that the identity drive is primary, stands the seeming dependence of identity upon physical survival. This would seem to be especially the case, in the here and now, for those who do not look for a continued existence after death. They might be supposed to say - "If I cease to exist, how can I have an identity?" This, however, misses the point. It confuses securing identity with the continued consciousness of it.

There is, what might be called, "the atheist's salvation". It is a sense of having done all things well and so of having joined a cosmic club or of having fulfilled a cosmic code. The atheist might say "It is done, I know who I am". It is not dependent upon the individual remaining conscious of it.

I conclude that religion is primarily concerned with meaning and value and with the securing of these. That is with the identity drive, rather than with anything in the realm of the physical. The points made above all lead in that direction.

In the end, however, the evidence for this position must lie in its greater explanatory power when dealing with the phenomena generally regarded as religious. That is, with its power to survive the test of being the beginning point for a scientific study of religion.

Suffice it to say, that I believe science to be man's most organized attempt to maintain and realize his physical potential, religion to be his most organized attempt to develop and maintain identity. In this view of religion I follow Whitehead and Rümke. I summarize its operation as follows:

Within normal human development there lies a psychological experience associated with a move that is biologically indicated. This is the move of ceasing to be primarily a member of one's own family in order to becoming the potential nucleus of a new family. It is an experience which varies greatly from culture to culture and indeed in some cultures it is tailored for the individual by rites of passage. It must, however, exist in all of them.

The awareness of individuality, of having become an ego over against all that is non-ego, that is, the awareness "that I am", leads inevitably to the quest to know "what I am" and hence to a dependence upon the world-out-there. Self-knowledge is not possible in a vacuum. Rather, it is the obverse of the question "What is all-that-out-there?". [5]

In all societies, but to a very variable extent, the answer to this question comes to the young pre-packaged. In some cases the conditioning may be so successful that a strong sense of individuality does not arise until the person becomes the oldest surviving member of his or her line and responsible for the decisions of the community. On the other hand, as in the contemporary West, what is offered may be much less structured.

It is in the latter situation that the young feel a pressure to go "jolling", so that they may gain experiences to say yes to and experiences to say no to.[6] For in saying A is real, B is not, C is better than D, individuals describe not only their world-out-there but themselves to themselves.

However structured or otherwise the answer, however immediate or universal its terms, the question "who am I" is the longest lasting question in life. There is no question more ultimate, no question more a candidate in terms of which to understand the religious quest, than this one.

If in the situation the answer to the question "what is all-that-out-there" should be *maya* (deceptive) then the problem becomes one of living with the experience "that I am", without being ensnared with an answer to the question "what am I", in terms of the immediate world. The point of departure however remains the same, the experience of individuality over against all-that-out-there.

In the process of human maturing the answer sought to the question "what am I" becomes ever more ultimate. Answers may, when the world out there seems to comprise of a collection of discrete possibilities, be in terms of such factors as hair style and favorite music group. To the extent that

---

[5] Existence, perhaps physical existence, is a *sine qua non* of awareness, but the awareness "that I am" is more closely related to the existence of identity than to physical existence. In the ultimate the awareness "that I am" and the knowledge "who I am" become one. If I am aware of an ultimate reality and I am not aware of my relation to it, "I am not", for all my physical existence.

[6] "Jolling", "jorlling", or "jawlin'" is a useful South Africanism, it is said to mean "doing nothing significant intensively".

experience draws together into a cosmos, so the answer will need to be in terms of more abstract ideals.

At all levels, identity depends on relationship. Even if it is by over-against-ness rather than by identification, I still require the other in order to know who I am. Even if I do not affirm the other, I must affirm the cosmos of which the other is part and seek to belong to that, if I am to develop an identity. Thus, the drive to establish an identity is necessarily a drive to belong. Even in the special case of withdrawal religion, in which an individualistic identity may need to be overcome, it is achieved by realizing one's identification with all else.

The drive to maintain whatever identity has been established is, even more clearly, a drive to belong. It is so, because I must seek to secure my relation to that which grounds my identity.

If I am not to exist in alienation I need to belong; if I am not to exist in ultimate alienation I need a mode of ultimate belonging.

The drive to establish and maintain identity is, in the end, a drive for ultimate belonging, which is why I believe the religious drive is *sui generis* and cannot be reduced to more basic elements. The *what* and the *why* of religious activity are one and the same. That is, they are the quest for, maintenance or realization of, belonging to the ultimately-real however that may be understood.

Belonging is not static. Belonging includes the creation of needs, not just the satisfaction of them. I have emphasized the need to secure identity and therefore to secure relationship with that which grounds it, but the other side of identity is all-that-out-there. The quest to know self is the quest to know reality. Reality is always open. The quest for belonging is not simply a quest for comfort. It necessarily includes a disturbing enquiry into the reality that one would belong to.

CONSEQUENCES FOR THE UNDERSTANDING
OF RELIGIOUS DISCOURSE

Earlier I said that I would have to return from time to time to say something more about religious discourse as the understanding of the nature of religious experience developed.

In chapter 4 I concluded that myth was a necessarily affective mode of expression for a necessarily unique experience. That can now be rephrased as: "a necessarily affective mode of expression for the conceptualization of the reality to which one would belong".

Also in chapter 4 I stated that myth is about reality as it is now, not as it was in some primal time or will be in some dreamed of future. It can now be made clear why this must be so.

If religion is concerned with belonging and myth expresses the nature of the reality to which one would belong, then it must express the nature of that reality as it is felt to be *now*. Not as it is thought to have been in some long lost past, nor as it might be hoped for in some remote future, but as it is felt to be *now*. Anything other than this may be history or wishful thinking, but it is not myth and not an expression of reality.

A sense of reality will have been shaped by history and it may have a place within it for a future hope, but neither of these is presently real. Reality is experienced now.

A METHODOLOGICAL REMINDER

In chapter 1 I sought to established what would constitute a scientific approach to the study of religion. I distinguished it from theology and phenomenology, that is, from the academic "doing" and "observing" of religion. I also distinguished it from the study of some particular aspect of religion taking place within a discipline whose primary concern lay elsewhere, perhaps with history or society, perhaps with philosophy or the functioning of the human psyche.

In succeeding chapters I engaged in a quest for what was needed to begin a scientific study of religion, namely, that "understanding of religion as a whole" which would be most likely to survive as the understanding which generates the most effective conceptual framework.

I assumed from the beginning, that the study of religion for its own sake and as a universal human phenomenon must begin with the experience of the individual. Only then could one turn to the study of religious traditions, to their nature and constitutive elements and to the processes of their generation and modification.

I assumed further, that the primary interest of anyone engaged in the scientific study of religious tradition would lie, not with whence a tradition's various elements were appropriated, or by what paths they had traveled, but with *why a particular belief or practice is or was important to a particular people at a particular time.*

In chapter 6 I endeavored to show why anyone who does inquire into "why a belief or practice becomes important", is led inevitably into the dynamic interrelation between the adherents' natural and historical context and the spectacles through which they view that context. Those spectacles include what they have already come to believe. In the complexities of this partially locked-in situation, the need for a structured approach to the study of religion becomes apparent.

In chapter 7 I arrived at the paradigmatic understanding of religion as the quest for, realization or maintenance of belonging to the ultimately real.

A methodological consequence of this understanding is that the study of religion, at its most general level, will be the quest to discover:

> how individuals-in-community, at their own moment in history, experienced reality and modelled it,

> how they organized to realize or secure their belonging to that reality,

> how and why this experience, modelling and organization, changed as the external circumstances changed.

In chapter 8 I begin the construction of a conceptual framework for the facilitation of this quest. In order to do this I step back from the inquiry into religion as it actually exists and engage instead in the theoretical task of "unpacking" the consequences of the paradigmatic understanding of religion arrived at in Part I.

PART II

A GENERAL THEORY OF RELIGION

Part II is a new beginning. What has gone before was intended to tease out some of the threads which comprise the complex tapestry of religion and to arrive at an essential definition of religion as a universal human phenomenon. Here the whole procedure is reversed. Instead of looking at examples of actual religious experience we take the particular understanding of religion arrived at in part I and explore its consequences. We explore the forms that religion, understood in that way, can take and the forms that it is likely to take when human experience changes in particular directions. This theoretical exploration does two things for us.

First, it generates a framework comprised of the varieties in which religion can exist and some expectations concerning the conditions in which they are likely to exist. Within this framework we can locate aspects of actual religious traditions, observe movements among them and assign possible reasons for the changes.

Second, it tests the understanding of religion with which we began. In using it, we are asking "does this understanding of religion enable us to hold together, in one conceptual framework, more of the phenomena generally regarded as religious than any known alternative? Does it do this more simply and more fruitfully than any alternative?".

For as long as the understanding of religion with which we begin survives this test, it will remain our "paradigm" for religion. A "paradigm" being the basic understanding which controls how the total conceptual framework is generated whatever other considerations may be drawn into it.

Part I was also intended to serve as a persuasive concerning the reasonableness of the point from which Part II will begin, that is, with the paradigmatic understanding of religion as belonging.

Nevertheless, Part II stands or falls on its own. Just as this approach to the scientific study of religion will only survive if people find it fruitful, so this particular paradigm must stand or fall on its own, for the proof of the pudding lies only in the eating. If this paradigm does not meet the test, that is, if it is not the best available understanding of the nature of religion as a whole because it generates the simplest and most fruitful conceptual framework in which the greatest variety of phenomena regarded as religious can be held together, then it is to be rejected.

CHAPTER 8

THE CONCEPTUALIZATION OF BELONGING

A TYPOLOGY OF RELIGIOUS TRADITIONS

THE CHAPTER MAY BE SUMMARIZED IN FOUR STATEMENTS.

Religion can be said to be the quest for, realization or maintenance of belonging to the ultimately-real.

The conceptualization of an ultimately-real to which one would belong can only take place within three basic paradigms for reality.

These three basic paradigms for reality generate three logically coherent types of religious tradition.

All religious traditions can be located in relation to these types. Not all religious experience can be located in relation to them.

This chapter, in which I reverse my previous procedure and thus commence a scientific study of religion proper, begins by restating the conclusion concerning the nature of religion reached at the end of chapter 7. That conclusion will be the starting point, what I have been calling the "paradigmatic understanding", for the generation of a conceptual framework.

A PARADIGMATIC UNDERSTANDING
OF
RELIGION

Religion is concerned with belonging. It is the quest for, maintenance or realization of, belonging to the ultimately-real, however that may be felt or conceived.

The ultimately-real is understood to be that to which the individual most feels the need to belong in order to give meaning to, secure, or otherwise enrich his or her existence.

Such belonging has two aspects:

a felt sense of the ultimately-real, together with a minimal conceptualization of the same, and

a mode of belonging to that ultimately-real

The latter will vary appropriately with the former.

The felt sense of the ultimately-real is distilled from the individual's total experience. At the cognitive level, it is the answer to the other side of the life-long question "Who am I?", namely, "What is all-that-out-there?".

Possible answers to the question "What is all-that-out- there?" are not unlimited. There are only three possible paradigms for (that is basic ways of modelling) the nature of an ultimately-real to which one would belong.

A fourth possible response, and in my view the only non-religious one, is that it is chaos, without integrity or meaning.

Whenever it is maintained that, beyond the individual, there is something on which he or she is dependent for the development and security of self-knowledge, then religion is present even though it be in an elemental form.[1]

---

[1] If one were only aware of Samuel Beckett's "Waiting for Godot", one could easily believe that he fell into my non-religious category. As one becomes more aware of the range of his work one comes to understand his enormous respect for human beings who contrive to go on in the face of absurdity. Humanity at least is worth belonging to.

Before I enter upon a discussion of the paradigms I must distinguish two terms that will recur. The distinction is between *affirming* experience of the immediate world-out-there as experience of the real, and of finding that experience to be *acceptable*. The first (affirmation) is a cognitive assertion and an aspect of a people's world-view. That is, it is part of what they believe about "reality". "Acceptability", on the other hand, may be informed by cognitive considerations, but is in the end an affective judgment, it is part of what people feel about their experience. Thus, to affirm experience of the immediate world-out-there as experience of the real, is not to affirm that it is felt to be acceptable. I will return shortly to how acceptability is judged.

To be in the position of affirming experience as real while at the same time finding it unacceptable is, of course, an unstable situation. A classic example of this was ancient Mesopotamia, but it is a situation to be found among the traditional religions of Africa.

While ancient Egypt was, by comparison, incredibly stable, the instability of Mesopotamia was what made it the cradle of the Abrahamic traditions. Enrichment being the test, the religion of Mesopotamia could only survive as long as it took some credible alternative to arise. [2]

Having made this necessary distinction I return to the main theme of the section, the three paradigms for reality.

THE THREE PARADIGMS FOR A REALITY
TO WHICH ONE WOULD BELONG

Humankind's primary response to the world-out-there is the uncomplicated monistic one, "this is the real". However it may be experienced (as harmonious or conflicted), however it may be modelled (as impersonal or personal), it is understood as a *whole*, a whole with many interacting parts. It will remain this way for as long as world-out-there can be affirmed as that to which one would belong, or if it cannot be affirmed, then so long as no other possibility is envisaged or believed in.

If total experience cannot be affirmed as experience of the real (in the sense of being that to which one would belong) and if the alternative model can be envisaged, the quest for belonging will lead to a splitting of experience, that is, to the conceptual separating out of that which can be wholly affirmed, from that which cannot.[3] I will refer to this conceptual split

---

[2] There is a further discussion of this in chapter 9, theme III.

[3] It appears to be clumsy, but it is necessary to speak of "affirming experience as experience of the real", rather than simply "affirming experience as being of the real". This is

as a "bifurcation". The modelling of this bifurcation can take two forms. It can be modelled as a divide between reality and its appearance or as a divide within reality itself.

In the first of these two forms of bifurcation, the reason the immediate world-out-there cannot be affirmed is understood to lie in the individual's perception. It cannot be related to as the real, because it is not apprehended, either cognitively or affectively, as it is in itself. In this model reality remains monistic, a unified whole.

In the second form, the bifurcation lies in reality itself. There is a now and a not-yet, a this and a that which transcends it, a real and an ultimately-real. This dichotomy in reality, modelled temporally and spatially, is expected to be overcome when this and the above come together and reality is experienced in its fullness.

Thus there are three paradigms for reality. The latter paradigms begin with a bifurcation built in, that is, they begin with the expectation of an unacceptable experience. The first paradigm begins without such an expectation and therefore every experience that is potentially unacceptable must be dealt with *ad hoc*. If it cannot be rendered acceptable or "explained away", it will make the model of reality feel unreal, destroying the sense that there is something to belong to. For this reason, traditions falling under this paradigm can become richly complex in both myth and ritual.

It is only in the paradigm which bifurcates reality where there is a necessity to distinguish between a real and an ultimately-real.[4]   When speaking of the other paradigms either term can be used because reality is one.[5]

---

because in the paradigm that I will be calling Withdrawal Religion, what one has experience of is conceptualized as real but the experience that one has of it is understood to be warped. Thus experience is affirmed as being "of the real" but experience is not affirmed as "experience of the real".

[4] This is also true of the terms "sacred" and "profane", to which Durkheim tried so hard and so unsuccessfully to give universal definition, and of the more modern usage, "sacred" and "secular". They might conceivably refer to the I-it and I-thou relationships and their appropriate language modes, but if they propose ontological referents, that is, if they propose distinctions between something existing out there, regardless of how humankind relates to it, then it is only an appropriate distinction in the secular world affirming paradigm.

[5] I have preferred, when speaking of religion in general, to use "ultimately-real" for that to which a sense of belonging is sought or is maintained by religious activity, for it then fits all three paradigms. In speaking of the monistic paradigms individually, I have preferred to use

Why a particular paradigm is chosen or comes to dominance within a culture may be accidental, but there seems to be evidence for predisposing conditions. For example, in relation to the events of biblical history leading up to the Sinai covenant, the condition which pressed the group toward choosing the bifurcation in reality itself was a socio-cultural disturbance which lead to geographic migration and thence to a sense of a lost past and a future hope.

It seems that when the important thing about time becomes some future event, rather than natural cycles, people put their god where their hope is. That is, they place the full availability of the divine in that future time when experience will be fully acceptable and affirmable as that to which they would belong ultimately. Because this ultimately real already exists, it is also modelled as being presently "above" or otherwise spatially removed. For such a model to be satisfactory, it must include the expectation that this and that which transcends it, will come together at that future time. I will return to these predisposing conditions in greater detail in the next chapter.

Before I move to the three coherent religious systems, I reiterate that there are three, and only three, possible paradigms for an ultimately-real to which one would belong.

THE THREE LOGICALLY COHERENT TYPES OF RELIGIOUS TRADITION

The three paradigms for reality give rise to some *necessary*, that is non-negotiable, consequential symbols including a mode of belonging. These symbols are non-negotiable in the sense that to reject them is to reject the paradigm.

The paradigms and their necessary consequential symbols give rise to sets of more *flexible* symbols. Flexible symbols are those that, being generated by one of the paradigms and its necessary symbols, belong to its set, but among which clear alternatives are available or upon which significantly different emphases are possible.

As soon as it is recognized that there are three possible paradigms the question is raised of a meta-paradigm, that is, of a value set that might enable one to choose between them. In the nature of things, this may be an affective possibility, but it cannot be a conceptual one.

---

the term "real" for that to which belonging is to be realized or maintained, in order to emphasize the monism.

These three sets of symbols, each including a paradigmatic symbol together with its necessary and flexible consequential symbols, correspond to the three logically coherent types of religious tradition identified in chapter 5. These coherent types of religious tradition are ideal, and no existing religious tradition may fit without remainder into any one of them. They will be seen to have incompatible modes of engagement with the immediate world-out-there and therefore to be mutually exclusive. Thus, they provide an adequate permanent frame in which the ever-shifting living traditions of the present and past can be located. 6

I previously labelled these coherent types (so as to reflect the way adherents understand and engage with their immediate world-out-there) as Nature Religion, Withdrawal Religion, and Secular World Affirming Religion.7 I will continue to use those labels and will capitalize their initial letters throughout the rest of this chapter.

The material which follows is not set out in a manner conducive to an easy first reading but for ease of reference. The three coherent types, the paradigms together with their consequential symbols, are set out in tables. The tables are not to be read on their own. Each entry in the left hand column of a table is also the heading of the explanatory and illustrative section of text in relation to which it is to be read. The material under each heading is relatively self-contained, but there is a logic in the order of their presentation and there will be an advantage, on first reading anyway, in following that order. There are some additional headings in the text which are not included in the tables. I begin with the basic variable that provided the justification for the labels chosen for the three types.

EXPERIENCE OF THE IMMEDIATE WORLD-OUT-THERE

This is the paradigmatic symbol. Each of the three forms that it can take grounds one of the ideal types of religious tradition. The response to this basic aspect of the types (what I will be calling the "mode of engagement") is likely to be the most visible factor to an outside observer.

---

6 Actual living traditions may, of course, include symbols picked up along the way, which are not consequential upon the paradigms, but have become culturally significant for some other reason.

7 The choice of these labels was explained in chapter 5.

In Nature Religion experience of the immediate world-out-there is affirmed as experience of the real.

In Withdrawal Religion, while the world-out-there is acknowledged as real, it is not experienced as it is in itself, therefore experience of it is not affirmed as experience of the real, but is regarded as deceptive and a snare.

In Secular World Affirming Religion experience of the immediate world-out-there is affirmed as experience of the real but as secular, that is, not as experience of the ultimately-real.

PARADIGMATIC SYMBOLS AND THE NECESSARY CONSEQUENTIAL SYMBOLS AND SOME OTHER FEATURES OF THE THREE LOGICALLY COHERENT TYPES OF RELIGIOUS SYSTEM			
1			
NON-NEGOTIABLE SYMBOLS AND FEATURES	NATURE RELIGION	WITHDRAWAL RELIGION	SECULAR WORLD AFFIRMING RELIGION
EXPERIENCE OF IMMEDI- *is* ATE WORLD-OUT-THERE	AFFIRMED AS OF THE REAL	NOT AFFIRMED AS OF THE REAL	AFFIRMED AS OF THE REAL BUT IS NOT ULTIMATE
REALITY *is*	MONISTIC	MONISTIC	DUALISTIC
CHANCE AND DETERMINISM	CHANCE EXCLUDED	CHANCE EXCLUDED	CHANCE, PRESENT
MODE OF BELONGING TO ULTIMATELY-REAL	ASSUMED must be maintained or repaired	ASSUMED needs to be realized individually [*]	to be SOUGHT individually
NATURE OF *is* ULTIMATELY-REAL [*] but see the text.	no rigid distinction between personal and impersonal		PERSONAL

REALITY

Both Nature Religion and Withdrawal Religion hold experience to be monistic and all that is experienced, therefore, to comprises the ultimately-real. If there are gods, then they are higher in the system than humans in the same manner as humans are higher than the animals, but they all belong to the same system. Secular World Affirming Religion is dualistic, there is an ultimately-real to which one would belong ultimately and there is the rest of experience. These two are quite different in kind.

As indicated, transcendence, the gap between the real and ultimately-real in Secular World Affirming Religion is modelled spatially (by the ultimately-real being above) and temporally (by its being future). The essence of the difference, however, is neither spatial nor temporal but concerns availability. The essence of transcendence is that the reality to which one would belong ultimately is not now *fully* available and that which is now fully available is not that to which one would belong ultimately. What is looked for is that future point in time at which this and that which transcends it will come together.

Transcendence has necessary consequences which, individually or in combination, give this type of religion its characteristic traits. It makes time linear, the ultimately-real personal, and belonging something that has to be sought. It establishes three actors, the individual, the real and the ultimately-real, and it establishes three pathways by which the individual might belong to the ultimately-real. I will return to each of these consequences later.

A monistic world-view must regard the cosmos as a closed system of cause and effect so that its supposed connections are almost mechanically conceived. That is, its connections are of the "If you press the button over here the bell rings over there" type. Thus in monistic traditions where experience of the immediate world-out-there is affirmed as real, magic is indistinguishable from aspects of religion. Each is a traditional science which offers knowledge of underlying cause-effect relationships which can be manipulated for advantage or disadvantage. If ritual does not work, it has to be because it was not performed correctly or some stronger force acted against it.

In traditions of the Nature Religion type, the spectrum of possibilities for the conceptualization of the powers-that-be moves from just such a mechanistic conception, through a quasi-personal vital force pervading all of life, to gods defined clearly in personal terms. Even in this last case, however, if the gods do not respond, it is more than likely that the necessary ritual was imperfectly performed. In a monistic system there has to be an explanation for every event.

CHANCE AND DETERMINISM

In monistic traditions there is no such thing as chance. Because everything takes place in a closed system, every event must have both a cause and a consequence.

In Nature Religion the community may absorb some of these consequences, but in Withdrawal Religion, with its necessary focus on the individual, the significant outworkings take place in the individual life that provoked them. It is then spoken of as *Karma*.

In the dualistic traditions, in an ultimate and philosophical perspective, the ultimately-real and the real together comprise a closed system. There is nothing acting upon these two from without. What has begun must run its course.[8] However, from the point of view of each of them in relation to the other, there is the possibility of new beginnings. Transcendence, the wholly otherness of the divine, and its consequent personal character, create a sense of freedom for humankind, *vis-à-vis* the secular and a sense of chance in any matter of less than ultimate import. From the human side this includes the possibilities of miracle (as distinct from magic) and of being forgiven, picked up and allowed to start again, the consequences of individual and corporate shortcomings having evaporated or having been absorbed by the divine.

THE MODES OF BELONGING TO THE ULTIMATELY-REAL

In Nature Religion belonging is assumed. It must be maintained or (should it become fragmented) repaired.

In Withdrawal Religion belonging is assumed, but each individual needs to realize that oneness.

In Secular World Affirming Religion belonging is not assumed, the transcendence gap intervening, and therefore it must be sought.

I say sought, rather than established, because belonging in this paradigm can never be considered a full belonging. The belonging that is sought would destroy the paradigm should it be achieved. The best that can be achieved, without threatening the paradigm, is the sense of a link that guarantees complete belonging in some future situation. In this paradigm the need to belong is, in fact, a need not-to- belong-fully. It must retain the sense of not-yet-ness.

Jewish people, for nearly 2000 years, said "next year in Jerusalem". Their ambivalence about going there when finally it became possible

---

[8] I return to this in chapter 12 in the section dealing with freedom and determinism.

has been characterized as neurotic, but it is a necessary feature of all Secular World Affirming Religion.[9] To have goals is always to be not-yet, to be alienated in part, and therefore to live with an existential guilt concerning the present and desire concerning the future. It is this that is the driving force of progress. It would be identity shattering to arrive, for it would destroy one's very sense of the nature of reality.

It is a consequence of the Secular World Affirming paradigm, in which belonging must be sought, that the individual adherent exists in a state of *essential* estrangement or alienation. When this is coupled with the goal orientation and the individual freedom and therefore responsibility which also belong to this paradigm, the continuing estrangement may be expressed as sin, and a sense of guilt enters in. With that, comes the need for some kind of a redemption.

Where responsibility is not stressed, as it is not, for example, in the Withdrawal Religion paradigm, with its *existential* but not essential estrangement, then the individual's situation might be likened to sickness, but not to sin. Although, being a permanent and universal state until realization is achieved, neither alternative is a very likely parallel.

In the Nature Religion paradigm where belonging is assumed and is assumed to be realized, fragmentation and disharmony can only be understood as a temporary existential experience. This experience is identical with sickness, and consequently the emphasis is appropriately laid upon recovering wholeness. Medicine and religion are one. Thus it was, that the sin-guilt emphasis of some Christian missionaries found no echo in Africa. On the other hand there should be no problem in Africa, as there is in the West, with putting together pastoral theology and pastoral psychology, the "religious" and the "secular" disciplines, for sin and sickness are one.

When I introduced the modes of belonging in the Secular World Affirming Paradigm, it was with the two logics of belonging familiar in the Abrahamic family and the sectarian alternative. I labelled them "direct cosmic belonging", "indirect cosmic belonging" and "compensatory", or "reduced reality belonging". The former two are logics of belonging. That is, they are the way in which people think of their relation to the ultimately-real. They do not consciously include a relation to the real, nor do they enable one to understand how that relation functions in individual identity. There is need, therefore, for a more discriminating way of locating the great variety of both overt and covert styles of religious belonging in this paradigm. This

---

[9] A B Yehoshua, "The Golah - As a Neurotic Solution" in *Forum on the Jewish People, Zionism, and Israel No.35.*

becomes possible with a small elaboration of the original schema and I introduce it here.

It is a consequence of transcendence that there are always at least two paths by which the individual may relate to the ultimately-real. It may be done directly, as it were face-to-face, or it may be done in relation to the real, as it were side-by-side or *sub specie aeternitatis*. In addition the divine may be understood to have established within the real (the creation) a bridgehead, in belonging to which one belongs to the divine. There are, therefore, three possible pathways. It is possible to locate all modes of belonging in relation to these three basic paths. I return to this in detail in chapter 11.

That belonging cannot be assumed, but must be sought, makes it possible to distinguish between a felt sense of belonging and what might be called "actual" belonging. To question whether a person *actually* belongs, as distinct from simply *feeling* that they belong, is a logical question. It is a question asked within a particular religious tradition and is concerned with the ontological status of the individual, that is, with what they believe they *are* rather than with what they feel or think. It relates to the tradition's "logic of belonging" and, within that, to the conditions upon which the individual may belong, and whether these conditions have been fully met.

This distinction, of course, is the reverse to that which exists in Withdrawal Religion. According to that type of tradition the individual always belongs essentially, that is ontologically, even though existentially he or she may not feel that they do.

THE NATURE OF THE ULTIMATELY-REAL

I have said that there is, at the popular level anyway, a tendency to characterize experience of the unique as personal. It feels that way. This is probably because our most typical experience of the unique is when we opt, in Buber's terms, to treat another person as Thou.

In the two monistic types, however, there is no rigid distinction between the personal and the impersonal. In Withdrawal Religion, logically speaking, the distinction should disappear and with it the more ultimate gods. In that paradigm one is inevitably on one's own, but the very nature of reality is on one's side.

On the other hand, in the dualistic tradition the distinction between personal and impersonal is a critical one. The relation between the ultimately-real and real is dependent upon it. This is because human beings are only familiar with two models of causation.

There is the mechanistic one, which one might picture as wagons in a train pushing and pulling one another, and the volitional model, with which we are all very familiar, but which we cannot picture. When I think of my arm moving, nothing happens, when I will it to move, it does just that, but I cannot picture the connection between what I think, that is the intention, and the nervous system which directs the muscles. Alternative models of causation, such as modern science has begun to explore, are certainly not of the kind that could hold a feeling of reality for ordinary mortals. Therefore, if causation cannot be modelled mechanistically, it must be modelled volitionally.

The transcendence gap in the Secular World Affirming paradigm excludes a mechanistic modelling. It therefore requires that the relation of the ultimately-real to the real be modelled volitionally. It follows that the ultimately-real must be conceived as quasi-personal, that is, as a god whose every act in relation to the real is an exercise of the divine will.

That there is no adequate alternative to a highly personal view of the ultimately-real within this paradigm has always created something of a problem. In this present time the necessity of having a credible symbol for the divine is being weighed against the cost of having one that is male or female, but I do not believe this to be the major problem. Given the frontiers of knowledge, particularly perhaps those of cosmic physics, it is difficult to see how the personal category can be sufficiently enlarged to contain a credible modelling of the ultimately-real.

It is not that modern western people can no longer believe in a goal toward which things are moving but rather that their notion of that goal has outgrown the personal category which contained it. Yet there is nothing to replace it. The more transcendence is emphasized the greater the pressure toward a personal sense of the divine, however remote it might be. Only an immanent modelling of reality can also be impersonal, but that is to lose the sense of a goal.

It is not only the relationship of the ultimately-real to the real that has to be understood volitionally, but also *vice versa*. Because, in this paradigm, belonging has to be sought and the ultimately-real must be conceived as personal, the individual's response to the ultimately-real must be a personal one. A personal response to volition is itself volitional. The structure of the belonging, therefore, is some sort of *covenant*.

A deity, that is, an ultimately-real modelled as personal, must also have a character. Thus, in the Secular World Affirming paradigm, there is a very different normal relation to reality than that which pertains, for example, in Nature Religion. In the latter, the individual, being firmly related to the immediate, has no need (save in the direst circumstances) to explore the nature of or relate directly to that which lies beyond. A general cosmic trust will suffice. In Secular World Affirming Religion on the other hand, the character of the ultimately-real must be known and lived with. Cosmic trust is not generally sufficient.

That there is a divine character and that the nature of the relationship between the divine and humanity is a covenant are necessary symbols in this coherent type. The nature of that covenant and the nature of the divine character are, however, second-remove symbols (with some flexibility).

The divine character is central to the manner in which the adherent of Secular World Affirming Religion relates to both the ultimately-real and the real. The three principal ingredients of divine character, expressed in images such as king, judge and father, may be summarized as sovereignty, righteousness and love. A shift in the balance of these three will have a major impact, not only upon the experience of belonging to the deity, but upon the whole religious tradition. Perhaps the most important difference between the three members of the Abrahamic family of faiths, Judaism, Islam and Christianity, is that they have traditionally emphasized a different one of these traits while acknowledging the importance of all of them. The distinction has not always held but it has done much to determine the overall ethos of each tradition.

In chapter 11 I will return to the character traits of the divine and will consider them in combination with modes of belonging to the divine, for together these two have major consequences for what might be called the quality of belonging, and therefore for the role that religion plays in life in general and mental health in particular. An indirect corporate belonging to a divine that is perceived to be high in sovereignty and love, is likely to be a very supportive relationship; while a direct and individual belonging to a divine perceived to be high in sovereignty and righteousness must be very demanding.

THE TWO TYPES OF BELONGING

I have spoken of the sense of belonging in very general terms but in fact it can take two significantly different forms. One may be called "identity" in which a lack of difference is the criterion of unity. The other may be called "complementarity" in which different functions within a wider inter-relation is the criterion of unity. Clearly, these are related to a distinction drawn earlier between a sense of unity likened to the impression made by the bowl of porridge, that is of sameness, and that likened to the impression gained from looking into a watch mechanism, a sense of unity generated by the fitting together of clearly distinguishable parts.

Identity is, as to the sameness which constitutes the relationship, essentially static. Complementarity establishes what each part requires from and must contribute to the others, which, on the personal and ethical level, would be needs and obligations. The elements that constitute it can always be changing and so it is more easily associated with personal relationship. Complementarity belonging necessarily has a strong cognitive content, whereas identity belonging tends to the affective.

In Nature Religion, complementarity *within* the whole is an important aspect of belonging, each part is real and immediate, having its own *telos*, its own purpose within that whole. However, there may also be the sense of a vital force interflowing all things which would contribute toward a sense of identity with the whole. Complementarity-belonging to the whole, insofar as this becomes conscious, cannot be purposive in Nature Religion, for the whole has no goal, but it can be structural for the whole can have a pattern.

In Withdrawal Religion identity is the only possible mode of belonging to the whole. Complementarity is excluded because the parts could not be known as they are in themselves.

In Secular World Affirming Religion belonging by identity is excluded as to essence, but remains as to form. There can be no present identity in kind, for that is excluded by transcendence. The personal modelling of the ultimately-real, however, makes belonging by identity possible, for example, as male, as parent or as having the experience of age. Belonging by complementarity, of course, as child, as female (where the ultimately-real is conceived as male) as one who has fallen and needs to be picked up, and many other such, is the more common. Thus, the dualism of the Secular World Affirming paradigm opens up the possibility of a dynamic complementarity belonging to the ultimately-real such as is not possible with the "totality" in the monistic traditions.

Complementarity need not be simple. It can be a belonging deep within a team, hierarchy, or other structure that is in turn related to the ultimately-real. However, the complementarity type of belonging to the divine raises a cognitive problem within the Secular World Affirming traditions. This is because it is difficult, if not impossible, to conceive of a complementary belonging which does not suggest needs in the divine.

This is a problem which haunts the theology of creation. If God needed the creation it suggests some imperfection in the divine. If the creation was not needed it suggests arbitrariness in the creative act. There are, however, needs that can be understood to arise from perfection itself, which is a static and therefore impersonal category. Perfection, it is said, can only change for the worse so it cannot change if it is to remain perfect. There are models that may succeed in avoiding this, for example, the need to externalize the possibility of suffering (or any passion) in an impassible divine if love is to have meaning, might be one of these.

Belonging to the real as distinct from the ultimately-real, in Secular World Affirming Religion, may be by identity, for example, a common creaturehood, but it is much more likely to be by a deeply structured complementarity. I will return to this when I deal with what generates a sense of meaning in life in each of the paradigms, and again in chapter 11 when I discuss aggregations significant for identity.

NOTE : THE REAL IN THE SECULAR WORLD AFFIRMING TRADITION

I must take a moment to deal with what it means to speak of all that is experienced (other than the ultimately-real) as "the real" in the Secular World Affirming paradigm. Primarily, it means that, as with the ultimately-real, its significance cannot be diminished without diminishing transcendence and thus beginning a move out of the paradigm. This has a number of inter-related consequences:

> *the real is such that something of the ultimately-real can be experienced through it*, otherwise it would not be the case that *the coming together of the real and that which transcends it, can be worked towards within it.*

If this were not the case then the ultimately-real might simply arrive at the end in a way that was discontinuous from this present experience. If that were so then the real would be simply a context in which one existed while awaiting rescue. Nothing could be known of the ultimately-real through it, nor even a language be learned within it appropriate to the communication of divine revelation. It might as well all be a dream. There would be *no significant this to come together with that* and one would have moved out of the paradigm.

TIME

In Nature Religion, because this present experience is the real and therefore a given, there is no question of beginnings or ends. Change, of course, is a feature of all life, but as it is not going anywhere it must be cyclical, or at least rhythmical or pulsating.

A seeming exception to the above statement in religious traditions of this type is a frequent concern with how existence or significant aspects of it took their present form. These are frequently referred to as creation myths but this is not helpful. They are not about the beginning of the real, but about changes within it.

PARADIGMATIC SYMBOLS AND THE NECESSARY CONSEQUENTIAL SYMBOLS AND SOME OTHER FEATURES OF THE THREE LOGICALLY COHERENT TYPES OF RELIGIOUS SYSTEM			
2			
NON-NEGOTIABLE SYMBOLS AND FEATURES	NATURE RELIGION	WITHDRAWAL RELIGION	SECULAR WORLD AFFIRMING RELIGION
TIME is	CYCLICAL biological, maybe astral	CYCLICAL rhythmic aeons	LINEAR
TEST OF QUALITY OF is EXPERIENCE	TEXTURE ONLY	TEXTURE ONLY	GOALS AND TEXTURE
GROUND OF is MEANING OF EXISTENCE	GRAND DESIGN (pattern)	GRANDEUR	GRAND DESIGN (purpose)
MODE OF ENGAGEMENT with world is to out there	FIT INTO	WITHDRAW FROM	TAKE HOLD AND SHAPE

In Nature Religion the conceptualization of time is not dominated by historical events, but by natural events and therefore by natural symbols. Such events are themselves part of what is conceived to be a cyclical reality.

Conceptualization of time usually reflects the seasons and their impact upon agricultural and pastoral concerns. It also reflects the human life cycle. It may reflect cycles manifested by significant aspects of local experience. Consider, for example, the role of the Nile in ancient Egypt. Particularly if life experience is chaotic and the day sky is a threat as much as a blessing, the cool order of the night sky may become a positive symbol, in which case the longer astral cycles may come to influence the conceptualization of time.

It is said of African society that it is backward thinking, that reality lies in the past and that it has little sense of future. There is some truth in this observation, but it must not be understood in a negative sense. In a monistic world-view there is no concern with a distant future but there is an immediate future to be shepherded in. The past is the known, the future is the unknown. The past is that on which the future is to be built. The past is a vital factor in determining the future. Care is always taken to link the present, concerned as it always is with the future, with what has gone before. Reality is one.

In a situation where goals do not govern individual existence and therefore specialization in terms of them is not available, identity, indeed prestige, is dependent upon present relationships and these include their history. Where and what one comes from is important in identity. A child's attitudes to life are mainly determined by her or his knowledge of the history of the family or clan or even the tribe as a whole. Rituals that link the new-born to the past are filled out in the telling of this history.

In Africa history rolled on. In common with other non-literate societies African people were not in bondage to a fixed version of their history. While the past was respected, so were the needs of those to whom the past was to be taught. History was told to communicate the values of the group to the new generation and to affirm them for the old. If circumstances reshaped values, the need to communicate values might reshape history. While not all myth is history, in this situation the telling of history functioned mainly as myth, that is, as the communication of the contemporary felt nature of reality.

In Withdrawal Religion time ought not to feature because all its indicators, although real, are deceptive. There can be no objective knowledge of a past or future, only experience of the individual's own quest for the realization of belonging. Time in the sense of succession, but not in the sense of duration, could be registered on a recognized path to realization.

Because all is real and is one, and because change is experienced, and indeed may account for the deceptive quality of immediate experience, cycles or pulsations may be understood to be an aspect of the real. Thus while the devotee may long for the still heart of reality, its pulsations may be recognized and be symbolized, not in aspects of the turmoil that is biological time, but in aeons, that is, the millions upon millions of years in which a whole cosmos might be deployed, re-absorbed and replaced.

In Secular World Affirming Religion time is linear. If the ultimately-real is to be unconditioned by the real, the real cannot share the eternal status of the ultimately-real. The ultimately-real being conceived in volitional terms, the dependence of the real upon the ultimately-real is expressed as an act of will, that is, as creation and destiny. Time and space, which also must not condition the ultimately-real, but which are in any case not conceivable without objects, are understood to be part of the creation. Time, therefore, has a beginning and a destiny.

It is not wholly accurate to speak, as I did above, of linear time as a consequence of the transcendence symbol. Certainly, once the symbol of transcendence has been established, linear time is one of its logical consequences. It is historical experience generating a sense of linear time, however, which renders the paradigm and its central symbol authentic and its adoption likely. Once the transcendence symbol has been established it creates its own sense of not-yet-ness, but it would only arise and could only survive in an experience which renders major involvement with a future goal desirable and its fulfillment credible.

Once the transcendence symbol has been established, finitude, beginning, and destiny is what prevents the real from limiting the ultimately-real ultimately. In experience, however, it is the other way around. It is a sense of linear time that gives an authoritative feel to the dualistic ontology.

THE EVALUATION OF EXPERIENCE

I now return to the question of how acceptability of experience is judged and for this purpose, to some further distinctions.

The first distinction to be made is that between an immediate and affective judgment concerning the *quality of present life experience* and a judgment that may contribute to the former but which must be distinguished from it, namely one concerned with the *meaningfulness of existence*. They are both factors in the evaluation of an engagement with life within a particular paradigm. The quality of experience may be judged solely by its present *texture*, that is, by how it feels now, or by a combination of *goals* and texture.

In a linear time world-view, individuals are able to set goals for themselves, or embrace goals authenticated by their being the goals of the wider society. They can then evaluate their lives in accordance with their contribution towards or success in terms of those goals. There is a trade-off here, in which present texture is sacrificed for the possibility of attaining some future goal. Goal orientation may be restricted should religions of this type also have a deterministic quality or should it be suggested that individual initiative may endanger salvation.

In linear time traditions, both goals and texture are available as tests for the quality of life, but one would be moving out of the type if goals did not play a major role. Goals need to be determined and described, and therefore goal-oriented traditions require a considerable cognitive content.

In a cyclical time world-view, present texture is the only available test for the quality of experience. In Nature Religion this would include harmony, health and prosperity. In Withdrawal Religion, because experience is deceptive, even the desired texture must be expressed negatively, for example, as the absence of suffering. There is a whole, and it is worth striving for a conscious belonging to that whole, but it is an unstructured and ineffable whole. It has to be the viewpoint of Withdrawal Religion that the only satisfying texture is the texture of detachment.

Within texture-oriented religion what is sought is a texture which is more or less immediate, whether social or personal. It is a goal of a sort, but a short term one.

In goal-oriented religion one is concerned with longer term goals; one generation sacrificing something of its texture of life for some gain in texture for succeeding generations.

Goal orientation and texture orientation, therefore, are not two distinct categories but rather the ends of a spectrum. The former as well as the latter must be described in terms of the texture sought if it is to be authentic.

When, within a basically goal-oriented tradition, there is a loss of faith in goals or no clearly authentic goals recommend themselves, then one must expect a seeking for texture as a means of evaluation of life, probably without learning the lesson of detachment.

It is not easy to find satisfaction in the quietude of texture after the excitement of goal orientation. Texture orientation, unlike goal orientation, must take the world as it finds it, and that is not usually unambiguous. For whatever reason, among those who have been goal orientated an emphasis on texture seems to create its own thirst. If ordinary texture will not suffice, then the move is to more way-out and violent textures and if and when the possibilities of a positive evaluation of life have been exhausted, to self-destructive behavior and oblivion.

One reason for the revolt against goal orientation is that goals are frequently competitive and, in terms of beliefs about them, dogmatic and divisive.

Within a goal-oriented tradition it is possible for the goals to become *pseudo*. This happens when some measure of progress toward a goal, or condition for the existence of a goal, becomes a goal in itself. Examples of these might be profitability, productivity, freedom, and equality.[10]

Another way of seeing this is to say that a further consequence of a loss of authentic goals is that pre-occupation with ideas like freedom, equality, and efficiency cease to be pre-occupation with goals and become pre-occupation with textures. People cease to be concerned with freedom to achieve a goal and not seriously with freedom from something, but rather

---

[10] One way of describing what is happening in such a situation is to say that there is a failure to describe the goals in terms of the texture of their end point, failing to say what one is going to do with the products, or the time saved, or to say free from or for what, or equal in what. To be authentic, goals must be described in terms of their end point texture, what it is that is being sought. The examples just given are not rational end points.

with the *feeling* of freedom. Likewise concern can be with the *feeling* of equality and with the *feeling* of efficiency.

THE GROUND OF MEANING OF INDIVIDUAL EXISTENCE
INDIVIDUAL ACHIEVEMENT OR PARTICIPATION IN A GRAND DESIGN

Related to the evaluation of experience by goals or texture is the question of the meaningfulness of life. For life to be meaningful one of two conditions must be fulfilled. Either there must be individual achievement, which may have to include individual survival beyond death,[11] or there must be the sense of a grand design in the reality to which one belongs.

If there is a sense of grand design then it is possible for individuals to understand themselves as a *pleroma*, that is, that which fills up something to completeness.[12] All individual entities are, in this sense, equal - without any one of them the totality would be imperfect. Meaning depends upon the grandeur of that to which one belongs, not upon the size of one's contribution within it. The king and the village idiot are each a *pleroma* in the Creation.

If there is no sufficiently grand design, then meaning must be supported by individual achievement, measured, one supposes, against the achievement of other individuals.

If one has the sense of a grand design, there is no pressure to believe in individual survival in order to maintain meaning. To have caught sight, for a single moment, of the grandeur of the design of which one is a part, however small, is sufficient to invest the individual's life with significance. If there is no such grand design, and meaning depends on individual achievement, then death presents a major threat to meaning.

---

[11] But see the comment on the atheist's salvation in chapter 6 (ii) and note 25 below.

[12] Thomas Aquinas introduces this idea when discussing the will of God in The Summa Theologica Pt.I Q.19 Art.6 "He (God) wills some things to come about necessarily and others contingently so that there may be a pattern (right order) of things for the *complement* (perfection) of the universe.".

For most of the Old Testament Biblical period there was no emphasis on individual survival. This was in keeping with their Mesopotamian origin but they had had plenty of opportunities to import or develop such beliefs had they needed them, and people were seeking such belief even in Mesopotamia. Only the sense of corporate destiny accounts for the lack of interest, when that diminished an interest soon developed.

In each of the paradigms, the meaningfulness of individual existence is a prerequisite for a sense of belonging. Once established, the sense of meaningfulness releases the individual from ego dependence upon each and every aspect of immediate experience and, as such, is virtually the sufficient cause of a sense of belonging in Withdrawal Religion. It is close to faith understood as trust, but it does not tell one who one is or how to relate to all that is not self and it is not, therefore, a sufficient cause of a sense of belonging in the other paradigms.

I have used the phrase "grand design" as though it were a basic variable, but it is not. It needs to be further broken down before it can be applied within each of the paradigms.

"Meaningfulness" in the West is usually associated with purpose but it does not have to be. The grandeur which provides the sense of meaning may not reside in a purpose but in a pattern or simply in a sense of "worthwhileness".

In the linear time world-view of Secular World Affirming Religion, "grand design" might refer either to the creation as a given, which is a relatively static sense, or to the divine hand in history, which would have a strongly dynamic (goal-oriented) sense. Meaning in the former sense is the result of belonging to a pattern, in the latter it is the result of having a place in a purpose. Both of these are strongly, what was called earlier, complementary-belonging.

Buddhism can be understood as an invitation to replace individual achievement and survival, as the ground of meaning, with "grand design" as "worthwhileness".

In this type, it might be supposed that "worthwhileness" would have to be experienced directly, but that is not entirely the case. Even in traditions in which experience of the immediate world-out-there is understood to be deceptive, it is nevertheless a manifestation of the real and experience of it may generate a sense of its potential richness.[13] The experience of being a

---

[13] In the early days of its move into television, the British Broadcasting Company recorded a number of programs the purpose of which was to fill gaps between scheduled programs of uncertain length. One of these programs was of swans swimming down the Thames. They could swim for one minute or for five. Another of these, and the one that serves my purpose here, was of a pair of hands working upon a lump of clay on a potter's wheel. The hands gradually moulded the clay into the shape of a vase of some beauty. One could almost feel the gasp around the country as the hands pressed it down into the lump and began again. The second shape was more beautiful than the first and one had a sense of relief until that too was suddenly destroyed. So it proceeded. The moral, if one would not be hurt by the destruction of each beautiful manifestation, is not to become attached to them, but rather to allow all of them to teach one of the potential richness in the permanent, if previously unattractive, lump of clay and the pair of ordinary looking hands.

pleroma is not available in this type because, in spite of what has just been said, belonging must be of the identity kind.

One can summarize the above by saying that "grand design" can be understood as "grand purpose", "grand pattern", or simply as a general "sense of grandeur".

In Nature Religion, just as belonging can be by identity, so the ground of meaning can be by a general sense of "worthwhileness" in the whole with which one identifies, or in the life force that pervades it. However, because the paradigm affirms the reality of individual entities, it is much more likely to be grounded in the grandeur of pattern. It cannot be in grandeur of purpose because present texture is what matters.

While the permanence of individuals is usually affirmed in traditions of this type, it is very much as part of the permanence of the whole. Individual permanence is not essential for the meaningfulness of existence, it is a bonus, but one that does not threaten the paradigm if emphasized.

In Secular World Affirming Religion, on the other hand, an emphasis on individual survival can threaten the paradigm. For the real may then only enjoy a limited reality as a "theater" in which individuals "perform" in the quest for individual approval and reward from the ultimately-real.

Essential to this paradigm is a "grand design" of the purpose kind and consequential within it, a "grand design" of the pattern kind. "Grand design" as general "worthwhileness" is excluded as the ground of meaningfulness, because belonging, as identity with the ultimately-real is excluded, save as to those limited aspects stemming from the personal modelling of the ultimately-real. Stress on belonging of the identity kind, as with stress on individual survival, tends to the diminution of the real, and therefore to the diminution of transcendence. Such options threaten the paradigm.

If individual survival after death, not individual permanence, is affirmed in this paradigm, then it must be by re-creation on the other side of the transcendence gap and therefore discontinuous in time; otherwise the real and the ultimately-real have come together and the paradigm is extinguished. That is to say, belief in immortal souls is not tenable in this paradigm but resurrection is.

In the modern western world, the difficulty of believing in individual survival lies in conceptualizing it in traditional, or indeed in any credible form. In a situation where the norm is to affirm the reality of immediate experience, that which cannot be conceptualized seems less than real. Therefore trust in the meaningfulness of existence based on survival is also hard to maintain.

If the Secular World Affirming paradigm is to retain its primary place in the West, something of the grand design needs to be restored to take the burden off individual survival as the sole ground for meaningful existence.

The flirtation with the Buddhist and reincarnational alternatives, alongside the traditional Secular World Affirming mode of engagement, is understandable as a quest for individual meaning, but in the end it is fragmenting.

MODE OF ENGAGEMENT WITH THE WORLD-OUT-THERE

THE MODE OF ENGAGEMENT AND THE MODE OF BELONGING

In world-views, where the immediate world-out-there is not the ultimately-real and, even more so, where the immediate is real but experience of it is deceptive, the mode of engagement with the world-out-there must be clearly distinguished from the mode of belonging to the ultimately-real.

Thus, in Secular World Affirming Religion the mode of belonging and the mode of engagement are different but are normally positively related.

In Withdrawal Religion the mode of belonging is an assumed belonging in the course of being realized. This process calls for a mode of engagement with the immediate world-out-there which is in fact withdrawal; that is, withdrawal of affective attachment, and also withdrawal from physical involvement insofar as this is possible and facilitates realization.[14]

In Nature Religion the terms mean one and the same thing, save that "mode of belonging" suggests a more ontological concern, and "mode of engagement" a more existential one.

MODE OF ENGAGEMENT AND ETHICS

Later I will need to use the term "ethics". I will use it to refer to the specific rules by which the community or individual members govern, ideally speaking, their relationship with themselves, each other and the world around them. Mode of engagement is the general relation of the individual and perhaps community, to the immediate world-out-there. Ethics, therefore, fills in the details of a mode of engagement. However, there may be other sources of ethics than the mode of engagement, including the mode of belonging where that is different. I will be considering below, the sources of ethics within the different paradigms.

---

[14] There are sub-traditions which are best located within this type which advocate *embracing* the physical as a path to overcoming its affective influence.

THE MODE OF ENGAGEMENT ITSELF

The Nature Religion paradigm requires that the ideal person conforms to the real, that is, fits into the rhythms of the natural order and maintains its harmonies. It is a life style of a corporate nature to be fulfilled individually and universally. It does not mean that nature is not to be used. Animals may need to be slain and trees may need to be cut down, but it must be done from need and with respect and consideration. Each entity is real and each has its own *telos*, its own essential nature to fulfil, and that is not to be needlessly frustrated. If it were the sense of a "grand pattern" would be weakened.

In the Secular World Affirming paradigm the immediate world-out-there is *secular* and so may be grasped and modified. It is *real* and therefore worth human involvement.

The human side of the covenant relationship is to seek to bring about the will of a personally conceived ultimately-real within the real, or at least not to hinder it. The willingness to initiate action depends upon a sense of complementarity with the divine and upon belief in the possibility of new starts and of forgiveness. Even in a highly deterministic view of providence there remains the obligation to cooperate with the will of the divine.

It can be said, therefore, that within this paradigm the ideal person is one who takes hold of the world-out-there, and seeks to shape it in accordance with the will of the ultimately-real. This may once have been limited to one's own life space and that of one's society and in relation to what would be conceived as righteousness. The advent of the technological ability to conform the physical environment necessarily includes that in the task and extends righteousness to include enrichment.

NOTE : THE IDEAL TYPES ARE MUTUALLY EXCLUSIVE

It should be clear from the preceding typology that any attempt to unify the world religions by selecting the best insights of each, or doing a world theology in any simple additive way, is out of the question. Even a theology of other religions, in any style that does not take account of the possible models of reality, is doomed to failure.

There is a common essence in religion. It is the quest to know the nature of the ultimately-real and to be related to it. Nevertheless, how that ultimately-real is conceived will not only radically affect the mode of belonging and all other consequential symbols, it will have major personal and social consequences as well.

Religious traditions falling into the different ideal types may have much to learn from one another in practice. How wonderful it would be if one could combine the individual self-discipline of the Withdrawal Religions with the community spirit of Nature Religion and the goal orientation of the Secular World Affirming traditions. However, in terms of basic orientation to the environment they are mutually exclusive; one cannot at the same time do more than one of, take-hold-and-shape, withdraw-from, or fit-into-rhythms-of the environment. These modes of engagement with the world- out-there are not reconcilable.

The mode of engagement is perhaps the most important factor in locating a person or culture within the paradigms, for in addition to its visibility and its exclusiveness, it is hard to avoid. While it might be possible to do without a conceptualization of the ultimately-real, it is hardly possible to do without a mode of engagement with the immediate world-out-there.

PARADIGMATIC SYMBOLS AND THE NECESSARY CONSEQUENTIAL SYMBOLS AND SOME OTHER FEATURES OF THE THREE LOGICALLY COHERENT TYPES OF RELIGIOUS SYSTEM			
3			
NON-NEGOTIABLE SYMBOLS AND FEATURES	NATURE RELIGION	WITHDRAWAL RELIGION	SECULAR WORLD AFFIRMING RELIGION
SOCIAL FEATURES 1 INDIVIDUAL or COMMUNAL	COMMUNAL centered	INDIVIDUAL universal	COMMUNAL solidary
2 SOCIAL COHESION	BEHAVIOR PATTERN	BEHAVIOR PATTERN	BELIEF PATTERN
3 SOCIAL COERCION	"LOVE" "FEAR"	n/a	"LOVE" "GREED"
SOURCE OF is ETHICS	HARMONY, INDIVIDUAL PURPOSE	REALIZATION, ONENESS	THE END, THE ABOVE
MODELLING OF SURVIVAL AFTER DEATH	ANCESTOR	REINCARNATION[*]	TO HEAVEN
RELIGIOUS is KNOWLEDGE	WISDOM	DISCOVERY OF A PATH	REVELATION

[*] but see the text.

SOCIAL FEATURES - GENERAL

Religion and the values employed in social construction or maintenance are so inextricably bound up with one another that it is possible to be unaware of the religious aspect or even to deny it.

In many parts of the Third World two balances are possible. There is the natural one in which people die when the population outstrips the food supply (perhaps sickness adds to nature's culling) and then the food supply suffices for a while. Then there is the "un-natural" balance in which one takes hold of the environment and seeks to change it, seeking to increase the food supply by scientific and mechanized farming and control the population by family planning. Almost any group of Westerners would regard the latter course of action as axiomatic even if they denied all allegiance to an Abrahamic faith.[15] They might be astounded to learn that such a course of action was not axiomatic to many and that to press such action upon other cultures, without at the same time offering the world-view of the paradigm which gave it birth, could be highly irresponsible. It would tend to the destruction of the world view which was the current cement of society without offering the necessary alternative.

Significant social values arise out of the character assigned to the ultimately-real and the manner of belonging to it, and also out of the consequences of these symbols for social involvement. Three examples follow:

SOCIAL FEATURE 1. *INDIVIDUAL OR COMMUNAL*

Nature Religion is essentially communal. The individual belongs to the ultimately-real in belonging to his or her community, both living and departed, and with it to the immediate world of experience and to whatever extends beyond. Belonging begins with the most immediate and most clearly defined and then moves out to include all that is known and unknown. That is, it begins with the individual center and moves out to include everything, but with decreasing definition. It is a *centered* communal belonging.

Withdrawal Religion is individualistic and therefore universalistic. All individuals, wherever and whenever they happen to exist, have the same task before them, that is, the realization of belonging. Ontological corporateness (that is, corporateness in reality itself) exists in this paradigm only at the level

---

[15] I will return to the involvement by members of a culture in a mode of engagement with the world-out-there, which would be the consequence of the culture's religion, even though they consciously reject the religious tradition. This will be found in the discussion of the cosmos paradigm in theme III of chapter 12 and in the discussion of pluralism in chapter 14.

of the unity of all things.   There may, of course, be the affective corporateness of a sort of spiritual slimmers' club, in which individuals constitute a support group for each other's individual quest.

Secular World Affirming Religion is essentially communal, but there may be an individual step, and there is certainly an individual aspect. That is to say, unless one was born into an indirect cosmic belonging tradition, one needs to join the tradition community. Either way, the individual needs to contribute to the direction of the whole.

The end point in this tradition, however, is the coming together of the real and the ultimately-real. It is usually symbolically expressed as a kingdom, that is a situation in which the will of the ultimately-real is fully complied with. To seek to bring it in, or at least not to hinder its coming, is the obligation on the human side of the covenant relation.

For a number of reasons this goal is essentially a corporate one. It involves the adherent's whole world-out-there and is a statement about reality, not about the individual. Also it is modelled as the will of the ultimately-real and offers meaning to the individual by participation in a process. This process may call for the sacrifice of much present texture without the promise of individual participation in the fulfillment.

The end point being communal, it cannot be conceived as being fulfilled by individual action nor in a single generation, but requires the formation of movements, perhaps institutions, of like-minded people.[16]   The mode of engagement therefore is "*solidary*" it consists in group action. These groupings will be at all levels and secular as well as overtly religious. In the Christian tradition they would include all levels from local congregation to the world wide church (and perhaps to the Abrahamic family) and from local community to nation state and to, say, the "free world". This solidary communal involvement contrasts sharply with the centered involvement of the Nature Religion paradigm.

While the Kingdom symbol functions as an ever updating model for social construction, and one that enjoys the authority of seeming permanence, the need for goals and for solidary functioning make it potentially a conflict model.

Individuals and groups, while being committed to the divine authority of their own opinion, may not agree on the paths to be pursued. Rather, they may seek to impose their views on the world at large, justifying war and oppression in the process.[17]

---

[16] That is, unless one postulates a Tao, a sort of cosmic integrator of individual efforts, but that would not take seriously the degree of human responsibility latent in this paradigm.

[17] It is interesting in the light of this to consider the contemporary tendency to depreciate prophetic religion in favour of the more mystical sort. See for example R C Zaehner,

On the other hand, Withdrawal Religion and even Nature Religion, tend to social neglect when judged from the perspective of the Secular World Affirming traditions. They seem to offer peace at the price of anarchy and of a social violence by default. The East sends gurus to the West proclaiming a peaceful religious life style. The West sends tractors, medicines and those who would care for the impoverished, to the East. Neither is necessarily preferable, nor is it clear that a balance between the two is the answer. To have an aspirin requires an extractive industry, a power industry, a chemical industry, and a distributive industry, quite apart from all the necessary financial and educational back-up. This suggests that it is all or nothing in many areas of life.

I have said that linear time makes possible, and an ultimate goal lends authority to, the evaluation of life in terms of its goals rather than its present texture. They also require that all relationships need to be understood diachronically as well as synchronically. The individual needs to have his or her present relation to the divine and his or her present activity in the world related to the future corporate kingdom. In the process, the community that is presently served needs to be related to the kingdom. If this is perceived as a secular community then some form of civil religion will be called for *(Pax Britannica* served such a role). If for some reason a civil religion is not possible or is unacceptable, and provided that they are conceptually separable, then the religious community may take the place of the secular community and be the sole link with the future kingdom. The church, for example, may be conceptualized as "the alternative community".

At all levels, present involvement with the real must be understood to contribute to the ultimate goal, or at the very least not to hinder it. This does not presuppose a blue-print for the kingdom, but it does presuppose that the relationship of the ultimately-real to the real be perceived as diachronic as well as synchronic.

NOTE : "KINGDOM" IN THE SECULAR WORLD AFFIRMING PARADIGM

"Kingdom" is a non-negotiable symbol although flexible as to content and, of course, name. It is non-negotiable because:

(i) it stands for the putting together of this and that which is above or not-yet (depending upon how the transcendence gap is expressed) at a future point in time, and

---

Concordant Discord,(London, Oxford University Press, 1970), p.21f.

(ii) it expresses this in terms of a volitional relation of a quasi-personal ultimately-real to the real.

Both of these are themselves non-negotiable within the paradigm.

One of the ways in which the symbol "Kingdom" is flexible lies in its perceived continuity or discontinuity with the present time. This in turn will have consequences for whether or not humankind can contribute to its coming or its form, and also to what extent, if any, the creation other than humankind will participate. How much these variations are orthodox within the paradigm is open to question. All manner of twists and turns have been employed in the attempt to have the advantages of both time and eternity, as for example, the widespread distinction between the eternal kingdom and a millennium.

Illustrative of the sort of pressures which might lead toward continuity, and vice versa, is the debate between Luther and Erasmus on human freedom. It was a debate about what constitutes human dignity, whether it be the height to which humanity is called or the ability to achieve it unaided. If one is near to shore and a strong swimmer, it is fine to be dignified with the belief that one can swim there. If one is in the middle of the sea, all one needs is to be rescued. Thus a situation that engenders self-confidence and relatively low aspirations will tend to an emphasis on continuity, while a lack of self-confidence or relatively high aspirations, will tend to discontinuity, that is, toward belief in a divine intervention in history.

At one extreme, when experience of life is unacceptable, because bad or insignificant, the creation may be seen as set for destruction or replacement, and the hope of the individual is to be saved out of it.

This diminution of the status of the real leads toward monism, to one reality not yet in possession, and therefore toward the Withdrawal Religion paradigm. Equally to view present experience as the ultimately-real (as can happen in some forms of mysticism, and in extreme forms of incarnational theology or realized eschatology) is also a tendency toward monism and a move out of the paradigm, this time toward Nature Religion.

There are moves which convert "Kingdom" from an eschatological symbol to one concerning the rule of the divine in the present. There is no problem with emphasizing immediate providence in this paradigm, but to do that to the detriment of a symbolic ultimate goal is to be sliding out of the paradigm.

Transcendence requires two realities, otherwise there is nothing to transcend or be transcended.

The symbol "Kingdom" can be understood to model the overcoming of present suffering, but with different emphases. The emphasis may be on a coming prosperity or justice, which things are compatible with present struggle and can constitute a conflict model. On the other hand the emphasis may be on peace which is not compatible with a conflict model, for ends and means begin to conflict and one begins to feel the cynicism of the "stamp out violence" slogan.

SOCIAL FEATURE 2.   *SOCIAL COHESION*

Belief, Behavior and Distinct Experience

Every group or community, if it is to remain such, must have a principle of cohesion. This will usually be a common belief pattern or a common behavior pattern or some blend of the two.

In certain circumstances this principle of cohesion may become experiences that are unrelated to the rest of life. These have the advantage of cutting across cultural, political and ethical differences and across the behavioral markers of social stratification.[18]

Because human beings generally seek to relate what they believe to their actual context, such distinct-from-life experiences cease to function cohesively when the situation which favoured them ameliorates.

Inner spiritual experience, not being public, is not a principle of group coherence unless it is accompanied by beliefs concerning the authentic nature of the experience and testimony as to its existence.

Belief-pattern, in its most effective form, is a logically interrelated set of consciously held cognitive elements which can be cashed in relation to the rest of life.

When the rest of life is experienced as alien or chaotic, and belief can no longer be cashed in terms of real life experience, cohesion may continue to be maintained by exchanges within an approved set of words. These words may have little logical coherence and no attempt will be made to find relation for them with aspects of the everyday world.

Equally, when a behavior-pattern community can no longer maintain traditional behaviors for some reason then its members may develop what

---

[18] One finds in Pentecostal churches a very wide social spectrum, men and women whose beliefs and behaviors in relation to the wider world differ enormously, united around a common but extraordinary experience.

appears to be a belief-pattern without longer term goals, simply for survival purposes. The purpose that these beliefs serve is neither direction nor an immediate belonging to an ultimately-real but rather the sense of community solidarity which arises when members testify to them. This sort of belief is what I earlier called flag words - words and phrases which are better described as verbal behavior-pattern than as belief. The texture of community solidarity which they create in a fragmented world is their sufficient justification.

There are two quite distinct kinds of behavior-pattern. There is the natural kind, in which ordinary activities and relations of life-world take on added significance, and there is the kind in which rituals are specially established and are clearly distinct from everyday activities. There are many behavior-patterns which fall between these, perhaps having begun as one and moved toward the other. I will be examining this process in the next chapter and then again in chapter 10. All ritually significant behaviors presuppose some belief, however minimal.

Hinduism is a familiar form of behavior-pattern. It is almost true to say that one can believe what one likes and still be a Hindu, provided that one keeps the lore of the caste. At the other extreme lies that type of protestant Christianity where the emphasis is on right belief, and where there is a constant enquiry to discover if the membership is "sound".

Belief and behavior patterns have different societal consequences.

Belief-pattern tends to be as divisive between groups as integrative within them. Behavior-pattern, particularly of the natural kind, tends to be undogmatic and tolerant of variety in belief and therefore to leave an inner privacy which is particularly important for people living in close community.

Behavior-pattern as the cement of corporate existence tends to maintain the social *status quo*. No one changes unless all change. Belief-pattern, on the other hand, is to be expected where there is a concern for social and geographical mobility. Belief, like inner spiritual experience, is carried within the individual and does not inhibit change to the same degree.

In Nature Religion in stable circumstances, participation in religion and therefore in society would be largely by the observance of a communal behavior pattern, that is, of a lore. Wrong, or missing belief, would not be a ground for exclusion. Behaviors for the maintenance of belonging would be indistinguishable from everyday life activity. Behaviors for the restoration of belonging would also be closely related to life activities, but might, where circumstances require it, become special and distinctive ritual.

In traditions of this type one finds prescribed relationships with kith and kin, with the ancestors and with the objects of nature, and there are rites of passage throughout life and beyond. Rites of passage seek to maintain or restore belonging at critical stages and are normally distinctive ritual. In stable and acceptable conditions, other ritual tends to be behavior-pattern within the normal life-world.

Withdrawal Religion, theoretically speaking, has no place for a principle of social cohesion. Insofar as one existed in practice, it would emerge from a relatively limited but strongly held belief at the level of the paradigm, and the common behavior of those engaged in disciplines leading toward individual realization.

In Secular World Affirming Religion both the volitional relation to an ultimately-real, and the goal orientation in the mode of engagement with the real, necessitate a large cognitive content, that is, the religion must be in major extent a belief-pattern. This is more the case in what I have called direct cosmic belonging than in indirect cosmic belonging, but it is true for both.

In spite of this pressure toward belief, traditions which are generally and overtly of the Secular World Affirming kind can, where the situation prompts it, become predominantly behavior patterns.

For example, in deprived communities, while Christianity of the protestant kind has tended to move toward distinct experience (pentecostalism), that of the catholic kind has tended to become a prescribed set of specifically religious ritual practices (baptism, going to confession and hearing mass, observing saints' days and other festivals) without too strong an emphasis on the purity of belief.

At the other end of the social scale, a caricature of the upper-class Englishman in favour of the *status quo* might be that he was an Anglican, able to sing the *Te Deum* without a prayer book whilst rattling the coins in his pocket, and nobody asking him what he believed from the day that he was confirmed onwards. If anything were to make him feel unaccepted in the Church it would be his bad manners. Manners are behavior-pattern.

Judaism and Islam, viewed from without, appear to have a rather nice balance between cohesion on the basis of behavior and of belief. They are not as dogmatic as much protestant Christianity tends to be, on the other hand they require the performance of symbolic acts.

SOCIAL FEATURE 3. *SANCTIONS FOR SOCIAL COERCION*
     "Love", "Fear", "Greed"

Apart from the habitual, all of humankind's other action would seem to be motivated by love (affection or simple altruism), or fear (of some diminution, exclusion or pain), or greed (hope of some enrichment or aggrandizement), or by some mixture of these. Love, fear and greed are extreme words for my purpose but they will serve. All religious traditions, as here understood, including forms of humanism, would look for the time when all the actions of humankind were motivated by love.

Withdrawal religion, as such, has no interest in social coercion. Precisely, it seeks escape from the situation where fear and greed, even affection, operate, but altruism, of course, is not excluded. To the degree that love fails, humankind, even in Withdrawal Religion cultures, must be motivated, if society is to exist at all, by fear or greed or both.

The so-called free world has tended to emphasize greed, whereas, to the outsider at least, the socialist world seems to have emphasized fear. Whether, in order to compensate for the failure of love, it is better to emphasize greed rather than fear is an open question. For the religious, the answer will depend on their understanding of the character of the ultimately-real and the mode of the individual's belonging to it, and also (together with the humanists) on which is most likely to encourage humankind to love.

My concern here is not with how individuals are motivated, but with what is the preferred motivation of a religious tradition, supposing that it has one, when love fails.

Nature Religion is essentially corporate. Each entity is real and has its nature to fulfil within the whole. To be aware of the rights and needs of all those "essential natures" at all times is the quality of the ideal person. The encouragement of self-interest is therefore contrary to the paradigm. It could only be acceptable if there were some *Tao*, some principle of the cosmos, guaranteeing the integration of individually directed strivings into an optimum whole. Traditions of the Nature Religion type, therefore, will tend to resort to fear for social coercion. The natural threat is that of social alienation and at its worst it is the context of the witch-hunt or other purging of the body corporate.

Secular World Affirming traditions will differ in this respect according to whether they are at the direct cosmic belonging or indirect cosmic belonging end of the scale.

Indirect cosmic belonging moves somewhat in the direction described for Nature Religion, in that the divine bridgehead already has something of the nature of the ultimately-real even though it is not yet the kingdom. What was said above, therefore, applies here in limited degree.

Direct cosmic belonging traditions stress the individual's need for belonging and individual responsibility within a solidary contribution to the coming kingdom. This has an affective affinity with individual rewards.

In both of these logics of belonging new starts are possible, and a god is acknowledged who can draw all things together into an optimum whole and who can reward individuals. Above all, the volitional nature of the relationship of the ultimately-real to the real suggests a volitional relationship in the other direction.

All of these factors weigh against the choice of the goad and in favour of the carrot.

Stated in another way, it can be said that, if freedom of choice is of the essence of the personal, and if the necessity to conceive of a personal ultimate real includes conceiving of an ultimately-real who grants freedom of choice to persons, then any level of fear that could be depersonalizing is excluded by the paradigm. The tendency therefore, to the degree that love has failed to motivate, would be to turn to greed rather than fear.

NOTE :   THE RELATIONSHIP BETWEEN THE THREE PAIRS OF FACTORS, BELIEF AND BEHAVIOR, GOALS AND TEXTURE, INDIVIDUAL SURVIVAL AND GRAND DESIGN

I have identified the following three pairs of factors together with their sub-types. There are some further things to be said about their inter-relation.

BELIEF	v.	BEHAVIOR
i) life related		i) life patterns
ii)"flags" pass over into ->		ii) special patterns
GOALS	v.	TEXTURE
GRAND	v.	INDIVIDUAL
DESIGN		SURVIVAL
i) purpose (inc. *pleroma*)		i) permanence
ii) pattern (inc. *pleroma*)		ii) resurrection
iii) grandeur (unstructured)		

Goal orientation is necessarily associated with a belief- pattern because goals have to be spelled out. One form of grand design is purpose and therefore goal related. These three, grand design (purpose), goals and belief tend to go together. When goal orientation weakens in a belief-pattern tradition, grand design may remain as the pattern type and be accompanied by a developed concern with texture.[19] In general, behavior-pattern will be

---

[19] The European Middle Ages moved quite strongly in this direction.

accompanied by a texture- orientation, but, as we will see in the next chapter, in a situation where life texture becomes unacceptable there may be a move to special behaviors for group cohesion and then to the increasing importance of belief.

If individual survival is *required* for meaning and is not simply a bonus, it means that "grand-design" in all versions is missing and therefore there are neither major supportable goals (corporate directions of striving), nor worthwhile texture, whether as pattern or unstructured grandeur. All that remains as a possible ground of meaning is individual contributions to and struggle for short term sectional improvements in texture. A death that was extinction would put an end to any meaning generated in this way.

Just as goals require belief so texture orientation and behavior patterns tend to go together, but belief and texture orientation is a possible mix, in which case one would need a grand design of the pattern type to ground meaning. [20]

Where a situation is in flux or otherwise unacceptable and a behavior-pattern in relation to life as a whole is difficult to maintain, and where it is difficult to gain common assent to a belief-pattern, then another principle of cohesion may come into use. That is, a common experience generated within the group itself and unrelated to the wider, fragmented or unacceptable context. Such common experiences have been referred to above. One is the seeming belief-pattern which is really made up of flag words, another is the extra-normal experience of the mystical or pentecostal kind. It is in these situations that one would be likely to find reliance upon individual survival as a ground for meaning, a sense of grand design of any type not being supported by experience.

SOURCES OF ETHICS

"Ethics", I have said, refers to the specific rules by which, ideally speaking, the individual or community govern their relationship with

---

[20] The world view of the educated classes of classical Greece might well be an example of this mix, as might Mao's form of Marxism, to the extent that the emphasis is on the texture of continual revolution rather than upon some utopian future. Both of these arose in texture orientated cultures. Some forms of African Socialism and African indigenized Christianity might also be said to be texture orientated with a belief-pattern principle of cohesion, but this is probably only so in a period of transition, goals are likely to gain in importance.

themselves, each other and the world around them. I am not here concerned with the rules themselves but with their sources in each of the paradigms. Until one has embraced symbols for the ultimately-real, that is, a paradigm (or paradigms together with what I will later call "bridging symbols") one cannot operate ethically.

In Nature Religion the sole source of ethics is the mode of belonging which is synonymous with the mode of engagement. It is developed by general agreement, that is, by wisdom, rather than logically from an overall goal, for the real is now. Each entity has its own purpose within the whole which must be respected. In a paradigm which affirms the immediate as real and reality as a unity, there is usually no need to enquire beyond the immediate.21

In each of the two bifurcated reality paradigms there are two sources of ethics that may conflict with each other.

In Withdrawal Religion the individual's action will be directed by his or her own need to achieve realization. On the other hand the paradigm affirms the unity of all things and, therefore, that to diminish any aspect of reality is to diminish self and is to diminish all. It is perhaps these two sources which lead to the enormous respect for present forms of life, other than one's own, that distinguish religious traditions in this paradigm. The potential conflict is well illustrated by the tension within Buddhism between what the Buddha taught concerning detachment and his example of compassion.

In Secular World Affirming Religion there are two ways of modelling transcendence, temporally (as future) and spatially (as above). Ethics, therefore, can arise from two possible sources, from consideration of action toward a revealed goal and from consideration of action under a revealed law. The former is usually spoken of as teleological ethics, and the latter as transcendental or sometimes deontological ethics, although the last term is better reserved for ethics done under the presupposition that it is possible to develop a purely rational ethic without a paradigm for reality.

Both types make it clear that an ethic requires a symbolic description of that which is not here and now, and both are driven by the desire to conform to the will of the ultimately-real. They could however conflict and either might supposedly be suspended by a more immediate revelation of the divine will.

---

21 This ethic, without a *telos* or a transcendent realm, is necessarily an empirical and, wisely, a communal wisdom. It reminds one of Aristotle's insistence, within his community, that one can recognize good men who are the norm and yardstick of what is good. Aristotle, *Nicomachean Ethics*, Bk.3 Ch.4. Each thing having its own purpose in the overall present, one does not need to seek a source of ethics in anything beyond what is experienced.

THE MODELLING OF SURVIVAL AFTER DEATH

If the question of life after death is raised and answered affirmatively by a religious tradition, then the belief that one will not cease to belong to the ultimately-real upon death will be modelled differently within the various paradigms.

In Nature Religion, where the ultimately-real is the present reality, the need is to remain - in a different state of being, perhaps as spirit or ancestor - but to remain. In this real and monistic world, death may be understood as one more rite of passage through which one must move before being harmoniously linked back into the totality of things.

In Withdrawal Religion the nature of the ultimately-real is cyclical manifestation and dissolution. To be part of it at a simple level, therefore, is to be reincarnated. At a more sophisticated level death (even a life) ceases to be a reality, for the individual is the all and the all is the eternal in which even the aeon cycles are negligible movements in the stillness.

In Secular World Affirming Religion where the ultimately-real is understood, in spatial terms, as across the gulf which divides Creator from Creation, life after death must be expressed, at least if it is to be eternal life, as going to be with God or as going to heaven.

Therefore the three statements, "When I die I will be an ancestor", "I will be reincarnated", "I will go to heaven", all affirm the same thing, that is, "When I die I will not cease to belong to the ultimately-real as I model it". The statements are not truth claims in conflict in the literal realm of discourse, but identical affirmations of faith within different paradigms for reality. Because the difference lies, not in the three statements, but in the three views of the ultimately-real, there could be no point in debating which of them was true, only perhaps which paradigm best expressed reality and that would not be validated in logic but in feeling.

THE NATURE OF KNOWLEDGE AND OF RELIGIOUS KNOWLEDGE
- THE LIMITS OF LANGUAGE AND KNOWLEDGE IN THE THREE TYPES

Understanding of the source and limits of knowledge (and of religious knowledge when that is different) is generated by the paradigm for reality and the paradigmatic type of religion. My present concern is with these different understandings. However, as no understanding of the nature and limits of knowledge can properly exist without a criterion for what shall constitute reality, I must begin by locating the more familiar criteria for reality in relation to the paradigms.

CRITERIA FOR REALITY

In this study of religion I have worked with the understanding that the real is that to which humankind wants to hang on in the long term. It is obviously a feeling judgment however much it might be informed by cognitive considerations. It is the only possible criterion if one wishes to include values, that is, ways of engaging with the physical world as well as the world itself, within the concept "reality".

Science operates with the criterion, which has the appearance of being value free, that reality is that which can be "handled" or more generally, that which is subject to empirical verification. Such an empirical stance is at home in both the Nature Religion and Secular World Affirming paradigms with their different emphases on the reality of immediate experience.

There is, however, another criterion of reality and one that has a respectable pedigree from Plato to the modern period. It is that "the most real is the most permanent". In all the paradigms the totality or the ultimately-real is permanent. With emphasis upon this criterion it becomes possible to suppose that the most real entities within immediate experience lie in the realm of ideas. Indeed the form of some object is always more permanent than its material manifestation, the idea of an attribute more permanent than its exemplification in a particular object.

The human intellect can obviously have knowledge of these forms, so it becomes possible to suppose that knowledge of them is not necessarily abstracted from experience of their concrete representations, but could be remembered or communicated from a more permanent realm of existence. The problem is that the only public referent of the language which serves to express these realities seems to be this shadow world of material realities.

The idealist view of reality is not perhaps the most popular today, yet, while mathematics enables humankind to predict and control the environment, it cannot to be written off too lightly.

Belief that access to reality lies in a *logos*, that is, belief in a rationality which pervades both human thinking and the human environment, could fit both the Secular World Affirming and the Nature Religion paradigms. In the latter it would be a given of experience, in the former it would require belief in a common source in the creator of both. If it were otherwise it could give rise to the positing of pre-existent souls or some other link between the real and ultimately-real, and that would diminish transcendence.

On the other hand, the sort of idealism that depends upon memories of pre-existence in a more permanent realm does not sit easily in any of the paradigms. It reflects, perhaps, a world in which the Nature and Withdrawal Religion paradigms co-exist. It is a sort of pragmatic Withdrawal world-view that wants to believe in unity with a greater but hidden reality, but does not wish to withdraw too far from immediate experience. It therefore dignifies immediate experiences as reflections, if only shadows, of some real distinctions in the more permanent realm. Withdrawal Religion is a radically empirical tradition, even though, insofar as the common language for conceptualization is grounded in common experience of the external world, there can be no trustworthy conceptual knowledge.

The paradigms for reality have consequences for all knowledge and to assume a form of knowledge that is not appropriate within a paradigm is to threaten it. Here, however, I am primarily concerned with religious knowledge

KNOWLEDGE WITHIN THE TYPES OF RELIGIOUS TRADITION

There is necessarily a variation in the understood nature of religious knowledge across the three ideal types. At the simplest level, the styles of religious knowledge can be described as Wisdom, Discovery of a Path to Realization, and Revelation respectively. I will consider each in turn.

i) Immediate Experience Affirming Religion (Nature Religion)

In Immediate Experience Affirming Religion all that surrounds us, the here and now, and that which is continuous with it, visible and invisible, is the real. Therefore there can be no difference between religious knowledge and knowledge in general. Each concrete entity is real, each has its own *telos*, its own role to fulfil within a whole that itself has no *telos*.

The source of knowledge in this paradigm is the exercise of radically empirical reason upon experience of the natural world and of the consequences of relationships therewith. It is both immediate and abstracted and is what is typically called Wisdom. The traditional respect for the aged has one of its sources here, for they are those with much experience.

Forms of *a priori* knowledge, that is, a rationality pervading both thinking beings and the rest of experience, or even a partly remembered knowledge gained at one's creation or in a previous existence, are not necessarily excluded. However, in a situation where the real is understood to be immediately available to the senses they are not likely to be the priority style under normal circumstances. It would be like seeking knowledge from some superior realm when one was in heaven. Only if the quality of immediate experience begins to cast doubt upon its own reality and therefore to challenge the paradigm, would a move to an emphasis on *a priori* knowledge be likely.

As long as one remains within the paradigm, immediate experience is not a lesser representation of a greater reality behind it. Rather it is the available part of the real and it is at one with whatever lies behind it. Nothing hides or deforms the experience of reality, therefore there is no path to a knowledge that is truer than that which presents in immediate experience.

In this type, while one may not have complete knowledge, what knowledge one does have is of the real, therefore one may suppose oneself to be speaking of reality in absolute terms. Thus literal language fails in this type only when one would speak of the unique, in particular when one would speak of the totality of experience. Language intended to express a total perspective cannot be literal. The symbolic representations of aspects of nature and society are, of course, not literal, but literal description of that which they represent shades over into the symbol and vice versa. I will return to this in chapter 10.

This type of knowledge tends to be democratic. The need in crisis for contact with spirits or ancestors requires that the agent in this, for example, a diviner, have a specialized knowledge. However, even he or she must be authenticated in the tradition and in general the function of religious knowledge is to prevent the crisis occurring.

The source of much biblical wisdom was the Nature Religion of Egypt. This seems to have entered Israel when, to some at least, the goal that had been out in front for centuries seemed to have arrived. The prophets fought the tendency to return to this type of religion when existence became settled and texture became a better measure of life than goals. They fought it again later, when the hope of a salvation in historic continuity with the present diminished. Wisdom is the natural form of religious knowledge in a situation where the present experience is possible of acceptance and there are no obvious or attainable goals.

I have usually dealt with Withdrawal Religion before Secular World Affirming Religion because it remains monistic. In this matter, however, what has to be said must be a final word and I will leave it until last.

ii) Secular World Affirming Religion

In Secular World Affirming Religion, with its secularization of the immediate environment and its transcendent monotheism, there are two quite separate areas of knowledge.

Immediate experience is real albeit not the ultimately-real to which one would belong. It is that in which the will of the ultimately-real is expressed and may come to be known. Experience of the real, therefore, grounds the language in which both the real and the ultimately-real must be modelled, but the ultimately-real, being unique, cannot be spoken of in literal language.

Because knowledge of the ultimately-real depends absolutely on the self-involvement of the ultimately-real in the real, knowledge of the ultimately-real must be modelled as revelation. This does not need to be conceived as verbal revelation. It is only necessary that the ultimately-real be known through its will operative in the real. Revelation owes nothing necessarily to its channel, nevertheless, respect for those learned in the revealed tradition tends to elitism in this paradigm.

All that could be known without a special revelation from the divine would be drawn from what is concerning the One who wills its existence. If one looks for special revelation of the ultimately-real in events, one must also believe in a providentially acting ultimately-real. What can be revealed is limited to the language that experience has generated. I will return to views of revelation in a moment.

A knowledge of the totality of the real could arise in part by summation of knowledge of its constituent elements, but that would not, as it would in Immediate Experience Affirming Religion, be knowledge of the ultimately-real to which one would belong. In this type, unlike the previous one, there is not just something greater behind immediate experience but something quite different in kind.

Knowledge of the ultimately-real can only be had *indirectly* through the real, not at its surface as is the case in Immediate Experience Affirming Religion. Knowledge of the ultimately-real is a "modelled knowledge" of that which lies behind the surface. The model generates a mode of engagement with that surface and therefore indirectly with whatever lies behind it. The model is verified if and while the mode of engagement generated is more enriching than any known alternative.

All knowledge of what one cannot observe directly through the senses, for whatever reason, is modelled knowledge. It has happened that things which were too small or too far away to see and therefore had to be modelled, have, with improvements in technology, come within the field of vision. Here, however, we are concerned, not with technical limitations, but with logical possibilities within the paradigm concerned, and with that which is conceptually excluded from all sensible knowledge (whether one is thinking of five senses or six) by the controlling view of experience as a whole.

Science, for good methodological reasons, assumes the continuity of the realm in which it operates, that is, it assumes a monistic environment. Philosophy must do the same for the realm in which it thinks. It may model other realities than the cosmos in which it operates, but it cannot think its way across a transcendence gap without destroying it. A philosophy which seeks to describe a transcendent god, insofar as it seems to have succeeded, will have destroyed transcendence and hence departed in that degree from the model of reality within which it regards itself as working.

If one remains within the model there is no way of thinking oneself across the transcendence gap. To the extent that one believes that one has succeeded in doing so, to that extent one has moved out of the paradigm.

Transcendence can only be maintained if knowledge of the ultimately-real remains modelled knowledge in the manner described above.[22]

In this paradigm it is not possible to assign value within the real without reference to how the ultimately-real is experienced and modelled. To deal with the real as though it were a "cosmos", that is a self-contained, self-explanatory, closed system of cause and effect, is appropriately the *method* of science. It cannot, however, provide the values that *drive* the whole scientific enterprise.

NOTE : *POSSIBLE MODELS OF REVELATION*

The self-revelation of the divine in Secular World Affirming religion may be understood in different ways. I have endeavored to show that in the classical Abrahamic tradition, knowledge of the ultimately-real must be understood to be distilled from or at least verified in, ongoing total experience. I have indicated the role of the prophet and the tradition community in that process. Such a view of revelation is only maintainable in a situation of transcendent monotheism (in a dualistic tradition it would hardly be possible to distinguished who was responsible for which event in history). It is also only maintainable when one believes the divine to be actively and purposively involved in history. When Israel's faith in a historical salvation waned two things happened.

The first I have already mentioned, namely some moved back toward Nature Religion and therefore to wisdom rather than revelation as the style of religious knowledge. If a transcendent god is to reveal himself through a creation at more than the impersonal level of designer, then somehow he has to be understood to inform the human mind of the meaning of what it sees. Under the pressure of that need, Israel personified the wisdom of God and understood, rather like the Greek concept of *logos*, the divine wisdom becoming incarnated in both creation and the human mind and ultimately in the *Torah*, the written word of God.

The second thing that happened was that some retained their hope in a blessed future, but came to understand it as discontinuous from present experience, whether of history or nature. God was nowhere to be found. To render revelation conceptually credible in this situation they personified the voice of God. So the revelation to St John the Divine, for example, came from The Voice not simply from a voice.

It should be clear that both of these variations suffer from the same defect that I attributed to Otto's faculty of divination. In general terms it is the problem of any intuitive understanding of revelation, if it cannot be

---

[22] The course of medieval philosophy, "launched" by Anselm and "wrecked" by Scotus and Ockham can be understood in this light.

tested against a sense of reality distilled from all the significant data received via the senses, there can be no knowing if or when it has gone maverick.

Once one has moved into a dualistic view of reality there exists the possibility (although not a logically consistent one) that the adherent perceives the bifurcation to be not simply between Creator and the creation (including human beings) but within the individual human being, such that the bodily-self lies on the side of the creation and the spiritual-self lies on the side of the Divine.

In such a model it could be supposed that religious knowledge was remembered or directly communicated knowledge, knowledge of the sort that the New Testament seems to suggest Jesus of Nazareth had during his earthly life. Nevertheless, *knowledge of* can only be *knowledge about* when it has to be communicated. Then it must be conceptualized and language enters. The meaning of language, particularly religious language, in all its subtlety of feeling, requires a sort of case law of complex past experiences for its expression. An informed pre-existent soul would be just as limited in its powers of communication as the fruit worm in the orange, even if those it was addressing shared its pre-existent experience but not a pre-existent language.

In this type of tradition, therefore, religious knowledge in its institutionalized expression must remain revelation in the classical sense. It is a divinely inspired interpretation of divinely inspired experience within space and time, whatever subliminal proddings there might be in addition, for this is the source of the language as well as the source of the message.

iii) *Withdrawal Religion*

In Withdrawal Religion the concern is with the realization of belonging. The immediate environment being transient and a snare, religious knowledge is typically the discovering of a path (a method or discipline) to realization, and of markers along the way. Neither age nor intelligence are necessarily involved in such discovery. The revered one is the discoverer of a path and also he or she who has travelled far along one and can therefore lead others.

In subsequent chapters I will undertake a more detailed breakdown of Nature Religion and the Secular World Affirming type. It is not possible to proceed in the same way with Withdrawal Religion because I am considering ways in which the ultimately-real and the adherent's relation to it can be modelled. In Withdrawal Religion, because the basic model of reality is a bifurcation between reality and the human experience of it, further modelling is excluded. There is a totality worth belonging to, but not a totality that can be known, even in part, by adding together experience of its bits and pieces. If all appearance is distorted there can be no experience, factual or affective, that can serve to ground a language in which reality and the human relationship to it could be described.

Because I will not be undertaking a detailed further breakdown of Withdrawal Religion I must say here why it has to take the forms that it does take. Some of the points made are quite demanding. They are not required for an understanding of the rest of the book.

SOME REMAINING ISSUES CONCERNING
THE WITHDRAWAL RELIGION PARADIGM.

The paradigm for reality which generates this coherent type of religious tradition poses two interrelated questions:

   a) What is it that causes the individual not to perceive reality as it is in itself?

   b) How may the problem be overcome and the existing state of belonging be realized?

Insofar as the latter question is independent of the former it resolves into a matter of the preferred technique to achieve realization. While it is undoubtedly the techniques which contribute the many sub-varieties in religion of this type, they are not logically determined and therefore cannot contribute to the sort of framework that I have been developing. I will, therefore, concentrate on the former question and begin by seeking to clarify the limits set to any attempt to conceptualize the problem before asking about its source.

THE LIMITS SET TO CONCEPTUALIZATION

Because in this type reality is not perceived as it is in itself, there can be no valid assumption that each individual perceives it in the same way, for there can be no external control on what is perceived. To the extent, therefore, that literal discourse is dependent upon a common perception of the external world, the world-out-there may be experienced but not spoken about literally. Nor can it be spoken of truthfully if spoken of directly. One cannot speak directly and truthfully, about that of which experience is distorted, in a language that takes its meaning from that same distorted realm. Knowledge of the immediate world-out-there can only be had in an indirect sense. One could report, for example, the affective conclusions that the world-out-there is attractive and that one's present relation to it is a source of pain.

Thus, while the tradition may be radically empirical, there can be no direct knowledge reliably conceptualized in literal style, by reference to entities comprising a common external world. It follows that knowledge of the real-in-itself can only be affective knowledge and equally, that there can be no knowledge of an ontological self, only the experience of a stream of experience. Knowledge cannot be said to be either *à priori* or *à posteriori* for it has a claim to reflect reality but not to convey truth. Thus there are no absolute truths, only what is held to be a path toward absolute experience of the real-in-itself.

The natural channel to knowledge of the real-in-itself is the underlying oneness of the individual with all else. The obtaining of such knowledge would be the result of penetrating the immediate to its ground and probably, because it is then at its most available, doing it in oneself.

If in a tradition, intellect was associated with an ontological self and that was understood to be united with the rest of reality, knowledge might be conceived to be *à priori* in a *logos* sense or simply memory of past experience, but the problem of expressing it would remain.

Conceptually, within this type there could be a literal language among those who have achieved, and who, perceiving eternal reality as it is, are logically in the position described earlier for the Immediate Experience Affirming type, but then reality could not be "seamless".

Any attempt to describe reality as a whole would, of course, remain in symbolic discourse. Even if reality is understood to be simple and therefore fully present in each of its manifestations, it remains unique. Such a limited literal discourse would not be literal beyond the group of those who have achieved. There could be no public reference for a literal language while the appearance of the immediate remained distorted.

Clearly, when a bifurcation is believed to exist there is a desire to overcome it. In the first instance, therefore, there will be a pressure, despite the limits set to conceptualization, to ask how the problem arises, even if in the end any solution must be justified empirically rather than logically.

THE SOURCE OF THE HUMAN CONDITION

The reason the individual does not perceive reality as it is in itself might be thought to lie either in the way in which reality manifests, or in some aspect of those seeking to perceive it, or in some combination of these two. There would be some consequential differences between them.

If the problem lies in the perceiver, then perception of each manifestation of reality and of every combination of manifestations - up to and including the whole - is distorted. If it lies in that which is perceived, say in the failure of the parts to reflect the nature of the whole, then perception of each manifestation is distorting of reality, as is every combination of manifestations up to but not including the whole. If reality is simple, then the problem cannot be thought to arise in this way, for then the whole must be available in each of its manifestations.

A much more important consideration is that if the problem does not lie with the perceiver then there is nothing that he or she can do about it and the paradigm would describe a situation with no solution. Conceptualization will begin, therefore, the other way.

If the problem lies with the one perceiving and if a reason is offered, as distinct from an empiric prescription for its cure, then it will depend upon how human nature or human functioning is conceptually divided up. In the West it is usually divided into cognitive and affective. Sometimes volition is added as a separate category, sometimes "to will" is simply understood to mean "to feel in a certain way about a certain conceptualized goal".

If one starts with the cognitive-affective divide and the problem is thought to be cognitive, then the problem may be pictured as either:

a) a failure of understanding, or

b) a lack of conviction that an understanding that is held is in fact true of the real, that is, a failure of faith or assurance.

In fact the latter presupposes the former because assurance concerning a cognitive understanding presupposes the understanding. Therefore to conceptualize the problem as a cognitive one must, in this paradigm, leave it without a solution, for the cognitive understanding is not available.

That aspect of the Hindu tradition in which the prescribed path to *moksha* is the gaining of certainty that *atman* is *brahman* does not fit without remainder into this type of religion. I will return to this when I discuss bridging in chapter 13.

In the end, the logic of this type demands that the problem in the human condition, if it is to have a solution, be conceptualized not only as lying in the perceiver, but also in the affective realm. It also demands that the possibility of knowledge of an ontological self be denied. Beyond that, knowledge must be empiric and not in the control of the logic of the paradigm.

If some stress continues to be laid on cognitive modelling, within the quest for an affective solution, it must be understood as an empirically justified technique and not as part of the logic of the paradigm. Thus, any further breakdown of the logic of the paradigm is a very limited exercise.

POTENTIALLY DISINTEGRATIVE FACTORS AND FACTORS LEADING TO THE NEGATION OF THE PARADIGM

Before I leave the logically coherent types of religious tradition it may be helpful to reverse the procedure that I have been following and to ask, not what a particular paradigm generates, but what threatens it.

In Nature Religion anything which fragments experience, whether in community or nature or between them (for example, any attempt to secure advantage which does not contribute to the advantage of the whole), threatens the paradigm. Thus the use of the powers-that-be (including medicines) in a sectional manner would be witchcraft. Natural disintegration, such as the death of those of full years or, if they were needed, the killing of an animal or the cutting down of a tree, would not threaten the paradigm, but lack of respect for the animal or the tree would threaten it.

In Withdrawal Religion anything which suggests that the appearance of the immediate world is the reality, or otherwise hinders individuals from coming to realization, threatens the paradigm. For example, anything which leads to despising   "life" - the ultimate reality in all experience - is threatening. Not, however, the disintegration of present forms. That is as natural as the creation of present forms.

In Secular World Affirming Religion anything which diminishes transcendence, that is, anything which suggests an ontological link between the real and ultimately-real, or anything that greatly enlarges or diminishes the importance of the real in relation to the ultimately-real and *vice versa*, will threaten the paradigm. The loss of the sense of a real goal to history would threaten the authenticity of the paradigm, as would the sense that the goal has arrived. For most people, the loss of the sense of the personal nature of the ultimately-real will threaten it.

This completes, for present purposes, the comparative development of the logically coherent types of religious tradition within the three paradigms for reality. A summary table appears on the following page.

THE THREE LOGICALLY COHERENT TYPES OF RELIGIOUS SYSTEM			
NON-NEGOTIABLE SYMBOLS	*NATURE RELIGION*	*WITHDRAWAL RELIGION*	*SECULAR WORLD AFFIRMING REL.*
EXPERIENCE OF IMMEDIATE WORLD OUT is THERE	AFFIRMED AS OF THE REAL	NOT AFFIRMED AS OF THE REAL	AFFIRMED AS OF THE REAL BUT NOT ULTIMATE
REALITY is	MONISTIC	MONISTIC	DUALISTIC
CHANCE AND DETERMINISM	CHANCE EXCLUDED	CHANCE EXCLUDED	CHANCE, new beginnings
BELONGING is TO ULTIMATELY REAL	ASSUMED must be maintained or repaired	ASSUMED needs to be realized individually	to be SOUGHT individually
NATURE OF is ULTIMATELY REAL	without rigid distinction between personal and impersonal		PERSONAL
TIME is	CYCLICAL biological, maybe astral	CYCLICAL rhythmic aeons	LINEAR
TEST OF QUALITY OF is EXPERIENCE	TEXTURE ONLY	TEXTURE ONLY	GOALS AND TEXTURE
GROUND OF is MEANING	GRAND DESIGN (pattern)	GRANDEUR	GRAND DESIGN (purpose)
MODE OF ENGAGE-MENT WITH WORLD OUT THERE	FIT INTO	WITHDRAW FROM	TAKE HOLD AND SHAPE
SOCIAL FEATURES 1 INDIVIDUAL or COMMUNAL	COMMUNAL centered	INDIVIDUAL universal	COMMUNAL solidary
2 SOCIAL COHESION	BEHAVIOR PATTERN	BEHAVIOR PATTERN	BELIEF PATTERN
3 SOCIAL COERCION	"LOVE" "FEAR"	n/a	"LOVE" "GREED"
SOURCE OF is ETHICS	HARMONY, INDIVIDUAL PURPOSE	REALIZATION, ONENESS	THE END, THE ABOVE
THE MODELLING OF SURVIVAL	ANCESTOR	REINCARNATION	TO HEAVEN
RELIGIOUS is KNOWLEDGE	WISDOM	DISCOVERY OF A PATH	REVELATION

I must now return briefly to religious experience in the individual in order to show the relationship between that and the coherent types of religious tradition developed above.

RELIGIOUS EXPERIENCE AND THE PARADIGMS

While all religious traditions may be located across the three paradigms for reality and the corresponding religious types, not all individual religious experience may be so located. One reason for this is that religion must be understood to include quest.

Religious experience may still be at the level of quest because no felt sense of reality has formed or because no symbols for reality have appealed to whatever felt sense has formed.

Another reason is that one may, as it were, have come out on the other side, by recognizing the paradigms to be precisely what they are, paradigms. Every paradigm is in fact a sort of *koan* which creates cognitive problems that force some of its adherents beyond it. Then religious experience will be a sort of cosmic trust, trust in a reality that will be less conscious to individuals than their own self-image which, to some degree, depends upon it.

There are, therefore, five distinct styles within which religious experience can be located:-

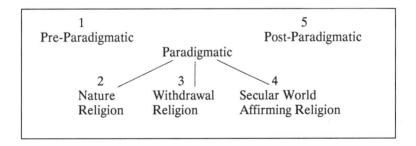

PRE-PARADIGMATIC RELIGION

Pre-paradigmatic religion implies that at least the quest to know "Who am I?", and therefore also "What is all that out there?", has begun. That is to say, that the quest to belong is under way, that the individual is not asleep or bound to mother's apron-strings. Should the individual be heir to some answer to these questions received on authority then, to the degree that it is accepted, the individual's religion would be paradigmatic. To the degree that it is felt to be questionable, it would be pre-paradigmatic.

It is not implied that the quest for religion in the pre-paradigmatic state is necessarily conscious. What is likely to be happening, apart from the search for identity, is the related process, that of experimentation with modes of engagement with the individual's world-out-there.

In order to go anywhere beyond this stage, it is required that a reasonably integrated felt sense of reality develops in the individual. To move into the paradigmatic stage the individual must find a set of symbols for reality which fit the felt sense and which are not unacceptable for some other reason.

It is possible to pass from the pre-paradigmatic form of religion directly into the post-paradigmatic. It is also possible to institutionalize religion as quest. Indeed, given the paradigmatic nature of religious knowledge, all religion which would be cognitive as well as affective must be understood as a continuing quest. The symbol of transcendence in Secular World Affirming religion forbids the absolutization of any understanding of the ultimately-real and of the paradigm itself. Complete knowledge, like salvation, lies in the future. It is, however, possible to admit an affective commitment to a paradigm without making it a cognitive absolute.

POST-PARADIGMATIC RELIGION

The post-paradigmatic form of religion is, as I have said, the one in which the paradigms are recognized for what they are, paradigms. Thus, even as the symbol set which is recognized as having the best fit with the felt sense of reality, the paradigm cannot attract the commitment that would be given to whatever was felt to be absolute. When I say that the paradigms are recognized for what they are, I do not, of course, imply that all persons whose religion is of this type are philosophers, only that they have:

(a) found an affective sense of belonging, (what I called a "cosmic trust") and

(b) stopped looking for a cognitive answer to the question "What is all that
    out there?".

This last may be because they do not feel the need for a cognitive answer, or because they do not think that there can be one, or because they think that they have one which is not religious; for example, that the world-out-there is a self-explanatory secular cosmos.[23] I will seek to unpack the implications of these positions later. For the moment it may be noted that while some sorts of agnosticism can be located within the post-paradigmatic form of religion, others are better understood within the pre-paradigmatic form. The post-paradigmatic form ought not to be confused with atheism, because in this form there can be no symbol of a divine to deny.

All people who are awake need a mode of engagement with their world-out-there. If this is conscious and cognitive it will, in post-paradigmatic religion, have to be expressed in terms of what, in paradigmatic religion, would be medial-axioms such as "All men should be treated as brothers" or "It is better to save life than take it", or in a set of more specific directives for action. I will return to this. Here it must be said that any mode of engagement implies some understanding of that with which one is engaging, whether it has become conscious or not. Post-paradigmatic religion, therefore, can almost always be located within a paradigm by implication of the individual's chosen mode of engagement with the world-out-there. [24]

Cosmic trust plus a consciously modelled mode of engagement with the world-out-there is, perhaps, the only present possibility for many critically-minded adults who wish to be integrated personalities. The modern western felt sense of reality tends to be monistic but within linear time, that is, it tends to what I will be calling the "cosmos paradigm".

Cosmic trust, in spite of its agnosticism about all-that-out-there, can have a strong sense of salvation. The sense of having done all things well, as I said earlier, can produce a sense of belonging to a sort of cosmic club or of having fulfilled a cosmic code. It might begin with the willingness to serve one's country to the death.[25] Such a sense does not require belief in survival after death. It has more to do with identity than with physical survival now or later.

Yet for all its attractiveness, cosmic trust is not a fully articulated position. It is not coherent as a basis for a logic of belonging and to settle for it obscures what is going on at the unconscious level.

---

[23] Post-paradigmatic religion is not only to be found outside the bounds of religious institutions. Individuals who are themselves in this position may nevertheless value an organization which will bring the next generation to cosmic trust and to an approved set of medial axioms. In fact one suspects that the majority of church goers in the western world might fit best in this category.

[24] See the development of this theme in chapter 14.

[25] There is an anonymous poem by a Russian soldier of World War II who is expecting to die, that catches just this feeling. Unfortunately I have not been able to trace it.

LOCATING INDIVIDUAL RELIGIOUS EXPERIENCE

I will return to the location of individual religious experience in the Appendix but for present clarity it is necessary to show the limitations of the five styles of religion just identified and say what other factors need to be added before one can usefully locate an individual's religious experience in relation to them.

An individual's religious experience may be located, in relation to the framework already developed, within one of the paradigms or with those who are still questing or with those who are post-paradigmatic. Alternatively, if we allow that a mode of engagement with the world-out-there implies a paradigm, then all except those whose mode of engagement is still tentative or lacks consistency, and those who are asleep and in no way engaged, are locatable within the three paradigms. The advantage of looking at individuals in this light is that, although they are not overtly associated with a paradigm, they can be expected to have adopted other of its aspects along with the mode of engagement and one is alerted to looked for them.

The location of individual religion in terms of these three or five possibilities, while interesting, is still crude, and there is a need to further break down the coherent types of religious tradition into the great variety of theoretical possibilities that they are capable of generating. This I will do in subsequent chapters. However, location within a framework of possible varieties of religious beliefs and practices is not sufficient to describe an individual's religious experience. There would need to be added something about the intensity of the sense of belonging already achieved and the intensity and directedness of the continuing quest. The individual would also need to be located within a spectrum of interpretive possibilities and a spectrum of attitudes that he or she might have taken up to the beliefs and practices.

The first spectrum comprises, at one extreme, the overtly religious possibility of understanding the paradigm as an ontological statement, a statement about how things really are, and at the other extreme, the overtly secular possibility of understanding the paradigm simply as a means of expressing that which is implied by a mode of engagement with the world-out-there. In between would be those for whom the paradigm was consciously a model, but a model that had gained in reality status because it "worked", and those for whom the paradigm had been an ontological statement, but who had begun to sense the difficulties of such a position.

The second spectrum comprises a set of possibilities determined primarily, it would seem, by the felt level of security. One end of the spectrum is characterized by trust and openness and the quest for reality, the other by closedness, certainty and a clinging to the "truths" that legitimate both belonging and the rejection of what does not belong. The former is the style of religious belonging that I have referred to as "cosmic", the latter is the style referred to as "reduced reality". As I proceed, therefore, I will be seeking to show, not only the greater variety of possible beliefs and practices within each paradigm, but also how these other factors might be assessed.

THE WAY FORWARD

The bare bones of a conceptual framework for the location and interrelation of elements of religious tradition and religious experience has now been established by "unpacking" the consequences of the paradigmatic understanding of religion arrived at in Part I. From this point on, the scientific study of religion is a three pronged enterprise. It must seek:

i) To expand and refine the framework.

ii) To use the framework to locate and explain religious phenomena

iii) To test in use the framework's power to locate religious phenomena widely, simply and fruitfully, and thereby to test the validity of the paradigmatic understanding which gave rise to it.

My primary concern in the remaining chapters will be to indicate how (i) above, that is, the further development and refining of the frame, might be undertaken. In the process of pursuing this further development of the framework, its uses will inevitably be exemplified and its integrating power indicated. Likewise, each time the conceptual framework is seen to include a phenomenon recognized as religious, the paradigmatic understanding from which the frame has been developed will be further vindicated. Nevertheless, my primary concern in the rest of this book is the development and refinement of the theoretical frame, not the use of it in the study of particular religious phenomena. I turn now, therefore, to a consideration of the processes by which the conceptual framework which has just been arrived at can be further extended and refined.

POTENTIAL MOVES FOR THE EXPANSION AND
REFINEMENT OF THE CONCEPTUAL FRAME

i) Expansion of the Coherent Types Within the Established Threefold Comparative Structure.

This would have to be done by seeking further significant elements that comprise a religious world view (which are not reducible to those already dealt with) and asking what form those elements would need to take to cohere within each of the types.

ii) Expansion of Each of the Types in Turn.

On the one hand, each type presents a special case and therefore the method employed for its expansion would vary. For example, in the secular world affirming paradigm, because belonging has to be sought, it can be asked "What conditions must be fulfilled for a sense of belonging to be established?". We can investigate, within this, the varieties of situation engendered by the relations of the "three actors" identified earlier, and the choice of emphases within the "three paths".

On the other hand, there is a tool for the expansion and refinement of the types which is available within all three paradigms. It is the principle

> If religion is the quest for, realization or maintenance of belonging to the ultimately-real then it follows that when religion changes it will do so in a manner that seeks the maintenance or restoration of the sense of belonging.

This means that it is possible to expose the varieties in which a type of religious tradition can exist by exploring, under various conditions of disturbance, the moves that are available to adherents of that type as they seek to maintain their sense of belonging. This is a very powerful tool. It can be used to explore the types *individually*. It is done by asking what moves are possible in the attempt to maintain or restore the sense of belonging in a situation of disturbance. The question may be asked in consideration of a major disturbance or of a minor one, an acute disturbance or a chronic one. It can be used to explore the *interaction* of the types by asking what moves are possible for the maintenance or restoration of the sense of belonging as one type impinges upon and threatens another. It can be used to explore *competition* between the types by asking what moves are possible as two or more types continue in side by side competition.

When one explores these questions a framework, comprised of the varieties in which each type can exist on its own and the varieties in which it can exist in relation to the other types, emerges. Each variety is associated with an exemplary set of conditions for its generation. The exploration also indicates the conditions under which one might expect to find a trend toward each of the types as a whole.

The framework, once generated, provides a powerful explanatory device for whatever might be found in the complexities of living traditions but whether it is the most powerful explanatory device and whether, therefore, its generating paradigm is the most adequate, can only be determined in competition with other paradigms.

In the process which has been begun in this chapter, of developing and in a preliminary way using and testing a conceptual framework the generation of which is controlled by a paradigmatic understanding of religion, we have gone beyond necessary foundations and are firmly engaged in the scientific study of religion.

Before developing a further breakdown of each of the types I turn to the general question of religion and change.

CHAPTER 9

RELIGION AND CHANGE

If religion can be said to be the quest for, realization or maintenance of belonging to the ultimately-real, then it follows that when religion changes, whether in response to socio-cultural change, or with an appearance of spontaneity, it will do so in a manner that seeks the maintenance or restoration of the sense of belonging.

It will be clear, from what was said about the development and expression of the felt sense of reality in chapter 6, that the relationship between socio-cultural experience and religious tradition is a two-way one. Change could be triggered at any point in the system. However, for the sake of clarity, that which follows has been simplified and experience, being the primary reality in religion, has been treated as the independent variable and tradition as the dependent one. That is to say, I have considered the influence of experience upon religious belief and practice, not the other way around.

Thus while, in general, my assumption is that wherever a disturbance is introduced into the system, moves will be made to preserve or reestablish the sense of belonging, for present purposes the assumption may be stated as follows:-

AS SOCIO-CULTURAL EXPERIENCE CHANGES SO WILL THE FELT SENSE OF REALITY. THEREFORE THE SYMBOLIZED SENSE OF REALITY, THE MODE OF BELONGING AND ALL OTHER CONSEQUENT SYMBOLS WILL ALSO CHANGE, IF AND AS NECESSARY, TO MAINTAIN OR RESTORE THE SENSE OF BELONGING.

Possibilities of change are almost limitless. What is offered here are three diverse themes, each interesting in its own right, but also chosen to exemplify the explanatory (and to some degree predictive) power of understanding religion as belonging.

The first theme describes identifiable stages in religious change, generated by moves to maintain the sense of belonging as the perceived level of socio-cultural disturbance increases, as the culture in question is threatened by another one.

The second theme examines the consequences of a rapid pace of change, of time-lag, and of identity preserving moves within a single tradition. Myth reflects reality, but once established, that is, once identities have an investment in it and social structures legitimate it, then it has a life of its own. Then it is possible in the short run, for experience and myth to come apart and to exist in conflict.

The third theme goes back to the most basic elements in religion to consider some limits upon change. In this case, limits set by constraints upon a community's choice of paradigm.

THEME (I)   *RELIGIOUS CHANGE IN SOCIO-CULTURAL*

DISTURBANCE   -   SOME IDENTIFIABLE STAGES

DEFINITION OF TERMS   -   By socio-cultural experience I mean the sum total of the individual's every experience of the world-out-there, which, although unique to the individual, will be very much controlled by the culture and social structures of which he or she is a product and in part a creator. It may, of course, include the experience of others, past and present, which the individual has made his or her own, including those of a religious tradition.

I will be using the word tradition in a more restricted manner than previously so as not to include prescribed relationships and behavior patterns belonging directly to the everyday life of the community. For this present purpose I include these only in the socio-cultural experience of which they are always a part.

Tradition in this restricted sense will therefore include:

(i) beliefs (including any which explain or lend authority to the prescribed relationships and behavior patterns that I have temporarily excluded from the term "tradition") and

(ii) specifically religious practices which are not ostensibly related to the everyday life of the community.

Clearly it can be difficult to draw lines in this area. Are rites of passage, for example, prescribed socio-cultural behavior or specifically religious practices? In general, however, the distinction is clear enough for my purpose.

Tradition is used, therefore, in the limited sense of an overtly religious set of words and practices, by which people express, conceptualize and communicate, their feelings for, and understanding of, the ultimately-real. This is done, recognizing that these same things may also be expressed in the activities and relationships of the everyday life of the community.

I have argued that feelings for the nature of the ultimately-real, what I have called the felt sense of reality, is in the long run distilled from, and certainly verified in, that which I am now calling socio-cultural experience. It will receive, in the short run, some modification from the religious tradition through which the socio-cultural experience is viewed. The tradition may itself have done much to determine the socio-cultural context.

Except perhaps in withdrawal religion, the individuals' felt sense of reality and their mode of belonging to it, will derive predominantly from either their socio-cultural experience or their tradition, or from some combination of the two. There must, therefore, be a fit in the longer run between the felt sense of reality and the socio-cultural experience, or in the short run between the felt sense of reality and the tradition, or the sense of belonging will be lost.

LEVELS OF DISTURBANCE AND STAGES OF CHANGE

Before introducing the actual stages, I must make it clear that all that is offered is a description of a number of stages of change in socio-cultural experience, together with a statement of what changes in belief and practice one might anticipate at each of them, from a consideration of the continued need for a sense of belonging.

I have set these stages out in the order in which they might take place in a situation where an incoming secular world affirming tradition *actively confronts* a nature religion tradition either as a primary concern or as a by-product of other (economic or political) concerns. Disturbance of the socio-cultural experience may not, of course, arise from the deliberate missionary activity of another culture, or indeed from another culture at all. It may be the result of a forced geographical migration, or a spontaneous mixing with other similar groups, sparking off a cultural migration, or any other of a host of internal or external pressures.

I will deal, in chapter 10, with the situation of a disturbed nature religion culture where there is *no* other tradition on offer. A third situation (in today's world the most common, as well as the most difficult to counter), in which a second culture does not actively confront but simply threatens to lure individuals away by its very existence, will be discussed with the modes of containment in chapter 13.

It is not implied that one has to begin where I do, nor pass seriatim through every stage described, nor that stages cannot be missed out, nor that the direction of change could not reverse. Still less is it implied that religion at the end of the series is somehow more advanced than religion at the beginning.

With these matters made explicit, I turn to the identifiable stages of religious change in socio-cultural disturbance.

(i) *THE STATIC STAGE*

I begin with a society which has experienced a stable situation for a considerable period of time and which has not developed a tradition of speculative intellectual enquiry carried out for its own sake by an elite minority, in the style of the Greek and later western philosophical and theological traditions. The characteristics one would expect religion to manifest in such a situation are that it would be predominantly:

(a) A behavior pattern. That is, it would consist in an established set of relationships and practices within the family, community and wider society, and with the natural order. Precisely because the sense of belonging is with every entity in experience, it tends to remain a behavior pattern. Change, other than the cycles of wider nature, would be marked by birth, growth and death in the family, or of significant members of the community and, insofar as there is belief in life after death, there would be prescribed relationships and practices with regard to the recent or otherwise significant dead.

The object of these relationships and practices would be the maintenance of unity, harmony and prosperity, that is, the health of the community and of the individual-in-community. Individual behavioral idiosyncrasies would tend to be controlled by "fear", that is social pressure, rather than by "greed", in the extreme situation, by accusations of witchcraft, for example. If a member threatens the health of the whole body he or she may be exorcised quite radically.

The community and family would have a hierarchical structure, group rather than grid in Mary Douglas' terms,[1] that is, there would be a corporate body sense in which feet would not complain against the head nor the head blame the hands if they became dysfunctional. It is no problem, for example, that a younger son would only approach the father through the eldest brother.

All the relational aspects of life would be essentially religious, for belonging begins with the immediate, which itself belongs to a less clearly defined beyond. Therefore the culture would be:

(b) Texture oriented. That is, the quality of life would be judged by its present texture rather than by some future goal. Each individual's life would be judged by his or her contribution toward or against the maintenance of the desired texture. It would also be:

(c) Immanentist. That is, the divine or powers-that-be would be felt to be present in the order of things as it exists, pervading all of life and maintaining the status quo.

(d) The tradition, in the restricted sense, would be weak, in that there would be little of it and failure in knowledge of the tradition would not be a ground for exclusion nor lead to a loss of the sense of belonging, as failure to observe the behavior pattern might be. The tradition would also be weak in the sense of lacking coherence. Such myths as existed in the tradition would appear to be unrelated to each other, even contradictory, because they would find their coherence, not directly with each other, but indirectly through the relationships existing between those parts of the socio-cultural experience to which individual myths related. So long as the society remained stable there would be no need for the myths themselves to manifest logical cohesion.

(e) Such myths as the religious tradition does contain would have had time to adequately reflect the qualities of the socio-cultural experience.

The members of such a community as I have described, with their sense of reality firmly integrated with their socio-cultural experience, would not be

---

[1] Mary Douglas, *Natural Symbols*, (London, Barrie and Rockliff, 1970).

open to any serious shift in their understanding of reality unless their socio-cultural experience was itself disturbed. In such situations, missionaries who brought a new tradition from another socio-cultural context and offered it in place of the old, would have little chance of direct success. Nevertheless, they would disturb the socio-cultural context in quite inadvertent ways.

Then again the society might be secure enough and innocent enough to be open, at what might be called a playful or a *cujus regio, ejus religio* level, to the reception of the traditions of another culture. These received ideas might only become central to their religion generations later. They might, for example, become deeply ingrained in identity by becoming significant in a struggle for liberation, as certain aspects of the Christian tradition did in the struggle of the British yeoman class against the aristocracy in the puritan period, or quite other aspects did in the struggle of the working class and peasants against the "men of property" in the evangelical revival.

While there is no doubt that in earlier times such stable societies existed, today the "static stage" is virtually an ideal concept. In any period, they would have ceased to exist as they observed themselves being observed, and today there can be few who do not feel observed. It has been suggested to me that another name would be appropriate for the stage where a society, confident in its own tradition, had become aware of other options, but was neither in need of them nor threatened by them. Conservative stage is, I think, the best suggestion, but as there is no significant difference, religiously speaking, between this situation and that which I have described for a truly static stage, I have not included it. I believe that it is sufficient to note the ideal nature of the static stage in today's shrunken world, but to recognize that its religious features could continue in a situation of low level disturbance.

(ii) *PROTECTIVE STAGE*

If the group described above underwent some disturbance of its socio-cultural experience then the expected effects in relation to the maintenance of a sense of belonging would be:

(a) a lessening of the sense of belonging derivable from the socio-cultural experience itself, and

(b) a corresponding increase in the importance of beliefs and specifically religious practice, that is, of tradition in the limited sense. The tradition could be expected to:

1) grow in extent,

2) be more consciously held,

3) become more coherent within itself (the coherence of those parts of the socio-cultural experience to which it relates having weakened), thus tending to move toward a more consciously monistic system even if it retained a place for evil forces,

4) become a criteria for inclusion in, or exclusion from, the group.

(c) the introduction of new behavior patterns. Such patterns tend first to be ones of avoidance in every day life and to be demanded of the individual rather than of the community as a whole. They are thought of as appropriate or ethical behavior, but are not directly necessitated by life itself. For example, they may relate to dress, to drink, to sexual relationship, to wearing red ochre, to dancing, even to the making or not making of noise. These patterns function to strengthen group identification and to provide a semblance of structure in a disintegrating socio-cultural experience.

From this protective stage, through to what I will call the paradoxical stage, a new behavior pattern, whether of commission or avoidance, would no doubt be preferred to the sweeping introduction of a belief pattern. An exception to this might be where increasing demand for social and geographical mobility of the individual is a factor in the new situation. This is because it would be more familiar in style, being more in keeping with the behavior pattern which functioned previously in the stable socio-cultural situation.

A particularly important, specifically religious behavior pattern of commission, is that of prayer. In a situation of increasing disturbance it is likely to be prayer for healing or wholeness. When in the process of change, tradition becomes detached from the contemporary socio-cultural experience, and older ritual practices (grounded as they were in a largely predictable experience) become less plausible, then resort may be had to prayer. Prayer is rendered the more appropriate by the divine becoming more transcendent and therefore more personal. Prayer as behavior pattern can easily move toward prayer as belief pattern, becoming more cognitive than earlier ritual practices, and therefore a more possible religious expression for the mobile individual.

Finally in this protective stage one would expect:

(d) a declining sense of immanence and a tendency toward transcendence.

This last point is the most fundamental for it relates directly to the paradigm for reality employed. I must remain with it for a moment.

To the extent that a present socio-cultural experience is disordered or unacceptable, one has no wish to see it continue. Rather, if such a hope can be maintained, one begins to look for a new future or a restored past.

If the hope cannot be maintained, then the quest for some other explanatory framework within which to reestablish meaning might lead toward a form of withdrawal religion. If a future hope can be maintained, the ultimately-real will be conceived as transcending the present socio-cultural experience and as being ahead, leading into the future.

Desired change of any kind will tend to produce an emphasis on transcendence and therefore a more volitional, personal aspect to reality.

It has been suggested that the move to monotheism, that is to transcendence, takes place when a people's world enlarges and the need of a more cosmic deity to deal with it is felt.[2] It is true that the scale of power must meet the scale of need. For example, a god with the whole world in his hand is vital in major social disturbance, a god immediate enough to be concerned with the aches and pains of individuals is equally necessary at virtually all times. Increasing scale, however, does not lead inevitably to monotheism. The evidence is otherwise. Transcendence gained emphasis when the Israelites left a highly cultured Egypt for small-group isolation, and again two and a half millennia later, when Christendom was busy breaking down into small states each wrapped up in its own new-found independence.

It is change itself, not increase in scale, that leads to transcendence. People place their god where their hope is, that is in the future. The need for a more cosmic sense need only lead to monism. Monotheism is dualistic as to reality, not monistic. The two must be carefully distinguished.

The socio-religious processes leading to these predicted changes might be something as follows:

> In the early stages of disturbance one would expect a tightening up of the existing behavior pattern. Then one would expect a rise of spokesmen seeking to maintain, proclaim and bring society into line with (what would be claimed to be) the old tradition, although this might include appropriate elements taken from elsewhere, even from an incoming threatening culture if these seemed to offer a stronger source of power or unity. These moves necessarily involve the growing importance of right belief.
>
> Then would come the exorcism from the communal body of those who, by their failure to conform to the general behavior pattern, or to

---

[2] Monica Wilson, *Religion and the Transformation of Society*, (Cambridge, Cambridge University Press, 1971) p.9.

subscribe to the beliefs or perform the specifically religious practices, weaken its power to provide a sense of belonging.

As the group's own symbols become less adequate and exorcisms more frequent, then meanings from the incoming culture might be given to the old symbols, or the incoming symbols and their meanings be taken over together. During this stage one would expect the old leadership to remain, becoming more authoritarian.

(iii) *SEARCH STAGE*

If the pace of change in socio-cultural experience is not too great and if, for other internal or external reasons, the group does not feel too insecure, it might not go far in the protective stage, but rather follow a path that could include accommodation with the tradition of any incoming culture. Then one would expect a general search, including within the incoming and disturbing tradition itself if there is one, for elements with which to understand its own gradually changing sense of reality. At the same time there would be a move to give new meaning to suitable elements of the existing tradition.

For the society at large, the search for new elements to meet new needs would be largely unconscious and go on gradually over a long period. In most situations, however, there are marginal individuals, or even marginal groups, who given their less than total acceptance in the existing society, might take quite active steps to accommodate to an incoming culture. Once such a move toward accommodation has been made, these people would be even less acceptable to those members of their own society who had not made the move. So, although accommodation may solve some immediate problems, it may also add to alienation and to the sense of chaos. If that is the case, there will be an even more pressing need to reformulate the symbolized sense of reality and to intensify the search for belonging. This will push such a people, beyond the search stage into a more fully developed protective stage or into the paradoxical stage.

(iv) *PARADOXICAL OR IRRATIONAL STAGE*

If the disturbance of the socio-cultural experience becomes so great as to border on the chaotic, then one can expect the religious tradition to move to the paradoxical or irrational stage. This stage is paradoxical or irrational in the sense that it is characterized by a situation in which:

(a) The religious beliefs and practices no longer gain their *authority* from their resonance with the socio-cultural experience, but from their success in creating the required sense of group belonging. This they do the better, precisely because they are independent of the chaotic or unacceptable socio-cultural experience. They become a haven in the midst of chaos by the limitation of the "really real" to experience within this overtly religious, acceptable and partially controllable context.

(b) The beliefs and practices no longer gain their *meaning* from their relation to the actual socio-cultural experience, although they may from a imagined one. The meaning arises from their place in the whole tradition, that is, in the set of beliefs and practices which have now become a sort of theological castle-in-the air.

(c) The meaning of the beliefs and practices is now less important than the fact that they are held in common, a form of words and acts which have authority, precisely because they succeed in creating a sense of belonging in much the same way as a flag might.

(d) What is believed is now less important than the *strength* with which it is adhered to.

or: (e) It is at the paradoxical stage that the other principle of cohesion, rather than those of behavior or belief, becomes a possibility, namely, a shared experience unrelated to the socio-cultural experience. Here, the highly emotionally charged religious meeting, charismatic experience and the charismatic figure find their place, and here again it is the strength of the allegiance to the experiences in their context that is self justifying, rather than the meaning ascribed to them.

This is the stage at which sudden and mass conversions become a possibility because:

(a) When the authority of the tradition depends only on its power to produce a sense of belonging, not upon its relation to a deep sense of the nature of the ultimately-real distilled from the socio-cultural experience, then one "flag" may be changed for another, provided that the change is complete.

(b) Whereas the new was completely rejected, now the old will be completely rejected. The intensity of loyalty to one "flag" is everything in the production of the sense of belonging, but which flag is virtually irrelevant.

(c) When changes have taken place such that the old socio-cultural experience seems irrecoverable, a move may be made to embrace the symbols of the culture which is causing the disturbance, or should there be none, or if their is resistance to them, then an active search for a new "flag", a third alternative, becomes a strong possibility.[3]

The paradoxical stage, however, will only last as long as experience of the socio-cultural situation remains unacceptable and no other way can be found to cope with it, because:

(a) the beliefs and practices begin to feel unreal as the need for them (as the sole supplier of the sense of belonging) recedes. This is because, to derive a sense of belonging to the ultimately-real out of a community sense of belonging requires the reduction of one's effective reality to that community and its activities. This closing down of experience would not continue for long, except for individuals of a particular psychological type, once the external situation had changed.

(b) such beliefs and specifically religious practices have a dogmatic quality which means that while they unite those who hold to them they are, in more general terms, divisive and

(c) people never seem to be comfortable in two unrelated worlds, but rather seek to integrate their experience.

Religion in the paradoxical stage will tend to be of the kind that I have previously called "reduced reality belonging" precisely because the cosmic sense has failed. There can be no tolerance of nice distinctions, for example, about levels of righteousness. Either one belongs to the group or one does not! The group is good! Others are bad!

Religion in the paradoxical stage has the world- view and language style of apocalyptic. It will be overtly concerned with the power rather than the character of the ultimately-real and may look for imminent intervention whether by divinities or ancestors.

Although the talk is about power and intervention, the underlying quest is still for belonging. This is clearly indicated by the fact that support for the charismatic type leader who arises in this situation is increased, rather than diminished when promises of divine or ancestral intervention are not fulfilled. In such situations the sense of chaos is increased by the failure of the predictions and the first response (traditional links being all in disarray) is to hold even more firmly to the figure representing a link with the ultimately-real.

My concern here is mainly with the whole cultural group under pressure and, of course, with those who lead its opinion, but as I have indicated, individuals of a certain psychological type, as well as marginal individuals and groups, may also embrace this style of religion. Individuals, however, are likely to be looking more overtly for *belonging*, that is for a secured identity

---

[3] It is in this way that Marxism has offered hope to many in the Third World who, feeling themselves oppressed by the Free World, have not been able to find sufficient ideological resources in their own traditions.

and for personal significance, than for *power*. They may speak in apocalyptic language of imminent divine intervention, but they may go on doing it for a very long time without manifesting any concern that it has not happened. Here we are not concerned with a real need for power but with the personal status or significance which the possession of *gnosis*, in this example, knowledge of divine purposes, conveys.

Generally, in this situation, individuals are more likely to move to pietism than to reduced reality belonging. I will be returning to pietism, but for the moment, it will suffice to say that what I mean is an increased concentration on relation with the ultimately-real and a consequential withdrawal of concern from the socio-cultural realm. It remains open and positive in relation to the rest of experience. Belonging is found solely in relation to the ultimately-real, not as is the case in reduced reality belonging, in the rejection or even hatred of that to which one does not belong.

Pietism can exist in individuals when the wider society is at any of the stages described here, but is not likely to be common in the static stage. In the protective stage it could be persecuted, if the group ethos is contrary to it.

(v) *THE INTEGRATIVE STAGE*

During the protective stage and beyond, tradition becomes more coherent in itself, that is, it tends toward what, in Christian circles, would be called a systematic theology, together with theologically justified practices. After a community has been through a period of intense upheaval it will almost certainly have a systematic heritage.

When the socio-cultural experience stabilizes, not necessarily to the point of becoming static, but at least to the point where change becomes reasonably predictable and where there is a sense of exercising some measure of control, then most people become impatient of beliefs that are not relevant to life. That such beliefs are systematically integrated is not sufficient. They begin to question the relevance of each belief and practice, that is, they want to know how beliefs and overtly religious practices relate to socio-cultural experience. There will now be a felt need for direction in the more controllable socio-cultural arena. The interest will shift, therefore, from systematic belief toward the specific ethical topics that are highlighted by the socio-cultural process, perhaps with a carry over into systematic ethics.

Should the socio-cultural experience again become relatively static, religion will tend to return to being a behavior pattern pervading all of life, rather than a pattern of specifically religious beliefs and practices.[4]

---

[4] I believe all of these stages are recognizable in the European theological history of this century.

I might illustrate this by returning to my caricature of English, particularly rural, Anglicanism of a generation ago. The most one would be asked for in belief and practice was general assent to a Catechism at Confirmation and an unsupervised requirement of attendance at Communion in the octave of the major festivals. The Church reflected the socio-cultural experience of the community. The squire sat in his box in the chancel, the gentry in the front pews, the laborers behind, the women of each group knowing their station and having different tasks in relation to altar linen, flowers, cleaning and contributions to harvest festival, etc. On the church walls the ancestors of the significant members were reintegrated into the socio-cultural experience. God was the immanent maintainer of the status quo. Only bad manners (a failure to observe the prescribed behavior pattern) would tend to exclude one from such a community. As a religious type there is little to distinguish it from the static monism with which we started, save that an elite few may continue to do theology or ethics of a systematic self-contained kind, regarded as a self-justifying intellectual game by the majority.

It is clear that different combinations may arise from the passage of religion through the paradoxical stage. If a form of conversion has taken place, that is, if one tradition has been exchanged for another then either:

the new set of symbols will gradually take their meaning from a new socio-cultural experience, or

the new set of symbols may take their meaning from a recaptured old socio-cultural experience.

If conversion has not taken place then either:

the old symbols may take new meaning from a new socio-cultural experience, or

the old symbols may regain meaning from the recaptured old socio-cultural experience.

In any case, if intensity of belonging to a single flag had been reached it would now relax and, if conversion has taken place, a renewed interest in one's roots may emerge, or, if conversion has not taken place, at least a polite interest in the other symbol set becomes a possibility.

I have written as though the community under discussion was, with the exception of a few marginal individuals, monochrome. Relatively speaking, that might be the case in a long stable society with a cyclical time world-view.

Just how religion settles down will depend upon the socio-cultural experience of individuals, and if that is not monochrome nor will the resulting religion be. It is very unlikely to be monochrome in a goal orientated society, however consistent the experience may have been, for it will almost certainly have developed social stratifications, each stratum having its own life experience. Thus, although I am speaking of how religion is likely to settle down after a shake up, I will be dealing with tendencies most of which would be present in any non-homogeneous community. Only those things that result from a rapid pace of change are likely to be different. Even in settled times there will still be a socio-economic stratification of life needs and therefore of religious expressions. I will return to this in chapter 11 when I consider how the individual's whole religious system is authenticated.

When a community has a strong communal sense, such as is typical of traditional Africa and of diaspora Judaism, its religion will tend to serve that communal sense and remain unitive.

When a society develops the strata which are almost a *sine que non* of goal orientation, or where two or more cultures mix, religion will tend to serve the interests, that is, conform to the experience of each sub-group. By way of example consider a society which in general embraces a secular world affirming type of religion.

For what becomes an established dominant group and therefore one in favour of the *status quo*, the situation will be much as described above for a settled nature religion culture. The ultimately-real will be an all pervading spirit, maintaining the texture and legitimating the structures of culture and society. Religion will tend to be universalistic and tolerant. It would probably, therefore, embrace an individual, that is universal, ethic for the world at large, but nevertheless have a strong corporate ethic in its own group. It would have a nice balance of individual and corporate advancement within its own group, but be strongly in favour of corporate advancement in relation to the whole society. That is to say, it will move to hierarchical rather than egalitarian structures, to group rather than grid relationships.[5]

The power of evil will not be taken too seriously, bad being simply a failure of the good. Its concern will be with culture (present texture) rather than with historical development. Religion will tend to be of the indirect corporate type and its expression to be in terms of the best in the culture (music, architecture etc.) and to favour ritual dignity.

For the next group down, the ones who feel that they can achieve advantageous change by their own individual efforts, the religious need

---

[5] Mary Douglas, *ibid*.

would be for:

> *change*, so the ultimately-real will remain out in front, that is, be transcendent, and

> *direction*, and therefore knowledge of the character of the ultimately-real, an ethic, will be more important than power, and therefore teaching more important than testimony or sacrament, and

> the present *freedom* to be at risk *vis à vis* the environment, which comes *inter alia* from belief in a determined (predestined) end which enables one to launch out into the fog of unknowing certain of coming to the other side.

Therefore, the socio-cultural experience (history) will be affirmed and allowed to inform the beliefs and will probably be addressed in prophetic style. That is, the relevance of belief to specific socio-cultural concerns (that is the mark of the integrative stage) will be a live issue. The religion will tend to be direct and individualistic, allowing individuals to be mobile units. The emphasis will be on self-discipline (righteousness) rather than love, and "greed" (self-enhancement) will be preferred to "fear" (social pressure) for social coercion. History, although likely to be finally determined, will be seen as continuous with what lies beyond it.

Social relationships will tend to be egalitarian, that is, grid rather than group, in which leaders are accepted only for specific purposes, unless they should happen to become symbolic of an espoused cause. There would be a stress on an individual ethic and individual advancement rather than upon their corporate counterparts. The religious expression would be concerned with self-discipline and the texture of individual life. The expectation being that "God blesses the righteous".

Members of a group who feel that they can achieve advantageous change but only by corporate effort, will differ from the above in that fellowship will be emphasized, social pressure will be more acceptable as a motive, divine power as well as character will be important. They will not see themselves as individually entering the top group but will be concerned with the reform of society as they experience it. Religious expression will be concerned with individual righteousness, but also loyalty to group and to the good of society.

For a group without hope of changing an unacceptable socio-cultural experience, the religious need is a thaumaturgical one. Experience of God is more important than knowledge of God, the power of the ultimately-real rather than its character. What matters is not teaching, but testimony to past and present super-natural phenomena such as healings, tongues and dramatic conversions. The socio-cultural experience (history) is not affirmed but looked to for examples of the ultimately-real's control over the forces of "evil" and its power to intervene in bringing about an historically discontinuous future in which "the last shall be first".

This, of course, is the apocalyptic religious type and remains in what I called the paradoxical stage. It tends to be corporate religion of a sectarian kind, creating a security group by clear definition of who is in and who is out. This, as I said, will be achieved by requiring "soundness" of belief and performance of, or abstention from, certain activities.

The pietistic alternative might exist at any of these levels.

THEME (II)   *SOME CONSEQUENCES OF RAPID CHANGE*

In the normal individual, there seems to be a constant attempt to harmonize what I called the felt sense of reality and its symbolization. If this is indeed the case, then in a situation which has been relatively static for a considerable period, there will be a high degree of fit between the socio-cultural context and the tradition (in the more inclusive sense of the word) of the wider society. It is not possible to say just what sort of a time scale one is involved with here and factors tending to facilitate or inhibit smooth change must be many and varied. What can be specified, are situations in which the time span has been too short or change has been too rapid, given the other factors in the situation, for the mutual adjustment to take place. I wish to describe two such situations.

Theologians, or in general, those religious functionaries who are responsible for keeping the tradition vital and relevant and thereby helping individuals to symbolize their own sense of reality, function by addressing themselves and their peers. This is quite natural, for they give priority to those matters which predominate in their own sense of reality. It would take a very deliberate effort to acquire a more universal standpoint and, having done so one would have lost one's audience. Contextual theology is not new, it may have become a little more consciously contextual.

Consider for example a Christian theologian belonging to a long dominant and affluent group who, when he brings the Christian gospel to bear upon his situation, must either legitimate the status quo or do what might be called "guilt theology". If he does the latter, he will emphasize the human responsibility of his group and of the individuals who comprise it, responsibility before God for the world in general and the underprivileged in particular.

Further, as he calls upon his not so Christian peers to manifest this righteousness, he will call upon his Christian peers and his Church to set an example, to be "a lamp set on a lampstand". The Church then tends to become an alternative community, that which sets an example to and even condemns, the wider society by its very presence.

This theology, because it emphasizes personal responsibility for the maintenance of eternal values, tends to become universalistic and ahistorical, concerned with life's present texture rather than its goals, and perhaps to neglect the needs of the ordinary church member with his family to provide for. Like the prophets of old prophesying in times of confidence and carelessness, they will emphasize the responsibilities of freedom and the conditional nature of the covenant relationship.

On the other hand, a theologian belonging to an oppressed group will do a "providence theology" of the liberation kind. He will emphasize, if there is any hope of it, exodus from rather than acceptance of the situation. He will look to the power of an historically active God, that is, to providence. He will tend to see only oppressors and the oppressed and not allow himself the luxury of distinguishing between righteous and unrighteous individuals within either group. He will see in his situation forces at work which, unbeknown to themselves, are instruments of the divine purpose such as were the Assyrians, Babylonians and Cyrus of old. These are forces to be co-operated with, not struggled against, whether they be Christian or quite otherwise.

He may, in order to recommend to his Christian peers, the non-Christian forces as the instruments of divine purpose, seek to show what is Christian in them by a another name. His concern will be with the goal of liberation rather than with the present texture of individual relationship and he will probably postpone consideration of the hoped for texture to beyond the liberation event. The Church is not an alternative community, a lamp set on a hill, but rather the salt or yeast in God's Kingdom of all the oppressed, for which purpose even the oppressor may be seen as oppressed (alienated) by his own situation and included in the hoped for liberation. Like the prophets of old, when prophesying in times of oppression and despair, they will emphasize the liberating providence and a divine acceptance that is unconditional.

These two groups stand at the extremes. In the middle stand those who feel themselves to be neither oppressor nor oppressed but, feeling themselves to be reasonably in control of their situation, look to their faith in the matter of taking hold of their world and shaping it and therefore for direction rather than power. Theology in this context might be called "knowledge of God theology" for it is concerned with ethics, not so much in the sense of eternal values by which the individual is judged, but rather as seeking to know the character of the historically involved God in order to understand what He would have humankind, his vice-regent, do next.

The Church in this view is primarily the bearer of the tradition which is understood to be the source of this knowledge of God. Even in this group, of course, there are differences. There is, in the lower end of this middle group, a desire to control the development of the whole society, exemplified by the theology of urban and industrial mission. In the upper middle group would be those who largely affirm the social *status quo* and desire to improve the lot of the individuals and perhaps families within it, exemplified by theologies associated with pastoral counselling and family life enrichment.

The problem is not that the trends that I have pointed to exist or that each theologian tends to think of his or her own theology as the authentic tradition, which indeed it may be for the particular situation, but that what I have said of the theologian may become true, in time, of an entire group, not just the strata discussed in the last theme.

The core of the sense of reality, as it is expressed in the theology, may in time become part of the world-view of even those who are not recognizably religious. It can become enshrined in the very structures of society, not least in the education processes.

A sudden change in the context of experience will not then be reflected easily by a corresponding change in the tradition.

The fact selection and valuation processes are such that a great deal of the change in a context may be filtered out and not, therefore, form part of the experience operating to modify the felt sense of reality. Behind the felt sense, as it were, stands the old symbolized reality corporately established as tradition, tending to keep the felt sense of reality unmoved by whatever new experience does filter through.

I will examine briefly two such sudden changes in context, the one in South Africa, the other in Israel.

In South Africa, the Afrikaner group, whose ancestors had struggled with nature and the indigenous people for a foothold in the land and then suffered reverses under British domination, developed in that process a providence theology appropriate to a situation in which they looked for liberation.

Representatives of the core of this group came to political power in 1948, took South Africa out of the British Commonwealth in 1961, and gained a reasonable parity with the English-speaking group in economic institutions by the late 1960s or early 1970s. Theology reflected some of the consequences.

Throughout these years of change and into the mid-1980s, the theology of the traditional Afrikaans-speaking group remained a theology of the kind usually associated with the oppressed, which laid great stress upon divine providence and upon the group and its cohesion. The individual in such a theology is important but he or she is not conceived apart from the group.

This theological outlook was reinforced by the *laager* situation in which Afrikanerdom found itself *vis à vis* the world at large. Yet within the local situation, the Afrikaner had moved into a situation of power and relative affluence. Thus the culture lag ensured that for two or three decades a providence theology was at work in a dominance situation. It was a situation in which the paternalism of that group toward other groups was the inevitable outcome.

Cultural inertia, however, is not the same in all individuals and a few Afrikaners, applying the Christian gospel to their situation, found a place in a knowledge of God theology, but many more found themselves doing guilt theology. This not only separated them from the majority of their own folk, but placed them in the eyes of that majority and indeed in their own eyes, in the same situation as their erstwhile oppressors, the English-speaking South Africans. They had become not only deserters but traitors.

The English-speaking guilt theology in South Africa fitted fairly cleanly into the type described above, which is why theologians in this group identified so easily with other theologians of the first world and could sympathize, if not empathize, with the third world theologians and the World Council of Churches. Their tendency was to set the community of faith over against society (which served to preserve its unity in a fragmenting situation) and to emphasize the importance of the individual and of the eternal values of love and justice. Thus they tended to neglect the pragmatic needs of the situation, not least the need for a common mind within the wider group, that is, for common goals, hopefully drawn out rather than imposed.

Resentment of this new and more immediate (than the earlier English variety) religiously legitimated paternalism, put pressure upon other groups to bolster pride in their own identities.

Those who could went back to their roots in other identifiable traditions, taking pride in rediscovering the riches of Black Africa or India.

Those for whom the situation was most difficult were those who had only the Euro-Christian culture that they shared with the dominant group. In many cases they had received their faith at the hands of those who now used it to legitimate their paternalism. These were members of the so-called Colored community.

For the majority of this group there was no way of affirming their own identity without affirming the tradition of the dominant group, nor of rejecting the tradition of the dominant group without attacking the core of their own identity.

Some, in the attempt to secure their identity, moved into Islam or into heterodox forms of Christianity, others established independent churches. The majority moved into a pietism in which political and social issues, if not neglected altogether, were not allowed to enter into the religious preserve which became entirely concerned with the individual's relation to the divine. Such a situation was a highly unstable one in which either increases or decreases in the perceived pressure could have engendered sudden and massive changes in allegiances.

The situation in Israel has some interesting parallels. People whose ancestors had been in diaspora for two thousand years and whose religion has been described as a formula for survival, suddenly in 1948, became the citizens of an independent state after what was, in comparative terms, a very brief struggle and one in which only a few of its later members were directly involved.

Having for centuries been almost constantly deprived of justice, equality and compassion, and seldom enjoying them in any security, these same virtues had been stamped deep into Jewish identity, alongside a concern for the whole House of Israel and for that which promised liberation, the Land of Israel.

It is said in Israel that Judaism taught them not to persecute while Zionism taught them not to be persecuted, the problem is to hold them together.

In a situation where preservation of the State could call for acts of reprisal against those who would destroy it and less dramatically but of equal significance, where full rights for non-Jewish citizens (given the birth-rates) could result in the State ceasing to be a Jewish one in the not too distant future; the preservation of Jewish identity and preservation of a Jewish State came into fierce competition. It was a competition that was divisive not only between but within individual Israelis.

The choices open to those, who would take the stresses out of their self understanding, were limited. It was possible to leave the State or to give up the tradition! Some did!

Among those who stayed with both State and tradition some opted firmly for the Land and with it, most frequently, for the corporate behavior pattern aspects of the tradition.[6] Others opted equally firmly for the ethical aspects.[7] A large group of those who felt torn apart by this situation opted for pietism, that is, many who had previously only a traditional attachment to religious observance, old and young alike, gave themselves to the performance of the mitzvot, leaving the destiny of the State in the hands of God.[8] Although

---

[6] For example the Gush Emunim, the Block of the Faithful.

[7] For example members of the Peace Now movement.

[8] The Ba'al T'shuva.

there will always be some who are natural pietists, this situation also appeared unstable and likely to survive only as long as those who had opted for the survival of the State held the political reins.

All of these groups, having settled for one aspect of the tradition and having rejected conflicting aspects, were free to prophesy with clarity from their chosen position. Others, who tried hard to hold the whole tradition (traditional symbols, ethic and piety) together, could say nothing without qualification and, not having an audience, fell silent. They felt themselves to be sidelined and seemed to others to be apathetic.

These are always the short term options in preservation of identity when rapid change of context produces conflicts within the tradition. One may opt out of a tradition, or out of the context (if that is possible) or opt firmly for one conflicting aspect of the tradition to the rejection of others, or opt into a religious quietism and thereby out of responsibility for the context.

THEME (III)   *CONSTRAINTS ON CHANGE - TWO CONTROLLING*

VARIABLES IN THE CHOICE OF PARADIGM

Religious change at the cognitive level is not unrestricted. It is bounded by the three paradigms for a reality to which one would belong, and by the possibilities of bridging between these paradigms. Bridging, being very much a corporate activity, will be discussed in chapter 13. What I wish to consider now is what controls the choice of paradigm at the most basic level.

In chapter 5 I introduced the idea of a logic of belonging. A logic of belonging is comprised of beliefs about the necessary links in a relational chain that attach the believer to the ultimately-real, they are cognitive entities.

There is evidence, however, that there is a connection between such cognitive logics and the felt appropriateness of individual beliefs. The necessary elements in these logical chains appear in the religious expression of people who seem never to have raised the cognitive question. This is not altogether surprising, for we are dealing with symbolic entities. I cannot explore the connection further, but I wish to note it in order to make clear that when, in what follows, I speak of the relation between elements in cognitive terms I do not intend to exclude the affective, far from it. The two are so interwoven at this level that I must assume both, even when speaking of one. Even when I am discussing meaning, I would have the reader be aware that the decision as to whether something is meaningful is an affective judgment as well as a cognitive one. Meaning in this context signifies not only that something is communicated but that it is appropriate and not trivial.

Because I am going to be concerned here with the meaning component of the sense of belonging I must say a preliminary word on the relation of meaning and belonging.

Belonging is more than meaning, there is alienation as well as anomie, but meaning is a necessary component of a sense of belonging.

I said earlier that meaning in a goal oriented world-view may be the same as purpose, but it is not so in a texture orientation. Purpose, is necessarily strongly cognitive. "Meaningful" may simply mean worth relating to and be largely an affective judgment. Meaningfulness, at this level, may be little more than the necessary condition for letting questions concerning the nature of the totality of things rest. Even the word "questions" should not be interpreted too cognitively. To question experience may be only the attempt to give verbal expression to what it feels like.

The question may not, of course, be asked. People may be asleep or too busy just surviving or, in an acceptable and relatively static context of experience, the existence of an answer may simply be taken for granted.

If the question is asked, then both meaning and belonging require a cosmic integration. "What is all that out there?" cannot be answered in bits and pieces. Unless the ultimate context is unitive there can be no way of assigning clear relations, and then meaning has disappeared. To say that all that out there is fragmented, is to say that there is no *other* to belong to, only accidentally related entities. The answer is also the other side of the answer to the question "what am I?", which must be integrated or there is no *me* to belong.

Before I return to the criteria for choice between the paradigms, I must reemphasize the distinction made earlier, between *affirming* experience of the immediate world-out-there as experience of the real and finding it *acceptable*. The former is an aspect of the belief system, the latter an aspect of present experience.

THE TWO VARIABLES

At the basic level of choice between paradigms, there are two variables in operation. The first has to do with the supposed context of experience, the individual's world-out-there, and is whether or not experience of the immediate world is affirmed to be experience of the real. The second has to do with the individual life, is it permanent or impermanent? *Felt permanence* is the real issue. Whether it be expressed in terms of souls, spirits, vital force or any other difficult to clarify concept, is not significant for this purpose.

Most peoples down through history have perceived the individual life to be permanent in one way or another. The most significant exception from our point of view, being the people of ancient Mesopotamia and their heirs in this, the various members of the Abrahamic family of religions. The sense of impermanence seems to have been as deeply ingrained in the people of Mesopotamia as the sense of permanence is in the people of Africa.

If experience of the immediate world-out-there is affirmed as experience of the real, it may be because it is felt to be that to which one needs to belong in order to secure and enrich one's existence or because, even though it is unacceptable, no alternative and better way of understanding the situation has arisen. Experience may be unacceptable because life is harsh and unpredictable or, as the evidence from ancient Egypt and the modern West suggest, it has become so predictable and struggle-free as to lack meaning. That is to say, its unacceptability can be in regard to both texture and goallessness.

I know of no situation in which a people, who have affirmed their immediate world-out-there as the real and found it to be acceptable, have not believed individual life to be permanent. This may be my ignorance or it may be an accident of history. It may equally be a consequence of the monistic sense which arises in such a situation, followed by the extension of the life cycles of nature to the individual life. It may arise, as is suggested by ancient Egypt and its elaborate cult of the dead, from the need to extend the possibilities of meaning beyond the tangible world should that not be sufficiently demanding to generate them. I think, however, that the most fundamental reason is that meaning is only possible in any world of experience if either the individual is permanent or otherwise survives death, or there is some grand design of which the individual is a part. The former is the simplest answer to the need for meaning in an acceptable world and may exist even when the latter solution is available. On the other hand a sense of design may generate cosmic trust, and cosmic trust, belief in continued existence, even though survival is not then necessary for meaning.

I now wish to consider the four possible combinations of the two basic variables in detail.

THE FOUR POSSIBLE COMBINATIONS OF THE TWO BASIC VARIABLES

(i) *Experience of the Immediate World-Out-There Affirmed as Experience of The Real   -   Individual Life Not Permanent*

The classical example of people who affirmed their immediate world-out-there as the real but who did not believe in the permanence of the individual life were the people of ancient Mesopotamia. By the time they become known to us they were affirming their world-out-there as real but not, as the texts of period make abundantly clear, because it was acceptable. Their religion had become a conflicted polytheism in which even the accounts of creation were conflict stories, and in which it was said that the gods gave life to men but retained eternal life for themselves.

It could be argued that even here there was a permanence of some sort envisaged, but so bad was the description of it that I believe it to have been only a literary device to make clear that there was nothing beyond which could be likened to life as it was experienced here, bad as that was.

These people lived at the confluence of the great rivers in a situation where nature was cruel and unpredictable (only the cool night sky, neither creating nor destroying, seems to have been predictable and acceptable) and the country was wide open to invasion. That their hope, such as it was, came to be placed in political structures rather than natural ones is also clear from the mythology.

Their options are clear - they could move and in the end many migrated around the fertile crescent. Some found an acceptable experience that they could affirm and they seemingly moved to a belief in the permanence of the individual life, others moved to a sense of a future and a this worldly purpose and thence to a bifurcation of reality, but not to belief in permanence. I will return to these.

For those who could not or did not move, what options were open to provide meaning?

Evidence of trade links with the western end of the fertile crescent and with the Indus valley suggests that they were familiar with beliefs of individual permanence. A reading of the most significant Mesopotamian text for our purposes, the Gilgamesh Epic, suggests on first thought a situation poised for change in world-view. They existed in a monistic system of cause and effect in which everything should have an explanation. Humankind suffered! There had to be an explanation!

There were two possibilities. Either humankind suffered due to its own failures or because of the whims or neglect of the gods. To over-emphasize the latter explanation was to diminish the gods who, bad as they were thought to be, were the only available powers. To get rid of their malevolence was also to deprive oneself of their possible benevolence.

Pragmatism suggested that the those who sufferered blame themselves and there is much of that type of explanation in the texts. But human fault could also be of two kinds. The first, being an innate inadequacy (and there is evidence for that line of thought) returns the ultimate responsibility to the gods who made them and is again diminishing. The other is the willful neglect by man of his duty to the gods. Such an explanation is fine in part but is not credible if it has to bear the whole weight of explanation for the human condition.

Such was the inadequacy of these explanations that it might indeed have been better to have diminished the gods right out of existence and to have moved to an impersonal view of reality. The question is why the world-view did not change as one would have expected.

One possibility would have been to attempt an explanation in terms of the permanence of individual life, but they did not do this. The reason I think is clear. In a monistic world there is nothing to be gained by adding to an unacceptable life what all the evidence would point to being an unacceptable after-life. Reincarnation, which is an attractive thought if one can affirm life, is precisely what the Hindu seeks to escape. Permanence is no gain if experience is bad.

The other possibility would have been to bifurcate reality. They already felt a deep divide between humankind and the gods, but they could not explain their adverse conditions satisfactorily by bifurcating reality because, being bound in a sense of cyclical time, they could have no future hope of the two paths coming together again.

Religion of this kind fits most nearly into the nature religion type, but in fact, it is a religion in transit and unstable for it has no adequate logic to explain the human experience.

(ii) *Experience of the Immediate World-Out-There Affirmed as Experience of The Real   -   Individual Life Permanent*

I said earlier why I believe the second of these variables usually follows from the first, and this will find support when the alternatives in (iii) and (iv) are considered for, as explanatory devices, they are much more complex and, in a literal sense, unnatural.

This present combination of the variables falls into the first paradigm offered earlier and as I said then, it is the *telos* of the other two, at least until people come to feel that goal orientation is good in itself and better than having arrived. This is not only the religion of most viable undisturbed societies, it remains deeply ingrained in Black Africa and in those in favour of the status quo, the example I used being that of the upper-class English.

Anything which does go wrong in this system requires explanation in immediate terms and a restoration of the harmony of the system.

(iii) *Experience of the Immediate World-Out-There Not Affirmed as Experience of the Real   -   Individual Life Permanent*

This combination falls into the second paradigm and the type of religion

I called withdrawal religion. It is typical of the religious traditions cradled in India.

If individual life is permanent, but immediate experience is bad, how can the situation be rendered meaningful? Clearly there is little to be gained by surrendering permanence, although the individualness of it might be surrendered if that would help the other possibility, which is to account for and suggest a way out of the unacceptability of immediate experience.

Again, bifurcation of reality is not available as a solution because time is experienced as cyclical and there is therefore no future hope of the two coming together again.

There remains bifurcation between reality and its present appearance. The immediate world is unacceptable and, because it is not seen as it is, is the cause of human suffering. The immediate word-out-there is real but experience of it is not.

Humanity's failure to apprehend reality as it is can be understood as a largely cognitive problem, that is, not knowing or feeling assured, that everything is one; in particular that I and the ultimate ground of being from which all comes and to which all returns are one. I addressed the two problems with this otherwise attractive solution in chapter 8 and I will only summarize them here.

The first is, that apart from "the one" being necessarily unique and therefore literal discourse concerning it impossible, the immediate world which provides the public frame for discourse is deceptive. One cannot know the real in concepts that are themselves deceptive. The second problem is "I". If all other immediate experience is of the real but is deceptive, then where is the logic for supposing that I am not deceptive. Therefore a cognitive explanation of the failure to apprehend reality as it is in itself is less satisfactory than the affective one which locates the problem in wrong feeling. The Buddhist tradition took the last logical steps in this paradigm locating the problem in feeling and reducing the self to five transitory qualities.

These cognitive and affective emphases parallel the two possible grounds of meaning. Either the individual survives, which suggests structure and therefore the cognitive emphasis, or there is something grand enough about experience for existence to be worthwhile simply by being a conscious part of it for a moment. The latter does not require structure.

(iv) *Experience of the Immediate World-Out-There is Not Affirmed as Experience of the (Ultimately) Real - Individual Life is Not Permanent*

This situation is one in which there is nothing to lose and everything to search for. Meaning requires only that one gain a sense of linear time, that is, of a future, together with a sufficient sense of the reality of the present context of experience, that the future can be known through it and worked for in it. That is, immediate experience is of a real but not of The Real, not what I have been calling the Ultimately-real. This represents a move into the third paradigm.

Simply to move to a belief in permanence would not suffice for meaning. To do so would be to move into the situation that the religions of India sought to overcome.

If the future directedness is seen, not only as the result of the individual's quest but also as part of a greater design, it is not necessary, for the purpose of grounding meaning, to move to a belief in individual permanence. This seems to have been the situation in biblical Israel until faith in a national and historical salvation waned.

If in the situation described, survival after death is added as a bonus to a meaningful existence grounded in a grand purpose, it must be by way of resurrection and not immortality because, in addition to the reasons indicated earlier, the individual's survival must be included in, not be separable from, that purpose. Otherwise the purpose is simply bypassed and ceases to be sufficiently grand.

I do not wish at this point to draw any conclusions from these logical constraints on change at the paradigmatic level. It is, however, a suggestive thought, that for an African to move from a traditional world-view into that of Islam or Christianity means giving up the sense of permanence and then going in search of it again, either as individual permanence or as a moment in a divine purpose. It is not easily done unless the immediate world of experience becomes unacceptable.

FURTHER BREAKDOWNS WITHIN THE COHERENT

TYPES OF RELIGIOUS TRADITION

The next two chapters are dedicated to drawing out greater detail in the consequences of the paradigms of reality and thereby setting out the varieties of tradition that could develop from each of them. This will be done for immediate experience affirming religion (nature religion) and for secular world affirming religion but not for withdrawal religion.

It is not possible to proceed further with withdrawal religion because the basic model of reality is a bifurcation between reality in itself and the human experience of the same. There is a totality worth belonging to but, all appearance being distorted, there is no experience, factual or evaluative, that can serve to ground a language in which reality and the human relationship to it can be described.

CHAPTER 10

A FURTHER BREAKDOWN OF IMMEDIATE EXPERIENCE AFFIRMING RELIGION (NATURE RELIGION)[1]

INTRODUCTION

Among the coherent types of religious tradition described in chapter 8 was the type, previously labeled Nature Religion, in which experience of the immediate world-out-there is affirmed as experience of the real. It was presented in very general terms and in a comparative context. I must now deal with it again, specifically and in detail, in order to explain the varieties in which it can occur.

The world-view of this type is not easy to enter and it may help to reiterate that it is the *telos* of the other types. Africans, whose traditional religion would fall into this type, have known little of the existential loneliness, the not-yet-ness, which drives adherents of the secular world affirming type of religion. It is no more surprising that cultures of this type could remain non-literate than that they seemed to new-comers to have no religion. One would not need writing or religion (as quest anyway) in heaven or nirvana.

Before entering upon the main theme of this chapter it is necessary to summarize and extend what has been said about myth. Clearly, this is not because myth is peculiar to this type of religion, for it is the sole means for the verbal expression of primary religious experience whatever the paradigm. Nevertheless, it is in the nature religion type where myth or other symbolic forms should be almost unnecessary in the ideal situation, that there springs up what seems to be the greatest number and variety of myths.

To understand why this is the case, one needs to recognize that the other two paradigms exist, only and precisely, because the unacceptability of experience has had to be dealt with as a whole. The basic divide between the

---

[1] A summary of the type and details of its features are presented in chapter 8.

ultimately acceptable and the ultimately unacceptable is built into their world-views and this has a number of consequences.

In these other two types, the very experience of unacceptability stands as evidence for the validity of the paradigm. In nature religion unacceptability ought not to be present. It stands as evidence against the modelling of reality and each unacceptable experience must, therefore, be dealt with as it arises. It is this episodic maneuvering to maintain the unity of experience that gives rise to such highly complex and fragmented mythology and to its associated ritual, when the world-view is threatened.

Myth that is generated within the other two types tends to become systematically integrated around the appropriate principle of bifurcation and the proposed means of overcoming it. Thus it is likely to appear more as a coherent theology or philosophy than as a collection of independent, perhaps conflicting, myths. It is therefore less readily perceived as myth, but myth it remains.

Because in this type immediate experience is affirmed as the real, and because there is no bifurcation to act as a buffer, myth must continually reflect any and every change in experience.[1] In particular, there is no escaping the fact that nature is destructive as well as creative and this ambivalence must be reflected in the world-view or it will not feel real. Sometimes the ambivalence is deliberately fostered, sometimes it is reduced to order, but somehow it must be reflected.[2]

For these reasons, and others that will appear, it is important that I enter a little deeper into the nature and functioning of mythical discourse before I enter upon a further breakdown of the types, and of the immediate experience affirming type in particular.

---

[1] A consideration of the extreme positions taken by the religious traditions of Ancient Egypt and Mesopotamia, even though they both fit fairly cleanly within this type, illustrates how readily nature religion adjusts to differences in life experience.

[2] Sometimes the ambivalence remains in each of the powers, as for example in Indra and Rudra, sometimes the powers are separated into creative and beneficial on the one hand and destructive on the other, as in Vishnu the preserver and Shiva the destroyer, although the latter retains some positive qualities. In Egypt, Seth seems to have remained the only destructive manifestation in an otherwise positive pantheon.

A particularly interesting technique for maintaining the ambivalence, while ordering it, is found among the Yoruba of Nigeria. The god Esu functions as a mediator, forerunner, messenger, perhaps "screen", for all the other deities including the high god, Olorun. Not all destructive powers are removed from the other deities but Esu clearly represents the ambivalence of nature that cannot be bypassed and little else besides.

A FURTHER CONSIDERATION OF THE NATURE AND
FUNCTION OF MYTHICAL DISCOURSE

Myth, I said earlier, is verbal symbol, a necessarily affective mode of discourse for conceptualizing and speaking about the unique. I presented it as the product of a largely unconscious felt sense of reality, seeking expression by grasping at symbols that felt right. I drew attention to the locked-in dynamic relationship between myth and experience, each influencing the other in the human quest to know reality as it is in itself. This served, among other things, to indicate that the same symbol, perhaps the very same words, might express different things in different traditions, even for the same individual at different times, and equally, that different symbols might express the same feelings. One cannot lift a symbol out of its context and hope to understand it.

I wish to re-emphasize that if religion is concerned with belonging, that is with identity and its securing, then myth, as the mode of discourse for the communication of the felt nature of the ultimately-real, must be seeking to express what reality is felt to be right now. That is, it must express that to which I wish to be related, as my continuing experience of it is now, good, bad or irrational, not as I once felt it to be or hope that it will be in the future, but as I know it now.

While myth is not history, if the reality expressed is not all-that-out-there, but rather the other side of the coin, the identity of the individual or the community, then history can be a quite basic expression of reality. How I got here and where I am going is one expression of who I am at this eternal moment. Nevertheless, where I was and where I will be are not now real.

Myth, because it is heavily identity significant, will not be given up easily and in certain circumstances people may go on using it, not because it reflects reality, but to generate a false or compensatory sense of reality. In that situation myth is dead but not lying down.

Myth, as well as passively expressing reality, serves to repair reality and to overcome its contradictions. It must do this, however, in a way that is credible. It may do it by seeking a longer perspective than that of the difficult moment, but it must express what is really experienced. Wishful thinking, an unsupported hope for a better tomorrow, does not satisfy. Myth, even of this secondary kind, is about now, for it is the present reality that must be repaired and the present sense of reality which must provide the means.

Apart from noting that much of the vocabulary of mythical discourse was borrowed by some analogy of feeling from the literal mode, I did not in the earlier discussion ask about the sources for, or choice of, the symbolic building bricks out of which myths are constructed or about what renders such choices effective.

It is convenient to deal with these issues by locating and exploring the sources of the similarity that scholars have noted in the myth and symbol of many cultures. When I have done this, I will return to the felt-sense of reality and its symbolization from a pool of possible symbols, in order to show the inter-relatedness of the sources.

UNIVERSAL SIMILARITIES IN MYTH AND SYMBOL

Scholars have long recognized that symbolic forms, including myth, have a basic similarity across time and space and that this goes far beyond what could be regarded as accidental. Some have sought to explain it by diffusion from a common source or sources. Some have seen it as a process of decay (as well as diffusion) from some early monotheistic purity. Clearly there is frequent borrowing of symbolic forms, but diffusion on its own, or even as a major factor in an explanation of the similarities, will not suffice. I will not, therefore, be concerned with diffusion. The paths that myths have travelled and whence they were appropriated, is no doubt an interesting study, but it is not my present concern.

There was a period when, probably under the influence of developments in the biological sciences, social scientists turned to evolution as an explanation of these similarities. Some pointed to an evolution in human mental capacities, others to evolution of cultural experience, including the means of production. Each stage was understood to give rise to symbolic material that manifested it own characteristics wherever and whenever it appeared.

Few today would wish to speak of a primitive mentality that was unable to conceptualize the high god of the monotheistic faiths, or one that was so strongly controlled by emotion that it turned its heroes into gods. Human mental powers may well have developed over millions of years, but in the time span of the myths of which we have knowledge, this is not a supportable explanation.

This is not to say that there has not been change. It is as idle to deny the possibility of change in human thought processes as it is to insist that all change is mono-directional and progressive. Cultural experience also changes, for example, the move to agrarian culture is reflected in myth far and wide. Whether, however, culture or even the means of production, can be said to change through a determined hierarchy of stages and whether, therefore, evolution is a suitable word, is not so clear.

It is my intention to consider the sources of these similarities in a different way and one that will include all that I understand to be valid in the preceding explanations.

THE SOURCES OF SIMILARITY

There are four factors which might be the generators of similarity in symbols.

The first is that profound experiences best express profound feelings about reality and are therefore used for that purpose.

The second is a possible universality of structures in the processes of human perception, conceptualization and communication, whether these be physically determined, logically necessitated, inherited, or simply culturally controlled.

The third is the consistency in the structure of the reality of which human-beings have experience in different times and places.

The fourth, which has been already stressed in this book, is that changes in the modelling of reality and of the ways of belonging thereto are constrained by the three paradigms.

In short, similarities in symbolic forms can arise from the sameness of what is out there to be experienced, similarities in how human beings do the experiencing, limits to how they can conceptualize the experience, and similarities in the language in which they choose to describe the experience.

These are not all static sources. In the symbols drawn from profound experience, as well as in the processes by which human beings experience, there could be patterns of change. Perhaps these would not be of such a determined nature as to justify the description 'evolution', but certainly such that they could account for some of the similarities.

The logical limits set to the modelling of reality would seem to be fixed, but new experiences and new insights might lead to widespread credibility for the sort of conceptualizations of reality that only physicists work with today.

It is, of course, the nature of what-is-out-there, including whether it is static or dynamic, that is of particular interest to religionists, whether they are adherents or students. Before that could be investigated, however, it would need to be disentangling from the consequences of the other sources of similarity. It is therefore necessary to consider all of them.

i) *Profound Experiences Best Express Profound Feeling*

Before we consider this potential source of similarity, it is well to be reminded that while myth employs profound experiences to describe reality, it is not concerned to explain each profound experience, but rather to describe the total reality to which humankind would belong. It may be that, at a second level, in a process of establishing or maintaining the integrity of reality, myth will have to account for aberrant behavior in some of these profound experiences. I will be considering these processes later in the chapter.

We must also note that profound experience is not necessarily the same thing as extreme experience. Extremes certainly focus things, but what they focus on is not necessarily the heartland of reality. Life and death, for example, are not simply extremes in opposition but a spectrum running from no life at all, through little life, all the way to life abundant. All of that spectrum is reality. In fact myth provides a way, while in an extreme situation, to stand back and to realize that the immediate is not the sole reality. This was one of the ways in which the biblical books of Job and Deuteronomy functioned. With these two caveats in mind I return to profound experiences as the building bricks of myth.

Myth could be woven out of symbolic language that gained its meaning from reference to experiences both trivial and unlikely. It would then require a very "hard sell" to gain the attention of those whose sense of reality it represented.

At those times when an escape is sought, and particularly when this is (as in the secular world affirming paradigm) to something which is discontinuous from the present reality, then myth may function best when employing unlikely images. In fact these may be necessary to express the discontinuity involved whenever faith wishes to speak of that which is held to be either before or after the space-time continuum. The apocalyptic literature of the Judao-Christian tradition exemplifies this.

Otherwise the profundity of the purpose, which is to facilitate a sense of belonging to the real, including the establishment of a secured ultimate identity, is best served by reference to profound experiences, not only because these carry over an accidental authority from the experience to the myth, so smoothing its acceptance, but also because they have the authority of being themselves undeniably real.

In the logically coherent type of religion, that affirms immediate experience as the real (nature religion), the real is in any case best represented by the profoundest aspects of experience. The telos of the other religious types being the world view of this one, it follows that reference to that which is familiar and significant and best serves this type, may best express the telos of the others.

Profound experience can, of course, be universal, merely widespread, or quite localized.

Birth, growth and death, male and female, light (day) and dark (night), sky and ground, sickness and health, are universal.

Hunger and plenty, flood and drought, heat and cold, sea and land, war/hate/selfishness and peace/love/generosity, power and weakness, order and chaos, heroism and cowardice, are near universal.

The experience of trees and plants tending to grow again when cut down while man and animals do not, and of the effectiveness of iron on the tips of spear or plough, are widespread.

Quite local but nevertheless profound might be the experience of what an inundation of salt water does to previously arable ground.

Should the profound experiences that a myth reflects be universal or local ones, that would be of interest when first observed but, being an accidental fact, it would be of little continuing significance to the student of religion. If, however, the discovery of universal features in myth were such as to contribute to the better understanding of the structures of human thinking, then that would be of considerable interest. It is still not the primary concern of the student of religion, but it is something of which all students of religion should be aware, lest it mask or otherwise interfere with the effects of that which is the primary concern. To this possibility of universal structures in human thinking I now turn.

ii) *Universal Structures in Human Thought*

A second possible source of commonality in symbolic forms lies in the universality of human thought processes and, if this can be separated, in human communication processes.

It may be that human beings can only perceive and conceive in certain ways. Clearly what they can perceive through sight and hearing is limited to certain wave-lengths and to certain frequencies. Other senses are equally limited. There are, therefore, realities that we have no way of registering directly and, it is reasonable to suppose, some that we cannot register at all.

Conceptualization also seems to be limited to certain categories of relationship. It is not clear whether this is because our mental filing system is not infinitely flexible but operates with a set of given pigeon-holes, or because, at a further remove, our processes of abstraction by which categories are established perform only in certain ways.

It is not clear to me, for example, whether the evidence, on the bases of which Jung proposed his collective unconscious and the archetypes, is a result of fixed features in human thought processes or abstraction from human racial experience.

Philosophers from Aristotle through Kant have struggled with the limits set to human thinking. In more recent times psychologists, structuralists, communication theorists and those concerned with artificial intelligence, have made us aware that, at a deep level but one at which some of the effects can be observed, perception, conception and communication are constrained. They may be constrained by the nature of our humanity, or by a grammar necessary to particular modes of conceptualization and communication, perhaps by racial memory, perhaps by a more immediate cultural conditioning. Among these contributors, structural analysis, which has made a major contemporary impact upon the study of myth, requires our special attention. I must diverge from the main theme to deal with it.

NOTE : STRUCTURAL ANALYSIS

Structuralists suggest that much of what is conveyed by language lies deep in its structure rather than upon the surface and that this structure arises from the human subconscious. Two continuing interests of structural analysts impinge upon the study of religion. The one is the analysis of narrative, the other the analysis of myth.

The structural analysis of narrative seems to provide a useful tool and not to raise extraneous problems. Narrative, after all, is simply a form within language. The structural analysis of myth is a more dubious enterprise. I will deal with narrative first.[3]

The Structural Analysis of Narrative

Corporate experience, as distinct from personal experience, can only be possessed in the categories of language and there can be no doubting the importance of such categories for any study of culture. I hold it to be beyond doubt, that just as there are rules within which meaning is conveyed at the level of the sentence, so there are rules or normative structures in operation at more general levels in the processes of communication.

People writing about structuralism have sometimes stressed a musical parallel. One musical note written without a frame means virtually nothing, just as the first audible note of a piece being played means nothing, but gains significance from what follows. So sentences and blocks of sentences are frequently such that they gain meaning in relation to other sentences and blocks of sentences.

It is clear that structuralists would affirm not only that that which comes after in a text gains its meaning from what has gone before, but also that that which has gone before is constantly modified by that which comes after. This means that, as with music, two hearings will not necessarily be the same, for what comes early in the piece will be modified by what came after in previous hearings, and that in turn will modify that which comes after in this hearing. It is a process that potentially continues until all extractable

---

[3] There is now a large body of literature in this field from both linguists and anthropologists and latterly biblical scholars, but one of the best ways into the field for the student of religion is still Jean Calloud, *Structural Analysis of Narrative*, Daniel Patte (trans.), (Philadelphia, Fortress, 1976).

meaning has been distilled.

The structuralist, then, needs to have in mind at one and the same time, the whole of the entity under consideration. This gives to the process of analysis a positivist feeling, a feeling of photographing a slice through time and fixing it. This ahistorical sense, however, is misleading, for it does not have to be a denial of change, nor of an interest in the processes thereof. It is the necessity of a method, moreover it would not be inappropriate to the analysis of myth. Myth, as was said earlier, is always a description of how reality is felt to be now. History certainly plays the major role in creating a sense of reality, perhaps in the long run it is the only significant factor, but neither history nor a future hope is of the essence of myth. Myth is an expression of reality, reality is now. Thus a method that holds the moment still is not alien to the study of myth, provided that in the back of the observers mind is always the knowledge that reality probably felt different a few moments before and will feel different again a few moments hence.

Having said this, it does not require structural analysis to tell us that places and times, characters and activities are defined as they go, or that the myth will be experienced differently if it has been heard before. Nor does it require structural analysis to tell us that a narrative is *inter alia* defining whatever or whoever moves the whole story, be it chance or fate, tao or deity, or simply reality. Where those concerned with religion and hence with myth would look to structuralists for a contribution and, for one perhaps that only they could make, would be in the area of how myth conveys profound feelings.

Meanings that emerge in the ordinary grammar of the sentences may, of course, be feeling cathected, that is, they may have feelings associated with them, but broader structures could also convey feelings. They could do this indirectly, by conveying some cognitive meaning that is itself feeling cathected, or they could perhaps do it directly without cognitive meaning intervening. If they do it directly, then it may be by reflecting feeling cathected structures in reality itself, that is the myth may be, as it were, onomatopoeic. On the other hand the structures may be purely conventional and communicate feeling by means of some structure that has come to connote the feeling cathected structures of reality or simply to connote the feelings themselves. Whether there are, or could be, structures that universally convey some particular feeling remains to be seen.

In the end, when the student of religion is concerned with myth, he or she is concerned only with meaning and feeling. Knowledge of how the meaning and feeling is conveyed is a secondary consideration; knowledge of the processes by which they are conveyed would only be significant if it contributed to a grasp upon meaning and feeling by those who, because they are not part of the culture, are not conditioned to grasp these immediately.

Meaning is essentially conscious, therefore any meaning that was revealed by analysis that would not grasp, or be grasped by any in the culture, is not a deeper meaning, but an invented meaning. Feelings too, are conscious, but what shapes how a person feels may be hidden deep in the unconscious and be communicated in ways that are not normally conscious. Students of religion are as interested in how people might be 'not conscious of not belonging' as they are in how people are 'conscious of belonging'. Therefore they have a primary interest in *what* is conveyed at both conscious and unconscious levels. *How* it is conveyed is not their primary interest.

The work done by structuralists on narrative suggests that it is a universally recognizable form, regardless of the culture or language in which it is located. The presence of that normative structure alerts one to, or confirms one in, the belief that what one is receiving is narrative and not some other form of discourse. It alerts one to what is to be expected of and to be done with the meaning and feeling possibilities communicated in the sentences. This would be different from the stance that a reader would adopt if he or she understood a text to contain legal or scientific material.

The structure is not always completed in a particular narrative but, such is its normative nature that when any part of it is present and recognized, the rest is expected. This sets up the possibility of generating meanings and feelings, including simply a questioning stance, when the normative structure is tampered with or left incomplete.

Although the analysis of narrative must begin with an examination of the content of many examples and therefore with real human experience, it ends up revealing the structural means by which human beings communicate about choices and value conflicts, abstracted from the time, place and individuals, which give a narrative flesh. In the end narrative appears as a structural form in the realm of language with real persons and real places deconstructed into timeless, spaceless contrasts. Narrative is an arena in which human beings can consider abstracted values.

Insofar as the student of religion has an interest in the level of abstraction at which the feeling for present reality is expressed, that is, whether the language is almost the literal description of representative parts of experience, both immediate and historical, or whether it has moved toward a more universal attempt to model reality's essential nature, he or she has something in common with the structural analyst of narrative.

The Structural Analysis of Myth

Myth, of course, may be narrative and be analyzed as such. There can be no problem with that, but the question is whether myth can be analyzed as myth. To do a structural analysis of myth *per se*, without first offering a definition of myth, means that myth is understood to be self-defined and presumably by its structural form.[4] I, on the other hand, understand myth to be a tool of religion and therefore to be defined by its function in relation to religion. Religion is the primary fact, not myth.

There have been many emphases in the scholarly understanding of myth, most of which appear to have a claim to truth, but none of which seem to have penetrated to the essence. When myth is treated as an aspect of religion, rather than being treated as though it were itself a primary human product, certain consequences follow.

In the first place it will be recognized that living myth is always part of a dynamic process, not that which has been caught in static textural form. In the second place it will be understood that myth can only be the product of an individual creator in a tradition community of one. Myth does not become myth until it is grasped as such by the tradition community. It may be spoken by one voice but it develops by a process akin to group psychoanalysis. It is a *corporate account of what reality feels like now*.

Those who have employed structural analysis in the study of myth and have demonstrated the presence of a complex structure in the myths chosen seem to have reduced myth to one of its secondary functions, namely the reconciliation of potential contradictions, the synthesizing of aspects of experience which are seemingly antithetical.[5] For this limited purpose there might well be a recognizable linguistic structure. There are a number of reasons why such a limitation of myth could have seemed authentic to those who engaged in it.

It could have seemed authentic because these were western scholars and therefore most familiar with that form of religion in which the overcoming of an alienated condition is the overall drive, an outlook reinforced in recent times by scholars who have associated religion with meaning-marginal situations. They chose to work for the most part, however, with religions where wholeness is assumed and upon material that represented attempts to maintain an integral sense of reality when that assumption was threatened.

The limitation could also have seemed authentic because scholars accepted the presence of myth and ritual, functionaries and artifacts within cultures, speaking loosely of them as religion, but not fully exploring the

---

[4] Indeed Lévi-Strauss claims that myth is universally recognizable. *Structural Anthropology*, Clair Jacobson and Brooke Grundfest Schoepf (trans.s), (London, Allen Lane The Penguin Press, 1968) p.210

[5] I have in mind Claude Lévi-Strauss and those who have followed him. If Hegel was right and reality is itself dialectical, then myth, as the description of reality, would reflect that quality, but that is not the same as using myth to overcome it.

nature, consequential varieties and dynamic quality of religion. It allowed them to treat myth as a static entity enshrined in the reports of field workers and other texts, rather than as an aspect of religion and therefore in a constant process of generation and modification. Far from myth being obviously myth to any observer, it only becomes myth when it is owned, as an expression of their felt sense of reality, by the members of a tradition community. It remains alive when it is constantly updated by an "healthy doubt". I will return to these processes later in this chapter and again in chapter 13.

Finally and at a more profound level, the limitation could have seemed authentic because one might understand all myth to be primarily concerned with establishing a frame of meaning. This is not the same as the need to symbolize the felt sense of reality, but its consequential output in a relatively harmonious experience would not be dissimilar. All meaning is conveyed in frameworks that enable distinctions to be made. The most basic form of this is a simple binary opposition, for example, east v. west, north v. south, high v. low, near v. far. These may then be included in further binary oppositions north-south v. east-west and vertical v. horizontal. To these may be added, before v. after, and a great variety of quality scales constructed of binary oppositions, hot-cold, hard-soft, bright-dull. Thus a network builds in which subtle meanings can be conveyed.

Given the way in which computer language is built from binary statements, it may well be that all human meanings are built from such basic binary oppositions. If this were the case, however, it would be true of all forms of communication, not just myth.

Myth, however, communicates very basic feelings in a solemn way and it is usually long matured, so that it reflects with precision what its adherents require it to reflect. It would not be strange, therefore, if myth manifested a structure of binary oppositions near the surface and near complete, while the language of more common discourse functioned with a mass of shortcuts, suggestions and approximations, in which the structure that established the possibility of meaning was all but lost. It would then be easy for the distinction between process and purpose to become blurred, that is, for the integration of binary oppositions into a frame for the communication of meaning, to become associated with the resolution of contradictions in experience.

There is indeed a large body of myth which represents the human attempt to overcome contradiction. It might very well be that this is the dominant overt concern in what has come to be regarded as mythic literature. To recognize a common structure in this body of myth, if it exists, would be important. Nevertheless, not all myth is concerned with this process of reconciliation, nor is such a structure the only manner of dealing with contradiction. Structuralism's dealing with myth has begun on a branch, not with the root.

Whatever the reason for its acceptance, the choice to restrict mythic literature to the sub-class of material concerned with the overcoming of significant oppositions is not supportable. One could hardly reduce the role of symbol to that of reconciling oppositions in experience. Myth is best thought of as symbol that has taken verbal form.

Even if there were no oppositions, there would be a need for identity and therefore for myth. Certainly the need for identity is emphasized by oppositions, but identity and a sense of belonging can equally be threatened by harmony, by having nothing to raise the consciousness of unity and belonging.

There are cultures where, far from a need for integration, there is a need to break out and where forms of antinomianism exist for just this purpose. These enable the adherents to stand outside the traditional understanding of the cosmic order for a moment and to know what it is like to be without it. There are also cultures where life is so smooth that, from time to time, deliberate risks are undertaken in order to test the quality of the belonging.[6]

Myth is the attempt to model the reality to which one would belong. Above all, it must reflect reality as it is experienced, conflicts and all, otherwise it may remain as narrative but it will cease to be myth. Myth may, as we have seen, in part and in the short term, modify experience, but it is always in dynamic relationship with life. It is not to be reduced to a *genre* of literature or a form in language.

What makes myth myth is not a matter of linguistics but of purpose. When, within that wider purpose, a particular problem has to be dealt with, namely the integration of seeming contradictions, then humankind may have a recognizable linguistic form for dealing with it, but it is not the only way.

The structure that is apparent in the type of literature which the structural anthropologists chose to identify with myth, seems to lie in the process by which the resolution of oppositions takes place. Thus it is a structure appearing in a text, which, if it goes beyond the establishment of a frame for linguistic meaning, is a structure imposed by one commonly chosen solution to a problem arising in a particular context and from a basic religious need. It is not the structure of a linguistic form such as is narrative, which universally provides the arena in which all values may be explored.

It has been seen that the drive for the integration of identity and for the integration of that to which one would belong may require that experience be divided into that to which one would belong and that to which one would not belong. In such a bifurcated world-view certain types of contradiction in experience, far from being an embarrassment, act to confirm the world view.

---

[6] See chapter 12, theme II (antinomianism), where I draw heavily upon Mary Douglas' study of the Lele.

Only in a non-bifurcated world view do all contradictions in experience tend to threaten it. In the end all mythic systems must seek to locate the real in total experience, but they do it in different ways, controlled by the drive to belong, not by a drive for integration of experience for its own sake. In the end, these "different ways" that I have called "paradigms for reality", are more basic than structural considerations in the interpretation of a myth and in its generation of feelings.

When myth is understood in these more general terms, as the verbal expression of the reality to which an adherent of a tradition would belong, then a whole variety of things fall into place. These things would not even emerge were myth to be defined negatively as a sort of cosmic repair kit to be called into operation when contradictions threaten meaning.

To deal, for example, with the problem of the potential fragmentation of the sense of reality within this more positive understanding of the function of myth, is to be able to show why myth proliferates precisely in those traditions where one might expect myth to be least developed.

Myth is first structured by the need it serves to model a reality to belong to. It is then limited by the paradigms for reality, and only after that might it be structured by a process for the integration of binary opposites. Thus, in summary, it must be said that the important contributions made to the understanding of myth by structural analysts would be even more significant if placed within a wider understanding of myth and, in the process, the word "myth" would be rescued from their clutches. Within this wider understanding, stories told to express the felt sense of reality will in many cases be analyzable as narrative. Even material, which first presents as a set of laws or as a recommended behavior pattern, might be analyzed as narrative, for it might well be understood as a story told about the ideal human life within a particular tradition.

I have dealt with the second possible source of similarities at some length because, while it is the one that is least directly related to religion *per se*, it is an area where there is a great amount of scholarly activity and it has the potential to distort priorities for the study of religion. The two remaining sources of similarity can be dealt with briefly.

iii) *The Structure of Reality Experienced*

The structure in reality itself is the ultimate concern of religion and of the student of religion, everything else is a peeling away of humanly imposed structure. Whether all-that-out-there (the context of experience) is sufficiently coherent to justify speaking of it as the real or as reality and, if so, what is its structure and whether there is change in the structure, are things that students of religion would like to know. Yet this must represent an aim rather than an achievable goal, for even if the effects of all imposed structures had been stripped away one could never know that that was the case. Nevertheless it is the aim that direct the quest toward an undistorted perception of reality.

iv) *Limits Set to the Modelling of Reality*

I have already discussed the limits set to modelling the reality to which one would belong. I will not repeat it here. It will suffice to note that, unlike the previous source of similarity, this one sets limits to how reality is *conceived* not to how it might be *perceived*. It will be seen that it is a special case of (ii) above or (ii b) below.

Interaction Between the Four Possible Sources of Similarity in Myth and Symbol

Similarities might also arise in the ways in which the four possible sources interact, for none of them is independent of the others. The mode of this interaction will become clearer if the sources are located in the diagram for the development and expression of the felt sense of reality set out in chapter 6.

The sources of the similarities in myth, I have said, may lie in:-

i) similarities in profound experiences, universal and near universal,

ii) regularities in human ways of a) perceiving, b) conceiving and, if different, c) communicating,

iii) the reality experienced and

iv) the limits set to modelling a reality to which one would belong.

If we relate these four possible sources to the model then it is clear that (iii) above (the reality experienced) relates to the context of experience but not as it is generally experienced. While it is a primary objective of human religious activity to know reality as it is in itself, human beings do not have direct access to the context of experience, but only to that which arrives to shape the felt sense of reality. There may be universal, permanent or dynamic structures in that context, but if there are regularities in (ii.b) above (human ways of perceiving), which in the model is nearest to the selection and valuation of raw data, then they will also manifest as regularities in experience.

Equally, it is clear that (i) above (profound experiences) relates to the pool of possible symbols, but what rendered them profound in the first place lies in the felt sense of reality, whether that be formed by personal experience or be received on authority. What renders them usable in the symbolization of the felt sense of reality, lies in a process that must be added to our former diagram between the felt sense of reality and the symbolized sense of reality.

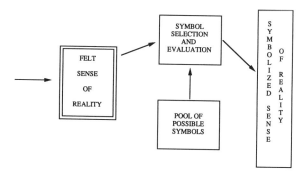

This process I have called the "symbol selection and valuation process". This stands, as it were, above the pool of possible symbols into which it dips. It is heavily and directly controlled by the felt sense of reality but it also relates to (ii.b) above (the processes by which human beings conceptualize experience). It must also operate with the constraints set by (iv) above (the paradigms and the logic of the coherent types of religion), but by what else? Almost certainly, insofar as it can be separated from the rest, by (ii.c) above (communication processes). This logic of symbolic language, this deep grammar for the communication of feelings is, as we noted, the interest of the structural analyst. It is paralleled by the interest of depth psychologists in the universality of non-verbal symbols.

Having located the possible sources of similarity in the model, the possible interactions between them will be apparent. One such interaction is worth special mention and for this I return to secular world affirming tradition and to its classical understanding of revelation as a moment in time in which God communicates to humankind information concerning, Himself, humanity and nature, and their interaction.

Such a view of revelation is threatened by what has been said about religious discourse. It is threatened both by the fact that language is limited by experience and that religious language needs a frame of meaning generated by a paradigm for reality that "feels real" before it can become significant. Therefore, before serious communication can take place a language needs to be developed that is adequate to the task, and experience needs to have created a felt sense of reality that validates a paradigm. Such a view of revelation is threatened by the fact that no tradition will grasp anyone whose felt sense of reality does not resonate with it. A felt sense of reality is not molded in a moment.

A view of revelation, that would not be threatened by what has been said, is that of a providence which acts to provide an experience that both generates a language and creates an appropriate feeling for reality and only then a situation and a catalyst that will put them together. The focus is usually on the latter, but it need be no more than a hint dropped in a market place of ideas, while the former is the longer and more wondrous task. There were some 450 years from Ur to Sinai. That this is contrary to the popular idea is simply because the process only becomes visible at the point where the symbols are taken hold of. Theology is concerned with the symbols when they have been grasped; science of religion is concerned with the processes leading to their meaning and credibility. Experience of the reality that is expressed in the symbol must long predate its conscious appearance.

Before I leave consideration of the processes by which the building bricks of myth are selected, it might be helpful to draw together the consequences of what has been said about myth, for a science of religion approach to the study of the myth in a particular tradition.

SUMMARY - AN APPROACH TO THE STUDY OF A TRADITION

The interest of science of religion, in the body of myth and ritual of a particular tradition community, lies with why a particular belief or practice is or was important to a particular people at a particular time. It is not concerned primarily with where a myth came from, or with classifications of myth based on profound experiences supposed to be universal or near universal, nor with regularities in human thought or communication processes, but rather with all that a particular people experience which is rooted in their own context of experience and processed by fact selection and valuation filters shaped by their own historical experience. This can only be arrived at by knowing the history and the mythology of the community concerned, and how the latter (the mythology) functions in context.

There will be two levels to this functioning:

a conscious level,
    that is, what people think the myth means, says to them, or does for them, and

an unconscious level,
which will include the structure of reality as that is experienced and
has become reflected in the myth. That is the structure which, at the
deepest level, makes the myth feel real.

I need say no more about the first level, save that it must be carefully and
responsibly elicited.

In regard to the second level, one needs to ask, not only, what is the
structure of reality presented by the myth, but also if the structure presented
could be one generated by that context of experience, given that it is
experienced through the spectacles of the existing model of reality. That is,
whether it is living myth rather than old myth of the community (or indeed of
any community) retained as history or just for entertainment. To know that,
and to get to the structure that is the primary concern, it is necessary to
escape the overlay of any structures which may be imposed by more universal
factors and to deal only with responses to differences in what is experienced
in the context in question. We must not be in the position of taking things
that are a universal feature of being human and drawing local conclusions
from them if there are no locally specific contributing factors. Equally we
must not let our awareness of universal features mask local factors which
would influence myth formation and modification in a similar direction.

Therefore, the scientist of religion is interested in:

i) the story content of the myth

   what profound experiences natural and historical does it reflect

   which of these are universal, or near universal, and which are
   specifically local

For this one needs to know the natural context and history of the people
whose myth it is. Insofar as it is possible, one also needs to reconstruct the
history of development of the symbols which are incorporated in the myth,
for again, we must not be in the position of employing present symbolic
meanings in the attempt to reconstruct earlier stages in the tradition's
development. In regard to what I have called profound experiences, it could
seem that while the attainment of this stripping away of more universal
features might require some effort, it would not pose a conceptual problem.
But things are not as simple as that. As the model in chapter 6 was intended
to show, what is believed modifies what is experienced and vice versa; they
are in dynamic relationship. If we ask, therefore, what makes profound
experience profound, the answer would have to include what is already
believed about the nature of reality.

The scientist of religion is also interested in :-

ii) the structure of the myth

within which of the coherent type or types   does the myth model reality and, if it is indeed types,

what attempts at bridging the types are present

are there structures present which represent attempts within the type or types to maintain the world-view; to explain (defuse), contain or reconcile contradictions in experience [7]

is there normative narrative structure present and if so, to what extent is it complete or has it been modified, and finally

what structures of experienced reality does the myth reflect, do these accord with what is known of the people's experience seen through their eyes

When we seek to separate out the structures that lie in human thought and communication processes there is an additional problem. The trouble is that the student is also human and therefore also functions within those categories and processes of thought. One of the most difficult things for human beings to attempt is to think about their own thinking.

Because of the difficulties involved, it is probably best for the student of religion, as distinct from those whose primary concern lies with human thought processes, to begin with the expectations of the model developed in chapter 6, that is, with the presumption that there is a self-contained causal nexus (comprised by the actual context of experience, myth, and the experience had; each in dynamic relationship with the others) and to look for all explanations there.

Nevertheless, different approaches are not mutually exclusive. Through the efforts of anthropologists, philosophers and those concerned with artificial intelligence,. some universal factors in human thinking have emerged, and these need to be taken into account by the scientist of religion interested in myth. Certainly the work of the structuralists cannot be neglected, although, as I indicated, the work on narrative is more central to the purpose than that on myth itself.

When the scientist of religion reports similarities and, in particular, similarities that have no adequate local explanation, data is offered in turn to those whose primary concern does lie with the human psyche and with

---

[7] I develop the ideas of "bridging" and "containment" in chapter 13.

processes of human thought and communication.

Knowledge of reality is basic to the religious quest and there seems to be no reason why one cannot have confidence that the nature of what-is-out-there does (in the long run) shape human expectations of it to the point where, to a significant degree, it can be experienced as it is in itself. Science of religion would assist in this quest insofar as it was able to separate out similarities in myth that are attributable to other sources and leave exposed that which results from humanity's attempt to express its experience of the real in every age and clime.

I now turn to discussion of the method employed in the body of this chapter.

METHOD OF APPROACH

The method employed for the main theme of this chapter is much the same as that employed in the previous one. I begin with the assumption that religion is concerned with belonging and, therefore, that it will change as and when necessary and in such a manner as to maintain or restore the sense of belonging. Therefore, the varieties in which a type of religious tradition can exist may be exposed by exploring, under various conditions of disturbance, the moves that are possible as adherents of the type seek to maintain their sense of belonging. If there is no disturbance there is little likelihood of religious change, although change may remain after disturbance, and processes of change that have been initiated by disturbance may continue or go into reverse when the situation has settled.

Two Situations of Change - An Alternative, or No

There are two broad situations in which change may take place. The first situation is that in which a tradition community is disturbed and where another tradition is on offer, whether or not the latter is linked to the disturbance. The other situation exists when a tradition comes under pressure and there is no significant alternative. I have partially explored the first situation in theme I of chapter 9 and will return to it when I examine the ways in which people, who find themselves in more than one world-view, seek integration.

In the second situation one is concerned with moves made to maintain or restore the sense of belonging within the logic of the type, or moves made, under pressure from within only, toward the logic of another type. In what follows I will only explore the possibilities of protective adjustments in this second situation.

Although I am considering responses within the limits of a single type, the stages identified in chapter 9 (in increasing levels of felt disturbance) will apply. Moves to preserve the tradition by closing ranks, such as might generate accusations of witchcraft and the exorcism of deviants, will remain a possibility even though there are no outside influences.

Two Aspects of Belonging: The Ultimately-real and
The Mode of Belonging Thereto

Belonging, I said, requires knowledge both affective and cognitive of the ultimately-real and a mode of belonging thereto. In this type, where belonging is both assumed and assumed to be realized, the distinction between reality and one's belonging to it can become blurred. It will serve my purpose, however, if I maintain the distinction.

Two Forms of Disturbance - Chronic and Acute

That which threatens the sense of belonging can present in two forms. It can be chronic, for example, as the result of adverse natural conditions, or it can be acute, the result of an isolated major problem such as drought or war. The effects of these may be very different, not least because in the latter case there is no time for gradual adjustment or elaborate solution, while in the former there is time to make preferred moves. A new and suddenly arising threat to belonging may have a more dramatic effect in a situation that is generally acceptable than in one that has organized to deal with the unacceptable over the longer term. In the extreme, the new disturbance may be (as to pace of change or degree of unacceptability) a last straw leading to the breakdown of existing structures and to major modifications. To deal adequately with such situations would take us into the realm of what is known as catastrophe theory. It will not be dealt with here.

Thus, I will be considering, for situations under either *chronic* or *acute* pressure and where there is *no other tradition* on offer, possible protective moves tending to the maintenance or restoration of:

   i) a unified sense of all-that-out-there, and

   ii) the mode of belonging thereto.

I) MOVES TO MAINTAIN A UNIFIED SENSE OF THE REAL

Scholars not infrequently present the cosmologies of traditions falling into the nature religion type in hierarchical manner with the high god (where there is one) at the top, followed by lesser deities or spiritual powers, followed by ancestral spirits. This indeed may be the way that adherents perceive the power relationship, but it introduces a dangerous hint of transcendence simply because transcendence is spatially modelled in the West. It also suggests that in such traditions the principal powers are thought to dwell above, which is certainly not the case universally.

I think it better to discuss the relationship of such powers-that-be in the manner in which they arise rather than in the way they are modelled once they have arisen.

I will therefore discuss the development of the varieties of tradition in terms of three possible perspectives on the adherent's world-out-there. I will describe these perspectives briefly, their detail will emerge in use. They are, the Actual Life-World Perspective, the Total Perspective, and the Symbolized Life-World Perspective.

THREE POSSIBLE PERSPECTIVES ON THE WORLD-OUT-THERE

1. Actual Life-World Perspective : This is the perspective in which each aspect of everyday existence is perceived as it exists in itself and in interaction with its neighbors. That is, without overt symbolic implications and without relationship to postulated entities or to the totality of things. This perspective exists in every culture, although in some it may be heavily overlaid by perspective 3.

2. Total Perspective : This is the perspective in which one might stand back from all the bits and pieces of life and seek to know what all-that-out-there feels like and, perhaps, to ask "What is it all about?". In the nature religion type of tradition the minimal conceptual answer would have to be that it is a closed system of cause and effect embracing a multitude of interacting parts and that it has a feel, if not a conceptualizable character, of its own.

This total perspective is always immediately available as an alternative perspective to the previous one although individuals may not always be aware of it.

3. Symbolized Life-World Perspective : This is the perspective in which significant aspects of the life-world are separated out and then given a symbolic content or relationship. It enables them to be reintegrated at a level beyond that of their actually experienced relationships. The different aspects may be personified, or given the characters and whims of beasts, or they may be conceived as vital forces that are neither personal nor impersonal.

The locus and role of each of these three perspectives will emerge as I explore the development of varieties within the type. Each perspective has its characteristic *style of language*. I will begin by considering the type in relatively ideal circumstances.

NATURE RELIGION IN IDEAL CONTEXT

Structure is absolutely essential in a world-view where goals are not available for identity formation. In an experience that is relatively stable and acceptable the need for belonging can be satisfied by participation in the structures of everyday life. These structures do not need to be overtly religious and, in a world with just sufficient struggle to impose them, they can be quite natural structures and thus, to a considerable degree, unconscious. In this situation identity, which may itself be largely unconscious until the individual is called upon to respond to novel situations, is established in terms of the existing natural and social orders.

If the struggle for individual and corporate survival is not strong enough to impose survival-related structures upon everyday life, structures may have to be invented. The entities to which they relate must, of course, be real, but the relations to them, and between them, can become highly elaborated for no other reason than to structure the life-world. For example, the sexes may be clearly separated and then the interaction between them prescribed in great detail; also who can do what, where and when, may be prescribed in relation to the village, the savannah and the forest, to animals, crops and crafts. What is generated is a mass of strongly sanctioned taboos (which to the outsider appear as a mixture of superstitions and manners) which serve no other obvious purpose than to provide and maintain the necessary structure where this has not been sufficiently generated by other pressing concerns.[8]

What all these situations have in common is that members of the culture can remain within perspective 1, and their language remain literal. Only in the case of the "invented" structures and where the sanctions go beyond those overtly imposed by the community itself need there be an appeal to a symbolic world, and even then it does not have to be conceptualized in detail. For many in the Western world an unspelled-out but omnipresent "other dimension" is sufficient to invest superstitions with authority. So it is with sanctions for "invented" structures. [9]

---

[8] See for example Mary Douglas' description of the life-world of the Lele of Zaire in *African Worlds*, Daryll Forde (ed.),(London, Oxford University Press, 1954), p.1.

[9] For an account of such structures among the Lele see Douglas M, in *Myth and Cosmos*,

This possibility (of an exclusive use of literal discourse) may seem to be in contradiction to my earlier statement that myth is the mode in which one speaks of that to which one would belong. This is not really the case however, for one does not belong to bits and pieces, but to a whole. In this situation the life-world would always have unquestioned edges and while the literal discourse spoke of the bits and pieces in focus, not of the penumbra beyond, the discourse would necessarily represent the whole and therefore have a symbolic dimension.

In such an acceptable situation there is no need to manipulate any particular aspects of the life-world, so the very activity of speaking literally can fulfil the function of myth, just as secular leaders can be the religious leaders, and religious ritual need not be different from ordinary life activities and not even consciously religious. There is, of course, no need for divinities or a high god. We will see in chapter 12 that there are clear parallels between this situation and the so called secularization that appeared when people found themselves in a relatively acceptable condition of life in the modern West.

In this ideal situation there would probably be ancestors, the living dead. These would be strongly individual and remembered if the culture happened to be at the individual survival end of the "ground of meaning spectrum" discussed in chapter 8. On the other hand, they would be absorbed into a nameless background unity if the culture was at the grand design end.

If individual ancestors are remembered they share with and go beyond the elders in general wisdom and perhaps in particular wisdom. For example, an ancestor may enjoy the reputation of having been a great hunter and continue to be consulted in such matters. They will almost certainly be regarded as having more immediate access to the powers within reality and they will enjoy a mediatorial role. If there are ancestors, there will almost certainly be those who have some special role or natural ability in communicating with them.

As was said in the last chapter, myth in this situation is likely to be weak in the sense that:

There will be little of it.

Belief in it, as opposed to conformity with the group's behavior pattern, will not be an important criterion for membership in the community.

It will not necessarily be very coherent in itself, because each myth refers to aspects of existence in the ordinary life-world and these have a felt coherence of their own.

Middleton J (ed) (Garden City New York, The Natural History Press, 1967), p.231.

The situation that I have been describing is indeed idyllic. Like a traditional view of heaven, it presupposes stability and a minimum of struggle. Thus, *inter alia*, an adequate and reliable gathering and hunting culture is the ideal norm for this type of tradition, and perhaps the only one in which an approach to what I have just described, could exist. However, the ideal is not available, there is always death and decay, and nature is frequently at its most destructive precisely where it is also the most prolific provider. For this situation to exist in actuality would suppose, not only an existing stable and acceptable situation, but also that it had never been otherwise, or at least that there had been a continuous history of acceptability for an extended period of time.

Nevertheless, there do exist situations where life is so ordered that its structures, "invented" or natural, can be taken for granted to the degree that, if the sense of belonging is challenged, the sense of structure is not sufficient to maintain it. Then it becomes necessary to refresh the sense of structure, perhaps by deliberately stepping outside of the structures for a moment. At a less dramatic level, it may be felt necessary to test the health of one's belongingness. I will return to these issues in the discussion of antinomianism in chapter 12. I turn now to possible adaptations of the ideal in a more realistic context.

NATURE RELIGION IN PROBABLE CONTEXTS - MOVES TO MAINTAIN THE UNITY OF EXPERIENCE

Probable contexts lie on a spectrum. At one end of the spectrum lies the situation that I have just described, which is religiously stable, and at the other end lies the situation in which the immediate life-world is affirmed as the real, but in which it is experienced as highly unacceptable. This is an unstable situation, and moves may be made toward a bifurcation of experience into that which can be affirmed and that which cannot, that is, toward a move out of the immediate experience affirming paradigm. These are the extremes and the rest of the spectrum may be filled in by considering responses to increasing unacceptability.

The unacceptability of experience which threatens the paradigm and therefore the sense of belonging can be either acute or chronic. I will deal with the acute form first.

Likely Responses to Acute Unacceptability of Experience

It is particularly in the acute situation, in which there is no time for segmental and preferred adaptations in the face of meaning threatening experiences, that a move to an increased consciousness of the total perspective described under 2. above is likely.[10] The unitive perspective is always an available alternative to the immediate and discrete one. If experience suddenly ceases to be coherent and ceases to support its being affirmed as the real, then the likelihood of standing back and asking, "What is the nature of all-that-out-there?" is great. This is not yet a cognitive question, it is the attempt to get the present unacceptability into a more holistic and therefore more real perspective and, hopefully, to come out with the *feeling* that experience as a whole can still be affirmed as the real.

Language will also change. Literal discourse will not serve to express consciousness of, let alone feelings about, the totality. As a minimum aid to consciousness of totality the ultimately real may be named. Feelings about it are likely to be expressed in art forms and in narrative myths.

This standing back and becoming conscious of the totality may itself suffice to preserve the sense of belonging. If it does not suffice then the belonging of cognitive human beings will require the support of a cognitive grasp on reality, that is, belonging will need to be modelled, where previously it had simply been accepted.

The modelling of belonging requires, as a first step, a cognitive frame in which reality is held together. In this case one or more aspects of the actual structure of experience will provide the cognitive frame for all of experience. That is, there will be a symbolic frame participating in that which is to be symbolized. These things, however, take time to develop and are therefore unlikely as responses to acute forms of unacceptable experience.

It is the constantly available possibility of moving into a total perspective that renders correct, both those who say that Africans always had a high god and those who say that they learnt it from Christian and Moslem sources. It is hardly possible that there could be a society which has not experienced an acute disturbance, such that people have stood back for a moment and establish a total perspective. This is why one finds awareness of an ultimate power, even in those societies that have been least disturbed and in which ritual relation to the immediate, probably including the immediate ancestors, usually suffices to maintain the sense of belonging. On the other hand, the nature of the totality as transcendent is not appropriate and its nature as personal is optional, so long as societies remain in the immediate experience affirming paradigm.

If one would relate to this whole, manipulate it and certainly address it, then it will tend to be conceptualized as personal. This question, personal or

---

[10] By preferred adaptations I mean those that use aspects of the natural order to heal the natural order. See the quotation from G J Afolabi Ojo included a little later in the chapter.

not, requires further comment because it relates to transcendence and is the real test of which paradigm is in operation.

Total perspective is necessarily unique and unique entities tend to have a personal feel to them. Thus, if people move into perspective 2, they will have a tendency to speak of the whole in personal terms. This means that one must get behind the language to the structure of the reality being expressed, if an experience being described in personal terms is to be fully understood.

When I discussed secular world affirming religion I noted that the ultimately-real had to be modelled as personal because, the transcendence gap intervening, its relation to the real could no longer be modelled as mechanistic and the only familiar alternative was a volitional relation.

When the ultimately-real becomes the focus and prime exemplar of the personal and the real is understood as its creation, the personal becomes highly valued and sharply distinguished from the impersonal. The impersonal may then, particularly by comparison with the monistic traditions, appear to be under-valued. One only has to speculate upon Walt Disney's contribution to the increasing difficulty that Westerners have with eating meat, to wonder if giving potatoes personalities could ever have a similar effect. One already finds invitations to sympathize with plants in their pain. That is to say, the divide between the personal and the impersonal in the secular world affirming tradition is so taken for granted, that its major impact is only recognized when the process somehow goes into reverse.

One expects that the more transcendence is emphasized in an existing religious tradition, the more personally will the ultimately-real be conceived. Conversely, the more transcendence is diminished by, for example, a philosophical determination to think one's way across the gulf of transcendence, the more the ultimately-real may be thought of as an impersonal force.

In the type of religious tradition that we are now considering there is no pressure to think of the ultimately-real as personal and, therefore, not the same pressure, as in the secular world affirming traditions, to make a radical distinction between personal and impersonal. The real is neither strongly personal nor strongly impersonal, and it may be modelled in either way and then easily pass over into the other and back again. Equally, it may be modelled as a vital force, perhaps more manifest in ancestors and chiefs than in ordinary folk and in some descending degree in animals, plants, rivers, the earth and stones, but nevertheless as being the essential presence in all of them. It is this understanding that makes African writers protest that, however much imagery may be drawn from aspects of life in order to speak of reality itself, Africans are not animists.[11]

It follows, for example, that arguments about which of the high gods of a

---

[11] See note 10 and the associated quotation.

number of traditions is the most personal, or most transcendent, cannot be decided simply on the evidence of the language used.[12] If one would speak of reality, symbols have to be drawn from somewhere and whether they are real or imaginary, animate or inanimate, from the human realm or the animal, may be almost accidental.

The really significant factor is whether volition is necessary in conceptualizing the relation of the powers-that-be to the rest of experience. This may be tested by asking whether chance really plays any part in the system and whether there is the possibility of new beginnings, or whether, in spite of personal language, the powers are controllable if one has the knowledge and one's rituals are properly performed. If the cause and effect nexus is closed, if *karma* dominates, whatever the language, there is no transcendence and the powers are not in any serious sense personal. If, on the other hand, the ultimately-real is predictable only on the basis of its known character and only when it is acting within that character, then transcendence is present and, however inanimate the language, it is best understood as personal. It will be appreciated that there is the possibility of carry over here and that if, for whatever reason, personal language is used of the real it would tend to inculcate a sense of chance.

All in all, one needs to look very closely at the expectations associated with ritual action to discover if transcendence is really present. One must ask whether the significant criterion of volition would have, of necessity, to be included in any accurate modelling of the reality to which the ritual relates. If so, transcendence is present, but if volition is not a necessary ingredient of the reality related to, transcendence is not present.

I return now to my main theme and to a consideration of what is likely to happen to the ideal model iñ a situation of chronic unacceptability.

Likely Responses to Chronic Unacceptability of Experience

I have not wished to suggest that the only possible response to *acute* unacceptability is the move to a total perspective, rather, that given the lack of time for adjustment, it is a likely move. In fact a beginning may be made upon any of the moves which are about to be discussed as possible responses to *chronic* unacceptability.

The situation at the acceptable end of the spectrum described above may be summarized as follows:

---

[12] See, for example, the discussion of the Yoruba and the Dinka in this regard, in Benjamin C Ray, *African Religions*, (Eaglewood Cliffs, Prentice-Hall, 1976), p.56.

Belonging being assumed, the need to belong can be met by an almost purely affective and largely unconscious grasp on all-that-out-there, that is, by a general sense of order and permanence in the background which is established and maintained by the rhythms of the natural order.

As one moves up the spectrum toward major unacceptability (beyond the move to a total perspective and the minimum cognitive support given by naming and expressing one's feelings about the whole) there will be moves to disarm the disintegrative effects, that is, to modify the unacceptable and to integrate that which cannot be modified.

Integration may be attempted by categorizing and accepting, as, for example, when a high infant mortality rate is dealt with by inventing a category of "those born to die".

Clearly, appropriate ritual helps to overcome felt fragmentation and as this becomes more necessary, ritual will become more distinctive and be less the everyday activity of the ordinary life-world. At this stage the *mode* of belonging will also need appropriate special devices specifically to give cognitive support to its maintenance or restoration. I will return to these below, but for the moment I wish to stay with the maintenance of the frame itself.

Earlier I had reason to contrast the experience of unity that one is not so likely to have when viewing a bowl of porridge with that which one is quite likely to have when looking into the back of a watch. I wish to recapture that imagery for a moment.

What I have been saying about acute unacceptability might be likened to coming across a lump in the porridge that triggers a standing back to consider the quality of the porridge as a whole. It may in fact prove to be relatively uniform and acceptable, but if an acceptable verdict on experience cannot be delivered simply by moving from the particular to the general, then one must seek to divide, distinguish and interrelate both the threatening and compensatory aspects. In that way a sense of unity, more like that generated by viewing the mechanism of a watch, may emerge. One has then moved into the third perspective identified above.

The motivation for this breaking down and interrelating will certainly include the desire to better know, and so manipulate the parts. However, what happens in the extreme cases when manipulation fails yet support for the system remains or increases, suggests that the maintenance of a meaningful unity, in that to which one would belong, is the paramount concern. The desire to control may or may not give rise to a personification of the aspects, but if it does it will also open the door to a tendency to move away from a closed system, in which belonging can be assumed, toward a situation in which it must be realized or established.

These processes take time and they serve their purpose best if they are a corporate activity. They are therefore only appropriate in the chronic situation, and it is in this sort of situation, and in order to prevent the logic of belonging fracturing, that the volume of myth increases and greater integration emerges among the myths that already exist. I return to a longer version of an opinion referred to above:

> ... multiplicity is a logical consequence of their (the Yoruba's) keen recognition of the numerous elements in their physical and biological environment, their awareness of the associated problems and their determination to solve the problems in the ways they know best, using the environment to counter its own problems most of the time. Both their polytheism and their anthropomorphism found a basis in the profusion and variety of the geographic environment. In spite of its derivation from these concrete objects Yoruba religion is not animistic. [13]

This quotation refers to a situation which might be said to be "chronically acute", a prolific environment that promises much and disappoints in the same degree. Its myth and its ritual, reflect this luxuriousness. [14]

Not every culture of this type has become as elaborate in its quest to maintain the unity of experience as that of the Yoruba, but Afolabi Ojo's statement is an excellent summary of what I have in mind when I refer to the overlay (even domination) of the first by the third perspective. This third perspective is a symbolized life-world, in which significant aspects are understood to be controlled by other aspects, and the closed system of cause and effect is conceptually maintained, despite conflicts in experience.

Before I turn to consideration of possible moves in the maintenance of the mode of belonging, it is appropriate to note the possible sources of symbols for the construction of the symbolic frame just discussed.

NOTE :   POSSIBLE SOURCES FOR THE ESTABLISHMENT OF
A COGNITIVE FRAME

Possibilities for a cognitive frame are limitless, but because it begins in

---

[13] G J Afolabi Ojo, *Yoruba Culture - A geographical analysis*, (London, University of Ife and University of London Press, 1966), p.183.

[14] The unacceptability of experience with which the Dinka of the Sudan had to cope was probably greater than that of the Yoruba, but it came on a more even keel and produced an effective but more austere response.

the actual world of experience and because it is better to modify the unacceptable than to have to integrate what cannot be modified, there is something of a hierarchy of sources appropriate to different levels and types of disturbance.

Possibilities for such a frame from NATURE *include:*
general aspects such as earth and sky, land and water, sun and cloud, seasons marked by ploughing and sowing, the night sky and astral seasons, life cycles, animal kingdom classifications or aspects of some particular type of animal or even the parts of an animal and, similarly, the plant kingdom.

Possibilities for such a frame from SOCIETY *include:*
aspects of the actual society as experienced, as well as aspects of society as conceptualized. If they are conceptual, then the societal concepts may be drawn from the natural world, for example the human body image extended to community. Equally they may be human political constructs such as kings, princes, nobles and commoners.

Possibilities for such a frame from
BOUNDARIES BETWEEN NATURE AND SOCIETY *include:*
those between village and forest, domesticated and wild, civilized and natural, rational and irrational, even cooked and raw.

All of those things of which the above are some examples, are immediately available to virtually all people. In more chaotic situations, however, significant aspects of both nature and society may so participate in the chaos experienced as to render them inappropriate (in their unmodified state) as symbols for integration of the whole. In that case more imaginative transformations will be required.

Possibilities if the frame is comprised of
ASPECTS OF NATURE AND SOCIETY PICTURED AS A SOCIETY:
These aspects would probably be personified, with family or power relationships reflecting the relationships of that which they represent in the natural or social order. They could be gods who founded or endowed cities (particularly if defence or the lack of a wider social order is the problem) or gods of storm, of river, of iron, of smallpox, or anything else significant in the natural order. They will represent the conflicts of the real world, perhaps as jockeying (hopefully within checks and balances) for power between themselves, and certainly they must represent the ambivalence of nature, as provider and

destroyer, if the system is to feel real. Their own identities and the meaningful order that is established between them, hold together whatever they represent in the actual world and establish a cause and effect nexus that can, to some degree, be manipulated.

I have been dealing with aspects of the real world isolated and interrelated in a symbolic way. There is a stage beyond this in which the actual is at one more remove from the symbols. For example the stars might be represented as powers existing in a cosmic society and thought to control rather than symbolize the other aspects of nature. Beyond this again would be a frame that is a purely imaginative construct.

Possibilities if such a frame is A PURELY IMAGINATIVE CONSTRUCT:
Unless it were also a reduced reality move and seeking to generate a sense of belonging by intensity of belief rather than by what was believed, any frame that was constructed, not of images drawn from a chaotic experience, but of purely imaginative entities, would still need to reflect the felt structure of experience if it were to feel real.

II) MOVES TO MAINTAIN A MODE OF BELONGING -

THE NATURE OF PARTICIPATION IN THE FRAME OF REALITY

The previous section was concerned with the frame, that is, with the nature and integrity of the reality of which the individual is a part. I must now consider how the individual participates in that reality and distinguish two aspects of this participation.

The first aspect has to do with what I earlier referred to as the ground of meaning spectrum, that is, with whether the meaning of the individual's existence lies in the grandeur of the totality in which he or she participates, if only for a moment, or whether it lies in the survival, in this case immortality, of the individual.

The second aspect of participation has to do with mediation, whether and how it exists.

These two aspects seem to be independent of each other, mediation being necessary or otherwise, which ever way meaning is grounded. The question of mediation is intimately related to the perceived nature of the real, that of the choice of a ground for meaning seems not to be.

THE INDIVIDUAL SURVIVAL OR GRAND DESIGN SPECTRUM

As I said in chapter 9, the individual survival or grand design spectrum appears to be one of the basic independent variables affecting the choice of a paradigm for reality, and therefore, to be an issue in all manifestations of religion. Even in astrology, the appeal may lie in the grandeur of cosmic affairs or in a knowledge of individual destiny.

In the type of tradition with which we are now dealing these possibilities tend to flow into one another because survival is, in any case, within the given order of things. Nevertheless, there can be very different emphases. Some may emphasize individuality, some the total order and some may fall in between by emphasizing, for example, the mini-design of family succession and such expediencies as Levirate marriage.

An emphasis upon individual survival would be likely to arise, where it had not previously existed, when the situation was threatened and the integrity or worthwhileness of the world-out-there, and therefore the sense of grand design, became less than credible. It is also likely that it would remain should the latter become credible again. On the other hand, in those stable situations in which immediate experience is affirmed as the real and it is felt to be acceptable, the evidence seems to be that there will be belief in the continued existence of the individual, even if it is not strongly emphasized as the ground of meaning.

The explanation of this common conjunction may lie in the fact that there can be few cultures in which, at some time or another, the integrity and worthwhileness of the totality has not been threatened. Alternatively, it may lie in the fact that in this world-view every individual part that comprises the reality is as much a given as the reality itself. That being the case, if the felt quality of reality is dominated by the cyclical return that pervades the rest of nature, and if individual survival is felt to be desirable, then it will feel authentic to extend belief in that direction.

I have referred to this as a spectrum and such it is. At one end there is a sense of the integrity and worthwhileness of the whole in which one participates that can generate a cosmic trust which does not call for a conscious concern with individual survival. At the other end, in a situation where without survival there would be no meaning, there is a strong emphasis on or an earnest (even frenzied) quest for some form of individual survival. In between there could be every blend of these. In all combinations there is belief in some form of survival but, because each is also part of a totality worth belonging to, individuality in the survival may not need to be emphasized.

There are, for example, cultures in which the individual is believed to have multiple "souls" which separate upon death, and cultures where it is believed that a soul may have multiple contemporary reincarnations.[15] To the extent that meaning is dependent on individual survival, this would be threatening, but to the extent that meaning is grounded in participation in the totality, this diffusion would be felt to be natural.

Somewhere in the middle of the spectrum would lie those cultures in which one could expect, as an ancestor, to be actively related to the living for about as long as living experience goes. That is, to be remembered for about three generations (chiefs and persons of greater "presence" being maintained in tribal memory somewhat longer) and then to blend into the undifferentiated background.

If experience becomes really unacceptable, then it becomes difficult to maintain any possibility, because on the one hand there is no totality worth belonging to, and on the other there is no reason why ancestral life in this reality should be better than present life in this reality. Neither possibility will ground meaning. Nevertheless, meaning is a prerequisite of belonging and so a struggle will take place to re-establish one or other ground, probably both, and a highly confused picture is the likely result.[16]

MEDIATION

Both the perceived need for and the nature of mediation in one's belonging to the real, will be affected by changes in the perception of the nature and integrity of that reality.

In this type of tradition belonging is assumed, and assumed to be realized and, in a relatively stable and acceptable experience, the sense of belonging is grounded in factors and relationships that are part of the ordinary life-world. Therefore, when disturbance does come the first move will be to restore the health (wholeness) of the community and the communities relationship with the natural order, that is, they will seek to ensure, in the ways just set out, the continued integration of the real.

Insofar as this fails or tarries, protective moves will be made in relation to the *mode* of belonging, and this will begin in a strengthening of the sinews that are already understood to hold experience together. One of these is the

---

[15] This is the case among traditional Yoruba and was the case in Ancient Egypt.

[16] Both the Yoruba and the Dinka exemplify this confusion. The Dinka's strong emphasis on being represented in descendants and the levirate arrangements that support this, as well as the unusually long line of remembered personal ancestors, point to the need to evidence the continued existence of the mini-grand-design that is the lineage through which the individual is linked into the grand-design that is the whole Dinka people in context.

family and extended family, to the clan and beyond. In situations of disturbance these relationships are likely to become more conscious and to be more consciously safeguarded. In situations of chronic unacceptability of experience they may even be duplicated in some way, so that each individual has two or more ways of belonging to the community.[17] In either acute or chronic disturbance one would expect the mediatorial roles of key figures such as the heads of households, the chiefs of clans, of immediate ancestors and of specially endowed individuals, to be further elaborated and emphasized. At levels of disturbance beyond the community's expectations of such functionaries special arrangements will need to be made.

If we now return to the relatively undisturbed situation, it can be seen that the first level mediators will be the practitioners of medicine whose function it is to eradicate the sickness (broadly understood) of individuals, of the community as a whole and of its relation to the total order.[18] At this level, when one speaks of medicine it clearly includes what in the West would be regarded as such, herbs and other specifics and psychology, but may go beyond that.

Also at the ideal level and at low levels of disturbance, there will be a need for someone to discover the inadvertent causes of disruptions in the harmony of existence, that is, a diviner of some kind. The task at more disturbed levels becomes a dual one.

On the one hand there is the attempt to remedy the problem by extending the scope and the power of medicine into what would be regarded in the West as magic or religion, but is still the attempt to use forces within nature to modify the unacceptable. Such medicine is about understanding and manipulating the causal nexus and is best conceived as an empirical

---

[17] A number of societies create a second way, other than biological descent, in which the individual belongs to the group as a whole. Sometimes these are actual, as with the Dinka where each person belongs to a clan but, more practically, to a sub-tribe and tribe arising from the herding groups and also to an age set. Sometimes they are imaginary but birth related, as among the Vakavango where one belongs not only to one's fathers line but, in many ways more significantly, to one of a limited number of clans having the name of an animal or sometimes a craft, membership of which one inherits from one's mother. The Yoruba have a divined second line. The child soon after birth will be taken to the diviner to discover which destiny soul he or she is a reincarnation of and from then on will maintain a strong association with others of the same origin.

[18] In chapter 12 I will consider the testing of one's belongingness and make reference to Mary Douglas' description of the role of the hunt among the Lele of Zaire, as the thermometer of society. If the "health" of the community is found not to be good, a healer, perhaps from another village, will be called in to restore it.

science that makes free use of symbolic entities. On the other hand there is, as we have seen, the attempt to integrate what cannot be modified or eradicated and to maintain the sense of belonging to the modified totality. The practitioner of medicine, therefore, both precedes and accompanies the mythical and ritual integration of that which cannot be modified.

At higher levels of unacceptability of experience the need to focus belonging will lead, not only to the discrete symbolizing of significant aspects of experience as described above and almost certainly to the establishment of orders of functionaries to relate to these and to perform the more complex manipulations, but also to the elaboration of sacraments. That is, to the identification of special times, places and objects, at and through which the powers within reality are felt to be more available.

When in the acute situation things become very chaotic, and mediation hangs by a thread, the need for effective mediation may be met by the charismatic figure, a person who is not one of the normal sinews of society, or if he or she is, then one who acts in a manner that goes beyond the normal. Mediation at such times is so important that if the charismatic figure fails to produce the material things promised, far from losing support, he or she is likely, in the short run anyway, to gain in both the volume and intensity of support. This, as was said previously, is because their failure increases the sense of chaos and therefore the need for a link to the real.

It is the need for mediation in these extreme circumstances which may call for extreme rituals such as human sacrifice or self-sacrifice, actual or mythical.

If the high level of unacceptability is chronic, the charismatic link is likely to become institutionalized and thus, together with special times, places and objects, to remain when the level of unacceptability of experience has settled down. This may be seen in the extreme rituals associated, for example, with those chiefs who have at some point in time become priest-kings. These rituals can seem bizarre when observed in more settled conditions.

This institutionalization of the practices entered into during high levels of unacceptability also accounts for extreme measures aimed at maintaining the mediatorial powers of chiefs and priests. For example that they commit suicide, arrange to be buried alive, or are otherwise disposed of when their powers fail.[19]

The contrived death of these mediatorial figures has another significance in a cyclical view of reality, that is, to close a beneficial cycle in order that it

---

[19] See for example, the arrangements made for "burial alive" of a chief of failing power among the Dinka.

might begin again.

It is for this reason that much heroic myth in Africa ends with the hero being killed or driven out by those whom his or her heroism has served, otherwise the story would be unreal, wishful thinking, or merely entertainment. It would not be a myth reflecting the structure of reality as it is experienced and therefore able to offer a grounded hope, and it would not enable the cycle to begin again.

While it has been convenient to separate out matters concerning the real and those concerning the individual's belonging to it, these are not usually separated in practice. For ritual, perhaps the very same ritual, will operate in both the felt integration of the real and in the maintenance of the mode of belonging thereto. It will serve to restore relationships as well as to rehearse those that exist.

It has also been necessary to speak of the roles that must be fulfilled, but of course, these may be fulfilled by the same person. The practitioner of medicine may be the link with the ancestors and the link with the ancestors may be the link with the symbolized aspects of the natural and social orders and perhaps beyond to the unitive focus of reality. On the other hand the more fragmented and conflicted experience is, the more this is likely to be reflected in the variety and the number of religious functionaries that the society will be willing to support.

CONTAINING THE UNCONTAINABLE

Because I have been exploring possible variations within a type, I have dealt with moves to maintain both the unity of experience and a mode of belonging. I have done this without reference to aspects of experience that resist explanation. However, in all traditions which do not enjoy the buffer of a bifurcation in the modelling of reality all experience has to be contained. All traditions of this type, therefore, must have a way of containing the inexplicable.

The destructive, as well as the creative can, as I have said, be natural and be contained within the order. That which cannot be contained in the order is irrational. In low levels of unacceptability this irrational destructiveness is frequently contained in the "hold-all" of witchcraft. Where unacceptability is high, where "the divine has no tears", the irrationality may need to be clearly contained within the divine itself. Such is the role of the free-divinity Macardit in the religion of the Dinka. [20]

---

[20] Godfrey Lienhardt, *Divinity and Experience,*(Oxford, Oxford University Press, 1961), p.81.

CHAPTER 11

A FURTHER BREAKDOWN OF

SECULAR WORLD AFFIRMING RELIGION

A PRELIMINARY ISSUE -
THE POSSIBILITY OF OTHER PARADIGMS

Because the secular world affirming type of religious tradition is generated by a paradigm in which reality itself is bifurcated, its very existence poses the question, "Can reality not be further fragmented, or can it not be divided in different ways?". It is a question that I must explore before proceeding with the principal themes of the chapter.

Provided that aspects of the real and ultimately-real were not mixed in the process, it would not remove a tradition from this coherent type if the ultimately-real were further conceptually sub-divided, or if the real were thought to have different levels, for then the further bifurcations would be contained within the basic one. Such attempts at further sub-division might create logical problems of their own, but if they were acceptable on other grounds they would not remove a tradition espousing them from the type. Divisions made in other ways represent a move out of the type toward one of the other paradigms or the attempt to have the best of two worlds by mixing aspects of the pure types. In a partial form, they represent what will be called "bridging" in the chapter after next. An example follows.

The human soul is sometimes thought of as part of the divine, that is, as an emanation, a "divine spark" within each individual. Alternatively the soul is thought of as created, but as nevertheless sharing the divine immortality.

In the first case the transcendence gap no longer falls between the divine and the creation including humankind, but within the individual human being. The soul in this instance belongs to the godward side, the body to the creation. In the second case it is not clear which side of the divide the soul lies. It would depend, perhaps, on whether having been created it was truly permanent or simply existed at the whim of the ultimately-real.

Such views of the human soul are attempts to overcome not-yet-ness in the individual while maintaining it in the general environment. Whichever form they take, these moves represent a mixing of paradigms. They weaken transcendence both by closing the gap between the individual and the ultimately-real and by diminishing the significance of the real. The real is no longer that by which one comes to the ultimately-real, because, ontologically speaking, one is already there.

This does not mean that such mixed traditions cannot survive, only that they are not firmly located in a logically coherent type and must pay the price of having a weaker logic of belonging. I will be dealing with the importance of these logics shortly.

There are no ways, other than that now being presented, in which reality can be divided such that a coherent type is created.

THE METHOD OF APPROACH - A FOURFOLD BREAKDOWN

I will not, as I did in the two previous chapters, seek to expose possible varieties by asking how the type could be modified to maintain or restore belonging when that is threatened. I will not begin that way because, in this type, belonging must first be sought. The preliminary enquiry, therefore, will be concerned with what the individual requires in order to come to a sense of belonging within this paradigm. Only at a secondary level will I be asking what moves might be made to maintain it.

Because the transcendence gap of the secular world affirming paradigm bifurcates the adherent's world-out-there, it also sets a scene with three actors - the individual, the real and the ultimately-real. Religion of this type is concerned with the re-relating of these three. This fact establishes a four-part structure for the study of these relationships, the themes of which are:

the nature of *the ultimately-real* and of the adherent's relation thereto

the nature of *the real* and the adherent's relation thereto
(This establishes the details of *personal identity*)

ritual, broadly understood, which serves to link, or express the link, between the ultimately-real and what is believed and felt to be the "self".

the *authentication* to the adherent of his or her whole religious system

This fourfold breakdown is more than just convenient, it is basic to an understanding of religion as belonging in the secular world affirming type. There has to be a Thou, there has to be an I, and there has to be an authentic means of holding them together. The Thou, of course, is the ultimately-real, distilled from one's total perspective on all-that-out-there and conceptualized as well as may be. It is experienced as an outer focus.

It goes without saying that knowledge of *the ultimately-real*, both affective and cognitive, is knowledge of that to which the adherent belongs. It creates the paradigm, sets the whole context and is the ground of value, yet knowledge of *the real* is no less essential.

Because the ultimately-real is known through and may be related to in the real, that too is part of the outer focus. But it is more than that. It provides the context for the application of value and therefore for the details of the individual's mode of engagement. That is, it establishes an identity that cannot be had in a vacuum and gives substance to the "this" which is seeking to belong to "that", the self which would relate to the ultimately-real, and it establishes the possibility of an inner focus.[1]

For some people, these two, the one which belongs and that to which one belongs, seem to be sufficient, but for most people they need putting together and their togetherness celebrated. This is the role of ritual, the most obvious, but not the most basic, aspect of religion.

Finally, there are a number of paradigms to choose from and many choices to be made within them, many ways of seeing the world-out-there (and therefore the self) and many forms of ritual expression. The question is, why is one particular set adhered to rather than another, that is, what authenticates for the adherent his or her whole religious system.

Clearly, a system is finally authenticated because it creates the required sense of belonging, but one must ask what gives it the ability and the necessary legitimation, to do that.

I will present all that is to be said in this chapter under these four headings.

I. THE ADHERENT'S RELATION TO THE ULTIMATELY-REAL

In chapter 5 I distinguished the corporate mode of belonging to the

---

[1] In withdrawal religion, the entity which belongs is logically reduced to consciousness, to the witness which stands behind even one's most intimate traits, viewing them also as part of the transient world out there. In the other paradigms that which belongs has an identity, created in its detail by its relation with the world-out-there.

ultimately-real from the individual mode, calling the former "indirect cosmic belonging" and the latter "direct cosmic belonging". I then distinguished these from reduced reality, or compensatory belonging, which becomes appropriate when a cosmic sense is not attainable. I am now going to consider these modes of belonging in greater detail for the differences are of major significance in an individual's experience of religion.

Most people in the western world participate in a nominalist world-view, that is, in a world of individual entities, in which the divine also is radically other than nature in general and humanity in particular. It is for this reason that a sense of cosmic belonging requires the establishment of some deeply felt links between all of these essentially disparate entities.

In secular world affirming religion it is possible to make a distinction between a sense of cosmic belonging and the sense of belonging to one's immediate community. It is a distinction which has become particularly apparent in the urban situation, when long established roots in family and community have been lost and there is a pressing need for the clear marks of belonging to a group. Then the religious community itself may function as a primary security group, from out of which the individual relates to the real, that is to the immediate world-out-there. In a uniformly Catholic village in a uniformly Catholic country, such a distinction would hardly enter consciousness. Nevertheless, religion can be seen as an attempt to satisfy both of these needs to belong, even where the distinction between them is not conscious. Where the difference is conscious, a tradition will hardly succeed at the cosmic level if it fails at the immediate level.

In indirect cosmic belonging, which I exemplified by reference to Judaism and the catholic forms of Christianity, there is already a community in existence. This community has an habitual pattern of relation to the world-out-there which tends to absorb the distinction between cosmic and community belonging.

It is primarily in direct cosmic belonging that a deliberate provision has to be made for relation to the real, as well as to the ultimately-real, if a cosmic sense of belonging is to be achieved. When the mode of belonging is direct, all externals such as ministry, sacraments, even a sacred literature could, in theory, be discarded and the emphasis laid upon an inner trust or spiritual experience. In practice, however, the direct relationship usually requires a great deal of support. If one is to know that the level of trust is adequate or that the spiritual experience is authentic, then both cognitive and community support are almost essential.

Faith as trust may be transmuted into faith as right belief. This makes it possible for the community to give its testimony to the individual that he or she is believing the right things and therefore meeting the requirements of belonging. It can also give its testimony to the authentic nature of inner experience more easily, if that also is transmuted into external consequential behaviors. The authority of the community to testify to these matters will lie in its ability to create the required sense of belonging. Overtly it is likely to be tied to an authoritative source, a sacred literature or a tradition, probably to an emphasis on literal interpretation or at least one that is controlled by a confession of faith. All of this is quite apart from the compensatory sense of belonging to the group, which the group must supply, if cosmic belonging is weak.

With the exception of the mystical extreme, if belonging is to be cosmic, it is also required that the adherent of a direct belonging tradition experience a sense of belonging to the natural world and to society at large. If this has the cognitive support of the religious community, it will be by means of an ethical system rooted in the approved belief.

All in all, even direct cosmic belonging requires a complex web of supporting relationships.

In chapter 8 I considered the mutually exclusive coherent types and some of their non-negotiable elements, the surrender or acceptance of which signal a move from type to type. I did not, however, consider the importance within these of a clear and coherent logic in the mode of belonging.

Modes of belonging include, whether consciously or not, logics of belonging, like those of the direct and indirect cosmic belonging referred to above. The elements which comprise these logics seem to turn up in acts of worship, whether they be in cathedral, synagogue or small independent church and even where a logic has not been consciously considered. It is the point at which the cognitive and affective aspects of religion coincide and it is these logics which provide cognitive support for the sense of belonging.

On the face of it, a logic of belonging would not seem to be of paramount significance. Any examination of world religions will show that most traditions operate with elements drawn from more than one of the different types and in the end, one is concerned with a *felt* sense of belonging which might be thought to be the product of wholly affective factors. Why then the importance of a clear logic? I must confess to not knowing the reason, but there is much evidence that it is so.

To speculate on the nature of the relationship between logic and felt coherence would take us far from the present theme, but the situation is not unlike the relationship existing between mathematics and the material world. The evidence for the relationship is omnipresent, but that the seemingly abstracted armchair manipulation of mental symbols should enable humanity to model and control its material world has seemed miraculous to many who think about it.

Humankind is cognitive and because, ideally, belonging moves ever to a more ultimate level, it would seem to require necessarily not just a logic, but a conscious logic. Long before the ideal level, however, some pressure seems to give rise to elements in a logic which may be quite unconscious to the adherents. It seems to me that this is the result of more than just an aesthetic appreciation for logical structure. There is a deep connection between logic and a felt appropriateness in the conjunction of symbolic elements and this may exist even when the cognitive logic is not conscious to those who adhere to the symbols. To those who look for it, the logic is there and evidence of its importance comes in many ways. In the next sub-section I will set out the elements of these logics and, in the following one, I will break down the modes of belonging themselves into the pathways that comprise them.

THE LOGICS OF BELONGING

There is a logic to a mode of belonging that transcends the traditional symbols in which it may be expressed, as well as such forces as the socio-economic context of the adherent. While one remains in the same mode of belonging, the same logical elements must be present.

THE LOGIC OF DIRECT COSMIC BELONGING

The logic of direct cosmic belonging requires:

i) a knowledge of the ultimately-real, (God)

ii) belief in the act of God which established the means by which individuals might belong to Him,

iii) the conditions of such individual belonging, and

iv) assurance that one has fulfilled and is fulfilling such conditions.

The religious institution will proclaim (i) to (iii), and those who have met the conditions in (iii) will insist that these conditions are preached to them, in order to establish (iv). For example, those who have experienced conversion, will (strangely to the casual observer) insist that the need to be converted in order to be saved be preached to them over and again. Assurance, that is (iv), is most easily attained in the case of a prescribed ritual behavior; progressively less easily, in the case of required ethical behavior, right belief, right spiritual experience, and trust.

The temptation of insecurity, to make a work out of faith and to ask if one is trusting enough, will tend to move the criteria of belonging back up this scale toward right belief and prescribed behavior. It also makes desirable the support group which can testify to the individual that his or her beliefs, or inner experiences, are such as to meet the conditions of belonging. All this in spite of the fact that the logic of direct cosmic belonging would suggest that the institution should constantly seek to render individuals self-sufficient and independent of itself.

THE LOGIC OF INDIRECT COSMIC BELONGING

The logic of indirect cosmic belonging requires:

> i) a knowledge of the ultimately-real, (God)
>
> ii) a belief in the act of God which established the institution or "bridgehead" in the world,
>
> iii) knowledge of the identifying features of the institution,
>
> iv) knowledge of the conditions for individual belonging to the institution and
>
> v) evidence that these conditions are fulfilled.

The religious institutions will proclaim (i) to (iv). (v) will follow automatically to the extent that it is a fulfilled ritual behavior pattern, otherwise assurance must be gained as in direct cosmic belonging.

THE LOGIC OF REDUCED REALITY BELONGING

The logic of reduced reality belonging requires:

> i) a knowledge of the ultimately-real, (God and frequently personified evil),
>
> ii) belief in the cosmic act which established the "good group" and the cosmic event which established the badness of the rest,
>
> iii) knowledge of the identifying features (symbols) of the group,

Beliefs will almost certainly be expressed in apocalyptic imagery, because the flight from the rest of experience necessitates the conceptualization of a radical gulf between this historical time and "the blessed future". This inhibits the use of literal discourse.

> iv) the terms on which one may belong to the group and
>
> v) evidence that these terms are being fulfilled.

In reduced reality belonging, the terms of belonging (iv) and evidence that one belongs (v), will coalesce in a *gnosis*, that is, in a recital of the group's apocalyptic mythology and in such "marks of belonging" as dress and food laws, rejection of dancing, television, alcohol etc..

The elements in belief required by these three logics are not negotiable and are therefore stable as long as one remains in a particular mode, although their symbolic expression may change. The logic of belonging must be clearly distinguished from the authentication of the whole system (from ritual expression to total paradigm) of which it is but a part. I will return to authentication later.

THE LOGICS IN PRACTICE

Many religious institutions, including most mainline Christian churches, operate with a mixture of direct and indirect belonging and the possibility of drawing the best from both worlds. Indeed the confessions of some churches combine a high ecclesiology with the faith principle. Few members of overtly protestant denominations, if asked how they belong to God, would not make some reference to membership of their church, soon after, or even before, a reference to faith. In addition, most religious institutions, even at the most stable of times, display elements of reduced reality belonging. Few groups can have been consistently secure enough not to have succumbed, at some time or another, to the temptation to bolster their own sense of belonging by dwelling upon the inadequacies of others. Yet, for all this mixing, there is evidence of the importance of a clear logic of belonging, particularly in situations of insecurity.

Among the Yorkshire and Lancashire parishes of the Church of England in the 1930s and 40s, only the relatively secure middle class parishes could afford the luxury of drawing the best from being both "catholic and reformed". The working class parishes of the industrial towns seemed to have moved toward either a clearly evangelical or a clearly Tractarian (that is, catholic) position, from which they regarded each other with the utmost suspicion. In more recent times, the so called charismatic movement, seems to have had less influence in churches where the model of belonging is either clearly direct or clearly indirect. Both pieces of evidence suggest that a mixed logic of belonging presents some difficulties for a secure faith.

In my view, much of the power of Luther's "by faith alone" doctrine to grasp its 16th century hearers lay in its logic. For when the image of the church as a divinely constituted entity (in belonging to which one belonged to God) had waned in the face of nominalism and other corrosive factors, there remained the question of how the individual should understand his or her belonging. Europe awaited either an individual and direct model of belonging or a revival of the corporate and indirect one. The reformation offered the former, the counter reformation achieved much toward the latter.

THE POTENCY OF A LOGIC OF BELONGING

The importance of simply having a logic of belonging, whether clear or not, is also well evidenced in both the individual and the community.

I have already indicated that the elements of a logic will appear in the religious expressions of groups who have never consciously sought a logic.

Later I will be looking at what happens when there is no dominant tradition, and how religious cultures generate bridging symbols in order that both individual identity and corporate strivings can remain united in situations where value systems compete. Not all bridging symbol is cognitive, but where it is, the out-pouring of bridging symbol serves the need for a logic of belonging which is as coherent as it can be in the given situation.

Earlier I described the secular world affirming paradigm as a conflict model. Another sense, in which it is this, has its roots in the manner in which people defend the symbols which constitute their logic of belonging. This defense is a generator of prejudice. Thus manifestations of prejudice, even when they have the appearance of having secular roots, may in fact have religious ones.

If my logic of belonging includes and is dependent upon my nation state and my sense of belonging becomes threatened, I am very likely to seek to "purify" my nation state in the attempt to get rid of all unaccountable and otherwise unacceptable fragments. It is all right if some of the people present belong to other nations provided that they do not confuse my identity by assuming that they belong to mine. The pressure for this "purification" comes from the need to define more sharply the nation state as a symbol in the logic of belonging and thereby render it more functional. For example, the most revealing form of anti-semitism is not that which is found almost accidentally in mass political movements with a need for someone to blame, but that which occasionally takes even the self-conscious Judaophile unawares. I believe that the root of anti-semitism, most difficult to recognize and to know how to deal with, lies in the significance that attaches to the logic of belonging.

The real root of Christian anti-semitism does not lie in the usually referred to New Testament passages concerning the implication of Jews in the death of Jesus, however much these may have been misused. The whole action, good and bad, takes place in a Jewish microcosm and the Romans were at least as much involved. Rather, it lies in the all pervasive fact that not only were Jesus and all his early followers Jewish, but that the whole Christian message only makes sense against the Old Testament background. That is to say, the Christian is utterly dependent upon a symbolic Jew and a variety of Jewish symbols for the logic of his or her belonging to the ultimately-real. This is likely to be resented by those Christians whose identity is formed to a significant degree by membership of some community other than the Christian one, for example, by membership in a nation state.

While the Christian logic of belonging is inextricably dependent upon Jews, from Abraham through Jesus to Paul, the Muslim logic, although acknowledging the past, is much more a new beginning. It is not surprising, therefore, that Jews seem to have suffered less from religious prejudice in Muslim countries than in Christian ones.

Because the roots of anti-semitism lie in resentment of dependence upon Jews (rather than upon members of one's own group) for salvation, it is less vigorous when the cost to Jews (of being such a symbol) is apparent. That is, when they are obviously observant or suffering for the faith. "It is more vigorous when they share my position, but are still different. Different, because they sometimes claim to be, but more important in this context, because I need them to be."

It is not surprising, therefore, that the pogroms in Russia intensified at the time when Jews were beginning to leave the shtetls and ghettos and were being assimilated into the wider society.

This way of understanding anti-semitism helps to explain a number of diverse associated phenomena. Being English, I had never quite understood the appeal that the stories of King Arthur held, until I came to consider logics of belonging. These stories serve to root British hearers in primeval time, that is, in an ultimately-real whose spokesman and functionary was Merlin.[2] They enable them to belong to the ultimate through a Briton, in a profounder sense than they do through any Jew. I do not doubt that Teutonic and Norse myths serve the same purpose in northern Europe.

Nor do I doubt that the respect of black people for black prophets who were seemingly "untainted" by contact with white missionaries, their desire to see Jesus as Black, or at least as Middle Eastern, even the antagonism that some diaspora Jews show toward Israel and Israelis, all stem from the same root, that is, the resentment felt against those upon whom one is dependent (as symbols in one's logic of belonging) if they are not clearly one's own. It is not easy to separate the Jew, the White or the State of Israel, that are my neighbors, from the Jew, the White or the State of Israel that are my symbols, or to refrain from imposing upon the former both my expectations and resentment concerning the latter.[3]

---

[2] I am sure that this is one of the things, though far from the only thing, that accounts for the popularity of Mary Stewart's trilogy, *The Hollow Hills, The Crystal Cave and The Last Enchantment*, (London, Hodder and Stoughton, 1979)

[3] There are other examples of this phenomenon, such as the pervasive pressure to turn the Jewish Jesus of history into a cosmic Christ or to emphasize the Spirit, even the frequent attempts to rediscover the "lost tribes" among one's own people.

It is my impression that there is a tendency among Black Africans to see and to reject modern Jews as Whites and to identify Arabs, understood as both black and semitic, as the proper inhabitants of Palestine and nearer somehow to Jesus and to the Jews of the Biblical story than are contemporary Jews.

THE THREE PATHWAYS -
BASIC ELEMENTS IN THE MODES OF BELONGING.

I introduced the modes of belonging with the two logics familiar in the Abrahamic family and the sectarian alternative. There is now a need for a more discriminating way of locating the great variety of both overt and covert styles of religious belonging. This becomes possible with a slight elaboration of the original schema.

In chapter 8, I said that it is a consequence of transcendence that there are at least two paths by which the individual may relate to the ultimately-real. It may be done directly, or via the real *sub specie aeternitatis*. In more traditional terms, one may relate to the creator directly or via that which he has created. Between these two is the other possibility of which I have spoken, namely that the divine is seen to have established within the creation a bridgehead, in belonging to which one belongs to the divine. This establishment of a bridgehead might be conceived as an emanation, a new creation within creation, or simply as election and endowment. These pathways may be represented thus:

Fig. 11.1

Path 1. is direct and individual.

Path 2. is indirect and usually corporate.

Path 3. is the possibility of relating to the ultimately-real side-by-side, rather than face-to-face, by relating to the real *sub specie aeternitatis*. This relationship with the real may have a number of different emphases. It can be cognitive, in a consuming desire to understand it; practical, in the desire to engage with it in a manner that is efficient and fruitful; ethical or political, in the desire to improve it; affective, in an outer mysticism; or aesthetic, in the drive to appreciate it.

Belonging may be modelled in an infinite variety of ways comprised by rejection or acceptance or any degree of emphasis on these three paths. If one includes a description of the balance between cognitive and affective emphases then all possible modes of belonging, within the secular world affirming type, can be located in this schema.

To be thoroughly cosmic, indeed to be orthodox within the Abrahamic faiths and retain a balance between the creation and saviour aspects of the divine, it is necessary to include path 3 along with either or both of paths 1 and 2. It is possible, however, to remain cosmic in spirit by an emphasis in depth within path 1 or 2 while neglecting the breadth offered by path 3. For present purposes we will call this pietist. It is a form of specialization within a cosmic sense of belonging, much as marriage is a form of specialization in one's relationships with others, that limits but does not deny the value of other relationships. The consequences of pietism may be an improved estimate of the rest of life, albeit one that might not be considered very realistic by the outsider. Whether one regards it as a form of what I have called reduced reality belonging depends on one's perspective. Likewise a concentration on path 3, with little beyond a cosmic trust in place of path 1, may, I believe, remain cosmic in spirit.

Which path is emphasized may not make much difference affectively, but cognitively and consequentially they are markedly different. An emphasis on path 3 is an emphasis on creation, an emphasis on path 2 is an emphasis on the Church or Israel as a new opportunity within creation, an emphasis on path 1 is an emphasis on the individual's relation as new creation or new endowment. These will clearly have different consequences for the adherents' priorities in relation to their world out there.

Reduced reality belonging of the sectarian kind may be understood as drawing cognitively on path 1, while it creates the affective benefits of the bridgehead in path 2 by an active rejection of path 3 in whole or in part. That is to say, that it compensates for the failure of a cosmic sense of belonging by creating an ingroup, the tightly knit quality of which is bolstered by denigration of the rest of life including, perhaps, other groups attempting the same move. It is the extreme case of all weak path 1 belonging which needs strong communal testimony for its survival. However, it steps out of orthodoxy to achieve it. It diminishes the real, therefore transcendence is diminished rather than emphasized.

Every tradition is in some sense a reduction of reality to the level of the manageable, even though it is a model for total experience. The problem is how to be part of universal humanity while remaining in ones own model with its strong sense of belonging. It is a particular case of the general problem of how strongly to draw lines in seeking to maintain both an identity and a sense of community.

Consider the following table in which possible combinations of Paths 1, 2 and 3, together with cognitive and affective emphases, exemplifies the broad range of religious types.

Paths	Examples of Religious Type		
1 and 3	Traditional protestant and pietist Christian and Muslim emphasis. That is, Direct Cosmic Belonging		
2 and 3	Traditional Catholic or Jewish emphasis. That is, Indirect Cosmic Belonging.		
1 + 2 + 3	Mixed D.C.B. and I.C.B., e.g. Anglican and, *de facto*, most protestant churches		
1 without negating 3	Forms of Pietism		
	(cognitive emphasis)	individual adherent as new creation, divine as saviour	
	(affective emphasis)	inner mysticism	
2 without negating 3	(cognitive emphasis)	traditionalism	
	(affective emphasis)	sacramentalism, mysticism Hasidism?	
3 only	(affective quietist)	nature mysticism if transcendence lost, then nature religion[*]	
	(cognitive quietist)	aesthetic or intellectual absorption, if transcendence missing, then cosmic trust	
	(cognitive activist)	political or practical absorption	
3 permeated by 2	Incarnationalism, tends to nature religion.		
1 + 3 with very high 1.	Tends to quietism and an abstracted, rose tinted view of the world-out-there. Divine as saviour emphasis.		
1 + 3 with very high 3.	Tends to ethical activism, the divine as creator emphasis.		

[*] Quietist and activist stances will be to some degree idiosyncratic, but are legitimated and partly controlled, by an understanding of the divine character.

There is little in the history of the Abrahamic family of religions to indicate that uniformity of emphasis within these pathways is either possible or desirable. Belonging may be experienced in any of them. There are, however, some tendencies to be discerned. For example, goal orientation, because it is highly cognitive tends to be associated with the individual and direct path, for that too can be highly cognitive. Strong texture orientation tends to be associated with the institutional path because both can be largely affective. Where the individual mode becomes textural, that is affective, it is almost certainly because the context has become that of mysticism. This displays a tendency toward one of the monistic types of religious tradition.

Goal orientation is difficult to relate to the institutional path because goals usually require individual mobility and, because they are cognitive, they can become dogmatic and to a degree divisive. Goal oriented communities tend to stress the importance of truth, texture oriented ones the importance of harmony.

Religion and religious institutions are, of course, notoriously conservative, understandably so because they relate to individual identity at the deepest possible level, but paths of belonging change and are sometimes no longer recognized as religious. I will not at this point enter into the whole question of secularization, but there is little doubt that much that has gone under that name is in fact a shift into alternative pathways rather than a move out of religion. I include in the next chapter a "parable of secularities" which is designed to make this point.

THE CHARACTER TRAITS OF THE ULTIMATELY-REAL:
SOVEREIGNTY, RIGHTEOUSNESS AND LOVE

I have said that within secular world affirming religion the ultimately-real is necessarily conceived as personal. It follows that such a deity must have a character and that virtually everything within this type of religion will be influenced by that.

Being modelled as personal, the ultimately-real must also be assigned a sex. I mentioned when I discussed the two types of belonging, identity and complementarity, something of the effect which the sex assigned to the ultimately-real might have upon the adherent's experience of that relationship. A personal divinity without sexual designation would be less than credible to most adherents, however desirable it might be thought to be for other reasons. A mother-father god is not easily credible and a god which is referred to as "it", is impersonal and within this type, therefore, not credible. Fortunately, I do not have to enter deeply into this issue for it will not impinge directly upon what I now have to say, provided always that the symbol for the divine remains credible and other than mechanistic. Here, however, I am concerned with those character traits which would apply equally to a divinity conceived as male or as female.

If one looks back to the major prophets of the eighth century B.C.E. one finds each of them emphasizing a different aspect of divinity according to their own predilections and the circumstances in which they prophesied. Isaiah emphasized sovereignty, Amos, righteousness and Hosea, love. These three principal ingredients of divine character have been expressed in a great variety of images such as king, judge and father. To the adherent they represent control and security, direction and consistency, benevolence and acceptance, respectively. Sovereignty and righteousness taken together represent demand, while sovereignty and love represents acceptance. Love can also, of course, be demanding, but that is not the primary content of the word, nor of the majority of biblical images used to represent it.

A shift in the balance of these three will have a major impact, not only upon the experience of belonging to such a deity, but upon the whole religious tradition. Perhaps the most important difference between the three members of the Abrahamic family of faiths is that they have traditionally emphasized a different one of these traits while acknowledging the importance of all of them. The distinction has not always held, but it has determined the overall ethos of each tradition.

Islam with its traditional emphasis upon the sovereignty of God has also a quality of kismet or fate. Man serves God but God is the initiator of action rather than man. So, although Islam shares the secular world affirming outlook, willingness to take hold of the environment and shape it is somewhat controlled by a deterministic emphasis on the sovereign will of Allah.

Judaism has chosen to emphasize righteousness. An observant Jew therefore seeks to obey the Law of God, to do the Mitzvot. Although Torah is understood to have been given for life, it is grace and not the legalistic thing which it is often interpreted as being, nevertheless it leads to a careful walk through life. The orthodox Jew has not been at risk *vis-à-vis* the environment.

Christianity has traditionally emphasized love, which has two consequences, the first being that salvation is a gift and not something to be earned, the other, that the human response to this is to love God in return. Love necessitates freedom and freedom demands responsibility. So, within Christianity, particularly within that part of the reformed tradition which laid heavy emphasis on predestination to salvation, the predestined one is not only free to, but also responsible for taking hold of the world and shaping it. Without the divine sanction such an attitude can, of course, become exploitative and indeed, destructive.

What is clear is that whichever characteristic is emphasized, all three are necessary to maintain the Abrahamic tradition and the importance of each having a champion may be seen in the following exercise to illustrate the significance of the balance between the three characteristics.

It will suffice to notice what happens when each characteristic is highly emphasized and each is neglected. None of the character traits could exist virtually on its own and still have significance, except perhaps a brand of sovereignty which would constitute the divinity as an undemanding, impersonal power and thereby cease to be traditionally Abrahamic. I will therefore consider them in pairs.

If one neglects love, then sovereignty and righteousness will constitute a demanding, legalistic and somewhat impersonal deity.

If one neglects righteousness, then one has an arbitrary deity who may be benevolent when and to whom his sovereign whim pleases.

If one neglects sovereignty, then one has an otherwise very attractive deity, but not one that is in control, a god without teeth, a religion that is well described as a "holy custard".

If all three traits are present, but one is greatly emphasized above the others, then there are other consequences which should be noticed.

If sovereignty were emphasized there would be a tendency for the divine to become impersonal, for events to be seen as determined and, unless the divine demand for action were particularly clear, for human response to be submissive and quietist. One would have an unbounded ultimately-real, that is, an arbitrary and immediate deity, unrestrained even by his own attributes of righteousness and love and probably having to be related to directly.

If righteousness were emphasized then conformity to what is conceived as righteousness could not only lead to an exceedingly careful walk through life, but might also become an end in itself. One would have a bound ultimately-real, structured by its own character frame (law), remote (only commands need be present), probably having to be related to indirectly.

If love (acceptance) were emphasized far beyond the others both direction and significance of life would be lost and anomie result.

THE QUALITY AND INTENSITY OF BELONGING

I will conclude this section by saying something about the *quality* of religious experience. This derives from a consideration of the effect upon the individual's relation to the divine of the two factors just considered (the character traits and the various pathways of belonging) as they occur in different combinations. In particular it is possible to place in a rough hierarchy the levels of demand and acceptance that would be experienced by an individual (in his or her relation to the divine) if he or she were to stand in each of the possible combinations of the variables.

Demand and acceptance seem to pull in different directions and therefore to be in need of existing in some balance, but they are not contradictory, as any observer of the parent-child relationship knows. Both are necessary in a healthy upbringing.

That demand and acceptance are not opposites can also be seen by consideration of the two factors in religious belonging that I have been considering. In terms of these, the most demanding religious experience would be that of direct cosmic belonging to a god conceived to be high in righteousness and sovereignty. The most accepting situation would lie in indirect cosmic belonging to a god conceived to be high in love and sovereignty. The least demanding would differ from the most accepting in that sovereignty would also be low. The least accepting would differ from the most demanding in the same manner, a situation in which even the demand has no support. Between these extremes lie a whole spectrum of possibilities.

Whether determined by this indirect and composite method or by direct enquiry, the levels of felt demand and acceptance within the sense of belonging are interesting indicators of its quality. Consider the following diagr⌐

Fig. 11.2

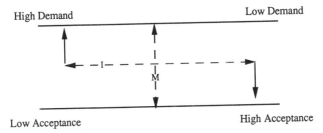

There is a felt level of demand scale running from high to low and a felt acceptance scale running parallel from low to high. Levels of demand and acceptance are indicated by the small arrows. "M" represents the mean between the levels of demand and acceptance. In any sort of relationship one would look for a balance here. In the individual's relation to the divine, if this mean were to move to the right, it would engender a loss of meaning. A move to the left, would give rise to a loss of freedom and incentive and therefore also of meaning. Demand with support is challenge, demand without support is oppressive, support without demand is devitalizing. I will return in a moment to the dimension marked "I".

This is the most useful pair of scales and the one most clearly related to these basic variables, but there is another pair which is directly related to the individual's perception of the nature of the ultimately-real and of the mode of belonging thereto. This is the pair, "sense of freedom and individual responsibility" over against "divine determination". While these may be logical opposites more clearly than in the previous situation, they are not necessarily opposites at the level of feeling. One may have a strong sense of individual responsibility and at the same time a strong sense of the divine orchestration of challenges and outcomes.

The movement of the mean of this pair is also significant, for it represents a calculus between meaning and security. Divine determination offers security but loss of meaning, while being out on one's own and responsible provides meaning at the expense of security.

NOTE : *RELIGIOUS INTENSITY*

The assessment of religious intensity is notoriously difficult and is quite impossible unless religious attachment has been clearly defined. Measures of religious activity such as attendance at services, time and money given, even as a proportion of what is available, do not measure the intensity of religion. They measure intensity of religious commitment, neither as the level of the sense of belonging achieved, nor as the intensity of quest for such a sense of belonging. They could even be inversely related to it and represent a frenzied acting out of a felt failure to belong that was so undirected as not even to constitute a quest for belonging. On the other hand, one cannot penetrate the real base of religion in the individual, that is, the felt sense of reality, so what does one do?

Personally I have used a measure constructed from the five factors, background, self-assessment, formal observance, private observance and the nature of world view held. I am now of the opinion that the most promising way into a measure of religious intensity is via the demand and acceptance scales.

If we return to the parental situation for a moment, the child who experiences little demand and little acceptance is virtually an orphan. The child who experiences high demand and high acceptance is in an intense relationship. The distance "I" on the diagram is, therefore, a measure of intensity of relationship. In this case if "I" is low, religious experience hardly exists, on the other hand it could also be too high for comfort, even for mental health.

The equivalent dimension, in relation to the freedom and responsibility scale over against the divine determination scale, is not such a good measure of intensity. For one thing, the logical issue enters in and separates the more affective person, who may at the same time feel intensely responsible and highly determined, from the more cognitive person who is likely to consciously balance them out. This measure of intensity as it has been presented, is only applicable to individuals who have consciously accepted the paradigm. However, if one were designing an intensity measure in a post-paradigmatic situation, where the mode of engagement with the world out there was to take hold and shape, it would hardly differ from this. It makes sense to speak for people in that situation of the felt demand and felt support of the cosmos, or simply of life, for it is not the feeling, but the cognitive modelling of reality which they reject.

II. THE ADHERENT'S RELATION TO THE REAL

My general concern in this section is with the adherent's relation to his or her world-out-there, which includes all things natural as well as societal. However, attitudes to things natural are strongly socially determined and for present purposes, therefore, I will be emphasizing the adherent's relationships in, with and through, social groupings.

In the previous section I discussed the possibility of relating to the ultimately-real by relating to the real *sub specie aeternitatis*, and indicated the number of different emphases that this might have. These, and the choices among the paths for belonging to the ultimately-real have implications for the adherents relation to the real, but the discussion would become exceedingly complex if I attempted to relate all that I now wish to say to each of the possible paths. I will for the most part, therefore, be restricting what I have to say to the quite general situation of the individual who believes in a transcendent and personally conceived ultimately-real, and to the consequences of that belief for his or her relation to the world-out-there and *vice versa*.

While most of the discussion that follows will be in external terms, that is in terms of the individual's relation to his or her world-out-there, and will therefore be reminiscent of what was said about path 3 belonging, the primary concern at this point is an internal one. It involves the consequence of that external relationship, namely the individual's sense of identity. There would be little point in a potential adherent having knowledge of the character of the "Thou", or of a pathway for belonging to the "Thou" if there were no sense of an "I" to belong. There can be some sort of a sense of identity without a sense of belonging, but there can be no sense of belonging, whatever the pathway, without the sense of a self to belong.

With these points in mind I turn to a consideration of the relationship between religion, identity and the adherent's world-out-there.

RELIGION, IDENTITY AND THE WORLD-OUT-THERE

Religion is concerned with the individual's participation in reality. Identity depends on how that participation has shaped one. Self-image (the conscious aspect of identity) depends on how one perceives that participation.

In discussing the method of approach for this chapter, I said that the world-out-there, in providing the detail of the individual's identity, gives substance to the other actor, the "this" which is seeking to belong to "that", the self which would relate to the ultimately-real. It is this which makes the need to deal with the question "Who am I?" a priority for humankind that is not far behind that of physical survival, sometimes even ahead of it. This means seeking for a unified identity and then, perhaps, having to make moves, including religious moves, for the preservation of that identity. Thus religion in this type is not simply concerned with the sacred but with putting sacred and secular together. It is about belonging at both the ultimate and immediate levels, and it is not sufficient for the student of religion to be concerned only with the adherent's relation to the ultimately-real. There is need also to be able to isolate the effective factors which determine the individual's relation to the real, that is, to the world-out-there as the individual perceives it.

IDENTITY AND BELONGING

Belonging is more than identity, but in the secular world affirming type of religious tradition, a sense of self is the *sine qua non* of a sense of belonging. An identity which fits the world-out-there is a necessary but not, in most cases, sufficient condition for a sense of belonging. One needs also the other things listed at the beginning of this chapter, including the ritual necessary to express and confirm belonging to whatever is felt to be the ultimately-real, as well as authentication of the whole religious system.

Here I am concerned with the role of religion in the formation of a sense of that self which has the potential to belong, its integration and its maintenance. The relation between identity, the world-out-there and religion-as-belonging is a complex and often circular one. Consider, without getting too involved in them, the four examples that follow. I will be returning to the same ideas later. I include them here to indicate why one must be involved with the sort of detailed analysis that occupies the rest of this section.

i) The power of the religious tradition to integrate the world-out-there and to create a sense of cosmic belonging depends upon its relation with the world-out-there legitimating the whole religious system. The only exception to this is reduced reality belonging, in which it is precisely its power to be a substitute for an unattainable cosmic sense that legitimates the system.

ii) Because identity is only obtainable in its detail in relation to a world-out-there, relation to the world-out-there has the power to inhibit or distort belonging. If identity is prevented from forming and one remains anomic, there is no self to belong. Likewise identity once formed may become fixed and potentially the seat of a false or alienated consciousness.[4]

iii) Individuals need symbols for the ultimately-real and for the relation of the ultimately-real to the real. These need to be such that they engender a cognitive integration and, more important still, an affective coherence and integrated evaluation of the various aspects of the otherwise fragmented world-out-there.

This entails a need for coherence in what are understood to be the divine attitudes to the created realm and may require theodicy. Theodicy frequently functions by offering an account of the divine purpose, that is, a providence tradition. Such a providence emphasis can come into conflict with the tradition's ethic, as it has in contemporary Israel.

iv) Adherence to a particular religious paradigm, is potentially identity threatening. This is because any religion in which adherents submit themselves to the distilled and conserved wisdom of the past must always be somewhat contrary to contemporary experience. However alert a tradition community may be to the issues of its own time, it cannot legitimately allow the present to be the sole or even the major contributor to the corporate understanding of the world with which it has to deal.

This conserved wisdom serves to structure identity and to liberate its adherents from the situation in which decisions can only be taken as

---

[4] Peter Berger has shown why religion, understood as a tradition handed on within an institution, is the most powerful force in overcoming anomie, and at the same time and for the same reason, a most powerful force in creating alienation. Peter Berger, *The Social Reality of Religion*, (London, Faber & Faber, 1968), p.87.

the result of subjective whim, or a narrow concern with the problems of the present. On the other hand, in times of rapid change and when a new context sets aspects of a tradition in conflict, it can also create major problems for the identity so structured. I considered two examples of this in chapter 9.

The foregoing paragraphs point in many directions. The rest of this section is dedicated to elucidating, developing and inter-relating the ideas that they contain.

A CONCEPTUAL EXPLORATION

I begin with a conceptual model intended to expose the relationship between religion, identity and goals (all carriers of values) and the factual possibilities of a given situation. It is a model which was developed in the first instance for better understanding of the situation in contemporary Israel and draws its illustrations from that source. It is again a case of "the worst first" and in terms of what will follow it is more important that the general reader concentrate upon the definition of the conceptual entities rather than upon the finer details of their inter-relation.

THE CONCEPTUAL ELEMENTS   (reference is to the conceptual model)

"A", the PARADIGM FOR THE ULTIMATELY-REAL plus "B", the MODE OF BELONGING, constitute religion in its most general sense.

"C" represents communally held values and their symbols and is here referred to as CIVIL RELIGION. In the literature concerned with civil religion at least three overlapping, but different referents of the term may be discerned. These are:

C1   This is the shared, largely sub-conscious value system of the community, by which events are judged, including civil religion in the second and third senses. This level of civil religion is largely unconceptualized until called into play in particular situations and even then may be defined only negatively in relation to the events in question - "we cannot stand for that". It is not therefore a known focus of unity as, for example, the symbols of civil religion in the second sense, yet it gives rise to what is perhaps the deepest sense of group unity once it is discovered to be shared. It is always operative through the ballot box and various market forces, without it being obvious to those participating. It is an intuitive grasp on this element that enables a leader, or even a songwriter, to select the right symbols for an effective input to C2 or C3.

Fig.11.3

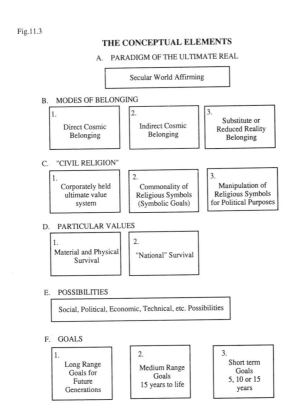

THE CONCEPTUAL ELEMENTS

A. PARADIGM OF THE ULTIMATE REAL

Secular World Affirming

B. MODES OF BELONGING

| 1. Direct Cosmic Belonging | 2. Indirect Cosmic Belonging | 3. Substitute or Reduced Reality Belonging |

C. "CIVIL RELIGION"

| 1. Corporately held ultimate value system | 2. Commonality of Religious Symbols (Symbolic Goals) | 3. Manipulation of Religious Symbols for Political Purposes |

D. PARTICULAR VALUES

| 1. Material and Physical Survival | 2. "National" Survival |

E. POSSIBILITIES

Social, Political, Economic, Technical, etc. Possibilities

F. GOALS

| 1. Long Range Goals for Future Generations | 2. Medium Range Goals 15 years to life | 3. Short term Goals 5, 10 or 15 years |

C1, rather than C2, is best understood as the core of corporate identity, although identity is bolstered by the conscious elements of corporate memory. Insofar as culture and state can be separated, C1 belongs with the culture, C2 with the state. C1 is clearly related to A and to B as set out above, but is filled out by the consequential mode of engagement with the rest of experience. It will be more affective and less cognitive than the tradition borne by the religious institution and not necessarily overtly religious at all. The appeal tends to be to values, that is, to ethical symbols, rather than to history and traditional symbols, when it becomes conscious.

C2. This is the usual meaning of civil religion when used in a non-pejorative sense. It is in the first place a set of commonly espoused symbols for corporately held values. Because the symbols represent the corporate vision, however, they are already related to existing historical possibilities and are therefore partly goals expressed as values (see under F below), or as medial axioms (for example equality, freedom, democracy, prosperity, survival of the State). Although the symbols may be drawn from religious tradition or the peoples historical experience, the values and goals that they enshrine are contemporary. The appeal is to both ethical and traditional symbols.

C3. This is the usual meaning of civil religion when it is used in a pejorative sense. However necessary it may be politically, it is a prostitution of the symbols, for it is the deliberate manipulation of religious symbols for political ends. C2 can very quickly become C3 when a situation changes, as when a liberation theology lingers once a group has moved into power. The appeal is usually to traditional symbols.

The formation of individual identity in the western world depends to a considerable degree on the individual's ability to set authentic medium and long range goals. Authenticity in this context normally requires that the society at large possesses established goals which the individual can relate to positively, or even negatively, but clearly, including a civil religion in the second sense (C2) and medium and long range goals (F1 and F2).

GOALS (F) arise by the bringing together of the general values in (C1,C2) and PARTICULAR VALUES (D) with POSSIBILITIES (E)

Among the most pressing particular values which may conflict with or reinforce certain aspects of general values, are material and physical survival (D1) and frequently, national survival (D2).

F3   This represents short term communal goals of say, 5, 10 or 15 years according to the matter being dealt with. Decisions made about these tend to be pragmatic, the choices being controlled by medial axioms from C2 if available, rather than by their superordinate values, otherwise by sub-group interests.[5] They can frequently be seen as temporary expedients. To be concerned with them, therefore, is not too great a threat to identity. A major emphasis on short term goals has been called the "magical approach", that is, the covert hope that if one deals with immediate issues the longer term problems will just disappear.[6]

F2   Medium term goals, say 15 years to a life-time, tend to be

---

[5] By medial axioms in this situation I refer to those generally accepted directions of development, or more vaguely defined community strivings, which, having become established, are largely unquestioned. Having become part of the flesh on the bones of the civil religion, they are something that the community stands for. They might, however, have little continuing relation to the more abstract values that the community lays claim to and which it supposes to have generated, or at least to be in keeping with, these lower level objectives.

[6] See for example, N Chabani Manganyi, "Soweto on my Mind" in *Looking Through the Keyhole*, (Johannesburg, Raven Press, 1981) p.147f.

hammered out in terms of the perceived real possibilities and the acceptable, if more pragmatic, values associated with civil religion in the second sense. Goals of this length affect the self evaluation of every participating individual and can therefore threaten identity. One cannot say of a goal of this length, if one is seeking it, "it is not really me".

F1 Long range goals, that is, those for which members of a generation may be prepared to sacrifice present texture of life in order to improve the lot of future generations. These will be to a considerable extent expressions of pure value because the material possibilities are much less clearly defined and therefore goals can hardly be formulated. Long term goals are inextricably bound up with identity and therefore with civil religion in the first sense, but they are far less easily threatened by the vicissitudes of the immediate situation, for they have not been cashed in terms of contemporary possibilities.

THE PRINCIPAL RELATIONSHIPS BETWEEN CONCEPTS (reference is again to the conceptual model)

C1 and E and where appropriate D1 and D2, would normally give rise to C2.
C2 and E would normally give rise to F2.
C1 and some attempted future projection of E would usually give rise to F1.
C2 and F1 have much in common, but C2 is more general, symbolic and contemporary in it expression, F1 is more specific and overtly future.
C3 is likely to occur, because it is more likely to succeed, when C1 is weak or threatened and when C2 is conflicted or undefined.
C1 tends to be ideal while C2 tends to be pragmatic.

If C1 and C2 are too much alike the society will tend to a sense of self-satisfaction and inertia and individuals to anomie.

If C1 and C2 are far apart, as D and E may force them to be, the probable consequences are manifold:

(i) A schizophrenic society with all the communicative and organizational problems which flow therefrom. (D, given C1 and E, may both demand and inhibit the formation or survival of C2).

(ii) A disintegration of and reluctance to reformulate civil religion in the second sense, together with a consequential reluctance to formulate medium term societal goals F2.

(iii) A weakening of the consciousness of group unity which would normally flow from a strong C2.

(iv) A feeling of threat to individual identity and to C1 where that has become conscious.

(v)   Either a rapid change in civil religion in the first sense and virtually an unselfing and therefore anomie, or a reactionary defense of it with concomitant alienation from other aspects of experience.

Indirect cosmic belonging B2 is the normative mode of belonging in any secular world affirming community with a strong sense of corporate destiny. If C2 does not form or if it disintegrates, then that to which one belongs in order to belong to the ultimately-real has a diminished reality. Adherents may then move toward either direct cosmic belonging B1, which would be further encouraged by, for example, the needs of a technological society for mobile individuals; but discouraged, if there were the lack of a wide group to testify to the authenticity of the individual's relationship to the ultimately real, and thus establish the cosmic sense of belonging. It might also move toward reduced reality belonging B3.

Identity, which may include everything from conceptions of the divine, nature to mother's traditional recipes, is rooted in the experience of and traditional symbols concerning A, B1 or B2 and perhaps B3. It is filled out in relation to life as a whole, while its corporate ethical content is basic to C1, it would normally have symbolic, this-worldly goals in F1. "Zion", "Pax Britannica", "The American Dream" were all such symbols. Should these symbols be dissolved in the seeming arrival of the reality to which they pointed or be otherwise broken, and if there are no obvious goals with which to replace them, then there is a potential conflict between the identity formed around them and the aspirations of the group in their contemporary context. Britain after the second world war and contemporary Israel are cases in point.
As with individual self-image, conscious corporate identity may be realistic, that is, what we see ourselves to be now; or idealistic, that is, what we strive to be. The former, if it were allowed to find expression, would closely relate to C2, the latter to C1.

Throughout the foregoing discussion I have been writing of corporate identity as though it were necessarily a unified whole, and of the nation state as though that were the only significant level of aggregation beyond the immediate family. I have therefore dealt with civil religion as though that were the only significant corporate value system, from the individual to the universal, in which people could participate,. This picture is still relatively true in modern Israel and until recently for "Afrikanerdom" within the South African state.[7] It was once truer for the nation states of Europe and North

America than it is today.⁸ In general, however, it is not true. I must therefore add to the concepts employed above the more universal notion of "an aggregation significant in identity". This will allow me to continue using the term identity, while recognizing that the value component of identity includes the perceived corporate identity of each significant aggregation in which the individual understands himself or herself to participate. Civil religion, in the total of the various meanings distinguished, is but the shared value system, the *sine qua non* of the group, which functions at the national level of aggregation. What has been said about nation and civil religion therefore will apply *mutatis mutandis* to all other significant levels of aggregation. I will speak, therefore, of aggregations, of levels of aggregation and of their appropriate value systems, rather than of civil religion. I must now clarify what I understand by a significant aggregation.

SIGNIFICANT AGGREGATIONS -
THE CORPORATE ASPECT OF IDENTITY

Adherents of a religious tradition are not simply individuals relating to the ultimately-real, the real, and the constituent parts of the real. They are social beings constituting, and constituted by, participation in any number of societies. I refer to these groupings as "aggregations" because the word has less inherited connotations than society.

A society, in the sense that I have been using the word, would be any level of aggregation, membership of which contributes to an individual's identity, an entity in which he shares a corporate identity as a result of which he will say I am an Israeli, a teenager, a radical, or an academic. Collectively, the aspects of civil religion distinguished earlier are but a special case of this collective consciousness which for Durkheim was the essence of religion.

Every such aggregation, insofar as it is not simply a collection of individuals, has its own value system - in fact its own religion - in Durkheim's

---

⁷ If, for example, the pressure were to be taken off Israel, sub-groupings such as Ashkenazim and Sephardim, the secular and the observant, and many other actual and potential political, economic and cultural groupings, would become very much more important for the identity formation of individual Israelis.

⁸ Ninian Smart points to the decline in significance of the Nation State in this regard and to the rising significance of both lower and higher levels of aggregation. Ninian Smart, *Beyond Ideology*, (London, Collins, 1981), p.208f.

terms. Thus belonging to an aggregation significant in identity necessarily means espousing a set of values which are felt to be significant for the survival of the aggregation.[9]

While the aggregation's values are for it an ultimate, in the sense that without them it reduces to a collection of individuals and ceases to exist as an aggregation, the importance of the values to the individual member depends upon :

> a) how important the survival of the aggregation is to the member concerned and

> b) what she or he feels about the roll of each value in that survival.

Thus, if I value the academic endeavor and I believe trust to be essential to that endeavor, then I will almost certainly consider it offensive for an academic to flirt with one who is currently his or her student.

In turn, the importance of the survival of an individual aggregation will be determined in part by its place in a wider horizontal and vertical integration, particularly the latter. Only in a reduced reality situation, where membership of a particular group compensates for a failure of belonging in the rest of experience, will this not be the case.

Part of individual identity will always be idiosyncratic and beyond my present concern, much of it, however, will be formed by participation in these corporate identities. Much of this shared value system lays hidden until some crisis calls forth a response, the universality of which may surprise the members of the aggregation, making the bond of group identity more conscious and a more powerful contributor to the self-image of each individual.

An aggregation, then, is simply a shared-values grouping. It might be as structured as "The Regiment" or "This Corporation", as relatively unstructured as "Academia", or as totally unstructured, by anything save the values themselves, as say, "Liberal".

There are some general things to be said about the size and definition of aggregations in relation to identity.

---

[9] On the face of it, aggregations significant in identity could be perceived in terms other than their shared values or goals, for example, they could be delimited by a bureaucratic structure or simply by accidental and habitual interaction. Clearly there are societies whose corporate values are more obvious than others, but all have values, even if it is individualism's very strong central value warding off all other corporate values. Even the accidental, if it became habitual, would have developed values that could be significant for identity. Without standing for something the aggregation could not be significant in identity.

Where identity comes under threat, there is need for the support of a tightly knit community. But in such a situation there can be a tension between identity and community. If I draw the lines between myself and others, between my community and other communities, too weakly I lack clarity of definition, if I draw them too strongly, I diminish the others in relation to myself and therefore their power to define me significantly. In general terms, the smaller the aggregations, membership of which most clearly defines who I am, the clearer can be my identity; the larger the aggregations the more strongly is my identity supported.

The aggregations significant for an individual's identity formation are at once part of the world out there and that through which she or he relates to it. One need not be pressingly aware of these significant aggregations unless loyalty to them is divisive or one feels irritation when some outsider criticizes them.

The religious institution is inevitably one of these aggregations for its adherents, while the individual's membership of other aggregations and his or her relation to all aggregations and their felt significance, will be influenced by religion. In addition, religion, as we will see, must assist in the integration of these aggregations.

What we have, therefore, is a situation in which, for many people in the modern world, a number of religions in Durkheim's sense of the word, contribute to one religion in the sense that I have been using it.

In order to gain an understanding of the role played by aggregations significant in identity (or the consequences of their absence) in both the individual and social aspects of religion, it is necessary to locate them within those processes in the life of the individual where religion functions and is authenticated. To this I now turn.

RELIGION, IDENTITY AND SIGNIFICANT AGGREGATIONS

I said earlier, that there is a need for the student of religion to be able to isolate the effective factors which determine the individual's relation to the world-out-there as she or he perceives it. A consideration of the aggregations significant for the individual's identity will enable a number of these effective factors to be identified. Among these factors will be:

i) the effective size of the world-out-there,

ii) it's significant levels of aggregation,

iii) whether a level of aggregation is weak or missing,

iv) whether conflicting loyalties arise in the individual because of participation in aggregations at different levels or the same level,

v) whether in consequence, the world seems coherent or disjointed - and if conflicted whether

vi) moves are being made to preserve or restore the integrity of identity - and lastly

vii) the quality which the overall experience of the world-out-there has for the individual.

I will enlarge upon each of these factors. I begin with a consideration of the features of the various aggregations significant to an individual, given that the sense of belonging sought is a cosmic one.

The Integration of Significant Aggregations
The achievement of a cosmic sense of belonging requires two features in aggregations significant in identity. It requires an integrated hierarchy of identifiable aggregations with conceptually manageable intervals and it requires compatibility of significant aggregations on the same level. I begin with the hierarchy.

A sense of cosmic belonging requires *inter alia* that I have a sense of belonging to a hierarchy of aggregations. For example, I need a sense of belonging to my family or immediate group, which in turn belongs, with other families, to my community; that my community, with other communities, belongs to the nation; that my nation belongs to, for example, the "Third World" or "West" and that to humankind; that humankind belongs to the whole created order and that to the ultimately-real. I stress that this is an example. A hierarchy there must be, but its constituent aggregations could be very different.

Consider the following hierarchy of significant aggregations to which an individual might belong. There are a number of consequences that derive from it.

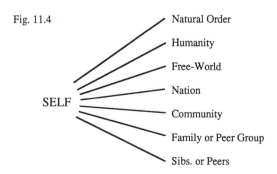

Fig. 11.4

SELF

Natural Order
Humanity
Free-World
Nation
Community
Family or Peer Group
Sibs. or Peers

Such an hierarchy of aggregations is the natural source of ethics. Each level promotes the understanding necessary for dealing appropriately, that is justly, with members of the aggregation below.

Consider, for example, how one could treat fairly any member of one's family without an image of what the family ought to be, or what one owes to one's own family over against the needs of other families, unless one has an image of what a community of families ought to be.

The desire to belong at the level above is what keeps one in relation to others on the same level while distinguishing oneself from them, even competing with them.

The desire to belong to the level above is the natural sanction for behavior at the level in question. Should one of these levels be missing or weak, there would be a sense of arbitrariness to whatever ethical directives emerge in the levels below the disjunction.

Values, even ubiquitous values, can, of course, be espoused in a purely idiosyncratic manner, the person concerned feeling or thinking them to be right. Otherwise values in which an individual acknowledges authority (as distinct from the super-added force) are ones that are perceived to be those of an aggregation to which the individual would belong. Thus the question of whether there can be universal human values, as distinct from drives for physical and identity survival, is related to how strong in individual identity formation an aggregation at the level of humanity could be, and how ubiquitous could be the perception of its values.

I drew attention earlier to the need of the individual in a secular world affirming tradition to link his or her individual belonging to the divine, to the corporate destiny symbolized as the kingdom. This, I said, was one of the roles of civil religion, but now it can be said that the whole integrated hierarchy of aggregations is what relates individual activity to the ultimate corporate goal.

It is sometimes suggested that a strong sense of belonging at levels below that of humanity is divisive and not desirable, particularly is this said of the national level, but then one would need a significant aggregation large enough to include all other people yet specific enough with which to identify. This is hardly possible. The potential aggregations Humanity, Christian, Marxist may be big enough but they are too vague. The need is for the "nest of boxes" sense that an integrated hierarchy of aggregations can provide.

In the secular world affirming paradigm it is a consequence of belief in a transcendent creator that one must recognize the desirability, if not the possibility, of understanding all aspects of experience in relation to their creator. This entails two things that are inter-related.

On the one side, there is a need for coherence in the understanding of the divine character as expressed in his attitudes to each of the levels of aggregation and to the natural realm, that is, a non-schizophrenic and therefore credible divine personality.

On the other side, there is a need, if one is to understand the character of the divine as coherent, that one's own understanding of the rest of experience, *sub specie aeternitatis*, also be coherent. Theodicy is the special task of theology when certain experiences are difficult to integrate.

I have written as though there is only one hierarchy, but there can be alternative hierarchies in the same individual at the same time, and these may be mixed and even interlace, contributing as may be to a sense of harmony or fragmentation.

Missing or Weak Levels of Aggregation

I have already had occasion to comment upon the effect of missing or weak levels of aggregation on ethics, but levels may be missing in different ways.

An individual's effective world-out-there, judged in terms of factors perceived to affect existence seriously, may be small, as is often the case among the deprived and disenfranchised of the world. In such situations, significant levels of aggregation extend from the family to the local community and the work community, but not very far beyond. This small world, however, may still be clearly related to the ultimately-real and therefore strongly cosmic. Such a limited world-out-there must not be confused with reduced reality belonging, for this unasked for situation can be open to growth and quite cosmic in spirit.

The tendency for those who struggle to remain firmly wedded to more immediate levels of aggregation, while those who are privileged develop a sense of belonging at more universal levels, is of course, not always the case. The oppressed can convert very rapidly from a concern with the immediate to a commitment to a highly universal ideal and to the sense of group belonging which goes with it. This is particularly true of the young, whose identities tend to be less stable.

Weak or ill-defined levels of reality set between the individual's immediate world and the ultimately-real are a more serious problem than an effectively small world-out-there, for these diminish the sense of cosmic belonging. There are minority groups who cannot affirm or feel part of a nation state or equivalent. These have no clearly defined level of aggregation feeding significantly into their sense of identity between the local community and humankind, save perhaps some vaguely defined entity such as "Third World". How clear and significant the entities "Black Peoples", "Women", "Workers" etc. are in individual identity formation and, therefore, in their sense of belonging, will vary from individual to individual. In general, however, they could not be expected to produce the same cosmic sense of belonging as might be possessed by an individual whose levels of belonging are securely "nested" throughout, for example, by one whose family is linked through "King and Country" to a community of nations and thence to mankind.[10]

If there are strong aggregations with a conceptual gap, a divide in the community may result. The Jewish community, for example, has been without a nation state for 2000 years. While in recent times, they have participated as individuals in other nation states, they have been somewhat insulated from that level of belonging by their Jewishness. So, while they have been free to identify less with national authorities, they have had no other significant level of aggregation between local community and that very real, but rather intangible entity, the "House of Israel". Jewish people, therefore, have had to opt to seek their sense of belonging on one or other side of the divide, that is by participation in the local community and probably in religious observance, or in that universal Jewish ethic which has characterized so many social reformers.

While the Jewish communities in the Diaspora might be marginal in the sense that they have not felt fully accepted by the dominant groups in the nations of which they have been a part, they are not marginal in the sense of having no equivalent or higher levels of aggregation to belong to. The so called "Colored" community of South Africa, however, have been marginal in this additional sense. Having been removed from the voters roll and not having Africanness or Indianness to fall back upon, members of that community have a major gap in their hierarchy between the local community and the wider Euro-Christian culture to which they belong. For some, belonging to Islam has offered an alternative aggregation, while others have turned the nation-state level into a strong anti-symbol. Still others call

---

[10] Consider in this regard the following extract from a hymn written by Dean A C Alington and quoted from the Shrewsbury School Hymn Book by Nevil Shute, *In The Wet*, (New York, William Morror, 1953).

> Lord God of Hosts, through whom alone
> A Prince can rule his nation,
> Who settest up Kings upon their throne
> And orderest each man's station;
> Now, and through ages following,
> This grace to us be given:
> To serve and love an earthly King
> Who serves our King in Heaven.

For King one might read Ruler or simply Nation.

themselves Black or Third World or even Khoikhoi (the original inhabitants of their part of Africa). Most have moved to a pietistic form of Christianity, but the gap creates a massively unstable situation, in which a ferment of attempts to remodel belonging to the ultimately-real exists at the individual, small group, and whole community levels; each seeking, creating or modifying myth for that purpose.

Conflicting Levels of Aggregation
In addition to the problem of weaknesses or gaps in the hierarchy, there is also the problem of the conflict which can occur between different levels of aggregation.

Durkheim could feel that his situation, in the intellectual world of Europe, was not unlike that of the Australasian Aboriginal people that he made use of in his study. Both presented an integrated situation within which he could speak of society as the soul of religion. Modern western man, particularly since patriotism lost its shine, belongs to many aggregations at both higher and lower levels than the nation, such as humanity, Europe, minority group, generation group. Thus, for many, military service has ceased to be the relatively uncomplicated obligation that it once was, but is seen to conflict with loyalties to aggregations both above and below the nation. It is all too easy for the individual's loyalties to be torn apart when the different levels of aggregation to which they belong come into conflict.

Alternative Hierarchies of Aggregations and Conflict at the Same Level
Having considered those things within a single dominant hierarchy that can place a stress on identity, I must now return to identities formed by parallel hierarchies. A second hierarchy may be a complete one, with its own aggregations at every level, each of them virtually independent of aggregations in the first hierarchy, alternatively the hierarchies may interlace. Religion, for example, can provide a hierarchy all the way from local congregation to world-wide church and beyond, that can either be highly independent or practically indistinguishable, from the secular hierarchy. Then again, the second hierarchy can simply be one or more loops on the dominant hierarchy, probably taking off from the level of the family and re-entering two or three levels above.

It is probably the case in relation to these co-existing hierarchies, that a single clear hierarchy creates the strongest cosmic sense at the conscious and cognitive level, while parallel or interlaced hierarchies create a stronger sense of belonging at the subliminal and affective level.

Competing aggregations at approximately the same level are fragmenting and one sees political movements seeking to overcome this. For one who is black, a feminist and a worker, each aggregation is potentially in conflict with the others. Some workers are men and white, some blacks are men and in favour of free enterprise, feminists straddle the whole economic ideological spectrum and include whites. Therefore one cannot totally endorse any group without being disloyal to the others. The symbolic common oppressor, the white male capitalist, may conjure up some sense of unity.

Clearly, religion has a role in the integration of aggregations, whether it be within a hierarchy or on the same level. I will deal with this later as an aspect of the role of corporate religion. If aggregations significant for identity cannot be integrated then the maintenance of a coherent identity requires that their aspirations be related *justly*. It may even require that an aggregation be rejected, or that its significance be drastically reduced. Religion may be called upon to legitimate all such moves.

For the religious adherent, the religious institution, apart from having a role in the integration of significant aggregations, will itself be one of these aggregations. In chapter 13 I will return to a consideration of aggregations in order to show the possible relations between a secular and a religious hierarchy of aggregations. At the moment, I wish to make the point that a sense of belonging to an aggregation significant for identity may exist at almost any level in the religious hierarchy or pervade all levels. For some the local congregation is what really matters. For example, they belong to St. Michael's and are almost accidentally Anglicans. If that is the case then St. Michael's will constitute an important part of their local community. Whereas others are Anglicans and almost accidentally belong to St. Michael's. At the top of the hierarchy it is possible to be a monotheist and almost accidentally a Christian, or a Christian and almost accidentally an Anglican. For others there is more of a balance in their belonging to each level.

In a crisis situation, an attempt may be made to substitute the religious institution for one or more levels of the secular hierarchy and to think of it as an alternative community.

IDENTITY PRESERVING MOVES IN RELIGION -
SECTARIAN REDUCED REALITY BELONGING, PIETISM AND UTOPIANISM

In a situation where the world-out-there cannot be integrated, identity may be threatened. Belonging requires the preservation of identity and moves will therefore be made to protect it.

In chapter 5, I introduce the idea of reduced reality belonging and had in mind what I will now be calling sectarian reduced reality belonging, or simply sectarian belonging, to distinguish it from other moves which might be thought to be reductions of reality, but which are not sectarian in spirit. In the second theme in chapter 9 I mentioned possible moves toward the preservation of the integrity of identity when, in a changing situation, aspects of a tradition come into conflict with each other and where involvement might decree a course of action at loggerheads with identity. In the situation discussed it was possible for some to give up the tradition, but that is not always easy nor is it without its costs.

I am now concerned, in the light of what has just been said about aggregations, to enlarge upon what has already been said about those identity preserving moves which can be made while remaining within the same tradition.

It is the case that distinct and opposing aggregations are likely to be formed around aspects of a tradition that have come into conflict. In one of the examples discussed earlier this conflict arose between, on the one hand, traditional symbols concerning people and land and, on the other, ethics. Related to these symbols, sometimes as their source, there is the other potential opposition discussed earlier, namely that between providence theology and what I called "guilt" theology.

I am going to concentrate here, however, not upon "choosing sides", but upon the other possible move; that of opting out of personal responsibility for the socio-political situation that has set aspects of the tradition in conflict and of opting into a form of pietism. I need, however, to add another term to those of sectarianism and pietism, namely utopianism, understood as a form of pseudo-activism. It will be useful to integrate two previous diagrams, in order to show the pathways for belonging and the levels of significant aggregations in conjunction.

Fig. 11.5

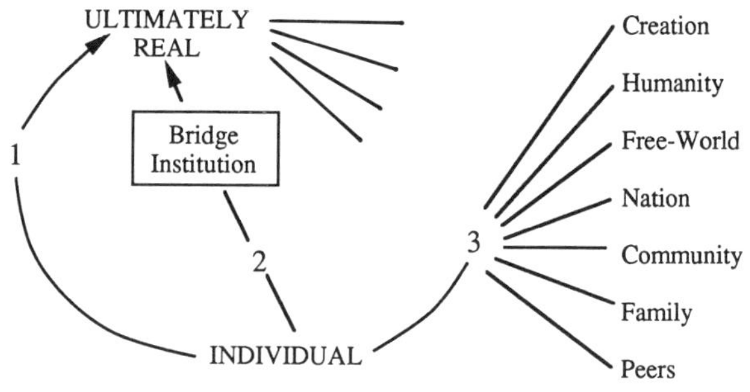

Pietism can be understood as a *neglect* of the possibilities of path 3 belonging, *sectarianism* as the overt *rejection* of these possibilities, *utopianism* as an *escapist selectivity* among such possibilities.

i) PIETISM

The least extreme religious move in the preservation of identity is to some form of pietism. This might be considered a reduction of reality but it is not sectarian in relation to the world. It is not a deliberate rejection of the rest of experience, but rather, such an emphasis on the individual's relation to the divine whether in the direct or indirect mode (path 1 or 2), that the rest of experience (potentially path 3) is no longer relied upon for a major contribution to the sense of belonging.

From a point of security in the divine care the pietist sees an abstracted and somewhat idealized world-out-there, particularly the natural order (creation), as being in divine control. Thus, while the world may be conceptualized as evil or at least as a temptation, "the devil's stomping ground", it nevertheless basks in a sense of security and harmony derived from the overtly religious realm. This "glow" effect is a frequent characteristic of pietism and gives people, who have nothing good to say about the world, a positively rose-tinted feeling about their future in it. Pietism does have its costs however. It means letting go of the quality of ethical demand in the character of the divine, or at least reducing it to personal ethics, with a consequent loss in the sense of individual responsibility and therefore of meaning - a "quietism" that tends to anomie.

In terms of the conceptual framework presented earlier, pietism is one way of avoiding involvement in identity threatening middle range goals. It is also a way of dealing with a missing, weak, or otherwise unacceptable middle in the hierarchy of significant aggregations, all of which situations threaten identity.

Pietism, as I have been using the word, must be distinguished sharply from the sectarian reduced reality belonging to which I turn next.

ii) SECTARIAN REDUCED REALITY BELONGING

The extreme religious move in defense of identity, one which for most persons can only be a short term solution, is the move to a sectarian reduced reality belonging, to the rejection (from reality status) of all experience save that which is to be had in the religious group itself.

While the description, reduced reality belonging could be applied to the *de facto* situation in pietism, here I am concerned with both a sectarian attitude and the *de jure* reduction of reality, both of which serve to legitimate and boost belongingness in the group.

As with pietism, so in sectarian reduced reality belonging, the religious tradition is used to legitimate a withdrawal from involvement in middle-range goals. Religion becomes privatized in the sense that it withdraws from the civil arena.

For both, the world-out-there is effectively reduced in significance by focusing reality in the religious experience, but the latter achieves much of its sense of religious belonging through exclusivity, by rejecting all path 3 possibilities of belonging. That is, it establishes an over-againstness in relation to the world-out-there, seeing it as evil, or at least transitory and of little significance, and looks to be saved out of it. It is this that creates the most obvious difference between the two moves. The sectarian move closes down the personality, whereas, as we have seen, pietism tends to give a "glow" to the rest of life. Either, therefore, might be described by a materialist as a false consciousness, but they have very different effects.

In most cases the sectarian move can only be a short term solution, even if the engendering situation does not improve, for it will not satisfy integrative human nature for long. Instead, moves may be made to "accept" the unacceptable, that is, to find some way of living with the problem situation rather than rejecting it. On the one hand there is the possibility of a cognitive justification of the unacceptable. Consider, for example, the explanation of the Jewish situation, "we are in diaspora because we sinned in the land", which potentially can turn every moment of suffering into a sacrament of relationship with the divine. On the other hand one of the ways of living with those who reject you is to join them in laughing at yourself, even to invite them to do so. Consider also the self-denigrating humor of the Jewish people, or the "coon" image in which the oppressed deliberately, but mockingly, act out the image imposed on them by the oppressor for his entertainment.

iii) UTOPIANISM

It will be clear that while path 1 and for the most part, path 2, function for identity and therefore for belonging solely as symbolic universes, path 3 can function either symbolically or in terms of outward relations.

People fall short of their ideals, but even then, symbolized relations to peers and family will not, in most cases, differ markedly from the actual relation. As one moves up the levels of aggregation, and as the individual's power to exert any modifying influence diminishes, so the gap between symbolic and actual relations widens, until, at the level of nation, the relationship must be entirely symbolic for most people and at the level of humanity symbolic for virtually all people.

It is possible to have an intense symbolic relationship with aspects of one's world-out-there at any level, either individually or collectively. The individual gains a sense of belonging and legitimation through involvement in much short term activity and mutual testimony concerning something vaguely defined which will bring about a rosy future at that level, that is, people indulge in much consideration of long term goals while steadfastly refusing to look the middle range consequences in the eye or even to discuss them. The result is that the calculus of benefits and costs to actual people does not impinge upon those considering. There is, therefore, no threat to their identity.

Activity of this kind remains evangelism for the values and symbols in question which may or may not bear fruit in actual involvements at some future time. Nevertheless, at the lower levels of the hierarchy of significant aggregations, possibly up to and including local community, it would be difficult, for an aware and rational individual, to maintain a symbolic engagement for any length of time which was not cashed in some actual involvement. Beyond that level it does become possible and the potential is created for what might be called a secular pietism, for it functions by a selective emphasis, not on the ultimately-real, but upon the more ultimate aspects of the real (perhaps *sub specie aeternitatis*) to the neglect of the rest of the real. I speak of it as utopianism, for it is a pseudo-activism and can be either consciously religious or consciously secular. Either way it can shade off into a recognized quietism, the consciously religious form of which finds expression in the pietism described above, the secular form in a fatalism.

Thus it is possible for those whose effective world is quite small, and those with a missing or unacceptable middle level in their hierarchy, to invest their identities in lower levels of significant aggregations both symbolically and actually. Alternatively they can invest their identities at some level or levels, from "nation" upward, at a purely symbolic level. Like pietism, utopianism can lead to a lack of real ethical demand and in the longer run, therefore, and in spite of much talk about values, to a reduced sense of meaning, that is, to anomie.

PIETISM, SECTARIANISM AND UTOPIANISM - ALIENATION AND ANOMIE

Pietism liberates its adherents to continue to function in their world-out-there with some sense of integration, and having idealized their relation with the divine they can accept their lot in an otherwise unacceptable world. Pietism, because it is affectively inclusive rather than exclusive, does not split the wider community. Forms of sectarianism, however, tend to divisiveness because their power to unite adherents is in direct proportion to their power to mark them off from all other groups, that is, sectarianism finds security in likemindedness rather than numbers. Pietism, on the other hand, can function with either or both, but thrives with a large support group. Pietism, therefore, best meets a community-wide need to overcome alienation, sectarianism best meets the individual's need to overcome anomie.

For sectarianism to function effectively the world-out-there has to be unacceptable *in toto*. While this may seem to be the case for many individuals it is not the case for many communities. In most situations some level of life can look rosy to some people, for example, where immediate and individual goals promise to be met, but where goals at the more remote levels of self-determination and harmony among nations do not so promise, nation and world may be regarded with considerable pessimism, while individual and local community life may be regarded optimistically. In that situation pietism, but not sectarianism, is a possibility.

A feature of the pietistic option, whether of the religious or "secular" kind, is that when those who have so opted are forced into temporary confrontation with middle-range worldly issues, there would seem to be no immediate going back to the pietistic position. For them there must be something more extreme. For those without worldly hope, it might be some form of sectarianism, whereas for those with hope, or with a sense of having nothing to lose, it might be strenuous socio-political action to change the unacceptable world whether from left or right.

UNIFICATION OF THE ADHERENTS RELATION TO THE ULTIMATELY-REAL AND TO THE REAL

Before I leave this section on the adherent's relation to the real, I wish to return to the concept of the felt sense of reality which was developed in chapter 6. I do this in order to relate what has now been said about the adherent's relation to the real with what was said in the previous section about his or her relation to the ultimately-real. The purpose of this is not simply to locate the relationships in a single frame but to display the religious entities which serve to link these two aspects affectively and cognitively. These are set out in the adjacent diagram.

Although I originally presented and will continue to deal with the felt sense of reality in external terms, that is, as being the individual's distilled estimate of the reality of (or in) his or her world-out-there, it must now be recognized that it includes all that is known of the self.[11]

---

[11] The dualistic traditions are essentially projective of the ultimately-real, it has to be modelled as above and future. In the other types also reality can be symbolized in a projected manner but frequently it is not.

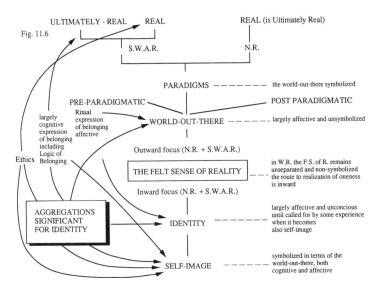

Fig. 11.6

Behind what is known of the self lies a center of pure consciousness, sometimes spoken of as "the witness", which has no content of its own, but enables us to stand outside everything that is consciously ours, even our most intimate traits, and view them from without. This requires that the felt sense of reality be thought of as being rather like a telescope opening up in two directions. The one end being directed toward what is perceived to be the external world, the other end toward what is perceived to be the inner-self. Aspects of the bodily-self may fall either way.

If one were employing this kind of image in withdrawal religion the telescope would not open up, the concentration remaining on the felt sense of reality.

In other traditions, such matters as time lag, rigidity of personality and traumatic experiences apart, the answer to the question "Who am I?", is the other side of the answer to the question "What is all that out there?". A cosmic sense of belonging depends upon a reflective relationship between what is felt to be the nature of all-that-out-there and what is felt to be the self. What is felt to be the self is not necessarily the same as the self-image in which it has been conceptualized, for that can become fixed as the felt sense moves on, then subsequent attempts at conceptualization can come as a shock. Nor are either of these quite the same as identity, for much of that is unconscious. Again, if these get far apart, it will call for major adjustments if and when novel aspects of identity are revealed in response to some new situation. It is important therefore, that consideration be given to the religious entities which link the self to the real and to the ultimately-real.

The linking religious entities to which I would draw attention may be located in the consolidated diagram and are as follows:

i)   a ritual expression of belonging, which links, at a largely affective level, the deepest aspects of the felt sense of self with the felt nature of the ultimately-real.

ii)   a cognitive (theological) expression, or logic of belonging, which links the paradigmatic and consequential symbols for the ultimately-real with the conscious elements of identity that comprise the self-image.

iii)   a cognitive directive for the mode of engagement with the immediate world-out-there, that is an ethic, although an ethic may include aspects of (ii).

iv)   the aggregations significant in identity formation and, of course, for self-image, are at once part of the world-out-there and also a means of corporate engagement with the world-out-there. In secular world affirming religion these may be understood to be secular or religious, but they remain part of the real, except for the religious aggregation in the indirect mode of belonging when it is perceived, in its essence, as directly related to the ultimately-real.

In settled conditions (ii) is likely to be weak and (iii) to be hardly distinguishable from (i). I have dealt with each of the above separately except for ritual. To that I turn in the next section.

III RITUAL : THE ESTABLISHMENT, CONFIRMATION
                                OR EXPRESSION OF BELONGING

THE FUNCTION OF RITUAL

In some individuals a sense of self, together with a general unspecific cosmic trust, seems to suffice for their sense of belonging. For others a sense of the self, together with a *sense* of that to which one belongs, (the latter not being conceptually defined) seem to be sufficient. These two are what I earlier called post-paradigmatic religion. For most, however, the sense of belonging requires that the two sides of the coin, the felt sense of the ultimately-real and the felt sense of self, be actively brought together. The self, of course, is a self only in relation to the real. Ritual, therefore, unites not only the self to the ultimately-real, but the real to the ultimately-real for the self. The drive to overcome the sense of ultimate alienation, or to prevent its occurring, is basic to religion. It is ritual, broadly understood, which performs this function. Ritual, therefore, although frequently the most obvious, is not the most basic aspect of religion. Without an adequate and coherent sense of self, without at least a felt sense of the ultimately-real, ritual is empty.

Ritual may, of course, have secondary functions. It may teach the adherent about the ultimately-real, it may help to refine the sense of self, it may serve to unite the tradition community and, particularly in secular world affirming traditions, it may be the instrument of worship, that is, of submission or adoration, but its primary role is as I have described it. Other aspects of religion may serve these secondary roles, but only ritual, including the logic of belonging, serves the primary role.

Overtly, ritual relates the individual to the ultimately-real but, as we have seen, both the sense of self and the sense of the ultimately-real are heavily dependent upon experience of the adherent's world-out-there. Ritual, therefore, is a point where everyday experience and symbols for the ultimately-real inter-act. In that inter-action each may give support to the other.[12] It is also a point of testing, for if the ritual does not feel real then one of the actors is wrongly or inadequately drawn, or the ritual itself is inappropriate.

THE DIMENSIONS OF RITUAL

As I have indicated the culmination, that is, the sense of belonging, is necessarily affective, but the steps toward it can be very different. Ritual is one such step, the performance of which may be by word or action. Ritual *words* may seek to promote a sense of belonging by a cognitive process, in which case it will operate within a tradition's logic of belonging, but on the other hand, the words may function primarily at the affective level. Ritual *action*, on the other hand, is likely to operate at the affective level, but it may also act out the logic of belonging and actually be a cognitive approach.

Usually word and action, the cognitive and the affective are mixed. This creates a whole range of possible ritual symbols, whereas at one end of the range, symbols overtly reflect the conceptualized nature of the ultimately-real and the mode of belonging thereto. At the other end, symbols display no overt conceptual relations, but function with an affective affinity, or simply with the authority of significant association, familiarity and trust.[13]

---

[12] Clifford Geertz emphasizes this function of ritual. Clifford Geertz, "Religion as a Cultural System", in *Anthropological Approaches to the Study of Religion*, Michael Banton (ed.), (London, Tavistock, 1966), p.9.

[13] There would be "significant association" if, for example, religious symbols that had

While symbols might be allotted a firm place within this range by the objective observer, they can operate at different points on the scale for different adherents. For children and new converts, all symbols, even the seemingly most cognitive, operate at the affective end, calling for trust rather than understanding. With growing awareness, however, the cognitive aspect of symbols will tend to be reasserted. Conversely, the cognitive meaning of a symbol may be lost, even to a whole community, while the symbol is retained at the affective level.

I believe that *Kol Nidre*, set at the beginning of the Jewish rite for the Eve of the Day of Atonement, once operated strongly at the cognitive end, but was not accepted as such by the authorities and now operates solely at the affective end. I will return to this when I discuss antinomianism in chapter 12.

If one does not need to rely heavily upon ritual in order to maintain one's sense of belonging, then one can remain at the affective level in one's knowledge of the ultimately-real and indeed, of the self. Nevertheless, ritual is greatly empowered by a logic of belonging. Once one has entered upon the cognitive aspect of belonging a clear self-image becomes important, for example, and at the simplest level, if in the logic of belonging the Christ is presented as one who offers himself to sinners, then the self-image of one who would belong to Christ must include sinfulness.

One encounters people who seem to live predominantly "in their heads", seeking in an extremely cognitive fashion what is, in the end, an essentially affective sense of belonging. What is affective and what is cognitive, however, is not always as apparent as it may seem. Prayer, on the surface, appears as relational and affective, but prayer as well as study could be understood as fulfillment of the terms of a logic of belonging and be a largely cognitive approach. On the other hand, study, which seems cognitive, can be the quest for enrichment of a personal relation and be motivated affectively. For most people to achieve and maintain a sense of belonging, some support is required from a logic of belonging. Even the ritual consumption of Grand-Ma's interpretation of traditional recipes on Jewish high holidays, would offer nothing but the possibility of gastronomic delight and togetherness, were it not for the logic of the immediate family's belonging to a wider family and beyond.

Ritual may be quite distinct from the activities of everyday life and therefore be recognizably religious. It may also be the case that aspects of the everyday behavior pattern perform the ritual function, albeit unrecognizable

---

simply crept up on people, or were previously the property of a community in a very general sense, gained a sense of great significance by being the rallying point in a struggle, much as a flag might.

as ritual and certainly as religious ritual. Ritual does not have to be institutional or overtly religious. Extra-ecclesiastical ritual, whether consciously religious or otherwise, also has its place.

For many in the contemporary West the ritual function is served by communing with nature, or by getting ones hands in the soil, or simply by some small job well done. It has always been served by music or other forms of art and by service of others, not only the distressed other, but by honing one's talents wherever they may lie, in order to offer one's best. It is served by relating to the one other, the "temporal thou" which for a moment fills one's horizon and stands for the "eternal thou". For most people, however, even if the ritual is not traditionally religious, it will need to be a moment of consciously putting the self and the ultimately-real together if it is to give rise to a consciousness of belonging, not simply prevent or assuage a sense of not belonging. That is to say, it needs to be ritual appropriate to path 3 belonging and therefore performed *sub specie aeternitatis*, even if the ultimately-real is modelled only as a sense of destiny.

Ritual is likely to be repetitive action, but it does not have to be. It may equally be a special moment of joy, sorry, wonder, or anything else that triggers a sense of integration.

THE CHOICE OF RITUAL SYMBOLS

The choice of ritual style can be largely controlled by historical accident, for example, churches which came into existence largely because a racial group was not admitted to leadership roles in the original church, reflected the original ritual forms very closely, a situation where independency was socially, but is not religiously, interesting. On the other hand the ritual forms are quite different in churches that came into existence to counter the social and economic aspects of deprivation or because the culture of the deprived group was not reflected in the life of the church.[14] In these the ritual forms are directly related to the expectations and deprivations of the originating life- world and to religiously significant factors. It is with the *religious* factors influencing the choice of ritual that I am here concerned.

Ritual symbols, I have said, seek an affective goal by either an affective or a cognitive means. Individual adherents will, at any point in time, have a cognitive or affective preference and, if free to shop around, can choose accordingly.

There are, however, rituals which are best suited for the participation of

---

[14] See for example, Glenda Kruss, *Religion, Class and Culture - Indigenous Churches in South Africa, with special reference to Zionist-Apostolics*, M.A. thesis, University of Cape Town, 1985.

adherents and those that are better suited to observation by adherents. In part, this is also a matter of preference, but this preference must work within a wider preference for a logic of belonging.

Clearly, indirect cosmic belonging has an affinity with an observer relation to ritual, for the logic demands that there be evidence of the presence of the bridging institution. Therefore, even while being present, one needs to be able to stand apart from the institution and be aware of it. In the Catholic traditions of Christianity the priesthood and the sacraments are the ligaments of the Body of Christ. In the Jewish tradition it is the Minyan and the Torah.

It seems strange, to those accustomed to a direct cosmic belonging tradition, to see Catholics "popping in" to hear mass or light a candle, or Eastern Orthodox or Jewish worshipers doing in the midst of their services most things they would do at home. This is not only possible within the logic, it is a means of reinforcing the logic. These are not a group of individuals simultaneously at prayer but the Body of Christ or the House of Israel at prayer. So long as the priest fulfills his role, or it can be presumed that the representative ten Jews are rehearsing the Torah, then all that is further required is that the belonging of the individual to the Body of Christ, or to the House of Israel is sufficiently evidenced.

In direct cosmic belonging the primary ritual must be of a participatory kind. There may however be secondary ritual aimed at assuring the individual that he or she is believing the right thing or experiencing the right thing. These would have an observational character.

If we put together the above options we have a four segment matrix comprised by the two scales cognitive-affective and observer-participant. Within this the ritual choices of all religious collectivities in the secular world affirming paradigm can be located. For example, traditional Catholic worship might be located as observer-affective, Presbyterian as observer-cognitive, Pentecostal as participant-affective and Brethren as participant-cognitive.[15]

---

[15] Donald Aeschliman used the four ideal types, Emotional Observer, Intellectual Observer, Emotional Participant, Intellectual Participant, to locate styles of worship in his study of independent churches. While most acts of worship were mixed, they could all be placed according to their predominant style on the matrix comprised by the two scales emotional-intellectual and participant-observer giving some indication of the mode or modes of belonging assumed by the worshipers and of the needs being met in the different collectivities. D R Aeschliman, *The Independent Churches of the Colored People of the Cape Flats*, Ph.D. thesis, University of Cape Town, 1983.

Some Limits and Preferences in the Choice of Ritual

Some general observations concerning likely choices between the cognitive and affective, and the participant and observer styles of ritual are possible. For the most part, affective and cognitive aspects will be combined in order to meet the needs of the whole person and it is probable that observation and participation will both be present to some degree. There are, however, some special circumstances that will shift this balance. Amongst these are the following:

i) I said earlier, that in situations of insecurity, mixed logics of belonging are inappropriate. Because the choice of participation or observation type is related to the logic of belonging, the same can now be said of mixed ritual. It is inappropriate in situations of insecurity.

ii) Sects need to legitimate their separation from the world-out-there and this will necessitate a large cognitive component in ritual.

iii) The offerings of religious institutions which cater for those who are seeking to cope with a chaotic and inadequate life experience will of necessity have a large affective component, since intellect is not generally sufficient under these circumstances, or chaos has defeated it.

Returning to the four emphases in ritual described above (cognitive and affective, observer and participant) it is informative to consider what sort of mixes occur in practice and to speculate concerning the reasons.

Religious institutions, in which ritual is mixed only on one axis of the suggested quadrants, seem to represent strangely different degrees of possibility. For example:

Institutions of the observer type which combined cognitive and affective aspects are common and popular. In normal circumstances they present only the slight problem, at the theological level, of whether one belongs by faith, cashed as right belief or as inner spiritual experience, or by sacramental initiation. This is probably because, the focus being upon the corporate body, both cognitive and affective elements are appropriate.

Institutions of the participant type, however, seems less able to combine easily the cognitive and the affective, perhaps because of the focus on the individual, who will have a preference for one or the other. The Quakers seem to be an exception who combine these aspects well.[16]

---

[16] Some Black churches in the U.S.A. whose roots lie in a strongly affective tradition but

For institutions of the cognitive type to combine observer and participant ritual roles represents a conflict between the corporate sense of indirect belonging and the individualism of direct belonging. This may be resolved in part by those with the corporate sense accepting as elders or the like, laymen with a strong individual participatory sense, or individual types accepting one or more of their number as charismatic leaders serving to link them with the Divine. One sees this last happening among Brethren from time to time.

Affective observer institutions require both long established symbols and some financial means. It would be difficult, therefore, for most affective participant institutions to add affective observer elements. On the other hand, affective observer institutions such as the Anglican Church, during the so called "Charismatic Renewal", added affective participant elements. This would either restore a waning authority in the church as the bridging institution of indirect belonging (if the Spirit now seemed to be moving in it) or, if the emphasis was on the individual and the direct mode of belonging, further diminish the authority of the institution.

The possibilities of the two sorts of institutions mixed at both levels are also strangely different:

The cognitive observer type with affective participation, while creating stress, has come to exist in many places, while the cognitive participant with affective observer elements, and vice versa, do not seem to occur at all. This last possibility represents the extremes of human-kind, the cognitive individualist and the affective communal type, those who seek order and those who need "highs". The Salvation Army includes both elements but one is mostly for the members, the other for the outreach.

IV THE AUTHENTICATION OF
THE ADHERENT'S WHOLE RELIGIOUS SYSTEM

The overall religious need, I have said, is to belong to that which is felt to be the ultimately-real and one must not lose sight of this positive *sui generis* need. In a chaotic world the dominance of this need can become clearly

---

whose current membership have very cognitive needs, combine the two by having a highly cognitive study group with a worship service that remains strongly affective. When a Bible study immediately precedes the service the switch in mood is quite dramatic.

apparent. Nevertheless there are different ways in which this need might be fulfilled. A question remains concerning the experiences that vindicate a particular paradigm, a mode of belonging and a style of ritual expression, enabling them to create a sense of belonging. What authenticates his or her whole religious system to the individual adherent? What makes it feel real? In the final analysis the criterion is enrichment, for that which will be authenticated in the long run as the most real is that which in the long run is felt to be the most enriching. Enrichment has to do with needs, perhaps with their creation, but certainly with their satisfaction.

Religion is conservative precisely because it provides the most universal frame in which identity is structured and because identity is the firm ground from which individuals relate to their world-out-there. Human beings are protective of both the relation and the identity. If religion does change, therefore, there is the presumption that the old form is no longer experienced as the most potentially enriching, that is, it no longer provides a strong sense of belonging to the ultimately-real. This in turn suggests that the religious system as a whole is no longer being authenticated by the provision of satisfactions in keeping with life's needs.

An individual's life needs are largely dependent upon those aggregations which are significant in his or her identity formation. If the system is to be authenticated and enabled to provide a sense of belonging to the ultimately-real the satisfactions provided by the religious system must conform to these needs. In order to enter deeper into an understanding of the authentication process, I need to distinguish three levels of need that are conceptually distinct (even though in certain circumstances, and as to content, they can be one and the same). These are:-

(a)   the *sui generis* religious need to belong to the ultimately-real whatever the nature of that may be felt to be,

(b)   life needs - that is, those needs that are generated by the individual's relation to his or her world-out-there which are culture and socio-economic status dependant, and

(c)   the needs satisfied by the religious system, in what I will call "blessings".

The importance of distinguishing these elements in the authentication process will be clearer, if I sketch their relationship at different levels of a hierarchy which exists permanently within most communities. This is a hierarchy of individual perceptions of the world-out-there, some perceptions exist as a result of psychological condition, some as a result of actual socio-economic circumstances. I will discuss the hierarchy in socio-economic terms.

In most societies there are those who feel the world to be a vale of tears over which they can exercise little or no control. Life needs are felt not to be met, nor are they expected to be met at any reasonable level. In such a situation the religious system can only be authenticated and the sense of belonging be maintained by blessings which are not related directly to life needs, but offer some alternative compensation.

"Blessings" is how some members of this group refer to the sort of experiences that I have in mind, so I have retained the term throughout. At this level blessings are distinct and therefore overtly "religious". As one moves up the scale, however, they become more overtly related to the needs generated by the socio-economic status, until, at the top, they become something akin to "religious culture". Blessings in reduced reality belonging tend to include the misfortunes of the outsiders.

At the deprived level, blessings usually relate to the immediate situation, even to the religious gathering itself, since there is little in which to rejoice outside. They tend also to be thaumaturgical, or experiences unrelated directly to the material dimension of life, for example, they may be testimonies to conversions, healings, overcoming the use of alcohol and, of course, signs of possession by the Spirit. They represent experience of divine power rather than of divine demand. The phenomena associated with pentecostalism serve this purpose.

Beyond these are those who feel that they can exercise some control upon their circumstances by corporate, or even by individual effort. For these, blessings will tend to relate to the rest of life and be more universal, reflecting an ordered world, in control or at least controllable.

If one looks to a corporate effort, then fellowship and loyalty to the fellowship is both a blessing and a virtue that will itself be blessed.

To the extent that improvement of life circumstances through a rugged individual effort can be envisaged, the blessings tend to shift towards the individual virtues. Hard work, sobriety, thrift and other forms of self-discipline, count both as blessings and as righteousness that will be blessed. If there appears to be evidence that righteousness is being blessed then the religious system will be authenticated and, other things being equal, it will create a cosmic sense of belonging. These virtues and blessings are evidenced in worship in the dignity of the service and sabbath-best clothing, the grandeur of the buildings and the education of the minister. Even indications of a certain affluence are likely to be encouraged.

Dignity and order are the evidence of belonging appropriate to an economic level where success is achievable at the cost of some effort. They are not simply the preference of a certain type of person.

As one moves further up the scale the blessings become less material, moving into such areas as status, meaning and direction of life, the solidarity and enrichment of family life, and thence to almost purely cultural forms of enrichment. Thus at the top there are those to whom life has come as a gift or for whom it is no longer a struggle. At this level, where material security already exists and the self justifying understanding of the group is self perpetuating, the only seeming life need is for the sense of belonging itself. Its achievement, therefore, is the only blessing that can authenticate the chosen religious system. If, at this level, the religious system is be experienced as authentic it can only be because it creates a sense of belonging by means of the best that is already available in the culture, in music perhaps, or in other art forms including the spoken word.

If belonging is not obtainable through the ritualization of what is best in the culture, perhaps because of an ascetic tradition, perhaps because of a stress on socio-political responsibility, then one can only return full cycle to those unusual and non-worldly experiences which are sought so earnestly at the other end of the spectrum. This is why the charismatic and pentecostal movements appear superficially similar but are not so in their elicitation. They ought not to be confused.[17]

The purpose in considering this hierarchy was to show that the three needs, that is, the need for a sense of belonging to the ultimately-real, the needs that are met by blessings, and immediate life needs, are each conceptually distinct, but that at certain socio-economic levels the latter two and even all three may coincide in content.

Enrichment, that is the meeting of life needs and the raising and meeting of further needs, is what in the long run authenticates any religious system. It is this which gives it a feeling of reality and thereby enables it to meet the specifically religious need for belonging. Only where life needs cannot be met, or are already met, is the need be belong to the ultimately-real the only blessing required, the only need to be met by the religious system. I am not here, of course, concerned with particular deprivations, but with the all pervasive fact that for religion to be real it must meet people in the great variety of their concrete situations.

---

[17] In certain circumstances, for example where material advantage engenders guilt, the need may be to go on hearing, even in prosperity, that god blesses the righteous. Guilt related needs may, of course, be deliberately generated so that their satisfaction may serve as legitimation.

CHAPTER 12

BELONGING AND NOT BELONGING

> I have suggested that humankind manifests a drive for belonging. There are also those, who in a variety of ways, manifest what appears to be a drive not to belong. I am obliged to explore this phenomenon. The exploration will promote a further examination of the individual and affective aspect of religion.

Throughout this book I have proposed the existence of a near universal drive to belong. This chapter deals with three manifestations of what might be thought of as a drive *not to belong*.

There is first, what seems to be the rejection of all religious belonging. In this age and in the western world, this has come to be called secularization. The term covers many different positions, but the apparent loss of interest in overtly religious belonging and the assumption that the secular world is the only reality available for belonging are central to it. Clearly there may be people who do not wish to belong in any sense, people who have a death wish, at least as social beings. Nevertheless, if Durkheim is right, in the majority of cases one should look under the surface of this phenomena for new religious forms.

Then there are those who, although rooted in a religious tradition manifest, from time to time, a need to break out. People who deliberately throw off the restraint of laws and norms. This tendency is referred to as antinomianism.

Finally, one observes a desire to assert independence even within a tradition. In the secular world affirming traditions this has been debated by philosophical theologians, at the ultimate level and at length, in relation to the seeming conflict between human freedom and divine omnipotence. I will focus on the same issue.

I will examine each of these levels of the seeming drive not to belong in the ascending order of their power to contradict the universality of the drive that I have proposed. That is to say, I will begin with people firmly rooted within a tradition who worry about their independence vis-à-vis the divine, then move to those who, while based within a tradition, find it necessary from time to time to break out, and finally consider those who seem to reject all forms of religious association.

The chapter serves a second purpose. I have noted that it is impossible to get directly at the real seat of religion in the individual, what I have called the felt sense of reality, for that is not fully available even to its possessor, nor can one know the feelings of another. The best that one can do is to describe contexts in which similar people might be expected to have similar feelings. This chapter provides a number of such contexts and therefore enables me to explore a little further the nature of the affective element in individual belonging.

In the process it will become apparent that the sense of belonging itself presupposes the possibility of not belonging, that belonging and freedom are not opposites, but rather that a significant aspect of a sense of freedom is the sense of a freedom to participate.

Before I begin on the three themes there are two preliminary issues which require attention. The one has to do with the *consequences* of not belonging, the other concerns what can sometimes be mistaken for the rejection of belonging, but is simply a testing of it.

TWO PRELIMINARY ISSUES

i) *Consequences of the Failure to Belong*
Most of what follows in this chapter, while it deals with phenomena which seem to set a question mark against the wisdom of understanding religion as a quest for belonging, will in fact show that these phenomena are best understood as aspects of that very quest. Because I lay such emphasis on belonging, it is important that I recognize that a cosmic sense of belonging is not easily obtained and that a myriad consequences of the failure to belong stand as evidence of this.

In the previous chapter, and within the consideration of secular world affirming religion, I noted that a sense of belonging requires three things; a sense of the ultimately-real, a sense of self, and a way of putting these two together. Clearly, belonging can fail on each of these levels. It can fail because there are not two entities to put together, or because for some reason one is unable to put them together.[1] Perhaps it is simply that there is no adequate or sufficiently authoritative ritual to unite them, but whatever the reason for alienation, it will have its consequences. I have already referred to some of these. I referred, for example, to reduced reality religion with its rejection, even hatred, of the world out there, as a substitute for an unobtainable cosmic sense.

Then Erik Erikson has pointed out the tendency in adolescents who are unable to form a socially acceptable identity to accept a socially unacceptable one, rather than have none at all.[2] This seems to me to have a parallel in the Christian pastoral practice of encouraging adherents to understand themselves as sinners and as part of a fallen humanity. If one would belong, it is more important to have an integrated self-image than a "good" self-image.

Others have noted that the great majority of dramatic conversion experiences take place during adolescence when identity is less stable. If one cannot grow into an integrated sense of self gradually, then one must do it by what has been called, "rupture and rapture".[3]

All of these in their different ways represent attempts to "force" an identity, or the sense of belonging itself, when these are not otherwise available.

One response to the situation of alienation is an inner anger which seems to have no source but which may give rise to violence, and perhaps to dramatic attempts to take belonging by storm. The anger of alienation may turn inward toward the self and manifest in the acceptance of a highly authoritarian religion, or even to forms of self punishment. It may also turn outward in a forced intimacy with or destruction of the environment.

It has seemed to me, that violence which is a consequence of failure in belonging, manifests most clearly in the area of ritual. This is not always ritual aimed at putting the self and the ultimately-real together. It may be ritual aimed at the integration of the self, and it can take many forms. If the

---

[1] See the last section of chapter 6 for examples of these reasons.

[2] See on Erik Erikson, Henry W Maier, *Three Theories of Child Development*, (New York, Harper Row, 1969) p.60.

[3] Earl H Furgeson, "The Definition of Religious Conversion" in *Pastoral Psychology Vol 16 No 156*, p.10.

problem is a fragmented self seeking to re-establish contact with what Jung called its "shadow", that is, with all the rejected options still subconsciously significant for the personality, then it might be facilitated by identification with the admirable but bad characters of the soap operas. It might be facilitated by the evangelist waving a Bible but speaking in lurid detail of nothing but the evil practices of "our fellow countrymen", or by a personal reaching out to people and situations which are regarded as sinful.

Irrational "ritual" may also comprise the taking of extreme risks, a sort of challenge to reality to own one, to force it into relationship. It can be the attempt to know intimately - to enter into - another human being as the representative of all-that-out-there. There is an account, which unfortunately I can no longer trace, of an army officer, in the events preceding the Russian revolution, trampling the body of a dead enemy shouting "I will know you", "I will know you".[4] That may be an extreme and rare response to alienation. I believe, however, that much person-to-person violence and, in particular, rape and other violent frontiers of the sexual relationship, are rooted, in the final analysis, in the failure of a cosmic sense of belonging.

I said earlier that the secular world affirming type of tradition, because it does not offer a full sense of cosmic belonging in the present moment, is to that degree a conflict model. It cannot offer the same amelioration of the tendencies that I have been describing that the other types can. To have a goal is to be not-yet-there and if it is a vigorous goal one can become very impatient.

ii) *The Testing of Belonging*

There is a need in the individual not only "not to be conscious of not belonging", which is all that can be hoped for in young children, but to be positively "conscious of belonging". Just as it may sometimes seem necessary to test one's limits to see if one is free, so it can be necessary to test one's belonging to see if it is still a reality.

In situations where life is relatively struggle free this testing can pose a problem. Where shall one look for evidence of belonging? In such situations one may need to challenge one's environment in order to see if it responds in a way that may be interpreted to mean that the powers are on one's side. This is not the same as the antinomian situation to which I will come shortly. In that, the need is to step for a moment right outside of one's belonging. Here it is simply a question of testing ones belonging when doubt about it has arisen.

---

[4] I believe this to be a paraphrase of something that Nicolas Berdyaev wrote but have not been able to rediscover its source.

Mary Douglas writes about a practice that was current among the Lele people of what is now Zaire, which illustrates just this point.[5] These people were not primarily a hunting people, rather, their economy was built around the raffia palm, and although meat was prized, they did not eat a lot of it and could have bred it for their own consumption had they wanted to. In any case the hunt did not produce very much, nevertheless, it was enormously important in their estimation and it involved them in all sorts of efforts and deprivations. The outcome was awaited with awe, and there is little doubt that this practice not only served (in the absence of opposition) to hold the community together, but that it tested the "health" of the village. It tested whether the powers were favorably disposed toward it. Such a practice could exist among these people precisely because they lived under an equitable climate in a relatively undisturbed and acceptable situation. It would make no sense in situations where each day was a struggle to survive and life's quality was continually at risk.

There is a similar presupposition behind the ancient practice of trial by ordeal. It may also be that included in the roots of the need to flirt with chance, whether with dice or guns or simply by sin, lies a subconscious need to test whether God or fate, life or the powers-that-be, will intervene beneficially on one's behalf.

THEME I - FREEDOM AND DETERMINISM

Normally a sense of freedom is required for volition and volition is an essential factor in both responsibility and the expression of commitment. Freedom, therefore, is the presupposition of ethics and of all voluntary relationships. Yet freedom is not what life is about. Life is about belonging.

Freedom and belonging are not opposites, but freedom of some kind, if only that of being able to imagine what it is like not to belong, is a *sine qua non* of a sense of belonging.

The Context in which Freedom becomes an Issue

Freedom is not a central issue in the world views of nature religion and withdrawal religion. Monistic systems are closed systems of cause and effect from which chance is excluded. The centrality of freedom is a consequence of, and problem for, secular world affirming traditions only. Freedom belongs

---

[5] Mary Douglas, "The Lele of Kasai", in Daryll Forde (ed.) *African Worlds*, (London, Oxford University Press, 1954), p.26.

in a complex with responsibility and with goals, with linear time, a personal deity and a final *goal*. This total complex is the product of transcendence.

Transcendence, and therefore freedom as a religious concern, entered the heritage of the Western tradition in the period between Abraham and Moses and received its symbolization at Sinai. Before that and still today, the alternative concern is with destiny, frequently one prescribed for humankind by the powers-that-be.[6]

Freedom is a basic presupposition of the Abrahamic traditions, but it would be empty as an end in itself. Freedom as an end in itself, is a pseudo-goal, just as efficiency, productivity, equality, are pseudo-goals when made ends in themselves. Any realistic consideration of freedom must ask from what and for what is freedom required. There are all sorts of freedoms, freedom to eat, to sleep in peace, to educate ones children, to be politically self-determined, and many more. The freedom with which I am here concerned might well be described as the freedom from God, for God.

The seeming conflict between the divine determination of events and human freedom is a recurring theme in secular world affirming religion. There are parallel issues in the largely monistic traditions, in the Gita for example, but it is never the same issue as that created by the transcendence gap of a secular world affirming tradition.

In a dualistic system there are always two ways of looking at experience. One of these is to see the real and the ultimately-real together as one total and therefore closed system with nothing beyond. The other is to see it as two actors over against each other, one of which has absolute freedom, the other a conditional freedom.

If, in the former and monistic way of seeing, a creator is thought to have set a creation in motion toward a predetermined destiny, then the situation can be likened to a billiard table upon which, a ball having been struck, all the balls are in motion striking each other and the cushions. The movements may appear random, but in fact every movement is determined in the first shot and could be calculated, provided that nothing outside the system interfered with it. So also with the creation. Once the creator has set it in motion there is nothing outside the creator-creation totality to "run interference" with it. Therefore the ensuing moves are, in principle, for ever predictable.

The other way of viewing a dualistic system is to consider the relation of the real to the ultimately-real. When freedom is the issue, this relationship has usually been reduced to the relation between an individual and the

---

[6] It remains a Jewish concern, in the "days of awe" following each new year, to be "inscribed in the book of life".

divine. In this aspect of the paradigm the relation is not mechanistic but volitional and to all appearances, each has freedom of choice over against the other. Chance can enter in and, if and when things go wrong, a genuine new beginning appears possible. This, however, is challenged by the monistic view of the paradigm and by belief in the absolute sovereignty of the divine, both of which set a question mark against the reality of human freedom.

Two Referents of the Word "Freedom"

It can be argued (in a debate concerning human freedom and divine omnipotence) that if the end of humankind is to love God then only a *feeling* of freedom is required, and that this cannot be in competition with divine omnipotence.

The above statement makes a distinction between what might be called structural freedom and psychological freedom. By psychological freedom is meant, that sense of freedom which is essential to any voluntary relationship but which can exist without structural freedom. Structural freedom is the actual freedom to do or to refrain from doing something and which is frequently said to be a necessary pre-condition of responsibility. That is, "ought" is said to imply "can".

In what I said by way of introduction, concerning the necessity of freedom for any form of commitment, I was not referring to structural freedom however, but to a *sense* of freedom *vis-à-vis* the powers that be. It is this that is required in order that a *sense* of responsibility and the *experience* of a voluntary relationship might also exist.[7]

In relation to these preconditions for a sense of freedom, it must be noted that science, because it operates methodologically within a monistic universe, helps to create a general sense of living within a closed system. Within the method of science, freedom is not a possibility, for it operates in a universe in which all effects are to be explained by relating them to a cause even though indeterminacy may sometimes serve as an explanatory model.[8]

It is for this reason that the human experience of freedom is such a slippery thing to deal with in the human sciences. If social science would

---

[7] In the culture of Mesopotamia, from which Hebrew culture emerged, there was much verbal acceptance of responsibility, that is, of self-blame in pleading with the gods, but it had no logic and no feeling of authenticity, for, far from having a sense of freedom vis-à-vis the gods, the people regarded themselves as the puppets of divine whim.

[8] This must be distinguished from the world-view that drives the whole scientific enterprise and its technological applications, which is anything but a closed system.

function as a hard science might, it must assume that man is not free in the sense of being structurally undetermined, but rather that for whatever he does there is a reason. Nevertheless, human beings experience freedom, at least at the level of feeling.

Much of the problem in the debate about freedom has been a failure to understand that we operate within two realms of discourse. Only structural freedom can be expressed in literal discourse, psychological freedom requires symbolic language for its expression. Human freedom, as it is experienced, cannot find expression within the scientific realm of discourse, because the very manner of scientific functioning which assumes discoverable relationships in a publicly established frame, excludes it. The feeling of freedom can only be expressed in the I-thou or mythological mode of discourse. To say that "ought" implies "can" may be a useful maxim in assigning responsibility in a court of law, but as a general principle it is a confusion between the two realms of discourse. "Can" belongs to literal discourse and "ought" to feeling discourse. There is no logical bridge between them. As Peter Berger concluded, we must have both the scientific presumption and the experience of freedom but we must keep a *kosher* kitchen and not "pour the milk of subjective insight over the meat of scientific interpretation".[9]

Whether or not social science can deal with it, the question remains, "Is it sufficient within the logic of the secular world affirming paradigm to say that human freedom must lie in the subjective realm, but not necessarily in the structural realm?" "Is it sufficient for the purpose, that an individual feels free, that she or he has a psychological freedom?" Perhaps it is.

Freedom and the Expression or Conceptualization of Commitment
As I said, freedom can hardly be supposed to be an end in itself. One can only be free relative to certain goals, and if one has no goals one cannot test whether one is free or not. Indeed, the very lack of goals may lead to a sense of unfreedom.
Within the Christian tradition the overt goal is to relate to God in love, and perhaps, in the end, this is true of all the theistic traditions. I must therefore explore further what was said earlier of traditions of this type - that love (or personal commitment at any level) requires for its expression, volition. Volition requires a sense of freedom. Consider the following:

If, while staying in a hotel, I order breakfast in bed and the waiter brings it, I get breakfast in bed, but if my children rise early and bring me breakfast

---

[9] Peter Berger, *Invitation to Sociology* (Harmondsworth, Penguin, 1963) p.144.

to bed, I receive breakfast and an expression of love. The one who was employed to bring breakfast would have to add some voluntary extra to achieve the same effect. An expression of love necessitates volition, but volition does not necessitate structural freedom only a <u>sense</u> of freedom, viz.

If A were to tell B that he would like to give him his gold watch as an expression of appreciation, it does not matter if A's wife has already given the gold watch away, or even that B knows that she has. All that matters is that A believes that he is free to give it and B knows that A believes it.

A further scenario, in which the gift has no possible material value to the recipient, may be useful. It is at the same time more appropriate to the human-divine relationship and makes the additional point that the distinction may be more easily accepted as an idea than it is in the situation.

A child saves a piece of a bar of chocolate to give to her father when he returns from work. The piece gets smaller and sticker during the day as the child goes back to it for another nibble. The father returns. The child, in rushing to give the chocolate to her father, drops it and the dog eats it. The child is heartbroken. For the father, who is probably relieved not to have to eat the sticky mess, the offering is complete.

The statement "I love you" is cashed in the willingness to sacrifice, not in the actual sacrifice. Whether Abraham was ever free to sacrifice Isaac or Ishmael is beside the point. Yet it is noted that in the biblical story Abraham is provided with a ram caught in a thicket, to offer in substitution, just as the father in the above scenario might provide a sweet for the child to give back to him. It is clear, that love or personal commitment at any level requires for its expression, perhaps also for its conceptualization, volition, that is, the willingness to do something, or to sacrifice something, for the object of the love or commitment. Such a willingness may not exhaust the meaning of "I love you" but its absence somehow negates the statement.

One normally seeks to express love through some external act over and above what is required. It may happen that structurally one is not free to perform the act, or the gift may not be available. It matters not. If the lover, believing that he or she can give or do what will be desired, wills to do so, and the beloved knows that he or she so wills, the love is expressed. This remains true even if the beloved knows that the gift cannot be made or does not in fact desire the object or act comprising the gift.

All that matters is that one believes oneself free to make the offering that is in mind. This sense of freedom is absolutely essential for any expression of commitment at any level, but if that sense of freedom disappears the purpose is defeated.

Volition has been made much of by Christian theologians. Paul Tillich treats the Fall as the point at which man becomes man; for, being removed from God, it becomes possible for man to *choose* to return. The possibility of a radically new relationship is established. Karl Barth spoke of the "impossible disobedience"; the state of freedom in which man actually believes that he is free to *choose* to exist apart from the very source and sustainer of his existence. For Soren Kierkegaard, volition being so central to his thinking, the very omnipotence of God is most clearly demonstrated in his power to give himself while taking himself away. The ultimate miracle is that the One who provides and maintains all things should not at the same time overwhelm humankind with his presence. [10]

Perhaps it follows from this that in these traditions a sense of freedom, *vis-à-vis* God, depends upon ignorance of God, of the self, and what the self can do in relation to God.

---

[10] Paul Tillich, *Systematic Theology vol 2,*(London, Nisbet, 1957) p.33ff.
Karl Barth, *Dogmatics in Outline,* (London, SCM Press, 1949) p.56f.
Soren Kierkegaard, *The Journals of Kierkegaard 1834-54,* A Dru (ed.) (London, Collins, 1958) p.113.

Gordon Kaufman has argued that the possibility of nuclear holocaust has radically changed the human situation. Humankind can now destroy their species and their world: they can prevent all their potential posterity becoming actualized: they can defeat what has been supposed to be the Divine purpose, at least for this planet. Such a sense of freedom they have never known, yet paradoxically they are not free, for they must change their consciousness or perish. In Christian terms they must become Christlike or perish, but what Christlikeness means cannot be known only from the past but must now take into account the new possibility.

Having moved from servanthood to sonship, humankind must now truly "come of age" with the recognition that God must be understood to intend them to share His status, even to be enabled to defeat the Father's purpose. No longer will it do to believe that while God has given freedom to human beings He has set limits to that freedom which would prevent them from destroying their kind. Such responsibility for human destiny is staggering and such as even Kierkegaard never dreamed of. It will demand a radical change in theology.

The above is how the author heard Gordon Kaufman, "The Nuclear Crisis: A Problem for Christian Faith" a public lecture delivered at the University of Cape Town, 1985.

Not only would theology change but so also would ritual. This new freedom and responsibility would have to be celebrated, that is ritually asserted, even while recognizing it as God-given. Perhaps the Kol Nidre, referred to earlier, set so appropriately in the Days of Awe, provides a model for this.

The Significant Freedom is not Indeterminacy, but Freedom to Participate

I have been arguing that it could be sufficient that an individual should be subjectively free, but there are others who seem to operate with the idea that humankind needs the dignity of being able to make "real" choices.

MacKay in arguing against the notion that a completely causal explanation of brain function, in physical terms, would make "the firm subjective conviction that we have free will" an illusion, seems to argue that man is free in what I have called structural terms. His argument turns on the individual being able to change his or her mind successively once the prediction of his or her action, on physical grounds or any other, is known. It can be illustrated as follows.

Suppose that one is proffered a plate with two apples on it, a red one and a green one. If one then takes the green one the person may say, "Oh yes! I knew that you would take the green one", at which point one may say, "Very well then, I'll take the red one", at which point the one offering the apples may say "I knew that if I said "I knew you would take the green one" you would then take the red one", so you say, "Very well then, I will take the green one". So it may go on. Provided there is communication between the two, there is a complete (structural) freedom of choice. One may take either apple and be perfectly free in doing so. [11]

The point that people can change their minds, was made a little more bluntly some 700 years earlier by Duns Scotus, when he said "a strict proof of the freedom of the will, that is the existence of a contingent course of action, could not be produced, but it is attested by immediate experience. If anyone were to cast doubt upon contingent conduct and events, he ought to be flogged until he should acknowledge the possibility of not being flogged."[12] These seem to suggest that the significant freedom is a structural indeterminacy, but this does not seem to me to be the case.

There is another illustrative tale which makes it clear that man's feeling of freedom is not to be tied to indeterminacy. It goes like this:

Consider a situation (not to be confused with any historical one) in which Caesar when in command of troops in Gaul has to make a decision whether or not to cast all upon a last battle, or to withdraw and fight another day. He must decide whether to cross a river, burn his boats and commit his army totally to the battle. He knows the situation in Gaul and he knows the

---

[11] Donald M MacKay, "On the Logical Indeterminacy of a Free Choice", in *Mind vol 69*, 1960, p.31f.

[12] Quoted in Reinhold Seeberg, *Text-Book of the History of Doctrines vol II*, (Grand Rapids, Baker Book House, 1961) p.149.

situation in Rome and the possibilities of going back there if he has been less than successful in Gaul.

Caesar's friends in Rome, or the historian looking back upon such a situation, would have very little problem in deciding what Caesar would do, they would give very long odds that Caesar would cast all on this one battle. It is, they would say, as good as certain, but it would feel a long way from certain to Caesar, for whom this was perhaps the most agonizing decision of his career.

Why is there this vast difference between Caesar and the rest?

The historian or the friend in Rome, looks at the situation in Gaul, the situation in Rome and he looks at Caesar's character. Putting these together, the decision follows as a matter of course. But Caesar considers only the situation in Rome and the situation in Gaul. Only at some less pressing time is he likely to speculate upon his own personality and what he is likely to do in hypothetical situations. In the midst of this decision he can engage in no such luxury. Rather, he considers the situation in Gaul and the situation in Rome and he then, as it were, plugs these into his unconscious. From the unconscious would be thrown up all the bits of evidence which he would need to weigh, in deciding for and against the crossing of the river and the burning of the boats. Even then, having brought into consciousness the various factors, he would still not go through a logical process of decision. All the considerations would be thrust back into the unconscious and he would wait in an agony of suspense for the decision to come to mind.

What he feels to be an agonizing exercise of free-will, is in fact no more, but no less, than the "plugging in" of the situation to his own personality.

What makes it seem like an agonizing exercise of free-will is the cost involved, the importance of the decision. The greater the potential cost the greater the consciousness of free-will. We may choose one of a number of pieces of rope and use it for all sorts of purposes without being conscious of the exercise of free-will in the choice, but if we have to select a piece of rope on which to go over the edge of a cliff then it may well seem like an agonizing decision.

Returning to Caesar and recognizing that from the outside the issue seems determined, we must ask whether Caesar would want it any other way. We don't usually seek to be indeterminate. Caesar would hardly have thought it a compliment if his friends had said "Caesar is inconsistent, you can never tell how he is going to decide next". On the contrary, we consider it something of a compliment if we are told that we are consistent people, not so consistent perhaps as to be considered "square", but one likes to be the sort of person who can be known from day to day.

When one asks for freedom one is not asking for indeterminacy or that one's personality should be fluid from moment to moment. What we are asking for is rather that the decision should be made through us, that it is we and not somebody else who should be "plugged into" the decision situation. That is to say, we are asking not to be free in the sense of indeterminate, but as belonging, as responsible in the making of the decision. A sense of freedom is what we experience when we are making a decision, when we are allowing a situation to be plugged into our personality, when, in short, we are being responsible.

Going back to the earlier discussion, what the individual would need vis-à-vis God, is to have a role in God's design, a place within His on-going purpose, to be what is called a "secondary cause". To be "plugged into" such a role, would provide a sense of freedom from God for God. 13

I do not wish to enter here into a debate on the body, mind, soul problem, or the relation of computers to human beings, but what we have been saying certainly excludes from the classical "Is that a person behind the curtain?" debate, the argument that a person is free and the machine is not. In fact it suggests that the difference lies in the area of self-consciousness, although it is not clear to me how one would test whether a machine was self-conscious. Perhaps in the evidence of a quest for belonging, for a securing of identity. This, however, takes me beyond where I wish to be for present purposes. I am here concerned only to show that individuals can have a subjective sense of freedom and that it is real. It is real in the sense that it is an experience to be had, particularly when one is a key to the possible resolution of a significant situation. It is real also in the sense that, as well as being affective, it may be effective in consequent action.

Freedom in the religious sphere is simply the necessary pre-condition for love or commitment and for this purpose freedom does not have to be structural, indeed, structural freedom in ourselves would simply be indeterminacy. In these terms God's omnipotent purposes and the human experience of free-will are in no way incompatible. Freedom does not have to be such that it would be in any way possible for humankind to upset the purposes of God, even though humankind may have to model it as such. 14

---

13 The problem which we have been addressing is not one solely for overt religion. Marxists, such as Rosa Luxemburg, who have wrestled with the tension between historical necessity and individual freedom, come to much the same conclusion. That far from being incompatible and calling for a quietism, historical necessity comes about through human beings with a sense of responsibility and therefore of freedom. Their freedom lies not in indeterminacy but in participating, that is in being the ones through whom the inevitable choices are made. James Miller, *History and Human Existence*,(Berkeley, University of California Press, 1979) p.125f.

14 See 9 above. The changes to which Gordon Kaufman pointed are at the level of

What Constitutes Freedom and what Restraint, is Context and Goal Dependent

Included among those who believe that freedom needs to be structural for human dignity are those who feel that God, in giving to human beings a sense of freedom which was not real in structural terms, would somehow diminish the works of His own hand. This, I think, supposes that to give freedom is the same as not restraining (for it is restraint that seems undignified) but this also is not the case.

Precisely because freedom is not always the opposite of restraint, a goal must be in mind before it is possible to say whether freedom does or does not exist. Consider the bringing up of children.

Parents place a child in a play-pen, not to take away freedom, but to give the child the freedom to grow, to become what it ought to become, rather than damage itself at the hearth or electrical source. Nevertheless, to enlarge the play-pen as the child grew would be to create a prison, so the now inappropriate bars are replaced by sanctions, that is, by threats and promises. "If you play near the fire you will be smacked", "If you stay away from the road this morning, I will take you to the play-park this afternoon".

There comes a time when such sanctions also become inappropriate, for the goal is that the child shall become independent and stand on his or her own feet, as friend of parent rather than child. To let go and so risk hurt to child and therefore to self, is the price that all parents must pay for that potential goal. This is the last cost. Only love may now remain as a sanction, that is, that the child knows that the parent is rendered sad or happy by his or her choices, and even this sanction must be veiled, lest it become a form of moral blackmail.

Freedom, therefore, is not an absolute. It is both goal and condition dependent. It can be the very opposite of the absence of restraint. Here again, what is required in the end is a *sense* of freedom. It is this that the good parent aims at, but cannot fully implement in the beginning without being less than caring. That freedom is not an absolute, but is goal and situation dependent and that psychological freedom is not dependent on structural freedom, was exemplified earlier by reference to the predestinarians. It is precisely those, who believe that their final end is determined who enjoy the greatest sense of freedom *vis-à-vis* the present, for they are sure of coming to their goal.

I have been dealing for the most part with the Christian tradition and of love, because in this regard this is the extreme case, nevertheless what has been said is true, *mutatis mutandis*, of all forms of commitment and of all the traditions falling within the secular world affirming paradigm.

---

feeling. It would still be the case that divine omnipotence would not be threatened by the sort of human freedom that is necessary for humankind's relation to the divine.

The logic of cosmic belonging in this paradigm, in which the Creator must be conceived as having a volitional relation to his creation, is that humanity's relation to the Divine should also be conceived volitionally. That is to say, belonging can never become absorption into the Divine, but rather requires that freedom be constantly reaffirmed and that God is for ever seen to be letting humankind go.

I conclude that the maintenance of a sense of belonging within the secular world affirming paradigm requires the maintenance of a sense of freedom. Without the goal of a personal commitment to a divine, the sense of freedom is hardly necessary, *karma* will suffice. Some religious traditions do in fact have rituals aimed precisely at a rejection of relationship with the ultimately-real so that it may be re-entered voluntarily and afresh. These are the subject of the next theme.

THEME II - ANTINOMIANISM

For a sense of freedom to exist it is necessary that, among the available courses of action, there seems to be the possibility of being apart, that is, of not belonging. A sense of freedom, however, requires only that one believe that one can choose that possibility, one does not have to do so. Individualism, the actual decision to be apart, goes beyond this.

On the face of it, all forms of individualism seem to be opposed to a drive for belonging and, if the idea of a universal drive to belong is to ring true in an individualistic world, something must be said about them.

Withdrawal religion is necessarily individualistic because there is nothing of experience which is not potentially deformed. The quest to belong is, in the last resort, a lonely one, however much one might organize mutual support groups along the way. Here there is no clash between an individualism, if it does not diminish others, and the quest to belong. It is of the nature of the paradigm.

In a secular world affirming culture, however, with its corporate goal within the real, and the consequential need for solidary functioning even within the direct and individual mode of belonging, any significant individualism would seem contrary to the logic of belonging. There are, of course, forms of individualism that are unrealistic and even pathological and which would indeed be contrary to any quest for belonging.

For the moment, however, I wish to look at a form of individualism which, while it can sometimes take extreme forms, is in fact part of the very quest for belonging. It is concerned with the refreshment of belonging. It would seem to apply, at some stages anyway, in all the paradigms.

The Tension Between Identity and Community

I have suggested on a number of occasions that identity cannot exist in a vacuum and that, even if it is by taking up a contrary stance, it must arise in relationship to the individual's world-out-there. This is true, but it is also true that identity requires one to mark oneself off from the other and, if the self image is to be precise, from the other who is most like oneself. This tension, between being part of a community while separating oneself out from it, exists at all levels. I need, as it were, to draw a line between myself and my peers, between my family and other families like it, between my community and other communities, and so on up the scale. I need to do it for all levels of aggregation significant for identity. Nothing significant is gained for self understanding by distinguishing oneself, or one's own, from that which is neither similar nor significant.

Identity, therefore, may be weakened in two ways. It will be weakened if the line between the individual or community concerned and the significant other is not drawn strongly enough. It will also be weakened if the line is drawn so strongly as to diminish the other, so that it ceases to be as significant. This might be expressed by saying, that one only gains really significant identity over against that which one includes in one's wider belonging.

Clearly this is a matter of balance. It goes almost without saying that I can lose my sense of identity and therefore of belonging by being too individualistic, but I can also lose it by having my individuality swallowed up in community. Then I can have *no sense of belonging*, only *no sense of not belonging*. This theme is concerned with a possible response to the experience of "being swallowed up in community".

Antinomianism as the Refreshing of Voluntariness

A consciousness of order and its significance requires that one be conscious of the possibility of chaos. The refreshment of the former depends on reviving the latter. In the same way, a sense of belonging supposes a consciousness of the possibility of not belonging, of being out there in the void, alone, without meaning, without security, without warmth. Not to be conscious of such possibilities, however unpleasant, is to cease to be consciously an individual center, but rather to be absorbed, indeed smothered, by that which is no longer appreciated nor even recognized. This lack of a consciousness of not belonging is the situation of the pre-puberty child in a stable home. To go beyond it, the sense of voluntariness must be established or refreshed.

In monistic traditions, where belonging is assumed, the consciousness of belonging requires only a consciousness of what it would feel like not to belong, in order to lift it out of the unity that I likened to porridge and into the unity that I likened to a watch mechanism. Belonging in a dualistic tradition requires all that was set out in chapter 11.

In all traditions it should be sufficient that one was once aware of what it felt like not to belong. In theory, in the dualistic paradigm it ought to be sufficient that there exist the consciousness that once there was a possibility of not belonging and that the choice was made to belong. In practice, however, neither of these seem to be sufficient to prevent a sense of belonging becoming, at worst, a sense of bondage and at best, a sense of inability to express what one wants to express, or to appreciate what one has.[15]

When a child is born and grows up in a family, its presence there *per se* conveys nothing. If, however, during the process of psychologically breaking out of the old family unit to become the potential nucleus of a new one, the child leaves home and then chooses to return, its presence there can become an expression of love, for it is volitional. He or she may not, of course, need to leave the home physically; all that is required is the sense that they are free to do so.

The first time establishment, of such a volitional basis to a long standing relationship, may be difficult enough, but having entered freely into a personal relationship, the maintenance of the sense of freedom, or better, the maintenance of the voluntary nature of one's presence in the relationship, is exceedingly difficulty, for we become bogged down in obligations. Once we feel that we cannot withdraw, a relationship is in danger of becoming a prison and then our presence in it no longer expresses love.

If in a marriage, for example, one could only have the courage to renounce the vows and declare them null and void, so that one could not only feel the loss, but also gain the sense of re-entering it voluntarily, one might gain the advantage which advocates of the informal marriage claim for it, namely, that their presence with their partner is a constant expression of their desire to be there, that is, of their love.

Frequently in voluntary relationships, we do not even risk asking the question "Do I still want to be here?" thus depriving ourselves of the joy of discovering that in fact we do, until the sense of bondage has become so great that the only solution seems to be to break out completely.

---

[15] In the face of the instability of the institution of marriage, some Christian pastors have sought to persuade married couples to periodically reaffirm their marriage vows, a practice largely resisted by the populace, presumably because it is psychologically counter-productive. If a couple still feel individual and in love, they reaffirm their vows all the time in a thousand different ways. If the pressure of obligation has already threatened the sense of volition, to reaffirm vows is to focus upon and thereby magnify the problem.

Because the mode of belonging is different in the three paradigms, the communal entity established by the relationship will be different and so may the form of any attempt to refresh the sense of belonging by recovering the consciousness of being an individual center. In each, however, it would require the self to transcend symbols on which it is dependent for identity and therefore for belonging. It would involve the short term abandonment, even deliberate rejection of a symbol or symbols, not because they are dead or objectionable, but precisely because they are overwhelmingly significant for the adherent.

AN EXAMPLE FROM IMMEDIATE EXPERIENCE AFFIRMING RELIGION

Mary Douglas poses the question "Can there by any people who confound sacredness with uncleanness?"[16]   Dirt, it is said, is matter out of place. Uncleanness in this context, is the result of contact with matter out of place, or of actions out of place, or even thoughts about the same. Sacredness, on the other hand, is that which creates or legitimates order. If this is the case then Douglas' question may be rephrased as "can there be any people who confound order with disarray and thus create chaos?" She answers her own question in the affirmative and cites the Lele adherents of the pangolin cult as an example.

The solemn ritual consumption of the pangolin (the giant scaly ant-eater) which is normally avoided as a living question mark against the human and animal categories which are the frame of meaning in Lele life, is said by Douglas to be "only one example, of which many more could be cited, of cults which invite their initiates to turn around and confront the categories in which their whole surrounding culture has been built up ...". She completes the sentence, "... and to recognize them as the fictive, man-made, arbitrary creations that they are."
The latter part of the sentence may not always be true, but I believe that the effect of rituals of this type lies primarily in the area that I have been discussing. One cannot refresh one's sense of belonging without refreshing one's sense of the possibility of, and something of the nature of, not belonging. To do this, one may have to fly in the face of norms.

The most general form of Douglas' original question can be expressed as "How do the religious learn again to appreciate that which their religious commitment supplies?" This, within the dualistic and therefore voluntaristic religions, becomes "How may a sense of voluntariness survive?" or "How shall the freedom to love survive the stranglehold of a sense of obligation?" or

---

[16] Mary Douglas, *Purity and Danger*, (London, Routledge & Kegan Paul, 1969), p.169f.

"How shall submission (which is only submission so long as it continues to be consciously voluntary) survive?". Submission, like love, is not a word that one uses of machines.

One looks therefore within the Abrahamic family for some parallel to the regular ritualized confounding of symbols central to identity, exemplified by the pangolin cult among the Lele, expressing in this case independence from a monotheos. Fiesta of various kinds is perhaps the nearest that Christian communities come to it, but this is more at the level of that joyful irreverence which one finds enshrined in the Jewish traditions associated with Simchat Torah and Purim, than a deliberate and overt confrontation with existing norms. Fiesta gives evidence of a need perhaps, but is little more than the letting down of one's hair and certainly far from a conscious and deliberate saying "no" to God. Not the "no" of unbelief, of course, nor the "no" which is perhaps the ultimate expression of trust in such heroes of the faith as Moses and the mythical Job, but "no" in the ritual sense that I have been discussing. What one is seeking is a sense of a new beginning and of enjoying the dignity of being an individual choosing to be in community, rather than being a cog enmeshed in a machine, in order that whatever one does for god or man shall be an expression of love rather than of servitude.

While restraint in not always the opposite of freedom, refreshing the sense of freedom requires rejection of whatever restraint is imposed by the relationship. Balance and moderation already suppose restraint and even the orgiastic is hardly sufficient release. In the Abrahamic traditions one would be looking for ritualization of outright conscious rejection of the normative relation to God. It seems that religious authorities in the Abrahamic family have set their faces against recognizing any such ritual within the orthodox fold.

The only ritual included within a liturgy which, in my view, once served this purpose, is the Kol Nidre, which stands at the beginning of the rite for the eve of the Day of Atonement in the Jewish prayer book.[17]

AN EXAMPLE FROM SECULAR WORLD AFFIRMING RELIGION

The Kol Nidre at the beginning of Yom Kippur, seems to stand for the determination not to devote the day to patching up a marred relationship but to discarding the old totally, so that one can enter into it anew and because one wants to do so.

Historically speaking, it is there because the populace demanded it. The responses of the Sages to its presence in the liturgy, included seeking to get

---

[17] For a similar opinion on the Kol Nidre see Karl Abraham, quoted in T Riek, *Ritual a Psycho-Analytic Study*, (New York, International Universities Press, 1958), p.218.

rid of it altogether, attempts at textual emendation and reinterpretations of its meaning. The drawn out conflict between the populace and the authorities reflects, paradoxically enough, exactly this need to refresh not only a legal standing before their god, but their love of him also.

It seems clear that whatever Kol Nidre might or might not mean in contemporary Judaism (in the Ashkenazi rite it has a haunting melody) when it was being fought for by the populace, the Kol Nidre was another example of those "cults which invite their initiates to turn around and confront the categories in which their whole surrounding culture has been built up". In this case it means confronting a structure of voluntarily covenanted obligations to God and to man for God, not only to regain a sense of the importance of the order itself, but also to re-establish awareness of the individual's volitional presence within that order.

The reason why this ritual survived in Judaism is that within Rabbinic Judaism there was always a mechanism for the populace to have its own way. Such was not the case within Christianity. In the Christian world their has been, as indicated in the previous theme, a strong emphasis on volition. In spite of this I do not know of any ritual in any branch of mainline Christianity that comes close to serving the purpose of volitional refreshment. The evidence of a need for such ritual expression is to be found in those antinomian movements which have, from time to time in the history of the church, advocated a deliberate rejection of accepted laws and norms. In an age when human defects are considered more as individual and social inadequacies than as sin in a legalistic sense, Christians and Muslims may come to recognize the renewing power of Kol Nidre, and consider what form its equivalent might take in their own traditions.

It is interesting to speculate on whether religion involving detachment, such as the various forms of Buddhism, might not require the opposite, that is, a symbolic excursion into attachment to regain the witness quality of the individual consciousness. The Hindu tantric ritual of The Five Forbidden Things, in which an adherent far along the path of renunciation is required to turn back in dramatic style, may be a case in point.

THEME III - SECULARIZATION

USAGE OF THE TERM "SECULARIZATION"

Anyone who can accept the framework that I have been proposing will recognize that when the word secularization is used to describe what has been happening to western religion especially when it is used to imply its failure, it is not necessarily good usage. The word secular, when used as the equivalent of profane and as the opposite of sacred, is only used rigorously when it is applied to the real as distinct from the ultimately-real in the secular world affirming paradigm. In that use it is descriptive and not evaluative.

It is many moons since Durkheim sought to distinguish clearly between sacred and profane. He finally threw in the sponge saying that it did not matter, for everyone knew what he meant, for the distinction exists everywhere. Which they did not! Because it does not! When Durkheim came to apply the distinction between sacred and profane it had been reduced to the distinction between social and individual, as these operate in each member of a society and, by extension, in the society itself. The distinction is very similar to the one Freud makes between Super-ego and Id. Important as that distinction is in human experience, it is hardly where one would look for the distinction between sacred and profane.

Durkheim was right about the universal feel that the distinction between sacred and profane has for anyone socialized in the secular world affirming paradigm, but in that situation it depends on a sense of transcendence. All that can give rise to it anywhere else is the distinction between the two stances (the I-it and the I-thou) and the two modes of discourse used to speak of them. I spoke of these in chapter 10 as life-world and holistic perspectives, but again, while these stances must be present wherever there is a distinction between sacred and profane, the distinction between sacred and profane does not exist everywhere that the two stances exist. It is transcendence that necessitates the distinction between sacred and profane, nothing else. If the distinction between the two modes of discourse is not understood, it is only too easy to confuse the relational and linguistic distinction with an ontological one as I believe Otto did. [18]

The confusion that exists in the usage of the term "secularization" requires that I stay with contemporary referents of the word, seeking to untangle the substantive events to which it points, before I can deal directly with the latter.

Generally speaking, writers on secularization have fallen into one of two groups. There are those who see it as a failure of religion and those who, like myself, see it as religion changing its form, which includes, if the moves are not conscious, the possibility that religion can become hidden. The two

---

[18] Rudolf Otto seems to me to reify the Numenous. *The Idea of the Holy*, (Harmondsworth, Penguin, 1959).

groups correspond to the two approaches to religion that I earlier associated with the schools of thought stemming from Weber and Durkheim. The larger group seem to be those who, for some reason, choose to regard religion as a relatively fixed thing in an otherwise changing society. What seem to be very different views about the current situation turn out, therefore, to be a matter of definition and perhaps also an indication of what particular interest area the writer comes from as he or she approaches the study of religion. The situation is not detrimental provided that one is constantly aware of the approach in use and of its consequences, but many do not offer a definition of religion, presuming that everyone knows what they are writing about.

It is all right, for example, to speak of secularization as individuals and institutions moving out from under the authority of religious symbols, provided that one makes it clear that one means symbols that are traditionally accepted as religious, and that this will always be happening in any dynamic society as the felt sense of reality shifts. It must also be clear that the symbols from under the authority of which the modern world is seen to be moving, are, in the sense in which I have been using the term, no longer fully religious. They must be dead or dying symbols. They may have been appropriated as "flag" symbols in times of insecurity; they may have functioned as bridging symbols in a time of transition that is passed; it may simply be that the felt sense of reality has undergone a major shift, but it is certain that they no longer serve to communicate the felt nature of the ultimately-real or how one belongs to it. If they did, one could not simply slide out from under their authority. One would have to justify it, or go into conscious revolt, not against the symbols, but against that which one felt to be the ultimately-real.

"Secularization" is used most frequently to refer to a movement or an ethos, a primary characteristic of which is the failure of religion. It does not usually allow that religion is changing, and it normally generalizes from the failure of the traditional religious form of a particular society. Nevertheless it could refer to the failure of religion in general, as well as to the failure of a particular form of religion to hold its erstwhile adherents. I must therefore deal with both.

SECULARIZATION AS THE FAILURE OF RELIGION IN GENERAL

The word secularity, used to imply a failure of religion in general, must be reappraised in the light of the possible styles of religion set out in chapter 8. Thus, one who fails to believe in a personal deity, or indeed in any transcendent reality, might still be included in the two monistic paradigms. One who fails to espouse any beliefs, that is any symbol set for the ultimately-real, may still be said to be religious in a pre-paradigmatic manner, or if they have a developed felt sense of reality and a cosmic trust, to be religious in a post-paradigmatic manner.

When considering the pathways of belonging in the secular world affirming paradigm, it became clear that an almost total concern with the natural order, such as would be regarded as secularization in the popular sense of the word, is not necessarily a failure of religion in the terms of that paradigm any more than it would be in nature religion. Similarly the fact that the language of a group becomes in all appearances secular may simply be because, in a mixed tradition situation, the use of sectional symbols in the public domain has caused embarrassment and substitutes have had to be found for them. [19] In certain circumstances religious symbols may disappear from a group not because they have become unimportant but precisely because they are valued and it does not feel right to employ them in the present situation.[20]

SECULARIZATION AS THE FAILURE OF RELIGION WITHIN A PARADIGM

While it is more difficult to regard people as having moved right out of a religious position than many writers suppose, there are many ways in which religion can fail in terms of a particular paradigm and I will return to these. Nevertheless, it is seldom appropriate to use the word "secularization" to describe failures of religion outside the paradigm which gave the word "secular" its meaning, and even within it there are problems.

Secularity in the nature religion paradigm could, I think, only be used of an attitude or activity which would use the powers-that-be for sectional ends, without respect for the good of the whole. In the extreme case, this is what distinguishes "medicine" from "witchcraft".

Secularity might be used in the withdrawal religion paradigm to describe the very state that religion of that type seeks to overcome, namely, relating to the immediate world as though it were permanent and to its appearance as though it were the reality.

These usages, however, would only indicate how far the word had been applied beyond its modern primary meaning of profane, for in a monistic world-view there can be no distinction between secular and sacred.

---

[19] The large, so called "secular" group in Israel, may be a case in point. It would be interesting to explore the new value language of this group, as I have suggested it would be to explore the process of new value language development in the United Nations Organization.

[20] See for example Shlomo Deshen, "The Varieties of Abandonment of Religious Symbols" *Journal for the Scientific Study of Religion 11:1.*

The term "secularization" appeared in the western world shaped by the secular world affirming paradigm, in which the real (as distinct from the ultimately-real) is secular and must remain so, if the paradigm is to be maintained. Therefore, in that paradigm, if the word "secularization" is used to imply the failure of religion, then to reduce the secularity of the real would, paradoxically, be secularization.

NOTE : *CRITERIA FOR DISTINGUISHING FAILURE FROM CHANGE*

When a religious tradition seems to be failing within its erstwhile paradigm, it is not easy to distinguish between situations in which religion is best said to be failing in some aspect of that tradition and those in which it is best understood to have moved, or to be moving, into another paradigm. The two most visible indicators are the mode of engagement with the world-out-there and ritual, the latter expressing the mode of *belonging* to the ultimately-real and therefore suggesting something of its nature.

Sometimes the evidence provided by these two is contradictory, and that in itself points to a degree of failure, but as an indictor of change greater weight must be given to the mode of engagement with the immediate world-out-there. This is because, while the mode of belonging seems more central to the paradigm and more clearly a statement of the nature of the reality believed in, the former is what people actually do in relation to the world in which they find themselves. The latter, in the extremes, may be locked into a somewhat fixed self-image or be swept along in a major shift in fashion, the former tends to reflect a community's view on what is life's most enriching course of action, which is perhaps the profoundest statement one can make about the nature of reality. If there is a clear mode of engagement, or even a lively debate about the right mode of engagement, then religion may have changed, but it has not failed.

Nothing of what has been said, concerning doubtful usage of the term "secularization", is meant to imply that religion cannot fail. If religion is understood as a sense of cosmic belonging or the quest for it, then, when belonging fails and the quest is absent, it fails. If belonging or the quest for it ceases to be cosmic, religion has at least been diminished.

When I was considering the *conceptual* aspects of belonging I made the point that, within the framework that I was employing, there was only one positively non-religious stance. That is, to say of all-that-out-there, that it is chaos, without coherence or meaning. If it is without coherence there is no significant other to relate to, if it is without meaning there is nothing worth relating to. There are however less conscious forms of the failure of religion in general, many of which I have referred to.

When discussing the development of the felt sense of reality I indicated a variety of reasons why one might not have religious experience, not least because one is asleep, or too involved in the bits and pieces of life ever to stand back from it, but also because one has not developed psychological independence (what H.C. Rümke called "becoming an ego") or, if one has, one cannot surrender back into relationship with all-that-out-there. [21]

When I dealt with post-paradigmatic belonging, I raised the question of whether either a cosmic trust or acceptance of the "cosmos paradigm" could suffice for belonging. By "cosmos paradigm" I meant an extension of the necessary methodological assumption of science (that the real is a self-explanatory closed system) into an ontology, while nevertheless retaining a linear sense of time and a goal orientation. Whether this could be a failure of religion in general needs further examination. It would certainly appear to be a failure of religion in the secular world affirming paradigm. I will return to cosmic trust and the "cosmos paradigm" later in the chapter because they merit special attention.

Having said that within the understanding of religion employed in this book there is less failure of religion than might be supposed, and that the term "secularization" is not well used outside the paradigm in which the word "secular" received its modern meaning and that even within it it is confusing, I must now acknowledge that "secularization" in its popular usage has a referent. Traditional forms of religion which served their adherents for so long that religion itself became identified with them, are now the object of ambivalence, puzzlement, neglect and rejection. That the reasons are complex is evidenced by the wealth of literature on the subject from both schools of secularization thought. Fortunately, my present concern is a limited one. It is to explore the degree to which secularization can be positively contained within the conceptual framework generated by an understanding of religion as belonging, and then, to the degree that it cannot be contained positively, ask whether its most significant form, the "cosmos paradigm", could in fact be a viable independent alternative. I begin by exploring secularization as a process of readjustment taking place within the quest for (or maintenance of) belonging.

SECULARIZATION AS ADJUSTMENTS IN THE QUEST FOR BELONGING

Secularization as adjustment, presents a spectrum of possible situations.

---

[21] See the final sections of chapter 6   and   H C Rümke, *The Psychology of Unbelief*,(London, Rockliff, 1952).

The spectrum runs from adjustments that have already taken place but which have not been recognized as remaining religious by those who speak of them as secularization, perhaps not even by those who have adopted them - through situations in which (while some serious rethinking and major affective re-adjustments are called for) solutions seem possible even if they are not immediately apparent - to those situations in which religion as belonging is seriously threatened and the manner of its maintenance is far from clear.

This last set of possibilities arises out of the actual and ideological elevation of individualism in what is referred to, in corporate context, as pluralism. I have not yet dealt specifically with corporate processes and therefore secularization, understood as adjustments in the quest for belonging at the corporate level, must await the discussion in chapter 13. It must suffice here to say that they are problems of such magnitude that their resolution seems to call for a widespread re-evaluation of the nature of religion, together with a determination to be involved overtly in the processes that religion has always served.

For the rest, if one examines some of the roots of the desertion of traditional forms, what emerges is that they are at least compatible with adjustments within the quest to belong, and are not necessarily its rejection.

I discussed earlier the development of a tradition within a community and the necessary roles that I labelled prophet, priest and pragmatist.[22] The processes of preserving and updating which went on within older religious communities no longer seem sufficient in themselves. Some of the reasons are obvious, some have already been referred to. I will simply list them.

> The process that I described cannot be hurried beyond a certain point and the pace of change seems to have overtaken them.

> Technology has shrunk the world so that history can no longer be conceived as taking place within a single tradition community, and yet the integration of traditions seems an insuperable task.

> The apparent success of modernization has set a question mark against received traditions.

> The recognition that the paradigms for reality are just that, paradigms. That all knowledge beyond the most immediate experience exists only within a paradigm and is therefore relative and socio-culture dependent.

Related to the above are some less obvious sources of dissatisfaction with the older forms. The first group of these have to do with various

---

[22] See chapter 3.

manifestations of rigidity, the second with misunderstandings of, or inadequacies in, symbolic language. I begin with rigidity and again in summary form.

i) *Rigidity of Institutional Forms*

In times of great insecurity whole communities can turn to their tradition looking for absolutes. They make it into a sort of castle, barring the windows and pulling up the draw bridge, and when the world changes for the better and they feel more secure, what seemed a fortress can be experienced as a prison. Then, instead of letting it change and flow into more appropriate forms, they flee it. When they again look for belonging, however, the movements to which they are drawn and the style of their relationship to them, appear very like the original.

The roles, which I have suggested must exist within any dynamic community, tend in stable times to become specialized and institutionalized as the community leaves its decisions to those who care to be involved. The result is that within the wider tradition community, there appear identifiable institutions which become the focus, and virtually the limits, of what is understood to be religion. When this happens there are consequences which lead people to neglect the religious forms that have been thus corralled. For example:

Exclusivity leaves those who are on the margin feeling left out.

When a variety of institutions claim to have the truth one inevitably asks, " Does anyone have it?".

When religion and the working world are thus separated and each claims a 100% commitment, religion will loose, for people must live.

This segregation of "religion" may lead not merely to secularization as the passive neglect of older religious forms but also to a positive secularity, to the obverse of pietism, that is, to the letting go of one end of the tension in order to preserve the integrity of identity and a sense of belonging. A deliberate not belonging to one sphere, in order to belong clearly to the other.
In the end, an active religious consciousness will break out of bondage that the segregation constitutes, driven by the loss of a sense of belonging or by a decline in its ability to express what it wishes to express.

Earlier, when discussing the variety of possible styles of belonging, I included a comment on the extreme use of the word secular in contemporary Israel. In that country there is a tendency to lump together, under the head "secular", all those who are not thoroughly observant nor yet traditional. The traditional are members of the folk religion who, while not thoroughly observant themselves, are prepared to acknowledge that that is the religious ideal. In an attempt to convince an Israeli academic colleague that there were other ways of being religious than making an ideal of ultra-orthodoxy I composed a "parable of secularities" in which I tried to show that what is called secularity may well be another mode of belonging. In particular, I wanted to say that an enthusiasm for the real may in itself be a way of relating to the ultimately-real.

It may be that in emphasizing the love of the father figure in the story rather than his sovereign righteousness, I have shifted the balance toward the Christian and away from the traditional Jewish understanding of the divine. Yet I feel that the story makes the general point, that before leaping to the conclusion that people are not religious one ought to ask what forms being religious can take and whether in the context concerned, a change in the mode of belonging has not taken place.

It has to be remembered that the Jewish people have been more or less permanently insecure for at least 2000 years and that Rabbinic Judaism is, *inter alia*, a "formula for survival". The tradition, therefore, may not be appropriate to the modern nation state of Israel, nor perhaps to situations of seeming security in other nation states. It is an interesting case study of a well constructed castle that has difficulty of flowing into other shapes. The "parable" follows.

THE FAMILY - A Parable of Secularities

Key:-
Orth or Morph represents the modern orthodox, that is those who look for change within the religious law to enable them to embrace modernity. Sec is a secular man.

Ultra and Dox represent different forms of the Super- Orthodox who are prepared to withdraw from much of modern life in order to maintain the traditional forms.   Mar and Nod will be self-explanatory.   Mat, the materialist, is in love with possession for its own sake.

A certain man had six children; Orth, or was it Morph, Sec, Ultra and Dox, Mar and Nod. Nod was asleep. When Rosh Hashanah came the father give to each child a present.

Orth or was it Morph, said "thank you Father", read the instructions and played with the present. From time to time he checked on his understanding of the instructions and from time to time returned to re-affirm his gratitude. The father was happy.

Sec, on the other hand, was so excited by his present that he quite forgot to say thank you and was so engrossed that he never did pay heed to the instructions but launched directly and enthusiastically into playing with it. The father laughed, shook his head and wondered at the child's naive trust but he was happy.

Ultra said, "thank you Father, thank you" and then "thank you Father, you're the greatest" and then "thank you" until the father became a touch nauseated and rather wished that the child would open his present.

Dox opened the present, carefully took out the instructions and read them, re-read them and read them again. The father could hardly be angry with the child, but he certainly became impatient.

Mar did not say thank you. He took the present but did not want to, he tore it open but did not play with it. He didn't not want the present but nor did he want it, either for its own sake or because it was a present, for he had a bitterness of spirit which could have been wickedness or it could have been sickness. The father did not know whether to be angry or to weep in his sadness and not knowing, wanted to turn away.

Nod, of course, was asleep.

You may ask about Mat, the child who never even noticed the father nor really played with the present but just grasped it to his chest. Well, if he exists, he doesn't really belong to the family, he is virtually an orphan. There is all the difference in the world between finding a flower lying in your path and believing that someone placed it there for you. However desirable it may be in itself it is more desirable as a gift. Which is why, although he sometimes becomes quite violent when he feels insecure, Mat is maybe another name for Nod.

Now, Morph-Orth being blessed, or was it cursed, with balance and insight, felt an obligation to his siblings. Having learned the advantage of following the instructions he wanted Sec to do so too, or at least accept his advice ere he hurt himself or damaged the present, and of course it would be nice if Sec remembered to say thank you.

Concerning Ultra and Dox he was ambivalent. Deep inside himself he sensed that they were wrong but he could not escape a grudging admiration; for the one seemed so much more grateful than he, and the other had studied in detail not only the instructions but also by now manuals on how to apply the instruction drawn up by those who had studied just such instruction in the past. He had even added a few logico-hypothetical consequences for himself. The very attractiveness of these two made him uneasy.

To Mar he tended to give the benefit of the doubt, called it sickness and underwrote a whole therapeutic programme.

Nod, of course, was asleep.

In Israel there are a number of Morph-Orth's busy disagreeing about the interpretation of the instructions and their importance relative to the present, a great many more Sec's and a seemingly growing number of various combinations of Ultra and Dox. In a young and partially self-selected society there are not many Mar's or Nod's. One hopes that Morph-Orth will seek to wake such Nods as there are, be more understanding of Sec and not allow Ultra and Dox to dictate the mode of belonging.

In more literal vein it must be said that if Mosaic orthodoxy lies within the secular world affirming paradigm, then there is a serious questions whether "ultra-orthodoxy" is in fact orthodox and not a form of reduced reality belonging. The context also enables me to re-make the point that religious activity may in fact be inversely proportional to the felt sense of belonging.

I now turn to the second group of situations in which secularization may well be understood as adjustment within the quest for, or maintenance of belonging. These are those concerned with the misunderstanding of, or inadequacies in, symbolic language.

ii) *Misunderstanding and Inadequacies of Symbolic Language*

The failure to understand that the language, in which primary religious experience must be expressed, is not literal language inevitably gives rise in a scientific ethos to either the overt rejection of the paradigm, or the need for those who retain a religious spirit, to live in two worlds. Frequently the more scientific a religious person is the more fundamentalist he or she is.

It is difficult, however, to remain in that position, particularly for those who become aware of what they are doing. The tendency is toward the post-paradigmatic state and a sort of cosmic trust. This is not necessarily to diminish religion, only to have difficulty with its conceptualization.

Secularization as the rejection of older forms, may also result from the difficulty many have with a personal deity. The personal category seems too small to contain all that modern people believe about the universe. The problem with the personal, however, is related to another and more profound problem, that is the loss of a sense of transcendence, coupled as it is, to the lack of a strong goal orientation. It is not clear which, if any, of these is an independent variable.

Christian moral theology was once a stern program of three elements. That is, a description of what people are now, what they should be, and a program for getting them from the first to the second. Now the *telos* has all but gone. The emphasis is on present texture, what Nietzsche stigmatized as a "morality of pity". The question is why?. Is the post-enlightenment growth of individualism a cause or a consequence?

Individualism is the only alternative for ultimate meaning when grand design disintegrates. There has been a tendency to flirt with Buddhist grandeur with no telos, but it is difficult to see how grand design cannot involve a telos, that is, be grand purpose, in a culture which for other reasons maintains its linear time and goal orientated world view.

It is not that a *telos* cannot be believed in. Marxists of the more traditional kind believed in a telos, even if it was defined for the most part in negative terms. Most people can accept movement toward a *telos* provided that it is sufficiently open to make their involvement worthwhile and is not of the blue print variety. Nor is there much problem with belief in an ultimately-real, even modern physicists flirt with that.

I suspect that the problem is that the *telos* became intimately wrapped up with a personal deity, while the view of the ultimately-real that is now necessary has grown beyond the limits that are credible within the personal. When one's world could be controlled by a nobleman beyond whom was a king, a personal deity behind that was quite credible. It is still credible to those who occupy a small world but many do not. What one needs is a larger than personal, non-mechanistic symbol, which will extend or replace the volitional one, yet remain credible and, when necessary, intimate. It is hard to imagine what it might be, for it remains fact that, where the mode of engagement is to take hold and shape, a sense of personal providence can be enlivening but a sense of impersonal providence (fate) is enervating.

As I said above, the widespread moves have been toward a non-specific cosmic trust or to the more cognitive position of the "cosmos paradigm". To an examination of the viability of these I now turn.

THE VIABILITY OF POST-PARADIGMATIC RELIGION (COSMIC TRUST) AND OF THE "COSMOS PARADIGM"

COSMIC TRUST

Post-paradigmatic religion, as a sort of cosmic trust and a commitment to an acceptable set of medial-axioms by which engagement with one's world might be controlled, seems an undogmatic, non-authoritarian and otherwise attractive alternative to any paradigmatic religion. Indeed, in a world which is coming to accept that all knowledge, save the most immediate and discrete, exists in paradigms and is therefore relative, it may be the only possible form for many. The question is, will it do? Will it serve the purposes, social and individual, that paradigmatic religion or even pre-paradigmatic religion have served in previous generations?

The first thing to be said about cosmic trust is that it is not a fully articulated position and to settle for it obscures what is going on at the unconscious level. Recognizing withdrawal religion as a special case, most people need an identity and all people need a mode of engagement with their world-out-there. Cosmic trust settles for identity in terms of values that are more arbitrary than they need to be and ignores the paradigmatic implications of the mode of engagement.

Identity does not have to be entirely conscious, nor does it have to be understood in ultimate terms. Religion understood as the quest for belonging, however, presuppose a *quest* for identity in the most ultimate terms possible, cognitively as well as affectively. A mature identity cannot be independent of values. Any set of values derived from a context, which is less than as total as one can make it, is unnecessarily arbitrary. If the principal values which generate one's whole set of values are to be expressed, then the nature of the context from which they are derived must also be expressed, which takes one back to the paradigm for reality.

If for identity purposes, a set of medial-axioms seems sufficiently authoritative in its own right, it can only be because one has been socialized in those values within a particular culture, the paradigmatic background of which has remained covert. I will return to the question of values when I discuss the idea of a self-sufficient secular cosmos.

With regard to modes of engagement with the world-out-there, I have said that there are only three and that these are, in the same person at the same time, mutually exclusive. One may either fit into, withdraw from, or take hold of and shape the world out there. People will normally select whichever of these is perceived to be the potentially most enriching, which already implies something about how reality is experienced. Why then should it not be made articulate?

It is clear that a mode of engagement can itself become a set of symbols to which ultimacy is ascribed. A method or a measure is made a goal in itself. It is this which creates the Illiberal Liberal and the Totalitarian Radical. It makes the pseudo-goals referred to in chapter 8, out of freedom and equality by not saying free for what or equal in what, and out of efficiency and profitability by not saying what is to be done with the time saved or the proceeds generated. The goal is not described in terms of end-point texture. The mode of engagement has become self-justifying. To close off at this point and not ask the question beyond, "What are the goals which render these the most enriching modes of engagement?", is simply arbitrary.

There is a great difference between recognizing the paradigms as paradigms, and the ultimately-real as ineffable in literal discourse and either rejecting or simply giving up the quest to know what is out there. If one does give up, then any value-set that one chooses to work with can well be described as ideological.

Values may be held tentatively by the individual who is seeking the most enriching way of engaging with the world out there, but that form of quest has ontological assumptions. As a minimum, it implies a belief that in all probability there are laws of relation to others, to the world and to self which can be discovered, and that the quest is an authentic human activity.

All knowledge beyond the immediate is modelled in some way, and to the degree that it is modelled it is projected onto the world-out-there by the human mind. Knowledge at this level is theory. Theory is tested finally, in its power to do for us what we have decided that we want it to do. Just because philosophers of science have made it clear that theory is projected - that it exists only within a particular paradigm - that the paradigm itself will survive only so long as it does for us what we want it to do better than any other contender for the paradigmatic crown - scientists have not given up doing science. They have not given up the belief that they are engaged with and in describing reality.

Religious knowledge is not different in this regard. The truth of the paradigm lies in its power to do for us what we need it to do, that is, to create the sense of belonging to the ultimately-real. It will only have power to do that if it is legitimated by its perceived power to meet life's needs in the most enriching way. Central to those life needs is the need for a mode of engagement. There is, therefore, a dynamic feedback in the system. The paradigm gives rise to a means of explanation and integration of the world-out-there, and to a mode of engagement with it. Insofar as these are assessed as enriching, the system and its paradigm are affirmed. Insofar as they are judged not to be enriching the system and its paradigm are brought under criticism and potential modification. Why then is the paradigm not acknowledged?

People do not generally live in a paradigmatic vacuum. There is no reason to suppose that life experience is such that it would continue to engender cosmic trust if no explanations of it were offered, and no mode of engagement advocated by a paradigm was forthcoming.

Religious knowledge is, of course, different to scientific knowledge in the language in which it must be expressed. It is my view, as I said above, that much of the rejection of the traditional religious paradigm in the West since the Enlightenment is the result of a failure to understand this fact. There have been many who, in remaining strongly goal oriented have retained the mode of engagement appropriate to the paradigm, but who could not accept in literal terms its necessarily symbolic language. Nor did they realize that in the final resort the modelling of reality is tested in experience and in feeling, not cognitively and abstractly.

THE "COSMOS PARADIGM"

I now come to the related issue of the viability of "cosmos" - a modern pretender to the paradigmatic throne. This goes beyond the gentle agnosticism of post-pardigmatic religion with its cosmic trust to the positive affirmation of an alternative paradigm.

Modern western man has found it enriching to engage with the bits and pieces of his world out there as though they together formed a closed, self-explanatory, and entirely secular system. Such is the method of science and it has borne much fruit. Science, far from embracing values, seeks to be value free. It all looks very wholesome.

However, when one seeks to take the same stance to reality as a whole as science takes to its parts, all is not well. The result of doing so is well pictured in terms of a series of transformations within the coherent types of religious tradition.

One must begin by imagining oneself to be in a nature religion world-view, then one must imagine that fact and value, the personal and the impersonal are separated out. The essence of the personal and the source of values are then removed entirely from the immediate world and placed across a transcendence gap. One is then in a secular world affirming world-view, with its goal orientation in linear time. Now one simply disposes of the transcendence gap and all that is on the far side of it. What is left is a Real, with no Ultimately-Real; a secular, closed system of cause and effect in linear time.[23]

This raises two questions. The first is the cognitive one of whether such a view of a secular self-contained cosmos in linear time is itself self-contained, that is to say, whether it is conceivable if the implications are fully articulated. The second question and (because people live happily without spelling out implications) the more practical one, is whether it would work and survive were it not parasitic upon the secular world affirming paradigm.

I am not here concerned with what is, I am concerned, on the one hand, with what can be fully conceptualized and, on the other, with the question, "would this world-view go on being what it is, functioning as it does, without the control of the transcendence half of the paradigm?". While the former is not my primary concern, I must say enough about the cognitive problem to make the issues clear.

---

[23] This is the general thrust of Henri Frankfort's presentation of the progress of myth from Egypt and Mesopotamia, through the Hebrew world, to the Greek.
See Henri Frankfort et al, *Before Philosophy*, (Harmondsworth, Penguin, 1949)

i) *THE COGNITIVE PROBLEM*

The word secular only has meaning in the secular world affirming paradigm, as the other side of the transcendence gap to the ultimately-real. For present purposes it is translatable into the word "mechanistic". A completely mechanistic universe is conceivable if one understands it as eternal, or at least as a given, in which one does not ask about its origin or destiny. However, if one understands reality in this way, then what is the meaning of linear time? It cannot be simply the accumulating revolutions of the sun or the seasons, for how are they not simply cycles returning ever and again to the same point. Linear time requires progress to some long-term goal or distance from some starting point, if it is to be different from cyclical time.

If a people were to inherit or otherwise come by a linear time world-view without a beginning or a destiny, it would only survive if it had some value for them which made it feel right (which is unlikely given that it is literally un-natural) or because they had some measure of progress, but that in itself would require a goal of some kind. Maoism softened the strong goal orientation of Marxism-Leninism with the notion of an ever present texture of continual revolution. It therefore had a more immediate affinity with the world view of pre-communist China. It is not an affinity that is likely to survive. Impetus from the West or from the revolution itself may carry this idea for a period, but then the question of motivation will arise. Why should each generation bother to break out of the myths and structures of preceding generations unless there is some gain from the effort? How shall one measure such gain without a goal, or without a sense of what I earlier called blessings, that is, without a sense of what the system is expected to deliver to enable its adherents to deal with life's needs. In short, any such attempt to justify change by an appeal to a texture of change rather than to goals is a deception and must run out of steam. The system will either begin to articulate goals or simply return to a concern with present texture. An illustration of linear time in spatial terms may help to make the issue clearer.

The answer to the question "what is that down in the cutting?" may be either "two long lengths of steel fastened to wooden beams" or "the railway from A to B".

These two answers - the one which confines itself to what is in view and which parallels what I have been calling present texture, and the second, expressed in terms of points of departure and destination - are both complete answers.

The answer "it is a railway line", which sounds complete on first hearing, is seen not to be if given a little thought. For either:

It means the same as the first answer if it has been agreed that all such bits of steel fastened to such wooden beams in that manner shall be called a railway line. In which case, as in all short-hand, one needs to know the code otherwise no information is imparted.

or

It is parasitical upon many such bits of information as the second answer offers and also on the faith that these two bits of steel do not come to an end immediately that they are out of sight.

Likewise belief in a self contained cosmos in linear time seems complete but is in fact parasitical upon belief in a beginning or a destiny.

ii) THE AFFECTIVE PROBLEM

Whether or not "cosmos" is fully conceivable, it is in fact the paradigm with which many attempt to operate. The question, "could it work and therefore survive without the secular world affirming paradigm in the background?", is a question with practical consequences. There are three issues here. The first (which I have already touched upon) has to do with the paradigm as a source of values - the second with the paradigm as a source of motivation - the third, with whether the cosmos paradigm can in fact support a cosmic sense of belonging.

Cosmos as a Source of Values

Values cannot arise out of scientific enquiry *per se*. [24]

While individuals will operate with medial-axioms or even with a "felt sense" for the greater part of the time, values which are not more arbitrary than they have to be, arise out of a consideration of the most total possible experience.

In my view the important values are not those arrived at by the remote giants of the philosophical tradition but those embraced, tested and refined by communities of people over extended periods of time. That is, by tradition communities operating within some paradigm for reality.

That values cannot simply be plucked out of the air is well illustrated by a continuing debate to be found within Neo-Marxism. It concerns the source of values for social construction.

---

[24] See the discussion in chapter 4 about the independence and interdependence of fact and value.

There are those who argue that simply to address oneself to correcting the obvious pathologies of the present stage of society is to be overly determined by that context. It is better to stand somewhat detached and decide what sort of society would maximize human flourishing and then to work for that. The other side then wish to know from what air will the values be plucked, at best they will be subjective, at worst metaphysical, even theological. Between subjectivity and the dominance of the moment, stands the process at work in a religious community. That is, the process of corporate commitment to, and the gradual development of, a value tradition.

The question is, could a similar development of a tried value system take place within a community embracing the "cosmos" paradigm.

It would require within the cosmos world-view (it being in linear time and a process of change) some focus around which values could develop and be integrated, as they are about the external ultimately-real in the secular world affirming paradigm. For values cannot arise out of economic or material processes alone, any more than out of any event taken in isolation, but only out of those situations that are understood as aspects of or challenges to a sense of reality distilled from the totality of things. That totality needs a symbolic focus.

The whole world-view would, of course, be tested as any other is by the enrichment or otherwise arising from the mode of engagement generated. It is difficult to see, however, what "cosmos" modelling of reality could carry the detail of goals and values embraceable in the notion of the will of God, or what modelling could attract the commitment necessary for the values to be lived, evaluated and preserved corporately. Perhaps the nearest is some symbolically permanent, but historically adapting, notion of a this worldly utopia, the rightness of striving for which is felt to be self-evident.

Cosmos as a Source of Motivation

The cosmos paradigm gains authority from the success of science, it being supposedly the world-view within which science operates. This view needs qualification.

A science which seeks only an understanding of the world-out-there, including the ability to predict, can and has existed within the nature religion paradigm. A science which seeks to go beyond understanding to "improving" the world out there has moved, or is moving, into the secular world affirming paradigm.

The science which many western minds see as evidence for the validity of the cosmos paradigm is of the latter kind. It is part of the process of taking hold and shaping the environment, and such a scientific enterprise cannot be value free. The value free scientific ideal applies only to the scientific observer as he or she records the total data of a limited phenomenon. The moment one has to select which data to record, value has entered into the observation of the phenomenon. Even before that, value entered into the selection of the phenomenon to be observed. Thus each bit of information in a physics text book may be value free, but what is included in the book, indeed in the total repertoire of physics, is anything but value free. It is the product of the invested resources of a great variety of individuals and interests.

We therefore face the situation that while the value free approach may lead to effective theories concerning particular phenomena, it may not lead to investment of energies in what could be the most important phenomena nor, in the end therefore, to the best theories. In short we face the fact that the separation of value from fact is only possible and profitable in the investigation and exploration of particular phenomena, the choice of the phenomenon and the profitability of our dealing with it are inevitably, questions of value. That aspect of the enlightenment ideal which extended a method appropriate to the laboratory to the whole of life and to life as a whole, I take to be effectively dead.

So we are returned to the question whether the cosmos paradigm can be a source of less than arbitrary values. This time, values for the choices that must be made concerning the investment of human energies.

Motivation not only includes the direction in which one might be moved but whether one is moved at all. While science as an approach to an immediate phenomenon may be value free, the total scientific enterprise, the whole quest and all the structures and resources which make it possible, are clearly goal oriented. Something moves them, and this takes us back to the question whether such an orientation could exist simply as part of the cosmos paradigm, or whether its presence there is not inevitably parasitic.

That human beings are in the long run moved to take hold of their world-out-there and shape it, will depend upon that being the most enriching mode of engagement. The mode of engagement has some cognitive implications at the ontological level and these might need to be conscious for the engagement to get under way, certainly for it to be as enriching as it could be once it was under way. These implications are that the world-out-there:

a) is worth relating to.

b) is secular, that is, that it *may be* taken hold of and shaped.

c) has a cosmic destiny involving a responsibility for humanity, that is, that it *should be* taken hold of and shaped.

and perhaps

d) that man is cosmically acceptable, predestined or forgiven, that is, that individuals can risk their eternal destiny in the manner in which they seek to take hold and shape it.

The first two factors are clearly present in the cosmos paradigm. The third may be sustained in the short term anyway, perhaps by making ultimates out of modes of engagement. The fourth, if it is necessary, as the evidence of history seems to indicate, is clearly not present in "cosmos" for that is inevitably karmic, a closed system of cause and effect.[25]

It is my personal conviction, that while the cosmos paradigm (which is but half of the secular world affirming paradigm) will suffice for some people in the short term, that in general and in the long term, it must reduce to some version of the monistic paradigms. It will then lose its goal orientation and cease to be the "cosmos" associated with the scientific venture as we know it.

Cosmos and Belonging

I have dwelt on the coherence of "cosmos" as a concept and as a generator of direction and drive, now I want to return to the sense of belonging and ask whether the cosmos paradigm can provide an alternative to the other paradigms for that purpose.

To belong does not always require meaning understood as the details of self-knowledge, or a positive mode of engagement with the world-out-there, but it will always necessitate meaningfulness, whether derived from individual survival or from grand design, and it will always tend to release the adherent from ego dependence upon any immediate piece of experience. I must ask, therefore, whatever one decides about its cognitive coherence, whether the cosmos paradigm can provide this. Could it's modelling of reality be affectively enriching to belong to if it existed on its own?

Because "cosmos" affirms the reality of the world of immediate experience but not transcendence, it has the appearance of being nearest to nature religion. I therefore begin with nature religion and ask what is the difference between it and the cosmos paradigm.

In nature religion reality is not necessarily personal but includes the personal. In the cosmos paradigm reality is impersonal in the sense that the personal has disappeared as a category other than as another way of saying 'human'. The personal is simply a quality of that particular material construction known as a human being. It might be said to include the idea

---

[25] I take this "freedom to be at risk vis-à-vis the world-out-there" to be a basic factor in the empirical evidence presented for the truth of Weber's Calvinism - capitalism conjunction.

that each human being is unique, yet most, if not all things are unique in
some sense. If to say something is personal is to say something different, it
must express an obligation or a belief that each human being should, unless it
is inappropriate for the specific purpose, be related to as unique. From where
in a secular cosmos could such a particular obligation arise?

In nature religion, time is cyclical and meaning may be found as a part of
a once-for-all *grand pattern*. In the cosmos paradigm there is a goal
orientation, time is linear and the final pattern is not yet available.

If a *grand purpose* could exist within the cosmos paradigm it would only
be as direction, not as destiny, that is, not as design or intent, for what is
there to have an intent when the personal has been removed from reality.

In a goal orientation, meaningfulness requires a cognitive grasp on that
to which one belongs. One cannot belong fully to that which is not-yet unless
it has the characteristic (one that is there in all three paradigms but is
strongly felt in a personal ultimately-real) of being a unity. The unity in this
case is that of an entity in process, as opposed to being accidentally related
bits and pieces caught up in a process. The meaning of "an entity" here
obviously has to do with a principle of continuity, with an expected
fulfillment not necessarily a known fulfillment, nor one that will then be a
static achieved-once-and-for-all kind, but a fulfillment whose arrival is
nevertheless built into the present entity. That is, it must be "a something"
going "somewhere" if it is to be not-yet but still "belongable" to.

For fulfillment to be built into the present entity, there must be
relationship between its parts, not a fixed relationship, it can be organic. That
is, if new things are added it cannot be as bricks to a wall, but must be via
digestion through a system. It is this that provides relationship through time
and guarantees that there are no absolute discontinuities.

This entity in process, or "a something going somewhere", is paralleled by
the individual soul of western tradition. If it were not individual and in need
of resurrection to survive, but a "spark" of brahman or life force, it could not
be not-yet save in a cyclical sense.

This not-yet-ness understood as an entity going somewhere, not simply as
chaos awaiting the accident of order, is what the symbol of transcendence
stands for. The nature of the entity in process does not have to be expressed
in the aggressively personal terms of intent. A vital principle will do, a sort of
D.N.A. providing a program for the system, always providing that it is not
"blind", that is, provided it responds as a whole system to input. (What in
personal terms, could be called caring.) If the whole system responds, there
must be a principle or principles for readjustment (a goal perhaps,
controlling the relation of sub-goals) and a response to negative feed back.

A principle of engagement (rather than a goal) might suffice for a while
in a conscious system in which it was believed that that particular mode of

engagement was likely to produce the best end, whatever that might be. In the longer term, however, there needs to be the possibility of assessing progress.

When such continuity exists there is something that can be trusted, that one can have faith in, and which can be related to directly for affective satisfaction. One ceases to be dependent on a cognitive grasp on the present configuration of the parts in process and stages in sub-processes for affective satisfaction.

Not-yet-ness requires this sort of an entity. Not-yet-ness can be posited of parts of a total system, or of the real if there is an ultimately-real, but a total system cannot be not-yet, for it must contain all that will be. What would it mean for a self explanatory cosmos with nothing outside itself to "respond to", "to define for itself its best end", or "to be not-yet". It will not do to think of it simply as a process working itself out, for then the beginning would have no explanation, and in that sense it would not be a whole in linear time, but something that was either eternal or having an uncaused cause.

A total reality, which is the sort of entity that can be belonged to, and a goal orientation do not go together. Cosmos is not a sufficiently coherent concept to provide a whole to belong to *meaningly*, only a brute fact to live alongside.

CHAPTER 13

THE CORPORATE ASPECTS OF RELIGION AS

BELONGING

Thus far in Part II the emphasis has been on the individual's sense of belonging to an ultimately-real and religion itself has been considered from the individual's view-point. It was appropriate to begin this way because, in the final analysis, whether or not a particular form of religion is authenticated depends upon its power to engender a sense of belonging and that can only be attested by the individual concerned. Now I must examine the corporate aspects, some of which are corporate for convenience sake, some by their very nature. There are three corporate faces to religion. I have already introduced aggregations significant in identity. The others are the religious institution and the tradition community. I will present what is to be said under these three headings.

There are aspects of religion that manifest corporately whenever that is possible. Therefore, if religion were to become entirely privatized it would still remain what it is, an essential aspect of being human, but it would no longer be recognizable as the religion we know. Clearly, there are desert islands even in the midst of large cities, where individuals may dwell by choice or otherwise, but for the most part human beings are social creatures and so religion has its corporate aspects.

There are corporate manifestations of religion which cannot be said to be essential to its nature. These, as it happens, are the more familiar ones.

They represent the way in which humankind has organized to meet the needs of the individual for a sense of belonging. They fulfill much the same role as do those associations of individuals bent on loosing weight, that is, they offer mutual support in the quest for an essentially individual goal. This is most obviously the case in withdrawal religion and the direct cosmic belonging form of the secular world affirming paradigm.

In the indirect cosmic belonging form of secular world affirming religion and in nature religion, corporateness is built into the logic of belonging. There has to be an entity in belonging to which one belongs to the ultimately-real, nevertheless, even here an overt corporate aspect cannot be said to be essential. The individual in a nature religion tradition who had no community would always have the natural order to belong to, and one could be a Catholic or a Jew in isolation if circumstances required it. In the latter case belonging would have to be via the mystical Body of Christ or mystical House of Israel without the support of any material reality.

There is, however, an aspect of religion that must be corporate when ever that is possible. This corporate aspect happens to be an unfamiliar one, and it is so because it does not have to be conscious and in most cases would not be acknowledged, for it is a quest for that which is conceptualized as a given. It is the quest for the nature of the ultimately-real and for the mode of humankind's belonging to it. Religion, therefore, is not only a matter of an inner subjectivity but exists in dynamic inter-relationship with an outward, cognitive and usually corporate aspect. Belonging, in cognitive beings, requires at least a minimal conceptualization of the ultimately-real, and the quest for that only makes sense as a corporate activity when that is possible. This quest for a conceptualization of the ultimately-real, even as a corporate activity, is not, of course, unrelated to the individual aspects of religion, for it must be tested within and requires feedback from the individual.

The topic will be dealt with in two parts. In this chapter I will distinguish and describe the different corporate aspects of religion. In chapter 14 I will consider the essentially corporate quest that I have just described.

It is my present purpose to draw out from the model of religion as belonging its expected corporate aspects. I will focus upon secular world affirming religion, for in this regard it is the case with the greatest variability and includes most of what might be said of the other paradigms.

Withdrawal religion is essentially individual, although the need for both continuity and mutual support in the individual quest has led to some institutionalization.

Nature religion is already essentially corporate and its adherents at one with their life-world. The institutionalization of oppositions within this extended family is abhorred, and traditions of this type, therefore, must provide non-divisive mechanisms for adjustment of the way in which the corporate sense of reality is symbolized when experience changes. This might take the form of permitting interruptions and alternative suggestions at the public recital of traditional myths, or by licensing the protests of certain individuals. The less that myth is the product of a single creative mind and the more it is the product of a process akin to corporate psychoanalysis, the more smoothly will it be owned by the whole tradition community and the less dramatic will be the experience of change.[1]

Some corporate aspects of religion have been introduced along the way and I summarize them here. They have included the development of a tradition and the roles of prophet, priest and pragmatist within that development, and also the variables which control a community's choice of paradigm. There are also consequences for corporate religion arising from what has been said about the individual aspects.

In general corporate religion must provide for:

    i) the individual needs of the members of the religious community,

    ii) the communal needs of the membership of the religious community and, insofar as that is distinguishable from a wider community, for

    iii) the needs of any wider community of which the religious community considers itself to be a part

    iv) the institutional aspects of the religious community itself.

I will summarize the corporate consequences of earlier material in relation to secular world affirming religion as I enlarge upon each of the above.

i) THE INDIVIDUAL NEEDS

The sense of belonging has three prerequisites:

    a) a felt sense of the ultimately-real and a minimal symbolization thereof,

    b) an adequate sense of self,

    c) the sense that these two are securely related,

and for this purpose that

---

[1] The process takes the communal form among the Vakavango of northern Namibia and southern Angola, which ensures smooth change. Traditionally it took an individual form at the Tswana Paramount's court where the oldest member of the community could send back a decision. (The Jester and the Prophet enjoyed a similar license.)

d) the whole religious system be authenticated to the individual adherent.

(a) and (b) include all that was said about becoming an ego - about acquiring the necessary experiences and an adequate symbol-set to ground identity, and about the development of the felt sense of reality and the integration of aggregations.[2] Ritual is the means by which (c) is achieved, expressed or repaired and is frequently a way in which (a) and (b) are developed or refreshed. All ritual which is not natural requires the authority of familiarity or an impressive institution and is strengthened by a logic of belonging. (c) also requires what Rümke called the ability to surrender.

ii) THE COMMUNAL NEEDS OF THE RELIGIOUS COMMUNITY

Corporate religion must provide a gathering, sifting, synthesizing, conserving activity in order that nothing of value in the experience of the community be lost and that it be made available to all. It must also establish a communal mode of engagement with the world-out-there, including a meta-value system within which competing interests in the wider world can be brought into a relative integration for community members.

iii) THE NEEDS OF THE WIDER COMMUNITY

Provision at the level of the community must include input into the mode of engagement of any wider community or communities of which the religious community feels itself to be a part. This would include some contribution to the higher level values which serve to unify the wider community's priorities. It might do this simply by recommending hegemony for its own values but, to the degree that it is not a reduced reality congregation, it must perceive itself to be making some offering at this level.

iv) THE INSTITUTIONAL ASPECTS OF THE RELIGIOUS COMMUNITY

Corporate religion must also provide for a self-understanding (ecclesiology) and all the consequences of desiring to be available to meet the previously mentioned needs in future generations, such as finance,

---

[2] It is not clear whether such an emphasis on integration is necessary in a non-linear world view. Chinese tradition, I am informed, finds little or no problem in having different religions for different aspects of life, but to the degree that a sense of cosmic belonging is maintained this may suppose a hidden meta-religion, providing a sense of the unity of all things, within which the overt religious systems operate.

physical plant, legal status, ways of training and authenticating its function-aries.

Before I begin to draw out further corporate consequences of understanding religion as belonging I must distinguish some different ways of viewing religion corporately.

THE THREE FACES OF CORPORATE RELIGION
- SOME PRELIMINARY DISTINCTIONS

There are three ways of viewing religion corporately, these are via:

I. *AGGREGATIONS SIGNIFICANT IN IDENTITY*

I have already dealt with these because, although they are indeed a corporate aspect, they are defined in and by the individual adherent.

II. *THE RELIGIOUS INSTITUTION*

The term "religious institution" I will use in its primary and limited sense to refer to those entities which are definable in external and public terms. Such bodies are usually self-defined in terms of membership or function. They include such things as constitutions, official texts and other relatively permanent symbolic representations, including habits of ritual; together with functionaries, and the infra-structure (physical, financial, legal and adminis-trative) intended to ensure the survival of the whole system. They will almost always have a membership, or if not, they will have a target group.

As I have defined religion, membership of an institution says nothing *per se* about the adherents' religious situation and not all the purposes served by a religious institution can be narrowly religious.

III. *THE TRADITION COMMUNITY*

I have already introduced and must now develop the term "tradition community". Tradition community relates most closely to what is generally spoken of as an -ism, for example, Judaism, Methodism, Jainism, but it is not easy to say precisely what these are. What for example, is Christianity, what and who should be included in it, what and who should be excluded from it?

In the short term a tradition community can be identified by the beliefs and practices generally held by its members, but in the longer term a tradi-tion community is not so easily delimited. Beliefs and practices change, and what was regarded as heretical in one generation may well be applauded as pioneering orthodoxy in the next. Like the membership itself, these things are transitory.

Nor can it easily be delimited by its allegiance to some basic key to the interpretation of life, that is, some text, person or event (for example, the Qur'an, Jesus, or Sinai), for this raises hermeneutical problems. There could be as many views of Jesus as there were original witnesses (to say nothing of the current faithful) and how many written accounts have not subtly changed their meaning.

Nor yet can it be delimited by the community otherwise defined, let us say by birth, for then the tradition itself could embrace everything and nothing.

There is some heuristic value in delimiting tradition communities in terms of logical consistency, that is, in relation to a paradigm and then by choices within the flexible consequential symbols. However, in dealing with living traditions, such a limitation can result in the exclusion of much that has been historically valued and is identity significant. For example, with these criteria in operation the Old Testament would surely be centered on the prophetic tradition, while much of the wisdom and apocalyptic traditions would have to be excluded as heretical.

A tradition community, while consisting at any point in time in its contemporary members, is best delimited by the processes going on within it, the processes that link the contemporary members, in their real life context, with their ongoing tradition. I exemplified such a process earlier by reference to the manner in which the Vakavango of Namibia created and constantly updated their communal myth.[3]

When, in another place, I discussed the development of a religious tradition of the Abrahamic type, I wrote of the creative interplay between a people's total experience and the concrete symbol, that is, the basic clue of the particular tradition, be it a book, person, or historic event.[4] I then wrote of the three roles necessary within the community for these processes to take place, labelling them prophet, priest and pragmatist. It must be said now that these roles might be established and filled without anything happening. It is, therefore, the processes, rather than the roles, that define a tradition community.

Within any tradition community there are processes at work which can take place either unconsciously, being naturally generated as people seek belonging; or consciously and therefore with a degree of organization and institutionalization. They must always be happening so long as the tradition community survives, even if episodically, but that is not to say that all within the community need to be aware of it. I begin discussion of these processes by returning to the three roles.

Within any vital religious tradition subject to socio-cultural change there

---

[3] See note 1 above.

[4] See chapter 3.

are roles being acted out. These are the roles of conserving, encapsulating and handing on the tradition (priest); of breaking its ideal essence out of old structures in the face of new challenges and attempts to compromise it (prophet); and the role of conserving the community without which there could be no adherents and no context for either priest or prophet (pragmatist).

The theological task is seldom considered to include the pragmatic role, for it can call for worldliness and compromise. Rather, theology subsumes the other two roles and then takes a stance over against the pragmatist. The role of the pragmatist ought not to be thought of as other than a contribution to the vitality of the religious tradition, for without it there might well be no community to bear a tradition. However, I am presently concerned to define a tradition community, not its champions.

The two roles other than the pragmatist, are of equivalent importance. Without the prophet there is no growth and without the priest there is nothing to grow. This polarity, and this is the point that I wish to make, partakes in another polarity which is present in every tradition whose adherents have become numerous and scattered across space and time.

This second polarity is that between what might be called contextualisation (I will be calling it "Incarnation" to stress its real individual, flesh and blood context) and the opposite of this, universalization (which I will call "Distillation", to stress the dependence of the process on the "mash" of human experience).

These two processes of gathering and redistributing the community's experience of living the tradition in context must always be present, for they delimit the tradition community. Where they do not exist there is no potential for continuity and, while there might be an abstracted tradition and even a community, there is no tradition community.

There is another pair of processes that must be present in all but the most logically coherent of dynamic tradition communities. This latter pair I will speak of as Bridging and Cleansing and will explain them later.

When one speaks of a tradition community, one speaks of individuals bound together by these two, or where necessary, four processes. The processes will almost certainly require some institutionalization of the tradition community itself, or the development of some institution or institutions within it.

THE THREE FACES ARE NOT MUTUALLY EXCLUSIVE

The three faces of corporate religion which I have just identified are neither mutually exclusive nor logically interrelatable for they are distinguished by unrelated criteria. Significant aggregations are determined in and by the individual; institutions are self-defining in external and public terms, they are what they are and do; while a tradition community is delimited by the processes going on within it and may then be named and tentatively described to distinguish it from others of its kind.

If it were said that the first face would be the primary concern of a psychologist and the second the primary concern of a sociologist, then the third face is the primary concern of any student of the corporate aspects of religion.

THE INTERRELATION OF THE THREE FACES

While sociologists could have criteria useful for their purposes for categorizing institutions as religious or secular, it would be a foolhardy student of religion who attempted such a categorization. All that one can do is to label institutions as religious when their members would regard them as such and they are therefore likely to be among the aggregations significant in identity.

One might adopt what seem to be less subjective criteria and define religious institutions as those institutions created or adopted by people espousing a religious tradition, so that the meeting of individual and corporate needs, particularly the overtly religious ones, might be better organized. Such a distinction, however, presumes to know when a tradition is religious without reference to the inner life of the individual and it serves little purpose in the study of religion.

An institution, any institution, may serve a religious purpose when it becomes an aggregation significant in the identity formation of a religious individual, or when it serves the processes essential within a tradition community. That is to say, an institution can only be said to be a religious institution when it relates to one of the other two faces.

Many tradition communities are closely related to a single identifiable institution, others embrace various institutions within themselves, for, to be what they are, they must have organized in some way for the continuity of both community and tradition. This requires some institutionalization if only the recognition of individual religious functionaries and the way in which they are validated. This validation may be no more than the recognition of the headship of a family, or simply age and a reputation for wisdom. It would, however, take something more substantial than these if all the processes mentioned above were to be facilitated in a secular world affirming context.

Because the processes of a tradition community may be episodic in operation, the question of whether a tradition community or sub-community exists (as distinct perhaps, from the episodic reemphasis of some feature of a wider culture) may reduce to a question concerning the existence of the necessary institutional arrangements for continuation of the processes.[5]

Aggregations significant in identity also have institutions associated with them, in fact many significant aggregations will have an institution as their principal external referent, that is, as the obvious public entity to which the individual relates. Nevertheless, the *aggregation* in every case, is the institution as it is *perceived* by the individual, not as it might be defined by others.

A tradition community is ill-suited to be an aggregation significant in identity, for its reality is a collection of processes and it is fluid. On the other hand, the members for the time being and the symbols that are the product at any point in time of the delimiting processes (including a name), as well as the institutions established to press forward these processes, can all become the external referents of an aggregation.

AN ILLUSTRATION OF THE IMPORTANCE OF DISTINGUISHING BETWEEN THE INSTITUTION AND THE TRADITION COMMUNITY

The study of religious movements has tended to follow existing institutional structures and to allow these to become descriptive categories. For example, when changes begin and remain contained within an existing religious institution, they would be spoken of as a reform movements. Such changes are distinguished from changes which begin within an existing religious institution but end up with a structure separated from the parent body. This would be spoken of as an independence movement. Finally, there are changes which seemingly begin *de novo*, without immediate connection with existing institutions, and are therefore described as new religious movements.

Such categories are far from being discrete. One can point to situations which would have to be classified as reform movements but which are to all intent and purposes independent churches continuing to exist within the old institutional shell. Similarly, there are seemingly independent churches which are only removed geographically from a parent church, and there are independent churches whose religious expression is so far removed from that of the supposed parent body as to be virtually new religious movements.

The term Independent Church is far from satisfactory. Where, for example, would one place that group of African Independent Churches which

---

[5] It is an interesting question, for example, whether Islamic fundamentalism represents a continuing sub-tradition community within Islam or whether there are symbols within the principal tradition which lend themselves to this manifestation when the context calls for it. If the former were true then one could expect greater deviance from the main tradition than if the latter were true.

in reality have two parent traditions? They can equally well be understood as new expressions of traditional African religion as they can of the Christian tradition. The nomenclature Independent *Church* masks this truth and the category *independent* expresses very little except a possible attitude of mind and a change in institutional structure, which can itself be misleading.

The very word independent means that the type is defined dependently. That is, we do not know what it is until we know from what more established or larger institution it is independent, be it ecclesiastical or secular. In fact no religious institution can be totally independent, any more than it can be totally spiritual in its interests. It must have material, economic and probably political concerns that link it with other institutions. Among these links is a process frequently at work between significant groupings within the wider society, whether religious or secular, namely the seeking of legitimation.

Any institution or movement which would survive or expand its influence must seek to align itself with the authoritative symbols of its context, or perhaps define itself over against such symbols, for these represent the life concerns of its members. As groups reach out, seeking the support of members of other groups, they will be seeking either to reinterpret or re-direct the existing symbols of such groups along their own interest lines, or be seeking to import their own symbols into those groups.

This exchange goes on all the time between different groupings to which individuals belong. To say where a symbol belongs within this interflow, and whether it is religious or political, is well nigh impossible unless one concentrates on what the symbol means to the different parties. Institutional structures are not the important factor, but rather what is happening within and between the inter-related tradition communities.

The label "new religious movement" is perhaps better than "independent church" but there are problems here also. For what is it that is new? There are new religious movements, which while discontinuous in time, really represent a reappearance in slightly different garb of long established traditions and which may even in time be reabsorbed into one of them. The fact that they may represent a new grouping of individuals, a new sub-structure within society, is not, in itself, of interest to the student of religion. There is always change. In a sense all religion is "new every morning". If the newness is suggested by an unusually high pace of change it would again not be of very great interest to the student of religion, although it might be to other social scientists.

It should be clear that if we would learn anything comparatively from reform movements, independent churches and new religious movements, then we ought to be working with the same variables throughout. To begin by separating movements on the basis of essentially non-religious factors must tend to defeat this *sine qua non* of comparative study.

In contrast, the present model offers a framework within which all varieties of religious change can be located. It does this both in terms of the specifically religious variables within the three paradigms generated by the central religious need to belong and in terms of the processes that delimit the tradition community. A summary of the questions that one might ask in locating a tradition community is included in the Appendix.

FURTHER CONSIDERATION OF THE THREE FACES

The greater part of this chapter will be taken up with a consideration of the processes at work in a tradition community and their consequences. Before I turn to that, however, there are some more things to be said about aggregations significant in identity and about institutions serving religious purposes.

I. *AGGREGATIONS SIGNIFICANT IN IDENTITY*

Two things remain to be said concerning aggregations significant in identity. The first has to do with the role of religion in the integration of aggregations in general, the second with possible hierarchies of religious aggregations and their inter-relation with secular aggregations.

These matters appear here, rather than in chapter 11, because they have implications for how the religious institution must organize itself to deal with other institutions. The religious institution cannot, of course, deal directly with aggregations, only with individuals and with other institutions. The importance of significant aggregations must be recognized and institutions must seek to be aware both of the institutions that are likely to become significant aggregations and of the individual adherent's perception of these institutions. What makes an institution into a significant aggregation cannot, as I said above, be other than how it is perceived by the individual.

RELIGION AND THE INTEGRATION OF AGGREGATIONS

In what follows the reader is referred back to the diagram in chapter 11 which combined a typical hierarchy of aggregations significant in identity with the pathways for belonging. I will be concerned here to show the role that religion must play in the integration of aggregations within this hierarchy as well of aggregations on the same level.

I begin by returning to the need described in chapter 11 to link the meaning of the individual's life to his or her sense of a movement toward a corporate destiny. I said that persons, for whom community and nation are significant aggregations, must be able to understand their own contribution to their community as being one to their nation, and their nation's contribution as being one to humankind, otherwise they must fail to see their own relation to God in terms of a coming kingdom. This requires some form of civil religion. The alternative is a sectarian or apocalyptic position in which the kingdom is understood to be in radical discontinuity from this present age. I must now say that the need for a civil religion is but a special case of the need for a theology at each level of aggregation.

The contribution of religion to the hierarchical integration of aggregations may in certain circumstances be a theodicy, but must certainly include an integrated theological understanding of each level of aggregation, otherwise in addition to the problems of a fragmented hierarchy dealt with earlier, the Divine, being perceived as schizophrenic, will be experienced as less than real. That is to say, the possession of integratable theologies of family and of humankind, of community and of the natural order, is as essential as having a civil religion.

Corporate religion's contribution to the compatibility of aggregations on the same level is equally important. By affirming membership of one unit in a group of units, I disclaim membership of the others. By saying that this is my family, community or nation, I say that others are not mine. However they remain part of my experience and must be explained, that is, I must know how to relate to them if my belonging is to be cosmic. Stated in the terms of the secular world affirming paradigm, I must see them all as God sees them.

Many such units which are not mine become mine at a higher level. Other families may be part of my community, or of those other communities which, together with my community, form a nation. Some, however, may remain outside all that I call mine and therefore my belonging will be less than cosmic. Theology, particularly theodicy, becomes the instrument by which one seeks to restore a cosmic sense, by accounting for that which is not mine even at the most ultimate level. It may in the end have to be seen as opposed by the divine. Most religion, therefore, manifests to some extent what I have called reduced reality belonging and it is perhaps timely to reiterate that this is a descriptive and not an evaluative title, save that it cannot be wished for as an ultimate goal.

Corporate religion's contribution to the compatibility of aggregations on the same level will need to be deliberate if it is to serve the individual adherent in his or her quest for a sense of belonging. The potentially competing goals of significant aggregations will need to be integrated, and to be seen to be integrated, as far as that is possible. Where it is not possible the competition needs to be rendered healthy, that is, it needs to offer opportunities for growth on both sides. There can be no inner sense of unity if loyalties to aggregations significant in one's identity tear one apart. It is here, of course, that the quest for justice enters. Justice is, above all, what makes it possible for loyalties to different aggregations to coexist.

To know what constitutes justice at one level, I have said, requires that we have an image of what the aggregation above ought to be. The desire to belong to the level above is what holds individuals or groupings in relation to each other even while they compete. Because for this purpose each level is dependent upon the level above, there can be no conceptualization of justice between the aspirations of aggregations on any one level unless the hierarchy of aggregations is itself integrated as far as it goes.

This returns me to the thought that, while the religious institution is inevitably one aggregation among others, its quest and its offering must include a meta-value system for the integration of aggregations in general. [6]

POSSIBLE HIERARCHIES OF OVERTLY RELIGIOUS AGGREGATIONS
AND THEIR RELATION TO OTHER AGGREGATIONS

One can, of course, have multiple hierarchies of aggregations significant in one's belonging. For many people a hierarchy of specifically religious aggregations exists alongside the sort of secular hierarchy that I exemplified earlier. These hierarchies could exist in complete isolation, but it is more likely that they will relate to each other at an appropriate level or even interlace at a number of levels. Religious and secular aggregations may virtually merge over a number of levels. In this regard the position of indirect belonging traditions is somewhat different from that of direct belonging traditions.

In direct cosmic belonging the local religious congregation may be one aggregation among the others which form the local community, or it may form part of a clear and largely separate religious hierarchy, or it may be part of an hierarchy that interlaces with the secular hierarchies. Thus particularly, but not only, in the case of a community with a single religious tradition the immediate religious collectivity may be virtually indistinguishable from the local community and, in addition, the denomination to which the local collectivity belongs may be perceived by its members to be a highly significant aggregation comprising the national aggregation. This was perhaps true for many in the Church of Scotland until quite recent times and indeed the national synod of the Church of Scotland still serves to express aspirations that elsewhere might be expressed through a parliament.

In indirect cosmic belonging, while the local congregation may again be indistinguishable from the local community,[7] or at least be seen to be a

---

[6] This in turn raises a question concerning the relation of world religions to one another and how one must view the various paradigms. The solidary aspects of religion are clearly divisive and compete with the unifying function, but on the other hand, a clear logic of belonging cannot be had in a mixed paradigm situation.

[7] Consider what contact with the institutional aspects of the church would be necessary

highly significant aggregation constituting it, in general the religious hierarchy will not interlace with the secular aggregations, but will interact with
them at every appropriate level.

Traditions which are "established", whether formally or informally, have
deliberately interlaced hierarchies. Thus religion and nation are symbolically
integrated for the British member of the Church of England, as are religion
and *volk* for the Afrikaner member of the Dutch Reformed Church. In
contrast would stand the Catholic or Jewish national of a largely Protestant
country, whose religious belonging stands apart from and even in some
conflict with the religiously identified state.

Thus indirect cosmic belonging can be dysfunctional in obtaining a
cosmic sense of belonging if both hierarchies of aggregations, the religious
and the secular, are acceptable to the individual but are themselves in some
conflict. It can be supportive of a cosmic sense of belonging in, for example, a
totally Catholic or Jewish community, or where the national level of
aggregation is weak or unacceptable as it is for certain minority groups. To
see the church as alternative community is to emphasize the importance of
the hierarchy of religious collectivities in one's sense of belonging. [8]

A few moments spent in considering the pathways in the adjacent
diagram may make these relationships clearer and will also enable me to
elaborate some further detail. The diagram reduces an almost infinite variety
of possibilities to some order but a grasp of its detail is not required for an
understanding of the rest of the chapter.

The pathways represented by the straight arrows without numbers or letters,
running up from "INDIVIDUAL" to "ULTIMATELY-REAL" are examples of the
most extended possible hierarchies. The one on the left is made up largely of
aggregations understood to be religious and the one on the right of
aggregations understood to be secular. The diagram is constructed to apply
particularly to direct cosmic belonging, while indirect cosmic belonging is
superimposed with a dotted line. I will deal with the latter first. The bridging
institution (here exemplified by "CHURCH"), is parallel to the levels

---

for someone in rural Spain or Italy to say meaningfully "I am a Catholic" and for the same to
be said in heterogeneous New York City. In the former the Church is an all pervasive quality
in the life of the community, whereas in the latter the Divine bridgehead is focused in a
building with functionaries and rites and in those who gather there. In order to support the
identities of its adherents in the latter situation the Church is pressed toward a sectarian stance
and away from catholicity.

[8] Because the sense of belonging is achieved only through membership of the group, with
even family and local community falling into insignificance, the sect in its extreme reduced
reality form is the ultimate alternative community. It could be said in this situation that there is
no other community significant enough to be an alternative to, which serves to emphasize that
a more orthodox understanding of alternative community would hold saviour and creator, and
therefore the religious and secular hierarchies of aggregations, in a more equitable balance.

"CHRISTIANS" or "DENOMINATION" in the basic diagram and there can be nothing significant above that level in the hierarchy before "ULTIMATELY-REAL". The secular hierarchy is not rejected and the institutional manifestation of the symbolic bridgehead might have a role in relation to nation, community of nations and to mankind (these are the indirect cosmic belonging equivalents of Paths Y and Z) but it could not be "as other nations" in this respect.

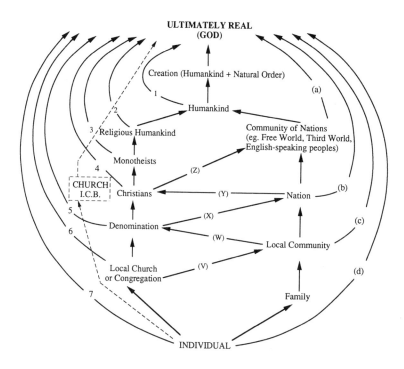

For adherents of an indirect belonging type of tradition, belonging via the secular hierarchy remains in parallel and does not intermesh, although it may seek to absorb the functions of the secular hierarchy.[9] In certain

---

[9] The State of Israel, to the extent that it is identified with the House of Israel or is

circumstances the local congregation, as well as being the immediate manifestation of the divine bridgehead, may also be a significant institution comprising the local community (the indirect belonging equivalent of Path V) and thence the nation.

In sectarian reduced reality belonging the individual belongs to his local congregation, which may or may not be associated with other congregations in a denomination, then that grouping belongs directly to God, all other pathways being irrelevant, the aggregations comprising them being understood to be under divine condemnation. Reduced reality belonging, therefore, is pathway 6 or perhaps 5, to the virtual exclusion of all else.

Path (7) coupled with the secular hierarchy is direct cosmic belonging. The religious hierarchy may or may not play a significant role in the sense of belonging. In pure direct belonging the rest of the religious hierarchy will be understood as institutions serving religious ends and relating to secular structures. If they contribute to the sense of belonging it is as part of the world-out-their and as such as part of identity. Most Christian denominations, however, are *de facto* mixed direct and indirect cosmic belonging, so that at least the lower three levels, that is, "LOCAL CONGREGATION" to "CHRISTIANS", will be significant for many as a symbolic manifestation of the bridgehead, in addition to whatever institutional significance they may have.

If (7) is the only significant path of belonging and is consciously religious we have mysticism or an extreme pietism. The equivalent form that is not consciously religious but is a sort of cosmic trust, I have represented by (d), for it is different to (7) in that the ultimately-real remains undefined. Path (d) differs from the end point of, say Buddhism, in that the secular hierarchy is also significant.

In a situation where there is but one religion in a community and particularly if it is also the established religion of the nation (formally or informally) then Path (W) may be significant. For example, the village, being indistinguishable from the local congregation, may be felt to belong equally to the wider Church and to the Nation.

Path (C) is only likely to be significant where a deliberate attempt has been made to create a utopian community, that is, to so control secular experience that it always renders plausible the religious tradition. Examples might be the early Mormon community, and some of those ultra orthodox Jewish communities which seem to have reduced the "House of Israel" virtually to their own community.

Path (5) or (4) can be significant without being sectarian, that is without rejecting the significance of the secular hierarchy, then they have become

---

understood as the long expected Zion, is an exception to this for those who are or feel themselves to be its own citizens, but it is a situation which engenders its own problems.

indirect cosmic belonging and the equivalent of the dotted line.

The link (X) can exist strongly where the religion is the religion of the nation, or of significant sections of it, or has been so historically, or where the adherent believes that it should be. It can be highly significant if coupled with Path (b) or, through community of nations, with Path (a). It is, of course, either religious nationalism, the belief that one belongs to a specially selected nation, or an elaborate civil religion. This special aggregation does not have to be a nation, it can be a race or language group or a group which perceives itself to be deprived or oppressed. Providence (e.g. liberation) theology may serve to create such an aggregation. It is a form of indirect cosmic belonging that has virtually absorbed the secular hierarchy. It frequently appears as a means of adding the corporate (kingdom) dimension to individual direct cosmic belonging.

This special aggregation may have an institutional manifestation, or when what is required is not security, solidarity or even purpose but rather the self-esteem provided by *gnosis*, it can be almost purely symbolic. To be British and therefore part of the English-speaking peoples and to believe in *pax Britannica* could be an example of the former type, while to adhere to the teachings of British Israel would be an example of the latter.

Path (4) coupled with a weak secular hierarchy and nothing above "CHRISTIANS" in the diagram, represents the "no salvation outside the church" position whether Jewish, Christian or Moslem. Path (3) likewise represents the position held by many liberal Moslems that all monotheists are acceptable to God. Path (2) represents the view that all religions are paths to God, while Path (1) distinguishes humankind from the rest of the finite creation in the sense of partaking in a special relation to the ultimately-real. It may do this, for example, by attributing immortal souls to them.

II. *THE RELIGIOUS INSTITUTION*

I will be considering later in this chapter and also in the next, processes which are required in the existence of the tradition community and processes that have traditionally found their home there, all of which have been facilitated by religious institutions. It will be suggested that humankind must now be involved in these processes overtly and self-consciously. This would require broader institutional form.

Earlier I summarized some of the things that the institution might be expected to provide in the individual's quest for belonging. It is in the area of ritual and the authentication of the whole religious system that the institution is least dispensable, but institutions recognized as religious have continued to be responsible for promoting all of the things mentioned above and there is clearly some advantage in having an institution with an overall concern for the individual's sense of belonging.

Nevertheless, one must ask, "Do all the various factors that contribute to the sense of belonging have to come from the same source and do they have to be integrated save in the individual?". Similarly one might ask of values beyond personal ethics, that is, of values for corporate engagement with the world-out-there, "Do they need to be integrated except in society at large?", that is, is a distinctive religious institution necessary? To this question I now turn.

It follows from the understanding of religion presented earlier, that:

> i) an institution, religious or otherwise, is not a *sine qua non* of a sense of belonging and therefore

> ii) the religious institution has no authority (of any religious significance) unless and until it has assisted the individual to a sense of belonging, or he or she has become convinced that it is the likely agent in a sense of belonging.

> iii) a religious institution could be antithetical to religion understood as the quest for a sense of cosmic belonging.

> iv) although the earlier statement about the factors necessary to a sense of belonging make it sound a very individual matter, such is not likely to be the case unless the individual exists in a social vacuum. The religious institution, therefore, if it is to fulfill its functions in relation to the individual, must also have functions directed toward the body corporate.

> v) the same institution would not necessarily have to be responsible for each of the three factors in belonging, the ultimately-real, the self and the ritual which relates them.

I will develop each of these points.

i) THE INSTITUTION IS NOT A *SINE QUA NON* OF A SENSE OF BELONGING

I indicated earlier, when discussing pre-paradigmatic and post-paradigmatic belonging, that it is possible to have a sense of relation with an ultimately-real without accepting an existing paradigm, or even without having sought to establish a paradigm of one's own and, of course, one can establish an identity without a recognizably religious paradigm for reality. It might not be optimum, but if one can manage without the structure of a paradigm one can certainly manage without the support of a religious institution.

ii) THE AUTHORITY OF AN INSTITUTION LIES IN
ITS POWER TO GENERATE A SENSE OF BELONGING

It has been said that theologians address various publics and in some cases this is undoubtedly the intent. No public, however, gives serious attention to an address unless the members of that public recognize an authority in what is said, or in the individual or institution addressing them. On the other hand, any individual or institution which succeeds in facilitating a sense of belonging has, potentially speaking, great authority.

It has come to be assumed that authority is somehow dependent upon relevance, relevance being understood in different ways in different contexts. Sometimes it means being involved with the rights and aspirations of those who regard themselves, or are regarded by others, as oppressed or deprived, that is, being involved with socio-political movements and with symbols such as peace and justice.

Sometimes a community can become so cause centered that it takes on a herd mentality, within which the members become impatient if they are dealt with as individuals. Then an authority will lie in enabling the group itself to have a more ultimate sense of belonging, but the group may be much shorter lived than the individuals that comprise it.

Sometimes the quest for authority means embracing the modern pluralistic world and endeavoring to touch all significant movements and avenues of enquiry. Religion then begins to look like an extension of the academic realm, in which it is the task of the institution to know everything happening in culture and society and to relate its adherents to it. There is a certain truth in this position and I will be returning to a concern with the whole of human experience and with ethics later in this chapter.

Nevertheless, relevance, certainly when that is understood as the opposite of concern for the inner needs of the individual adherent, is not where religious authority lies. Authority lies with the facilitation of a sense of belonging and, therefore, with the development of a coherent felt sense of reality, of identity, and with the bonding of these.

It may happen that the quest for relevance does lend some authority of the kind that facilitates belonging. If it does, it is because this primary need has not been otherwise sufficiently provided for, and because the process has aided adherents to integrate their sense of the ultimately-real, or to gain a better sense of their world-out-there and therefore of themselves, or has introduced an authentic area of ritual in which these two may be put together. In practice there is frequently an overlap between relevance and the power to generate a sense of belonging, but the priority must be right. Relevance, for its own sake, is not the same as a shift into what I called "path 3" belonging. The latter remains *sub specie aeternitatis*, precisely because the individual's belonging to the ultimately-real remains the priority.

One way of stating the difference is to say that what is offered by the institution must aim at ensuring that ritual (the putting together) succeeds and that the exercise is not simply one in social education or, worse, exhortation. The pressure upon functionaries to have members of their institution both be, and appear to be, relevant and on the side of the angels in relation to situations of social concern, can all too easily becomes counter productive of a sense of belonging. Ethical demands laid upon its membership by an institution which has not fulfilled the primary responsibility can only lead to a questioning of whatever authority the institution retains. Social concerns are relevant to the sense of the ultimately-real and to personal identity and it may be the case, therefore, that one cannot have a lively sense of belonging in socially problematic situations without a social concern. Nevertheless, one can have a social concern and seek to generate it in others, without having or generating a lively sense of belonging.

iii) THE INSTITUTION CAN BE ANTITHETICAL TO
A COSMIC SENSE OF BELONGING

The tension, between the need for and threat of the institution, is potentially present wherever religion exists in a social context. I have referred to the institutional needs of the tradition community and to the conflict in the roles of prophet, priest and pragmatist who serve these needs. This presents the problematic nature of the relationship between individual religion and the institution in its most complex form. The institutional needs I will return to, here I am concerned with the threat that the institution poses to religion understood as the individual's quest for a sense of cosmic belonging.

Religion of the individual spirit, that is religion as quest and perhaps as cosmic trust, need not always have the same form. It can flow into many appropriate forms as situations change, but it offers little external support or internal structure.

Religion of the institutional kind offers both structure and support. Belief, authenticated by the institution, offers both an internal frame and a mode of engagement with the world-out-there, while institutional ritual offers an authenticated link with the ultimately-real. Thus the institution can liberate the individual from a pressing concern with both identity and belonging and so provide a sense of freedom in relation to life in the here and now.

On the other hand, institutional religion can lead to a sense of pressure from the community. It can lead (returning to an image used earlier) to a sense of being gathered into the same castle with the draw-bridge up, into a fortress which once provided security but which, in a new situation, feels more like a prison.

In the end, the consciousness of belonging is an individual concern. Any institution, therefore, which represents a direct and individual style of belonging, should be constantly seeking to work itself out of a job in relation to its current members. Its purpose is to establish them in a relation with the ultimately-real and then to let them go. It would have to do this, of course, while gearing itself up to serve future generations. This, however, does not seem to happen. Rather the institution seems to operate in such a way as to embrace the greatest number, or otherwise to extend and maintain its influence.[10]

The religious institution's power to hold adherents lies in its provision for a number of their needs. It is therefore appropriate to examine the pros and cons of a number of these need-provision complexes which have the potential either to inhibit the individual's sense of belonging and to advance it.

a) "Plug-in Modules" for Identity

The institution offers a sort of "plug-in module" for the more ultimate aspects of identity, as well as a "spin off" contributing toward identity's more immediate aspects. Such modules may be the best with which busy people can allow themselves to become involved. Against this, it might be thought desirable that people should develop their own sense of reality and construct *de novo* their own symbol set to fit it. To do that, however, individuals would not only have to initiate and press forward the development of their own felt sense of reality, but also develop, or borrow and learn, a symbolic language, or at the very minimum, acquire ritual modes of expression having some existing authority. If symbols are to arise having any authority for the individual, let alone any ubiquity, the process cannot start anew in every individual and generation.

On the other hand, as things are, each institution has its own language, or at least its own dialect, and there is little attempt made to help individuals discover which is the best, or even to explore criteria for what that best might be. Even academia (which seems to be growing apart as each discipline develops its own language) remains more conscious of the need for its quest and its language to be universal than the overtly religious institution does.

In the best of all possible worlds the "plug-in module" of which I spoke, would encompass positive engagement with the whole range of aggregations likely to be significant for identity. In the worst possible world it would be an alternative, albeit shrunken, reality to belong to. This reduced reality thinking, an Israel within Israel, is a sort of formula for survival in times of chaos, but if it becomes the norm of an institution then people will flee it when times are more secure.

A danger, not only in the chaotic situation but throughout, is that it if the

---

[10] J M Yinger, *Religion in the Struggle for Power*, (North Carolina, Duke University Press, 1946).

habit of institutional reliance develops it can become the norm to grant easy acceptance to less than adequate "plug-in modules". If that happens, then, when some pressure for self-awareness develops or simply when the fashion changes, the institution will be perceived to have been inadequate.

b) "Kingdom" as a Model for Social Construction

African traditional society offers an example of resistance to institutionalization. Fluid groupings which gather around individual functionaries, serve the religious needs. As heirs to this stand the indigenous independent churches with their fluid multiple membership which, far from being sects, represent a protest against divisions between church and church and between sacred and secular. The preference for the one party state reflects this same resistance to institutionalized oppositions fragmenting a community understood to be an extended family.

In contrast to this stands secular world affirming religion with its corporate end-symbol "the kingdom", which functions as a model for social reconstruction. It is a symbol with an aura of permanence, but which is constantly being updated as to content.

Whether one has in mind simply the righteous society or also physical improvements, to seek the kingdom entails taking hold of the world and shaping it. It cannot be achieved by individuals, so it must be structured institutionally in what has been called solidary style, each group competing with the other to establish the kingdom of its own view. It is necessarily in some degree a conflict symbol and therefore a potential threat to individual belonging. This will be the case particularly when a long deprived community which has come to believe in an imminent "kingdom" within a strongly world-rejecting, reduced reality tradition, moves swiftly into a position of relative power. The symbol that was solely a means for satisfying, under adverse conditions, the drive for the maintenance of identity, may now become in addition a vision for satisfying politically, or even militarily, the drive for a physical and material "place in the sun".

c) The Individual and the Kingdom

I said earlier that in this paradigm individuals need to have a sense that their present relation to the divine and their present activity in the world are somehow integratable into the future corporate kingdom. For this purpose the present community which they serve must be conceptually related to the kingdom. There is, therefore, some pressure, not only to turn the nation state into a significant aggregation, but to give that aggregation institutional form. To the extent that the nation does become a religious institution the individual's sense of belonging is vulnerable to its continuing adequacy for that role.

iv) THE SENSE OF BELONGING AND SOCIAL EXISTENCE

Although it cannot be said that a recognizable and self-consciously religious institution is necessary to religion in general, some institutionalization seems to be required if individuals are to be a community. In fact it is difficult to see how, in normal circumstances, some institution could fail to exist. Any group of people sharing a religion automatically comprise an institution at some level. The tradition they adhere to, not only links them to the ultimately-real, but also influences their relation to each other and their world-out-there. Not only does the group inevitably lend authority to shared beliefs and practices, but it provides a means for adherents to locate themselves in immediate status and in ultimate significance. It may, of course, go far beyond this and provide for all sorts of material needs as well. Three ways in which social existence presses the quest for belonging toward institutionalization are indicated below.

a) The Need for a Corporate Symbol Set

In any paradigm, the individual, and certainly the social individual, needs symbols for reality. Without such symbols there is no way to conceptualize reality, to communicate about it, or to pass from feeling to action, whether that be for change (in the secular world affirming context) or for maintenance (in the nature religion context). That is to say, without symbols there is no possibility of dealing with values in a way that amounts to more than the expression of immediate preferences. Still less is there a possibility of arriving at anything like a common mind about value priorities. The more universal the quest for common values the less possible it becomes if one does not have adequate symbols for reality. One role for an institution, therefore, is the preservation, updating, elaboration, integration, communication and application, of a symbol set for reality, a corporate value language.

Whether humanity could ever arrive at one ubiquitous symbol set, that is, whether some single model of the ultimate is possible or conceivable, and whether it would be good for growth toward the best model of the ultimate to have only one symbol set in the penultimate situation, are questions beyond the scope of this book.

To have a symbol set is not simply to be aware of it, but to live it, that is, to have some level of commitment to it. As I have said, medical practice offers a model for this, namely, to operate firmly with what one knows at the time as though that were the truth of the matter, but always being alert to the outcome and to alternatives, so that one might be wiser the next time.

This commitment to a dynamic relation between the symbol set and the experience of the community requires some form of institution. For it is only an institution which can offer a communal statement on the role of the tradition community in the life of the individual, together with symbols for the development and maintenance of that community and of the community's relationship to other communities.

b) Social Critique

An ever unfolding vision, whether as a goal, or as a critique of the present, can hardly be provided by the whole community, for even in Marxist countries the Party has needed to be in some sense over against the State. The institution that offers the vision, however, may do it as from within the ranks of that which is criticized, emphasizing the critical role of the religious institution, or as clearly from the outside, which again establishes the religious institution as alternative community.

The extreme case of the religious institution operating from within is the established religion of a nation state mentioned earlier, whether establishment be *de jure* or *de facto* and whether it be Marxism or one of the overtly religious traditions of the Abrahamic family.

c) Other "Religious" Causes

Any cause that moves people has a religious overtone. At the extreme of experience war has a religious overtone. This is because a cause tends to integrate both the self and that upon which one's attention is focused. It tends to render the focus "neighborless and seamless". The relation between a religious institution and the wider community, therefore, can rarely be a clear one, there are always "causes".

Christianity, in Augustine's time, formalized a distinction between the spiritual and temporal authorities that went far beyond the ancient licence of the prophet. Judaism seems to have embraced the notion while in diaspora, but not yet to have integrated it into the religious tradition. Islam seems still to reject the notion. Either way, to be adherent and citizen is frequently to have loyalties divided between institutions, both of which are religiously significant if not overtly religious.

v) DIFFERENT INSTITUTIONS MIGHT PROVIDE FOR THE THREE FACTORS IN THE QUEST FOR BELONGING - THE ULTIMATELY REAL, THE SELF AND THE RITUAL LINK

It is clear that while religious institutions, as popularly understood, have been involved in all three aspects of belonging, they have not been the sole contributors, save, of course, where religion and life-worlds were coterminous.

If religion is about belonging, and if essential to that is how reality feels to and is conceived by the individual, then it follows that the universities, once overtly religious institutions, have never ceased to be centers of religion in this second aspect. For they have never ceased to be involved in asking about the nature of reality and certainly in shaping how people feel about it. Educators, as well as psychologists, consciously make an input to identity, and all sorts of movements, including the political, contribute to the mode of engagement. Even the ritualization of the relation between the self and reality is not wholly absent from the academic world.

Nevertheless, one supposes that the overtly religious institution will continue to be marked by its provision of ritual, including a theological concern with the logic of belonging. This would always be the case, of course, where the religious institution symbolizes the bridge institution in an indirect cosmic belonging tradition.

In summary it can be said that both the nature of the ultimately-real and of the self are intimately bound up with the nature of the real and with one's mode of engagement with it. These, in turn, are intimately bound up with one's society and culture. Therefore, although it cannot be said, even within the divided reality of the secular world affirming paradigm, that a recognizable and self-consciously religious institution is necessary, some form of institutionalization there must be, even though it may not be deliberate or even conscious, nor even recognizably religious as that is presently understood. I will return to these matters in the next chapter.

THE FORM OF THE RELIGIOUS INSTITUTION

Such institutionalization as does take place may happen in seeming spontaneity under the pressure of the drive to belong, or be the result of deliberate action. Either way it can take many forms. I begin with the membership aspect.

The institution may have an exclusive and clearly defined group of adherents who, as members, have a minimal relationship with the wider society. At the other extreme the institution may be coterminous with the society, or with some significant parts thereof. In between lies the institution that is a tradition community within a tradition community, in which the functionaries and enthusiasts shade off into members of the wider community. This sort of institution provides ritual opportunities, education in the tradition, including its ethical values, and a pool of possible symbols for all who wish to take advantage of them.

Then the institution may be perceived by its adherents as lying anywhere along what might be described as a spectrum from sacredness to secularity. It may be understood as an bridging institution of divine origin or election; as an outcropping into the here and now of what reality is or is to be (a foretaste of the kingdom); as a society in which individuals gain mutual support in their individual quest for the same goal; or simply as an unfortunate but necessary organizational adjunct to the individual's quest for belonging.

The significance of emphasizing these distinctions will become clearer when the processes that delimit the tradition community have been elaborated and the importance and authority of a "center" explained.

III. *THE TRADITION COMMUNITY*

Something to be avoided, is the tendency to deal with traditions as though they exist on their own, as though people come to them and leave them, as though they are abstract things comprising symbols and rituals. Symbols and prescribed rituals can exist in books but there are no traditions without adherents.

The symbols and rituals of a tradition can all change, whereas the community is continuous. The community, however, changes its members. What, therefore, identifies the community? Earlier I said it was certain processes and gave them a name, but I did not at that time describe them in any detail. To this I now turn.

Every dynamic tradition whose adherents are scattered far and wide needs a process which will:

i) prevent individual communities growing further apart in their understanding of the tradition,

ii) help sub-cultures to be constantly breaking down and reformulating their traditions ere they become fossilized and left behind,

iii) maintain mutual understanding and respect between adherents in different contexts

iv) enhance the creative power of the tradition by the distillation and integration of adherents' experience across time and space.

Thus the ligaments of the community are those processes which knit together the experience had in contemporary context with received beliefs, and the individual members of the moment with the tradition. Even these processes may change their form, but they cannot change their essential function if the community is to survive. Without these processes there is no tradition community and no living tradition. To focus on the symbols associated with a tradition is to miss the point. A tradition community can only be effectively delimited by the processes going on within it.

These processes may not operate continuously. In most developing traditions there will be periods of experience that provide a challenge to the existing orthodoxy and these will be followed by moments of recrystallization of the tradition. The processes will be smoother in non-literate cultures, for in these history "rolls on" as the recounting of the past unconsciously serves the purpose of communicating present values. In non-literate cultures, the updating of the tradition is unhampered by earlier crystallizations fixed in texts. Whether smooth or episodic, however, the processes will take place. In all but the logically purest traditions, these processes exist in two pairs.

THE TRADITION COMMUNITY PROCESSES

Incarnation and Distillation are the twin-processes that actually constitutes a tradition community out of the sub-communities that comprise it. Even the most monolithic tradition will have sub-communities, family units, for example, or even just responsive individuals.

Bridging and Cleansing are the twin-processes that must go on in any community with mixed paradigms (which most are) and perhaps also in communities where experience within a paradigm is unacceptable and a reaching outward has begun.

INCARNATION AND DISTILLATION

The published deliberations of the Vatican and the World Council of Churches are not renowned for their ability to "grab" the faithful in the pews. What is not always understood is that they would be failing in their purpose if the situation was otherwise.

Within every dynamic tradition there is a double process that moves between the poles of contextualisation and universalization. For the reasons given earlier, I labeled this incarnation and distillation.

Incarnation

If the beliefs of a tradition and its other symbolic forms, for example its art and music, are to participate significantly in the individual's sense of belonging then they must exist in what is sometimes called ideological form. That is to say, they must have an inevitable rightness about them which will depend upon their being enmeshed in the individual's own culture or sub-culture. In other words, their reality must be evidenced by some concrete aspect of the individual's experience. That concrete aspect must be sufficiently established for the individual to have forgotten that its existence, and certainly its interpretation, was as likely to have resulted from the idea enshrined in the symbol as vice versa.

Perhaps the simplest statement is to say that a symbol exists in ideological form when a culture would unconsciously socialize those growing up in it, into the belief that what the symbol represents is true, right or best.

The local expression of a tradition is in bondage to a pool of possible symbols, which have received their formulation under the pressure of particular needs, and in circumstances which established their ideological character. A tradition expressed in such a body of symbols serves to unite the local adherents, but, precisely to the extent that it is truly localized, it tends to be divisive between localities. It will also be limited in its growth to the possibilities of its own immediate situation.

Nevertheless, a tradition needs to be incarnated in a real flesh and blood context, and in the end in an individual existence, before it can be used, tested and refined in life, for only there can it grow in the pasture of experience.

If it were left like that however, growth in every community and indeed in every individual would be growth apart. In a tradition community it is not left like that. In a tradition community there is some form of center, something with which each concrete situation is in dialogue, ensuring that the experience is not lost and its interpretation is not divisive, but rather that the essence is distilled in the language of the center and integrated with all that has existed before. This is the other side of the double process. This is distillation.

Distillation

Distillation is the universalizing aspect of the process. It is the drawing out and the integration of the essence of each concrete development. Each experience needs to be understood for what it is in its own context, then the essence of that experience needs to be re-expressed in the symbols of the universal community and related systematically to other such symbolic expressions, whether of the present or of the past.

The process cannot stop there. If the universalized tradition is to mean anything in the local situation it must once again be incarnated.

Distillation enriches the content of the tradition and develops its creative power in human existence. Incarnation makes it relevant. A community that does not engage in both may be relevant, but creatively powerless, or potentially creative and irrelevant.

These two, incarnation and distillation, are directions of striving in a total ongoing process. They are not goals that are achievable once and for ever and they must take place whether the tradition is virtually pure in terms of the paradigms, or very mixed. I will come to the mixed situation shortly. In summary it can be said that:

the *task of incarnation* means taking the "universal truths" from the "timeless heart" of the tradition and making them meaningful and relevant, in some real context, at some point in time. It will include *inter alia*:-

i) translation into locally meaningful words and symbols.

ii) the establishment of rituals that enshrine in word, symbol and symbolic act, the logic of belonging, such that a sense of belonging is powerfully inculcated.

iii) the development of a mode of engagement with the world-out-there as it is perceived in the locality, expressed perhaps as attitudes of a divine being to locally specific possibilities.

iv) the theological integration *sub specie aeternitatis* of aggregations, both hierarchical and on the same level, that are significant in the adherents identities. This will call for integratable theologies of the person, the family, community, work, nation, etc..

the *task of distillation* involves, in its fullness, consideration of the experiences of all local incarnations and the drawing from them and expressing in an integratable language of the center their timeless, universal lessons concerning the nature of the ultimately-real, the mode of belonging thereto and whatever can be said, in the most general terms, about humankind's mode of engagement with each other and the world-out-there.

THE DISTILLATION CENTER

Distillation must take place around some sort of a center. This universalizing center needs to be seen as having authority because the universalized statement is not distilled from one experience only but ideally includes them all, and thus, in the process of its re-incarnation, can easily be felt to be alien in every particular locality. In a context rich with diversity of experience the center must inevitably be *contra mundum* in the process of integration, and will be experienced as such in many different worlds.

The center of a tradition community can take many forms, but a center there must be if the tradition is not to lose its creative power or its relevance. This center may take the very fixed form of founding documents and texts derived from succeeding moments of recrystallization. It may take the form of an actual or symbolic person also perhaps with crystallized utterances (pope or constitutional monarch), or it may be as flexible as that supposed ability of the common mind to know what is right which is to be found in the Common Law tradition. In the latter case, it is the developing tradition itself which is the center with which the concrete peripheral situations must maintain a dialogue. The functioning of this sort of center is facilitated by an agreed process for determining what the tradition is at any point in time, including, in this example, law reports, precedents and the jury system.

The periphery and center need not always be in dialogue directly, particularly after a period of stable experience. The history of European Judaism, for example, contains periods in which recent codifications of Rabbinic responsa functioned adequately as the *de facto* center, until major social disturbances created new experiences and drove the functioning center back towards its roots in Talmud and Torah.

As with the center, the processes also have taken different forms. In the Catholic world it has been possible to achieve two incarnations in the same locality where this was necessary. The Hierarchy has been able to identify with the needs and aspirations of the ruling group in some particular place, while an Order of Religious has, as it were, taken off its shoes and identified with the poor and the struggling. Such identification could be the more whole-hearted, because the relation of the Hierarchy and the Order at the local level could be little more than formal. This would always be possible because each feeds into, draws upon, and finds its deepest unity in the Vatican, and in an understanding of Papal authority, of tradition, and recently, of a revived manifestation of the conciliar nature of the Church. A center needs to be both symbolic and functional. Rome is the focus for both in the Catholic tradition.

The World Council of Churches has come to serve as a distillation center for many protestant denominations, although those in the pews, because they have not yet relaxed into the process, frequently find it irritating that the pronouncements of the Council have so little immediate relevance for their situation.

In the protestant world, before the need for a more deliberate ecumenism was felt, an understanding of the nature and role of the Bible served as the center, and it still does for many. This understanding, which is *mutatis mutandis*, that of the Jew for the Law of Moses, the Muslim for the Qur'an and the United States Supreme Court for the Constitution, is that all that is necessary for salvation is contained in the revered document, out of which new light and truth will continue to break as humankind in its concrete situation submits to its authority and enters into dialogue with it. Not all tradition communities are overtly religious but all are concerned with values.

In most cases, but particularly if change is rapid, if the dialogue with the periphery is to become actual, a center needs not only its central symbols but also its priests and its prophets, that is, its functionaries, for the two-way flow has to be both initiated and structured.

The center also needs to be trustworthy. This in turn means that if one aspect is fluid some other aspect needs to have a sense of permanence. In the

U.S.A., the Constitution and its interpreter the Supreme Court, supply this trustworthiness. Beyond them, those who service and those who administer justice seem to be free to be involved in political and free market processes to a degree that the British, for example, find staggering. On the other hand, trustworthiness in the British tradition (which has no written constitution) is provided for by the traditional norms concerned with guaranteeing and projecting the impartiality and incorruptibility of the servants and dispensers of justice, which to North Americans must seem incredibly stuffy.

Something has to lend an aura, so if the image of one aspect loosens up something else will tighten. It would be interesting to discover if American tolerance of the human failings of its lawyers and lower courts was greater in periods when the image of the Supreme Court was more conservative.

A study of what constitutes the center in Islam, which obviously functions well in spite of its seeming informality, could be very informative.

COMPLEX TRADITION COMMUNITIES

Neither traditions nor communities are as a rule monolithic. Even traditions, that are largely controlled by one paradigm operate at different levels, with the result that there are tradition communities within tradition communities, much like a child's set of nested barrels.

For example, in the Christian context, one might consciously belong at one and the same time, albeit with varying intensities, to different aggregations such as the local congregation, the district, the national church, the international communion, the protestant grouping, the Christian faith, the Abrahamic family of faiths and perhaps beyond. Each of these levels representing to some extent a distinct tradition community, with its own adherents and the three roles to be fulfilled, while each level is also subsumed into the levels above.

At every level save the extremes therefore, theology, while tending in particular situations to do one or the other, must participate in the whole incarnation-distillation process. Even the local level must make itself available to the distilling process, while the universal level must keep an eye on the need for re-incarnation of its handiwork.

The World Council of Churches, as a center of the Protestant tradition seeking a greater level of universality, is inevitably concerned with distillation, while African theology, for example, is clearly incarnational, for it is directed to a particular people, in a particular context at a particular time. On the other hand African theology includes an attempt to universalize the many forms of African Christianity, indeed of the whole African religious experience. To the extent that it succeeds, it will make these available to the distillation process at the level above.

Complexity lies not only in the community, it can also lie in the tradition.

I have assumed until now that the tradition community works within a single dominant paradigm, but tradition communities are not usually so well defined, or so simple. They can embrace a mix of paradigms, or a single paradigm tradition can, under pressure, reach out toward one of the others. Beyond simply living with it, there are three ways of coping with such divergence, I will call them containment, allocation and bridging.

CONTAINMENT

Containment is the encapsulation of intruding elements of an alien world, which would otherwise threaten a community's sense of reality, within symbolic and ritual sub-sets of the home tradition. The capacity of different traditions to encapsulate different types of incoming material will vary greatly, as the example to be given shortly will make illustrate. Clearly, it is related to manifestations of what others have called the "transformative capacity" of a tradition operating at low levels of disturbance.[11]

It general it can be assumed that "containment" will take place most satisfactorily in a strongly integrated tradition community, in which a wide range of significant aggregations is effectively held together, and where appropriate institutionalization already exists.

In chapter 9 I considered some levels of disturbance, identifiable in terms of what was likely to be happening within them in order that the sense of belonging might be maintained. Containment would be an appropriate ploy, if the amount of foreign symbolic material admitted to the system were small, in the protective and search stages and, of course, in the integrative stage in situations where conversion to the incoming tradition had not taken place. If the amount of foreign material were more substantial then allocation or bridging would be called for. Containment would not be appropriate in the paradoxical stage.

In a situation where the threatening tradition was not actively pressing, but simply luring individuals away, containment could remain the sole ploy (beyond treating incoming elements of the foreign tradition and those who embrace them as deviant) for a considerable period of time. All established traditions will have methods for the containment of frequently experienced lower level threats to world-view. Containment can take different forms according to the perceived permanence, benefits and scale of the elements that would otherwise threaten the world-view. This is best illustrated by reference to a particular situation.

In Southern Africa, as elsewhere, the individualism of the urban

---

[11] For transformative capacities see Eisenstadt's generalization of Weber's Protestant Ethic thesis in his *The Protestant Ethic and Modernization*, (New York, Basic Books, 1968) p.9f. See also his reference to Gershom Scholem's earlier work with this concept.

industrial situation has been both a continuing lure and a threat to traditional rural communities. The community's first line of defence would be to treat involvement in the urban situation as it would any other deviant behavior. When the necessity or advantage of being involved in the industrial sphere had been recognized, however, an individual's choice to be so involved could no longer be treated as deviant behavior. It might still be possible to see it as undesirable and to hope that it would be temporary, it might then be *contained* within the sub-set of symbolic understanding and ritual behavior associated with war - dangerous, necessary and hopefully *ad hoc*, calling for strengthening and protection beforehand, purification and rejoicing when a warrior returns, hopefully with spoils.

If involvement is seen as longer term and of continuing benefit, then it could be included in the symbol and ritual sub-set associated with the hunt, even the long duration elephant hunt, should these be available in the experience of the community; or, in certain areas and frequently associated with river travel, there are sub-sets associated with trading journeys. All these are dangerous aspects of life, but permanently undertaken and advantageous. For a pastoral community, without such experiences, war might have to remain the containing sub-set, but transformed into a more permanent militarism, in which many or all of the young men will be expected to participate. Becoming a migrant worker could now be encapsulated within the rite of passage of becoming a hunter, a journeying trader, or a warrior, a step beyond that of simply becoming an adult.

When many have experienced the urban industrial world and perhaps also received education at the hands of those with the city's world-view, the scale of the problem is enlarged. Now there needs to be symbolic and ritual spaces where involvement in that individualistic world is legitimated in its own right, rather than as hunting or trading. One needs a "plug-in module" from that other world (or one that will serve the same purpose) legitimating individual initiative, but in such a way that the overall communal world view is not threatened. It might be a call for individual effort to speed the coming of a not too distant Kingdom or a Classless Society, but in some way it would have to be the restoration of true community.

In the urban areas, independent churches provide many of the social and welfare aspects of life that are essential characteristics of the traditional community, whereas in the rural situation these churches provide containment. A unit of the alien world-view which supports individual initiative is taken over and domesticated as far as possible without destroying that quality, so that it might be directed to bringing about an imminent return to ideal conditions. Containment might, of course, be required in the urban situation also, depending on to what extent the membership's dominant world-view is still the traditional one.

If one were looking for evidence of containment within these churches, one would be looking for apocalyptic language that stressed the proximity of the Kingdom and true community, rather than divine power or the inversion of present power relations, or anything else that might lead to quietism rather than to individual initiative. In this situation the emphasis would not, as in the paradoxical stage, be world rejection, but rather the containment of a linear time, goal oriented module within an immediate experience affirming, communal world-view and ritual.

When the "plugged-in modules" begin to flow together, that is, when the scale of influence of the incoming culture enlarges to the point where there are simply two world-views in competition with each other, then the need is for allocation, or more likely, for bridging. This last might also begin in the independent church, but the need for greater influence and therefore for unity in approach and also for continuity, is likely to move the independents toward integration, or move their members toward the mainline style of church.

ALLOCATION

Allocation is one of two processes that may take place when two or more traditions exist side by side in the same community. Traditions can come to co-exist in the same community in a great variety of ways, but whatever the origins of the traditions, all sub-groups may in time come to accept substantial elements of each tradition. These elements may coexist in an uneasy tension, or they may somehow be allocated to their own life space. If that is the case, then people come to inhabit multiple worlds on a more or less permanent basis. Alternatively the traditions may be bridged, as I will explain shortly.

Allocation may be just a *modus vivendi* but it suggests that there exists at least the sense of a whole, in which the different frames of social existence participate. For example, one tradition may come to serve the need to belong to the wider community, while another serves the needs of family and local community, still another may serve the needs of production and other forms of work. This is not a case of élite and folk religions which are adhered to by different strata in the same society, but rather a single people who adhere to different traditions in different compartments of life. Such a situation may, of course, be the result of an élite and a folk religion having come together.

The religion of Europe is still in many areas a mixture of an élite form of Christianity shaped by monarchs, monks and the younger sons of great houses and the "superstitions" of the masses. All might dutifully go to church on Sundays and for the major life events, but maintain their sense of immediate group belonging, as well as the sense of a hidden dimension in everyday life by, for example, not putting shoes on a table, or by not setting sail or uttering the word "pig" on a Friday. This divide within a shared religion goes back into antiquity.

In Mesopotamia it was the custom to owe allegiance not only to the high gods at the level of the state, that is the gods to whom the king would relate in the great national rituals, but also to covenant with a god at the level of one's own concerns. Thus, they would covenant with the gods of agriculture, crafts, fertility and health, in much the same way as a Catholic might develop a devotion for a particular saint beyond simply calling upon an appropriate one in times of special need.

Such a situation is not only the result of living in different social or economic worlds but represents the ongoing human condition of having needs at very different levels. It is, as was said earlier, a matter of scale. When personal insecurity is the result of national insecurity, one needs a god with "the whole world in his hand". When a child is sick, such a god may be altogether too grand and remote and his concern for the problem less than credible. Then comes the need for a more immediate agency whose concern would be credible. The large scale needs tend to integrate the powers-that-be, everyday needs to divide them, while devotional needs can tend either way.

I have been considering overtly religious traditions in potential conflict with one another. It is important, however, to remember that not only recognizable religious traditions, but each aggregation significant for the individual's identity, will have, in Durkheim's sense, a religion. I have said something about reconciliation of these in the same paradigm, but, where the dominant traditions in a community are mixed, the value systems of the aggregations may also be dependent on different paradigms and be potentially in conflict.

Integration beyond that of allocation appears to be unnecessary in a non-linear world view since there is a presumption of unity in the background. Chinese tradition, I am informed, has had little or no problem in embracing different religions for different aspects of life, but this may suppose a hidden meta-religion in which time is non-linear and which is sufficiently dominant to maintain the sense of unity and thus a sense of belonging.

In a goal oriented community, however, competing traditions need to be held together or they will tear their adherents apart. The more goal oriented and dynamic a community is, the less will allocation serve to hold together diverse traditions. If individual and corporate identity is to be possible, if life-worlds are to feel coherent and community values to be reasonably integratable, ways must be found to bridge the competing logical systems.

BRIDGING

In all dynamic situations where traditions of different types or sub-types exist together the development of bridging myths, or alternatively the embracing of bridging symbols, becomes the appropriate means of integration. If a relatively integrated tradition includes elements from more than one paradigmatic type then it will also include this additional type of symbol, holding together, as well as can be, the irreconcilable elements.

I considered earlier the importance of both an integrated sense of self and a clear logic of belonging for the individual's sense of belonging. Perhaps the most widespread evidence for these needs lies in the bridging which takes place when a clear logic is not otherwise available. Without bridging there can be no sense of belonging.

While scholars can speculate on the importance of a common mind and the freedom that it gave to the body corporate in the development of the West, the degree to which the corporate mind is indeed common in Third World situations is an immediate and pressing problem.[12] Without effective bridging, a mixed tradition cannot give rise to a clear and relatively unambiguous communal mode of engagement, let alone the details of corporate priorities.

There has always been bridging between incoming and indigenous religions and between élite and folk religions. There was bridging on the grand scale between Athens and Jerusalem, then between Christianity in Neo-Platonic garb and resurgent Aristotelianism and, in our time, there is bridging between western Christianity and the world-view of Africa. [13] [14]

---

[12]   This is an element in the interface of Calvinism and capitalism and indeed in the development of the U.S.A. before pluralism "rescued", from a relatively monochrome value system, those individuals who had come to regard it as a straitjacket.

[13]   There are affinities between Plato and some Hindu thought. I think this to be the case because they were both moving in a world-view in which nature religion and withdrawal religion were bridged. I will return to the case of Hinduism, but I would like to consider the situation of early Christianity seeking, insofar as it remained in the Hebrew world view, to co-exist in the Hellenistic world, and choosing to operate in a neo-platonic world-view.

Platonic thought, as I said, might be considered to have been nature religion bridged with withdrawal religion, and although there were divides within its universe it remained essentially monistic.

Christian thought was predominantly secular world affirming with some harking back to nature religion in the Wisdom tradition and a tentative reaching out toward withdrawal religion in the Apocalyptic tradition.

Platonic thought was idealist, it found reality in ideas, in the universal "forms", rather than in the experience of particular concrete things. As such it had affinities with any tradition in which the source of religious knowledge had to be revelation. The universal forms would not seem conceptually far removed from ideas in the mind of a transcendent, providential divinity. In fact, however, they are very far removed.

Philosophy, insofar as it is a quest to understand all things in relation to each other and to the whole, must itself operate within a monistic universe, that is, within a single space-time continuum. Dualistic reality limits the philosophical enterprise to the realm of the real, the ultimately-real being transcendent is quite other than the real. Insofar as one supposes oneself to have thought a path across the transcendence gap, one has reduced the significance of

Thus in any mixed tradition where insecurity has been experienced, certainly in the indigenous responses to incoming traditions, one would expect to find:

i) elements that belong to logically coherent systems and are non-negotiable in relation to the other systems

ii) bridging elements.

Analysis of living traditions needs to look for each of these elements.[15]

Such mixed traditions, while not providing the most secure sense of belonging, may have "transformative capacity" to a greater degree, for they are essentially less stable and already have resources for coping with divergence. [16]

---

transcendence in the model and, to the extent that one has succeeded, the paradigm in operation has become one of the other two.

The whole bridging process between Christian and Hellenistic thought, therefore, was not only a dance between all three paradigms, but also a dance between the philosophical quest for understanding of the ultimate and that which is incompatible with it, namely, the affirmation of transcendence. Real awareness of that incompatibility had to await the outworking, in the later Middle Ages, of a dramatic incursion by the philosophy of Aristotle into Christianity's relatively well adjusted co-habitation with Neo-Platonism in the 13th. century.

The direction of Aristotle's philosophy was from the experience of concrete particulars upwards. It, as it were, invited one to go on to an ever-receding boundary. It did not begin at a seeming boundary in the realm of ideal forms that could be "fudged" over the transcendence gap.

If one accepts that much of the Christian literary deposit that Thomas Aquinas was heir to, was bridging material between the two already internally bridged traditions of Hellenism and Hebrew Christianity, then Aquinas' mammoth effort was directed to the re-bridging of what these had become. This he had to do within the framework of Aristotel, wherever, and insofar as, the latter had destroyed the credibility of the Neo-Platonic.

[14] For African bridging theology in action see Gabriel M. Setiloane, *African Theology: An Introduction*. (Johannesburg, Skotaville, 1986)

[15] Consider, for example, movements which developed in India in response to the secular world affirming paradigm during the European presence there. One would expect them to have elements drawn from all three types and bridging symbols intended to hold them in some sort of unity. Clearly there would be pre-existing bridging symbols holding the earlier nature religion and the élite withdrawal religion together, and then bridging symbols between this complex and the incoming secular world affirming system. Bridging symbols might also develop directly between key nature religion and withdrawal religion symbols and the secular world affirming symbols.

[16] See note 11 above .

Where two traditions exist together on a more or less permanent basis, what I have called bridging symbols will themselves become elaborated and integrated into what might be called a bridging tradition. To be Jewish and American has required symbols for "Jewish-American-ness", particularly in recent decades when Jewish Americans have had to respond as both Americans and Jews, to media reports of events in Israel. With such symbols in existence, if the American Jew feels torn apart at least he or she feels part of a similarly affected group. Just how strong and integrated a tradition this is, and how strong similar traditions in other nation states can be, is evidenced by the difficulty Jews, who move from one country to another, have in feeling at home, not only in the country concerned, but in its Jewish community. It is further evidenced by the readiness with which Jewish emigrants from the same background associate in their new country even where language is not an issue.[17]

Forms of Bridging Symbol

Bridging symbol can take many different forms. It can be a story, probably independent of the traditions that are competing, that is strongly integrated in itself and in which elements of old and incoming traditions are firmly woven together. The King Arthur cycle is of this type linking the older world-view with the Christian one. Bridging symbol can also be a vaguely defined mystical or historical entity such as "Ethiopia" or Presta John, linking Christianity and the Black experience. It can be a charismatic individual, present or past, linked in some way to the adherents and to both traditions, such as Ma-Redebe the faith-healer of the Transkei, or Ntsikana the Black Xhosa prophet.[18] It can, in the short term anyway, be some powerfully emotional or habitually established ritual or ritual figure, or even a powerful argument (e.g. theodicy) directed to the affective linking of elements that do not logically belong together. It can be a symbol taken from one tradition and reinterpreted to conform to the other, for example, the shift from the Jesus

---

[17] Bridging traditions are not, of course, large scale phenomena only. Traditions, frequently with elaborate initiation ceremonies, developed in university colleges and such like small scale situations, have long served to hold together newcomers from diverse backgrounds. These traditions have to die and be reborn, or at least to go through traumatic changes, when the diversity of background suddenly increases to include strong but previously unrepresented traditions.

[18] See Janet Hodgson, "The Faith-Healer of Cancele", *Religion in Southern Africa vol 4 no 1.* and her "Ntsikana - Precursor of Independency?" in *Missionalia vol 12 no 1.*

of history to an all pervasive Christ spirit, conformable to both Buddhism and the traditions of Africa.[19] This last sort will be less obviously bridging symbol for it functions precisely by denying that there is a real gulf to be bridged.

CLEANSING

Cleansing means discarding (or storing away against future need) bridging symbols that no longer function for that purpose and therefore do not seem to belong (perhaps in retrospect may seem never to have belonged) to the tradition.

When the situation has moved on and new bridges are required, the old bridging symbols become so much "unnecessary baggage" needing to be cleaned out. If they are not cleaned out they can become a source of confusion and division, or become places to hide for the insecure and retrogressive. To retain such symbols, as seemingly significant for the living tradition, could only inhibit clarity in the logic of belonging and coherence in any associated ethic.

In the past, bridging was not thought of in these terms, the symbols employed were not always as flexible as they might have been, and deliberate cleansing of the erstwhile sacred has never been easy. This brings me to a special problem and to the issue of responsibility in the exercise of bridging theology.

Responsible Bridging

There is a sense in which the symbols of the logically coherent types can almost be left to look after themselves. Bridging symbols, however, given the context in which they exist, are probably going to be temporary. When introduced they must grasp the adherents of the mixed tradition and, if they do this successfully, they will become significant in identity formation. How then shall people be persuaded to give them up when there is no longer need for them?

Because a community may well need to be weaned from them, and because some symbols are more flexible than others, bridging symbols need to be created and offered responsibly to the community. Optimally, bridging symbols should be such as allow change to take place smoothly and then fall into the background when they are no longer needed.

Bridging symbols tend to become fixed in a community if they take doctrinal form, or if they become the "flags" around which a movement of

---

[19] In the extreme, a charismatic figure may be all that is left to symbolize belonging, in which case his or her failures may, in adding to the chaos, actually increase the number and intensity of the adherents. See, for example, Janet Hodgson's two part article on Nxele, *Religion in Southern Africa vols 6:2 and 7:1.*

socio-political or economic liberation gathers, for then they become rooted in identity and long afterwards cannot be surrendered easily. The more flexible forms of bridging symbol are myths (stories not doctrine), histories and living individuals who, even after their deaths, may be the source of a fluid, developing tradition. Such symbols are easier to reinterpret or set aside as the need arises. [20]

Thus the process of bridging and cleansing implies a number of things for the theological venture. There is need to distinguish clearly between the task of drawing out and clarifying the implications of a particular tradition which may or may not be logically coherent, and that of providing the bridging myths and alternative symbolic interpretations necessary in times of transition or merging. There is also the task of discarding or returning to storage all such symbols once they have served their purpose. Finally there is the need to be alert to hidden consequences, among the pressures and the enthusiasm for bridging.

It is important to be aware that, in the last resort, bridging is logically impossible, and that a clear logic of belonging and a fully coherent ethic are only possible within a single paradigm. Thus bridging is always logically deceptive and it can, without appearing to do so, destroy important elements in a tradition. To take the historic Jesus, for example, and to turn him into an immanent cosmic christ, or even into the universal suffering man, so as to fit a monistic world-view may have affective appeal, but it destroys meaning in the symbol of incarnation. In a monistic world-view incarnation makes no sense, but in the secular world affirming paradigm it is this symbol which forges an eternal bridge between the real and the ultimately-real and does it without divinizing the real. This watering down of the symbol of incarnation could be a desired consequence, but one must be aware that it is a consequence.

Bridging as Outreach

Bridging, as it has been presented, supposes strong traditions rooted in two or more paradigms within the same community. It does not have to be like that. It can begin as a reaching out from within a tradition which has been firmly entrenched in a single paradigm, but where something is felt to

---

[20] It will be clear that bridging symbols which take verbal form in creed or confession are likely to be very inflexible, while those which center on the activities of a charismatic person, or on the understanding of the life of an historical figure, will be open to a variety of interpretations and therefore be more flexible.

The tradition stemming from Ntsikana shows tremendous flexibility. See Janet Hodgson, "The Symbolic Entry Point", in G C Oosthuizen (ed), *Religion Alive*, (Johannesburg, Hodder and Stoughton, 1986).

be missing or where life experience is unacceptable.

In chapter 11, I attributed the mixing of beliefs concerning resurrection with those concerning immortal souls to the desire to overcome not-yet-ness in the individual while retaining it in the environment at large. It is a stealing of attractive symbols from an otherwise undesirable paradigm. It must give rise to bridging, albeit in a partial form, in order to hold the disparate elements together. By bridging as outreach, however, I have something more elaborate in mind.

In a situation where the existing dominant paradigm or paradigms no longer feel real, and where the experience of the community puts it under the sort of pressure that would move it towards one of the other paradigms if the community were familiar with it, then bridging may take place. In this case, however, it will not be bridging between two known paradigms, but rather an outreach from the existing tradition toward a model of reality that is as yet unknown.

In situations of this type one would expect an intense threshing around for a way to deal with the unacceptable quality of life and the resulting picture to be complex and difficult to interpret. The following illustrations, however, seem to be clear manifestations of bridging as outreach.

One way of understanding developed Hinduism (in which, in the midst of an experience that is of the transitory the *atman* retained permanence, and in which all experience is *maya* yet the solution proposed had a considerable cognitive component) is that it is a bridge from nature religion toward withdrawal religion. When the full logic of the latter appeared in Buddhism, there was a partial backlash to the outreach because a major threat to withdrawal religion is that the world should feel good again. Thus Buddhism had either to withdraw from the world in the ascetic sense, (Theraveda) or do its own bridging back toward the world affirmation of nature religion (Mahayana).[21]

It cannot be said that Japan did not know of secular world affirming

---

[21] Once bridging-out has begun, insecurity will press a tradition toward as clear a logic of belonging as may be established, in this case toward the pure withdrawal religion paradigm. On the other hand a clear logic of belonging can be very demanding in its clarity, and once the sense of insecurity subsides there is likely to be a swing back. One sees these swings not only between paradigms but also, for example in secular world affirming traditions, between the direct cosmic and indirect cosmic modes of belonging that I exemplified earlier, and even between demand and acceptance in the divine character, either of which provides a clearer logic than some uncertain balance between them. Not only the Protestant reformation but also Islam, in their pristine condition, might be understood as a swing to a logical but demanding clarity in the secular world affirming paradigm which was to receive some tempering in times of relative security.

traditions, but they almost certainly had unacceptable associations. Therefore, when a creative rather than an imitative technology came to dominate Japanese society, and it became a personal commitment to take hold of the environment and shape it, instead of individuals moving in any number to the known but foreign forms, new religious movements developed. Many of these new movements, while taking off from within the older traditions, clearly reach out toward the secular world affirming paradigm.

RELATIONSHIPS BETWEEN THE TRADITION COMMUNITY PROCESSES
- THE TASKS OF THE COMMUNITY

Incarnation and distillation must take place whether a tradition is pure or has mixed paradigms. In a mixed tradition bridging theology will need to be involved in both incarnation and distillation. Clearly bridging and incarnation have a strong affinity, for they are both concerned for the present needs of individuals and for communities in their own particular context.

In a mixed situation, distillation must necessarily be concerned with whatever bridging has taken place in order to render the most effective bridging symbols ever more ubiquitous, for the more powerful a bridging symbol is at the local level, the more potentially divisive it is between localities. Nevertheless, distillation ought to be concerned less with the immediate needs of individuals and more with the tradition in itself and therefore with cleansing, with the need to discern what are the non-negotiables of each paradigm and what, therefore, are the currently significant bridging symbols.

The task of the theologian, or equivalent religious functionary, in a local mixed tradition situation, is first to seek to create or maintain in individual adherents a sense of belonging to whatever they feel to be the ultimately-real. The second is to guide, draw out and reconcile to as common a mind as can be achieved, the values necessary in corporate existence. These tasks will require bridging and cleansing activities in relation to:

the nature of the ultimately-real

the mode of belonging

the identity of the individual and the community

the corresponding modes of engagement with the world-out-there

the ritual whereby the sense of individual belonging and the community values are created and reinforced

In order that each of these tasks might be fulfilled adequately those engaged in the theological bridging exercise must:

receive what is offered from the more universal level of both traditions seek to incarnate these received truths

assist in the process of bridging

seek to distill a bridged theology

make that bridged theology available to be distilled at the more universal level

PARADIGM SHIFTS AND THE DEVELOPMENT, CHALLENGE
AND RECRYSTALLIZATION OF A TRADITION

The process of incarnation and distillation may be likened to "place", that is, they are about a center and a periphery, about the relationship between the hub of a tradition and the outposts where sub-traditions are hammered out in the real world. It is, as it were, the continual expansion and contraction of the tradition, its heart beat, and it can be organized and institutionalized, but within this process there is another. This second process has to do with "time", that is, with periods of time (chronos) but more, with moments *in* time (kairos), and with ways of seeing.

When we looked at individual religion we considered the relationship between experience, the felt sense of reality and the symbolization of reality. The symbolization of reality takes place in paradigms, sometimes uneasily mixed, and in sub-paradigms. As experience moves on, so the felt sense of reality shifts and the symbolized reality adjusts to take account of it.

Within a given way of seeing, however, one can only shift so far. After that, one is pressing the edges, or making all sorts of unnatural contortions within it, in order to give an account of experience and how one feels in relation to it. The paradigms or sub-paradigms are then ready to shift, waiting only for the opportunity and the trigger.

An individual's "way of seeing" at this level does not change easily and therefore smoothly. Identity investments are too strong for that to be the case. Rather, the pressure on the old way builds up until, when it finally comes, the change takes place by "rupture and rapture" rather than by growth.

What is true of the individual is true of the tradition community, save that the community is more conservative than the individuals that comprise it, for corporate change requires that all must change or nothing changes. When change does take place it is the sort of societal experience that creates widespread anomie or alienation and such phenomena as the generation gap.

The tradition is the spectacles, through which the community views what is happening to it. It shapes both the fact and valuation filters through which the community's experience is received. After a time, it may happen that the tradition can no longer contain the experience which has been received through those lenses. Then the situation becomes like a super-saturated solution awaiting a little more salt or some speck of dust; poised, until some trigger initiates precipitation into new crystal forms. With its re-formed spectacles the community enters upon its next era of experience and perhaps upon reviewing its past.

It is possible to discern in the biblical period, for example, four such major periods of experience, followed by moments of re-crystallization, viz. the centuries of migration that led up to Sinai, the heroic period that climaxed with David and Solomon, the national decline and prophetic re-think that ended in Babylon, and the attempted reconstruction under near continuous domination that ended with the fall of Jerusalem. Each period ended in a recrystallization of the tradition. The last period ended with two, the one Rabbinic, the other Christian, but the process did not stop there.

This process, by its very nature, is not easily institutionalized. Such changes in a whole community require extraordinary constellations of events. Fear tends to cause people to cling to what they have, but clearly, the loss of a world which resonates with one's world-view necessitates reconstruction. Periods of confidence would be liberating in this regard, as would moments of corporate gratitude, although the short lived nature of such an experience would require a charismatic figure or group to carry through major change. Moses at Sinai fits this pattern. It may be that a people's logic of belonging has died under the pressure of experience and there is a widespread thirst for a new logic. I see the followings gained by both Siddharta Gautama and Martin Luther in this light.

The best that one could hope for by way of organization of this process, if indeed ordering it could be regarded as advantageous, is that through an awareness of the processes at work and of the paradigmatic nature of all modelling of reality, a greater willingness for earlier experimentation with new ways of seeing might lead to a smoothing of the changes.

BRIDGING AND THE METHODOLOGICAL CHOICE

Bridging is so important that it may well be the case that the greater part of the symbol deposit of long established religious traditions consists of bridging material. Certainly this would cast light on Toynbee's historical assertion that the great religions emerged when major civilizations impinged on one another.[22] Clearly these would be periods in which prolific creation of bridging symbols could be expected. Equally, under the pressure of the need for integration, there might also be periods in which the competing

---

[22] Arnold J Toynbee, *Civilization on Trial*, (London, Oxford University Press, 1948), p.(v).

traditions were themselves radically cleansed, stripped down as far as possible toward paradigmatic purity, leaving those features that would contribute to the new bridging process. If competing traditions cannot be reduced to their basic paradigms then one ends up looking for symbols to bridge bridging symbols.

If Toynbee was right, we are heirs to theological and ethical edifices built, not on the solid ground of a single paradigm, but on first attempts to bridge them. Those with the time, the patience and the historical and linguistic skills may have a field day in the complexity of such deposits, tracing logical connections and historic dependencies, resolving conflicts, systematizing and revealing hidden riches to the contemporary gaze. All of which may be very far removed from anyone's felt sense of reality, and ill-fitted to be a substitute for that symbolic conceptualization of the real which ought to be in the process of being tested in the community's contemporary engagement with its world-out-there. If the reader has had difficulty identifying my suggested coherent types with his or her experience of living religion, here lies a reason. The human condition is such that the theological deposit of a tradition may contain more by way of bridging material than elements drawn from the coherent types.

The volume of bridging material presents the same sort of problem to the student of religion as does reduced reality belonging. The problem being that elements of the sectarian form of belonging are so widespread that colleagues have had difficulty with my insistence that it is a substitute for an unobtainable cosmic sense and not religion in the same way that the cosmic forms are. They asked, "How can you take what is probably the majority form and give that the substitute status?".

It is important to recognize that the choice is a methodological one and that it implies, at this level, no derogatory value judgment upon any type of religion or religion substitute. It is solely that it provides the simpler model for explaining phenomena, usually regarded as religious, by relating them to each other and to other significant aspects of experience. Nevertheless, once one has defined religion judgment becomes automatic, for one has established criteria, and some phenomena will measure up to them better than do others.

If, for example, one emphasized the first half of my definition and said that religion is the quest for, realization, or maintenance of belonging, then the drive for an ultimate and secured identity would have become the primary factor in religion, and the measure of a particular tradition would have become the degree to which it facilitates that endeavor. Thus some forms of religion, while being the best that can be achieved at the time and in the given circumstances, may not contribute to the experience of belonging as fully as others do. One would not wish for the sectarian stance as a long term solution. Not even sectarians, one supposes, would wish for the eternal provision of "evil" so that the "good" might enjoy a stronger sense of belonging over against it.[23]

Likewise the identification of symbols as bridging symbols, constitutes a judgment on a less than coherent tradition. There is little doubt that the drive for belonging is best served by a tradition that is logically coherent and not in need of bridging symbols. Bridging symbols must always be secondary, for they are not of themselves an attempt to speak of the ultimately-real, rather, they are an attempt to hold together symbols which themselves represent that attempt. Thus, of the two types of material to be found in most religious traditions, that which belongs to a coherent type is primary, both methodologically and in the light of the long term need for a sense of belonging. That which serves a bridging function is secondary, even if it should constitute the majority of a tradition's literary deposit.

Finally in this chapter, I return to my definition and to its second part. The quest that drives the tradition community processes is not for a sense of belonging for its own sake, but for a sense of belonging to the ultimately-real, however that may be experienced. Identity, and therefore belonging, cannot appear to be invented, it must feel real. Experience is virtually without limit; conceptualization, however, is limited to the three paradigms and then to what ever can be done to bridge them. This raises the question of what would be the most fruitful attitude to the paradigms and what is the possibility of more universal processes of distillation in the human quest to grasp reality. Has the world not become, or is it not in the process of becoming, a single tradition community with sub-traditions within it, and should there not be equivalent processes across all tradition communities of the processes that I have described within them?

I have little to say about this issue at the *overtly* religious level, except that it is difficult to imagine what sort of center and institution could command the necessary authority for a wide-spread incarnation process to take place or to forge the necessary symbolic language. Distillation is potentially much less offensive, but without a center it could not happen, and without incarnation it would hardly be worth while. What could and does take place at a level that is not overtly religious is quite another matter.

I have already addressed the consequences of humankind opting for no paradigm, but for a cosmic trust or for some variety of the cosmos paradigm.

---

[23] In the shorter term this is not an uncommon feature but it creates a strange long term logic. For example, so much of the structure and belief of the Zulu-Zion type churches is concerned with warding off the effects of highly active evil spirits that there is almost no way of picturing the community with no more evil spirits be overcome. J P Kiernan read a paper which, as I remember, was entitled "Do Zulu-Zion Churches need Belief in Evil Spirits?" to a conference convened by the Institute for the Study New Religious Movements and Independent Churches of the University of Zululand, February 1985.

Beyond that, it seems impossible to say whether humankind would benefit most if people believed that only one paradigm could be right (presumably the one they already espouse), or whether each should be loyal to their own while believing that others are valid, or even that we should all use each of the paradigms where they seem most appropriate and then seek to bridge them. Nevertheless, I believe that a science of religion ought to at least address the pros and cons of these options.

One could not, in any academic sense, ask the question "Which is the best paradigm?", the answer to which could only emerge in history as people "voted with their feet". There are, however, two related questions which can be asked, namely, "How could one organize to facilitate the quest for the best paradigm or paradigms?" and "What circumstances would favour, or what experiences would count as evidence for or against, the various paradigms?". The second of these questions I dealt with indirectly but extensively in chapter 8 and in a way that was more direct, but confined to the issue of constraints, in theme (III) of chapter 9. The first question, "How does one facilitate the quest for the best model of reality and of humankind's relation to it?", is the subject of the next chapter.

CHAPTER 14

"THE QUEST FOR THE BEST"

> I have suggested that the primary aspect of religion is the individual's need to belong to the ultimately-real. I now come to what I believe to be the second essential aspect. It is generated by the first and it is the quest by individuals-in-community for the best model of reality and for the best model of how the individual belongs to that reality.
>
> In this last chapter I explore religion as humankind's quest for this best model of reality and for the best model of the individual's belonging thereto, both of which are related to the quest for the best mode of engagement with the world-out-there. In short, I explore religion as the "quest for the best".

APOLOGIA

Early in the book, I indicated that I held a positive view of the role of religion. I meant by this that I understood that humankind, in any event, needed to deal with reality as a whole and that religion is traditionally the way in which they have done this. One consequence of this understanding is that it makes sense to ask how well the various religious traditions, singly and overall, have organized to do it.

This positive approach to religion is in sharp contrast to those studies which adopt what is called a methodological atheism and which suspend not only the existence of god, but any interest in the nature of reality as a whole. While this may seem to serve the purpose of unbiased observation, it leaves the study without any frame for its evaluation or for the extension of its significance beyond the immediate matter studied.

If one does not allow a positive role to religion in its own terms and on its own scale, as being, for example, a quest to know and relate to reality, one is virtually deciding that nothing essential can be determinative of its presence. Certain aspects of and processes within human individual and social existence are designated as religion, by custom or decree, and then studied as such.

In the approach that I have employed, one might wish to say of particular religious processes that they have or have not led to beneficial consequences.

In the alternative approach the implication seems to be, that if the products of the processes that have been named religion were to be deconstructed, no healthy person or society would miss them. They are related to nothing beyond themselves. I find this unhelpful as a starting point, for while in the end it could conceivably be true, *prima facie* it is against the evidence of human history. To start there is to assume that one knows what religion is or, alternatively, that it does not matter, for no serious understanding of what religion is is being tested. What follows is an exploration of an understanding of the corporate aspect of religion that is commensurate with what religions lay claim to be.

THE QUEST FOR THE BEST MODEL OF REALITY AND OF HUMANKIND'S RELATION THERETO

In the processes of incarnation and distillation, of bridging and cleansing, the logically coherent types within a mixed tradition will covertly compete for the title "most enriching paradigm". In this competition, which is an essential feature of the long run quest for enrichment, lies the greater need to re-relate the competing paradigms at every stage. In this in turn lies the importance for individuals, institutions and the community as a whole, of a bridging theology. It is this whole process, this covert "quest for the best", that I now wish to examine. It includes many individual and institutional activities that would not normally be regarded as religious. To see why this is so I must reiterate some earlier statements concerning the cognitive aspects of religion.

THE COGNITIVE ASPECT OF INDIVIDUAL RELIGION

The individual possesses religion affectively in the first instance and then to varying degrees cognitively. Sometimes dependence upon the cognitive is very small, but sometimes, when experience is conflicted or will not for other reasons support a sense of belonging, dependence on the established symbols of a belief system can be very great.

When discussing the quest for belonging, I referred a number of times to the importance for the individual of passing from the affective level to the cognitive. In particular I emphasized the importance of a logic of belonging, saying that an adequate sense of belonging in cognitive beings requires at least a minimal conceptualization of the ultimately-real and of the mode of one's belonging thereto.

In more general terms I said that symbols are necessary if the individual would conceptualize or communicate his or her experience, or would pass from feeling to considered action and particularly if that considered action is shared with others.

The body corporate, on the other hand, can only possess religion, as religion, cognitively. Feelings, even of mass events, are private. They might be shared, but if they are, that cannot be known. Only the concepts in which people seek to express their feelings can be known to be shared.

Thus all of religion that can be known to be shared, apart from some artifacts, memories and practices (which would themselves need to be identified as religious), is a set of external symbols. Not even the details of a symbol's significance for another individual can be known to be shared.

THE CORPORATE GENERATION OF THE COGNITIVE ASPECT OF RELIGION

The discussion of the corporate aspect of religion in chapter 13 focused largely on corporate support for the individual's quest for belonging. In the process of that quest, the quest that we are now considering, for the best model of reality and of humankind's belonging to it, is generated.

Identity has to feel real. It will only feel real if it is an identity generated within an understanding of reality which itself feels real. That sense of reality and its conceptual modelling only has a chance of feeling real if it is recognized as the best available.

If a cosmic sense of belonging is available, then the best available sense of reality will be one based on the widest possible experience and upon the most thorough human attempt to distill and model it. That means a corporate attempt to both distill and model reality, or if it should be the product of an individual's insight, then the validity of that insight would have to be corporately verified. Therefore, to the extent that a cosmic sense of belonging is possible, the quest for the best sense of reality and the best modelling thereof is necessarily a corporate one.

If a sense of cosmic belonging is not available, what constitutes the best modelling of reality may have to be judged, however it is arrived at, simply on its power to create a sense of belonging in that situation. It will still need to be corporately attested, if that is possible, but it will be in a reduced reality context.

THE COGNITIVE ASPECT OF RELIGION AND THE
MODE OF ENGAGEMENT WITH THE WORLD-OUT-THERE

The validity of a modelling of reality, I have said, is tested through the mode of engagement which it generates, and that in turn is tested by its long run power to enrich humankind.

I have said that each of the three basic paradigms have their own mutually incompatible mode of engagement and that within each of these there are sub-modes of engagement. For example, within secular world affirming religion, the degree to which one takes hold and shapes, or the style and timing of the taking hold and shaping, will be influenced by one's view of the divine character.

There is, therefore, an interplay between the individual's felt sense of reality, the nature of reality expressed in the symbols of the community, and that implied in the (largely communally determined) mode of engagement with the world-out-there. In a stable situation, with time for adjustment, there should be no significant tension between these but in a situation of rapid change there can be considerable tension between them.

CHANGE AND THE QUEST FOR THE BEST MODEL OF REALITY

It follows from what was said earlier that if individual religion is the quest for belonging then the form of affective religion and, in the longer run, the form of any related religious institutions will change, as and when necessary, to maintain or restore the sense of belonging.

Within this process, insofar as the mode of engagement is found to be minimally enriching and seems to work better than any known alternative, the model of reality which gives rise to it will feel real. If on the other hand, the mode of engagement has to be adapted to be enriching, then the model of reality will also have to be adapted if it is to remain authentic. That is to say, the tradition concerning the nature of the real and of humankind's relation to it, will change as the roles of prophet, priest and pragmatist are played out in the processes of distillation and incarnation and perhaps also of bridging and cleansing.

Therefore, change (and in the secular world affirming paradigm, the sense of transcendence) sets up a dynamic process that is, consciously or otherwise, a quest, at the most general level, for the best paradigm. At the more immediate level it is a quest for the best elaboration of the prevailing paradigm or paradigms, into which the adherents are partially locked.

Therefore to know the ultimately-real cognitively is not, when it can be otherwise, an individual quest. It builds in the growth of a tradition and in a community feeling its way forward. It emerges, in the long run, in the successes and failures for each individual, of the individual and corporate modes of engagement that are recommended by the tradition.

Some institutions may seek to limit this dynamic, by limiting the degree to which changes in the wider world can impinge upon the adherents of their tradition. [1]

Having reiterated what I needed for the purpose, I am now in a position to return to my earlier suggestion, viz. that much that contributes to the quest for the best modelling of reality arises in activities other than the overtly religious.

THE QUEST FOR AN OPTIMUM MODE OF ENGAGEMENT AND ITS ONTOLOGY, OVERT OR IMPLIED

In any dynamic tradition community, that is a community in which the symbolized felt sense of reality of the adherents is being distilled, integrated and re-incarnated, there will be a relationship between the ontology, that is the modelling of reality, and the mode of engagement with the world-out-there.

While the process may not be a conscious one, the ontology comes to expression in any overtly religious community in whatever description is given to the ultimately-real or, where appropriate, to the real and the ultimately-real. The process is not, however, limited to overtly religious communities.

In a sense, everyone who is awake is seeking to optimize their mode of engagement with the world-out-there. Any considered mode of engagement with the world out there implies an ontology, that is, it presupposes some understanding of the nature of the reality with which one is engaging.[2] In a pragmatist view of truth, the result (enriching or otherwise) of that engagement provides the only possible evidence for the validity of the ontology.

Even belonging of the reduced reality kind, implies an ontology, although it curtails the dynamic relationship in which the ontology would be continually and empirically tested in the mode of engagement with the world-out-there. It substitutes, instead, an engagement with a fixed and manageable projection.

---

[1] I understand the Amish communities of the U.S.A. and the ultra-orthodox groups in Israel to have engaged in this protective practice.

[2] I understand W van O Quine to hold this view, but he is not responsible for what I have done with it. It is my understanding of a public lecture delivered at the University of Cape Town more than a decade ago.

This empirical evidence, that is, the result of the engagement, cannot help but be evaluated data, and that it is evaluated, returns us to the ontology, to the ultimate frame of values. It also indicates the partially locked in nature of the whole corporate process of engagement and evaluation as a quest for the nature of reality. It parallels, of course, the locked-in nature of the development and expression of the individual's felt sense of reality set out in chapter 6.

This quest for the nature of reality and for its best modelling has not been a conscious aspect of most religious traditions. Generally such matters have been presented as a given, either as revealed or as the possession of the group from time immemorial. Adherents of withdrawal religion traditions consciously seek the best experience of the real but not its modelling.

We have perhaps entered the period of history in which the quest for the best mode of engagement must, for some at least, become consciously a quest for reality. That is, the model of reality implied in any mode of engagement must become conscious. Should the majority become conscious of its nature it would, of course, take a major shift in attitudes for the process to work at all. For we are not concerned here with an ethic generated in philosophical abstraction, but with a value system embraced, and to varying degrees lived, by whole communities and, in its varieties, by sub-communities. Unless it is lived it is not tested: to live it, is to be committed to it.

The difficulty, as we are presently conditioned, is to be committed to a mode of engagement without the authority of the prior understanding of the ultimately-real which generates it. That is to say, it is much easier to be committed to a mode of engagement if one believes that the conception of reality that generates it is already a description of the ultimately-real and not just a model in the process of being tested, however long and probing that process may already have been.

Nevertheless, a process of testing it is! However consciously committed to the finality of a revelation once given a community may be, the history of religion shows development.

Commitment to the view that all is contained in the Law of Moses or the American Constitution, far from curtailing the quest, sets up the structure within which a community explores reality through an ever greater elaboration and refinement of a basic paradigm, the nature of which may move far in the process. The "once givenness" is a symbol that renders commitment possible and provides the threads of continuity.

One might say traditions grow because it is assumed that they do not need to grow, they only need to be lived; or the best form of the quest is one which, for most folk anyway, is least consciously such.

In summary it can be said that:

> "religion as the individual quest for belonging must include, wherever it can, the corporate quest by the same individuals for the corporate and individual modes of engagement with the world-out-there that most enrich individual experience. These modes of engagement necessarily include a modelling of reality, overt or implied."

POTENTIAL INHIBITORS OF THE QUEST

The process that I have described may be inhibited by any number of factors. Anything which prevents the formation of tradition communities and anything which prevents the free flow of the data of experience within and between such communities will inhibit it. I cannot deal with many of these situations, but to deal with two in particular will further contribute to an understanding of the functioning of tradition communities. These two represent the extremes of delimitation in which communities can exist and still be tradition communities.

At one extreme is the community in which a tradition is so strongly held that the rest of the world is virtually shut out and the reduction of reality stifles the process. At the other extreme, are traditions that are so loosely delimited that they flow into one another and thus give rise to a pluralism in which no tradition is seriously embraced and therefore tested.

The former possibility I have already dealt with in other contexts and little needs to be added here. It is the latter possibility which appears in the contemporary West as a major threat to the process.

THE TOO STRONGLY DELIMITED TRADITION COMMUNITY

There would be no tradition communities at all if there were no opting for a paradigm or paradigms, and to opt for a paradigm is itself a form of reduction. There are, however, different ways of doing it. The differences are not dissimilar to those between pietism and the sectarian, reduced reality belonging, discussed earlier. The one, for all its specialized commitment to a single path, remains open, the other closes down.

As with enthusiasm for one path so enthusiasm for one paradigm will give the individual a context of belonging. It will contribute to the testing of the paradigm and it will reveal its possibilities to any who would observe it. On the other hand, to enhance belonging by the aggressive rejection of other paradigms contributes nothing of long term value. It offers a less dynamic engagement with one's own paradigm, there is less possibility of enrichment arising in an honest comparison with others, and it adds nothing to an understanding of the nature of the paradigms as paradigms.

Such reduction of reality is not always *de jure*, it can be simply *de facto*, that is to say, there are religious institutions which bear a reduced reality tradition, and there are religious institutions that bear a tradition which is the deposit of an intention to be cosmic but whose adherents have found it necessary to embrace the tradition or the institution itself in a reduced reality style.

Reduced reality belonging may also exist in the environs of a pre-paradigmatic situation in which the tensions of the cosmic quest have been avoided and an individual has opted to identify with one constellation of relatively coherent elements to the exclusion of all that competes with it.

It might well be argued that to assert the cosmos paradigm, as distinct from embracing a simple cosmic trust, is a reduced reality form of post-paradigmatic belonging.

Reduced reality belonging, whether in relation to pathways within the secular world affirming paradigm or in relation to paradigms in general, may be the best that can be done in a crisis, but not as a long term solution.

THE TOO WEAKLY DELIMITED TRADITION COMMUNITY
- PLURALISM

The problem posed by pluralism is that there is no exploration of modes of engagement, and hence no evaluation of paradigms, when there is an inclination among individuals, perhaps even a pressure upon them, to stand apart from any particular tradition community.

This would to be a problem for all tradition communities for, however universalistic their beliefs, the survival of the tradition requires a solidary approach to the survival of the community that bears it. Secular world affirming religion, however, is solidary by nature and pluralism threatens it at the level of what feels real, not just at the level of whether the processes of tradition development can function. However, it is with this last question that I am presently concerned.

In order to see how pluralism might threaten the corporate quest for the best mode of engagement with the world-out-there and its appropriate model of reality, overt or implied, one must first recall what that process calls for.

It calls for an authoritative center, both to facilitate the processes of distillation and incarnation and to maintain a sense of the corporate reality in the tradition community.

It calls for factors related to the processes themselves. These are a language of the center, respect for the received tradition, and a means to achieve integration of the old with the new.

One must then ask what is meant by pluralism, but that turns out to be one of those things, more easily recognized than defined, which calls for an "unpacking" rather than a single definitive statement.

Clearly pluralism implies a community but, on the face of it, it has to be one that is not delimitable by reference to a common or dominant culture, value or belief system. Such a community might be called a pluralistic society.

Pluralism, however, might be used to refer to a community in which there is indeed a dominant controlling value, namely the value of self-determination for the individual or individual sub-group. This situation has been called a culture of pluralism. [3]

The pluralistic society is obviously the antithesis of a tradition community, whereas a culture of pluralism is not necessarily so. In fact a culture of pluralism must have an overt ontology or an implied one very near to expression. If the culture had grown in secular world affirming soil it would be no longer one in which much ethical detail could be filled out, but it would almost certainly be one in which the ultimately-real was perceived as having given freedom to humankind to the point of deciding their own good and their own bad, not simply of obeying or not obeying a divine law.

Whether the value of pluralism (self-determination) could, on its own, suffice for the creation of that set of shared societal goals that makes for the freedom of the body corporate is doubtful.

If one now relates these two meanings of pluralism to the factors called for, if the "quest for the best" is to be a viable process, the outcome would seem to be as follows:

In a culture of pluralism the unity of emphasis upon individual freedom could provide a symbolic center of high authority, perhaps supported by a contemporary view of a constitution and its interpreting body, or by its being regarded as the very essence of the community in question. It could not however provide   detailed content of a broad received tradition to be incarnated. Thus it may have different symbols for the same paradigm and unbridged bits of different paradigms in areas remote from the primary value of individual self-determination.

The aggregations to which people belong, the value systems of which are significant in their identities, will no longer be clearly integrated or even integratable. This must reduce the possibility of a cosmic sense of belonging.

One could then expect intense small group belonging which would lend clarity to identity, coupled with a whole-group sense of belonging associated with the controlling value, which would provide a wide base for the support of identity. There could, however, be little in between these extremes holding them together.

---

[3] See for example the sub-title of David Tracy's *The Analogical Imagination*, (London, S.C.M.Press, 1981).

If the processes of incarnation and distillation were to be enabled to continue informally in such a situation, it would require at least a horizontal integration of smaller group belonging, that is, an integration of aggregations significant in an individual's identity. Mobility would also require that membership of an aggregation was perceived to depend more on what one brought to it and therefore might transfer to another, rather than upon anything in the aggregation itself.

Nevertheless it is not impossible that distillation and even incarnation might proceed, not through nested aggregations, but through movements within the community having an inter-related membership, some as formal as feminist or ecological movements, some as informal as the provision of and testing the market for, popular music. Translation would then be taking place, not into a language of the center, but into a number of inter-linked languages which between them would carry the enriched tradition. The inter-linking of these languages would require that there be forums in which common understandings of value symbols might be generated.

Returning to consider the pluralistic society, there would seem to be neither a content center, that is a respected received tradition, nor a symbolic center and therefore no impetus toward the development of interlinking forums. On the other hand one has to ask whether there can really be such a thing as a pluralistic society?

At the overt level of symbol sets and paradigms, the answer is obviously yes! At the covert level of the mode of engagement with the world-out-there, the answer is almost certainly no! This is because in most of its ramifications, the mode of engagement is corporate and cannot be escaped from, any more than its "benefits" can be avoided by individuals and individual groupings within the community. This is an important consideration.

Pluralism could be the result of bridging out in one or more directions when a corporate mode of engagement was no longer experienced as beneficial and the earlier dominant paradigm came under pressure. In that situation it would be difficult for individuals and sub-groups to shift the mode of engagement substantially. It would be almost impossible to test an alternative paradigm because its mode of engagement would not be operative, save in a very superficial way in immediate environments.

If the older dominant mode of engagement of a pluralistic community is not seriously under pressure, and if there is a corporate mode of engagement which is accepted in general terms even if the details are constantly being tidied up, then one must ask if the pluralistic society is not really either a cosmic trust looking for different experiences by playing with other traditions, or a form of pre-paradigmatic religion in which the quest (for a paradigm) has become institutionalized.

These latter situations suggest a position of relative security, because the assumption that an emphasis on the liberty of the individual frees people for a richer sense of belonging in community could only ring true in security. Where the sense of security is weak, the importance of having a corporately supported clear logic of belonging increases and plurality inhibits this.

They also suggest a situation without strong corporate goals, for the freedom of the individual is won at the expense of the unity of the corporate mind and therefore of corporate freedom of action.

THE COVERT QUEST FOR REALITY

I said in discussion of the religious institution, that while religious institutions as popularly understood have been involved in all aspects of belonging, it is clear that they have not been the sole contributors. Rather, if religion is about belonging and that in turn is associated with how reality feels to and is conceived by the individual, then the universities and such like institutions, have never ceased to be centers of religion.

The universities of the western world, once overtly religious institutions, have never ceased to be involved in inquiring into the nature of reality and how best to speak about it and certainly in shaping how people feel about it.

In addition those who have an overt interest in facets of reality lie all sorts of movements, from the theatrical to the political, who contribute to an ongoing examination of humankind's mode of engagement with its world-out-there and its outcome. For most of these the model of reality remains implied, but that does not prevent their activities from contributing to the quest for the best modelling. It only means that their contribution remains covert.

This is not to say that recognizable religious institutions no longer contribute to the quest for the best modelling of reality. They have retained their own academic centers even though they are ones with limited concerns. More important, they have served the ritual function and for the most part have kept this in line with the felt sense of reality of those who continued to avail themselves of that function. This in itself facilitates the process.

However, while traditional religions are not going to cease their traditional activity, their adherents are not sufficiently representative or sufficiently at the points where new challenges to received values need to be met to perform the task on their own. The activities of traditional religions could not now adequately serve the quest for the best.

In chapter 11 I drew attention to the characteristics of what I called a society's short, medium and long range goals. All are value laden, the latter are almost pure values. The different agencies that I have mentioned along the way, as participating in the quest for the best, do so across these different time perspectives. Commercial interests in a free market are probably the most tenacious and effective pollsters of a society's shortest term goals.

Politicians seeking election might wish to represent goals that are a little longer. The legal system (in societies which have approximated to the democratic for a sufficient length of time) is where one would expect to find enshrined the longest term values other than those of the overtly religious institutions. All are partners in the quest for the best. Religion and Law being so close that at times they are hard to distinguish. Theater and literature explore the whole spectrum. Nevertheless, there is need for something more deliberate, more systematized, more integrated.

The modern university is deeply involved in the quest for the mode of engagement that most enriches humankind, though most would not wish to state it that way. In particular, the social sciences have been added to the traditional humanities and they, while again not seeing it that way, have developed tools by which enrichment, whether personal or social, can be assessed. If pluralism constitutes a threat to the ongoing quest for the best mode of engagement and the modelling of reality, then the processes of academia (broadly understood) offer some hope for its continuation. On the surface, of course, they may seem to be totally withdrawn from such a quest.

The confusion I spoke of earlier in relation to science in general certainly afflicts the social sciences. The quest to be value free in the gathering and evaluation of data, which makes methodological sense in relation to an already chosen experiment in a carefully controlled environment, makes no sense at all at the level of what motivates the whole scientific enterprise and very little sense at the level of the experiment chosen. The latter is particularly the case in the social sciences.

The justification for academia, and that which binds its disparate parts together, is nothing less than the quest for an understanding of what does and does not enrich humankind in its habitat. This surely includes modes of engagement, whether we are considering the lessons from history or the contemporary possibilities. [4]

While it might be argued that paradigms in the hard sciences are not deliberately sought, but arise in the process of theory building, perhaps the time has come for the West, its academics and in particular its social scientists, to make the quest for what enriches humanity an overt one. This would involve them in becoming conscious of a valuing process in which they are inevitably involved and which would in turn require that they became conscious of the continuing quest for the most enriching form of the major paradigm within which they operate. In my view this remains academic so long as the stance of quest is maintained.

---

[4] It has been suggested to me that "the sole object of academia is to seek out the truth for its own sake". I do not know what that means, unless it is that such a style of engagement is the potentially most enriching, but that takes me back to the position that I stated.

That the whole technological and social science activity presupposes a current preference for the secular world affirming mode of engagement is clear and to deny it is simply to be obscurantist. This denial seems to arise in part because of the desire to believe oneself value free and in part because the relationship between fact and value, science and religion, is misunderstood.

There is a sense in which academic disciplines, especially those that are applied disciplines with human subjects such as medicine, psychology and social work, are tradition communities. They cannot avoid evaluative processes and they organize to establish norms of good practice. These, however, are segmental and therefore open to a level of subjectivity that might be avoided by recognizing that values exist in paradigms and sub-paradigms and that the quest is not for the evaluation of particular values but for the most enriching paradigm or bridged paradigms and the options within these.

One is looking for evaluation of the experiences of these tradition communities at a level that includes them all. How one would organize and institutionalize such a wider process of distillation without infringing other freedoms is difficult to say. I must, however, explore what might facilitate the process.

FACILITATING THE QUEST

A world wide Brahmin class is today out of the question. A massive international organization for the integration of the quest, is out of the question. What is not out of the question is that the international academic world should consciously accept the role that I have outlined for it. They fulfil it now, in part, unbeknown to themselves. It must become a conscious and priority task to discover what engagements, within given contexts of experience, humankind has found to be enriching and what have been diminishing, and what this implies for the nature of the reality with which we are engaged.

I therefore hope to see this largely covert aspect of the academic enterprise become overt. It would also serve to relate the separate disciplines to each other and to those other aggregations in society which today fill the role that I have ascribed to religion.

Humankind ought not to be nibbling its way forward, for, as I have suggested throughout, what humans believe in the more ultimate realm of values, enjoys, *mutatis mutandis*, the same status as the paradigmatic understandings which have governed the scientific enterprise. It requires a different mode of discourse, but it is equally a quest for the best model of what lies behind a surface through which one cannot see.

I must face the fact, of course, that for many, value-free truth is not a dead dream and also that the consequences of it are deeply ingrained in the structures of the West and in particular in the academy. It is religion which is considered dead by many, or at least removed into a highly personal sphere, therefore the commitments that the process calls for may not be forthcoming. If, however, the commitments are forthcoming to any degree, then, in the facilitation of the quest, there lies a special role for the discipline of religious studies.

The Role Of Religious Studies

The discipline of religious studies is inevitably involved in the search for as ubiquitous and as precise as possible a language for the expression of value. This is not only because it constantly seeks understanding of other traditions but because becoming a normative scientific discipline involves the search for just such a language in which to speak about the object of its study. Insofar as such a common language can be developed it will provide an essential pre-condition to universalizing the quest for the best modelling of reality.

Religious studies also has a potential role of integration within its sister disciplines. I want to speak of a real integration around goals, but first I think it is worthwhile to dwell for a moment on the *sense* of unity within the social sciences.

There is a way in which physics makes the "*the sciences*" a recognizable entity. However well other sciences may explain at their own level, there is always a deeper level of explanation to be found in physics, which pressing more and more to the micro level, has drawn more and more of the material order into a single explanatory system.

The quest for controlling values begins at the opposite end and seeks to grasp the nature of reality in the most total possible perspective before it begins to locate the particulars of life within it.

Insofar as the humanities and the social sciences come to understand their activity as including the quest for that which most enriches humankind in context, and insofar as that is understood to necessitate the continuing quest for the most enriching overall paradigm, then religious studies might quietly accept the role that physics has in the hard sciences, for it is the discipline concerned with the most ultimate level of that quest.

It has been a problem in the social sciences to know when theory is good theory. To know it, one needs to know when one is succeeding and for that, one needs a goal. There are, of course, a myriad of *ad hoc* sub-goals, but to espouse the quest for what enriches humankind in context could provide that overall goal and serve to restore self-confidence in the social sciences.

A science of religion might have two aspects. The one I have been engaged in, is the theoretical one and it asks about the nature and possibilities of religion. It could also be an applied discipline. If it became applied it would be concerned *inter alia*, with evaluating the contenders for the best model of reality, or as least of the best mode of engagement with whatever is out there. That is, it would become a sort of meta-theology, or better perhaps, a metaphysics but not as that has been understood in the past. It would not take place within a single paradigm of reality or within a single bridged tradition, nor would it operate entirely at the level of abstract thought appropriate in the idealist tradition. It would be a metaphysics as empirical as physics, a metaphysics to which sensible evidence was appropriate and also, therefore, all the tools of the social sciences.

The discipline of religious studies has not yet entered into its own quest for the most enriching paradigm for reality. Perhaps it never will, but hopefully it will do more than simply observe. It could become a clearing house between the findings of the social sciences and those of the tradition communities (overtly religious and otherwise) who are engaged (consciously or unconsciously) in the "quest for the best", keeping each aware of the others and engendering a sense of unity of purpose.

THE CENTRALITY OF ETHICS IN TRADITION COMMUNITY PROCESSES

I have now completed what I wish to say in broad terms about the "quest for the best". However, I have been presenting the mode of engagement as the central factor in that whole process without making it clear that, as it is entailed by a paradigm for reality, a mode of engagement is a very general stance. Before it can constitute the human relationship to the world-out-there, the evaluation of which vindicates or otherwise the paradigm, it must be filled out in its detail by what would generally be called an ethic.

I have at a number of points in the development of this model referred to ethical matters, now I must address them specifically in order to make clear the ramifications of the process that I have been discussing. First, I must say what kind of ethics I have in mind.

RELIGIOUS, PHILOSOPHICAL, AND COMPARATIVE ETHICS

In my understanding of religion, the theological task (or whatever that task might be called in other traditions) is grounded in an empirical ethics. That is to say, a religious empirical ethics is the only instrument by which a model of what lies behind the surface of experience can be verified.

As distinct from traditional metaphysics and philosophical ethics, this sort of ethics can only arise within, or in relation to, a tradition community.

Religious ethics is not primarily a deductive task, still less is it a legacy from the remote philosophical giants who may or may not have tried to live what they taught, but it is the value system embraced, lived, developed and tested in a tradition community. Thus the religious ethicist, as with the prophet, can only expect to be heard within his or her own tradition community.

The language in use is not literal language, so there can be no general appeal to a logic framed, for example, as rules of contradiction. Nor can there be any appeal to history, for the past is only the source of symbols not the point of their verification.

It will be apparent that within this understanding of religion there is no such thing as a non-religious empirical ethic which is not simply a settling for medial-axioms which themselves need further justification. For if the raw material of ethics arises in the application of the felt sense of reality, and whatever has been spelled out deductively from its appropriate paradigm, to the world as experienced, and this is done so as to maximize the enrichment of experience, then such an ethic is always a religious ethic.

Values derived in a philosophical ethic, as is the case with all values, only have authority for an individual if and when they become the perceived values of an aggregation to which the individual would belong, or for some idiosyncratic reason they become identity significant.

To do comparative ethics, which I understand to be a branch of comparative religion and to suffer from all the same cross cultural communication problems, important though it is in the development of a language for speaking about values and valuing beings in the most ubiquitous and precise terms, is not to do ethics. There is no meta-point above a tradition from which one can do ethics authoritative for anyone save the self. Whether humanity itself could ever become a really significant aggregation and have the institutions necessary to constitute it a tradition community, is another issue.

It follows that comparative religious ethics is not best focused upon the giants within traditions, but upon those value systems embraced and lived by communities, in order to discover what, in context, including the world-view, has in the long run enriched and what has not.

RELIGIOUS ETHICS - GENERAL

Religious ethics is what the community of believers does or would do in relation to aspects of its world-out-there, in response to being preached, in Karl Barth's phrase, "the language of Canaan", that is, in response to hearing the basic myths of its tradition.[5] It is the community's preferences in the detailed filling out of the mode of engagement.

It is, as we have seen, a dynamic process in which the myths themselves are modified within the limits set by the non-negotiables of the paradigm or, if more than one paradigm is involved, by the non-negotiables of the paradigms and by whatever bridging system is in operation.

In this area the task of the religious ethicist would be primarily the distillation, integration, systematization and, perhaps, hypothetical reapplication, of such responses.

The purely deductive task, that is, the drawing out of the conceptual ethical consequences of the paradigm, is not unimportant. It represents a significant aspect of the "preaching" process, responses to which, the ethicist is concerned to integrate. It also contributes a framework for that integration. Together these ethical tasks lubricate the process with which I dealt in the main part of this chapter and they facilitate at the corporate level, what Rümke spoke of in individuals, as healthy doubt. That is, they force the community to constantly review the fit between its myths and its experience, its paradigm and its mode of engagement with its world-out-there.

Ethics must begin from both ends, the totality and the concrete, for to do ethics is to locate an act or intention within the widest possible understanding of reality. The ethicist must press his or her community in both directions.

That the widest context of value within human reach can never be ultimate does not justify giving up the quest and settling for what appear to be reasonable medial-axioms. For such medial-axioms are not truly medial. They are little more than slogans that reason easily sets questions behind and nor do they have the authority of experiment. The only experiment which can lend authority to values is long term commitment to and experience within a tradition, the experimental findings of which, are the established preferences of the tradition community.

There is undoubtedly pressure upon ethicists to conform to caucus opinions, but if one asks how many ethicists function with the tools of the social scientist and seek to distill from communities their established preferences, the answer is few. The people who are concerned, not with how people say that they value, but with how people actually do value, are not usually ethicists, but politicians before an election, marketing and advertising concerns, and those who present the theater and publish the books that the less realistic create.

In this understanding of religion, the religious ethicist might operate much as scientists do, in the faith that out there there are laws to be learned. In this case, laws of optimal relationship between individual and individual, between the individual and the world-out-there and between the individual and him or herself. Those laws, if one wished to integrated them, would call

---

[5] Barth K, *The Humanity of God*, (London, Collins, 1961) p.59.

for explanations, explanation could only take place within a paradigm or, less satisfactorily, within bridged paradigms.

Secular world affirming religion, I said earlier, because of its transcendence gap and consequent goal orientation, must have a significant belief content. Not only is it necessary to have an adequate symbolization of the ultimately-real and its relation to the real, including humankind, but of humankind's mode of engagement with the real. That mode of engagement being solidary and goal oriented can only be possessed conceptually. Theology, and in particular theological ethics, provides this ongoing conceptualization.

RELIGIOUS ETHICS IN RELATION TO RELIGION AS BELONGING - A SUMMARY

Religious ethics is empirical ethics, it is an essential part of the process in which the paradigm is elaborated and tested and of all the sub-processes that flow from that. Therefore:

i) Religious ethics is enunciation of the details of the mode of engagement with the real

as such it contributes to the symbols available for the construction of self-image.

ii) Religious ethics is enunciation of the details of the character of the ultimately-real and behavior (including attitude) in relation to that ultimately-real

as such it refines the logic of belonging, the conceptual element in ritual.

iii) Religious ethics is essential content of the processes of distillation and incarnation.

iv) The need for a coherent ethic in both individual identity and corporate action is the drive behind the bridging and cleansing processes.

v) The conceptualization of the source or sources of ethics will vary with the paradigm

this in turn establishes the type of ethical system.

vi) In the secular world affirming paradigm, the integrity of identity requires integration of values (commitments) as between the aggregations in the hierarchy of significant aggregations, integration of values (aspirations) between aggregations on the same level, and justice between the aspirations of aggregations that cannot be integrated.

vi) In the secular world affirming paradigm the hierarchy of significant aggregations is the natural source of ethics and of the sanction that empowers them.[6]

How the entities should relate at any level is controlled by what one understands that the level above should be. The sanction for ethics is the maintenance of identity, in this case the need to belong at the level above. Consequently:

a) The hierarchy of aggregations significant in identity must be integrated conceptually, that is, theology must make an input at each level and overall. Theodicy may be necessary for integration both on the same level and in the hierarchy. There is also a need to establish a theological and ethical relation to those aggregations that are "not mine". [7]

b) One would look within the hierarchy for the central "preferences of the believing community".

c) While individual adherents will operate with medial-axioms or even a "felt sense" for the greater part of the time, much of these will be comprised or shaped by the values of significant aggregations.

d) The importance of such a value to an individual will depend upon how important it is believed to be in the survival of an aggregation and how important the survival of the aggregation is held to be.

e) There can be no values having a corporate authority that are not the perceived values of an aggregation to which one would belong.

---

[6] See chapter 11.

[7] As one thinks ones way through the levels of aggregations the complex inter-dependence of ethics and theology clarifies.

POSTSCRIPT

A general theory of religion could never be complete, but this one has reached the stage where its basic elements are in place and what remains is further applications of the same principles to other data, the appropriation and reinterpretation of work done in other theoretical frames, and the exploration of a myriad of frontiers. I will not be doing any of those things here.

I do, however, wish to say something about the consequences of the theoretical position established in this book for the discipline of religious studies and for tradition communities.

CONSEQUENCES FOR THE DISCIPLINE OF RELIGIOUS STUDIES

In chapter 1 I suggested that religion could and should be studied at a variety of levels and that each level has its own kind of criteria for what shall count as a valid statement, and also that these levels of study ought to be mutually supportive within a single conceptualization of the religious studies enterprise.

Not only for the sake of its students, but also for colleagues in the humanities and social sciences, there needs to be a sustained quest for a holistic understanding of the subject. A deliberate attempt at integration is particularly important in the study of religion because the contributions of the many different interests at work, while important in themselves, have tended to fragmentation and to an increased sense of diffusion in a discipline which already has an intangible object of study.

Where students are exposed, in the same situation, to the findings of what I called doers, observers and explainers, the quest for integration would be met, if:

> a) some equivalent of the categories, doer, observer and explainer, and of the schema relating them, became a more overt aspect of the total program,

b) the place of a particular course or module in such a schema were carefully stated, indicating its strengths and also the aspects of religion that it fails to address and

c) courses were offered, parts of which deliberately sought to give to a student the sense of involvement in the quest for a unified conceptual framework.

The last of these proposals is the most controversial for it proposes that the overall ethos of academic religious studies be not that of a single religious tradition, nor the epoché of phenomenology, but that of a science of religion.

It is after all, at the level of a science of religion, that is, at the level of explanation, that the discipline of religious studies comes into its own. At the level of observation all detached participants add to the common stock of data. At the level of explanation it is vital that one is dealing with religion as a whole and that the quest for an understanding of religion itself be the primary motivation.

Certainly one would have to take great care to maintain the thrust for epoché at the stage of observation, and certainly one would need to be clear at all times that the modelling of reality is a theological task that can only be carried out and tested within a tradition community and that the "glamour" of the meta-levels is parasitic upon it.

On the other hand, while a phenomenological consciousness is threatened by both theology and science of religion, science of religion cannot escape its dependence upon both theology and phenomenology.

Theology may not enjoy being exposed to the scrutiny of science of religion but it can hardly help gaining from it, for while theology is concerned with the modelling of reality, science of religion is concerned *inter alia* to model theology, that is to model the modelling of reality. The foundational level can hardly help but be refined by exposure to the meta-level.

It is science of religion, therefore, that can best offer an academic context to the other two. Where departments are joint ones they should be established on that understanding.

CONSEQUENCES FOR TRADITION COMMUNITIES

It may seem somewhat *ultra vires* for the author of a general theory of religion to address the concerns of theologians, ethicists and other functionaries of tradition communities, but there are consequences of this theoretical position for living religious traditions which ought to be stressed. Perhaps it might be excused on the ground that the motivation throughout has been a pastoral one.

Having said of theologians and ethicists that they share with the scientist of religion, over against the phenomenologist, the construction and testing of models; one should perhaps return to an early remark and say that "to suggest that reality is understood by creating mental models of it, is not to say of whatever is out there, that it cannot be worthily engaged with as though it were the entity that it is modelled to be". Since scientists became aware that their knowledge of the physical world is largely a projection of the human mind they have not ceased to believe that what they are engaging with is real.

The choice of the paradigm within which one does one's modelling is the most important aspect of the whole conceptual venture, for it sets the limits within which knowledge can exist. For one thing the choice determines what shall count as data, so that, for example, if the paradigm for religion were belief in a god much of the data of Buddhism would not count as religious data. The paradigm for religion that has been suggested in this book would include beliefs in gods as data but in addition would make psychological data on identity, alienation, and what might occur when identity or its securing fail, relevant. This would not have counted if the paradigm were belief in a god. On the other hand debates concerning whether the creation is eternal or has a beginning, without reference to the fact that the two ideas belong to different paradigms for *reality*, could not find a place within this paradigm for *religion*. I have already noted that the different statements concerning what happens to the individual surviving death cannot be dealt with as truth claims in conflict.

The point is, if the present paradigm for religion should prove persuasive it will inevitably have consequences for the theological venture.

At the level of the congregation the most important lesson of this theoretical position is that theology or its equivalent is primarily a helping profession, helping the adherent to a sense of belonging. If that fails, all else fails. There will be no one around to be instructed, exhorted or cajoled.

The most important lesson at the level of the denomination, that is, of the tradition community looking inwards and perhaps to its own wider whole, is to become conscious of the need for distillation and incarnation and to organize to achieve them.

The most important lesson at the level of inter-faith relations, that is, of a tradition community looking outward, is of the limits set to dialogue.

The second of these is an institutional matter and I have nothing to add to what I said earlier. The other two need further explanation.

THEOLOGY AS A HELPING PROFESSION

There are numerous consequences of returning to the understanding that the primary task of theology is to assist the individual adherent to gain a sense of belonging to the ultimately-real and I have chosen to recall two. The first has to do with the need to speak of the totality of experience, the second with the nature of the language in which it is spoken about and, therefore, with the manner of its verification.

There is a tendency for theology and particularly theological ethics to address particular issues, and that is fine within limits, because religion has consequences for all the bits and pieces of life, but if religious discourse begins and ends with the bits and pieces of life it fails to be religious discourse. Primary religious discourse, the foundation, legitimation and spring board for all else which those speaking from within a tradition might wish to say, is concerned with the totality of experience. The question that is primary to religious discourse is, "what is all-that-out-there and how do I relate to it?".

One suspects that it is not simply the desire to be relevant, or to argue cogently, that leads theologians and ethicists to deal with the bits and pieces, but rather that they have become embarrassed to be found using non-literal discourse and perhaps ashamed to draw upon the inherited tradition at the entangled interface where the two modes of discourse meet. Thus they end up discussing observed facts in the light of some generally accepted medial-axioms and their own preferences. Such a process does not deserve the name of theology or ethics and falls far short of what the great traditions have to contribute to humankind.

That we cannot speak of the primary object of religious concern in literal discourse does not mean that there is nothing to speak about, nor that we should be ashamed to speak about it.

It is not a necessary consequence of the fact that we cannot speak literally of the totality that the only reasonable thing to do is to act as if it was not there, to deal only with its bits and pieces, perhaps trying to integrate them, but never jumping the gulf between the modes of discourse and attempting to speak of the totality itself. Still less does one have to go to the solipsist extreme of supposing that the religious reality exists only in subjective experience. It is entirely reasonable to suppose that there is something out there. It is entirely reasonable to ask what it is, not only as a multitude of bits and pieces, but also as a totality.

Not only that which is spoken about, but how it is spoken about, constitutes a problem for adherents of a religious tradition.

In order that they might be able to accept from their tradition community its modelling of that to which they would belong, individuals need to be weaned from the now deeply ingrained feeling that truth is what is historically true. While history is the laboratory of any tradition community seeking the best model of reality, the historical veracity of a particular understanding of a particular moment of history is not more relevant to that process than any other. That this weaning would not be easy becomes clear when one contemplates the problem for modern Westerners of being committed to that which they can only speak of in symbolic discourse.

Clearly children, and at times even the most intellectual of people, have no place for the distinction between literal truth and irreducible symbol. We all need simply to feel that it happened, the exodus, the empty tomb, and God speaking. We have no wish to be liberated from our "superstitions".

Nevertheless, the time has long been around when the cost of not being aware of the distinction is very high. The widespread education of critical faculties to the point where it becomes clear to most people, at a very early age, that religious beliefs are not literally true, tears people apart at the point where their felt sense of reality meets their cognitive faculties. Rümke's healthy doubt ceases to be healthy. Symbols for the felt sense of reality are checked, not in feeling, but against the bits and pieces of incoming sense experience (where symbols for physical reality are appropriately checked). The symbols are then found wanting. The sense of reality, however, goes on grasping at them in order to find expression.

It is not only the presently "unchurched" who fail to understand religious language. I noted earlier the many who feel drawn to religion, even the self-consciously religious, who have the disturbing experience of suddenly feeling outsiders to a religious conversation and of asking themselves what all these words mean, words which they may use themselves on other occasions.

There is a need for the critically minded to know when and why each mode of discourse is in operation and, because no one likes to live in two realities, it has to become clear that the divide lies at the level of language and not primarily at the level of experience.

The above problem does not only exist in present conversation, but also in the inherited tradition. Sometimes surgery is a necessity if a body is to remain healthy and perhaps the time has come for some radical cleansing and cutting away of the entangled growth at the interface between the modes of discourse.

Returning to the problem of commitment to that which can only be spoken of in myth, I again point to the scientists who, having come to the realization that most knowledge exists only in humanly constructed paradigms, have not ceased to do science, nor, because they have discovered that they can never possess absolute truth, have they ceased to believe that that with which they are engaged is real and worth relating to. In fact they continue to act and indeed feel, that the best they know at any point is the truth (which for all practical purposes it is) even while being alert to discover a better truth, knowing that it could mean a dramatic and painful shift in paradigm.

In the same way, there can be no shame in remaining committed to the symbols with which one grew up, or later came to recognize as those which resonated best with one's felt sense of reality, provided that there is a "healthy doubt" in operation, for there is no better way to operate.

THE LIMITS SET TO INTER-FAITH DIALOGUE

If dialogue is to be something more than polite conversation or an exercise in paternalism, it must be *back-to-back* dialogue and carried out for the purpose of *self-enrichment*. It has to be *self*-enrichment, because the moment that I seek to benefit the other, I impose my way of feeling, if not my way of understanding. Back-to-back is best illustrated from stages in the relationship of people in love.

When people fall in love they tend to put each other on a pedestal and experience the demand of living up to the supposed level of expectation which that creates. Sometimes they run away from it, not because they are no longer in love, but because they can no longer stand the stress. Mercifully, lovers tend to get married and have a child, or at least get a dog. Then love evolves to have a side-by-side possibility, in which mother and father are bound in a mutually unquestioning relationship in their shared love for the child and each parent and the child in their shared love for the other parent.

This looking out together at the same world has been suggested as the model for dialogue but it is not adequate, for it is not the same world. Even the common features of birth and death are not necessarily experienced in the same way. Nor is it adequate any longer as a model for the relationship of love, not in the urban West anyway, where the possibilities for self-fulfillment make it exceedingly unlikely the two will be looking out on the same world many years into marriage.

What one needs is what I called a back-to-back relation, in which mutual enrichment takes place as each overhears the other speaking, in their own terms of their own world-out-there, as they experience it and as they model it. The condition for being there to hear is that one also speaks so as to be heard.

Dialogue cannot be more than this in my understanding of religion. Anything I take from another paradigm, short of the whole, is no longer what it was. That is not to say, however, that it cannot enrich me nor that I could not come close to knowing what it is like to live in that other world of experience, particularly if the effort is made toward a common language at levels where that is achievable. What I cannot know is when, or the degree to which, I have actually come to know what the other's world is like, for there is no meta-position to provide a bridge.

APPENDIX

LOCATING RELIGION

A - THE MAPPING OF INDIVIDUAL RELIGIOUS EXPERIENCE

At the end of chapter 8 I indicated how an individual's religious experience might be located within the framework then developed and indicated what other factors must be needed. The further breakdown of the coherent types that has been undertaken makes it possible to locate much of an individual's religious experience in terms of variables that are assessable.

Thus, the religion of an individual can be located as pre-paradigmatic, paradigmatic or post-paradigmatic or, if it is allowed that the mode of engagement with the world-out-there implies a paradigm, then within one of the paradigms. Within these, the person may be located in relation to all aspects identified within the further breakdowns of the paradigms, including the defensive positions which may be adopted if belonging is threatened.

It was said in chapter 8 that a more complete mapping would have to include a number of intensity measures, together with location within a range of possible interpretive possibilities and within a range of possible attitudes that can be taken up to the beliefs and practices of religion. I repeat these here for the sake of completeness.

The range of interpretive possibilities comprised, at one extreme, the overtly religious possibility of understanding the paradigm as a statement about what actually is, and at the other extreme, the overtly secular possibility of understanding the paradigm as a means of expressing that which is implied by the mode of engagement with the world-out-there. In between were those for whom the paradigm was consciously a model, but a model that had gained in reality status because it had proved enriching, and those for whom the paradigm had been an ontological statement, but for whom that perspective had come into question.

The attitudinal spectrum comprised possibilities determined primarily by the felt level of security. The spectrum was characterized at one end by quest, trust and openness and by a looking for "reality", and at the other end by certainty (concerning what is in possession), by closedness and by a hanging on to "truths".

Other assessments necessary to complete the picture were the intensity measures. It can now be said that these are three rather than two. They are:

a) the intensity of the existing sense of belonging

b) the intensity of the quest

c) the intensity of the need for belonging

(a) refers to the "aliveness" of the existing felt relationship with the ultimately real such as was discussed under the heading of demand and acceptance in chapter 11, its opposite is not a sense of not belonging but the absence of "life" in a relationship that is presumed to exist.

(b) is a measure of the intensity with which belonging, or an increased level of belonging, is being sought. It would almost certainly have a conscious element but not necessarily be overtly religious. If it is not overtly religious then the clearest indicator would be the drive for identity and perhaps for its securing. At a more recognizable but not yet overtly religious level it would include a quest for a sense of the nature of reality. At the overtly religious level it would include a quest for the appropriate paradigm together with an effective ritual for holding the self and the real together.

(c) is the experience of not belonging, of an existential alienation, such as was discussed early in chapter 12. It may be conscious and directed, and therefore be the drive behind (b), or it may result in a non-directed threshing around or even violence. Its opposite is not a sense of belonging but the absence of concern, frustration or anger, when a relationship is not considered to exist.

While (a) must be testified to by the person concerned, (c) might well be denied and its assessment depend entirely upon the observer. Thus in a problem situation (a) and the non-directed form of (c) might be assessed to exist in the same person at the same time.

B - QUESTIONS TO BE ASKED IN THE LOCATION OF
A TRADITION AND OF A TRADITION COMMUNITY

The following is a summary of the questions that one would ask of a tradition and of a tradition community in attempting to locate them. One needs to locate not only the tradition, the beliefs and practices, but also the processes in which these beliefs and practices are reviewed, conserved and extended.

LOCATING THE TRADITION

It is possible to locate within the developed framework of religious entities all varieties of religious tradition and, therefore, to detail change in these traditions in relation to these entities.

One would need to know where a tradition is in relation to, and whether changes are taking place at the level of:

i) *the paradigms*

If the tradition is mixed one would also need to ask whether it contains bridging elements and if so what is the nature of these.

ii) *the mode of belonging*

iii) *the mode of engagement*

iv) *blessings*

v) *ritual and of ethical expression*
(Ethics, of course, is controlled at the most general level by the mode of engagement, and then to a considerable degree by the aggregations significant for identity. The term "ethical expression" as used here refers to the locus and style of ethical concern, that is, to the size of the adherents' effective world and to where they are on the quietist-interventionist scale in relation to it, and the form that any intervention takes.)

Changes at a higher level in this table will almost certainly require changes at all lower levels but not necessarily vice versa.

Within (i) above there are three possible sub-levels involving:

a) movements from the pre-paradigmatic to paradigmatic, from there to post-paradigmatic or perhaps straight from pre- to post, and, if confidence in the position is lost, movements in the reverse direction;

b) movements between paradigms calling for bridging symbols and other mechanisms of integration during change;

c) changes among flexible consequential symbols within a paradigm.

Some of the more subtle differences in each of these sub-levels are exemplified below:

i.a) *Pre-Paradigmatic, Paradigmatic, Post-Paradigmatic*

Whether people are in a state of quest, belief, or a paradigm rejecting cosmic trust may seem to be a highly individual matter, but it can have corporate significance.

For example, I think that it is highly probable that, among the new religious movements that sprang up in the U.S.A. in the 1960s, there were those which represented the rejection of the prevailing paradigm, not in favour of another, but rather for a position of institutionalized quest. Equally, I believe that those associations of committed humanitarians who reject all religious dogma together with groups who have been wrongly understood, even by themselves, as primarily heirs to the Eastern religious tradition, may be best thought of as belonging in the post-paradigmatic category. This would particularly be the case if they have a clear mode of engagement with their world-out-there, other than withdrawal. I would think it necessary to include such movements in the pre- or post-paradigmatic categories, in addition to those in the latter category, who are there with their eyes wide open having settled for a mode of engagement and a cosmic trust.

i.b) *Movements between Paradigms*

It is here that most of the new expressions of religion which arise out of a blending or clash of cultures fit.

If a move between paradigms which is not pressed by an encroaching dominant culture or the lure of an attractive one takes place, then one must expect that the previously dominant paradigm no longer has affective affinity with the felt sense of reality. Some of the new religious movements in Japan seem to represent a move from nature religion and withdrawal religion into the secular world affirming paradigm, pressed, not by an encroaching religious culture, but by the fruits of such culture, namely industrial technology with its goal orientation and its "take hold and shape" mode of engagement. As with the first generation Black worker in urban South Africa, it is possible, for a period and at a certain level of involvement, to earn in one culture while living in another. In the longer run, and when participation involves a responsibility for creative expression which requires a real identification with the overall purpose, such a divided world-view becomes unacceptable, and the quest for a single controlling paradigm inevitable.[1]

---

[1] It is significant that the outburst of new religions in Japan accelerated after the war when technology had ceased to be imitative and had become creative, and that it is Africans who become managers, or personnel or training officers, for example, who most feel the tension of the two cultures.

In the other direction, the Western World of recent decades has shown a marked interest in the withdrawal and   nature religion paradigms, presumably because of a loss of goal orientation and with it the feeling that reality is progress.   A goal-orientation may weaken for various reasons. Goals may fail, turn sour or simply cease to grasp people, in which case if a move is made toward another paradigm it is likely to be toward that of withdrawal religion.   There may also be the feeling that the goals have been achieved, in which case either boredom or just the sense of loss may lead in the same direction. On the other hand where life seems satisfying though static, a move to the nature religion paradigm is possible.

On a more cognitive plain, the unobtainability, suggested by both science and economics, of goals basic and still desirable within the present Western system, press the mind toward the meaningful but not purposeful logics of Buddhism or Tao.

i.c)   *Change of Consequential Symbols within a Paradigm*

All symbols within a coherent system are consequential at some level of remove upon the paradigmatic symbol, but here I am concerned only with those that are sufficiently central for changes in them to put pressure on the paradigm. Many symbols are pressed to adapt by changes in the context, for example, symbols with corporate implications come under pressure in a situation where there is the need and possibility of individual mobility. These changes, however, may or may not put pressure on the paradigm itself.

Moves which threaten paradigms are summarized in chapter 8. If, for example, the quasi-personal modeling of the ultimately real in secular world affirming religion comes under pressure, the credibility of the paradigm is threatened. On the other hand if those elements which comprise the divine character (sovereignty, righteousness and love) shift in balance, it will not threaten the paradigmatic symbol, but it could have a major impact on the quality of belonging, the ritual expression, and the ethic. The stern and sometimes cruel righteousness, associated with strong symbols of transcendence in the churches of Victorian England, contrasts strongly with the loving tolerance and immanence found in the same churches of the present day, but it does not of itself greatly pressurize the paradigm.

ii)   *Change at the Level of the Mode of Belonging*

The mode of belonging at the most general level is controlled by the paradigm for reality of which it is a central consequential symbol, but there are alternatives within these.

In the nature religion paradigm a different perception of the nature of the cosmos calls for a different outworking of the mode of belonging. Belonging is always assumed, but in an harmonious cosmos this calls only for care in its maintenance. In an alien and fragmented cosmos it calls for constant appeasement and manipulation of the powers that be.

I indicated earlier, when discussing the possible paths by which the individual might model his belonging to the divine in the secular world affirming paradigm, and the variety of combinations to which these possibilities give rise, that one would expect moves toward a clear unmixed logic of belonging in times of felt insecurity.

iii) *Change at the Level of "Blessings"*

I have defined Blessings as that which authenticates for the adherent his whole religious system from paradigmatic symbol to ritual expression. I place them above ritual and ethical expression in this hierarchy because I believe that the expected blessings control the latter, rather than the other way round. Even above this level, while the paradigms are a given and the options are consequential upon them, the meeting or otherwise of life-needs related to the blessings can cause the adherent to affirm, reject, or swop the whole paradigm or certain options within it.

The hierarchy of blessings associated with socio-economic level and set out in chapter 11, is expressed in secular world affirming terms, but one must also ask where the "proof of the pudding" is likely to be in the other paradigms.

To understand religious movements it is vital to understand shifts in what authenticates them to their adherents.

iv) *Change at the Levels of Ritual and Ethical Expression*

Ethical expression in the secular world affirming paradigm will be modified by the perception of the real and in particular by the size and constituent aggregations of the adherents' world-out-there. For many, ethical concern does not go far beyond the family, the local community and the work place. If it is forced to do so, for example by a wider politicization, it may challenge faith in the whole paradigm.

Ritual expression in the secular world affirming paradigm may be largely a behavior pattern or the rehearsal of a belief pattern. I have suggested elsewhere situations where behavior pattern will move toward belief pattern, but whatever form it takes, ritual must reflect the whole logic of belonging from the paradigmatic symbol down.

One of the most readily apparent differences in ritual expression has its roots in the cognitive or affective preference of the adherents. Changes which take place at the level of ritual expression, therefore, may reflect changes at higher levels in the hierarchy of possible changes that I have been discussing, or they may simply be concerned with changing fashion including swings between the dominance of the cognitive and the reassertion of the affective.

LOCATING THE TRADITION COMMUNITY PROCESSES

Having located a tradition, it is then necessary to examine the processes in which the beliefs and practices are or were reviewed, conserved and extended, that is, it is necessary to locate the tradition community processes. For this purpose one would ask:

i) Is the tradition dynamic? That is, were processes of distillation and incarnation going on within the tradition community at the time in question, and, in a mixed tradition, were there processes of bridging and cleansing, or lower level integration, also in operation? If so, then:

ii) were the observed processes continuous or episodic?

iii) what comprised the distillation center or hierarchy of centers? That is, viewed from the point of attempted incarnation:

In what did authority lie?

What was the *symbolic* center?
What was its nature?
What was its content?

Was there an *institutional* center, if so, what was it?

What were the channels in and out?
Who were the functionaries?
What were its tradition resources?
To what degree was the form of the institutional center symbolic and in that sense continuous, and to what degree was it *ad hoc*?

If the tradition was mixed then one would have to ask what level of the possible integrating processes was at work. One would also need to know whether the processes:

i) were informal, or lay in institutions or with significant individuals?

ii) were continuous or *ad hoc*?

iii) were coterminous with the distillation center or centers, or were based elsewhere?

INDEX